Developmental Psychopathology
From Infancy through Adolescence

Fourth Edition

Charles Wenar
The Ohio State University

Patricia Kerig
James Madison University

Boston   Burr Ridge, IL   Dubuque, IA   Madison, WI   New York   San Francisco   St. Louis
Bangkok   Bogotá   Caracas   Lisbon   London   Madrid
Mexico City   Milan   New Delhi   Seoul   Singapore   Sydney   Taipei   Toronto

McGraw-Hill Higher Education

A Division of The **McGraw-Hill** *Companies*

DEVELOPMENTAL PSYCHOPATHOLOGY: FROM INFANCY THROUGH ADOLESCENCE, FOURTH EDITION

This book is printed on acid-free paper.

4 5 6 7 8 9 0 DOC/DOC 0 9 8 7 6 5 4 3 2

ISBN 0–07–069617–9

Editorial director: *Jane E. Vaicunas*
Executive editor: *Mickey Cox*
Editorial coordinator: *Sarah C. Thomas*
Senior marketing manager: *James Rozsa*
Senior project manager: *Marilyn Rothenberger*
Senior production supervisor: *Mary E. Haas*
Coordinator of freelance design: *Rick Noel*
Photo research coordinator: *John C. Leland*
Compositor: *York Graphic Services, Inc.*
Typeface: *10/12 Times Roman*
Printer: *R. R. Donnelley & Sons Company/Crawfordsville, IN*

Cover/interior designer: *Maureen McCutcheon*
Cover photo: © *Tony Stone Images, Photographer Kevin Anderson*
Photo research: *Connie Gardner Picture Research*

Library of Congress Cataloging-in-Publication Data

Wenar, Charles, 1922–
    Developmental psychopathology : from infancy through adolescence/
Charles Wenar, Patricia Kerig. — 4th ed.
        p. cm.
    Includes bibliographical references and index.
    ISBN 0–07–069617–9
    1. Child psychopathology. 2. Adolescent psychopathology.
I. Kerig, Patricia. II. Title.
RJ499.W396   2000
618.92'89—dc21
                                            99–21568
                                    CIP

www.mhhe.com

To Blanche—for her love and care

Charles Wenar

My warmest thanks to Philip Cowan for setting me on the pathway to developmental psychopathology; to Charles Wenar for his wisdom, grace, and generosity; to Anne Hungerford for helping words to fly onto the page; and to Katalina Bartok for providing the net underneath. Last, first, and always, to Bob, my beloved husband and dearest friend.

Patricia K. Kerig

About the Authors

Charles Wenar

Charles Wenar is professor emeritus of psychology at The Ohio State University. He headed both the developmental area and the clinical child program in the department of psychology there. A graduate of Swarthmore College and State University of Iowa, Dr. Wenar was both a clinician and a researcher at Michael Reese Hospital, the Illinois Neuropsychiatric Institute, and the University of Pennsylvania. His two previous books and numerous articles, as well as his research on autism and on negativism in healthy toddlers, attest to his long-standing interest in both normal and disturbed children. In 1986, Dr. Wenar received the Distinguished Professional Contribution Award of the Section on Clinical Child Psychology of Division 12 of the American Psychological Association for his meritorious contribution to the advancement of knowledge and service to children.

Patricia K. Kerig

Patricia K. Kerig received her Ph.D. in clinical psychology from the University of California at Berkeley with a specialization in children and families. She completed an internship at Stanford Children's Hospital, and was a postdoctoral fellow in clinical child psychology at the University of Colorado Health Sciences Center. Previously a faculty member at Simon Fraser University, she is currently an Associate Professor in the doctoral program at James Madison University. She is also an actively practicing clinician. Her research honors include the Brodsky/Hare Mustin Award from Division 35 of the American Psychological Association and the New Contribution Award from the International Society for the Study of Personal Relationships. She is the author of a number of scholarly works on the topics of risk and resiliency in children exposed to interparental conflict, violence, divorce, and traumatic stress.

Contents

Chapter Four

Autism: A Severe Deviation in Infancy

Chapter Five

Infancy Through Preschool: Insecure Attachment, Oppositional-Defiant Disorder, and Enuresis

Chapter Six

The Preschool Period: Attention-Deficit Hyperactivity Disorder and Learning Disabilities

Chapter Eleven

Psychopathologies of the Adolescent Transition: Eating Disorders and Substance Abuse

Chapter Twelve

The Developmental Consequences of Mental Retardation

Chapter Thirteen

Risks of Physical Illness and Brain Damage

Chapter Fourteen

Risks in the Family Context: Child Maltreatment and Divorce

Chapter Fifteen

The Risks of Ethnic Minority Children

Chapter Sixteen

Psychological Assessment

Chapter Seventeen

Intervention and Prevention   383

Preface

The Developmental Approach

The unifying theme in all editions of this text is that childhood psychopathology should be regarded as normal development gone awry. Thus normal development becomes the point of departure for understanding childhood disturbances. The basic challenge is that of discovering what forces divert development from its normal course and what forces either sustain the deviation or foster a return to normality. Because of this unifying theme, an entire chapter (Chapter 2) is devoted to the normal development of ten variables relevant to understanding the various disturbances to be discussed subsequently: attachment, initiative, self-control, conscience, cognition, anxiety, sexuality, aggression, peer relations, and work. The roots of a given disturbance in normal development are then presented; for example, autism is related to the normal development of infants, and reading disability is related to the normal process of learning to read. A pedagogical advantage of Chapter 2 is that students from diverse backgrounds such as education or social work can all be equally well informed concerning the development of the ten crucial variables.

Another consequence of the developmental approach is that, with some exceptions, the psychopathologies can be arranged in a rough chronological order rather than in the usual descriptive categories such as "behavioral disorders" or "emotional disorders." Autism originates in infancy, anxiety disorders in middle childhood, and eating disorders in adolescence. This arrangement, in turn, is another way of helping students to "think developmentally."

Not everyone agrees with the developmental approach used here. For some, developmental psychopathology consists of describing a given psychopathology and then dealing with the issues of etiology and prognosis. However, even though such an approach may involve charting the "developmental pathways" of various disturbances, it is basically the same as that used in descriptive psychiatry. In both instances the *crucial connection to normal development* is neglected.

Reasons for the Current Revision

MAJOR ADVANCES IN RESEARCH

Since the previous edition, a number of areas have generated a particularly impressive body of research.

The organic context. The astounding technological advances in the study of the brain (see Chapter 13) have resulted in major advances in understanding the correlates and causes of psychopathology. The text discusses these advances as related to specific disturbances. However, it also notes that, as frequently happens, research with children has lagged behind that with adults, and methodological weaknesses hamper the replicability of findings. Psychopharmacological advances are also systematically covered along with their relative effectiveness when compared with other kinds of treatment.

Attachment. Insecure attachment lies on the interface between normal and deviant attachment. While clearly not a psychopathology, it might be considered a risk for developing various disturbances. A special section (see Chapter 5) is devoted to reviewing the general literature on insecure attachment while attachment is also covered in discussions of specific disturbances.

Conduct disorder. Despite the fact that conduct-disordered children are all given the same label, researchers have recently developed reliable and clearly defined typologies of conduct disorder (see Chapter 9). The origins, developmental course, and treatment of the disorder differ according to whether children's antisocial behavior is overt versus covert, destructive versus nondestructive, or childhood-onset versus adolescent-onset. In addition, a distinct group of conduct-disordered children has been identified whose personality characteristics—callousness, remorselessness, lack of empathy—have earned them the chilling label of psychopathy.

Longitudinal research. The developmental psychopathology perspective has alerted researchers to the crucial need for longitudinal research that allows us to observe patterns of continuity and change over the life span (see Chapter 3). The dilemma, however, is that a life-span study requires the entire life span of the investigator! Nonetheless, the harvest of a number of long-term longitudinal studies is now being reaped. Important new research is emerging about the etiology and course of many disorders, including depression (see Chapter 7) and conduct disorder (see Chapter 9), as well as about the aftermath of traumatic experiences, such as maltreatment and parental divorce (see Chapter 14).

NOTABLE PROGRESS

While not quite as impressive as the research advances just described, notable progress has been made in a number of areas. *Peer relations* are finally coming into their own as important variables in understanding various psychopathologies. The development of peer relations is covered in Chapter 2, while the research is systematically covered in discussing specific disturbances. Research is bringing to the fore certain variables that underlie psychopathological development, including *emotion regulation* and *transactions* between parents and children. *Comorbidity* is no longer regarded as a confound hampering the understanding of "pure" cases but is regarded as a condition to be studied and understood in its own right. *Anxiety disorders*, after years of neglect, have begun to generate a lively research interest. An integrative model of this research is presented in Chapter 8. *Lack of progress* is also noted particularly in the area of *ethnic minorities*, where the national concern over the plight of various groups has done little to stimulate a sizable body of research on childhood psychopathology (see Chapter 15).

EXPANDED COVERAGE OF TOPICS AND CONCEPTS

The current edition expands the coverage of the *family systemic* approach, as well as modern psychodynamic approaches such as *object relations theory* and *psychodynamic developmental theory*. Barkley's model of *ADHD*, which both integrates the empirical data and conceptualizes the basic deviation in this psychopathology, has been added (Chapter 6). *Boxes* have been introduced for the first time to deal with topics that are of interest but are somewhat peripheral to the main presentation—for example, knowing the best treatment does not guarantee that children will receive such treatment (Chapter 5), or the way political pressures and parental concerns affect the data concerning the prevalence of learning disabilities (Chapter 6). In addition, *case study* material is presented in the form of vignettes and boxes. For example, Chapter 17 includes transcripts of real-life therapy sessions to illustrate each of the therapeutic modalities described.

PEDAGOLOGICAL FEATURES

Overall organization. The overall organization in terms of *contexts*—specifically, time and intrapersonal, interpersonal, superordinate, and organic variables—provides a consistent framework for ordering the sprawling research literature. In addition, each psychopathology is systematically presented in terms of a set list of *topics*; namely, definition and characteristics (including prevalence, gender, and socioeconomic and racial differences), comorbidity, developmental course, etiology, and intervention. *Key terms* ap-

pear in bold in the text and are included in a glossary at the end of the book. There are frequent *summaries* throughout each chapter, presented either in written form or as figures. Such summaries have the advantage of being more detailed and relevant than an overall, global summation at the end of the chapter. An *instructor's manual*, including additional references for case studies and illustrative films, discussion/study questions, and suggested examination questions is available for the first time.

For the Student

The goal of the present edition has not changed-namely, to enable the student to "think developmentally" about psychopathology as it unfolds from childhood through adolescence. A number of features of the new edition have been designed to provide students with a clearer pathway through the material. For example, more figures have been included in order to illustrate research findings and conceptual models, the visual appeal of the book has been increased, and key terms have been put in bold print. In addition, boxes have been added in order to provide more detailed information, to explore issues and questions raised by the research, or to bring the material alive through case studies. Review articles are often cited so students can have access to more detailed presentations of

research than is possible within a given chapter. Also there are references to literature on topics which, while important, had to be excluded because of space limitations.

Acknowledgments

We appreciate the help of many colleagues who contributed information, encouragement, and clarification to the text. In particular, Jerry Winer was an unfailingly helpful colleague in addition to being a good friend, while Mike Vasey was an invaluable aid since he seemed always to know what we did not know.

We are also indebted to many individuals at McGraw-Hill, including Sarah Thomas who steadfastly shepherded us through the valley of reviews, revisions, and deadlines. Marilyn Rothenberger, the senior project manager, was well-organized, responsive, and kept us on course. Mickey Cox, our executive editor, oversaw the many aspects of the project. Linda Biemiller, the copyeditor par excellence, cut the Gordian knot of many sentences and freed the sense of them. Connie Gardner was responsible for the photographs that enliven the test and Diane Kraut helped considerably by obtaining permissions. Marketing was in the capable hands of James Rozsa. Mary Haas and Rick Noel are responsible for the attractiveness and readability of the new layout.

Finally, we are grateful to the many reviewers of this edition. We were impressed by their thoroughness and profited greatly from their comments. In particular, we would like to thank the following individuals:

Reviewers

Sandra Azar *Clarke University, MA*

Gordon Forbes *Millikin College, IL*

Laura Freberg *California Polytechnic State University–San Luis Obispo, CA*

Paul J. Frick *University of Alabama, AL*

Lisa Green *Baldwin Wallace College, OH*

John Grych *Marquette University, WI*

Eric Johnson *Presbyterian College, SC*

Marjorie Hanft Martone *Eastern Illinois University, IL*

Terri Shelton *University of North Carolina-Greensboro, NC*

M. L. Corbin Sicoli *Cabrini College, PA*

Paul Silverman *University of Montana, MT*

Tara Wass *University of Denver, CO*

The Developmental Approach

Box 1.1

What Is the First Question You Ask?

You are a clinical child psychologist. A mother telephones your office frantic over the sudden personality change in her boy. "He used to be so sweet and then, out of the clear blue sky, he started being sassy and sulky and throwing a fit if anybody asked him to do the least little thing. What really scared me was last night he got so mad at his brother, he ran at him and started hitting him with all his might. His brother was really hurt and started screaming, and my husband and I had to pull them apart. I don't know what would have happened if we hadn't been there. I just never saw anybody in a rage like that before."
What is the first question you ask?
You are at a cocktail party and, after learning that you are a clinical child psychologist, a former star-quarterback-turned-successful-business-executive takes you aside. After

some rambling about "believing in sexual equality as much as the next fellow," he comes to the point. "Last week my son turned to my wife and announced that when he got old enough, he was going to become a girl. When my wife asked him where he got a crazy idea like that, he said that he thought boys were too rough, and he liked to be with girls more. I know he's always been a 'mama's boy,' but I'll be darned if I want any son of mine to have one of those sex changes done on him."
What is the first question you ask?
You are a clinical child psychologist conducting an initial interview with a mother who has brought her daughter to a child guidance clinic. "She has always been a sensitive child and a loner, but I thought she was getting along all right—except that recently she has started having some really strange ideas. The other

day we were driving on the highway to town, and she said, 'I could make all these cars wreck if I just raised my hand.' I thought she was joking, but she had a serious expression on her face and wasn't even looking at me. Another time she wanted to go outside when the weather was bad, and she got furious at me because I didn't make it stop raining. And now she's started pleading and pleading with me every night to look in on her after she has gone to sleep to be sure her leg isn't hanging over the side of the bed. She says there are some kind of crab creatures in the dark waiting to grab her if her foot touches the floor. What worries me is that she believes all these things can really happen. I don't know if she's crazy or watching too much TV or what's going on."

What is the first question you ask? The first question is the same in all three cases: *How old is your child?*

Overview

The three vignettes in Box 1.1 illustrate the key hypothesis that informs this text: that child psychopathology can be understood as *normal development gone awry*. Psychopathology is behavior which once was but no longer can be considered appropriate to the child's level of development. Whether the described behaviors are regarded as normal or pathological depends upon when they occur in the developmental sequence. All three of the behaviors in the vignettes presented above are to be expected in toddlers and preschoolers but would be suspect at later ages. In the first example, it is not unusual for a docile infant to become a willful, negativistic, temperamental tyrant during the "terrible twos." If the child were 10, however, his attack on his brother might well represent a serious lapse in self-control. Likewise, in the second example, it is not unusual for preschool boys to believe that they can grow up to be women, because they have not grasped the fact that gender remains constant throughout life. And finally, ideas of omnipotence and a failure to clearly separate fantasy from reality are part of normal cognitive development in toddlers and preschoolers; their presence from middle childhood on suggests the possibility of a serious thought disturbance and an unhealthy lack of contact with reality.

At the applied level, the *developmental framework* underlies the child clinician's deceptively simple statement, "There's nothing to worry about—most children act that way at this age, and your child will probably outgrow it"; or its more ominous version, "The behavior is unusual and should be attended to, since it might not be outgrown." A considerable amount of information concerning normal development must be mastered before one can judge whether the behavior at hand is age-appropriate or whether a suspect behavior is likely to disappear in the course of a child's progress from infancy to adulthood. Further, knowledge of development alerts us to the fact that some problem behavior is *normal* in the course of life; in fact, the absence of misbehavior might constitute a reason for worry. (See Figure 1.1.) The 2-year-old who is not distressed by separation from the mother, the 3-year-old who never says "No," the adolescent who never experiments with new roles—children such as these might warrant a second look.

Before we set out to analyze child psychopathology as normal development gone awry, there are a number of preliminary matters to consider. First, we must present a general *developmental framework* in order to examine various characteristics of development itself. Then we must select those *developmental variables* that are particularly important to the understanding of childhood psychopathology and trace their normal course. Our vignettes, for example, suggest that the variables of self-control, sexual identity, and cognition should be included in the list. We must also select the *theoretical models* that will contribute most to the developmental approach. As we examine various disorders, we shall discover that there are many variations on this theme of psychopathology as developmentally inappropriate behavior; therefore, we shall constantly be seeking the specific developmental scheme that best fits the data at hand.

Calvin and Hobbes   by Bill Watterson

Figure 1.1   Excessively Normal Behavior?

We shall also come across some unexpected exceptions for which the developmental framework itself does not seem to hold. Lastly, we shall examine the **developmental psychopathology** approach, which attempts to integrate these different perspectives.

A General Developmental Framework

Our general developmental framework includes the time dimension along with four *contexts* of development: the intrapersonal, interpersonal, superordinate, and organic.

Time

Some psychologists anchor change in *chronological time*. For example, Gesell and his associates (1946) link crucial behavioral changes to chronological age. In tracing the child's relation to the parents, Gesell describes age 6 as a time of high ambivalence toward the mother, with cravings for affection being followed by tantrums and rebellion. Age 7 is calm and inward; the child is companionable, sympathetic, anxious to please. Age 8 is stormy again, with the child demanding the mother's attention while being exacting, rude, and "fresh," while 9

marks a return to self-sufficiency, eagerness to please, and affectionate behavior.

A different way to conceptualize change is in terms of **stages of development**; Piaget's cognitive theory and Freud's psychosexual theory are two prominent examples of this approach. Stage theories are more concerned with change itself than with chronological age. Typically, they make two assumptions: (1) stages represent qualitative reorganizations of behavior rather than "more of the same," and (2) the sequence of stages is unalterable. Thus, something new emerges at each stage, and the order of emergence is fixed. For both Piaget and Freud, the question "How old is the child?" is not as important as "What stage is the child in?"

A characteristic of stage theories is that they often regard the *transition between stages* as a time of increased tension, unrest, and even reversion to less mature behaviors. Freud's psychosexual stages have this characteristic, and Piaget describes the child's return to immature ways of thinking during cognitive transitions. Stage conceptualizations stand in contrast to radical environmentalism, which claims that stability or instability is primarily the consequence of the experiences the child is having. The important point for our discussion is that normal development may entail built-in times of stress and upset; for example, the transitions from infancy to the preschool period and from middle childhood to adolescence are two potentially stressful periods. Knowing when disturbed behavior is part of normal growth helps the clinician decide when to tell a parent, "Most children act like that, and yours is likely to outgrow it."

There is another aspect of the time dimension. Our developmental framework implies that in order to evaluate the meaning and import of an event in a child's life, it is essential to know not only what happened but also at *which stage of development* it happened. A lengthy separation from the mother, for example, may have few adverse effects in early infancy before an attachment to her has developed but may trigger a dramatic reaction after an attachment has been formed. Being hospitalized becomes progressively less upsetting between 2 and 12 years of age and also may have different meanings, with the younger children being distressed over separation, for example, and the 4- to 6-year-olds fearing mutilation or death or viewing hospitalization as punishment.

While earlier perspectives on development proposed that there were **critical periods** during which negative effects have pervasive and irreversible effects, the current view is less deterministic and foreboding. Now it is believed that there are **sensitive periods** during which particular developmental issues come to the fore, when they are both most vulnerable to disruption and most open to amelioration (Cicchetti, 1993).

The Intrapersonal Context

The **intrapersonal context** concerns variables within the person—personality characteristics, cognitions, emotions, and so forth. This context will figure most prominently in our discussions of psychopathology, since it contains the greatest amount of developmental data. We must give careful consideration to which variables would be the most useful to study for a particular child. Traditional behaviorists would persuade us to deal exclusively with manifest behavior and to avoid all mentalistic or inferential concepts; Freudians urge us to examine the child's ego strengths and monitor the battles between id and superego; Piaget reminds us not to neglect ego-

centrism and the balancing act between assimilation and accommodation; Erikson points to the centrality of ego identity.*

The choice among conceptualizations has important clinical implications. The behavioral viewpoint leans toward a statistical and social approach to psychopathology—since there is nothing in behavior itself which designates it as abnormal, such a judgment must be based on the behavior's infrequency or on the fact that a given society chooses to label certain behaviors as psychopathological. In another society the same behavior might go unnoticed or even be regarded as a special gift. The psychoanalysts' approach, on the contrary, maintains that behavior is important only as it furnishes clues to the child's inner life; psychopathology is not a matter of behavior per se, but of the meaning of such behavior. The frequency of masturbation in adolescence, for example, is not as important as the stage-appropriateness of the fantasies that accompany the behavior.

Because our primary goal here is to understand the intrapersonal context rather than to champion a particular conceptualization of it, we use various theories to the extent that they throw light on the psychopathology at hand. Such eclecticism assumes that no single theory offers a satisfactory account of all of childhood psychopathology, while various individual theories may offer conflicting but useful accounts of specific disturbances.

The Interpersonal Context

Interpersonal variables are concerned with interactions among individuals. There are two important interpersonal contexts of child development: the family and the peer group. Among *family influences*, the parent–child relationship figures most prominently in our discussions since it is generally assumed to be the most important in determining normal or deviant development and has been most thoroughly investigated. We will consider different normal patterns of parenting and the children's behaviors associated

*It would be helpful for the reader to have the kind of general familiarity with the major developmental theories that can be gained from introductory texts in child development; see, for example, Berk, 1999.

with them, as well as such pathological extremes as neglect and physical and sexual abuse. In addition, we will look at the family systemic perspective, which highlights qualities of the whole family that influence the behavior of individuals.

Peer relations also play a significant role in normal and deviant development, although they are only now being given the attention they deserve. In our discussions we explore positive peer relations, such as popularity and friendship, and also their negative counterparts, such as rejection and isolation.

The Superordinate Context

Superordinate variables deal with aggregates of individuals taken as a unit, such as the group, social class, and culture. We will discuss the role of social class in general and poverty in particular in producing psychopathology. In addition, as we shall see in Chapter 15, cultural background is a superordinate variable that significantly affects all other contexts, as well as the risk for becoming disturbed and the definition of psychopathology itself. Thus, a number of cultures traditionally emphasize the dominance of the male rather than equality of the sexes, while in others obedience and conformity in the children are valued over self-assertiveness and independence. In some cultures symptoms are internalized or expressed as physical symptoms to a greater degree than in others, while beliefs in malevolent spirits are more common and therefore regarded as less psychopathological.

The Organic Context

The **organic context** involves various characteristics of the human body that are relevant to understanding deviant development: genetics, mechanisms involved in the body's functioning with particular emphasis on the brain, and factors determining those innate individual differences called temperament. The effects of psychological disturbances on the organic body will be central to our examination of the eating disorders bulimia and anorexia nervosa. Reversing the direction of influence, we will also consider the psychological consequences of physical illness and brain damage. Additionally, the role genetic factors play in various psychopathologies and mental retardation will concern us.

Interactions

We have been discussing these contexts of development as if they were static entities, but in fact, they are in constant *interaction* with one another. For example, the context of time interacts with all other contexts, which in turn interact with one another. Parents who are 25 years old when their daughter is born are not at the same stage in their development as they will be at 40 when she enters adolescence. In a like manner, the casual, improvised peer group of the preschool period differs from the adolescent clique, which vies with parents as the arbiter of taste in clothes, music, language, and social behavior.

In sum, our developmental framework entails the interaction of variables both at a given point in time and over time. The framework itself is presented schematically in Figure 1.2.

Models of Child Psychopathology

The developmental framework we have presented is designed to be general and comprehensive. It is intended to serve as a means of organizing what might otherwise be a bewildering array of variables used to account for a given psychopathology. It also is sufficiently general to embrace the specific theories of psychopathology that we are about to present.

There are, at present, a variety of theories that provide models of the **etiology** (origins or cause) of childhood psychopathology. While having distinctive features, the models are not necessarily incompatible. Some share common features. Others are complementary. Still others have irreconcilable differences. Each has merit; none is totally satisfactory. Therefore, we must reconcile ourselves to living with diversity and partial truths. In our own presentation of models, we concentrate on those features that will be relevant to our subsequent discussion of various psychopathologies.

The Medical Model

The **medical model** is associated with the organic context. Historically, it was a step forward in the scientific study of psychopathology because it replaced

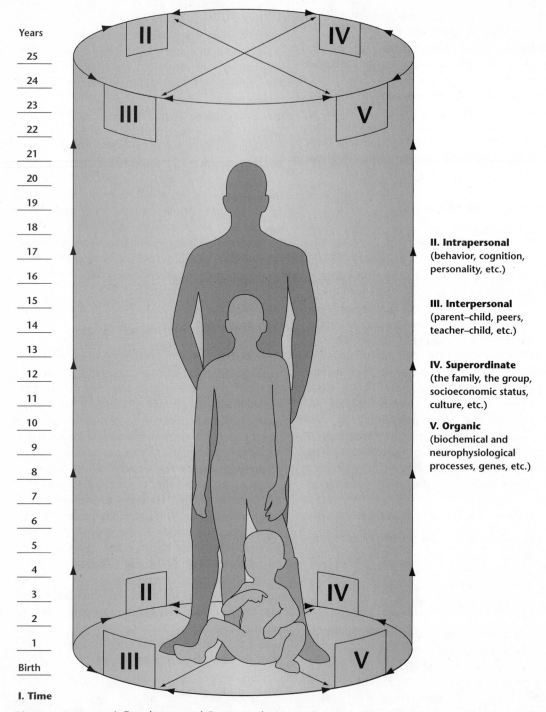

Figure 1.2   A Developmental Framework. Note: Contexts II to V Interact at All Points in Time As Well As Over Time.

the demonology of the Middle Ages. However, by its subsequent exclusion of all other etiological factors in the nineteenth century it became a roadblock to progress. Currently, the organic emphasis is more temperate and is buttressed by a more substantial body of empirical findings than it was 100 years ago. The present-day medical model consists of two components. The first involves the general hypothesis that certain psychopathologies result from organic dysfunctions. The second involves classifying psychopathological behavior in the same way as physical diseases—namely, in terms of diagnostic entities.

Organic Factors In Psychopathology

There is evidence that organic factors play a major role in certain kinds of adult schizophrenia and depression and in certain kinds of mental retardation and schizophrenia in children. Organic factors have also been implicated in the etiology of autism and in certain kinds of antisocial acting-out behaviors, hyperactivity, and learning disabilities in children, although the evidence varies in definitiveness. Further, a given psychopathology—depression, for example—may have an organic basis in some cases but may be psychogenic in others.

There are three specific models of organic etiology. In the first, *genetic* factors are responsible for the appearance of a given psychopathology. Research has centered around three related areas of inquiry. The first of these concerns *which psychopathologies* have a significant genetic component; for example, there is compelling evidence for a genetic basis of certain kinds of schizophrenia. The second area concerns the *mode* by which a genetic abnormality is transmitted. This involves tracing the path from gene to behavior and understanding all the mediators involved. The third area concerns the extent of *heritability* in a given psychopathology. Extremists maintain that genes per se determine the abnormal behavior; moderates counter that only vulnerability to a psychopathology is inherited, while its actual appearance depends on environmental conditions. For example, one child may become schizophrenic because a genetic vulnerability interacts with a series of traumatic life experiences, while another child with the same genetic vulnerability may make an adequate adjustment because of a sympathetic, caring family. (See Rutter et al., 1997, and Goldsmith, Gottesman, and Lemery, 1997.)

Proponents of the *biochemical* model seek to discover the biochemical agents that contribute to the etiology of psychopathological behavior. Again, schizophrenia has been the most frequently targeted disturbance, each new advance in medical science leading to new hope that the psychotoxic agent has been discovered. When bacteria were found to cause physical disease, it was also suggested that they were involved in mental illness; then attention shifted to viruses and, most recently, to alterations in the metabolism of certain brain chemicals, or *neurochemicals*, particularly a group of naturally occurring neurochemical substances called monoamines. Despite promising leads, the gap between chemistry and behavior, as between genes and behavior, is far from closed—and the assumption of a direct causal relation is a highly oversimplified one.

The *neurophysiological* model assumes that abnormal behavior is due to brain pathology, whether inherited, congenital, or acquired. Obviously, it overlaps with the genetic and biochemical models but includes other etiological agents such as intrauterine disease, premature birth, or traumatic brain insult. What this model does is make brain functioning the key to understanding psychopathological conditions.

At the most general level, the medical model is part of the quest to build a bridge between human behavior and human physiology. The quest is an ancient one and is currently being facilitated by astonishing advances in modern technology. However, to claim at this point that psychopathology is "nothing but" organic dysfunction would be as erroneous as claiming that it is "nothing but" a problem in adjustment. The organic context interacts with the intra- and interpersonal contexts, and knowledge of this interaction is necessary if progress is to be made in understanding the etiology of psychopathology.

The Medical Model of Diagnosis

Psychopathologies, like insects and flowers, are so diverse that viewing each separately would be overwhelming. In order to simplify their task, therefore, investigators assume that there are classes in nature and that keen observation will reveal what these classes are. But the medical model has always entailed more than a descriptive classification; diagnosis has implications for both *etiology*—the origins of the problem—and *prognosis*—the likely outcome. (We pick up this topic in Chapter 3). It is the former that is most troublesome. Emil Kraepelin, who published the landmark classification of adult psychopathologies in 1833, set the stage by assuming an organic etiology for each class of psychopathology. While it is an erroneous overgeneralization, the equation "classification = diagnosis = organic etiology" lingers on, particularly in the professional skirmishes between psychiatrists and other mental health professionals.

The Behavioral Model

Three characteristics distinguish behavioral psychology. First is the assertion that *observable behavior* comprises the basic data of a scientific psychology. The more radical theorists would limit psychology to the responses organisms make to environmental stimuli, excluding all mentalistic nonobservable variables such as thoughts, images, drives, and memory traces. More moderate theorists admit inferential concepts under two conditions: that such terms can be defined behaviorally and that their introduction facilitates the fundamental goals of predicting and controlling behavior. Next, behaviorists favor *research* conducted under highly controlled conditions, the laboratory experiment being the technique par excellence for establishing the necessary and sufficient conditions for producing the behavior being investigated. Third, behaviorists assume that a limited number of *learning principles* can account for a wide array of behavior in animals and humans. True, there are other forces at work—genetic, instinctual, maturational, temperamental—but the acquisition, maintenance, change, or elimination of much behavior can be adequately and concisely accounted for in terms of learning principles.

Principles of Learning

The three principles of learning that form the basis of the behavioral approach are classical conditioning (also called respondent or Pavlovian conditioning),

operant conditioning (also called instrumental conditioning), and imitation (also called modeling or observational learning).

In **classical conditioning** a stimulus that innately elicits a response (e.g., a snarling dog will elicit fear in a child) is successively paired with a neutral stimulus (e.g., the sound of the dog-house door opening). After a given number of pairings, the previously neutral stimulus comes to elicit the response. Such associations may explain the origins of phobias, i.e., irrational fears related to an object that is not in and of itself threatening.

In **operant conditioning** the organism operates upon or does something to the environment in order to achieve a given result. In essence, it is a process by which an organism learns to associate certain results with certain actions it has taken. These results may serve to increase or decrease the likelihood of the behavior's being repeated. The term used to designate an increase in the likelihood of occurrence is **reinforcement**. In positive reinforcement, behavior is followed by a reward; for example, the father of an 8-year-old treats his son to an ice cream cone after he has completed his chores. In negative reinforcement an aversive stimulus is removed; for example, a 10-year-old girl is excused from mowing the lawn for a month after improving her grades. The two terms used to designate a decrease in the likelihood of a behavior's being repeated are extinction and punishment. In **extinction** the reinforcement maintaining a response is removed; for example, upon her therapist's advice, a mother no longer gives in to her 4-year-old's demands every time he has a temper tantrum, and the tantrums disappear. In **punishment** a response is followed by an aversive stimulus; for example, a 3-year-old is denied dessert when she colors the walls with her crayons.

One consequence of punishment is particularly relevant to our interest in psychopathology. Once exposed to an aversive stimulus, an organism will try in the future to avoid reexposure, a process called **avoidance learning**. Avoidance learning is a double-edged sword. It protects the organism from a repeated encounter with a possibly harmful situation; for example, once burned, a 2-year-old does not continually touch the burner of a stove. But avoidance learning can also lead to unrealistic avoidance of situations after they are no longer noxious; for example, an adult may be terrified of his reasonable, benevolent boss because, as a child, he was brutally beaten by his father. Thus, avoidance prevents the individual from adopting new behaviors which are appropriate to changed circumstances.

The third learning principle is **imitation**, which involves learning a new behavior by observing and imitating another person's performance of that behavior. Thus, without any direct parental tutelage preschoolers will pretend to clean the house or hammer a nail as their parents do or will answer the phone with the exact words and intonation they have heard adults use. Children whose parents, peers, and communities model nonconstructive behavior are likely to develop antisocial ways of behaving.

Normal and Abnormal Behavior

The behaviorists' credo is that *all behavior is one* and—once allowance has been made for genetic, maturational, and temperamental factors—all behavior conforms to the basic principles of learning just described.

The *developmental dimension* is introduced in terms of age-related changes in societal expectations for behavior. In our society, a child should be toilet-trained toward the end of the preschool period, should be able to cope with school by the beginning of middle childhood, should function independent of parents by the end of adolescence, and so on. Other societies have different requirements and different timetables.

Some children grow up with the kinds of learning experiences that maximize their chances of making a successful adaptation to environmental demands, while others have experiences that minimize such an outcome. In the latter instance, behaviorists prefer to talk in terms of "*maladaptive*" rather than "abnormal" behavior to avoid any suspicion of a qualitatively different developmental outcome. Implicit in their stand is also a *cultural relativism*: what is adaptive in one society may be maladaptive in another.

In addition to being cultural relativists, behaviorists have a penchant for quantification which leads them to define psychopathology as deviations in the *frequency or intensity* of behavior. According to such a definition, psychopathologies can be grouped in terms of behavioral deficit or excess. In **behavior deficit**, behaviors occur at a lower frequency or intensity than is expected within society, so the child's social, intellectual, or practical skills are impaired. Autism, learning disabilities, mental retardation, and even juvenile delinquency are examples, the last resulting from deficient behavioral controls. In **behavior excess**, behavior occurs at a higher frequency or intensity than is adaptive to the standards of society. The hyperactive child who is in a continual state of excitement, the compulsive child who repeatedly washes his hands, and the anxious child who is constantly terrified by real and imagined dangers all show signs of behavior excess.

In addition to categorizing types of maladaptations, behaviorists have also conceptualized traditional psychopathologies in terms of learning principles. Depression may be interpreted as the result of extinction, in which significant positive reinforcements are withdrawn and the person becomes passive and hopeless. Autism, with its imperviousness to the human environment, may result from a failure of parents to acquire secondary reinforcing value.

Social Learning Theory

Social learning theorists such as Bandura (1986) expanded the scope of behavior theory in a number of ways. For one, Bandura countered the charge that behaviorism makes the individual into a mere recipient of environmental events. He proposed a process of **reciprocal determinism**, by which the person and the environment come to influence one another. He also views individuals as having an active role in determining their responses to the environment.

Bandura also expanded behavioral theory to include attention to *cognitive variables*, such as symbolic representations of experiences, expectancies, and problem solving. Bandura maintains that external events affect behavior through intermediary cognitive processes which "partly determine which external events will be observed, how they will be perceived, whether they leave any lasting effects, what valence and efficacy they have, and how the information they convey will be organized for future use" (Bandura, 1977, p. 160). His concept of **self-efficacy** reflects the fact that individuals come to anticipate not only that a given behavior will produce a given outcome, but more important, they also come to estimate whether they can successfully execute such a behavior. Such an expectation of mastery affects both the initiation and persistence of coping behavior. Thus people fear and avoid situations they believe exceed their coping skills, and they behave assuredly in those situations which they believe themselves capable of handling. Therefore, self-efficacy influences both the choice of activities and persistence in the face of obstacles.

While the cognitive dimension to social learning theory is an important contribution, one significant limitation is the lack of attention to developmental differences. Thus, we must turn to cognitive developmental theory—exemplified by the work of Piaget—to further understand childhood psychopathology.

Cognitive Models

Cognitive Developmental Theory

Piaget is one of the major figures in developmental psychology. Although much of his work focused on the development of cognition, Piaget and others that followed him have applied his research to the understanding of psychopathology. (See Cowan, 1978, and Piaget, 1981.)

Piaget makes the assumption that cognitive development proceeds in a series of orderly, fixed stages. Each stage is qualitatively distinct, and no higher type of thinking can evolve until the child has gone through all the preceding stages. The timetable may differ from child to child, but the order can never vary. (One of the clearest and most succinct expositions of Piaget's theory is found in Chapters 1 and 2 of Piaget, 1967.) Fundamental to cognitive growth is the schema (the plural is "schemata"). A *schema* is a building block of understanding, a sort of blueprint that helps the child to understand and predict the environment. The nature of the child's schemata will change over the course of development as the child's capacity to reason becomes more sophisticated, complex, and abstract.

For example, during the first two years of life the child is in the **sensorimotor stage**, so called because the vehicles for understanding are sensation and motor action. When presented with a novel object such as a rattle, an infant may determine its properties by placing it in the mouth or shaking it. Incapable of symbolization, except toward the end of the period, infants and toddlers must explore and learn by acting directly upon the environment and by using their senses. A significant development in this period is that of **object permanence**. For the first few months, infants give no evidence of missing an object they can no longer see or hold. Thus the world exists only when they are acting upon it or perceiving it. Only gradually do infants come to realize that objects exist regardless of their own actions or perceptions—objects exist "out there" as part of the environment, while actions exist "in here" as part of the self. This represents a giant step toward separating "me" from "not me."

The **preoperational** stage lasts from approximately 2 to 7 years of age and marks the appearance of *symbolic functions*. The most obvious manifestation of symbolization is language, which develops rapidly in this period. However, the preschooler tends literally to believe what he or she sees. Consequently, something that *looks* different *is* different. Piaget's well-known documentation of this thesis is the *conservation* experiment. If, before their very eyes, water is poured from a wide squat glass into a tall narrow glass, preschool children will claim that there is now more water. It looks like more, so it must be more.

The **concrete-operational** stage extends from approximately 7 to 11 years of age. The triumph of middle childhood is that children are capable of understanding the world in terms of reason rather than in terms of naive perception. They grasp the notion that objects conserve or maintain their identity despite changes in appearance. Although realistic, the child's thinking is still tied to concrete reality and bound to the here and now.

The **formal-operational** stage begins around the twelfth year and lasts into adulthood. In this period general ideas and abstract constructions flourish. The ability to draw conclusions from hypotheses rather than relying totally on actual observation is called *hypothetical-deductive* thinking. Adolescents can go wherever their thoughts lead them. They discuss, they write, they ruminate. They create a philosophy of life and explain the universe. They are also capable of being truly self-critical for the first time because they can reflect on and scrutinize their own ideas.

In order to understand the origins of psychopathology in Piaget's scheme, we must consider the processes that account for cognitive growth and progression through these stages. According to Piaget, development is fueled by the child's attempts to adapt to the environment. Adaptation occurs through two psychological processes: assimilation and accommodation. *Assimilation* refers to the incorporation of new information into an existing schema. For example, the boy accustomed to playing with his affectionate siblings may approach the first child he encounters in day care with an enthusiastic hug, assuming this new child fits his schema of "kids are great fun!" *Accommodation* refers to the alteration of a schema to take into account new information. Thus, if the new child backs away in alarm at the unexpected hug, the hugging boy may adjust his schema to a more realistic one of "*some kids are great fun.*"

In general, cognitive development is characterized by a balance, or *equilibration*, of assimilation and accommodation. Assimilation gives the world some predictability and provides the child some context in which to place new experiences so that they are not bewildering. Accommodation allows the child to take in new information and expand his or her understanding of the world. However, problems may arise when accommodation and assimilation are used to the exclusion of one another. Exclusive use of assimilation, for example, might interfere with new learning, resulting in the child's making faulty assumptions and distorting information so that it fits with preexisting notions. At the extreme, the child who is overly reliant on assimilation may be lost in fantasy, trying to bend the world to his or her own wishes. On the other hand, exclusive use of accommodation would result in the child's constantly changing his or her schema to fit with new stimuli. In the extreme, the overly accommodating child may lack a cohesive sense of self (Cowan, 1978).

Piaget's theory has generated an impressive body of research that confirms some aspects and disconfirms others. More sophisticated experimental techniques show that Piaget underestimated the infant's cognitive capacities: for example, object permanence is possible earlier in infancy than Piaget postulated. By the same token, altering tasks to make them more familiar can produce realistic rather than illogical thinking in the preschooler. Piaget's concept of stages also is hotly debated. For example, there are those who maintain that cognitive development is gradual and continuous rather than marked by qualitative advances. There is also a group of neo-Piagetians who prefer to retain and modify the theory, which, they claim, contains too many valuable and valid insights to be discarded (Lourenco & Machado, 1996).

Social Cognitive Theory

More recently, *social cognitive theorists* (also called social information processing theorists) have expanded Piaget's concepts in important ways. For example, Dodge (1993; Crick & Dodge, 1994) uses the concept of the schema to study children's behavior in the interpersonal domain. He emphasizes the fact that schemata are stable mental structures that incorporate children's perceptions of self, their experiences in the past, and their expectations for the future. Therefore, based on the lessons they draw from past experiences, schemata color children's perceptions of events, and thus their response to those events. For example, depressed children display a pessimistic *cognitive style* that draws their attention to all that is negative and consistent with their low expectations. Consequently, they behave toward others in ways that promote rejection, fulfilling their worst prophecies. In a similar manner, conduct disordered children display a hostile *attribution bias* that leads them to perceive others as ill-intentioned toward them and thus as deserving a response in kind. When conduct disordered children's aggression does in fact fuel others to respond negatively to them, their hostile schema is confirmed. The social cognitive perspective makes an important contribution to the understanding of the development of depression and conduct disorder, as well as informing effective interventions for those children, as we will see.

Psychoanalytic Models

Classical Psychoanalysis

The *classical psychoanalytic* school of thought is concerned with discovering the dynamics—the basic motives, the prime movers—of human behavior. This concern with intrapersonal forces clearly sets psychoanalysts apart from the behaviorists, with their concern for the environmental factors that shape behavior, and cognitive psychologists, who focus primarily on conscious processes and reason. As with the other approaches discussed so far, our coverage of Freud's work will not be comprehensive; instead, we will concentrate on the two aspects of classical psychoanalysis most relevant to understanding childhood psychopathology—the structural and psychosexual models.

The Structural Model   Freud's tripartite conceptualization of the human psyche—**id**, ego, and superego—is known as the *structural model*.

According to classical Freudian theory, the **id** is the source of all psychic energy, which in turn derives from biological drives. Among these, **libido** and **aggression** are prepotent in their implications for personality development. The drives of the id are alogical, demanding immediate and complete satisfaction, and its thought processes are irrational and magical. Developmentally speaking, the infant is an id-dominated creature, concerned only with reducing the tensions generated by physiological needs, having no capacity for delay and no awareness of the realistic parameters of the world he or she has entered.

At about 6 months of life, the **ego** arises from the id's need to balance gratification with reality. Unlike the id, the ego is endowed with *ego functions*, such as perception, memory, and reasoning, which enable it to learn realistic means of satisfying the id. The ego also is the source of the **defense mechanisms** that help a child tolerate intense emotions and cope with anxiety.

The third structure, the **superego**, comes into its own at about 5 years of age. The superego contains the moral standards which the preschooler takes over from his or her parents and which becomes an internalized judge of right and wrong behavior. In

case of transgression, the superego punishes the child with guilt feelings. The superego can be absolutist and implacable, demanding strict obedience to its standards of proper behavior. From middle childhood on, then, the ego must find ways of obtaining as much id gratification as reality will allow without arousing the superego, which in its way is as irrational in its demands as the id.

In structural terms, therefore, psychopathology is a matter of *internal conflict* and imbalance between id, ego, and superego. If the id is excessively strong, either because of innate endowment or a weak ego and superego, the result is impulsive aggressive or sexual behavior. If the superego is excessively strong, the result is overly inhibited behavior in which the child is tortured by guilt feelings for the slightest transgression, real or imagined.

The Psychosexual Theory   Freud's **psychosexual theory** assumes that eroticized intimacy exists throughout the life span, adult sexuality being only the culmination of a process begun in earliest infancy. Freud assumed that there is an inevitable progression in the parts of the body that predominate as sources of pleasure. These are familiar to us as, in turn, the oral, anal, phallic, latency, and genital stages. Equally important, each progression of libido is accompanied by a psychological change in the intimate relations with the parents or primary caretakers.

During the **oral stage**, feeding is associated with the first emotional attachment or object relation. This initial intimacy is particularly potent in setting the tone for future intimacies. Sensitive, loving caretaking engenders a positive image both of mother and of self; caretaking marked by distress and frustration will engender an image in which love is mixed with anxiety and rage. In the **anal stage**, conflicts over autonomy and parental control of behavior are primary. If parental training or discipline is punitive, unloving, or coercive, the toddler becomes rebellious and stubbornly resistive or anxious and overly compliant. The **phallic stage** in boys is associated with the wish to be the exclusive love object of the mother, which results in rivalry toward the father. This is referred to as the **Oedipus complex**. Resolution of the Oedipus complex requires that the child relinquish this infantile wish for exclusive love and, through identifying with the same-sex parent, content himself with the idea that "I am not your rival, I am like you." The *latency* stage offers a period of relative calm in which attention is turned to mastery of developmental accomplishments other than sexuality.

In adulthood, mature *genital* sexuality is a psychological achievement that involves components of the early stages of psychological development. From the oral period comes the need for and ability to provide tender care; from the anal period comes a willingness to negotiate the many areas of adult responsibility; from the phallic period comes pride in achievements and a desire to share those achievements with the partner; from the Oedipal period comes confidence that one is as good as the next person. Further, mature sexuality entails a mutuality, a givingness, and an appreciation of the partner's point of view that is counter to the egocentricism of the early stages.

Psychosexual theory contains a rich source of clues as to both the nature and form of psychopathology. **Fixations** lay the groundwork for psychological disturbances, either because they hamper further development or because they increase the possibility that, having progressed, the child will return to the fixated, less mature stage. This latter process is called **regression**. Excessive fixations can result either from inadequate gratification, such as inadequate love during the oral period, or excessive gratification, such as an overprotective parent during the oedipal phase. The stage at which fixation occurs determines both the severity and the kind of psychopathology. In general, the earlier the fixation, the more severe the psychopathology, so a child who is either fixated at or regresses to the oral stage is more disturbed than one who is fixated at or regresses to the anal stage.

The concept of *defense mechanisms* is another important contribution psychoanalytic theory makes to our understanding of development. The nature of the defenses used to ward off anxiety—whether primitive or sophisticated, rigid or flexible, brittle or robust—gives us important clues as to the person's emotional maturity and level of functioning.

As a developmental theory of psychopathology, the psychoanalytic model has no peer. Yet it is also mentalistic, inferential, exceedingly complex, peppered with contingencies, and lacking just those clear behavioral referents and accessibility to tightly controlled research that behaviorists claim are essential to a scientific psychology. It is also generally the case that neither the preferred method of investigation, namely psychoanalysis, nor the data it produces are subjected to empirical scrutiny. But to conclude, as some have done, that psychodynamic concepts are unscientific because they cannot be tested by the usual controlled procedures is unjustified. Psychoanalytic theory has generated more research than any other personality theory, and while older reviews claimed that the theory was totally lacking in scientific credibility, a recent review found it to be faring surprisingly well (Greenberg & Fisher, 1996).

Ego Psychology

Freud himself was most interested in exploring the motivational aspects of his theory, in particular the sexual and aggressive drives and the workings of the unconscious. The **ego psychologists** made a major revision in the classical theory by postulating that the ego initially is endowed with its own energy and can function autonomously rather than being subservient to the id. The emphasis of ego psychologists such as Erikson (1950) is on the reality-oriented, adaptive functions of the psyche. In addition, Erikson enlarges the interpersonal context of development from the nuclear family to the larger society.

Briefly, Erikson's developmental model focuses on stages of *psychosocial* development, which closely parallel Freud's stages of psychosexual development. Each of these stages represents a crisis, the resolution of which sets the individual on a particular developmental trajectory.

During the first year of life, the quality of the caregiving environment contributes to the child's sense that the world is either a safe and loving place or a disappointing and dangerous one. This is the crisis of *trust versus mistrust*. In the second year, conflicts with caregivers over such emotionally charged issues as toilet training can lead children to develop a sense of either self-pride or self-doubt; this is the crisis of *autonomy versus shame*. In the

4th to 5th year, the way in which the Oedipus complex is resolved can contribute to children's comfort with their own impulses or else the sense that they are fundamentally "bad" for having such desires. This is the crisis of *initiative versus guilt*. At age 6, children begin to confront the tasks of school and socialization with peers, contributing to a sense of either competence or inadequacy; this is the crisis of *industry versus inferiority*. The last stage of Erikson's we will describe is associated with adolescence, in which the tasks are to form a clear sense of identity and a purpose in life. This is the crisis of *ego identity versus role confusion*.

Erikson's framework enhances our understanding of psychodynamic development by laying out a clear progression of stages and the tasks that must be accomplished for the child to proceed through them apace, as well as by pointing out the social context in which child development takes place. We will refer to his work at many points, particularly when we consider the developmental challenges associated with adolescence.

Object Relations Theory

A "third revolution" in psychoanalytic thinking is represented by **object relations** theory. Object relations actually refers to a diverse collection of psychoanalytic perspectives that share an emphasis on the importance of affectionate *attachments* in human development. Relatedness—in essence, love—is seen as the primary motivator of human behavior quite apart from Freud's primitive drive of sexual gratification. The label "object relations" refers to the relationships with people—the objects of our affections—that determine what kind of individuals we become. (For more detail, see Greenberg and Mitchell, 1983.)

A major figure in this tradition is John Bowlby (1973), whose theory of attachment has had a powerful influence on the conceptualization of normal and deviant development and has generated considerable research. We will refer to his work in subsequent discussions, and we will describe the development of attachment in more detail in Chapters 2 and 5.

A second important figure is Margaret Mahler, whose theory provides much of the bedrock for object relations (Mahler, Pine, & Bergman, 1975). Over

the course of the first 3 years of life, Mahler proposes, children go through a developmental process called **separation-individuation**, which takes place in a series of stages.

At birth, Mahler believes the child cannot differentiate between self and other. Lacking a sense of difference between what is internal and external, the child is aware only of fluctuations in experience, of good states and bad states. This is termed *normal autism*. Within the first 2 months of life, however, there is a dawning recognition that there is a caregiver who responds to the infant's needs. However, the infant experiences the self and caregiver as being joined, as two parts of one organism; Mahler refers to this as the **symbiotic phase**. Inevitably, however, there are moments when caregiver and child are not in perfect synchrony. By about 4 months of age, such experiences—of delay, frustration, mismatched goals—help the child to recognize that the caregiver is a separate person with her or his own feelings and intentions. A crucial sign that the child has entered this **differentiation phase** is a preferential smile, which indicates both recognition of the caregiver and a specific bond to her or him. Toward the end of this stage, the infant shows stranger anxiety, indicating that the caregiver is clearly differentiated from other adults.

The next phase begins at about 8 months, ushered in by the development of crawling. For the first time, the infant can move under his or her own steam and is intoxicated with his or her own abilities and sense of omnipotence. A new world of exploration opens up to the infant; however, the caregiver is still at the center of it. The child moves in ever-widening circles around the caregiver, returning to this "safe base" at regular intervals in order to "emotionally refuel" through physical contact. Mahler calls this phase **practicing**, to reflect the infant's active experimentation with independence versus attachment. Games involving going away and coming back again are a source of great pleasure and fascination for the infant: saying "bye-bye," playing peekaboo, running away from the caregiver while looking back to make sure she or he is following to swoop the infant up.

The bubble, however, is burst in the middle of the second year of life. Two developments contribute to the child's move to the next phase. First, there are the beginnings of representational thought, with which comes a greater awareness of the vulnerability associated with being separate: for example, if one wanders away, one might get lost; if mother does not follow, one might not be swooped up into her loving arms. Secondly, as children experience more bumps and bruises in their encounters in the world, there is a deflation of the feeling of omnipotence. This is an emotional turning point for the child as well as for the caregiver–child relationship. The child who needs the caregiver's attention and protection is also frustrated and resistant to her or him. The **rapprochement** phase is marked by ambivalence toward the caregiver, as the infant alternates between clinging to the caregiver and pushing the caregiver away. Everyday frustrations yield to mood swings and temper tantrums. Children at this stage show strong reactions to separation from the caregiver, including protest, anger, depressive mood, and inability to play in the caregiver's absence.

Central to object relations theory is that the child's sense of self develops in the context of the relationship with the caregiver. The quality of that relationship communicates important messages about the child's own worth and the trustworthiness of others. Thus, the child's major task in the rapprochement phase is to develop an *internal representation* of the relationship. Children who experience warm and sensitive care internalize an image of the loving parent—the "good object"—and therefore of themselves as lovable. In contrast, children who experience poor parenting internalize an image of their caregiver as angry and rejecting and come to see themselves as unworthy and incapable of inspiring love.

All children sometimes feel anger or frustration with their caregivers, and all parents are sometimes "bad objects" who disappoint their children. Therefore, some negative feelings are inevitable during development. However, the magical thinking of preoperational children leads them to misbelieve that their negative thoughts and feelings can have real consequences. For example, young children are likely to believe that their anger can actually harm someone, destroying the loving mother or transforming her into the bad object of their fears. Because the child has trouble holding onto a sense of security about the mother when she is absent, rage at the

mother can be frightening. A child who thinks "I wish she'd go away" might worry "What if she does go away?" In such a case, ambivalent and angry feelings toward the mother interfere with the ability to sustain a positive image of her in the child's mind, threatening the internal image of the good mother and with it the child's positive self-image and sense of security.

In order to protect positive internal representations from these strong negative feelings, Mahler proposes that during rapprochement children defensively split their experience of the caregiver into good and bad images, as if there were two caregivers in the child's emotional world—the one who is the source of comfort and good feelings and the one who is frustrating and depriving. Similarly, the sense of self is split in two—the child who is good and lovable and the child who is bad and evokes the caregiver's ire. Thus, **splitting** is a defense mechanism that protects the infant's positive internal representations from feelings of anger and aggression. Thoughts of the loved and loving caregiver—and the lovable self—are safely locked away from negative emotions.

While splitting is a normal part of the young child's development, it is a primitive defense that does not allow us to experience ourselves and others as fully fleshed, complete persons. Therefore, the final stage of separation-individuation requires that we overcome it in order to achieve emotional **object constancy**: the ability to integrate both positive and negative feelings into a single representation. Thus, it is possible to be angry with the caregiver and yet still love her or him, to be disappointed with oneself and yet still believe one is a worthwhile human being. Object constancy is related to but is significantly different from Piaget's concept of object permanence. They have in common the fact that, like object permanence, object constancy depends on the *cognitive* capacity to recognize that an object out of sight still exists. However, object constancy goes further in requiring the recognition that an *emotion* we are not currently experiencing—for example, affection for someone who has just enraged us—still exists.

A criticism of Mahler's work, as indeed of most psychoanalytic theory, is that it is based on clinical observation and speculation rather than objective data. Most recent work on self-development in infancy suggests that revision of this formulation may be in order. For example, evidence suggests that normal infants do not begin their lives lacking any sense of separation between self and other. Rather, from the very beginning of life infants demonstrate an emergent capacity for self-organization as well as for engaging in the complex choreography of interpersonal relationships (Stern, 1985). However, while Mahler's theory may not be an accurate depiction of *normal* infant development, it appears to be a useful way of describing the origins of some forms of *psychopathology*. (See Greenspan and Greenspan, 1991. Fonagy and associates, 1995, evaluate psychoanalytic theory's contributions to developmental psychopathology.)

The Family Systemic Model

The last major theoretical orientation we describe is the family systemic perspective. While many other theories acknowledge the importance of family relationships, what sets the systemic model apart is that it views the entire family as the unit of analysis. The **family** is conceptualized as a *system*, a dynamic whole that is greater than the sum of its parts. Systems have certain characteristics. For example, they are coherent and stable, and they have a self-righting tendency, termed *homeostasis*, that allows them to maintain their structure even in the face of change. Like psychoanalytic theory, the systemic perspective is composed of many different schools of thought, but in this case the core idea that unites them is that individual personality is a function of the family system. We will concentrate on the work of Salvador Minuchin and colleagues (1974, 1996), whose perspective is called *structural family theory*.

According to Minuchin, one of the ways in which being part of a family helps us to develop is by allowing us to participate in a number of different relationships simultaneously. Within the larger family system, there are naturally occurring *subsystems* that join some family members and differentiate them from others. For instance, the parents form a *marital* subsystem, which is based on the complementary roles that husbands and wives

fulfill: to be a romantic couple, to raise their children, and to play a leadership role in the family. *Parent–child* relationships comprise another subsystem, based on the nonreciprocal needs and responsibilities that parents and children fulfill for one another; for example, while children turn to their parents for comforting and advice, and parents expect their authority to be respected, the reverse usually is not the case. *Siblings* form yet another subsystem, based on their shared status as the children in the family. Yet siblings, too, are differentiated from one another; for example, special privileges might be granted to the eldest child and extra latitude to the youngest. Thus, through the various roles they play, family members simultaneously experience feelings of belonging and feelings of independence from others.

What allows these subsystems to function well are the **boundaries** that separate them. Clear boundaries differentiate the subsystems from one another, define the roles of individuals, and allow family members opportunities to meet their developmental needs. Appropriate boundaries are also permeable and adaptable; that is, they allow both emotional contact and independence, and change as the needs of family members change over development. For example, the parent–child relationship should become more reciprocal and egalitarian as children enter young adulthood.

Failure to maintain appropriate boundaries can cause families to become confused and dysfunctional. For example, overly *rigid* boundaries foster separation between family members or maintain strict role differentiation among them: "father knows best," "children should be seen and not heard." While rigid boundaries can foster a sense of independence and self-sufficiency, they can also make it difficult for family members to reach across barriers to communicate their feelings or obtain emotional support. Individuals may feel lonely and unsupported in rigidly structured families and may lack a sense of belonging.

At the other extreme, absent or unclear boundaries result in **enmeshed** relationships. Family members who are enmeshed do not differentiate between one another, even between parent and child. Mutuality and togetherness are emphasized at the expense of individuality and separateness. While family members may enjoy the feelings of belonging and sharing that ensue, extreme enmeshment may interfere with individuals' freedom to have their own autonomous thoughts and wishes. An attempt by a family member to individuate may be perceived as a threat to the harmony of the family system and thus may arouse anxiety or resistance. For example, the youth in an enmeshed family who expresses a desire to go away for college may precipitate a family crisis.

In Minuchin's view of family structure, the heart of the family is the *marital subsystem*. The kind of intimacy, emotional support, and mutuality that characterize a healthy couple's relationship is unique; for example, the emotional needs an adult romantic partner fulfills are different from those fulfilled by parent–child and sibling relationships. Therefore, Minuchin especially emphasizes a need for clear boundaries around the marital dyad. When this boundary is violated, children become involved in their parents' marital relationship in inappropriate ways, and psychopathology may develop. Minuchin describes the different problematic family systems as *rigid triangles*, which may take one of three general forms, described next (see also Kerig, 1995).

First, a **parent–child coalition** arises when one parent involves the child in an alliance that excludes the other parent. Such a relationship occurs when a parent encourages the child to behave disrespectfully to the other parent, or it may take the form of an overly intimate and enmeshed relationship between one parent and the child. This family dynamic may create a *parentalized child* who is burdened by the assumption of such developmentally inappropriate tasks as offering emotional support and acting as an intimate confidante to a parent. Minuchin gives the example of a family in which the unhappily married mother becomes depressed. The oldest daughter takes over preparing meals and caring for her younger siblings, covering for the mother so the father won't know the extent of her dysfunction. A number of negative consequences follow from this scenario. Because the daughter has taken on responsibilities beyond her years, she begins to feel stressed and overwhelmed. In addition, because the younger siblings do not have direct access to their mother and cannot receive the care and attention they need from her, they begin to misbehave. Further, because the parents aren't communicating directly with each other, they cannot resolve their marital problems. In sum, while the intentions of the parentalized child are good and her self-sacrifice might help the family to cope in the short term, in the long term the family is an increasingly distressed and unhappy one.

In the second type of rigid triangle, called **triangulation**, the child is caught in the middle of the parents. In this case the child attempts to maintain a coalition with each parent, either to be a peacemaker or go-between or in response to pressure from parents to side with one or the other. Minuchin describes this as the most stressful family dynamic for the child, whose attempts to be close to either parent may be interpreted as disloyalty by the other. This family form may be particularly evident during conflictual divorces, such as in the "tug of war" over child custody (Buchanan, Maccoby, & Dornbusch, 1991).

The third kind of triangle, **detouring**, is the most subtle of the triangular family forms because there may be no apparent conflict between the parents. Instead, they may insist that their marriage is "perfect" and that the only problem in the family is their child's disobedience or delicate nature. As Minuchin got to know this kind of family better, however, he noticed that the parents never spent any time together as a couple but rather devoted all their time and energy to caring for their child. Then he began to observe covert ways in which the parents supported and encouraged their child's problems. Further, the only time the parents acted conjointly is when they were responding to their child's "special needs." It became apparent to Minuchin that in such cases having a troubled child was meeting some need for the parents.

Minuchin concludes that some unhappily married couples attempt to avoid acknowledging their marital problems because they do not know how to resolve them; instead, they try to deflect attention from them or detour around them. Having a troubled child, therefore, serves a function in the family by providing the parents with a problem external to their relationship on which to focus their attention. Because they are united when attempting to respond to their "problem child," detouring allows the couple to maintain an illusion of harmony. Further, detouring couples are motivated to covertly reinforce children's behavior problems in order to maintain the homeostasis in the family system. The detouring may take two forms: *detouring-attacking* when the child is viewed as troublesome or "bad" and *detouring-supportive* when the child is viewed as needy or delicate. The child in this family triangle is called the *identified patient* because he or she is the one who is overtly symptomatic.

Minuchin's perspective widens our scope of vision to include the larger context in which child development takes place. Not only is the individual psychology of the child important, as well as his or her relationship with parents, but the entire *family system* is important and must be taken into account. Another important implication of the family systemic approach is that the location of psychopathology is not in the child, or even in the parents, but in the *relationships among them*. Lastly, the systemic perspective reminds us to take a *functional* approach to interpreting problem behavior. An aggressive, acting-out child may appear to be disturbed; however, another possibility is that the child's misbehavior serves a function in the family system, perhaps representing an attempt to meet appropriate developmental needs in a pathological environment. Thus, the family systems perspective fits well with our definition of psychopathology as normal development gone awry.

Comparing and Integrating Models

There are many points of *divergence* among the models we have presented. Freud was primarily concerned with drives, the unconscious, and mental events, while ego psychologists concentrate on psychosocial adaptation, and object relations theorists emphasize the primacy of interpersonal relations. Traditionally, behaviorists wanted to banish the intrapersonal context with all of its mentalistic baggage, substituting an environmentally oriented objective psychology. Cognitive psychologists reintroduce mental terms such as schemata in order to

understand how children interpret their experiences with the environment.

There are also some points of *convergence*. For example, even such apparently opposing models as object relations and family systems theories agree that relationships are central to personality development. Further, each of these models has undergone its own developmental process, which in many cases has led to an expansion of common ground shared with other models. The medical model no longer couches issues dichotomously as, for example, heredity versus environment. Instead, there is a recognition that organisms develop in an environmental context that interacts with and affects organic variables. The psychoanalytic model has shifted from emphasizing the intrapersonal to appreciating the interpersonal context, while the behavioral model has changed in the opposite direction. With the increasing overlap and convergence among the different models of psychopathology, the possibility of—and need for—a unified model emerges. Developmental psychopathology represents the beginning steps toward creating such an integrative model.

Developmental Psychopathology

Developmental psychopathology is not a theory in and of itself; rather, it is an approach to understanding the emergence of psychopathology over the life span. (Our review follows Cicchetti and Cohen, 1995, except where noted. The classic paper is Sroufe and Rutter, 1984.) Developmental psychopathology is an *integrative* approach that incorporates different theoretical perspectives under one umbrella to produce an understanding of the development of the whole person (Achenbach, 1990). (See Figure 1.3.) Instead of focusing only on behavior, cognition, unconscious processes, and so forth, the developmental psychopathologist pays attention to each of these variables in order to understand how they contribute to the formation of psychopathology—or of emotional health. Although a number of definitions of developmental psychopathology have been offered, they often overlook the latter point, that both adaptive and maladaptive

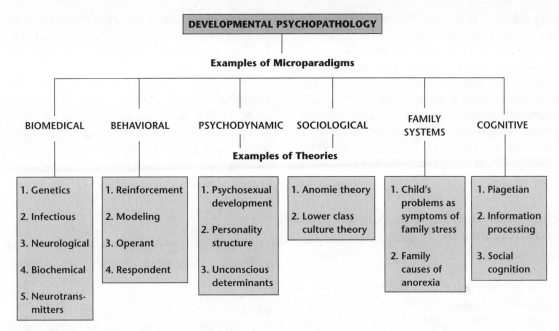

Figure 1.3   The "Umbrella" of Developmental Psychopathology.

From T.M. Achenbach Conceptualization of developmental psychopathology. In M. Lewis & S.M. Miller (eds.), *Handbook of Developmental Psychopathology*. Copyright 1990. Reprinted by permission of Plenum Publishing Corporation.

development are relevant to the field. Therefore, we offer the following as a concise definition:

Developmental psychopathology is the study of the developmental processes that contribute to the formation of, or resistance to, psychopathology.

Now we turn to the specific features that define the parameters of the developmental psychopathology approach.

The Organizational Perspective

Although developmental psychopathology does not follow any unitary theoretical model, it is guided by an *organizational perspective* (Cicchetti et al., 1988). First, the organizational perspective views the human organism in a *holistic* way, as an integrated and dynamic system in which all domains of development—the cognitive, social, emotional, and biological—are in continual interaction with one another. Second, development itself is considered to be *hierarchical*; psychological growth is a

process of increasing complexity and organization, such that new structures emerge out of those that have come before.

The key to understanding development in this perspective is to attend to the tasks at each stage of development—termed *stage-salient issues*—that must be confronted and mastered. Whether these issues are resolved in adaptive or maladaptive ways influences future adaptation. Erikson's ego theory provides a good example of this construct; for example, whether the infant resolves the first developmental crisis by forming an attitude of trust or mistrust toward the world will influence his or her capacity to satisfactorily resolve the salient issues of the next stage.

The implication of the organizational perspective is that stage-salient issues affect the individual in such a way that their effects are carried forward into the next stage of development. Thus, previous areas of vulnerability or strength may influence the way in which individuals handle stress and crisis and may shape the way in which they adapt to future life challenges. However, the consequences of previous stage-salient resolutions are *probabilistic* rather than *deterministic*. In other words, while previous development might have a shaping or constraining effect on subsequent adaptation, increasing or decreasing the likelihood of psychopathology, such an effect is not set in stone. Many intrapersonal and environmental factors might intervene in order to change the course of development.

The Continuum Between Normal and Abnormal Development

Another important characteristic of developmental psychopathology is that it assumes that there is a *continuum* between normal and abnormal development. Underlying every life course—whether it is a healthy or maladaptive one—are the same fundamental developmental principles. Therefore, it is important to have a clear conceptualization of adaptive development in order to understand how development might go awry (Sroufe, 1990). The challenge is to understand *why* development takes one path rather than the other in the case of an individual.

Risk, Vulnerability, and Protection

Risk Factors

A **risk** is any condition or circumstance that increases the likelihood that psychopathology will develop. (Kazdin et al., 1997, summarize the literature on risk factors.) There is no comprehensive agreed-upon list of risk factors, and they span all contexts. In the organic context risk may involve birth defects, neurological damage, inadequate nutrition, or a parent who has a disorder with a known genetic component. In the intrapersonal context risk may be in the form of low intelligence, low self-efficacy, or poor self-control. In the interpersonal context risk may take the form of parental neglect or abuse or poor peer relations. In the superordinate context risk may arise from poverty. While single risks have limited predictive power, multiple risks have a cumulative effect; for example, children with two alcoholic parents are more than twice as likely to develop problems as are children with one alcoholic parent.

Vulnerability

While risk may determine disturbance directly, **vulnerability** is the term used for factors that intensify the response to risk. A helpful way to distinguish the two is in terms of the statistical concepts of main effects versus interactions (Zimmerman & Arunkumar, 1994). A risk factor is associated with an increased likelihood of psychopathology for all children exposed to it; thus, it emerges as a main effect in statistical analyses. (See Figure 1.4.) A vulnerability, in contrast, increases the likelihood of psychopathology *particularly* for those children who are susceptible to it; thus, it emerges as an interaction effect.

Rutter (1990) identifies a number of vulnerability factors. Gender is one; for example, while both boys and girls are adversely affected by family stress, boys have a higher rate of behavior problems than girls. Temperament is another vulnerability factor; children who are difficult to care for are more often targets of parental irritability, criticism, and hostility than are easily managed children which, in turn, increases the risk of subsequent disturbance. Rutter's list also includes the absence of a good relationship with parents, poor planning ability, a lack of positive school experiences, lack of affectionate care, and poor social skills. Further, at the superordinate level, children whose personal characteristics do not match societal expectations—such as the shy child in a culture that values boldness—may be more vulnerable to risk.

Protective Factors and Resiliency

Since not all children who are at risk become disturbed, the challenge for researchers is to discover the factors that promote or maintain healthy development. These are called **protective factors**, and the children who make a good adjustment in spite of being at high risk are called **resilient**. Protective factors within children might include good intelligence, an easygoing disposition, and the presence of com-

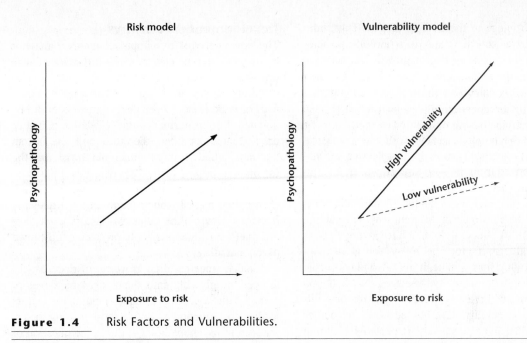

Figure 1.4   Risk Factors and Vulnerabilities.

petencies valued by themselves or society, whether they be academic, athletic, artistic, or mechanical. Protective factors in the family might include the presence of a loving, dependable parent; a parenting style characterized by a combination of warmth and structure; socioeconomic advantage; and social support from an extended family network. Protective factors in the superordinate context might include involvement with prosocial institutions, such as the church or school (Masten & Coatsworth, 1998).

Protective Mechanisms

Rutter (1990) proposes that we go beyond listing protective factors to attempt to understand what *accounts* for the protective power of such variables; for example, what is it about intelligence or socioeconomic advantage that protects against psychopathology? The term he uses for these processes is **protective mechanisms**, and he has identified four of them on the basis of theory, observations, and empirical research.

The first mechanism, *reduction of risk impact*, means that variables act so as to buffer a child from exposure to risk. For example, negative peer influ-

ences are powerful risk factors for children growing up in gang-ridden neighborhoods. However, parents who supervise and regulate their children's peer group activities and who guide them in their choice of play and friendships can reduce the likelihood of delinquency.

The next mechanism is *reduction of negative chain reactions*. Protective factors may provide their effects through their influences on relationships. For example, a temperamentally easy child is less likely to be the target of his stressed parent's anger; consequently, the child is less likely to develop behavior problems, thereby de-escalating the parent's stress and lessening the anger. Thus, a vicious cycle of negative reaction from parent to child is averted.

Next, factors that *promote self-esteem and self-efficacy* help children feel they can cope successfully with life's problems. These qualities are enhanced by secure and supportive personal relationships and by task accomplishments, such as school achievement, that foster self-confidence.

The fourth protective mechanism is *opening of opportunities*. Development involves many turning points that offer a chance to reduce the impact of risk factors, and the resilient child is the one who takes advantage of these opportunities. Thus, adolescents who choose to stay in school allow themselves more opportunities for growth and achievement than dropouts do, and those who pursue their unique artistic talents or interests have more opportunities for personal fulfillment than do those who deny their talents and "follow the crowd."

Table 1.1 provides examples of risks, vulnerabilities, protective factors, and protective mechanisms derived from the literature. However, it is important to keep in mind that no variable *inherently* falls into one category or another. A particular variable can be construed in different ways, depending upon how its effects unfold. While poverty acts as a general risk factor for many forms of psychopathology, for example, it may also play the role of a vulnerability factor by increasing the likelihood that a child will react negatively to a stressor. Children whose families have few economic resources may be the most negatively impacted by certain stressful life events, such as a house fire in which all their possessions are lost.

Developmental Pathways

The emergence of psychopathology over the life course is conceptualized in terms of **developmental pathways**, or trajectories. The initial question in constructing a pathway is this: At what point in time and for what reasons does development begin to be diverted from its normal course? Not all at-risk children become disturbed; therefore, both the factors that make children more vulnerable to risk *and* the factors that protect them from risk must be uncovered. In those cases in which protective factors are outweighed by risk and vulnerability, the question becomes, How do the latter two factors work their mischief over time in order to produce a full-blown psychopathology?

Finally, since children grow out of disturbances as well as growing into them, charting developmental pathways involves understanding the factors leading to extinction as well as those leading to persistence of psychopathology; this is the question of *continuity versus discontinuity*. The final challenge is to explain the data in terms of developmental

Table 1.1   Examples of Risks, Vulnerabilities, Protective Factors, and Protective Mechanisms

Context	Risks	Vulnerabilities	Protective factors	Protective mechanisms
Organic	Genetic disorders Pre-and perinatal influences Neurological damage Inadequate nutrition	Difficult temperament	Easy temperament	

Intrapersonal	Low intelligence
	Low self-esteem
	Low self-efficacy
	Low self-control
	Insecure attachment
		Gender
		Poor planning ability
			Intelligence
			Competence
			Sociability
				Reducing risk impact
				Reducing negative
				    chain reactions
				Promoting self-esteem
				    and self-efficacy
				Opening up
				    opportunities

Interpersonal: Family	Marital or familial
	    disharmony
	Abuse or neglect
		Poor relations
		    with both parents
		Lack of affectionate
		    care
			Positive, stable care
			Competent adult
			    models
			Parental supervision	

Interpersonal: Peer	Antisocial peer
	    network
		Poor social skills	Positive relationships
			    with peers	

Superordinate	Poverty	Personal characteristics
		    that clash with societal
		    ideals/expectations
			Positive relationships
			    with other adults
			Cultural tolerance
			    for diversity	

Sources: Masten and Coatsworth (1998), Robins (1972), Rosenblith and Sims-Knight (1992), and Rutter (1990).

principles and to understand the mechanisms and processes responsible for propelling the child from one step to the next along the path to a particular disorder (Sroufe, 1997). In addition, sometimes pathways cross to produce **comorbidity**, or the co-occurrence of two psychopathologies. In the past, clinicians tended to focus on a single disturbance and researchers tried to study "pure" cases, regarding the existence of other psychopathologies as potential confounds. However, it has become increasingly clear that certain disturbances, such as anxiety and depression or conduct disorders and hyperactivity, frequently occur together.

Developmental pathways involve more than simply charting a particular behavior over time. Sometimes the behavior itself changes over the course of development. For example, aggressive behavior in childhood predicts not only adult antisocial acting out but also adult alcoholism and schizophrenia. In certain instances, the changes in behavior involve what are called **transformations** (Sroufe, 1990). This means that there is continuity in an underlying disorder while its behavioral manifestations change over time. For example, an insecurely attached infant may be overly independent of the mother but in preschool may be overly dependent on the teacher. The inferred insecurity is consistent but is expressed differently at different ages (see Chapter 2).

The implications of developmental pathways for prevention and intervention are significant. The more we learn about the earliest risk factors, the better able we will be to design effective preventive programs. And at least for those psychopathologies showing a progression in seriousness of disturbance, earlier intervention is likely to result in more effective treatment. In our subsequent examinations of specific psychopathologies in the chapters ahead, we will chart developmental pathways and give more detailed accounts of the examples cited above.

Although the terms are not used consistently in the literature, we will reserve *developmental pathways* to refer to research that charts the journey children travel to a disorder; for example, how does a child come to be depressed? In contrast, the term *developmental course* will be used in reference to the progression of the disorder once it has developed; for example, what does the future hold for the child who is depressed? Developmental course is also referred to as *prognosis*; however, "prognosis" is a term derived from the medical model that implies that disorder is a fixed and static state. Because the developmental psychopathology literature yields much evidence for variability and diversity of outcome, we have chosen "developmental course" as a preferable term.

Equifinality and Multifinality

Equifinality refers to the idea that a number of different pathways may lead to the same outcome (Cicchetti & Rogosch, 1996). For example, a variety of factors may lead to the development of depression, including genetics, environmental stress, and cognitive style. In contrast, **multifinality** states that a particular risk may have different developmental implications, depending on such contextual and intraindividual factors as the child's environment and his or her particular competencies and capacities. So, for example, loss of a parent may result in depression in a child whose previous relationships with caregivers have been marked by insecurity, but it may result in conduct disorder in a child who faces additional environmental stress such as exposure to family violence.

Multideterminism

Following from the notions of equifinality and multifinality, developmental psychopathology proposes that the etiology of any psychopathology is **multidetermined**. The search for a single cause—as in "juvenile delinquency results from neglectful parents"—is simplistic and futile. Rather, psychopathologies have multiple causes.

The Question of Specificity

As we have noted, developmental psychopathology models have become increasingly complex, recognizing the interactions amongst multiple factors in the origins of a disturbance. However, the multiplicity of factors implicated in each psychopathology creates a new problem, that of *specificity*. The specificity question refers to whether a particular risk factor is *specific* to the development of a particular disorder, as opposed to increasing the likelihood of some sort of *global* psychopathology. For example, as we will see, certain risk factors—such as insecure attachment—may be precursors to such different forms of child psychopathology as depression, suicide, anxiety, conduct disorder, and substance abuse. Therefore, the question remains as to whether knowing about a given risk factor, such as a history of broken parent–child bonds, is helpful in predicting a child's developmental outcome beyond a rough notion of "bad input, bad output."

One of the snarls we encounter in attempting to untangle the specificity question is that most of the research devoted to identifying risk factors has focused on only one particular disorder; for example, a particular study might ask, Is insecure attachment a risk factor for childhood depression? The problem with this strategy is it does not tell us whether that same risk factor might predict other forms of psychopathology equally as well. Thus, one researcher's discovery of a relationship between insecure attachment and depression needs to be interpreted in the light of other research demonstrating that insecure attachment is a risk factor for conduct disorder. There is a need for studies that look at multiple risk and protective factors, as well as multiple outcomes, in order to discriminate between specific and general effects. (For an example of this kind of design, see Asarnow et al., 1994.)

Transactions

An additional concept that helps us to understand how multideterminism in psychopathology comes about is that of transactions. A **transaction** can be defined as a series of dynamic, reciprocal interactions between the child and his or her family and social context. Rather than viewing etiology as a matter of simple linear cause and effect—due to organic factors, such as genetics, or interpersonal variables, such as parenting style—developmental psychopathology sees development as a function of a complex interplay between the child and the environment over time (Cicchetti et al., 1988; Sameroff, 1995).

Let us look at an example. A mother gives birth to a delicate and premature infant, which is a source of some anxiety. Her anxiety during the first few months of the child's life causes her to be hesitant and inconsistent in her parenting. Subsequently, the child develops some irregularities in his sleeping and eating habits, making his temperamental style a more difficult one. This difficult child taxes the mother's parenting skills even more, and she begins to withdraw from interaction with him. As he enjoys less interaction and verbal stimulation with his caregiver, the child develops language delays that affect him when he enters preschool. Thus, a complex developmental sequence can be seen, in which parent and child both influence one another's behavior (Sameroff, 1995). (See Figure 1.5.)

There are three important features of transactions that help to define them. The first is that the nature of the transaction *changes over time*. This means that a particular kind of relationship, such as that between the parent and child, is the product of a series of exchanges during which they gradually shape one another's behavior over the course of development. Thus, the observation the clinician makes at any given moment—that the mother responds with helpless distress to her youngster's oppositionality, for example—is the product of a long history of their influence on one another. The second feature of transactions is that they are *reciprocal*, which means that development is not simply a factor of a combination of influences, some arising from the child and some arising from the environment, but rather that the child and environment influence one another, each changing as a function of the other. The third feature of transactions is that they are *dynamic*. There is a "live" quality to them in that something new happens in the chemistry of the relationship. In the case of parent behavior, for example, Sameroff (1994) states, "In order for a genuine transaction to occur, the parents must be influenced by the infant's behavior to do something they would not have done if the child had behaved otherwise" (p. 7).

Transactional processes do not always lead to negative developmental outcomes. Consider the following clinical scenario concerning a severely depressed mother and her young child: When initially observed, this girl had a tendency to be somber and reserved, herself showing some signs of emerging depression as would be expected of a child of a depressed parent. However, during her early struggles to learn to

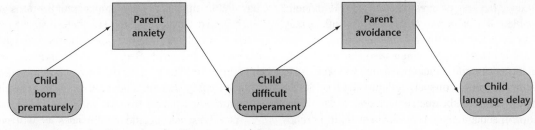

Figure 1.5   An Example of a Transactional Process.

From: A.J. Sameroff. General systems theories and developmental psychopathology. In D. Ciechetti and D.J. Cohen (eds.) Developmental Psychopathology. Vol 1: Theory and Methods. Copyright 1995. Reprinted by permission of John Wiley & Sons, Inc.

dress herself, the toddler discovered that there were behaviors she could perform that could coax a smile from her mother. For example, when her mother was distressed, the child might come into the room in outlandish getups—her father's boots on her feet, her mother's panties on top of her head. The mother began to respond more warmly and positively to the child, who in turn began to increase her repertoire of "silly" yet heartwarming behaviors. The feeling that she was a successful parent helped to lift the mother's depression, while the experience of being "mother's little sunshine" brightened the child's affect. Thus, through the transactions between them, mother and daughter shaped one another's behavior in more adaptive ways. Despite all the risks associated with maternal depression, the mother and child developed a positive relationship, which decreased the mother's depression and increased the daughter's chances of staying on a healthy developmental course.

In sum, like the family systems approach, developmental psychopathology perceives psychopathology not as something a person "has" but rather as the result of a series of successive adaptations to the environment (Sroufe, 1997). Further, transactions can provide a powerful tool for intervention in cases in which they can be interrupted or redirected.

Conceptualizing Childhood Psychopathology

As we have seen, the different models of psychopathology have different ways of conceptualizing childhood disturbances. It will be helpful to review the major conceptualizations here since we will be returning to them in our subsequent presentations.

Behavioral Deficit and Behavioral Excess

The major way of conceptualizing childhood psychopathology in the behavioral model is in terms of behavior that differs from that which is socially expected in terms of a significantly lower or higher frequency or intensity. The former is called a *behavioral deficit*, the latter a *behavioral excess*. While the developmental dimension is not explicit in the definition, it is implicit since the expectations of society change with the age of the child (e.g., oppositional behavior flourishes in the toddler period, declines in middle childhood, and increases in adolescence). As norms for expected behaviors change with age, so do criteria for judging behavior as a deficit or an excess.

Psychopathologies of Timing

The psychoanalytic model conceptualizes psychopathology in terms of problems in timing that significantly interfere with the normal course of development. *Fixation*, also called developmental arrest, is the persistence of normal behavior beyond the point at which it is developmentally appropriate. *Regression* is the return to developmentally early forms of behavior that are no longer appropriate.

In later discussions we will consider three more psychopathologies of timing: developmental delay, asynchrony, and precocity. In **developmental delay** development proceeds at a pace significantly slower than normal. In **asynchrony** there are markedly uneven rates of progress among developmental variables. For example, children with autism may speak in grammatically correct sentences and yet say things that are meaningless to the listener. In such cases, the communicative aspects of speech lag behind the ability to grasp grammatical rules. Finally, **precocity** involves an accelerated rate of development that can be associated with psychopathology. An example of precocity is the attempt by substance-abusing youth to take on adult roles and responsibilities before they are developmentally prepared for them.

The Quantity Versus Quality Distinction

Most conceptualizations of psychopathology claim that there is continuity between normal and deviant behavior. The disturbed child is not a "breed apart" but has much in common with well-functioning children. Thus, psychopathology is regarded as a *quantitative* departure from normality. Both the be-

havioral and psychodynamic conceptualizations are quantitative. However, there are some disturbances that seem to have little or nothing in common with normal development. Because of the discontinuity, it is impossible to extrapolate from one to the other. In such cases the psychopathology is regarded as *qualitatively* different from normality.

As we discuss specific disturbances we will systematically raise the question of what conceptualization(s) best fit the research findings and will frequently refer back to this summary.

Having outlined our general developmental framework, we are now ready to describe the normal development of the intra- and interpersonal variables that will have a bearing on our subsequent discussions of the various childhood psychopathologies. Then, in Chapter 3, we will be able to build a bridge to the psychopathologies themselves and learn which ones tend to persist and which ones tend to disappear with time.

Chapter **Two**

Normal Development

If we are to understand childhood psychopathology as normal development gone awry, we must first chart normal development. But having decided not to follow any one of the current models in favor of a looser, more inclusive framework, we still need a conceptual guide for selecting variables to discuss. Fortunately, it is possible to draw up a list of variables crucial to a child's well-being so that, if anything goes radically wrong with any one of them, we can seriously consider the possibility that the child is disturbed.

First there is a group of variables binding the child to the human environment. Prominent in this group is the bond of love that develops between infant and mother in the first year of life, which is called *attachment*. Throughout childhood and life the ability to feel deeply about and become attached to another individual lies at the core of the human experience. Attachments that become erotic result in *sexual relationships*. At a more moderate and diffuse level, the human bond may be expressed in *peer relations*. If something goes rad-

ically awry with any of these bonds—if, for example, the loving overtures of a parent are met with rage or profound indifference, if sexual intimacy is a source of terror rather than pleasure, if the child is socially isolated and friendless—we would rightfully be concerned.

Another basic variable involves *initiative*, or self-reliant expansiveness. The bright-eyed infant scanning the environment for new and interesting sights epitomizes this urge to explore and to master. In many of their ventures children are free to follow their own interests; but increasingly with age they are required to stay with a task whether or not they want to. We shall call this combination of initiative and necessity *work*, the special setting for work during childhood being the classroom. If, instead of having initiative and the capacity for work, the child is apathetic or distracted or fearful of any kind of venturing out, or if there is a persistent, self-defeating rebelliousness at being told what to do no matter how benign and reasonable, again we have cause to be concerned about the child.

Perhaps the most obvious variable for us to examine is *self-control*, with the issue of control of *aggression* looming particularly large. Socializing children often involves curbing their preferred behaviors; with time, children take over this monitoring, controlling function themselves, eventually adding another mechanism, the *conscience*, which is specifically concerned with judging the moral content of behavior. Self-control also involves the generation of *anxiety*, which serves as one of the principle deterrents to performing socially disapproved actions.

Finally, it is essential for the child to understand the physical and social environment as well as himself or herself, a variable we shall call *cognition*. Reality can be distorted by magical ideas in the first few years of life because of cognitive immaturity. It is essential that these distortions be replaced by realistic understanding; the persistence of bizarre, magical ideas—such as a 10-year-old's belief that he can hear through his belly button and can control television pictures by his thoughts—is a sign of disturbed development.

In sum, the ten variables we have selected in our developmental approach to childhood psychopathology are attachment, initiative, self-control, conscience, cognition, anxiety, sex, aggression, peer relations, and work.

Attachment

The bond of love between parents and child is pivotal to development throughout childhood. We shall refer to **attachment** in many of our discussions of psychopathology—the failure of attachment to develop in infancy, the rupture of attachment by death or divorce, the contamination of attachment with excessive anger or anxiety, the atrophy of the bond through neglect. It is essential, therefore, to understand how attachment is established in infancy and how it develops throughout childhood.

The Formation of Attachment

Human beings have the longest period of helpless infancy of any species. In order to survive they must be cared for by more mature human beings for many years. Thus, attachment takes place in the caregiving situation; the kind of care infants receive influences, to a significant degree, the kind of attachment they form. While most of our information comes from the infant's attachment to the mother, psychologists have begun to recognize and investigate the importance of father–infant attachment as well. (For a summary of research on attachment, see Field, 1996.)

The development of attachment to the primary caregiver follows a reasonably predictable course. Neonates are initially programmed to respond to stimuli emanating from other people. By 2 weeks of age they prefer the human voice over other sounds, and by 4 weeks prefer the mother's voice over other human voices. In the second month, eye contact is established. Between the third and fourth months, these precursors of attachment reach a cognitive and emotional climax: the pattern of stimuli comprising the human face is perceived with sufficient cohesiveness and detail to be distinguished from other patterns of stimuli and, equally important, is a source of special delight. The percept "people" and the affect "pleasure" are fused into what is called the *social smile*. The social smile is indiscriminate and hedonistic: infants light up when anyone hits upon that combination of grimacing and vocalizing and bouncing and tickling which delights them. On their part, adults will go through all kinds of antics to elicit such a smile. The simple fact that delighting the infant is highly rewarding to the adult is one of the strongest guarantees that an attachment will be formed.

Between the sixth and ninth month, indiscriminate responsiveness gives way to *selectivity* as infants show a strong preference for the mother and other special caregivers. This inner circle of caregivers can elicit greater delight than anyone else and can most readily comfort the infant in times of distress. In addition, two negative affects come to the fore. The first is *separation anxiety*, which arises when the mother or other special caregiver leaves. *Stranger anxiety*, or the fear of unfamiliar persons, is not actually as prevalent at this age as it was once believed to be. However, the indiscriminate pleasure that marked the era of the social smile is replaced with a more cautious, wary response to unfamiliar adults.

Sensitive caregiving involves stimulation as well as comforting.

Separation anxiety has implications for many aspects of normal and deviant development. First, intense *anxiety* is part of normal development. Indeed, there are those who claim that the absence of such anxiety is suggestive of deviant development; for example, some children reared in impersonal institutions will subsequently respond to anyone who shows them affection while failing to form an enduring relationship and being unaffected by loss. We also learn that, from the beginning, intense affection and intense anxiety over loss go hand in hand. Dare I love deeply and risk abandonment? is a question that comes up throughout life and that each individual must answer in his or her own way. Certain delinquents are difficult to help because they fear that if they let themselves become emotionally attached to a therapist, the therapist will desert them as other adults have done in the past.

Hostility is also a consequence of attachment, although it has received less attention than anxiety. In reunions after separations, such as hospitalization, it

is not unusual for infants and toddlers first to ignore their parents and then to become unusually angry and touchy for the next few days or even weeks. Infants and toddlers are cognitively incapable of grasping the reality of the situation, such as the fact that the separation was for good reason and unavoidable; all they can understand is that they needed the mother and she was not there. In their eyes she becomes a "bad" mother and the target for anger (see Bowlby, 1973).

Thus we see that attachment, even in its normal manifestations, is never purely positive; it is inevitably a mixture of love and anxiety and fear and anger. It is when the negative components begin to dominate that the chances for deviant development are increased.

Caregiving

A few comments concerning caregiving are relevant to the discussions to come. The traditional image has been that of the mother caring for a totally helpless, passive infant. However, there is now convincing evidence that an infant from the beginning actively takes in and tries to cope with his or her environment (see Sroufe, 1996). Each infant also has a particular *temperament*—an individualized tempo and activity level, a characteristic mood and adaptability, a special set of vulnerabilities and resiliencies, preferences and dislikes (see Rothbart, Posner, and Hershey, 1995). Psychologists have verified what parents have known for many years— namely, that certain infants are temperamentally easy to care for while others are difficult, regardless of the kind of care they receive. Thus caregiving is now viewed as an interaction between parent and infant in which each has to accommodate the other. If all goes well, the result is a mutual enhancement of development in which not only the infant grows but also the parent grows in terms of her or his caregiving skills, feelings of competence, and sources of gratification.

Caregiving itself is conceptualized as a combination of *comforting* and *stimulation*. Comforting and relieving the infant's distress are the basis of the traditional view of caregiving. More recently, however, attention has turned to the caregiver's role as stimulator. The very fact that he or she is human means that the parent is a source of fascinating and delightful visual and auditory stimuli for the infant. The parent is also a mediator of stimulation, bringing the infant in contact with a variety of interesting sights and sounds such as rattles and rings and mobiles. The sensitivity to the infant's needs and the promptness and appropriateness with which the caregiver responds to them are more important than the sheer amount of time he or she spends with the infant. And through comforting and stimulation, the parent provides both the emotional security and the varied environmental input necessary to normal development.

Caregiving influences the kind of attachment that will develop. If parents are sensitive in their caregiving, if they are alert to the infant's needs and react quickly and appropriately, the infant is more likely to develop a *secure* attachment. A securely attached infant responds positively to his or her caregivers and, because of their consistency, is confident they will be there when needed. Such infants develop a loving, trusting relationship. Closeness does

not result in dependency and clinging, however; on the contrary, securely attached infants explore the environment confidently. Well-cared-for infants are also apt to develop a positive self-image and confidence in their ability to cope successfully with problems as they arise. There is evidence, for example, that the securely attached infant becomes the effective problem solver as a toddler and the flexible, resourceful, and curious preschooler who is enthusiastically involved with school tasks and peers (Bretherton, 1996).

On the other hand, deviations from sensitive caregiving result in a number of kinds of *insecure* attachments, which we will review in Chapter 5. We will return to the topic of secure-insecure attachment again when we discuss the extremes of deviant caregiving represented by abuse and neglect in Chapter 14.

Another reason attachment is important is that it is a prerequisite for successful *socialization*. Infants and toddlers have no natural desire to be neat and clean or to respect property; on the contrary, they want to explore and mess and possess at will. Why, then, should they ever give up the pleasure of immediate gratification? Because the love of the parents is at stake. The behavior that the parents regard as good is rewarded with love; the behavior that they regard as bad is punished by the withdrawal of love. In normal development, toddlers and preschoolers for the most part acquiesce, because the love they receive compensates for the autonomy they lose. But already we can sense the possibilities for abuse of parental love. Suppose parental demands are excessive and entail total subjugation, as may have happened during childhood in someone who became anorexic (Chapter 11)? Or suppose demands are made with inadequate compensations of love, as may have happened during the childhood of someone who became a juvenile delinquent (Chapter 9)? We would rightly suspect that chances of deviant development would be increased.

Finally, attachment is linked with *exploration*. Securely attached infants explore the environment confidently because they are venturing out from a "secure base." Insecurely attached infants are either hesitant and uncertain or defensively avoid the caregiver thereby depriving themselves of what should be the caregiver's growth-promoting mediations. Thus, attachment sets the stage for the self-reliant expansiveness that we call initiative, which, as we shall soon see, is the pivotal development of the toddler period.

Attachment—the need to maintain proximity, distress upon separation, joy at reunion, grief at loss, and security seeking—may be an important component of subsequent affectional ties. It plays a part in friendship (Cassidy et al., 1996) and is a central feature of adult sexual partnerships (Hazan & Shaver, 1994).

Initiative

If attachment is central in the first year of life, **initiative** is central in the second. Toddlers literally and figuratively stand on their own two feet and turn their backs on their caregivers. Intoxication with a newfound sense of power propels them into a stage of willfulness and negativism. The same 2-year-old who, a few months ago, was terrified at the mother's departure, now counters her every request with an imperious "No!" For her part, the mother finds that she must increasingly restrict her child, who is into everything and all over the place. Thus begins the conflict between freedom to do what one wants and conformity to the requirements of society, a conflict that will last a lifetime.

Origins of Initiative

Initiative in the toddler period has a number of roots in infancy, the primary ones being *curiosity* and *exploration*. The old image of the infant's life as totally dominated by physiological needs such as hunger, thirst, and sleep is erroneous. (The landmark article is White, 1959.) As soon as there are periods of alert wakefulness, neonates begin exploring their environment. Their searching eyes and receptive ears lead the way, followed increasingly by motoric exploration as they outgrow their initial clumsiness. In the first month of life exploratory behaviors are remarkably mature, characterized by orientation, concentration, perseverance, gratification with success, or annoyance at failure. Infants are as hungry for stimulation as they are for food, their endless

fascination undergirding the giant steps taken in comprehending their environment.

But infants not only want to take in the environment; they want actively to *control* it as well. When 8-week-old infants who were placed in a specially designed crib discovered they could make a mobile move by turning their heads, they repeatedly did so with great glee (Watson and Ramey, 1972). Around 20 weeks of age infants begin to take the initiative in establishing, sustaining, and renewing contact and interaction with the mother, lifting their arms in greeting, clinging to her, following her when they are able to crawl. Other evidence of an early need to control are the many "battles" between mother and infant: 8-month-olds who have had the experience of holding the bottle, thereby taking feeding "into their own hands," may strongly resist attempts to make them drink from a cup. The "battle of the bottle" is subsequently replaced by the "battle of the spoon," as 1-year-olds insist on feeding themselves, although their ineptness results in bringing oatmeal to the nose or ear or hair as often as to the mouth. And just over the horizon—during the toddler period—lies the "battle of the potty."

There is an important *cognitive* component to this desire to control the environment. Neonates are too immature cognitively to grasp the relation between their actions and environmental events. By the middle of the first year the connection has been established, but—and this is the important point—it is an unrealistic, magical one. After discovering that their vigorous, jerky movements can make a mobile on the crib dance, they proceed to repeat these movements and look at the television set or the clock, expecting them to dance also. Again, infants whose attentive parents come when they cry initially believe that their cry actually produces a parent's presence. But how could it be otherwise? How could infants grasp the reality of the sequence—that the father was in another room, that he heard the cry, that he could decide to ignore it or come to the infant, and that he chose the latter? While unable to grasp reality, infants can make sense of their immediate experience, which is, "I make jerky movements, objects dance; I cry, father appears; ergo my actions alone cause environmental events to happen." In short, infants have an *omnipotent* concept of causality. While such thinking would be a sign of severe psychopathology in adolescence, it is not only developmentally appropriate in infants but represents a significant advance over the prior period, when the notion of causality itself was not grasped (see Piaget, 1967).

The desire to venture out in infancy continues into the toddler period, with locomotion opening up a whole new world for the toddler to explore and master. It is important to underscore the spontaneous, intrinsically rewarding nature of this exploration, in contrast to the socializing parents' directives and prohibitions, many of which go against the grain. Also, as toddlers explore they continue to develop the concept of the *self-as-agent*, and as their explorations are successful and pleasurable, they develop self-confidence and a healthy self-pride. This self-reliant venturing out, which we call initiative, has variously been labeled autonomy, mastery, competence, and independence by others. While the definitions may vary, all the terms share an emphasis on the self-as-agent and on expansiveness.

We now have a better appreciation of why anything that impedes the toddler's self-reliant exploration is apt to be resented and resisted. Typically, such resistance takes the form of *negativism*, which may be an active noncompliance (shouting "I won't" or throwing a tantrum) or a passive noncompliance (ignoring the parent or doing nothing). Evidence indicates that the toddler will bridle no matter how sweetly reasonable the parent is (Wenar, 1982). Just as the self-centered infant knew only, "Mother is not here when I need her," the self-centered toddler knows only, "My parents are preventing me from doing what I want to do." The terrible twos are, by and large, of the toddler's own making. By the same token, exasperated parents can take comfort in the fact that, while nothing they do will prevent or shorten its reign, negativism is usually "outgrown" in a couple of years.

We have emphasized the toddler's physical venturing forth because it sets the stage for the conflict between compliance and defiance which will figure so prominently in our discussion of psychopathology. However, not all initiative is physical. Producing varied sounds seems to have an intrinsic appeal, and the toddler soon learns that certain sounds, made either fortuitously or in imitation of adult speech, have the magical property of eliciting responses of great delight from parents. "Baby's first word" typically becomes the occasion for rejoicing. The toddler also learns that words as well as gestures can be used to communicate, subsequently realizing that they are also more versatile and require less effort. In addition to their communicative value, words and language play an important role in self-control and cognition. Subsequently, when we turn to the psychopathologies, we shall learn that the absence or breakdown of communicative speech plays a crucial role in two of the most severe childhood disturbances—autism and schizophrenia (Chapters 4 and 10).

Developmental Course of Initiative

The toddler's fascination with objects continues throughout childhood. "What is it?" and "How does it work?"—questions first asked about ordinary household objects—are asked about objects in the wider physical environment and, eventually, in outer space. In the realm of tools, the toy hammer is replaced by the tool kit, the blunt scissors by the sewing machine, the toy cash register by the computer. The 10-word vocabulary of the 19-month-old increases to the 80,000-word vocabulary of the first-year high school student. In the social realm, playing house with the preschoolers next door develops into the complex gangs and cliques of adolescence.

Initiative has important consequences for the self. First, discovering what one can do plays a central role in *self-definition*. The 3-year-old who announces excitedly, "I can jump," and the high school sophomore who says, "I was elected class treasurer," have defined themselves through their various ventures. Second, children who succeed in their ventures are accruing a sense of *self-worth* and pride. Such healthy self-love can be as important as a healthy love relation with another person.

Objective studies of self-worth or self-esteem provide us with an account of its development in terms of progressive differentiation (see Harter et al., 1997). Before middle childhood, children cannot verbalize a general self-esteem, although they do differentiate two separate kinds, one deriving from being socially acceptable, the other from being competent. They fail to differentiate specific sources of self-esteem within these categories, however, so being good at schoolwork, for example, is fused with being good at sports. By middle childhood a *global sense of self-worth* begins to emerge along with three specific areas of competence: *academic*, *physical*, and *social*. Adolescence brings the additional areas of *close friendship*, *romantic appeal*, and *job competence*. However, these areas have different import or salience; making all A's or being beautiful may mean everything to one child but be a matter of indifference to another. Thus, salience is closely linked with self-worth: children with high self-worth are competent in areas that are important to them, while children with low self-worth are not competent in areas that are important to them (Harter, 1986). From middle childhood on, self-evaluation is also closely related to behavior: academic self-esteem predicts school achievement, curiosity, and motivation to take on challenges, while social self-esteem is related to being liked by peers.

Adolescence may be a period that presents special problems in regard to initiative. The adolescent must negotiate the transition from dependent child to independent adult, a transition made difficult by conflicts at many levels. Parents, for their part, want their adolescent to take on responsibilities, earn money, date, and be popular, but they also want to retain their role as guides to proper conduct and as decision makers. And adolescents themselves are ambivalent about independence. Physically, sexually, and intellectually they are young adults, not children; they have the capacity to work and devote themselves to an ideal; they are socially sensitive and can form meaningful friendships. Yet they also sense that they might lack the experience, judgment, and psychological maturity to use such assets appropriately. Finding a niche in a complex society and mastering the intricacies of vocational and sexual relations are often a matter of trial and error. Setbacks are apt to bruise their egos and remind them that, if they are no longer children, they are also not quite adults. When all the conflicts within and between family members boil over, the last of the normal battles of childhood is fought—the battle of the generations. The parents view the adolescent as wild, disrespectful, and amoral, while the adolescent sees the parents as old-fashioned, self-centered, and lacking in understanding.

Like attachment, initiative is fundamental to normal development. A significant diminution of initiative is an ominous sign, while a lack of initiative, as evidenced in autism, indicates severe psychopathology. Curiosity, which lies at the heart of initiative from earliest infancy, requires the ability to focus attention on interesting stimuli on the task at hand. When there is a deficit in this ability to pay attention, healthy initiative may be replaced by the scattered behavior of the hyperactive child (Chapter 6). A special kind of loss of initiative called *learned helplessness* may underlie the defeatist attitude that characterizes depression (Chapter 7). Both the normal negativism of the terrible twos and the normal transitional problems of adolescence can become exaggerated to the point where they block further growth (Chapter 5) or, in the case of adolescence, eventuate in drug use and abuse (Chapter 11).

Self-Control

In a number of psychopathologies, **self-control** figures more prominently than any other single variable. In early childhood, control of bodily functions is a basic aspect of self-control. Toddlers may fail to learn to control their bladders and continue to wet their beds at night or, less frequently, their pants during the day. Eating may get out of control, leading to obesity at one extreme or self-starvation even to the point of death at the other (Chapter 11). When self-control is excessive in middle childhood, the groundwork for certain internalizing disorders is laid; when self-control is weak, acting-out behavior such as aggression and conduct disorder may result (Chapters 8 and 9). Therefore, it is essential that we understand the development of self-control from infancy to adulthood and the factors that enable the child to achieve normal self-control.

Factors Involved in Self-Control

Socialization

The exploring toddler reaches for a vase on the living room table. Her mother rushes in and yells "No!". She withdraws. She may reach again, and again be scolded. The pattern is repeated many times.

Figure 2.1   Internalization, "For Better or Worse."

Source: © Lynn Johnston Productions Inc./Dist by United Features Syndicate, Inc.

Eventually, however, as the toddler approaches the vase and begins reaching for it, she suddenly stops, shakes her head, and even says, "No." Then she withdraws. She never again reaches for the forbidden vase. She has achieved self-control. However, teasing out the factors involved in this achievement and understanding how they work is far from simple. Let us examine certain important ingredients.

As our example suggests, there are *rewards* and *punishments* on the path to learning self-control. These may be physical: a toddler who puts his toy away at mother's request may get to lick the chocolate-pudding bowl, while another toddler who colors the wall with mother's lipstick may go without dessert. Rewards and punishments may also be psychological. As we have just seen, *attachment* en-

ables parents to bestow love for conformity to their directives; it also enables them to withdraw love when disobeyed, thus creating a situation akin to separation anxiety in the child. Thus the child's concern about being love-worthy is a major force in the motivation to seek parental approval and avoid parental disapproval by complying with socializing directives. Ultimately, however, the goal is not that children be guided merely by concern for external rewards and punishment but rather that they come to *internalize* parental values and, therefore, be intrinsically motivated to behave in prosocial ways (see Kochanska, Aksan, and Koenig, 1995.)

In rewarding and punishing the child, parents convey more meaning than they intend, since they are also serving as *models* of either controlled or uncontrolled behavior. Children are adept imitators. A parent can be taken aback on hearing a toddler, during a pretend telephone conversation, turn around and shout, "Be quiet! Can't you see I'm on the phone?" in an exact duplication of the parent's own words and tone of voice. (See Figure 2.1.) In certain instances, modeling or imitation may serve to undermine socialization; for example, a father who punishes aggression by beating his child serves as a model of uncontrolled behavior.

Cognitive Variables

A host of *cognitive variables* are involved in self-control. At the simplest level, toddlers must be able to grasp *cause-and-effect* relations and remember what behavior leads to reward or punishment; only then will they be able to apply past experiences to the situation at hand. They must then be able to integrate fragmentary experiences into guiding *principles* of behavior. *Language development* plays a pivotal role in the process of achieving higher levels of self-control. The simple "No" becomes, "Mustn't touch"; and then, "That's Jimmy's truck, not yours"; and finally, "You shouldn't take other people's things without asking them first." As the directives become increasingly complex, they guide behavior in an increasingly wide variety of situations. And as the cognitively developing child can both verbalize these directives and grasp their meaning, built-in controls become increasingly effective (Kochanska et al., 1996). Since "saying things to oneself" is one aspect of thinking, we can see why thinking is regarded as the ally of control: the very fact that the child must stop and think serves to check immediate action, while the content of the thought itself serves to guide behavior into socially acceptable channels. As thinking serves its delaying and guiding functions, control is enhanced.

Emotion Regulation

Lastly, self-control involves an aspect of emotional development termed **emotion regulation**. Thompson (1994) defines emotion regulation as the ability to monitor, evaluate, and modify one's emotional reactions in order to accomplish one's goals. Thus,

emotion regulation requires the capacity to identify, to understand, and, when appropriate, to temper one's feelings. This might involve *inhibiting* or subduing emotional reactions; for example, children might breathe deeply or count to 10 in order to calm themselves in the face of distressing feelings. But emotion regulation also may involve *intensifying* or maintaining emotional arousal in order to meet a goal. For example, children might "pump up" their anger in order to gather the courage to stand up to a fearsome bully; or children might enhance positive emotions by recalling or reenacting a pleasant experience. In essence, emotion regulation allows the child to engage in *self-management*—to be, as one child put it, "boss of my own self."

As Cole and colleagues (1994) point out, emotion regulation can go awry in two ways: through *underregulation* or through *overregulation*. In other words, the inability to express one's feelings can be as problematic as the inability to control them.

Although the concept of emotion regulation is being introduced here under the heading of self-control, it is also an essential component of many other developmental variables will we discuss. For example, emotion regulation is central to coping with *anxiety* and moderating the expression of *aggression*. Similarly, the child's ability to control extreme states of negative and positive arousal allows *peer relations* to go smoothly. We will encounter the concept of emotion regulation in our review of the literature on a number of forms of psychopathology, including depression, conduct disorder, and eating disorders, as well as the consequences of abuse. (For more detail see Cicchetti and Izard, 1995.)

Parental Discipline

One of the most influential typologies of parenting style is the one developed by Baumrind (1991). She views two independent dimensions of parenting as essential: warmth/support and control/structure. By assessing parents on these two dimensions, she derives four parenting styles.

The **authoritarian** parent is high on structure but low on warmth; consequently, this parent is demanding, controlling, and unreasoning. The implicit

The origins of self-control.

message is, "Do what I say because I say so." If parents discipline in a punitive, rejecting manner, their children tend to become aggressive, uncooperative, fearful of punishment, and low on initiative, self-esteem, and competence with peers. The **permissive** parent is high on warmth without accompanying structure. This parent is undemanding, accepting, and child-centered and makes few attempts to control. The result may be a dependent, irresponsible, aggressive, "spoiled" child. **Authoritative** parents, in contrast, are high on both warmth and structure. They set standards of mature behavior and expect the child to comply, but they are also highly involved, consistent, loving, communicative, willing to listen to the child, and respectful of the child's point of view. Their children tend to be self-reliant, self-controlled, secure, popular, and inquisitive. Lastly, the **neglectful** parent rates low on both warmth and structure; consequently, this parent is described as indifferent, uninvolved, or self-centered. Lax, unconcerned parenting is the breeding ground for antisocial behavior. Self-centeredness on the parents' part is associated with self-centeredness in the children, along with impulsivity, moodiness, truancy, lack of long-term goals, and early drinking and smoking.

The literature on parental discipline furnishes several leads as to which kinds are detrimental. Extremes of rejection, brutality, neglect, and permissiveness should be avoided. An inconsistent alternation between neglect and harsh punishment is apt to result in antisocial behavior; the child receives no love to make self-control worthwhile, while parental punitiveness foments rebellion and serves as a model of impulsive hostility. Excessive indulgence with few restrictions is apt to produce children who are impudent, demanding, and disrespectful tyrants at home, are bossy and uncooperative with peers, and have few friends.

Developmental Trends

To tell infants to "wait a minute" when they cry or to punish them for having a bowel movement makes no sense. It is only in the *toddler* period that requirements for self-control begin to be developmentally appropriate. Such requirements are apt to precipitate the angry storms, temper tempests, and shouts of defiance of the terrible twos and threes. Gradually, however, the storm subsides. Not only are controls being strengthened but affective investments are being diversified, with the intense involvement with parents and siblings now being supplemented by extrafamilial adults and peers. Diversification aids modulation, so the *preschooler* is increasingly capable of managing feelings that are becoming increasingly manageable.

The *school-age* period between 6 and 9 years of age is the high point of self-control. The early anxieties and jealousies within the nuclear family, the accommodation to peer groups, and the transition from home to school have all been weathered, and no comparably dramatic new adjustments need to be made. Children of this age are variously described as conforming, practical, industrious, self-motivated, and self-controlled. They have more insight into their own behavior and the behavior of others than they did formerly and are more orderly, organized, and persistent. They are less aggressive and possessive than before, while the tendencies to blame and ridicule, to be greedy and possessive, or to snatch and steal are all on the wane. There is also a general tendency to be more inward rather than acting on the feelings and impulses of the moment.

The calm of middle childhood is broken by the physiological changes and dramatic growth of *puberty*. The period between 12 and 14 years of age may

be marked by turmoil: some preadolescents are confused, touchy, negativistic and solitary, aggressive, deliberately provocative, and resistant to authority. Little wonder that some developmentalists have seen a similarity between this period and the terrible twos, even while recognizing that the preadolescent is vastly more complex. *Adolescence* itself is not so dramatically unstable, although, as we have seen, the many problems involved in the transition to adulthood still make it a time of vulnerability rather than stability in regard to self-control (see Rutter, 1996).

Moral Development

Self-control evolves from parental prohibitions epitomized by "No" and "Wait." *Conscience* develops from parental evaluations typified by "good boy" or "bad girl." It is this added element of evaluation that makes conscience a special kind of control mechanism. Because conscience is a complex psychological creation, we had best describe it before discussing its development.

What Is Conscience?

Conscience involves *thinking*, *feeling*, and *behaving*—understanding what is morally right or wrong, feeling appropriate satisfaction or guilt, and acting in a moral manner. But this is the description of the ideal, integrated conscience. In reality, one element can overshadow the other two: the devil can quote scripture, people can feel righteous or guilty over acts that have nothing to do with morality, and moral behavior can serve immoral or amoral ends.

A special word should be said about the feelings originating in the conscience. Interestingly, we have a ready label for the negative affect accompanying transgressions—**guilt**—but we have no such label for the positive affect accompanying obedience, so we will arbitrarily call it *self-satisfaction*. Both affects derive from the parental evaluations of "good" or "bad"; the former implies that the child is worthy of love, the latter that he or she is not. Because of the bond of love, being love-worthy is a source of one of the greatest pleasures of early childhood, while not being love-worthy subjects the child to intense anguish. As toddlers and preschoolers develop, they begin to internalize these two judgments; they judge their own behavior as good or bad. And as they say "good boy" or "good girl," "bad boy" or "bad girl" to themselves, they also experience the same pleasure and anguish that accompanied parental evaluations. The pleasure becomes self-satisfaction, the anguish becomes guilt.

Already we can sense the importance and potential dangers of guilt. Certainly guilt is essential to normal development, but the preschooler's negative self-judgment enters the scene long before it can be employed judiciously. This raises the possibility of all kinds of problems. Let us look at the developmental picture to find out why.

The Development of Conscience

Piaget (1932) provides the richest documentation of the cognitive distortions that characterize *moral reasoning* in the preschool period and the beginning of middle childhood. Elaborating and expanding on Piaget, Kohlberg (1976) reconstructs the stages of moral development in the following manner: At the *preconventional* level, children evaluate actions in terms of whether they lead to pleasure or punishment. Those resulting in rewards are good; those resulting in punishment are bad. During the *conventional* morality stage, the child adopts the conventional standards of behavior to maintain the approval of others or conform to some moral authority such as religion. Thinking is absolutist and inflexible—right is right, wrong is wrong, and there are no extenuating circumstances or mitigating considerations. In the *post-conventional* or principled stage, children judge behavior in terms of the morality of contract and democratically accepted law, of universal principles of ethics and justice, and of individual conscience, holding themselves personally accountable for moral decisions. Between 6 and 16, the preconventional level gradually declines while the other two levels increase, although only about one-quarter of 16-year-olds have achieved the highest level.

Although we know that the tyrannical conscience changes, we do not know why. Piaget emphasizes the importance of the cognitive give-and-take during *peer interaction* as counteracting the rigid authoritarianism of early moral reasoning, but the evidence has not been clearly supportive. The parent who confronts the child with such simply stated challenges as, "How would you feel if someone did that to you?" may help the child think of transgressions in terms of all the parties involved. Social learning theorists emphasize the importance of parents as *models* of moral behavior, of their *reinforcing* moral behavior in their children, and of their combining punishment with *reasoning*, as is done in authoritative parenting. When the mystery concerning the agents of change has been solved, we will be in a better position than we are now to ensure that normal children "outgrow" their primitive conscience and to help disturbed children who continue to suffer needlessly from its tyranny. (See Grusec and Goodnow, 1994.)

Up to this point we have been dealing with the thinking aspect of conscience, not with feeling or acting. Children show *guilt* as early as 3 years of age, but we know little about it in the preschool period. We do know that the conditions eliciting it change during middle childhood. Young school-age children are concerned primarily with punishment rather than with guilt over transgressions. Thus they have an externally oriented conscience. Subsequently, the theme of confession increases and is a kind of halfway house between externally oriented fear of punishment and internally oriented guilt. Children are inwardly troubled and driven to confession, even if they could get away with the transgression, because of what others might think of them. However, confession can also be used manipulatively by children learning the trick of saying "I'm sorry" in order to forestall punishment. It is only in the preadolescent period that true guilt in the sense of an internal judgment and self-criticism appears. Punishment or even the love and opinion of others are not central; rather, preadolescents are concerned with the damage done to their own self-image and self-respect. (See Tangney and Fischer, 1995.)

Conscience, like self-control, can be either too strong or too weak. Excessive guilt has been implicated particularly in the obsessive-compulsive disorder and in depression, while antisocial children with acting-out behavior may have an externally oriented conscience concerned only with the fear of getting caught and being punished. We shall deal with these deviations in Chapters 7, 8, and 9.

Cognitive Development

The aspect of *cognitive development* most pertinent to understanding the relation between normal and psychopathological development is the separation of the self from the social and physical environment—what has been called the separation of the "me" from the "not-me." Within this general domain, we shall explore the development of causal thinking and the concept of egocentrism, both of which will figure in future discussions.

Causality

An adolescent girl who will not speak for fear that feces would come out of her mouth, or a young man who always sleeps on his back in the belief that, if he did not, he would turn into a woman, would be regarded as psychopathologically disturbed because they are convinced that they can cause events which, in reality, are beyond their control. This magical notion is called **omnipotence**. Yet omnipotence is not the creation of the mature mind—many concepts of causality are initially magical. Piaget tells us that, between 5 and 8 months of age, the infant is beginning to grasp the idea that events, rather than being discrete, are related to one another: if A happens, then B is likely to follow. Yet infants mistakenly believe causal relations are dependent on their own activity. We have already seen two examples of such omnipotent thinking: infants who believe their cries produce the parent's presence and those who believe their bodily movements can cause any object in the room to jiggle and dance.

Let us now consider the implications of *magical thinking* for early development. The first six years are unmatched in terms of intense affect and fateful beginnings: attachment brings with it anxieties over loss; socialization requires the control of initiative, anger, and sexual behavior; evaluations in terms of good and bad are internalized and become sources of self-satisfaction and guilt; and, as we shall soon see, peers place their special demands on social participation. All of these momentous events occur at a time when the child is cognitively incapable of fully understanding the reality of what is happening. Distortions are likely to occur. If, for example, a 5-year-old girl's parents are going through a

stormy period in their marriage marked by quarreling and accusations, the child might not understand the reality of the situation (indeed, how could she?) but instead might distort it, believing her own "badness" to be the cause of disharmony. Thus omnipotence can create fears and guilts that have no basis in reality. As we shall see in Chapter 14, physically abused children can blame themselves for the pain inflicted upon them, while, according to psychoanalytic theory, cognitive distortions of reality lie at the heart of anxiety disorders (Chapter 8).

Egocentrism

Piaget defines **egocentrism** as conceiving the physical and social world exclusively from one's own point of view. Consequently, characteristics of the self are used to define or interpret characteristics of the objective environment: the me is confused with the not-me.

Egocentric thinking appears at all stages of cognitive development. The infant believes the very existence of objects depends on its actions. For preschoolers, egocentrism has an important social consequence in that it prevents them from understanding that each person has his or her own point of view. The ability to view the same situation from multiple vantage points—for example, to see an episode of classroom cheating from the viewpoint of the boy who cheated, the boy who was pressured into helping him cheat, and the teacher responsible for disciplining the classroom—represents a giant step forward in cooperative social interactions. In fact, a lively research interest has sprung up around what is called social **perspective taking** and its consequences for social behavior.

Social perspective taking has its own progressive stages; for example, 3- to 6-year-olds seldom acknowledge that another person can interpret the same situation differently from the way they interpret it, whereas 7- to 12-year-olds can view their own ideas, feelings, and behaviors from another person's point of view and realize that other people can do the same in regard to them. However, as was true of conscience, there is a gap between cognition and behavior, and psychologists are trying to tease out the variables responsible for translating social perspective taking into prosocial functioning (see Selman, Schultz, and Yeates, 1991). As we shall see, social perspective taking enters into the discussion of a number of psychopathologies, particularly conduct disorder (Chapter 9).

Egocentrism makes its last childhood stand in early adolescence. Piaget assumed that times of cognitive transition are times when primitive modes of thought are apt to reappear. One aspect of egocentrism may be expressed as *self-consciousness*; if someone laughs on the bus while the adolescent boy is fumbling to find the correct change for the fare, he is certain that he is being laughed at. Another aspect of the adolescent's egocentrism is the belief that ideas alone will win the day and that their ideas hold the key to solving the world's problems—if only the world would listen!

Recent research has cast doubt on many of Piaget's findings concerning egocentrism. It has been shown, for example, that preschoolers will adjust their language according to whether they are speaking to younger or older children. Thus they are not as locked in to egocentric thinking as Piaget would have us believe; rather, they shift back and forth, at times being able to see a situation from the viewpoint of others, at times not. However, in most studies contradicting Piaget's findings the task has been simplified so as to make it more congruent with the child's cognitive level. Life itself does not treat children so sensitively. Rather, children are confronted with perplexing and disturbing questions regardless of their ability to understand them: Why did mother die? Why do I suffer a painful illness? Why do my parents yell at each other all the time? Why am I beaten brutally, or neglected, or seduced? We can speculate that, under such conditions, children's thinking might show the kind of irrationality Piaget describes so well. (For an extensive critique, see Gelman and Baillargeon, 1983; for a rejoinder, see Lourenco and Machado, 1996.)

Information Processing

Information processing is a model of cognition that is an alternative to Piaget's model. It is concerned with analyzing the processes by which information is gathered and used to solve problems.

Using an analogy relating cognition to the information processing of computers, the model has two components, which correspond to computer hardware and software. The first traces the intervening steps between environmental stimulus and behavioral response. The stimulus input initially impinges on the sensory register, such as vision or audition, and then goes to short-term memory. This is working memory and is the setting for active information processing. From here information goes to long-term memory for more permanent storage as memory traces. The second component contains the control processes that are involved in selecting, monitoring, evaluating, and revising information so that it can be appropriate to the problem at hand.

Dodge (1986; Crick & Dodge, 1994) applied the information-processing model specifically to *social problem solving*. Here the sequence runs as follows: encoding social cues, forming mental representations of and interpreting those cues, searching for possible responses and deciding on a particular response from those generated, and, finally, acting on that response. The second step of cue interpretation involves the important psychological process of *attribution*. An attribution is an inference about the causes of behavior. Dodge's thesis is that, in disturbed children, the cognitive process is either distorted or deficient. Aggressive children, for example, attribute hostile intent to the behavior of others even when such behavior is benign or accidental. Aggressive children generate more aggressive responses and expect aggression to be effective in obtaining rewards and increasing self-esteem (Quiggle et al., 1992). We will return to social information processing when we discuss aggression in Chapter 9.

Anxiety

While **anxiety** has diverse definitions, its conceptualization as *anticipation of pain* is most relevant for our purposes. The concept itself originated with Freud, who used the term "signal anxiety" to designate the moderately painful anticipation of a noxious situation that warns, "Danger ahead!" Forewarned, the child can take steps to avoid reexposure to the situation. As we have seen in our discussion of self-control, anxiety lies at the heart of socialization, with the child forgoing various pleasures to avoid the pain of parental discipline. (See Silverman and Kurtines, 1996.)

The Developmental Picture

We will briefly outline the development of anxiety. (See Vasey, Crnic, and Carter, 1994.) Certain fears, such as fear of loud noise and fear of unexpected movement, seem to be *innate*, while the fear of strangeness enters the picture in the second half of the first year. Such primitive fears decline in the *preschool period* as other, experientially based ones appear. Here we find the fear of doing "bad" things and of failure, of traffic accidents and fires. However, unrealistic fears, such as of imaginary animals and characters, also appear for the first time.

In *middle childhood* the trend toward realistic fears continues: fear of bodily injury and failure increases, while fear of giants and ghosts declines. However, irrational fears—such as fear of snakes and mice, of nightmares and fictional characters—are still present. *Adolescence* brings with it new, age-appropriate fears, such as sexual fears, concerns over money and work, and concerns over war. The fear of failure is heightened, again as would be expected. Irrational fears are now infrequent but do not altogether disappear; adolescents can be afraid of the dark, of storms, of mice and snakes, or of cemeteries.

In sum, the development of fears reflects the increased realism of children's thinking and their developmentally appropriate concerns along with the gradual decline in irrationality, although the latter never completely releases its hold.

Defense Mechanisms

Freud stated that anxiety can become so painful that certain maneuvers are undertaken to defend the individual against it. A primitive defense is **repression**, in which both the dangerous impulse and the ideas and fantasies associated with it are banished from consciousness. In essence, the child says, "What I am not aware of does not exist"; for example, a girl who is frightened of being angry with her mother no longer is aware of such ideas and feelings after repression. If repression is insufficient, **reaction for-**

mation might be called into play, so that the child thinks and feels in a manner diametrically opposed to the anxiety-provoking impulse. Continuing our example, the girl now feels particularly loving toward her mother and would not dream of being angry. In **projection**, the forbidden impulse is both repressed and attributed to others; the little girl might be upset that "all of the other girls" she knows are sassy and disrespectful to their mothers. In **displacement**, the impulse is allowed expression but is directed toward a different object; for example, our little girl becomes angry with her older sister or with a teacher.

The danger of defense mechanisms is that they might persuade the individual that a distorted image of reality is an accurate reflection. The child who claims to have no hostility toward her parents on the basis of repression is as convinced as if, in reality, the relationship were an unusually congenial one. If defense mechanisms prevent reality testing by protecting the child from facing his or her fears, are they not pathogenic by their very nature? While acknowledging their potential danger, Anna Freud (1965) sees no inherent incompatibility between defense mechanisms and the general goals of socialization. Neatness and orderliness, which might be a reaction formation against the messiness of the toddler period, can be an adaptive, serviceable defense through adulthood; a political activist who is displacing anger toward parents onto anger toward entrenched political corruption still has a useful and meaningful direction to his life. In addition, the healthy child can use defenses flexibly, relying on them to manage a particularly painful episode in development but discarding them when they are no longer needed. It is when defenses become *rigid*, *pervasive*, *and extreme* and when the child's repertoire of defenses becomes unduly *limited* that they are in danger of jeopardizing future growth.

Recently, research has documented the emergence of the defense mechanisms over the course of development (Cramer, 1991; Safyer & Hauser, 1995) and across different levels of psychological maturity (Bond, 1995). Taken together, this research suggests that defenses can be construed along a *developmental continuum*, ranging from those that are primitive—and associated with poor adaptation if used exclusively and rigidly—to those that are mature, and associated with high adaptive levels. This continuum is represented in the Defensive Functioning Scale, one of the Proposed Axes for Further Study in DSM-IV (1994). (See Table 2.1.) Defenses at the *high adaptive level* are those that allow for a balance between conflicting motives and maximize the accessibility to consciousness of thoughts and feelings. An example of an adaptive defense is humor, which allows a person to acknowledge something painful without being devastated by it. At the *low adaptive level* are those defenses that interfere with the child's perception of objective reality, such as psychotic denial.

The Dual Nature of Anxiety

Anxiety, like other variables we have discussed, can either promote or block development. On the positive side, it prevents constant reexposure to painful and destructive situations; it raises the level of motivation, enabling the child to make maximal use of abilities; and it engenders defenses that may be socially adaptive and growth promoting. However, anxiety can also perpetuate inappropriate, self-defeating defenses and can bizarrely distort both thought and action. Consequently, anxiety will figure prominently in our discussions of psychopathologies.

Sexual Development

Sexuality has been approached from a learning-cognitive point of view and from an affective point of view. Infants, lacking innate knowledge, must learn to classify themselves as boys or girls. This classification is called **gender identity**. In addition, society prescribes which behaviors and feelings are appropriate for boys and which are appropriate for girls, and children must learn such appropriate **gender-role** behavior. Finally, *sexuality* involves

Table 2.1   DSM-IV Defensive Functioning Scale and Definitions of Defenses

1. **High adaptive level**: allowing conscious awareness of feelings and ideas and promoting a balance between conflicting motives **Humor**—emphasizing the amusing or ironic aspects of a conflict or stressor **Sublimation**—channeling potentially maladaptive feelings or impulses into socially acceptable behavior
2. **Mental inhibitions or compromise level**: keeping potentially threatening ideas and feelings out of awareness **Isolation of affect**—separation of ideas from the feelings originally associated with them **Repression**—expelling disturbing wishes, thoughts, or experiences from conscious awareness
3. **Minor image-distorting level**: distorting one's image of self or others so as to allow one to maintain self-esteem **Devaluation**—attributing exaggerated negative qualities to others so as to minimize their importance **Omnipotence**—perceiving self as being superior to others in order to fend off feelings of vulnerability
4. **Disavowal level**: keeping unpleasant or unacceptable impulses, ideas, affects, or responsibility out of awareness **Denial**—refusing to acknowledge some painful aspect of external reality or subjective experience **Projection**—falsely attributing to another one's own unacceptable feelings, impulses, or thoughts
5. **Major image-distorting level**: creating gross misattributions or distortions in the image of self or other **Projective identification**—falsely attributing to another one's own unacceptable thoughts or feelings and behaving in such a way as to engender in the other person those very thoughts or feelings **Splitting**—compartmentalizing positive and negative experiences so as to block one side of ambivalence from awareness
6. **Action level**: dealing with stress by acting or withdrawing **Acting out**—giving vent to conflicts through action so as to avoid experiencing upsetting feelings **Passive aggression**—a facade of overt compliance that masks covert resistance, resentment, or hostility
7. **Defensive dysregulation**: using defenses involving a pronounced break with objective reality **Delusional projection**—formation of fixed delusional belief system revolving around one's own projections **Psychotic denial**—extreme denial of perceived external reality resulting in gross impairment in reality testing

Source: Adapted from DSM-IV. Copyright 1994 American Psychiatric Association.

intense erotic pleasures which, at the very least, must be controlled through socialization or which, if psychoanalytic theory is correct, form the leading edge of major personality developments and changes in interpersonal relations.

Gender Identity

The typical 2- to 3-year-old male child has grasped the idea that "boy" applies to him, and he can correctly answer the question, "Are you a boy or a girl?" However, he does not comprehend the real meaning of the label, nor has he grasped the principle of categorizing people by sex, relying instead on external cues of size, clothing, and hairstyle. Remember that the preschooler is still cognitively in the preoperational stage, literally believing what he sees, so his categorizations by sex are on the basis of manifest differences. Because children this age are incapable of conservation (understanding that objects remain the same even when their appearance changes), they also believe that as appearances change so do essences—things that look different are different. Consequently, for a child this age it seems perfectly possible for boys to change into girls and vice versa just by altering their clothes, hairstyle, and behavior to that of the other sex. (See Golombok and Fivush, 1994.) And, to the boy in our third vignette in Chapter 1, it seems perfectly possible for a child to grow up to be a "mommy" or a "daddy" regardless of his or her present status. It is only at around age 6 or 7, when conservation is cognitively possible, that children grasp the idea that gender is permanent and immutable. They also come to realize that the genitals are the crucial factor determining gender.

Gender Roles

Every society prescribes behaviors and feelings appropriate and inappropriate to each sex. Traditionally in Western society, boys should be dominant, aggressive, unsentimental, stoic in the face of pain, and pragmatic; girls should be nurturing, sociable, nonaggressive, and emotionally expressive. The message was inescapable: parents knew it, advertisers knew it, television directors knew it, gym teachers knew it, car salespeople knew it. Now that

there is a strong movement afoot to change the traditional stereotypes and foster equality between the sexes, the same social forces are being mobilized to send the new message. Society is never subtle about an issue so important as gender role. Along with the stereotypes go rewards for conforming to and punishments for deviation from the prescribed role. In fact, it was society's punitiveness toward women who deviated from their traditionally prescribed role which eventually led to the rebellion against the narrowness of the prescriptions themselves.

In spite of the feminist movement, gender stereotypes have remained remarkably consistent over the past three decades (Ruble & Martin, 1996). Children as young as 3 years of age can classify toys, clothes, household objects, and games according to social stereotypes, and preschoolers do the same with adult occupations. As thinking becomes less concrete and more inferential in middle childhood, psychological characteristics such as assertiveness and nurturance are added to the list. While awareness of stereotypes increases, acceptance of them declines (Alfieri, Ruble, & Higgins, 1996).

So far we have been dealing primarily with knowledge of stereotypes. Very early in development there is also a preference for gender-stereotypical behavior. Children aged 2 to 3 prefer stereotyped toys (trucks for boys, dolls for girls) and would rather play with same-sex peers. In middle childhood boys increasingly prefer gender-typed behavior and attitudes, while girls shift to more masculine activities and traits. This is an example of boys being more narrowly gender-typed than girls. "Sissies" are teased, whereas "tomboys" are tolerated.

Social learning theorists point to the many ways culturally prescribed gender-typed behavior is reinforced. While the role of women has changed dramatically since the 1960s, parents' differing expectations of their sons and daughters have remained essentially the same. Fathers play more vigorously with their infant sons than with their infant daughters. In the toddler and preschool periods boys receive more physical punishment, are rewarded for playing with gender-typed toys, and are encouraged to manipulate objects and to climb. In middle childhood parents interact more with the same-sex child. Also, boys are reinforced for investigating the community and being independent, while girls are supervised more and rewarded for being compliant. In general fathers are more narrowly stereotyped in their behavior than are mothers, which is one reason boys are punished for deviations more than girls are (see Lamb, 1997). Finally, both teachers and peers, in numerous obvious and subtle ways, exert pressure for conformity to social stereotypes.

Erotic Pleasure

In addition to learning gender roles, children also have erotic experiences of intense pleasure when stimulating their genitals and are curious about anatomic differences and intercourse. Having already discussed psychosexual development (see Chapter 1), we shall focus here on the literature describing the development of *erotic pleasure*.

The *infant* boy's erect penis unmistakably points to the presence of at least one precursor of adult sexuality in the first year of life. The toddler may derive sporadic pleasure from genital stimulation, and by the preschool period the child practices masturbation as a source of pleasurable sensations, looks at the genitals of adults and peers, and asks questions concerning anatomic sex differences and the origin of babies. Erotic feelings may be aroused by the tickling and teasing and generally pleasurable excitement of caregiving during the toddler period. A mother may become concerned when her preschooler wants to masturbate while lying in bed with her, or a father may realize that his little girl is becoming too excited by "riding horsey" on his foot. While informed parents no longer react to sexual behavior with threats to cut the boy's penis off or with terrifying visions of the insanity or depravity that will be the fate of the girl who masturbates, even the most enlightened parents must inevitably require a certain amount of self-control. Typically, the parent wants to curb socially disapproved expressions of sexual behavior without alienating the child from natural feelings and curiosities. Instead of labeling the child as bad, the parent conveys the message that there is a proper time and place for sexual behavior.

Boys during *middle childhood* talk and joke about sex in their gangs, sometimes experimenting with mutual masturbation, while girls talk more about love and have powerful sexual fantasies, although engaging less in actual experimentation. Sexual curiosity is evidenced by an interest in peeking, seeking pornographic or sex-education books, and exchanging information with same-sex friends. Middle childhood is also the time of peer group segregation between boys and girls, fostered by the fear of being teased for interacting with members of the other gender (Maccoby, 1990).

Puberty ushers in physiological maturity, the period extending from around 8 to 18 years of age for girls and from around 9½ to 18 years of age for boys (Conger & Galambos, 1997). The complexities of sexuality now clearly occupy center stage. At the simplest level, there is the matter of obtaining accurate information. Because society does not always provide ready access to factual material, the adolescent is apt to accumulate both correct and incorrect information and to have areas of uncertainty and ignorance. In the search for personally gratifying sexual techniques, however, instructions in lovemaking are of limited value, each partner having idiosyncratic sources of erotic arousal and having to adapt to those of the other. Thus adolescents are dealing not merely with the awkwardness of inexperience but also with individual differences that make the same technique pleasurable to one partner and repugnant to another. And because intense pleasures are at stake, frustration readily becomes rage, and insensitivity touches off anxiety or disgust. In addition, each sexual venture involves the question, "What kind of sexual being am I?" Adolescents know that society will judge them, and they in turn will judge themselves in terms of the success or failure of their ventures. Most important of all, sexuality is part of the questions, "Whom can I love?" and "With whom can I share my life?" Such questions transcend those of information, technique, and social criteria of adequacy. In sum, the adolescent is searching for a physically and psychologically fulfilling relationship with another person as well as for sexual gratification.

Aggression

While there has been a notable relaxation of controls on sexual behavior, as evidenced by earlier sexual experiences for both boys and girls and the prevalence of unmarried couples living together, concern over the control of **aggression** keeps pace with the increasing rates of violence in society. Given its potential consequences, uncontrolled aggression is a much more serious problem from a prognostic point of view than is excessive inhibition (Chapter 9).

There is no consensus concerning the definition of aggression. We define it here as behavior that has injury or destruction as its goal, and anger as its accompanying affect.

The Developmental Picture

Infancy

Anger can be differentiated from general distress in the 6-month-old baby and is marked by crying and by random and overall body movements such as kicking, flailing of the arms and legs, and arching of the back.

The Toddler-Preschool Period

The period between 1 and 4 years of age is the high-water mark for unvarnished expressions of rage, the developmental trend being from explosive, undirected outbursts of temper to directed attacks, and from physical violence to symbolic expression of aggression (Parke & Slaby, 1983). Thus temper tantrums that include kicking, biting, striking, and screaming peak at around 3½ years of age and gradually decline. The more directed expressions of aggression such as retaliation are negligible in the first year but increase over time, until about one-third of the outbursts of 4- and 5-year-old children are of this nature. Concomitantly, verbal forms of aggression such as name-calling, arguing, and refusals also increase.

The descriptive picture makes sense in light of what we have learned about development. The infant cannot be angry *at* anyone because the independent existence of others has not been grasped; directed anger becomes possible only after the object concept is understood. While the toddler can intend to aggress, the idea that an attack actually hurts does not register until around the third year of life. Thus only from 3 years of age on is the child capable of meeting all the criteria of our definition of aggression. Subsequently, attack becomes less physical and more verbal and "psychological." While it would be comforting to believe the transition from physical to verbal aggression represents an intrinsic diminution in aggression rather than merely a change in form, this does not appear to be the case. A blow to self-esteem can be as painful as a blow to the face; a humiliation can be as destructive as a beating.

The meaning of aggressive behavior itself changes according to the intra- and interpersonal context. In certain emotionally unstable children, extremes of aggression alternate with extremes of withdrawal and fearfulness. On the other hand, vigorous social participation and the formation of mutual friendships also increase the incidence of aggressive behavior. Thus, while aggression solely as a desire to harm and destroy may be undesirable and aggression accompanied by withdrawal and fearfulness may be part of a general emotional instability, aggression that results from a high level of sociability may be regarded as innocuous or even healthy.

Middle Childhood

After the preschool period, aggression in the form of a crude physical attack in reaction to the immediate situation declines, and children's behavior becomes progressively more intentional, retaliatory, and symbolic (Hartup, 1974). Children are concerned with getting even and paying back in kind, while their aggressive repertoire proliferates: bickering, quarreling, teasing, and swearing abound, along with bullying, prejudice, and cruelty. Their increased cognitive sophistication enables them to differentiate intentional from accidental provocations and respond less aggressively to the latter. In keeping with the development of conscience, children now can be troubled by their outbursts. To counterbalance this gain, their increased time perspective also enables them to hold a grudge and have both more delayed and sustained aggression than was possible in the preschool period.

Unregulated emotion.

Adolescence

The early phase of adolescence, often called pread-olescence, is a generally unstable time. The more infantile modes of expressing anger, such as stamping feet, throwing objects, and crying, may reappear for a while and disappear subsequently. In adolescence verbal expressions of anger predominate, such as sarcasm, name-calling, swearing, ridiculing, and humiliating. Sulking frequently follows an angry outburst. The situations evoking anger resemble those of middle childhood: unfair treatment, encroachment on rights, refusal of privileges, being treated as a child, and being incapable of achieving a goal.

The Management of Aggression

Generally, parents should be affectionate and serve as models of self-control. Love-oriented discipline and reasoning along with consistently prescribed standards of behavior favor control of aggression, while punitiveness, rejection, neglect, and incon-sistency undermine it. The heightened arousal characterizing aggression should be channeled into alternative, constructive behaviors; it can motivate the sprinter, the satirist, and the social reformer, as well as the delinquent. Attention should be paid to the problems underlying aggressive behavior—the feeling of being unloved, the humiliating sense of insignificance, the self-loathing. The aggressive child, in turn, should be helped to find constructive ways of coping with anger and to focus on its source (Berkowitz, 1990). We will say more about aggression when we discuss its pathological extremes in Chapter 9.

Peer Relations

Peer relations are a potent predictor of subsequent psychopathology. (See Cicchetti and Bukowski, 1995.) In our discussions we distinguish a general interest in peers, which we call *sociability*, from *groups*, which are organizations of individuals possessing norms or values regulating the behavior of the individual. (For further reading, see Parker et al., 1995.)

Early Peer Relations

There is no lack of dramatic developments in the first six years of a child's life, but we shall treat such developments summarily, because they have yet to be linked with psychopathology. Two-month-old infants are interested in looking at one another, and by 10 months of age there is a more varied and sustained reaction expressed in mimicking, patting, hitting, and imitation of laughing. By 15 months of age affection appears, and by age 2 there is participation in games, although the toddler's short attention span and limited ability to communicate and to control the behavior of others gives sociability a fleeting, improvisational quality.

Clearly, all early social behaviors are less stable and intense than attachments, and for good reason. Peers have no interest in assuming the caregiving role of relieving distress and providing stimulation; nor do they have the caregiver's skill in responding quickly and appropriately to needs. However, they have one inherent advantage over adults in that, being at comparable developmental levels, they are naturally attracted to one another's activities. Whereas a parent may love a child for what he or she is, peer attraction is based on mutual interests. Peer relations are important not because they represent diluted versions of attachment but because they add a new dimension to development.

A number of changes take place in the preschool period. Positive exchanges such as attention and approval increase, although sharing and sympathy do not. Competition and rivalry are also on the rise, while quarrels are fewer but longer. More important, immature or inefficient social actions are becoming more skilled; for example, there is greater speaker–listener accommodation so that a child begins to talk *to* rather than *at* another child, and collaboration begins to emerge in social problem solving. Cooperativeness, respect for property, constructiveness, and adaptability are the basis of general social attraction. The preschooler who is highly aggressive, quarrelsome, or dictatorial; who refuses to play with others; or who is dependent on adults for attention and affection rates low on attractiveness and sociability (Musun-Miller, 1993). Friendships now have that combination of sharing and quarreling which will characterize them throughout childhood.

Sociability

Sociability, the interest in the larger world of peers, comes to the fore in middle childhood. Research on sociability often is based on an assessment of children's *sociometric status*; that is, the way that they are perceived by peers. (See Bukowski and Cillessen, 1998, for a comprehensive review.) Four types of children emerge from sociometric studies: accepted, rejected, neglected, and controversial. The child who is *accepted* by other children is resourceful, intelligent, emotionally stable, dependable, cooperative, and sensitive to the feelings of others. *Rejected* children are aggressive, distractable, and socially inept in addition to being unhappy and alienated. Moreover, they are at risk for being school dropouts and for having serious psychological difficulties in adolescence and adulthood. *Neglected* children, who are neither liked nor disliked by peers, tend to be anxious and lacking in social skills. Finally, *controversial* children are perceived both positively and negatively by others. These children are often troublemakers or class clowns, yet they possess interpersonal skills and charisma that attract or impress other children.

Among the many determinants of sociability, two social-cognitive and one affective variable will figure in our future discussions. We have already dealt with the role of **social perspective taking** in the development of conscience, and it is easy to see how it would also facilitate sociability by countering self-centeredness. The second social-cognitive variable is *social problem solving*, which is concerned with conflict resolution. As we have seen, it involves a number of social-cognitive skills: encoding and accurately interpreting social cues, generating possible problem-solving strategies and evaluating their probable effectiveness, and, finally, enacting the chosen strategy. Young children's strategies are impulsive and designed to meet their own needs; such strategies include grabbing, pushing, and ordering other children about. Older children take the needs of others into account and are inclined toward persuasion and compromise (Selman and Schultz, 1988). **Empathy**, the affective component of sociability, involves both an awareness of the feelings of others and a vicarious affective response to those feelings. Toddlers have been observed to respond empathetically to the distress of others, for example, by giving a crying child a favorite toy (Thompson, 1987). Empathetic responses increase with age. The range of eliciting stimuli also increases, broadening eventually to include general life conditions rather than immediate distress, as in concern for the poor or the sick. As for the psychological significance of peer relations, Sullivan (1953) claims that the shift from "me" to "we" is aided by the mutuality and equality of peer relations. In the context of sharing, children learn what Sullivan calls accommodation: instead of thinking of themselves as unique or special, as they might at home, they begin to learn how to get along with others.

There is another important dimension that sociability adds to the child's development. At home the child has to be love-worthy because affection and obedience lie at the heart of the parent–child relationship. With peers the child must be respectworthy, which is a matter of proven *competence*. Children must expose themselves to comparisons with other children in regard to athletic ability, manual skills, resourcefulness in suggesting and implementing interesting activities, and so on. They are valued in terms of their actual contributions to the activities that peers themselves value.

The Group

Middle Childhood

The insubstantial, play-oriented groups of the preschool period become the middle childhood gang, which, by the time children are 8 to 10 years of age, is sufficiently potent to compete with the family in terms of interest, loyalty, and emotional involvement. The child begins to subordinate personal interests to the goals of the group, tries to live up to group standards, and criticizes those who do not. Thus, "we" becomes more important than "I." The gang no longer needs to rely on stereotyped games and activities such as hopscotch or jump rope but is sufficiently autonomous to respond to general suggestions such as "Let's make a clubhouse" or "Let's give a party." Names, insignia, and secret passwords help give the gang a special identity. In addition to being identifiable social units, gangs traditionally have been segregated by sex, with boys being action-oriented and girls being sociable in their interests.

The gang advances the sense of belonging. It offers training in interdependent behavior, encourages venturing out further than the individual could go alone, and through its cohesiveness buttresses the individual member's self-control.

Adolescence

Group involvement reaches a high point in adolescence. The adolescent group is an autonomous social organization with purposes, values, standards of behaviors, and means of enforcing them. In its stability and differentiation it resembles adult groups rather than those of middle childhood. Conformity peaks in 11- to 13-year-olds and gradually declines; it is greatest in those adolescents low in status among their peers and high in self-blame.

Adolescent groups vary in structure and nature. There is the small, close-knit clique, whose members are bound together by a high degree of personal compatibility and mutual admiration. The crowd, a larger aggregate than the clique, is concerned with social activities such as parties and dances and does not demand the same high personal involvement the clique requires. Crowds vary in status, and being a member of a high-status crowd is one of the surest ways to gain popularity. An important function of the crowd is to provide a transition from unisexual to heterosexual relations. The clique still survives and requires more loyalty than the crowd. It is often hostile to adult society and has a specific goal: sexual, athletic, delinquent, and so on. It retains its emphasis on adventure and excitement as well as on the formal trappings of organization, such as name, dress, and initiation ritual.

Peer relations are an important influence on children's development.

These groups serve as the adolescent's primary bridge to the future. They provide a sense of belonging, which is especially important during the period of transition between being a child and being an adult. They help adolescents master uncertainty by prescribing behavior, right down to what clothes to wear, what music to listen to, and what language to use. They provide both provocation and protection in changing from same-sex to heterosexual relations. Finally, they support individuals in their opposition to their parents. This does not imply that the majority of adolescents are rebellious and alienated; the battle of the generations is fought only fitfully, and many values of the group, such as cooperation, self-control, and dependability, are congruent with or even reflections of parental values (see Conger and Galambos, 1997).

What mars adolescent groups is their rigidity and demands for conformity. Adolescence is a high-water mark for group prejudice, when caste and class lines are sharply drawn, and inclusions and exclusions are absolute. For all their rebelliousness against adult society, adolescents are more slavishly conforming to the group than they have been before or will be in the future. In short, in middle childhood and especially in adolescence there is a narrow group-centeredness, which is the counterpart of the child's earlier egocentrism. Perspective and flexibility, evaluation of individuals in terms of personal worth, loyalty without chauvinism, social commitments that transcend immediate group interests—all these lie in the future.

As we shall see, peer relations play an important role in both conduct disorder and drug abuse. However, there is a question as to whether they play a leading etiological role. Does the juvenile gang force its members to defy the law whether they want to or not, or do angry, defiant youths seek out juvenile gangs? Does peer pressure cause drug abuse, or are adolescents who become addicted those who are particularly disturbed to begin with? We will return to these questions in Chapters 9 and 11.

Work

We usually think of **work** as something that adults do. It is important to the adult's self-esteem and self-concept. What defines work is *requiredness*: the necessity to complete tasks regardless of whether they are intrinsically interesting and whether one "feels like it." Using this definition, it is evident that children also have work they must do, such as performing household chores. But even for those who help out at home, the principal work of childhood is school. Just like their parents, children must arrive on time each day, apply themselves to tasks assigned to them, and forgo their immediate pleasures in order to comply with the requirements of those in charge.

Work in Middle Childhood

Unfettered initiative is the toddlers' paradise. They can do what they want just because they want to do it. As we have seen, socialization, with its "no," "wait," "good boy" and "bad girl," is an intrusion, although sensitive parents try to preserve initiative while requiring self-control. The next major development in regard to initiative is *school*. As with socialization, children cannot choose not to go to school, nor can they choose not to learn what they are supposed to. With the introduction of requiredness, initiative takes on an important characteristic of adult work—work is something you do whether you want to or not. Ideally, work will be intrinsically rewarding and pleasurable, but these characteristics are not essential.

There are other aspects of school which make it a halfway house between the free exercise of initiative and the constraints of adult occupation. School is often the child's first encounter with a superordinate organization empowered to make significant decisions concerning the regulation of his or her daily life. The boy entering kindergarten, for example, is among children he has not chosen to be with; he is also with an adult on whom he has no special claim and who may feel obliged to show him no favoritism. His physiological needs cannot be gratified at will since neither the refrigerator nor the toilet is available on demand. Rather, there are schedules and rules that apply to all. Thus school is an impersonal environment compared to home.

What is more, the products of children's efforts are evaluated as never before. Children are with an adult whose principal function is to scrutinize what they do and help them do even better. Grades introduce an element of public evaluation; not only the teacher but parents and peers as well have knowledge of the quality of the children's products. "Right" and "wrong" enter the picture and take a place alongside "good" and "bad" as preconditions for adult approval or disapproval. In sum, school is product-oriented. Schoolchildren add "student" to the list of self-characterizations, and their success or failure in this new role contributes significantly to their self-esteem.

School failure figures prominently in discussions of psychopathology. Both the future delinquent and the future schizophrenic might be variously described as disruptive and inattentive in class, defiant and truant, for example, while the devaluing of achievement in school is an important factor determining drug use in adolescence (see Chapter 11). There are also learning-disabled children who fail to fulfill their potential despite being motivated to do so (see Chapter 6).

Vocational Choice and Identity in Adolescence

In addition to being students, adolescents begin to think of themselves as potential workers. The complexities of vocational choice are such that exploring them will continue into young adulthood. The job market itself is complicated and constantly changing, and today's adolescents probably are as poorly prepared for a vocation as they are for mature sexual behavior. The world of work has its own structure of class- and sex-appropriate occupations, its hierarchy of prestige, its requirements for occupational preparation. But work is not only doing a job; it is relating to others as well. In fact, more jobs are lost for interpersonal reasons than for lack of skill and inadequate preparation. Coworkers may have conflicting needs—to dominate and protect, to destroy and seduce, to expand and conserve, to placate and manipulate. The desire for a congenial interpersonal setting introduces an unpredictable element into the adolescent quest because there is no sure way of knowing how the individual's idiosyncratic needs will mesh with those of fellow workers.

Along with *interpersonal factors*, *intrapersonal factors* are important in choosing a vocation. Ideally, adolescents' interests, values, and talents should all find full expression in the work they choose. Yet development itself decreases the probability of such a harmonious outcome. Vocational self-knowledge lags behind other cognitive developments, and most high school seniors make important choices concerning education or work on the basis of little accurate information concerning their aptitudes. Fortunately, they have progressed in other areas, so the unrealistic idealism of middle childhood, such as an airy dedication to "helping others," has been replaced by a realistic set of vocational values.

In sum, adolescents must engage in a long period of trying to define their vocational as well as sexual selves. In a special form of reality testing, they set out to discover the most rewarding fit between their peculiar set of ideals, values, and talents and the world of work. Because the work they do will be an important aspect of self-definition and self-esteem, more is at stake than just finding a "good job."

Interestingly, the adolescent's search for a vocation in the broad sense has much in common with Erikson's (1968) well-known concept of the adolescent search for **identity** (see also Marcia, 1993). For Erikson, the adolescent's question of "Who am I?" is closely related to the question, "What can I do that will be fulfilling?" Similar intra- and interpersonal variables are involved. Adolescents bring with them a unique constellation of aptitudes, interests, values, and personality traits, which are their heritage from their personal past. Their occupation must offer an opportunity to continue and fulfill this special heritage so that what they value most will be valued by others, whether such "others" are the nation, an industry, the neighborhood, or a handful of close friends.

The instability of the adolescent period makes this search for identity a difficult period of trial and error, with two inherent dangers. At one extreme there may be *premature* occupational choice, with the adolescent perhaps latching on to a stereotyped image of "successful executive" or "prestigious doctor," only to be trapped in meaningless activities. At the other extreme, uncertainty becomes pervasive and immobilizing, causing the adolescent to bog down in what Erikson calls *role diffusion*. However,

such untoward outcomes need not be discussed now. In successful vocational choice, as in successful socialization, the individual wants to do what is required by maturity. If he or she can no longer live in the toddler's paradise, it does not matter; finding fulfillment in the adult world is far better.

There are also important cognitive changes in adolescent identity. Ask schoolchildren, "Who are you?" and they are apt to answer in *concrete* terms, giving details such as their address, physical appearance ("I'm tall"), play activities ("I'm good at baseball"), or possessions ("I have a bike"). Adolescents, by contrast, are more *abstract* ("I'm ambitious"), future-oriented ("I want to be a doctor"), *interpersonal* ("I like people"), and concerned with psychological *traits* ("I'm all mixed up") and *ideologies* ("I'm a liberal"). The development here is not an additive process in the sense that complex, abstract ideas are added on to simple, concrete ones. Rather, adolescents conceive of themselves differently, with prior descriptions either dropping out or becoming integrated into a more complex picture (see Harter et al., 1997).

While we have introduced the concept of identity in relation to vocational choice, it is important to many other topics we have discussed, such as self-control, sex, and relations to parents and peers. In fact, it will be the central organizing concept when we examine the risks and psychopathologies of the adolescent transition (Chapter 11), and the special challenges ethnic minority adolescents face in achieving a positive identity (Chapter 15).

Developmental Integration

Now we will integrate the information about developmental pathways presented in Chapter 1 with the ten developmental variables just discussed. To do this we use the case of a hypothetical girl named Zoey.

Zoey's mother went through a postpartum depression when Zoey was born; consequently, her attachment to her mother was colored by insecurity (*attachment, slight deviation*). While this did not constitute a major problem, she tended to react strongly to changes in her environment (*temperament, vulnerability*). When Zoey was 8 years of age, she experienced an increase in familial disharmony when her parents began arguing violently (*inter-parental conflict, risk*). However, her good relation with her father enabled her to take the stress in stride (*parent–child relation, protective factor*).

When she was 10 years old, Zoey's parents divorced (*risk*), and she was placed in her mother's custody. At this point, a number of behavior problems began to develop. The principal behavior was angry outbursts and argumentativeness with the teacher (*aggression, severe deviation*). Although initially a friendly child, Zoey began to be regarded as a troublemaker by peers, whose rejection of her inspired hostile acting-out directed toward other children (*transactional process*). Consequently, her popularity declined (*peer relations, moderate deviation*). However, at age 12 she was transferred to a new classroom where she made friends with two other girls who formed a special group of outsiders (*peer relations, protective factor*). With her mother she was chronically sullen (*attachment, continued moderate deviation*), although there were outbursts of temper tantrums and name-calling, especially after she came home from visits with her father. Her angry outbursts were usually overreactions to ordinary frustrations of everyday life; she was not spoiling for a fight by imagining everyone else was against her (*cognition, normal since there was no distortion in regard to attribution*). She went from being a B student to being a C student at school, and, while she acted bored and sardonic, she did not give up on school entirely (*work, moderate deviation*). Rather than doing homework, she concentrated on drawing and sketching, a hobby she had shared with her father, becoming quite skilled and covertly enjoying being praised (*initiative, normal since the decline at school was compensated for by an increase in hobbies*). She and her friends talked about sex, masturbation, and other pubertal changes, and, while wary of boys, she was no more so than a number of other shy preadolescent girls (*sex, normal*). She was properly but not excessively troubled over her outbursts (*conscience, normal*) and was not excessively anxious (*anxiety, normal*). Finally, while her self-control had declined

significantly, it had not collapsed altogether. She was not an impulse-ridden child, driven to strike out at the slightest provocation; rather, she was "basically a good kid" in the grips of a problem too big for her to handle (*self-control, moderate deviation*).

When she was 14 years old her mother remarried, and, with time, Zoey established a good relationship with her stepfather (*protective factor*). Her problem behaviors gradually subsided, and development began to shift to a normative pathway. However, she continued to be cool and "standoffish" toward her mother and made a point of finishing high school early so that she could move away from home as soon as possible (*attachment, continued deviance*).

To summarize, this vignette indicates that the degree of deviation from normal development is a function of how *severe* the disturbance is both within and across the developmental variables and the *duration* of the disturbance. It is also a function of the *balance* between risk, vulnerability, and protective factors. Zoey's story also demonstrates that a disturbance may not envelop all of the child's personality—or even all of a given variable. As we have noted, it is important for the clinical child psychologist to assess areas of intactness and resources as well as deviations, especially when planning remedial measures.

Our challenge in the coming chapters is to construct developmental pathways for the various classifications of childhood psychopathologies. First, for a given classification we must to discover which of the ten variables have been adversely affected and to what degree of severity. Then we must discover both the balance between risk, vulnerability, and protective factors that produces psychopathology and the balance that enables the child to overcome the disturbance.

Before doing this, however, we must become acquainted with the psychopathologies themselves and develop a general understanding as to which are apt to continue into adulthood and which are apt to be "outgrown." These are the matters that will occupy us next.

The Bridge to the Psychopathologies

In Chapters 1 and 2 we established a general developmental framework and provided a working knowledge of the variables we will use to investigate psychopathology as normal development gone awry. In this chapter we begin to focus on the psychopathologies themselves. We first discuss the way normality shades gradually into psychopathology both conceptually and empirically, then discuss the major psychopathologies of childhood, and finally summarize longitudinal studies of normal and disturbed children to show which psychopathologies tend to persist and which tend to be outgrown. In Chapters 4 through 12 we go on to explore selected psychopathologies.

The Conceptual Bridge

Time and again in our previous discussion we have seen that the same variables that facilitate development have the potential to impede its course. Attachment goes hand in hand with separation anxiety, which, if exaggerated, may undermine a preschooler's self-reliant expansiveness; initiative can become a self-defeating noncompliance in which the child strikes out at all authorities, even those who can be genuinely helpful; self-control can become a prison, and conscience a punitive inquisitor; realistic anxiety can become unrealistic terror; peer groups can mercilessly torment the outsider; schoolwork can become drudgery. This affinity between growth and failure to grow is our first, tentative support for viewing psychopathology as normal development gone awry. Note the word "tentative," since we have yet to put the view to the test in regard to specific psychopathologies.

In fact, one of the major unresolved issues in the study of psychopathology concerns the continuity or discontinuity between normal and disturbed behavior. Is all pathological behavior on a continuum with normal behavior? For example, is a phobia just an exaggeration of normal fearfulness? Is delinquency just an exaggeration of minor antisocial acts (such as the mischievous stealing of hubcaps)?

Or do we find, particularly among the severe psychopathologies, certain kinds of behaviors or certain patterns of development that have little or no counterpart in normal behavior and normal development? We should keep this issue in mind as we examine specific psychopathologies.

Diagnosis and Classification

One purpose classification systems serve is to parcel an unwieldy mass of information into meaningful and manageable units. However, they do more than help place a given child in a given category: they are points of departure for exploring *etiology* on the one hand and *prognosis* on the other. Thus the diagnosis of adolescent schizophrenia should carry with it implications as to causative factors and consequences, both in regard to the chances of outgrowing the disturbance and the effectiveness of therapeutic intervention. At present, we are far from realizing such an ideal goal.

While classification may be essential, children rarely fit neatly into a single diagnostic category. Consequently, *multiple diagnoses* are often preferable to a single diagnostic label. The clinician should also take into account acuteness or chronicity based on the history of the disturbance, evaluate the severity of disturbance, specify the developmental period the child is in, and describe the specific behaviors that comprise the psychopathology.

The current scene in regard to classifying childhood psychopathologies is a lively one. Clinicians concerned with the adequacy of traditional systems for diagnosing children have raised a number of criticisms, particularly in regard to whether such systems pay sufficient attention to developmental considerations. As part of our discussion we will examine alternative strategies to traditional clinical diagnosis.

The Traditional Approach: DSM

The various editions of the **Diagnostic and Statistical Manual of Mental Disorders** (DSM) are in the tradition of classification based on naturalistic observation. The tradition has primarily been carried on by psychiatrists and relies heavily on the observational skills of the clinician for its implementation. The most recent version of the DSM is DSM-IV (American Psychiatric Association, 1994).

Features of DSM-IV

Goals

The highest priority of DSM-IV is to be a useful guide to determining the need for clinical services by providing brief, clear, and explicit statements of the criteria defining diagnostic categories. Additional goals are to facilitate research, improve communication among clinicians and researchers, and provide an educational tool for the teaching of psychopathology. To meet those goals, the authors strove to ensure that DSM-IV's contents were supported by empirical research, and were not bound to any one theoretical orientation.

Definition of Psychopathology

There is no generally accepted definition of psychopathology, as our survey of models has shown. The authors of DSM-IV do not pretend to resolve the knotty issue of conceptualizing psychopathology but settle for stating their own criteria for what is termed a **clinical disorder**. According to DSM-IV, a clinical disorder is a *"clinically significant behavioral or psychological syndrome or pattern that occurs in an individual and that is associated with present distress (e.g., a painful symptom) or disability (i.e., impairment in one or more areas of functioning) or with a significantly increased risk of suffering death, pain, disability, or an important loss of freedom"* (p. xxi).

The authors of DSM-IV are careful to state that disorders, not individuals, are being classified. Thus, the manual never refers to "a schizophrenic" or "an alcoholic," as if the psychopathology were the person; instead, it uses such phrases as "a child with schizophrenia" or "an adult with alcoholic dependency." The distinction is a simple but a significant one, which we also have adopted in this text.

Objectivity and Behavioral Specificity

DSM-IV strives to avoid the use of terms that are inferential, theoretical, and open to multiple interpretations. Instead, *behaviorally specific* terms are used that can be objectively described and operationally defined. For example, "Fights more frequently than agemates" is more specific than "Has destructive impulses." To take only one example, separation anxiety disorder is defined in terms of ten behavioral criteria, including unrealistic worry about possible harm befalling major attachment figures, repeated nightmares involving the theme of separation, and persistent reluctance to be separated from major attachment figures.

Reliability

Reliability refers to the consistency of results obtained from using a diagnostic instrument. An instrument that would place the same child in different categories when used by two different clinicians would not be very useful. One criterion of reliability is the consistency with which a diagnostic instrument functions at two points in time, or *test-retest reliability*. More frequently, however, diagnostic systems use *interobserver agreement*, in which two experts are asked to evaluate the same child at the same point in time.

In his review of studies of reliability of DSM-IV, Cantwell (1996) concludes that acceptable reliability has been demonstrated for most of the major diagnostic categories. However, reliability is greater for more general categories, such as anxiety disorder, than for more narrowly defined subcategories such as social phobia or generalized anxiety disorder. There is also evidence that clinicians are less reliable than are researchers who undergo specific training to use the diagnostic system in a standardized way. One reason for poorer reliability in practice is that, while DSM provides lists of various criteria that must be met to diagnose a particular disorder, there are no precise rules for determining when a criterion is met, nor for how to evaluate and integrate various sources of information. Thus, if one clinician uses a parent report to judge whether a symptom is present, another interviews the child, and a third relies on a score on a formal psychological test, they might well reach different conclusions.

Validity

Validity is crucial to the utility of a measure. It indicates the extent to which the measure assesses what it claims to assess or, in this case, the extent to which

a diagnostic system does, in fact, correctly classify disturbed children. There are a number of different ways in which evidence for validity might be demonstrated. There is *content* or *face* validity, which is the degree to which the content of a diagnostic category has an obvious relation to what is being evaluated. In the case of separation anxiety disorder, the three behavioral criteria mentioned make sense on the face of it. Ideally, the criteria should also be analyzed statistically to test whether they do, in fact, cluster together. *Concurrent* validity compares the current evaluation with some other contemporary criterion; for example, the diagnosis of a reading disability based on parental report could be compared with scores on a reading achievement test. *Predictive* validity compares current evaluations with some future criterion; for example, children diagnosed with schizophrenia in middle childhood should continue to be more disturbed as young adults than children diagnosed with school phobia. *Construct* validity is the relationship between a diagnostic category and other variables that should be related to it theoretically; for example, children diagnosed with conduct disorder should perform poorly on measures of self-control, such as the ability to delay gratification. And, finally, *discriminative* validity is the extent to which clinical features are unique to the disorder in question and differentiate it from other similar disorders. For example, the diagnostic criteria should help to distinguish children with separation anxiety disorder from those who are depressed. This corresponds to the important clinical task of *differential diagnosis*.

Validity is difficult to establish, given that there are few independent criteria that can be used for predictive or concurrent validation studies. However, Cantwell (1996) notes that advances have been made in the attempts to obtain external validation of the DSM-IV disorders, although the study of child psychopathology has lagged behind that on adults in this regard. DSM-IV has a stronger *empirical basis* than its predecessors, and thus corresponds better to the research evidence regarding different forms of psychopathology. This evidence was obtained from comprehensive reviews of published literature, from reanalysis of studies containing information concerning diagnosis, and from field trials in which data on 6,000 participants were analyzed in terms of reliability and validity of diagnostic criteria. The resulting five-volume DSM-IV sourcebook provides documentation of the decisions reached concerning the classifications and their behavioral components.

Other evidence for external validity is suggested by the fact that there are different predictors and correlates of certain syndromes of disorders, as well as studies demonstrating continuities over time. For example, research has shown that the three kinds of childhood depression described in DSM-IV—Major Depression, Dysthymia, and Adjustment Disorder with Depressed Mood—have a different age of onset, course, and recovery. In addition, the fact that individuals diagnosed with a particular disorder respond differentially to treatments designed specifically for that disorder lends credibility the system used to diagnose them.

Comprehensiveness

DSM-IV is substantially more comprehensive than previous versions in its coverage of childhood disorders. In addition, DSM-IV supplies information concerning a host of characteristics of a given disorder where such information is available; for example, prevalence, age of onset, course, predisposing factors, differential diagnosis, laboratory findings, and specific age, cultural, or gender-related features.

Multiaxial Classification

Five Dimensions

Instead of assessing only in terms of the presenting problem, DSM-IV uses a **multiaxial classification** system to evaluate the child comprehensively in terms of five dimensions.

Axis I: Clinical Disorders; Other Disorders That May Be a Focus of Clinical Attention   This axis contains most of the disorders with which we will be concerned. The DSM criteria for those disorders will always be included in our discussions.

Axis II: Personality Disorders; Mental Retardation   This axis is concerned with conditions that affect functioning in a pervasive manner, including

personality disorders and mental retardation. It can also be used to indicate problematic personality characteristics that do not meet the criteria for a full-blown personality disorder, such as maladaptive and rigid use of defense mechanisms.

Axis III: General Medical Conditions   This axis includes general medical conditions that are potentially relevant to the understanding or management of cases: for example, injuries and infectious diseases, diseases of the nervous system or digestive system, and complications of pregnancy and childbirth.

Axis IV: Psychosocial and Environmental Problems   This axis includes negative life events, familial or other interpersonal stresses, inadequacy of social support, and environmental deficiencies or difficulties that make up the milieu within which the child's problems developed. (See Table 3.1 for a summary of relevant categories.)

Axis V: Global Assessment of Functioning   This is the clinician's judgment of the overall level of functioning. Such information is useful in planning treatment and measuring its impact. The judgment is made in terms of a Global Assessment of Functioning (GAF) Scale, which goes from superior functioning (100 points) to persistent danger of hurting self or others or persistent inability to maintain minimal personal hygiene (1 to 10 points). (See Table 3.2 for a condensed version of the GAF.)

Sample Multiaxial Evaluation

A multiaxial evaluation might look like this:

Axis I: Major Depressive Disorder; Reading Disorder
Axis II: No diagnosis
Axis III: Hypothyroidism
Axis IV: Parent–child problem (neglect of child)
Axis V: GAF = 35

DSM-IV also explicitly deals with *multicultural* considerations. First, there is a new section describing culturally specific symptom patterns, preferred idioms for describing distress, and preva-

Table 3.1   Examples of Axis IV: Psychosocial and Environmental Problems

Problems with Primary Support Group. These include death of a family member; health problems in family; disruption of family by separation, divorce, or estrangement; removal from the home; remarriage of parent; sexual or physical abuse; parental overprotection; neglect of child; inadequate discipline; discord with siblings; birth of a sibling.

Problems Related to the Social Environment. These include death or loss of friend; social isolation; living alone; difficulty with acculturation; discrimination.

Educational Problems. These include: illiteracy; academic problems; discord with teachers or classmates; inadequate school environment.

Occupational Problems. These include unemployment; threat of job loss; stressful work schedule; difficult work condition; job dissatisfaction; job change; discord with boss or coworkers.

Housing Problems. These include homelessness; inadequate housing; unsafe neighborhood.

Economic Problems. These include extreme poverty; inadequate finances; insufficient welfare support.

Problems with Access to Health Care Services. These include inadequate health care services; unavailability of transportation to health care facilities; inadequate health insurance.

Problems Related to Interaction with the Legal System/Crime. These include arrest; incarceration; victim of crime.

Other Psychosocial Problems. These include exposure to disasters, war, other hostilities; discord with nonfamily caregivers (e.g., counselor, social worker, physician); unavailability of social service agencies.

Source: Adapted from DSM-IV. Copyright 1994 American Psychiatric Association.

lence; for example, in certain cultures depressive disorders are characterized by a preponderance of somatic symptoms rather than by sadness. Next, there is an index of culture-bound syndromes that are found in one or only a few of the world's societies. The index includes the name of the condition, the cultures in which it is found, a brief description of the psychopathology, and a list of possibly related DSM-IV disorders.

Limitations of DSM from a Developmental Perspective

In many ways DSM-IV represents an impressive accomplishment. However, one significant shortcoming is its failure to acknowledge the *developmental dimension* within disorders. DSM-IV assumes that the diagnostic criteria are essentially identical across development, whereas research increasingly indicates that this is not the case (Cantwell, 1996). Evidence suggests that the symptom picture of a disorder changes with age. For example, younger children with separation anxiety disorder worry excessively about separation from their attachment figure and have nightmares, while older children pri-

marily have physical complaints and are reluctant to go to school. Motor disturbances are more characteristic of younger boys with attention deficit hyperactivity disorder, while older boys with the disorder are characterized by inattention.

Developmentally oriented clinicians have been offering similar criticisms across several generations of DSM revisions. As long ago as 1965, Anna Freud observed that the two criteria fundamental to diagnosing clinical disorders in DSM—*subjective distress* and *impairment of functioning*—are not appropriate for children. The most seriously disturbed children—for example, those with autism, schizophrenia, or conduct disorder—may be oblivious to the fact that they have problems and may experience no subjective distress. Instead of being "disturbed," such children are better characterized as "disturbing" to others. Regarding the second criterion, children do not have a consistent level of functioning. Given that they are still in the process of developing, it is normal for their abilities to wax and wane and fluctuate significantly. Therefore, Anna Freud proposed that only one criterion could help to determine whether a particular behavior or symptom was an indication of psychopathology in a

Table 3.2   Selected Levels of the Global Assessment of Functioning (GAF) Scale

Code (Note: Use intermediate codes when appropriate, e.g., 45, 68, 72.)

100 91	Superior functioning in a wide range of activities, life's problems never seem to get out of hand, is sought out by others because of positive qualities. No symptoms.
80 71	If symptoms are present, they are transient and expectable reactions to psychosocial stressors (e.g., difficulty concentrating after family argument); no more than slight impairment in social, occupational, or school functioning (e.g., temporarily falling behind in school work).
60 51	Moderate symptoms (e.g., flat affect and circumstantial speech, occasional panic attacks) OR moderate difficulty in social, occupational, or school functioning (e.g., no friends, unable to keep a job).
40 31	Some impairment in reality testing or communication (e.g., speech is at times illogical, obscure, or irrelevant) OR major impairment in several areas, such as work or school, family relations, judgment, thinking, or mood (e.g., child frequently beats up younger children, is defiant at home, and is failing at school).
20 11	Some danger of hurting self or others (e.g., suicide attempts without clear expectation of death, frequently violent, manic excitement) OR occasionally fails to maintain minimal personal hygiene (e.g., smears feces) OR gross impairment in communication (e.g., largely incoherent or mute).
10 1	Persistent danger of severely hurting self or others (e.g., recurrent violence) OR persistent inability to maintain minimal personal hygiene OR serious suicidal act with clear expectation of death.

Source: DSM-IV. Copyright 1994 American Psychiatric Association.

child: *whether it interferes with the child's capacity to move forward in development.*

A classic paper by Garber (1984) proposes a developmental framework for the classification of psychopathology in childhood, arguing against the "adultomorphism" inherent in DSM's tendency to apply adult categories to the problems of children. Garber states that clinicians need to devise developmentally sensitive criteria for diagnosing children, and also need to find a way to acknowledge the processes of change that create a context for children's behavior. Bemporad and Schwab (1986) echo this point, decrying the fact that, in attempting to avoid all theory, the authors of DSM also ignore the developmental perspective, overlooking the point that development is not a theory but a basic fact. Further, it is not only children who change over time. One of the child's tasks throughout development is to respond in age-appropriate ways to a changing environment. By focusing on superficial descriptions of behavior, DSM ignores the complex nature of the transactions and adaptations that affect individuals as they move through development (Jensen & Hoagwood, 1997).

Volkmar and Schwab-Stone (1996) offer yet another criticism of DSM-IV from a developmental perspective. Given how dependent children are on their caregivers, the interpersonal context must play a significant role in childhood psychopathology. However, problems arising from troubled family relationships are not considered clinical disorders in DSM-IV. Therefore, some of the most common concerns that bring children to the attention of mental health professionals—abuse, neglect, bereavement, family dissolution—are placed in DSM-IV in a somewhat vaguely defined category of "V-Codes," which may not be seen as priorities for treatment.

Lastly, Cantwell (1996) points out that classification systems such as DSM have not coped well with the *comorbidity* problem that frequently arises in studies of childhood psychopathology. It is difficult to know whether multiple diagnoses are accurate—whether they result from a lack of clear distinctions between diagnostic categories or whether they arise from different early expressions of various forms of psychopathology during development. Cantwell describes alternative classification schemes that sometimes have found more successful ways to address these problems, including the ICD-10 (World Health Organization, 1997), used widely in Europe, and the criteria specific to young children devised by the National Center for Clinical Infant Programs (Zero to Three, 1994).

Cantwell's conclusion echoes that of Garber twelve years earlier: "Developmental aspects of child and adolescent psychopathology will have to be given much greater consideration in future classification systems" (p. 9).

The Multivariate Statistical Approach: CBCL

In contrast to the *categorical* approach used by DSM, in which children are classified in terms of whether or not they "have" a disorder, other approaches are *dimensional*, rating children on the extent to which they show symptoms or problem behavior consistent with a particular diagnosis. One objection to categories is their all-or-none quality; for example, a child either is or is not depressed, and if he or she is, the clinician must decide whether the degree of disturbance is mild, moderate, or severe. The dimensional approach is compatible with the idea of continuity between normality and psychopathology, with the number of symptoms providing a measure of the severity of the deviation from the norm (Achenbach, 1995).

One strategy for assessing children's problems dimensionally is the *multivariate statistical approach*. The basic format is simple: Collect specific behaviors used in describing psychopathologically disturbed children; eliminate the infrequent, redundant, and obscure ones and subject the rest to statistical techniques designed to determine which are highly related. The statistical technique frequently employed is called *factor analysis*, and the related behavioral items are called *factors*. After examining the content of the interrelated items, the investigator assigns each factor a label. Such labels may resemble those used in traditional diagnosis, such as "delinquent" or "hyperactive"; however, they should not be regarded as equivalent until empirical evidence has shown them to be.

To illustrate the multivariate statistical approach we shall concentrate on the work of Achenbach (Achenbach, 1991; Achenbach & McConaughy, 1997). Achenbach's first step was to collect descriptions of pathological behavior from psychiatric case histories and from the literature. Through a series of preliminary studies these were reduced to 118 items that formed the Child Behavior Checklist (CBCL). Here are some examples of items on the checklist: argues a lot, complains of loneliness, does not eat well, runs away from home, has strange ideas. Another set of items dealt with competencies and were used to construct additional scales, but they will not concern us now.

Next the CBCL was filled out by parents of 1,800 children referred for mental health services, and the results were factor-analyzed. The analyses yielded both narrow-band and wide-band factors. The narrow-band factors included specific **syndromes**, or behavior problems, such as depression/anxiety, somatic complaints, social problems, aggressiveness, and delinquency. Two examples of narrow-band syndromes are Withdrawn, and Aggressive Behavior. The Withdrawn scale contained the following behavioral items: would rather be alone, secretive, shy, sulks, stares blankly, and won't talk. The Aggressive Behavior scale contained these behavioral items: destroys own and others' things, disobedient in home and school, argues, fights, is mean, and threatens others.

Several of the narrow-band syndromes grouped together to form two wide-band factors. The **Internalizing** factor comprised Withdrawn, Somatic Complaints, and Anxious/Depressed; the **Externalizing** factor comprised Delinquent Behavior and Aggressive Behavior. The internalizing-externalizing distinction describes two very different symptom pictures. Anxious children, for example, generally are well-behaved but are tormented by fears or guilt. They suffer inwardly, internalizing their distress. On the other hand, some children act out their problems in relation to others, thereby externalizing their distress. It is important to note, however, that internalizing-externalizing is a dimension of behavior, not a typology of children. While some children fall at either extreme, many of them demonstrate mixtures of both elements; that is, children can be both sad and aggressive, or have a "nervous stomach" and steal.

To obtain norms, the CBCL was next administered to 1,400 nonclinical children matched for age, sex, race, and socioeconomic status with the clinical population, and percentiles were calculated for the scores in the various narrow- and wide-band syndromes. With data from the normal and clinical populations it was possible to determine cutoff scores, below which the child would be considered within the normal range and above which the child would be considered disturbed. These cutoff scores were at the 98th percentile of scores for the total population. Thus a boy with a score of 1 on the Schizoid scale would be at a point equivalent to 69 percent of the population and therefore within normal limits; however, the same boy's score of 26 on the Aggressive scale would be higher than 99 percent of the population and deviates significantly from normal. These norms differ by age and gender. For example, girls generally are rated lower than boys on aggressiveness and therefore the cutoff score for

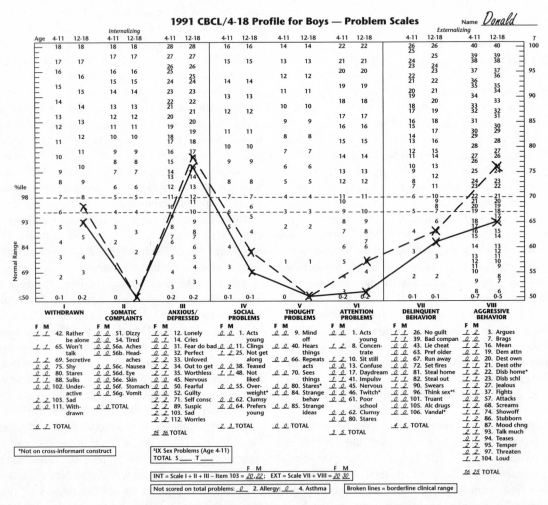

Figure 3.1 CBCL Profile of a 13-Year-Old Boy. The Solid Line Represents the Father's Report and the Dotted Line Represents the Mother's Report.

Source: Achenbach, 1991

girls is lower. A girl with a score of only 20 on the Aggressive scale would have a higher score than 98 percent of her peers and thus would be considered to be in the clinical range.

After scoring all eight narrow-band scales, one can obtain a profile indicating which scales are within normal limits and which exceed them. A hypothetical child might be within the normal limits for the internalizing scales of Withdrawn, Anxious/Depressed, and Somatic Complaints, while exceeding the norm in the externalizing scales of Delinquent Behavior and Aggressive Behavior. Figure 3.1 presents the profile of a 13-year-old boy using the parent-report version of the CBCL.

Because using computers to generate syndromes is quite different from using clinicians, it is interesting to compare Achenbach's factors with the diagnostic categories of DSM-IV. The approximate relationships are summarized in Table 3.3. DSM-IV is more differentiated; for example, it distinguishes two degrees of depression (major depression and dysthymia) and has a special diagnoses for subtypes of anxiety disorders such as separation anxiety. DSM-IV also contains diagnoses not found among Achenbach's syndromes, most notably anorexia nervosa and bulimia nervosa, specific learning disabilities, and autism. This last omission illustrates the difficulty statistical techniques have in capturing rare but important disturbances.

It is easy to understand the appeal of the statistical approach for those who value precision. Test-retest reliabilities are characteristically satisfactory, while the behavioral nature of the basic data gives them a palpability the more inferential diagnostic systems lack. As an added bonus, the CBCL and similar instruments are great time-savers compared with the traditional diagnostic procedures.

The combination of behavioral specificity and statistical manipulation does not guarantee precision, however. To begin with, objectivity in behavioral evaluation is a matter of degree (Drotar, Stein, & Perrin, 1995). While it is true that the statement "Is disobedient at home" is more objective than "Has a problem with authority figures," the former still requires a judgment. Thus the same behavior a mother might regard as disobedient in her son might be dismissed by the father as being "just the

Table 3.3   Correspondence Between CBCL Scales and DSM-IV Diagnoses

CBCL Scales	DSM-IV Diagnoses
Anxious/Depressed	Generalized Anxiety Disorder
	Major Depression
	Dysthymia
Delinquent Behavior	Conduct Disorder
Aggressive Behavior	Conduct Disorder
	Oppositional Defiant Disorder
Attention Problems	Attention-Deficit/Hyperactivity Disorder
Somatic Complaints	Somatization Disorder

Source: Achenbach and McConaughy, 1997.

way boys are." Behavioral ratings depend on who does the rating and the situation in which the behavior occurs: parents, teachers, and professionals may all disagree in rating a particular child, because they evaluate the same behavior differently or observe the child in different settings. In fact, Achenbach, McConaughy, and Howell (1987) found that, while agreement *within categories* of informants—such as parents, teachers, mental health workers, peers, and the children themselves—was reasonably high, agreement among informants in *different categories* was low. For example, the mean correlation between parents was .59, but the mean correlation between parents and teachers, mental health workers, peers, and the children's self-ratings ranged from .24 to .27. While the latter correlations were statistically significant, they were too low to have clinical utility.

The fact that information providers often have discrepant views of the same child is not a problem confined to multivariate statistical assessment but is present in all assessment procedures that rely on multiple sources of information. However, we do have a few leads as to what sources would be most valid for some particular psychopathologies. There is some evidence that parents and teachers are better informants in regard to externalizing symptoms, such as disruptive behavior, hyperactivity, inattentiveness, and oppositional-defiant disorders than are children, who tend to underreport them. On the other hand, children's own reports are more informative about internalizing symptoms such as anxiety and depression (Cantwell, 1996). This is an issue we return to in Chapter 16, when we discuss strategies for coping with multiple sources of data and divergent information about the same child.

The Classifications: Health and Normal Problem Behavior

If we are to treat psychopathology as normal development gone awry, we must anchor our thinking in a definition of normality. Moreover, we must have an idea of the problems and problem behaviors inherent in normal development, since normality never means problem-free.

Healthy Development

Since the various DSMs do not define healthy development, we must rely on another classification, the so-called GAP Report (Group for the Advancement of Psychiatry, 1974).

The GAP Report states that there is no single criterion for health; rather, a number of functions are involved. In *intellectual* functioning, health involves "adequate use of capacity, intact memory, reality-testing ability, age-appropriate thought processes, some degree of inquisitiveness, alertness, and imagination" (p. 220). Healthy *social functioning* involves an adequate balance between dependence on others and autonomy, a reasonably comfortable and appropriately loving relation with adults and other children, and an age-appropriate capacity to share and empathize with peers. Healthy *emotional functioning* involves an adequate degree of emotional stability, some capacity for self-perspective, some degree of frustration tolerance and sublimation potential, along with some capacity to master anxiety and cope with conflicting emotions. Healthy *personal and adaptive functioning* requires a degree of flexibility, a drive toward mastery, an integrative capacity, a degree of self-awareness, a positive self-concept, and the capacity to use fantasy in play constructively.

Note that the definition makes frequent use of the qualifying phrases "a certain degree of" or "some capacity for." As clinicians we would prefer more exact statements so that our evaluations would be less subjective, but such objective criteria for health lie in the future; the definition reflects current reality. On the positive side, the GAP Report does not present an idealized picture of the "normal, well-rounded child," with the implication that any deviation from such an ideal is suspect. Indeed, what is impressive about normal children is how much "deviance" they can take in stride!

Finally, the GAP Report emphasizes the importance of stage appropriateness of development. There should also be a general "smoothness" of development, as contrasted with alternating periods of exceptionally slow and rapid growth. And finally, there should not be excessive discrepancies in growth among the components of health, as seen, for example, in the pseudomature 6-year-old whose adult behavior effectively blocks peer participation.

Normal Problems and Normal Problem Behavior

Normal development involves both problems and problem behaviors. To take one example of the latter: one study found that about half the children in kindergarten through grade 2 were described as "restless," while another study found that a similar percent of 6- to 12-year-olds were described as "overactive." While both of these behaviors are part of the syndrome of hyperactivity, it would be incorrect to assume that half the children were hyperactive, since they have neither the clustering nor the intensity and chronicity of problems that would interfere with adaptive functioning. On the other hand, it would be equally foolish to deny that restlessness and overactivity constitute a problem both at home and in school.

Campbell (1989) outlines some typical nonpsychopathological developmental problems during the infancy and preschool period, which are described briefly in the next few paragraphs.

The "Difficult" Infant Studies of individual differences in infants, or infant temperament, have shown that some are easy to care for while others are difficult. The latter tend to be irritable, slow to adapt to change in routine, intense and negative in their reactions, and irregular in their biological functioning. If cared for sensitively, infants can "outgrow" this difficult phase; however, if caretakers are impatient and intolerant, or change routines abruptly and often, the chances of behavior problems in the toddler period are increased.

Insecure Attachment   We have already described the concept of secure and insecure attachment and reviewed the evidence that the insecurely attached infant may be at risk for problems in the area of initiative and social relations. However, such problems are not inevitable and can be minimized by sensitive caregiving. In Chapter 5, we will review the evidence.

The Defiant Toddler   Disciplinary problems and uncertainty as to when and how to set limits are the major concerns of parents of toddlers. In most instances the problems are stage-specific, leaving no residue. However, parental mismanagement, say, in the form of overcontrol, may increase the likelihood that problems will develop and persist.

Aggression and Withdrawal in Preschoolers   Aggressive behavior toward peers is a common complaint of parents and teachers of preschoolers, with boys being more aggressive than girls. However, as with other behavior problems, there is no need to read ominous portents into such aggressiveness unless it is coupled with mismanagement by parents or a discordant family situation. Social withdrawal, unlike aggression, is relatively rare and has not been satisfactorily studied. There is tentative evidence that the shy, quiet child is less at risk for developing behavior problems than is the disruptive one, but such risk may be increased in extreme cases when combined with other internalizing problems such as separation anxiety or dysphoric mood.

The Classifications: The Psychopathologies

For this overview we will follow the classifications in DSM-IV, providing summaries only of those specific psychopathologies that we will subsequently discuss in detail in later chapters.

Adjustment Disorder

We describe **adjustment disorder** first because it forms a link between the normal problems just described and the more serious psychopathologies to come. The symptoms of adjustment disorder emerge in reaction to a recent identified stressor. The symptoms are significant enough to interfere with social, academic, or occupational functioning and are in excess of the normal expected reaction. Adjustment disorders may occur with depression (sadness, hopelessness), with anxiety (nervousness, separation fears), and with disturbance of conduct (aggression, truancy). However, the symptoms do not persist longer than six months after the termination of the stressor, thus marking the boundary between adjustment disorders and other more persistent disorders.

Disorders of Infancy, Childhood, or Adolescence

As for the more serious psychopathologies, DSM-IV distinguishes between disturbances that are specific to children and those that are essentially the same for children and adults. We present those in the former category first.

Mental Retardation

Mental retardation is defined as significantly subaverage intellectual functioning (i.e., an IQ of 70 or below) and concurrent deficits in adaptive functioning such as self-care, social skills, and personal independence.

Learning Disorders (Academic Skills Disorders)

Learning disorders include *reading disorder*, *mathematics disorder*, and *disorder of written expression*. In each instance, the academic ability is substantially below that expected given the child's chronological age, measured intelligence, or age-appropriate education.

Pervasive Developmental Disorders

The primary disorder here is **autistic disorder**, which is marked by a qualitative impairment in social interaction (e.g., lack of social or emotional reciprocity, impaired use of nonverbal behavior such as eye contact and gestures to regulate social interaction), gross and sustained impairment in communication (e.g., delayed or total absence of spoken language, stereotyped language, absence of imaginative play) and restricted, repetitive, and stereotyped patterns of behavior, interests, and activities.

Attention-Deficit and Disruptive Behavior Disorders

The disorders included here were formerly listed under separate categories. They have been subsumed under a single classification because of the frequency with which they overlap.

Attention-Deficit/hyperactivity disorder is characterized by a number of inattentive behaviors (e.g., being easily distracted, having difficulty in following through on instructions, frequent shifting from one uncompleted activity to another) and by hyperactivity-impulsivity (e.g., acting before thinking, inappropriate running and climbing, fidgeting, having difficulty waiting in line or taking turns).

Conduct disorder is characterized by repetitive and persistent patterns of behavior in which either the basic rights of others or major age-appropriate societal norms or rules are violated (e.g., initiating fights, using weapons that can cause serious physical harm, stealing, setting fires, truancy).

Oppositional defiant disorder is marked by a pattern of negativistic, hostile, defiant behavior (e.g., loses temper, argues with adults and defies their requests, deliberately annoys others, lies, and bullies).

Elimination Disorders

In this category we will only be discussing **functional enuresis**, which is defined as repeated voiding of urine into bed or clothes at a chronological age of at least 5 years.

Separation Anxiety Disorder

Separation anxiety disorder is characterized by excessive anxiety concerning separation from those to whom the child is attached: for example, unrealistic worry about harm befalling an attachment figure, refusal to go to school in order to stay with an attachment figure, refusal to go to sleep without being near an attachment figure.

Reactive Attachment Disorder of Infancy or Early Childhood

Reactive attachment disorder is characterized by disturbed social relatedness (e.g., excessive inhibition or ambivalence, or diffuse attachments manifested by indiscriminate sociability with relative strangers) due to grossly pathogenic care, such as neglect or frequent change of caretakers.

Disorders of Both Children and Adults

The following disorders either have the same manifestations in children as in adults or can be made applicable to children with a few specific modifications.

Substance Abuse

Substance abuse is a maladaptive pattern of substance use leading to clinically significant impairment or distress. Among its various manifestations are an inability to fulfill major role obligations at work, school, or home because of the substance use.

Schizophrenia

Schizophrenia is a severe, pervasive disturbance consisting of delusions, hallucinations, disorganized speech, bizarre behaviors, and the so-called negative symptoms of flat affect, avolition, and alogia. Among the different types of schizophrenia are the *paranoid type*, marked by delusions or hallucinations, and the *disorganized type*, marked by disorganized speech and behavior and inappropriate affect.

Mood Disorders

A **major depressive disorder** is defined in terms of a depressed mood, weight loss, insomnia, psychomotor agitation or retardation, feelings of worthlessness or guilt, indecisiveness, recurrent thoughts of death, and markedly diminished interest or pleasure in activities. It occurs in single or repeated episodes. **Dysthymic disorder** designates a chronic state of depression lasting at least one year. (The third major category, bipolar disorder, is characterized by mood swings from depression to mania; however, it is extremely rare before puberty, and we will not be discussing it in detail.)

Anxiety Disorders

There are many anxiety disorders, but here we describe only those we will be discussing in later chapters.

Specific phobia is a fear cued by the presence or anticipation of a specific object or situation (e.g., flying, heights, animals). The phobic stimulus is avoided or endured with marked distress. While adults recognize the unreasonable nature of the fear, this is not true of children. We will be particularly concerned with **school phobia**.

Obsessive-Compulsive disorder is characterized either by obsessions, defined as recurrent thoughts, impulses, or images that are intrusive and inappropriate and cause marked anxiety or distress, or by compulsions, defined as ritualistic behaviors (e.g., hand washing) or mental acts (e.g., counting, repeating words silently) that a person feels driven to perform in response to an obsession or according to rigidly applied rules.

Posttraumatic stress disorder results when a person has experienced an event involving actual or threatened death or injury to the self or others. Among the many symptoms are persistent reexperiencing of the traumatic event (e.g., through recurrent, intrusive, distressing recollections), persistent avoidance of stimuli associated with the trauma (e.g., inability to recall aspects of the trauma or a diminished range of interests or activities), and persistent symptoms of increased arousal (e.g., difficulty falling asleep, irritability, difficulty concentrating).

Eating Disorders

Anorexia nervosa is an intense fear of gaining weight even though the individual is underweight, an undue influence of body weight on self-evaluation or denial of the seriousness of current low body weight, and a body weight less than 85 percent of that expected. **Bulimia nervosa** is marked by recurrent episodes of binge eating along with a sense of lack of control over eating during the episode. Self-evaluation is unduly influenced by body shape and weight, while weight is often normal.

Table 3.4 relates the various psychopathologies to normal development.

Longitudinal Studies

The issue of the persistence of disorders is one aspect of the general problem of *continuity*, which lies at the heart of developmental psychopathology. The discussion of personality variables in Chapter 2 demonstrates that continuity is not a simple matter of the constant recurrence of a specific behavior. Developmental forces reshape manifestations of the same variable; for example, in aggression, the toddler's temper tantrum becomes the highly organized vengeance of rival street gangs. At the very least, manifest behaviors must be organized into *categories* relevant to psychopathology, and the developmental course of these categories must be charted.

Such a model is still too simple, however, because it only allows room for categories of pathological behavior to continue or to disappear over time. In reality, one kind of psychopathology may be replaced by another: an enuretic preschooler may become a depressed underachiever in middle childhood; a truant from school may turn to drug abuse; or a psychotic adolescent may pull together and become an adequately functioning obsessive-compulsive adult.

Finally, continuity must be evaluated with and without *therapeutic intervention*. As we shall see, certain psychopathologies are responsive to remedial measures, while others are not. Understandably, the more severe the disturbance, the more difficult it is to alter its course.

Before reviewing longitudinal studies of the continuity of psychopathological behavior, we must discuss the methodological issues involved in conducting longitudinal research (see Loeber and Farrington, 1994, and Rutter, 1994).

Research Strategies

The Retrospective Strategy

A time-honored method of gathering developmental data is the **retrospective strategy**, in which inquiry is made about the past history of a disturbed child or adult in order to reconstruct the origins of the psychopathology. Most often this is done

Table 3.4   The Relation of Various Psychopathologies to Normal Development

Chronological time	The Context of Time					Attachment	Initiative and work	Self-c...
	Developmental periods	Piagetian stages	Freudian stages	Ericksonian stages	Separation-Individuation stages			
Birth	Infancy: 0–12 months	Sensorimotor: 0–2 years	Oral	Trust vs. mistrust	Normal autism Symbiosis	Social smile, 3–4 months Attachment: separation anxiety, anger, 6–9 months	Exploration; self-as-agent; battle of bottle and spoon	Not re Regul: excita 4–6 m
1 year	Toddlerhood: 1–2½ years				Differentiation	Secure vs. insecure		
2 years		Preoperational: 2–6 years	Anal	Autonomy vs. shame, doubt	Practicing		Willful negativistic; battle of the potty	Low: "terrib twos"
3 years	Preschool age: 2½–6 years				Rapprochement		Expansion of skills	Increa:
4 years					Beginnings of object constancy		Concrete self	
5 years			Phallic Oedipal	Initiative vs. guilt				
6 years	Middle childhood: 6–11 years	Concrete operations: 6–11 years	Latency	Industry vs. inferiority		Fluctuation	School: requiredness, impersonality, product orientation	High
7 years								
8 years							Psychological self	
9 years								
10 years								
11 years	Preadolescence: 11–13 years	Formal operations: 11 years on				Vigorous denial		Low
12 years								
13 years	Adolescence: 13–18 years		Genital	Identity vs. role diffusion		Emancipation	Vocational choice; identity	Increa
14 years							Abstract, future-oriented self	
15 years								
16 years								
17 years								
18 years	Young adulthood: 18–20 years			Intimacy vs. isolation		Rapprochement		High
19 years								
20 years								

Personality Variables*							
Conscience		Cognition		Anxiety	Sex		
gnitive	Affective	Casuality	Social, self		Gender	Erotic feelings	Psychosexual development
		Omnipotence of action		Innate			Mouth libidinized; object relation
							Anus libidinized; autonomy
			Egocentrism	Innate declines			
realism: te, rigid nventional	Guilt (Freudian theory)	Omnipotence of words; precausal thinking		Dark, imaginary creatures, etc.; defense mechanisms (timetable uncertain)	Determined by external clues; changeable	Masturbation; sexual curiosity	Genitals libidinized; exhibitionism; castration anxiety; Oedipus complex
ty of ration; ntional ty	Punishment is sole concern		Social perspective taking; cooperation; communication; reflection	Realistic and imaginary, supernatural dangers	Determined by genitals; immutable		Diminution of sexuality
	Troubled; confesses; others' reactions are important		Social problem solving				
cepted principles	Guilt: self-oriented regardless of others	Realistic grasp of physical casuality		Age-appropriate: prestige, sex, responsibility, etc. Some unrealistic fears		Central concerns: information, techniques, adequacy, love	Revival of earlier conflicts
							Integration of previous stages into mature love

*Each entry marks the beginning of a continuous developmental process.

Table 3.4 (continued)

Chronological time	Personality Variables (continued)*			
	Aggression	Social Relations†		
		Sociability	Friendship	Groups
Birth	Rage differentiated from distress (6 months)	Interest in peers		
1 year	Peak for uncontrolled aggression; age-appropriate provactions		Unreciprocated "friendships"	
2 years		Empathy		
3 years	Intentional attack, tantrums, retaliation			
4 years		Cooperative play	Insubstantial, activity oriented	Insubstantial play groups
5 years				
6 years	Increasingly verbal-symbolic, intentional, retaliatory; age-appropriate provocations	Accommodation to others; respectworthiness	More sustained, other oriented; superficial	Gangs: identifiable units
7 years				
8 years				
9 years				
10 years				
11 years	Immature modes reappear, e.g., tantrums			
12 years				
13 years	Verbal expressions predominate: name calling, sarcasm, etc.; age-appropriate provocations		Sustained; personalized; sharing, frank, critical	Stable groups with potent control: clique, crowd, gang
14 years				
15 years				
16 years				
17 years				
18 years				
19 years				
20 years				

*Each entry marks the beginning of a continuous developmental process.

Onset of Psychopathologies†

prior to age 3

n deficit/
tivity disorder:
ge seven

─Reactive─
attachment
disorders of
infancy and early
childhood

ion anxiety disorder:───────
ol period

─Oppositional defiant disorders:───────
3 years.

─Conduct disorder:───────
preschool through
adolescence

─Separation anxiety disorder:───
preschool thru middle childhood

nal enuresis: 5 years───

─Phobias: childhood thru─
adolescence

Learning disorders:
beginning school years

phobia: 7 years───

─Obsessive-compulsive─
disorder: middle child-
hood thru adolescence

Schizophrenia: childhood onset

─Substance related disorders:───────
early adolescence

─Suicide: increases in───
adolescence

─Schizophrenia: adolescent───
onset

a nervosa:───────
ence

─Bulimia nervosa: adolescence───

Depression: any age
Brain syndrome: any age
Mental retardation: any age
Posttraumatic stress
disorder: any age
Adjustment disorder: any age

†Age of onset not given for all psychopathologies.

through interview of the parents of the child or other knowledgable adults. However, despite the widespread use of interviews among clinicians and researchers alike, these data are of questionable reliability and validity. In order for a parent to be a satisfactory informant, he or she must accurately observe the behaviors a clinician will deem important (without foreknowledge of what behaviors these might be), preserve the observations in memory over a considerable period of time, and recall them intact on being questioned. Such an image befits a computer better than it does a human being, who is apt to distort information at all three stages even when the parent and child are psychologically sound—let alone if they are disturbed. While retrospective data may offer initial leads as to which intra- and interpersonal variables may be fruitful to study, their reliability is poor and therefore they should be used only with great caution (Henry et al., 1994).

The reaction against retrospective data has spurred an interest in techniques that are *prospective*; that is, they follow children over time. The interval between assessments should be sufficient to capture general developmental trends, and the evaluations should be independently conducted by individuals who are more objective than parents. Three of the most popular strategies are the followback, the follow-up, and the cross-sectional models, all of which eliminate a number of the deficiencies of retrospective data, although they have limitations of their own.

The Follow-Back Strategy

Like the retrospective approach, the **follow-back strategy** begins with a population of disturbed children or adults but obtains data from a previous time period via records kept by observers other than parents, such as school records, teachers' assessments, child guidance case studies, and court records. For example, one study examined the medical records of homicidally aggressive children in a child psychiatry inpatient unit for evidence of head injuries or seizures. A control group should also be selected, say, from the next name in the list of classmates or clinic patients, in order to narrow the variables relevant to the psychopathology being studied. For example, one might find that parental death, while

hypothetically an important precursor of psychopathology, occurred no more frequently in disturbed children than in a control group.

Advantages   The follow-back study has the advantage of allowing the investigator to focus immediately on the target population, while being flexible enough to permit the investigator to pursue new etiologic leads as they emerge.

Limitations   The follow-back strategy has a number of limitations. The data may be *uneven* in quality and availability, with some records being comprehensive and reflecting a high degree of professional competence, and others being skimpy and distorted by conceptual or personality biases. The data also tend to be very *general*—for example, number of arrests, decline in school grades, intact or broken family, number of job changes—lacking both the detail and the interrelatedness of variables found in an in-depth evaluation.

Other problems concern design and *population bias* in particular. Clinical populations may not be representative of disturbed children in general. Parents who seek professional help for a child with a school phobia, for example, may be different from those who do not, so findings from a clinical population cannot be generalized to all parents of phobic children. Likewise, children who are arrested may not be a representative sample of all youthful offenders, because police officers have their own biases as to whom they arrest and whom they let go.

More important, reliance on child guidance and court records biases the data in terms of *accentuating pathology* and *exaggerating relationships* found at time 1 and time 2. To illustrate: One follow-back study indicated that 75 percent of alcoholics had been truants, compared with 26 percent of healthy individuals—a highly significant difference—but a follow-up study revealed that only 11 percent of truants become alcoholics, compared with 8 percent of the nontruant population that became alcoholic. Thus truancy can have a variety of outcomes, and its particular association with alcoholism is too weak for predictive purposes. In general, follow-up studies, which capture the variability of development, show fewer relations among time 1 and time 2 variables than do follow-back studies, which select individuals who have already developed a particular disturbance.

The Follow-Up Strategy

The ideal method of charting children's development is the **follow-up strategy**, in which children enter into the study in their early years and are followed into the next developmental period—or even into adulthood. An example of this is the Cambridge Youth Study (Farrington, 1995) in which inner city boys were initially assessed at age 8 and then reassessed at ages 10, 14, 16, 18, 21, 25, and 32. The resulting longitudinal data can reveal which children develop what psychopathologies, together with the fate of the population with and without intervention. Instead of being at the mercy of extant records as with follow-back studies, the investigator can ensure that data will be gathered by well-trained investigators using the best available evaluative techniques.

Advantages   A major advantage of the follow-up study is that prospective longitudinal data allow the researcher to sort out the relationships among variables. For example, evidence that psychopathology in children of divorce was present *before* the breakup indicates that the divorce alone was not the cause; rather, the more likely culprit is the long and bitter process of marital dissolution that leads up to divorce (Rutter, 1994). Although no longitudinal design can demonstrate *causal* relationships—a true experiment in which variables are controlled and manipulated is necessary for that—prospective data allow investigators to test the plausibility of hypotheses about antecedent and consequent relationships.

Limitations   Despite its advantages, the follow-up study has a number of limitations. Such research is extremely *costly* in terms of money and expenditure of effort. A major problem, as Loeber and Farrington (1994) point out, is that of *time*: the investigator ages at the same rate as the participants and therefore one must live to a ripe old age indeed in order to reap the rewards of a life-span longitudinal study. On the other side of the equation, participants are difficult to retain in a study for such long periods of time. **Attrition** occurs when investigators lose track of participants; worse, participants may drop out selectively, with the most disturbed, unstable families or children tending to be the ones who move frequently or become uncooperative. Thus researchers may be faced with a dwindling number of people in the very population they are most interested in studying. Population *selectivity* is another problem. Because most psychopathologies are rare, large numbers of children must be evaluated at time 1 to ensure a reasonable number of disturbed ones at time 2. As one solution, many investigators begin with a disturbed population or with a population at risk for developing a given psychopathology, such as infants of schizophrenic mothers, who have a greater likelihood of becoming schizophrenic than do infants from an unselected population. However, such selectivity may introduce the same population bias we noted in the follow-back design.

Moreover, the follow-up study is *rigid*. Once having selected variables to study, the design does not allow the investigator to drop some and add others as results from relevant studies come in or as new theories and concepts come to the fore. Moreover, new measurement techniques may be devised which are superior to the ones in use; however the researcher cannot use them without losing comparability to the old data in the data set.

One final problem with the follow-up studies is the so-called **cohort effect**; one cannot assume that groups born in different eras are equivalent, since the time of birth may significantly affect development. Children born in times of war or depression are not necessarily comparable to those born in times of peace and prosperity, just as children born before the advent of television or the feminist movement grew up in an environment very different from that of those born afterward. Thus the results of a 30-year longitudinal study may or may not be applicable to the current population of children.

The Cross-Sectional Strategy

The **cross-sectional approach** to gathering developmental data consists of studying different age groups at one point in time. The chief *advantage* of this approach is that of time in that developmental differences can be studied without waiting for participants themselves to age. However, among its *disadvantages* is, again, the cohort effect. Although these groups may be equated for all the variables thought to be important, they cannot be equated for differential experiences they might have had because of their time of birth. For example, the parent–child relationships of a group of 14-year-old boys who grew up during the Vietnam war might differ significantly from those of a group of 7-year-old boys who grew up after the war. Thus age and environmental events are confounded.

The Accelerated Longitudinal Approach

One solution to the confounding of developmental effects with cohort effects is the **accelerated longitudinal approach**, also known as the longitudinal, cross-sectional approach. In this design children at different ages are studied as in the cross-sectional approach but then are subsequently followed until the children in the younger groups are the same age as those in the next older groups. For example, Stanger, Achenbach, and Verhulst (1997) assessed seven cohorts of Dutch children ages 4, 5, 6, 7, 8, 9, and 10 every 2 years for a period of 10 years. In this way, both within-cohort and between-cohort differences could be assessed. For example, the 4-year-old girls were compared with 6-year-old girls at time 1 and then again at time 2, and their scores at age 4 were compared to their own scores at age 6.

Among its *advantages*, such a design allows researchers to compare the age trends obtained cross-sectionally with longitudinal data. The saving in time is obvious: a longitudinal study that would have had to follow the 4-year-olds for 14 years can now be accomplished in half the time. However, as with any design, this one has *limitations*. These include the difficulty in equating groups and the likelihood of selective loss of participants across groups.

Evaluation of Research Strategies

While the follow-up and follow-back strategies are an improvement over the retrospective approach, neither is a panacea. Because of its flexibility, the follow-back strategy is most suited to generating hypotheses. Leads as to possible significant antecedents can subsequently be accepted or rejected as they are put to further tests. However, follow-up studies, because of their ability to monitor the child's development while it actually occurs, provide the most convincing data concerning change. This strategy also comes closest to testing causal relations among variables, although because it is correlational rather than experimental, it cannot actually establish causation.

One final cautionary note: The designs of follow-up and follow-back studies have only recently received the attention they deserve. Consequently, our reviews of longitudinal research will include studies using varying degrees of methodological sophistication and thus generating results with varying degrees of conclusiveness. While containing important leads as to the developmental course of childhood psychopathology, many of the findings reviewed should be regarded as tentative.

Empirical Findings

In our subsequent presentations we will explore longitudinal studies of specific psychopathologies. At this point we will present a basic overview of the findings of these studies. First, we examine evidence for continuity among psychopathologies, including those that are consistent within categories of behavior and those that change from one classification of psychopathology to another. Then we present evidence for discontinuity, including the psychopathologies that the child "grows out of" or "grows into" by adulthood. Our primary concern is with long-range predictions from childhood into adulthood, although we occasionally explore developmental trends within childhood itself. Finally, we examine resilience.

Continuity

The three deviations with the greatest degree of continuity from childhood to adulthood are aggressive behavior, the psychotic disorders, and severe mental retardation.

Aggressive behavior after 6 years of age becomes predictive of subsequent antisocial behavior in the adolescent period. For example, Fergusson, Horwood, and Lynskey (1995) followed a large sample of children from age 7 to age 15 and found that only 14 percent of children classified as having externalizing disorders demonstrated remission. Specifically, disobeying the teacher, cheating, unpopularity because of fighting and quarreling, and frequent truancy from school are predictive of what is popularly called juvenile delinquency. Anxious symptoms such as nervousness, nail biting, bed-wetting, and thumb sucking are unrelated but not incompatible with becoming a delinquent, since some delinquents rate high on the anxiety-withdrawal dimension.

Aggressive behavior in adolescence, in turn, is predictive of a host of acting-out behaviors affecting every area of the adult's life; such behaviors include criminality, vagrancy, excessive drinking, marital friction, promiscuity, and gambling.

Pervasive developmental disorders and *psychoses*, which include autism and schizophrenia, have a gloomy prognosis, although even in these cases one-quarter to one-third of the children make an adequate adult adjustment with or without treatment. The deviant behavior of those who do not recover may change while still remaining in the psychotic category; for example, around one-quarter of those who fail to recover from psychosis demonstrate clear evidence of organic brain pathology, even though none was discerned earlier. Finally, the prognosis for schizophrenia in adolescence is as poor as it is for the early psychoses.

Schizophrenia provides an interesting example of continuity of *disturbance* but discontinuity of *behavior*. In adults, schizophrenia is characterized by emotional withdrawal, anxiety, and thought disturbances in the form of delusions and hallucinations, while none of these characteristics are found in children destined to become schizophrenic in adulthood. There is no evidence that the shy, withdrawn child is apt to develop schizophrenia—or any other adult psychopathology. On the contrary, the at-risk child evidences both acting-out and withdrawal behaviors and is characterized as unstable, irritable, aggressive, resistant to authority, seclusive, friendless, and given to daydreaming. The conceptual bridge between such behaviors and adult schizophrenia remains to be built.

Discontinuity

Discontinuity can occur in a number of ways. The first of these is as a function of *development* itself. Aside from the early psychoses and severe mental retardation, problem behavior in the toddler and preschool period tends not to be a good prognosticator of subsequent disturbances. Such unpredictability is congruent with the fluidity of early development. Around 6 or 7 years of age predictability increases, with children with many symptoms at one age tending to have many symptoms later as well.

In general, *internalizing symptoms*, such as moderate anxiety, tend to be less stable across development than are externalizing symptoms. Other symptoms that tend to be "outgrown" by adulthood include nervous habits such as nail biting, sleep disturbances, and eating problems such as food pickiness and refusal to eat (but not obesity and anorexia). Internalizing symptoms also tend to be highly responsive to treatment, further indicating that their course is not rigid or fixed. However, we cannot paint too sunny a picture. Clinically significant levels of anxiety and withdrawal *do* predict later patterns of internalizing disorders (Ollendick & King, 1994; Achenbach et al., 1995b). Therefore, it is a matter of relative degree: while *stronger* evidence is found for discontinuity in internalizing disorders than in externalizing disorders, there is evidence for continuity in internalizing as well. (See Box 3.1.)

On the other side of the coin, continuity in externalizing disorders is also not absolute; *discontinuity* can be found as well. For example, Fergusson, Lynskey, and Horwood (1996) assessed whether disruptive behavior in middle childhood predicted conduct disorder in adolescence, using a large sample of New Zealand children followed from age 3 through adolescence. While children with early disruptive behavior were 16 times more likely to develop later conduct disorder than other children, 12 percent showed a discontinuous history. Among those showing discontinuity, 5 percent with early disruptive behavior were no longer symptomatic in adolescence, while 7 percent without early behavior problems developed an adolescent conduct disorder.

In addition, complex *patterns* of continuity and discontinuity are found when samples are studied more closely. For example, McGee and colleagues (1992) report other findings from the New Zealand longitudinal sample. Analyzing just the data from

Box 3.1   **Are the Problems of America's Children Getting Worse?**

We frequently hear it said that things are worse now than in the past. Is this true when it comes to childhood psychopathology? Achenbach and Howell (1993) set out to answer this question by comparing rates of maladjustment in children over a 13-year period. Parents' and teachers' reports on the CBCL were obtained from large samples collected at multiple sites across the United States from 1976 and 1989. The authors found that there were significant increases over time in all problems reported, and that these were not limited to a particular area of functioning; children demonstrated increases in both internalizing and externalizing disorders over the 13-year period. In addition, the proportion of children in the clinical range increased on all scales, particularly Attention Problems, Internalizing, and Externalizing. Over 18 percent of the sample scored in the clinical range in 1989, as compared to only 10 percent in 1976. Children's average competence scores also decreased.

The investigators also compared the rates of maladjustment shown by the U.S. sample with those found in other countries, including Thailand, Australia, Puerto Rico, and Holland, and found that cross-culturally the 1989 U.S. rates were not significantly higher. Further, demographic variables did not account for problem behavior, which did not differ according to child age, gender, ethnicity, or socioeconomic status.

While this study showed evidence that changes *have* occurred, it does not answer the question of *why* they occurred. Subsequently, Stanger, Achenbach, and McConaughy (1993) examined the risk factors associated with the development of adjustment problems over a 3-year period in a large national sample of children. Disturbance was accounted for by the presence of multiple risk factors, the most powerful of which were child attention problems, parental stress, and a need for mental health services on the part of any family member. Whether these risk factors increased in prevalence and intensity during the period from 1976 and 1989 is not known; if so, that would provide one potential explanation for the increase seen in children's problem behavior. What other factors do you think might have come into play?

age 11 to age 15, they found that girls who demonstrated anxiety or depression at time 1 were 6.2 times more likely to have anxiety or depression at time 2 than were girls without earlier internalizing problems. Girls' externalizing problems revealed no such continuity. In contrast, boys who demonstrated conduct problems at time 1 were 4.2 times more likely to have an externalizing disorder at time 2. Remarkably, boys who showed *internalizing* problems at time 1 were 5.8 times as likely to have an externalizing disorder at time 2! The authors speculate that *mediating factors* associated with gender—peer pressures, societal expectations, the quality of parent–child relationships—may cause these different developmental trajectories to come about. Evidence for other mediating factors comes from Fergusson and colleagues' (1996) study of externalizing disorders. Children whose early behavior problems remitted had fewer of the risk factors—including economic disadvantage, family conflict, learning problems, and low self-esteem—that predicted continuity in other children.

Data from McGee and colleagues' study illustrates two additional issues in the continuity-discontinuity conundrum. For example, examination of just those children diagnosed with attention deficit hyperactivity disorder showed that only 10 percent were given the same diagnosis in adolescence, thereby suggesting relatively low continuity. However, only 25 percent of these children were problem-free in adolescence, as compared to 75 percent of their peers. Thus, while there may be discontinuity in a *specific* disorder, continuity may be expressed in terms of an underlying vulnerability to psychopathology *in general*. The question of *specificity* raised in Chapter 1—whether a risk factor or preexisting disorder is a predictor of one specific disorder as opposed to being a predictor of psychopathology in general—is one we will encounter again.

The second point these data illustrate is the importance of assessing *multiple risk factors* and *multiple outcomes* when attempting to assess continuity and developmental pathways. As we noted in Chapter 1, this is rarely done, since most researchers focus on one particular disorder or predictor at a time. This strategy leaves us vulnerable to either overestimating—or, as in the case just cited, underestimating—the extent to which knowledge about the past can help to predict a child's developmental outcome.

Discontinuity in well-functioning children. Even psychotic children who have the gloomiest prognosis are not all fated to become disturbed adults. But if disturbed children can "outgrow" their psychopathology, can normal children "grow into" disturbances as adults? The evidence suggests that this possibility exists. For example, while the Berkeley Growth Study did not specifically address the issue of psychopathology, it was concerned with the kind of adjustment children made as adults. Some gregarious, vigorous, cheerful adolescent boys became tense, touchy, hostile men, and some bright, motivated, mature adolescent girls grew to be isolated, rigid, depressive women (Block & Haan, 1971). Therefore, yet another type of discontinuity is the change from healthy beginnings to subsequent psychological disturbance.

The idea that certain well-functioning children are at risk for becoming disturbed is a perplexing but important one. The developmental approach requires an equal concern with "growing into" as with "outgrowing" psychopathology; however, few data are available to help us understand this phenomenon. Just what are the telltale signs indicating that all is not as well as it appears to be? Some insight into this kind of discontinuity can be gleaned from Fergusson and colleagues' (1996) study of externalizing disorders. Those without behavior problems in childhood who went on to develop later conduct disorder were more likely to associate with delinquent peers in adolescence. Therefore, just as with the transition from a pathological to a normative course, unexpected negative outcomes may be accounted for by *mediating factors* within and external to the child.

Resilience

An in-depth study of resilience was conducted on the Hawaiian island of Kauai. Werner and Smith (1992) evaluated 505 individuals in infancy, early and middle childhood, late adolescence, and early adulthood. True to the interactive model, they conceptualized resilience as the balance between risk and protective factors. *Risk factors* included poverty, perinatal stress, and parental psychopathology or discord. Most of the low-risk participants became competent, confident, caring adults, while two-thirds of the high-risk participants had delinquency records, mental health or severe marital problems, or were divorced. The authors were particularly interested in the remaining third of the high-risk group who became competent, confident, caring adults.

The authors were able to isolate three clusters of *protective factors*: (1) at least average *intelligence* and *personal attributes* that elicited positive responses from family members and other adults, such as robustness, vigor, and a sociable temperament; (2) *affectionate ties* with parent substitutes such as grandparents or older siblings, which encouraged trust, autonomy, and initiative; and (3) an external *support system* in church, youth groups, or school, which rewarded competence.

The authors were also able to chart the complex *interactions* among protective variables at a given point in time and the ways in which these interactions set the stage for subsequent developments. We can only sample their findings. Active, sociable, temperamentally easy-to-care-for infants elicited more positive responses from their mothers at age 1 and from alternative caregivers at age 2 and had a wider network of caring adults in middle childhood. In addition, positive parental interactions with the infant were related to greater autonomy and social maturity at age 2 and with greater scholastic competence at age 10. Scholastic competence at 10, in turn, was positively linked with a sense of self-efficacy at age 18 and to less distress for adult men and a greater number of sources of emotional support for adult women, including spouse or mate. Scholastic competence at 10 was also positively related to parental education. This interaction of intra- and interpersonal variables over time nicely fits the general developmental framework we presented in Chapter 1.

Finally, the authors were able to determine the relative weight of risk and protective factors in contributing to the favorable outcome in the high-risk group. Overall, rearing conditions were a more potent determinant of outcome than prenatal and perinatal complications, while the intrapersonal qualities of competence, self-esteem, self-efficacy, and temperamental disposition were more important than the interpersonal variables of parental competence and sources of support within and outside the family. These intrapersonal qualities, which we call *initiative*, enabled the participants to take advantage of the opportunities for growth that life offered them at various turning points, such as joining the military in order to gain educational skills or becoming an active member of the religious community in order to find a social support network in adolescence. While manifested in different ways at different developmental periods, initiative itself was continuously present from infancy until adulthood.

Resilience Versus Invulnerability   Luthar (1993) makes an important observation about studies of resilient children. While earlier work referred to these children as *"invulnerable,"* this term implies an imperviousness to harm that does not characterize them accurately. For example, Luthar noted subtle ways in which resilient children in her study still carried a legacy of their adverse upbringing. While resilient individuals were less likely to behave in ways that labeled them as troublesome to others, they still showed signs of being inwardly troubled: 85 percent of them had significant symptoms in the areas of anxiety and depression. By the same token, many resilient adults in Werner and Smith's (1992) sample had stress-related health problems such as migraines and backaches, as well as feelings of dissatisfaction with their lives in general, in many cases related to the burdens of caring for their nonresilient parents and siblings. Thus, resilient children are not invulnerable, and their good social functioning may come at some personal cost. (For further discussion of issues regarding the study of resilience, see Cicchetti and Garmezy, 1993.)

Summary and Evaluation

This overview of diagnostic categories and longitudinal studies helps us appreciate the special fund of information a professional must have to make knowledgeable statements concerning diagnosis and prognosis epitomized by the statement, "Most children of this age act like this and your child will outgrow it," or the more ominous statement, "The behavior is unusual and your child should receive special help." We now have at least a working idea of what the psychopathologies are, when they are apt to appear, and the chances of their continuing, changing into other psychopathologies, or disappearing with time.

We have also ventured in a preliminary way into the realm of prevention and treatment. The longitudinal data suggest that special efforts should be directed toward eliminating or ameliorating the early psychoses, severe acting-out behavior, and mental retardation. Ironically, these are the very disturbances that are responsive only to the most heroic therapeutic efforts and can be prevented only in special instances.

Also troublesome is the ethical issue of providing psychotherapy for those children who are apt to "outgrow" their deviant behavior without treatment. In such cases intervention is not needed to forestall even greater and more intractable trouble in the future—one of the bedrock reasons for treating children. Rather, the clinician must find other grounds for recommending treatment, such as a humanitarian concern that children should not suffer unduly, even if such suffering is temporary. Parents also have the right to be informed before treatment that the chances are in favor of the child's outgrowing his or her disturbance. They should also know that a probability statement is not a guarantee, because there is always the possibility that a particular child will continue to be disturbed. With such information parents can make an informed decision whether to agree to treatment for their child.

The longitudinal overview has also dispelled any notion that children are easier to treat than adults. As with adults, some children respond readily to treatment, while others are highly resistive.

The decision to become a professional helper should be made on the basis of wanting to help children and finding such help intrinsically rewarding, not on the basis of an expectation that the task will be an easy one.

We are now ready for a detailed exploration of selected psychopathologies. As much as possible we will take them in chronological order, from a development standpoint. However, since depression and schizophrenia may appear at different points in development, we have located them to reflect the concentration of research in the infancy to middle-childhood period in the case of depression, and the concentration of research in the middle-childhood period in the case of schizophrenia. In all cases we will use the information about normal development provided in Chapter 2 to answer the question, How can this psychopathology be understood in terms of normal development gone awry? How deviations from normality at one point in time affect future development will also be discussed. This dual concern requires reconstructing the natural history of the psychopathology. Finally, the issue of the efficacy of psychotherapeutic measures in curtailing further deviance will be addressed. However, a systematic examination of psychotherapy will come only after we conclude our exploration of the psychopathologies.

Autism: A Severe Deviation in Infancy

What lies at the heart of human development in the first two years of life? The establishment of the bond of love, surely, and curiosity, and symbolic communication culminating in speech. And what if all were wrenched from their normal course? We would rightly predict severe psychopathology. One such psychopathology that could result is **autism**, the subject of this chapter. We will first outline autism's behavioral manifestations and effects on subsequent development. After that we will raise the seemingly simple question mentioned in previous chapters—How can this psychopathology be understood in terms of normal development gone awry?—and find how complex the answers are.

Definition and Characteristics

Definition

Early Description

In his classic paper Kanner (1943) delineated the three essential features of early infantile autism. The first is extreme *social isolation* and an inability to relate to people. For example, in a face-to-face situation a girl with severe autism will not look at you or even away from you; rather, she will look *through* you. If you put her on your lap, her body will not accommodate to yours; instead she will sit as if you were a chair. If she needs you to do something, say, open a door, she will take your hand (rather than taking *you* by the hand) and bring it in contact with a doorknob. It is as if you do not exist as a person but, at best, as a thing.

The second characteristic of autism is a pathological *need for sameness*. This need applies both to the child's own behavior and to the environment. Often the child's activities are simple, such as sitting on the floor and rocking back and forth for long periods of time, or twirling his or her shoelaces, or running up and down a hall. Sometimes the activities resemble complex rituals, such as the activities of a 5½-year-old who takes a toy truck, turns it on its side, spins a wheel while making a humming noise, goes over to the window, looks out while drumming his fingers on the sill, and then returns to the truck, only to repeat the exact same sequence over and over.

The need for environmental sameness can be expressed in a number of ways; for example, the child must have the exact same food and plate and utensils, or wear the same article of clothing, or have the same arrangement of furniture. The intensity of the need is evidenced not only by the rigidity of the behavior but also by the child's panic and rage when attempts are made to alter the environment even in minor ways, such as providing a different food or moving a chair to a different part of the room.

The third characteristic of autism is either *mutism* or *noncommunicative speech*. The former will be lifelong for 50 percent of the population (Klinger and Dawson, 1996). Noncommunicative speech may include echolalia (exact repetition of words or phrases spoken by others with no effort to comprehend their meaning); using phrases or sentences that are irrelevant to the situation (for example, while repeatedly flushing the toilet, a girl with autism suddenly said, "The hamburgers are in the refrigerator!"); extreme literalness (for example, when taught to say "Please" to get a cookie, a boy with autism would use the word only when he wanted a cookie, as if "please" and "cookie" had become inseparably linked); and difficulty using the first-person singular pronoun, with the child typically referring to himself by name (for example, "Jack wants to go out" rather than "I want to go out") or using "you" instead of "I" (for example, "You want to go out"). (For a study of use of pronouns, see Lee, Hobson and Chiat, 1994.)

DSM-IV Definition

The DSM-IV summarizes the current view of the basic diagnostic features of autism. (See Table 4.1.) Note that Kanner's three core criteria for autism—social isolation, mutism or noncommunicative speech, and a pathological need for sameness—have stood the test of time, although there are certain modifications and elaborations in regard to specific manifestations.

Associated Features

There are other behaviors that may be present in autism but are not essential to it. Children with

Table 4.1   DSM-IV Criteria for Autistic Disorder

1. Qualitative impairment in social interaction, as manifested by at least two of the following:
   a. Marked impairment in the use of multiple nonverbal behaviors such as eye-to-eye gaze, facial expression, body postures, and gestures to regulate social interaction
   b. Failure to develop peer relationships appropriate to developmental level
   c. A lack of spontaneous seeking to share enjoyment, interests, or achievements with other people (e.g., a lack of showing, bringing, or pointing out objects of interest)
   d. Lack of social or emotional reciprocity
2. Qualitative impairments in communication as manifested by at least one of the following:
   a. Delay in, or total lack of, the development of spoken language (not accompanied by an attempt to compensate through alternative modes of communication such as gesture or mime)
   b. In individuals with adequate speech, marked impairment in the ability to initiate or sustain a conversation with others
   c. Stereotyped and repetitive use of language or idiosyncratic language
   d. Lack of varied spontaneous make-believe play or social imitative play appropriate to developmental level
3. Restricted repetitive and stereotyped patterns of behavior, interests, and activities, as manifested by at least one of the following:
   a. Encompassing preoccupation with one or more stereotyped and restricted patterns of interest that is abnormal either in intensity or focus
   b. Apparently inflexible adherence to specific, nonfunctional routines or rituals
   c. Stereotyped and repetitive motor mannerisms (e.g., hand or finger flapping or twisting, or complex whole body movements)
   d. Persistent preoccupation with parts of objects

autism are frequently healthy and appear to be intelligent, judging by their facial expressions. They also may have excellent rote memory and may perform remarkable feats of remembering names or tunes or pictures. They are also more at home and content in the world of physical objects than they are in the interpersonal world.

Finally, autism is often associated with self-injurious behavior such as head banging or hitting, slapping, scratching, or biting oneself, although such behaviors are also found in children with other disturbances.

Characteristics

Age of Onset

Although autistic behavior may be noted in early infancy, it can also appear after a period of up to 30 months of normal development. Oddly enough, its appearance at this later date is not necessarily associated with any particular precipitating event.

Prevalence

It was previously believed that the frequency of autism was low, ranging from 4 to 6 per 10,000 children. More recent studies place the frequency between 6.6 to 13.6 per 10,000 children (Gillberg, 1991). Differences in findings may be due, in part, to how narrow or wide a definition of autism is used (Vicker and Monahan, 1988).

Gender and Socioeconomic Status

More boys than girls are diagnosed with autism, the ratios ranging from 2.6:1 to 5.7:1 when Kanner's criteria are used (Gillberg, 1990). While it was initially thought that autism existed only in the middle class, subsequent studies have shown that it is found in all classes (Gillberg, 1990).

Comorbidity

Based on his observation that the children looked intelligent and some could perform impressive feats of memory, Kanner inferred that children with autism were of average intelligence and that their disturbance was responsible for their functioning at lower levels. Subsequent research proved him wrong. Between 76 and 89 percent have impaired intelligence,

The social imperviousness and manneristic behavior of the autistic child.

with IQ scores falling below 70. Children with autism are better at nonverbal, visual-spatial tasks than at verbal ones. Their IQ is also very stable, being predictive of future academic and work achievement (Klinger & Dawson, 1996).

Autism can also coexist with known organic brain pathologies. Both grand mal and psychomotor seizures develop in about one-third of the autistic population, with the first few years of life and adolescence being peak times (Gillberg, 1988).

Developmental Course

One would correctly predict that so severe and pervasive a disturbance occurring so early in life would have ominous implications for future development. As adults, fully 60 percent of children with autism will be completely dependent in all aspects of life. Between 5 and 15 percent will achieve a satisfactory social and occupational adjustment (Lotter, 1978). Typically they cope with life by scrupulously sticking to the rules of acceptable behavior. Work and play have the same quality of being learned by rote without the freedom to vary and improvise that comes with full understanding. They are devoid of empathy and seem generally indifferent to sexuality (Paul, 1987).

No communicative speech by 5 years of age and an IQ below 60 are poor prognostic signs, along with early seizure onset and possibly seizure onset in adolescence (Gillberg, 1991). Those who do achieve communicative speech by 5 years of age and have average intelligence have only a 50-50 chance of making an adequate adjustment (Rutter & Garmenzy, 1983). Thus, the prognosis is poor under the most favorable conditions, and the overall prognosis is worse than that of other severe childhood disturbances, such as schizophrenia and mental deficiency.

Quantitative Versus Qualitative Differences

Note that DSM-IV uses the term "qualitative" when describing impairment in social interaction and communication (see Table 4.1). Whether psychopathology represents a quantitative or a qualitative difference from normality is a perennial question. Generally speaking, the *quantitative* view is more prevalent: phobias are regarded as extremes of normal fears, delinquency is viewed as an exaggeration of normal adolescent rebelliousness. The three major developmental models of psychopathology—fixation, regression, and developmental delay—are quantitative. DSM-IV's description of autism in terms of *qualitative* impairments implies that autistic behavior has no counterpart even in the behavior of younger, normal children and that the developmental sequencing of behavior does not follow that charted for normal children.

To evaluate the quantitative versus qualitative issue, Wenar and colleagues (1986) compared the development of 41 children with autism between 5 and 11 years of age with that of 195 normal children between 3 months and 5 years of age, using a standardized observational technique called the Behavior Rating Instrument for Autistic and Other Atypical Children (BRIAAC). The investigators found that severely autistic children's obliviousness to caretaking adults, their minimal expressiveness, their disinterest in or fleeting exploration of objects, their unresponsiveness or negative reaction to sound, and their indifference to social demands all

indicated an imperviousness to the social and physical environment that had little counterpart in normal behavior and development. In a like manner Dawson (1991), in discussing early socioemotional development, concludes that in certain cases both the surface behavior and the function or need it fulfills may be unique to the autistic child, and parallels in normal developmental patterns may be difficult to find.

Etiology: An Overview

A Simple Formula

There is a simple formula for understanding the primary features of autism: the major pleasures and interests of normal infants are *aversive* to ones with autism.

In the first weeks of life a multitude of factors conspire to make the *adult human* the most attractive and pleasurable stimulus for the normal infant. For example, the human voice quickly becomes preferred over all other sounds, and the patterning of the face, particularly the eyes, holds a special fascination; moreover, the infant learns to adjust his or her body to that of the caretaker when held and to anticipate relief from distress when the caretaker comes into view. Next, the need for *variable stimulation* lies at the heart of exploration of the environment, and the infant is nicely constituted to seek ever more complex challenges as the simple ones are mastered. In autism, the very basis of social and cognitive development is undermined, so avoidance and repetition replace approach and expansion.

While this formula may serve as a general orientation to the etiology of autism, it glosses over the many specific deviations characterizing autistic behavior that have come to light through research. The roots of autism are complex, and the search for a single key that produces autism is as futile as searching for a single key that produces normal development.

The psychological roots of autism are largely unknown at present. Strictly speaking, an etiological agent should precede autism in time and be the necessary and sufficient condition for producing it.

Etiological agents should also be differentiated from behaviors that represent other manifestations of the disturbance and behaviors that result from the disturbance. Because autism is rare and appears so early in development, such fine distinctions cannot be made at present.

The Search for Autism-Specific Functions

Autism is a pervasive developmental disorder; that is, a wide range of psychological functions may be adversely affected. Just what are these functions and how do they relate to the defining characteristics of autism?

Let us look at the first question concerning *what psychological functions are deviant*. Because the behavior of children with autism deviates so widely from normal, we can raise the question of whether they actually *perceive* their environment as normal children do. For example, some children with autism prefer mouthing or smelling or touching objects to looking at them. Thus, they seem to be taking in the physical environment through the more primitive senses of touch and smell rather than through the more advanced sense of vision. Could this be one clue to understanding their other deviant behaviors? Is their preference for physical objects over people due to a problem in *attention* or to a difficulty in *processing the information* that characterizes the complex and variable behavior of humans? Is their need for sameness due to a deficiency in *initiative*, and is their imperviousness to others due to an *affective* blunting? This is only a sampling of possible answers to the question of what functions have been adversely affected. All of them seem plausible, but their validity can only be answered on the basis of empirical data.

Our search is complicated by another requirement—the psychological functions must be *specific* to autism. As we have seen, many children with autism also are mentally retarded. Therefore, deviant functions that also are characteristic of mental retardation can not be regarded as essential to accounting for autism's defining features. In children with autism there also must be certain functions that develop normally and thus must be eliminated as specific to autism.

Fortunately, investigators have cast a wide net in their exploration of psychological functions, so there is a considerable body of research that will help us decide which characteristics are specific to autism, which are shared by children with mental retardation, and which are part of normal development. We will present this research a bit later in our discussion.

Organization of Research Findings

We have organized the research findings in terms of their relevance to the three defining characteristics of autism—social isolation, mutism or noncommunicative speech, and pathological need for sameness. However, this parceling into characteristics should not be taken to mean that the deviant functions affect *only* a given characteristic. Recall that our developmental model is an interactional one in which variables do not exist in isolation. Thus, one would expect that a deviant function that leads to social isolation would also affect communicative speech, which is basically interpersonal; or again, a deviant function involved in the pathological need for sameness would hamper the development of increasingly complex social relations. Thus our organization of research findings is, in part, a matter of convenience, since tracing the multiple interactions would unduly complicate our presentation.

Social Isolation

Autistic children's deviant transaction with their human environment is one of the most striking features of their psychopathology, and the research on the interpersonal context is extensive. We have divided the literature into two broad developmental periods: the infant and toddler period and the preschool and middle childhood period. Recall that autism develops in the first 30 months of life when the basic dimensions of human relatedness are being established, which is why we discuss this period apart from the rest of childhood.

The Infant and Toddler Period

The relation to the caregiver is central in this period. In the case of autism a number of factors conspire to divert development from its normal course.

Gaze Pattern

While normal neonates are not capable of establishing *eye contact* until the end of the first month of life, the ability to do so is an important step in the bonding process: mothers typically react with pleasure and say (wrongly) that the infant now "knows her." By 6 months the infant will initiate social contact through gaze, while infant and caregiver engage in coordinated patterns of engagement and looking away. Toddlers use gaze to signal the completion of their own vocalization and to invite the partner to speak (Volkmar and Mayes, 1990). Thus gaze plays an important role in a number of early social interactions.

The gaze of children with autism is deviant. In extreme cases they look through or past the adult, thus preventing the development of interactional patterns mediated by gaze. Studies of older children with autism who have established some sort of ability for eye contact find that the eye contact lacks the nice *complementarity* of normal glance exchange. For example, children with autism are more likely than those with mental retardation to look elsewhere rather than at adults and to look less at adults during one-to-one interactions (Buitelaar et al., 1991; Volkmar & Mayes, 1990).

This deviant use of eye contact is also involved in the clinical observation that children with autism treat others as objects rather than as people. Phillips and colleagues (1995) studied how children with autism and normal children used adults to get an out-of-reach toy on a shelf. While the autistic group used the adults less frequently (by trying to climb on the shelf by themselves, for example), they did gesture appropriately by pointing or pulling the adult toward the shelf; what they did *not* do is use eye contact as did the children in the normal group. This lack of eye contact may give the impression that the adult is being treated as an object because most people equate eye contact with being recognized as a human being. Recall that, when infants first are able to establish eye contact, the mother wrongly concludes that the infant "knows her."

Affect

The social smile appears at around 2½ to 3 months of age in normal infants and plays a major role in binding the infant and caregiver in mutually pleasurable exchanges. In severely disturbed infants with autism, the social smile is conspicuously absent. Moreover, while 30- to 70-month-old children with autism look and smile at their mother as frequently as do normal children, they do not combine smiling with eye contact in a single act, and they are less likely to smile in response to the mother's smile. Thus they are not deficient in the quantitative expression of affect but rather in its *communication*. This baffling uncoupling of affect and gaze in children with autism may account for the fact that their mothers smile less at them than do mothers of normal children (Dawson et al., 1990).

Vocalization

The human voice is innately attractive to the neonate and, by 2 to 4 months of age, normal infants and their mothers engage in patterns of simultaneous and alternating vocal exchanges that may be the precursor of later verbal communication. While there are few studies of children with autism concerning vocal communication, their characteristic mutism, evidenced by lack of babbling, blocks this avenue of social interaction.

Social Imitation

In normal infants social imitation is present shortly after birth. In children with autism there is a significant impairment of imitation of other people's movements. Incidentally, such imitation is correlated with the subsequent development of social responsiveness, free play, and language. Individuals with autism between 8 and 26 months of age can imitate facial expressions but often have to go through a number of bizarre and mechanical responses, indicating how difficult this behavior is for them. (For a more detailed presentation, see Klinger & Dawson, 1996.)

Initiative and Reciprocity

When responded to contingently by sensitive caregivers, normal infants soon begin to take the initiative in eliciting responses. This, in turn, can lead to simple back-and-forth sequences which mark the beginning of reciprocity. For example, when the mother pauses after delighting her infant daughter by tickling her tummy during diapering, the infant might flail her arms and legs, signaling that she wants more. In this way a sequence of pleasure-pause-signal-pleasure is established, which continues until mother or infant tires.

The most direct evidence concerning initiative in autism comes from a study of home movies of eight infants who subsequently became autistic. There was a decline in social play in the second year, with the children being passive recipients of adults' playful overtures rather than actively interacting with them (Losche, 1990).

There is another precursor of social reciprocity called **joint attention behavior** that has been of considerable interest to researchers. The normal 6- to 9-month-old will look between an object and the caretaker, as if to say, "Look what I am looking at." This is called *referential looking*. Toward the end of the first year of life, the normal infant starts using gestures, such as pointing to an object when a caregiver is present or holding an object up for the caregiver to see. Rather than attending to an object alone, the infant now tries to attract the adult's attention so that the interest can be *shared*. Note that the infant is assuming the initiative and the goal is sharing. The infant is not signaling in order to get an adult to do something the infant cannot do, such as bringing a toy which is out of reach.

In low-functioning preschoolers with autism there is a deficiency in both gestural and referential looking, whereas in high-functioning preschoolers with autism the deficiency is in gestures only. There is also evidence that when joint attention behavior occurs in children with autism, it is not accompanied by the sharing of positive affect as it is in normal children and those with Down syndrome. (See Kasari et al., 1990, and Roeyers, Van Oost, & Bothuyne, 1998.) Thus, referential and gestural behaviors are *socioemotional* ones, and autism robs them of the affective signals of smiling and laughter that play such an important role in reinforcing the adult–infant interplay (Mundy, 1995).

There is more at stake here than a specific social gesture, since joint attention behavior is concurrently associated with language development and is a significant predictor of future language acquisition in autism. (For a more detailed presentation of joint attention behavior, see Klinger & Dawson, 1996, and Carpenter, Nagell, & Tomasello, 1998.)

Attachment

While it was once thought that children with autism were incapable of forming an attachment, recent studies using the Ainsworth Strange Situation showed that 40 to 50 percent of those studied were securely attached, which comes close to the 65 percent found in the normal population.

However, it would be a mistake to conclude that there are no differences between the autistic and the normal populations in regard to attachment. Behaviorally, attachment in children with autism is interspersed with their characteristic repetitive motor movements such as hand flapping, rocking, and spinning. Their behavior is also more variable over time than it is in normal populations, although it does not differ from that of children with mental retardation (Dissanayake & Crossley, 1997).

There is another issue here. Attachment is often measured in terms of responses to separation from and reunion with the mother. Such behaviors are regarded as so critical to the survival of the species that they have been programmed into the infant by evolution. Thus one would expect them to be highly stable. However, attachment involves more than these behaviors aimed at seeking and maintaining proximity. It also involves a *working model*, or mental image, of the mother and of the mother–child relationship. This kind of complex mental image is probably beyond the cognitive capabilities of young children with autism (Capps, Sigman, & Mundy, 1994). Thus, while the child with autism may have a working model of mother as someone who is a source of security and pleasure, it is doubtful that this child can evolve an image of the mother as a person in her own right, with her unique thoughts, motives, desires, and personality.

Compliance and Negativism

There is evidence that children with autism are compliant to requests if such requests are within their intellectual grasp. Thus, they can respond appropriately when they are in a predictable, highly contingent, structured environment. Also, in spite of the fact that they have been described as being excessively negativistic, there is no evidence to support such a claim (Volkmar, 1986).

Table 4.2 presents a summary of the research on social isolation for the infant and toddler periods.

The Preschool and Middle Childhood Period

At around 5 years of age the more extreme manifestations of social isolation diminish in children with autism, although the general picture is still one of significant deviation. We now turn to the motivational-affective factors associated with this deviation and then to a discussion of the reciprocity that lies at the heart of normal social interaction.

Motivational-Affective Factors

The motivation to be an *active participant* in the social environment, which is so strong in normal children, is weak in those with autism. Parents report that their children have less interest in peers, for example, and do not join them in play or imitate them (Parker et al., 1995).

On the affective side, clinicians have described children with autism as lacking in *empathy*, the process by which a person responds affectively to another as if he or she were experiencing the same affect. In normal development empathy has been observed in preschoolers, although it might appear even earlier. In one of the few objective studies, Yirmiya and colleagues (1992) found that even nonretarded children with autism between 9 and 16 years of age performed less well than normal controls on empathy-related measures. Case histories on adults who no longer have the classical autistic symptoms (but still are not normal) note that this deficiency persists; for example, at times such adults may be bewildered when trying to understand how others feel, or they may be socially awkward, failing to realize when a tactful glossing over of a painful truth is preferable to embarrassing honesty.

Reciprocity

Reciprocity requires a finely tuned give-and-take between individuals. Senders must adjust their messages to what they infer to be the receivers'

Table 4.2   Social Isolation: Interpersonal Variables in the Infant and Toddler Period*

Gaze: Looking through or past adults in interaction	AS
Positive affect: absent or not coupled with gaze	AS
Vocalization†: mutism	AS
Social Imitation: impaired or difficult	AS
Initiative: passive recipient	AS
Reciprocity:	
Deficient joint attention behavior	AS
Deficient shared affect	AS
Attachment:	
Attachment behaviors intact but variable	AMA
Working models deficient	DN
Compliance and negativism	AMA

*AS=specific to autism; DN=below normal but mental retardation not controlled for; AMA=age-appropriate or mental-age-appropriate.
†Data meager.

level of comprehension, while receivers must be able to grasp the message that has been sent. Moreover, each subsequent message must be adjusted to the content of the previous one. The messages themselves can be both verbal and nonverbal, the latter including gestures, tone of voice, and body language. It is not surprising that reciprocity, which begins so early in life that it becomes automatic much of the time in normal children, presents major obstacles to those with autism. In fact, an inability to fully participate in age-appropriate reciprocal social interaction may persist throughout their lives (Baron-Cohen, 1988). Since we will cover the difficulties with verbal messages later in the sections on language comprehension and communication, we will now turn to the literature concerning the *nonverbal* aspects of social interactions, specifically dealing with receptive and expressive difficulties.

Receptive Difficulties

Children with autism know that people exist independently of them and understand that people are agents of action in regard to physical objects; for example, they understand that people can cook food and drive cars (Rogers and Pennington, 1991). However, they are less able than are normal children to recognize the face or voice of a familiar individual from photographs or sound recordings, perhaps because they do not attend as closely to people or because of a cognitive difficulty in processing complex social stimuli (Boucher, Lewis, & Collis, 1998).

But what about their ability to understand the *feelings* of others? Most of the studies in this area involve recognition of facial expressions of emotions as depicted either in photographs or drawings. Hobson, Ouston, and Lee (1988) found that adolescents with autism were able to sort photographs of faces according to mood (e.g., happy or sad) just as well as a group of children with mental retardation. However, the autistic children's criteria used for sorting the expressions were unusual: when given the choice of sorting according to expression or according to the type of hat worn by the people in the photographs, they chose the hat more often than did the children with mental retardation, suggesting that they found expression less salient.

In everyday life, emotions are not expressed by a face in isolation from the rest of the body, and it is this integration of information from diverse sources that proves difficult for many children with autism. The technical term for this integration is *cross-modal perception*. The basic studies were done by Hobson (1986a, 1986b), who found that children with autism were less capable than those with mental retardation in matching facial expressions of various emotions to the appropriate vocal and bodily expressions. Thus, the fact that people look and sound and act in special ways when displaying the basic emotions of happiness, sadness, anger, and fear is not readily grasped. However, there are a sufficient number of negative findings to cause some investigators to question whether recognition of affect is a primary deficit rather than being a result of a difficulty with cross-modal perception in general (Ozonoff, Pennington, & Rogers, 1990).

Finally, there is evidence that children with autism understand the *causes* of emotions, at least at a simple level; for example, they understand the relation between situations and affect in that one feels happy at a birthday party and unhappy when one falls down. They also understand that desires cause emotions in that the fulfillment of desire leads to positive affect, while frustration leads to negative affect. Thus, a child who wants candy and is given some is happy; a child who cannot find her mother is sad.

Turning now to the understanding of gestures, what little objective data there are indicate that children with autism do as well as children with mental retardation in recognizing simple instrumental gestures such as pointing, moving the finger to indicate "come here," or putting the finger to the lips to convey "Be quiet" (Attwood, Frith, & Hermelin, 1988; see also Baron-Cohen, 1991).

Expressive Difficulties

Clinical observations suggest that, while preschool children with autism evidence the basic affective reactions of pleasure, wariness, and rage, they lack the more highly developed ones such as shame, affection, and guilt, which are usually present by 2 to 3 years of age in normal children (Dawson & Galpert, 1986). It is worth noting that these highly developed affects require a greater degree of cognitive elaboration than do the basic affects—for example, guilt requires an understanding of right and wrong. In the interpersonal realm, 2- to 4-year-old children with autism display less positive affect interacting with adults than do developmentally delayed children (Mundy & Sigman, 1989b). Subsequently, a dearth of facial expression, poverty of bodily gestures, and lack of modulation in expressive aspect of voice give an impression of woodenness.

In an objective study, Attwood, Frith, & Hermelin (1988) found that adolescents with autism were no different from normal and retarded children matched for mental age in regard to using instrumental or action-oriented gestures (just as they were no different in understanding such gestures, as we have just shown). However, they never used gestures expressing *feelings* concerning the self or others, gestures such as hugging and kissing another child, putting an arm around another to console or as a sign of friendship, or putting the hand over the face to express embarrassment. Such social gestures, unlike instrumental ones, require knowledge of how another person feels along with an expression of one's own feelings and desires.

Cognitive Variables

Two cognitive variables that lie at the heart of reciprocity are *perspective taking* and *theory of mind*.

Perspective Taking   Piaget claimed that the infant views the physical and social environment in terms of the self, a phenomenon he calls egocentrism. Gradually, however, the developing child is able to view the environment from the perspective of others, to see the world through other people's eyes. This ability is called perspective taking and is crucial to the ability to communicate and engage in reciprocal social interactions. (See Piaget, 1967.)

There is evidence that children with autism have unevenly developed perspective-taking ability. Reed and Peterson (1990) compared 12-year-old children with autism with a group of normal children and a group with mental retardation, matched for mental age, on two kinds of perspective-taking tasks, one *perceptual* and the other *cognitive*. The perceptual task required the child to imagine what another person could see when looking at an object from that person's vantage point. For example, there were various toy animals on a turntable and the experimenter, who was sitting across from the child, requested to see parts of the animals' bodies such as their nose or tail. To comply correctly, the child had to rotate the turntable until the animal was in the correct position in terms of the experimenter's perspective.

The cognitive task, the other part of this research, required the ability to assess another person's belief. The situation used is called **false belief** and requires the child to infer what another person knows and does not know. In this particular setup the experimenter used a variation of the "Sally–Anne" experiment of Baron-Cohen, Leslie and Frith (1985) in which dolls act out the following sequence: Sally and Anne are in a room together; Sally hides a marble in a basket and leaves the room; Anne transfers the marble to a box; Sally returns. (See Figure 4.1.) The experimenter then asks the child the crucial question: Where will Sally look for the marble? The child must understand that Sally will act on her belief even though it is no longer valid. A correct answer indicates that the child has distinguished what he or she knows from what the doll knows. In Reed

and Peterson's (1990) study, the children with autism performed as well as the two control groups on the perceptual tasks but *not* as well on the cognitive ones. However, the evidence in regard to false beliefs is not totally consistent. Tager-Flusberg and Sullivan (1994), for example, show that children with autism did as well as those with mental retardation if the task was simplified by making it significantly shorter and less complex.

Theory of Mind   While developmental psychologists have extensively explored children's understanding of their physical and social environment, they have only recently turned their attention to studying children's understanding of the content and function of mental life, such as what perception, memory, intentions, or dreams are and how they function. The term used for this study of the understanding of mental life is **theory of mind**. (See Wellman, 1988, 1993.)

Researchers have explored certain aspects of the theory of mind in autism. (See Baron-Cohen, 1995. Yirmiya et al., 1998, discuss the issue of autism-specificity.) The aspects that will interest us most are those affecting reciprocal interactions, which, as we have said, require each participant to make inferences concerning the other's mental life and to adjust communication accordingly. We will discuss the difficulty autistic children have in grasping the mental lives of others, particularly their beliefs and desires, and how these difficulties affect their thinking and communication.

We have already discussed false belief, which involves inferring what others do and do not know. This can be viewed in terms of either perspective taking or theory of mind, since the two concepts overlap. Let us explore how false beliefs relate to another characteristic of children with autism that we have noted, namely, their tendency to be *literal* in their thinking. For example, if, at the dinner table, a parent says to a child with autism, "Can you pass the salt," the child is apt to answer, "Yes," interpreting "can" as "are you able to." Such literalism can be scary: a girl with autism was terrified when a nurse asked her to "Give me your hand" because she thought the nurse literally wanted her hand (Frith, 1989).

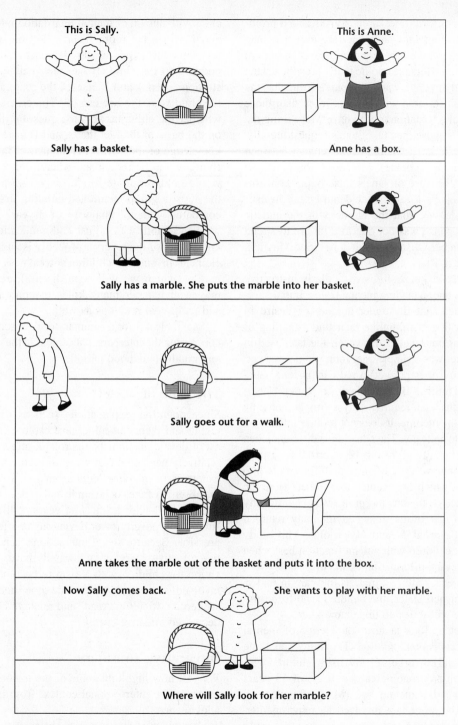

Figure 4.1   The Sally–Anne Experiment.

From Frith, U., Autism. Explaining the enigma 1989, Cambridge, MA, Basil Blackwell Inc.
Figures copyright by Axel Scheffler, 1989.

Now let us turn to research, considering a proto-typical situation. Jane and Mary are together. Jane puts a cookie in the cookie jar and leaves the room; Mary then transfers the cookie to the breadbox. Jane returns and says, "I want a cookie. Bring me the cookie jar." Children with autism, more than those with mental retardation, opt to have Mary bring the cookie jar because they take Jane's request literally. They do *not* infer that there is a discrepancy between desire (wanting a cookie) and request (bring me the cookie jar) because of Jane's false belief concerning the cookie's location. Incidentally, the investigators made sure that the children in the autistic group's response was not due to a failure to attend to or remember what had been done. (See Mitchell, Saltmarsh, & Russell, 1997.)

The research on *desire* is particularly instructive in terms of understanding mental states. Initial studies indicated that the understanding of desire in children with autism, unlike their understanding of beliefs, was unimpaired. However, the task used in these studies was a simple one: John wants a red car; John gets (or does not get) a red car; is John satisfied? As Phillips, Baron-Cohen, & Rutter (1995) point out, this task requires only a simple matching of goal with outcome. It does not require inferring a mental state of desire. The situation is different when desire is implicit and has to be inferred; for example, Matt jumps into the water and Tony falls into the water—which one wanted to get wet? Here the performance of the autistic group was significantly inferior to that of the matched mentally retarded group and normal 5- and 6-year-olds. This study shows that children with autism function best when all the relevant information is manifest and overt; when inferences are required, as they are in understanding mental states, the children tend to be impaired. We will return to this theme later.

Now let us look at how knowledge of mental states affects *communication*. The study was done by Perner and coworkers (1989) using children with autism with a chronological age (CA) of 13 years 6 months and a mental age (MA) of 6 years 2 months. The procedure involved an experimenter, two collaborators, A and B, and a toy bee that could make flying motions and nod its head. The experimenter demonstrated the flying motions to the

child with autism or mental retardation while A but not B was in the room. Then A left on some pretext, and the experimenter demonstrated the bee nodding to the child. B has seen neither demonstration. Then A and B entered the room and asked the child what the bee can do. The crucial issue is whether the child answers the question differently on the basis of the fact that A and B have different knowledge of the bee; for A an answer in terms of flying would be redundant, whereas either answer would be appropriate for B. Only 12.5 percent of the autistic group mentioned nodding first to A as compared with the majority of 3-year-olds. This weakened ability to adjust communication to the knowledge of the receiver probably is an important element in autistic children's weakness in pragmatics (which we will soon discuss), although it may well hamper many kinds of communication and reciprocal relations as well.

See Table 4.3 for a summary of research findings concerning the interpersonal context in the preschool and middle childhood period.

The Role of Affect

Since cognitive explanations such as perspective taking and theory of mind have captured the interest of developmentalists, the role of affect has been relatively neglected. Yet we have seen a number of examples of *affective blunting* in social situations: the absence of the social smile and of delight in joint attention behavior in the first years of life and the subsequent poverty of or deviations in affective expression. Because social interactions lack the positive affective charge they normally have, the motivation for children with autism to become socially involved is reduced. At the same time such children are more difficult to "read" and relate to because of decreased affective cues.

Integrative Summary

We will now highlight some of the major developments in the interpersonal context from infancy to adolescence.

A number of factors act as obstacles to developing reciprocal interactions in the infant and toddler periods. The deviant gaze, vocalization, and social

Table 4.3   Social Isolation: Variables in the Preschool and Middle Childhood Period*

Interest in peers: low	DN
Empathy: low	AS
Reciprocity, receptive variables:	
Understanding others as agents of action:	
adequate	AMA
Recognizing familiar voices and faces: low	DN
Understanding feelings of others: low†	DS
Understanding instrumental (action)	
gestures: adequate	AMA
Understanding causes of emotions: adequate	AMA
Reciprocity, expressive variables:	
Basic affective cues: intact	AMA
Advanced affective cues: low	DN
Positive affect: low	AS
Using instrumental (action) gestures: adequate	AMA
Using expressive (affective) gestures: low	AS
Perspective Taking	
Perceptual: adequate	AMA
Cognitive (false beliefs): low†	AS
Theory of mind:	
Literal thinking: high	AS
Understanding desire: low	AS
Communication: low	AS

*AS = specific to autism; DN = below normal but mental retardation not controlled for; AMA = age-appropriate or mental-age-appropriate.
†Evidence disputed.

imitation of children with autism hamper the development of early social exchanges with the caregiver. The lack of sharing for the pleasure of sharing is indicated by the meager number of joint attention behaviors—for example, the rare occurrence of simple interactive activities such as peekaboo. (In the next section we will discuss the problems with communication through language.)

The deviant nature of affect in children with autism further hampers the development of interpersonal relations. There is very little of the delight in social exchanges seen in the first year of normal development; thus, a potent incentive to engage in such exchanges is missing. The social smile is either rare or detached from its communicative function. Children with autism are also deficient in empathy, which, in normal children, provides a direct access to the feelings of others. On the positive side, children with autism comply with requests which

are appropriate to their mental development and are no more negativistic than mental-age-matched normal children.

Since the findings concerning the preschool and middle childhood period are complex, an overview might be helpful. The understanding of the physical environment in children with autism contrasts with their understanding of the social environment. They function adequately in dealing with the former and also with the readily perceived manifestations of the latter. Thus, for example, they can see the connection between a happy expression and a birthday party. However, they are deficient in the more inferential aspects of social understanding—that the birthday girl feels happy as well as looking happy, and that she has her own fantasies, expectations, and thoughts about the party. In fact, children with autism have been humorously described as pure behaviorists, going no further than their perceptions of human behavior will lead them.

Knowledge of others in children with autism is satisfactory or appropriate to their mental age level when such knowledge is derived from external cues alone. Thus they recognize the independent physical existence of people and know that others can initiate actions; they also grasp the relation between situation and affect. At a more inferential level they can assume the perspective of others in regard to viewing the physical environment. However, inferences concerning the social environment—those concerning what other people know and believe and desire—present difficulties even when allowing for autistic children's mental and linguistic deficiencies. For example, while children with autism can understand people as agents of actions who can do things for them or give them pleasure, they are deficient in inferring what other people do and do not know. They understand and use instrumental gestures involving action (such as "Come here") or gestures involving their own need satisfaction (such as "Get me that") but they do not use expressive gestures involving their own or other people's feelings. Their understanding of other people's expressions of affect presents a mixed picture. Children with autism can categorize basic facial expressions correctly, but the integration of face with vocal and bodily cues is difficult.

An Erroneous Hypothesis: Mother-Engendered Autism

For a number of years it was popular to regard the mother as the cause of autism. She was described variously as cold, obsessive, intellectual, disturbed, psychotic, depressed, or immature. Consequently, the theory went, the mother was unable to provide the infant with the kind of sensitive care essential for healthy psychological development. A popular phrase used to epitomize her was a "refrigerator mother"—a phrase that was cruel and ultimately turned out to be unwarranted.

Subsequent objective studies proved the hypothesis of mother-engendered autism to be erroneous. Mothers of children with autism are not significantly different in their personality characteristics and attitudes toward their children from mothers of children with handicaps other than autism (McAdoo and DeMyer, 1978). At the same time, evidence has accumulated pointing to the strong organic basis for autism. Currently there is no reason for parents in general and mothers in particular to blame themselves for their children's psychopathology. Caring for an autistic child is difficult enough without the additional weight of undeserved guilt.

Noncommunicative Speech

In this section we first examine various intrapersonal components of language, including syntax and semantics, and then proceed to discuss language's interpersonal function of communication. (For a detailed account of autistic language as normal development gone awry, see Schopler & Mesibov, 1985; unless otherwise noted, our presentation follows summaries of objective studies found in that text.) We will not discuss mutism because it has received scant attention.

Symbolization and Pretend Play

Children with autism have trouble comprehending the basic concept of *symbolization*. The idea that sounds such as words can represent an object or activity lies at the heart of speech, and it is just this idea that is difficult to grasp. One kind of symbolization that has been studied in autism is *pretend play*. In pretense a piece of paper can become a plate of food, a stick can become a gun, or the child can become a tiger. In each case one thing stands for or symbolizes another.

In normal children there is an orderly progression from simple forms of play, such as stacking blocks or using one block to push another; through more complex forms, such as using a spoon to feed a doll or dialing a toy telephone and bringing the receiver to the ear; to pretend, or what is called symbolic play. A study by Sigman and coworkers (1987) found that children with autism had the same range of play as did normal toddlers but spent more time on the simpler forms.

However, most of the research has required children with autism to produce pretend play spontaneously. When they are provided with prompts, such as the investigator's asking, "What can you do with these [toys]?" or "Can you pretend to give dolly a drink [from an empty cup]?" the performance of children with autism was comparable to that of children with mental retardation (Charman & Baron-Cohen, 1997). These findings suggest that there is *not* a basic inability to pretend in children with autism but rather that they are not as *motivated* to pretend as are other children.

Syntax and Semantics

Syntax is the way words are combined to produce meaningful sentences. The evidence indicates that while children with autism may lag behind normal children, they are no different from children at a comparable intellectual level. In both production and understanding, children with autism display mastery of a variety of grammatical rules. The girl who said, "The hamburgers are in the refrigerator" while flushing the toilet repeatedly was not communicating, but her sentence was grammatically correct (see Tager-Flusberg, 1989). Moreover, children with autism follow the same developmental course in the acquisition of syntax as normal children do (Tager-Flusberg et al., 1990).

Semantics involves the meaning of words and sentences, and it is here that the autistic flaws appear. When dealing with concrete objects, children with autism may be developmentally delayed, but no more so than a comparable group of children with mental retardation. For example, they know that the category "fish" includes a bluefish and a shark, might include a seahorse, but would not include a padlock. Thus children with autism do not acquire idiosyncratic word meanings, but show the same pattern of generalization of meaning as children at a comparable developmental level (Tager-Flusberg, 1985).

However, words that are not anchored in *concrete reality* present difficulties. While the normal toddler's vocabulary contains a wide range of experiential and social terms, such as "bye-bye," "all gone," "up," and "dirty," the vocabularies of children with autism typically relate to static aspects of the environment such as inanimate objects and food.

This general difficulty with words that do not refer to concrete objects produces an attendant specific difficulty with relational words. While the normal preschooler easily masters such relational words as "big" and "small," the child with autism has great difficulty, tending to treat them as absolute qualities, so that "big" becomes as much a characteristic of a given object as is its shape. By the same token, active verbs that refer to some clearly perceived ongoing event, such as eating, are more easily grasped than ones that have no specific physical referent, such as "want," "like," and "believe." Prepositions such as "beside" or "in" are troublesome because they are not characteristics of objects but denote relations among objects.

The pronouns "I" and "you" present special problems because they have shifting referents depending on the speaker rather than consistently designating a single person. Thus, children with autism may refer to themselves by name rather than by "I." Finally, multiple classifications of single objects may be baffling. For example, "white chair" may present problems because all chairs are not white and all white objects are not chairs.

Thus, we can see progressively complex steps in learning language. The simplest rule is this: one word, such as "chair," stands for one object. Relational words, such as "on" or "I," are difficult because they do not refer to a single object or person. Multiple classifications of a single object may also be baffling because they go beyond the simple one-word-per-object rule. (For a detailed presentation of semantic problems in autistic children, see Tager-Flusberg, 1989.)

Communication

Speaking is more than understanding and ordering verbal symbols, however; it is communication as well. Normal infants are quick to grasp the notion of communication via expressive sounds. Within the first 3 months they can take turns vocalizing with their caregiver and, by the end of the first year, they can vocalize to indicate needs and feelings as well as to socialize.

The socially isolated child with autism has no such need to communicate. It has been noted, for example, that children with autism are impoverished in their use of gestures to communicate even when such gestures are within their repertoire (Prior & Werry, 1986). Thus the cognitive problem of symbolization is compounded by a motivational problem of disinterest.

Pragmatics

Even when children have mastered the basic rules of combining words into meaningful sentences, they still may have trouble with **pragmatics**, that is, the social context of language, which involves learning when to say what to whom in order to communicate effectively and to achieve an underlying objective. In fact, pragmatic deficits are found even in high-functioning children with autism, suggesting that such deficits are specific to the disturbance. Thus children with autism have been described as talking *at* others rather than talking *with* them in the sense of engaging in reciprocal exchanges. In addition they do not explain matters well, often failing to fill in all the information that the listener needs to follow what they are saying. For example, they may launch into a topic which interests them at the moment, without finding out whether the listener shares that interest or even is familiar with the topic (Volkmar, 1987).

Language Mismatch

Finally, what sets autism apart from retardation and language impairments is a mismatch between syntax and semantics or between syntax and pragmatics. The "echo-box" quality of autistic children's speech means they store in memory and later repeat in appropriate syntactic structures words that have little or no meaning to them. Children with autism also produce sentences that are grammatically impeccable but that have no relation to the social context, so that syntax is unrelated to pragmatics. Such disjointed development is very much at odds with the progression of normal speech, which is characterized by synchrony among the various components, with children knowing the meaning of what they say and knowing the rules for using words to communicate to others (Swisher & Demetras, 1985).

Language Comprehension

The social isolation that characterizes autism adversely affects language comprehension because such comprehension in the first few years depends heavily on social interaction. In normal 8- to 12-month-olds, language comprehension grows out of social exchanges between caregiver and infant. Commands such as "Give me the spoon" are given typically when the infant is handing the parent the spoon, while parents frequently call for attention by saying "Look" and "See" when the child is already attending. In short, language comprehension is initially a kind of *overlay* on already meaningful social behavior.

Children with autism, with their social isolation and odd interests, make it difficult for caregivers even to set the stage for language comprehension. This difficulty continues into the toddler and early preschool period since language comprehension continues to be closely tied to the social context. (See Schopler & Mesibov, 1985.)

Summary

Children with autism understand syntax to the point of using grammatically correct sentences. While they can understand concrete words, abstract words and ideas often elude them; for example, they have difficulty with relational words, prepositions, pronouns and multiple classifications of single objects. The children's social isolation results in impoverished communication with an autism-specific disturbance in regard to pragmatics. The disjointed nature of language development is also a distinguishing feature of autism, with the discrepancy between syntax and

Table 4.4   Functions Involved in Noncommunicative Speech*

Symbolization:	
Pretend play:	
ability: adequate	AMA
motivation: low	AS
Syntax: adequate	AMA
Semantics:	
Words for concrete objects:	
adequate understanding	AMA
Abstract, relational words and multiple	
classifications: inadequate understanding	AS
Communication:	
Motivation: low	DN
Pragmatics: low	AS
Synchrony among components: low	AS
Comprehension: low	DN

*AS = specific to autism; DN = below normal but mental retardation not controlled for; AMA = age-appropriate or mental-age-appropriate.

both semantics and pragmatics being particularly striking. (See Table 4.4 for a summary of the findings on noncommunicative speech.)

Pathological Need for Sameness

Executive Functions

Until recently, research on autism concentrated on its social and, to a lesser extent, its language abnormalities. The pathological need for sameness or what we would call the pathologically low initiative was neglected. This neglect is being remedied by interest in **executive functions**. (For a comprehensive discussion of executive functions, see Pennington & Ozonoff, 1996. Unless otherwise noted, our presentation is based on this article.)

Definition

Executive functions underlie *flexible, goal-directed behavior*. They consist of a number of components: *planning*, or goal setting; *working memory*, or maintaining information in an activated state in order to guide cognitive processing; *set shifting*, or flexibility in discarding inappropriate in favor of appropriate means of achieving a goal; and *inhibition*, or the ability to hold in abeyance strongly competing but inappropriate behaviors.

Measures

A frequently used measure of executive functions is the Wisconsin Card Sorting Task (WCST) in which the child first learns by feedback from the experimenter whether color, shape, or number is the "correct" sort of 10 cards. Then the experimenter changes the "correct" category without telling the child. The critical measure is how long the child perseverates in the incorrect sorting. For example, after the child has learned that color is the "correct" way to sort the cards, the experimenter shifts to shape as the "correct" sort and records how many sorts it takes the child to make the shift. The WCST is regarded as a measure of set shifting or flexibility. Flexibility, in turn, is the opposite of perseveration, in which the child persists in an incorrect response after the correct one is available.

The Tower of Hanoi is used as a measure of planning ability. This is a ring transfer task requiring children to plan a sequence of moves transferring an initial configuration of rings on a peg into a tower of rings of decreasing size on another peg. In moving the rings, larger ones cannot be placed on top of smaller ones.

Research Findings

Deficits in performing executive functions tasks have consistently been found in individuals with autism of all ages and all degrees of severity of disturbance. Thus, children with autism made more perseverative mistakes than did children in control groups on the WCST, even when the task was simplified by telling them when the "correct" response was going to be changed. They also made more perseverative errors than children with conduct disorder or attention-deficit hyperactivity disorder, even though these two groups are also deficient in executive functions. Performance on the Tower of Hanoi task correctly classified 80 percent of a mixed group of children with autism and children without, while tasks of memory and perception of emotion did no better than chance in classifying the two groups. (See Pennington and Ozonoff, 1996.)

Problems

The agreement among research findings just described is impressive—and refreshing. There are problems, however. First, executive functions deficiencies are *not* exclusive to autism but are found in other disturbances as well (Ozonoff & Strayer, 1997). This is to be expected in light of the omnibus nature of the definition of executive function. However, research findings suggest that the *severity* of disturbance is unique to autism.

Another possibility that is beginning to be studied is that the pattern of deficiencies among the component parts of executive functions may differentiate autism from other disturbances. Thus, there is evidence that high-functioning individuals with autism are impaired in working memory as compared with normally developing controls. On the other hand, inhibition is intact (Ozonoff & Strayer, 1997). This latter finding is particularly promising because poor motor inhibition is a core problem in children with attention-deficit hyperactivity disorder (see Chapter 6).

Sensory Overload and Organizing Information

Sensory Overload

Children with autism may be *hypersensitive* or *hyposensitive* to stimuli, often with an unpredictable fluctuation between the two. To take some examples from audition: Adults who are no longer autistic have described hearing like having "an open microphone that picked up everything" or being deluged by sound. Parents describe their children with autism as having mild to severe distress reactions to certain ordinary sounds. In fact, abnormal reactions to sound differentiate such children from those with mental retardation in the first two years of life. On the other hand, their hyposensitivity to sound may be so profound that they are mistakenly thought to be deaf.

Autobiographical accounts also contain references to a generalized *sensory overload*, such as being bombarded by bright lights and unpredictable movement or being overwhelmed by the noise and confusion of large gatherings. It may be that, when faced with such an environment, the children might seek the safety of repetitive, low-intensity sensory stimulation, such as humming the same note over and over or concentrating totally on the movement of a spinning coin. In short, the pathological need for sameness is a defense against being overwhelmed by ordinary environmental stimuli.

Organizing Information

Another specific problem children with autism have is in coding and organizing stimuli in terms of *rules* and *patterns*. The amount of information from the social and physical environment impinging on any individual at any given time is prodigious. What prevents normal children from being overwhelmed is the fact that information is not random but is patterned and meaningfully organized. While normal children are particularly adept at reducing information to manageable proportions by organizing it according to patterns and classes of events, children with autism are deficient in this respect. For example, when a series of five black rectangles of differing sizes were presented in random order and the children were asked to arrange them from smallest to largest, the performance of children with autism was inferior to that of children with mental retardation (Hermelin, 1976). One can speculate that their repetitious, stereotyped behavior is an attempt to establish islands of predictability and stability in a potentially overwhelming environment (Frith & Baron-Cohen, 1987).

Accounting for the Characteristics of Autism

By way of summary, we will highlight the research that is particularly germane in accounting for the three characteristics of autism. The purpose is to present an overview rather than an exhaustive account of relevant research findings.

Social Interaction

Initially, children with autism are deficient in the three aspects of normal development that bind infants and toddlers to the social environment: orienting, imitation, and joint attention. Subsequently,

the cognitive difficulty in inferring the mental life of others (theory of mind) along with problems in inferring emotions from bodily cues reinforce the children's social isolation. Research shows that the impairment is specific to social situations rather than being general in nature. From the point of view of the social environment itself, others find it difficult to respond to children with autism because of their decreased or deviant expressiveness and communication.

Language

In autism, the children's difficulty with symbols in general and with deriving meaning from semantic information in particular are major impediments to language development, while their difficulty with perspective taking blocks the communicative use of speaking, as well as pragmatics. What remains to be accounted for is the characteristic mutism.

Need for Sameness

Executive functions, or the ability to generate and sustain flexible, goal-directed behavior, has emerged as one of the most potent variables in differentiating autism from other disturbances, although much needs to be learned concerning what patterning of its component parts is peculiar to autism. At a more speculative level, repetitive behavior is seen as a means of coping with a hyperarousing physical environment and a bafflingly complex social environment.

Conceptualizations of Psychopathology

We have encountered two new conceptualizations of normal development gone awry. The first is that of a qualitative difference, in which the behavior of children with autism has little or no counterpart in normal development. Here we find obliviousness to the caregiver and disinterest in exploration, both of which characterize severely disturbed children with autism. In the second new conceptualization, deviance lies in the relationships among variables rather than within a single variable itself. We will call this deviation asynchrony. Progress among variables is disjointed, with some variables proceeding at a normal pace while others lag or follow an idiosyncratic course. While asynchrony has been noted in the clinical literature (see A. Freud, 1965), it is now being verified in objective studies of language development in children with autism (e.g., in the discrepancy between syntax and semantics) or in their uncoupling of gaze and communication.

Etiology: The Organic Context

Genetic Factors

There is no doubt that genetics plays an etiological role in autism. The question is, how much of a role? Evaluating the same data, Klinger and Dawson (1996) conclude that there is genetic transmission in "at least some cases of autism" (p. 326), while Rutter and coworkers (1993) claim it plays a major role, with autism being the most strongly genetic of all multifactorial psychopathologies. Such disagreement among experts only shows that data even from well-designed and well-executed studies are rarely definitive. For purposes of exposition we will present Rutter's "strong" case bearing in mind that it is not a conclusive one.

Twin Studies

As is always the case, the most convincing genetic data come from comparing monozygotic (MZ) with dizygotic (DZ) twins, one of whom is autistic. (Our presentation follows Bailey, Phillips, & Rutter, 1996.) Three general-population twin studies yielded concordance rates of 36 percent, 91 percent, and 39 percent for the MZ twins and 0 percent for DZ twins, indicating a "very strong genetic component" (p. 93).

Furthermore, two environmental conditions that might have contributed to the high concordance were ruled out. The first was obstetric complications. These were either minor or no greater than those found in nonautistic infants with congenital anomalies. Incidentally, this finding concerning the noncontribution of obstetric complications can be generalized to all children with autism.

The second environmental factor was congenital rubella. Initial studies suggested that congenital rubella in the mother during pregnancy increased the incidence of autism in their children. However, further research indicated that both the clinical description and the course of the children's disturbance were atypical; for example, such children tended to "outgrow" their presumed autism.

The Autistic Phenotype

Further evidence for a strong genetic component in autism comes from the finding that the nonautistic MZ twin had some autistic characteristics but to a lesser degree. These characteristics included some type of cognitive deficit, usually involving language delay, and persistent social impairment. Only 8 percent of the MZ co-twins were without such cognitive or social disorders compared with 90 percent of the DZ pairs. These studies suggest that the autistic phenotype extends well beyond the traditional diagnosis, involving characteristics similar to autism but markedly different in degree.

The Nature of Transmission

Having made a case for a strong genetic factor in autism, Bailey, Phillips, and Rutter (1996) speculate as to the nature of the genetic transmission. Because of its complexity it is not likely that autism is caused by a single genetic abnormality but is more likely due to *genetic heterogeneity*—that is, different genetic abnormalities that all lead to the same clinical picture. The model of transmission, therefore, would involve multiple interacting genes rather than a single gene operating in a Mendelian fashion. The number of genes involved in various hypothetical models range from two to ten. At present, however, there are no strong candidates for what genes these might be.

Neurological Factors

The task of bridging the gap between brain and behavior is easiest when there is a circumscribed disturbance on the behavioral side that can be related to a known characteristic of brain structure or functioning. Autism is a far cry from this model of simplicity. Autism is a pervasive disorder, and the many psychological functions affected are affected in a selective rather than in a wholesale manner; for example, in language, semantics suffers more than syntax. On the organic side, Dawson (1996) lists no fewer than 5 neural substrate that might be involved in the major symptoms of autism such as orienting to social stimuli and motor imitation.

In light of complexity on both sides of the psychophysiological equation, we cannot expect simple and certain answers to the question of the relation between brain and behavior. To complicate matters, *replicability* of neurobiological studies has been relatively poor, with further research tending to disconfirm rather than confirm initial findings. (See Bailey, Phillips, & Rutter, 1996.) A number of studies have been poorly designed—for example, failing to control for age and mental retardation (Peterson, 1995). In light of the uncertainty of findings, we have chosen to sample the studies to illustrate the kinds of research being done, giving preference, whenever possible, to studies having clear relevance to autistic behavior. The three categories of studies are neuroanatomical, which are concerned with deviations in the structure of the brain, and neurological and neurochemical studies, which are concerned with deviations in brain *functioning*. (For a more comprehensive and critical presentation of neurological studies, see Bailey, Phillips, & Rutter, 1996, and Pennington & Welsh, 1995.)

Neuroanatomical Findings

Neuroanatomical studies suggest various *malformations* during early development. For example, Courchesne and colleagues (1988), using magnetic resonance imaging (MRI), found that individuals with autism had cerebellar hypoplasia (i.e., diminished size) that was not associated either with mental retardation or with abnormalities in the pons or midbrain. This damage, in turn, adversely affects neuronal systems directly connected with the cerebellum, including those regulating attention and motor imitation, both of which have been implicated in the etiology of autism.

Autopsies performed on individuals with autism have not revealed any gross structural abnormalities, but there is suggestive evidence of an unexpected increase in brain weight—unexpected because the usual finding is a decrease in brain weight in mental retardation. These data, in turn, suggest a more pervasive abnormality in brain development than previously had been supposed (Bailey, Phillips, & Rutter, 1996).

Finally, there is research relating autistic symptomatology with dysfunctions in the brain system specializing in social cognition. The amygdala (which is part of the medial temporal lobe) in particular has been linked to a cluster of early autistic symptoms, including social orienting, motor imitation, joint attention, and empathy (Dawson, 1996).

Neurophysiological Findings

Electroencephalogical (EEG) abnormalities have been found in about 50 percent of individuals with autism, although there is no pattern that is specifically diagnostic. However, there are atypical patterns during language and motor imitation tasks and reduced power in the frontal and temporal lobes but not in the parietal region.

Event-related potential (ERP) measures brain activity in response to specific stimuli, with the P3 component being considered a measure of attention to novel, unpredictable stimuli. Studies have shown a reduced P3 component in individuals with autism (Klinger & Dawson, 1996).

Neurochemical Findings

Neurochemical studies of autism search for abnormalities in **neurotransmitters** (the "chemical messengers" responsible for communication among nerve cells). Findings in regard to the neurotransmitter **serotonin** have rather consistently shown an elevated level in about a quarter of individuals with autism. While the significance of this finding is unclear, it might be a factor in deviant brain development (Klinger & Dawson, 1996).

Summary

Pennington and Welsh (1995) summarize the neurological findings by stating that consistent structural or functional correlates of autism have not been established as yet. Moreover, instead of searching for focal lesions, it would be more fruitful to think in terms of a *disturbed neural system* that plays a central role in integrating behavior and that can be disrupted by a variety of changes in brain development. In this evaluation by Pennington and Welsh we see the biological counterpart of our psychological approach to understanding deviant behavior. Recall that we are no longer searching for the single cause of a given disturbance; instead, we deal with a system of interacting variables both within and among contexts.

Intervention: Progress in Treatment

Significant progress in treating children with autism has been made in the past decade or so. In reviewing eight intervention programs, Dawson and Osterling (1996) found that approximately 50 percent of the children who received intervention services were placed in regular education elementary school classrooms. Across programs *IQ improvement* ranged from 19 to 30 points, with an average gain of 23 points. This means that the children progressed from being in the severely mentally retarded range to the moderately mentally retarded range, an achievement made more impressive when one recalls how fixed IQ is in untreated children with autism. In a similar review, Rogers (1996) found significant gains in *language*, with 73 percent of the children having useful speech by the end of the intervention period. *Social relations* were also improved. For most programs gains were accomplished within one to two years of intensive preschool intervention. Preschool was the period of choice since there is evidence that younger children with autism profit more from intervention than do older ones. The two programs with a longitudinal component reported that the gains were maintained for years after the intervention program ended.

Program Similarities

All the programs have five particular features in common (Dawson & Osterling, 1996): (1) Treatment focuses on a broad range of autistic behaviors, including attention and compliance, motor imitation, communication, appropriate use of toys, and social skills. (2) In light of the difficulty children with autism have with generalization, specific strategies are needed for generalizing newly acquired skills to a wide range of situations; for example, skills learned with the therapist would be implemented by the parent at home and then by the teacher in school. (3) The teaching environment is highly structured with a low staff-to-student ratio. In addition, the daily schedule is highly predictable. This emphasis on structure and predictability is necessary because of the children's stormy affective reactions to novelty and change. (4) There is a high level of family involvement, with parents serving as therapists or cotherapists. (5) Particular attention is paid to developing the skills needed to make the transition from the program to a regular preschool or kindergarten classroom. (Rogers, 1998, presents a methological critique of studies of effectiveness. See Howlin, 1998, for a review of treatment of autism from a practitioner's viewpoint.)

Program Differences

While having a number of features in common, the programs use different techniques. For illustration, we describe here two contrasting methods of remedying the language deficiencies in autism, both of which have an impressive record of success.

Lovaas (1977) employs an operant conditioning model that relies heavily on imitation and reinforcement. For example, the therapist models and reinforces words and phrases until the child gradually acquires a repertoire of language. The meaningful use of language is accomplished by two programs. In *expressive discrimination* the child is reinforced for making a verbal response to an object, such as correctly labeling a cup when it is presented. In *receptive discrimination* the stimulus is verbal and the response nonverbal, such as correctly responding to "Give me a cup." Sequences are carefully graded so that new ones are based on mastered material.

By contrast, a program called TEACCH (Treatment and Education for Autistic and related Communication handicapped Children) (Schopler, 1994, and Schopler, Lansing, & Waters, 1983) is based on principles of normal language acquisition and development. The motivational aspect of teaching is handled by making language relevant to the children's own interests and showing them that words are powerful means for getting people to act in a desired way. For example, "ride" is taught as a means of obtaining a favored bicycle, *not* as a rewarded label to a picture, as Lovaas would do. Comprehension is aided by teachers' simplifying their language and supplementing it with gestures. Finally, as is done with normal children, language is integrated into on-going activities and is supported by as many contextual cues as possible, rather than being taught as an isolated skill.

Psychopharmacology

While a number of medications have been tried on children with autism, such as antipsychotics, stimulants, antidepressants, anticonvulsants, and vitamins, none has proven to be successful in remedying the primary symptoms of autism. They are best regarded as adjuncts to other kinds of interventions. (See Jakab, 1993.)

While this concludes our discussion of autism, we are not ready to leave the infancy period as yet. There is a considerable body of research dealing with insecure attachment *not* as a psychopathology but as a *risk factor* increasing the probability that some future psychopathology might develop. We need to examine this research before going on to psychopathologies of the toddler and preschool periods.

Infancy Through Preschool: Insecure Attachment, Oppositional-Defiant Disorder, and Enuresis

As noted in the previous chapter, we have more to explore concerning the infancy period in order to do justice to the literature on insecure attachment, a topic that has generated an impressive body of research. It is also worth repeating that insecure attachment is not a psychopathology but rather a risk factor. In fact, as we shall see, the evidence indicates that it becomes a risk factor only in conjunction with other risk factors such as poverty. In and of itself, insecure attachment should be regarded as a normal variation on attachment.

Later in the chapter we will turn to the toddler period, first presenting an overview of normal developments that will be germane to understanding the psychopathologies that follow—namely, **oppositional-defiant disorder** and **enuresis**.

The Risk of Insecure Attachment

Patterns of Attachment

Before taking up the reasons for regarding insecure attachment as a risk factor it will be helpful to describe in greater detail than was done in Chapter 1 the patterns of attachment and the caregiving associated with them. In most but not all studies the caregiver has been the mother. (Unless otherwise noted, our presentation follows Main, 1996.)

Patterns of attachment are primarily derived from observing the infant, the caregiver, and a stranger in a setup called the **strange situation**. The observations take place in a laboratory where infants experience a sequence of prearranged separations and reunions with the caregiver along with interactions with a stranger. The critical variables are the infants' responses to *separation* and *reunion*, along with their *exploration* of various attractive toys that have been placed in the laboratory.

The first pattern is called secure attachment, and the remaining four are called insecure attachments. We will describe each pattern and the kind of caregiving associated with it.

Secure Attachment

Securely attached infants explore the environment freely in the caregiver's presence. They may or may not be disturbed by separation and will limit exploration in the caregiver's absence. They may greet the caregiver positively upon reunion or if distressed, will contact her, be readily soothed, and return to exploration. Around 55 percent of infants in a normative population are securely attached.

Caregiving is marked by *sensitivity* to the infant's needs. Specifically, the caregiver correctly "reads" the infant's signals and responds quickly, appropriately, and with positive affect.

Avoidant Attachment

In cases of **avoidant attachment** the infants seem to be precociously independent. They rarely show distress upon separation and ignore or avoid the caregiver upon reunion. While they seem to be preoccupied with exploration to the exclusion of human contact, they actually explore less than the securely attached infants. Around 20 percent of infants from a normative population show this avoidant pattern.

Caregiving is marked by *distancing* and an absence of comforting combined with *irritability* and *anger* during closeness. Avoidance is the infant's attempt to cope with the painful consequence of such parenting.

Resistant Attachment

In contrast with the avoidant infants, the ones with **resistant attachment** are preoccupied with the caregiver. They are extremely upset by separation but, upon reunion, angrily resist attempts at closeness or show an ambivalent pattern of demanding to be picked up followed by angrily pushing the caregiver away. Preoccupation with the caregiver significantly limits exploration. Around 10 percent of infants from a normative population show this resistant pattern.

Caregiving is marked by *unpredictability*—the caregiver is excessively close at some times and uninvolved or irritable at others. This instability has its roots in the mother's unrealistically high expectation that she can be all-loving and all-protective; the inevitable frustration of this expectation by the realities of infant care results in withdrawal and anger (Mayseless, 1998). Resistance is viewed as

infants' attempts to capture the attention of the caregiver, while anger results from the frustration of inconsistent care.

Disorganized/Disoriented Attachment

Infants with the **disorganized/disoriented attachment** pattern act in an inconsistent or odd manner. They may have a dazed expression or wander around aimlessly or seem to be fearful and ambivalent in the presence of the caregiver, not knowing whether to approach for comfort or avoid for safety. Unlike infants with avoidant and resistant attachments, these infants do not seem to have developed a consistent strategy for dealing with the caregiver. Around 15 percent of infants in a normative population display this pattern.

Caregiving is marked by the use of *confusing cues*, such as the caregiver's extending her arms to the infant while backing away. (See Lyons-Ruth, Zeanah, and Benoit, 1996.) The caregivers are basically frightened and confused individuals who expect the infant to fulfill their frustrated needs for comfort and protection. In short, the role of infant and caregiver is reversed (Mayseless, 1998).

Controlling Behaviors

This most recent addition to the patterns of insecure attachment seems to grow out of the disorganized/disoriented pattern in the toddler period, although it does not necessarily replace that pattern. The essential feature of **controlling behaviors** is a reversal of roles, with the child taking over the adults' functions. This reversal may be expressed negatively in bossiness and imperious directives or positively by exaggerated solicitousness concerning the caregiver's welfare.

Data on caregiving are sparse for this pattern, but there is some evidence that controlling behavior is found in children of *physically abusive* parents.

Table 5.1 summarizes the findings concerning attachment.

Variability in Patterns

As our developmental model requires, attachment should be regarded as the product of interacting variables that change over time. Thus the patterns of attachment are not permanently fixed nor are they due

Table 5.1   Summary of Findings Concerning Attachment

	I. SECURE ATTACHMENT	II. AVOIDANT ATTACHMENT	III. RESISTANT ATTACHMENT	IV. DISORGANIZED/ DISORIENTED ATTACHMENT*	V. CONTROLLING BEHAVIOR*
A. STRANGE SITUATION					
1. Separation	May or may not be disturbed; limits exploration	Rarely shows distress	Extremely upset		
2. Reunion	Positive greeting or readily comforted if disturbed	Ignores or avoids caregiver	Resists closeness or ambivalent mixture of demand for closeness and pushing caregiver away	Inconsistent and odd behavior; e.g., acts in a dazed, fearful, peculiar, or contradictory manner	Role reversal with child taking care-giver's role in one of two ways: Negative—bossy, imperious directives Positive—exaggerated solicitousness
3. Exploration	Freely explores	Preoccupied to the exclusion of human contact	Limited		
4. General Characteristics	Secure, trusting, emotionally expressive	Precocious independence	Preoccupied with caregiver	No consistent strategy for dealing with caregiver	
B. CAREGIVING	Sensitive: quick, appropriate, warm response to infant's needs	Distancing combined with anger or irritation when close	Unpredictable; responds in terms of own needs or feelings of the moment	Confused cues or inappropriate responses to infant	

*Attachment behaviors not associated with any particular phase of strange situation

exclusively to the specified caregiving. While the various kinds of attachment show stability, for example, they also may change, especially as environmental conditions change. Or again, while there is a relation between security and sensitivity of care, it is a modest one allowing for the influence of other parenting variables such as management and control, as well as family, socioeconomic, and cultural variables. (See De Wolff and van IJzendoorn, 1997.)

Insecure and Psychopathological Attachments

The various patterns of attachment described above were derived from studies of normal populations of infants. Historically, however, these studies were preceded by ones concerned with the effects of *maternal deprivation* on development. Research on institutionalized infants in particular showed that their normal development was significantly jeopardized (see Chapter 14). These infants clearly belonged to a *clinical* population because of the severity of their disturbance.

Moreover, it was this research on institutionalized infants that served as a background for DSM-IV's classification of *Reactive Attachment Disorders of Infancy and Early Childhood.* The behavioral manifestations are (1) excessive inhibition, hypervigilence, and highly ambivalent and contradictory responses (such as responding to caregivers with a mixture of approach and avoidance or exhibiting frozen watchfulness); and (2) diffuse attachment manifested by indiscriminate sociability and an inability to form an individual attachment. The behaviors must be the result of either *neglect* or *frequent change* of caregivers. (We will return to this classification in Chapter 14 when we discuss child neglect and abuse.)

As Zeanah (1996) summarizes the situation in regard to risk and psychopathology, the DSM-IV classification refers to an extremely impaired subgroup of infants whose insecure attachments are due to neglect or frequent changes in caregiving. However, most insecure attachments are not so extreme in their manifestations nor are they a product of such deviant caregiving. Thus they should be regarded as *risks within the realm of normal variability of behavior*. (Zeanah, 1996, has also devised a classification of infant disturbances that integrates the DSM-IV classification with the insecure attachment literature.)

Insecure Attachment and Psychopathology: The Conceptual Bridge

Insecure attachments are not miniature versions of later psychopathologies. Why then regard them as risk factors? After all, infants differ in many ways—in temperament, sociability, resilience, curiosity—and we accept such differences as defining their individuality with no ominous forebodings of their being "at risk." However, there are good reasons for singling out attachment, as we will explore in the discussion that follows.

General Risk Factors

We will first look at the variables involved in attachment that suggest insecurity is a risk factor (a more extensive presentation of these concepts can be found in Carlson and Sroufe, 1995) and then discuss the rationale for linking specific insecure attachments with specific disturbances.

Security   The affective heart of attachment is *felt security*. Our evolutionary history has programmed infants to associate proximity to the caregiver with safety and security, and separation from the caregiver with danger and anxiety. A host of early behaviors—such as crying, signaling, clinging, visual, and, later, motoric following—act in concert to achieve the goal of closeness to the caregiver. (See Chapter 1.)

Exploration   Motor maturation enables the older infant and the toddler physically to explore the environment. Attachment makes it possible for the infant and toddler to *explore from a secure base*, venturing out confidently but also being confident that, in times of danger, distress, and fatigue, the caregiver will be available for protection and comfort.

Working Models of the Caregiving Relationship
As symbolic representation plays an increasing role in development, the infant and toddler can represent the caregiver and caregiving mentally. This image is called a *working model*, which both reflects past experiences and involves expectations as to the security, trustworthiness, and pleasure of future intimate relationships. Thus, for example, the toddler with a secure attachment will tend to be open and trusting, one with an avoidant attachment will tend to be guarded and standoffish, and one with a resistant attachment will tend to be clingy, demanding, and petulant. In each case past experiences with caregiving have left their imprint on the children's mental life, and this imprint produces different expectations concerning what future close relations will be like.

The Self   In the toddler period attachment enhances the development of *self-confidence* and *autonomy*. Exploring from a secure base helps create an image of the self as capable of taking on new challenges while also being able to turn to others for help when the demands of tasks exceed the ability to master them. More important, the security of attachment, with its protection from potentially overwhelming anxiety and rage, counteracts initial feelings of infantile helplessness while fostering a view of the self as being in control of affect. One term for this control factor is *emotion regulation*, which allows the free expression of feelings without the need to inhibit them out of fear. Finally, through being well cared for, the infant and toddler develop an image of the self as being *love-worthy*.

In sum, attachment involves core intra- and interpersonal affective and cognitive variables. It is therefore reasonable to assume that, if the process goes awry, the infant's and toddler's development might be at risk for being diverted from its normal course.

Empirical Validation of Risk Factors   The above ideas concerning the centrality of attachment are backed up by a number of objective studies. There is evidence that securely attached toddlers and preschoolers, as compared with insecurely attached ones, have greater inner security and greater feelings of self-worth and self-reliance. They are more affectively expressive and responsive to others, are more flexible and resourceful in response to challenges, and have better control of their feelings. This last characteristic contrasts the brittle independence and affective overcontrol of avoidance attachment and the dependence and excessive display of fear and anger characteristic of resistant attachment. (See Carlson and Sroufe, 1995.)

Risk for Specific Disorders

In addition to providing a rationale for why insecure attachment should increase the probability of becoming psychologically disturbed, there have been attempts to relate specific kinds of insecurity to specific disturbances. However, the arguments in this case have not been so persuasive.

Let us consider externalizing problems, which include conduct disorder and aggression. These problems have been related conceptually to avoidant attachment. (Our presentation follows Goldberg, 1997, unless otherwise noted.) The argument goes as follows: The distant, irritable caregiver produces a view of others as uncaring and untrustworthy in terms of being available when needed. In addition, anger from the frustration of unmet needs is displaced on to others. The result is acting out antisocial and aggressive feelings. On the other hand, it can equally well be argued that avoidant attachment should increase the likelihood of internalizing disorders such as anxiety and depression. After all, infants' feigned indifference to the caregiver represents an attempt to cover up their feelings; for example, there is physiological evidence that they are as aroused as are securely attached infants even while they act as if they are indifferent. It is this tendency to keep one's feelings, especially negative ones, to oneself that is a central feature of internalization.

The same ambiguity marks the conceptual link between resistant attachment and subsequent disturbances. Some psychologists have argued that it is resistant infants who, because of their preoccupation with maintaining the caregiver's attention, become fearful of exploring, isolated, and withdrawn. Thus they should develop into internalizers. But it can be equally well argued that the ready display of the negative affects of anger and anxiety is much more congruent with "acting out" (externalizing) behavior.

A final complication involves the classifications of internalizing and externalizing themselves. One might think that they are discrete categories so that a child is *either* one *or* the other. In reality the two overlap considerably, so that a child with a conduct disorder, for example, might be both anxious and guilty. Thus, while specific predictions concerning insecure attachments are given in terms of "pure" cases of internalizing or externalizing behaviors, overlap is more common. When it comes to empirical testing of these predictions there is already considerable "noise" in the system. Consequently, there is a certain tentativeness to the research findings, as we will soon see.

The developmental model. It is important to remember that we should not expect a fixed relation between insecure attachment and subsequent psychopathology. Such a relation would indicate a single-variable model that states, "Given X, Y will follow." Rather, the child's fate depends on the particular combination of subsequent *risk* and *protective* factors that characterize the developmental path.

Insecure Attachment and Psychopathology: The Evidence

Overview

The evidence concerning the hypothesized relation between insecure attachment and subsequent disorders is mixed. While there are some impressive confirmatory studies, other findings have been positive but qualified (such as a relation's being found for boys but not girls or being found in data from teacher ratings but not from parental ratings). Finally, there are a small group of studies that failed to find any relationship at all. (See Goldberg, 1997, and Zeanah, 1996.)

Two comments are in order here. First, the number of studies is limited, especially in light of the complexity of the problem. Thus, a more definitive statement concerning the relationship between attachment

Box 5.1

The Group Versus the Individual

One of the continuing sources of tension between the researcher and the clinician is the fact that the former looks for generalizations concerning populations of children while the latter deals with individual cases. While it may be helpful to know that, in general, an insecure attachment places an infant at risk, the clinician must answer the question, Is that true for this particular child? The interactive model, with its emphasis on contingent relationships among variables rather than on a single generalization, can help bridge this gap between research and practice. As Radke-Yarrow and coworkers' (1995) study shows, a close positive relationship may be dangerous for the child *if* the mother is seriously depressed, while the distancing of an insecure attachment may protect the child from the potentially damaging influence of an emotionally unstable mother. While research findings may never be as individualized as the clinician would want, the interactive model brings the laboratory closer to the clinic than does the single-variable model.

and specific psychopathologies is not possible at present. Second, results need to be evaluated in terms of the research strategy used. Data from longitudinal studies, in which attachment is observed and classified in infancy and the population subsequently evaluated for psychological disturbances, yield the most convincing data and therefore should be weighted more heavily. Cross-sectional studies, in which attachment is assessed in a population that is already disturbed, yield less convincing findings because the psychopathology itself might alter the nature of the attachment and because attachment patterns themselves may change over time. One longitudinal study, for example, found that only half the infants maintained the same classification by 4 years of age (Goldberg, 1997).

At a general level, the empirical findings support our developmental model of insecure attachment as a risk factor producing psychological disturbances *only in interaction* with other variables. For example, studies that find a relationship between insecurity and subsequent disturbance have been done on high-risk populations (e.g., children reared in poverty or in chaotic home environments); studies of low-risk populations have failed to find a relationship (Greenberg, et al., 1997).

Radke-Yarrow and coworkers' (1995) research nicely illustrates the point concerning interaction among variables. First, they found that insecure attachment alone at 1.5 and 3.5 years of age was *not* directly related to disturbance when the children were 6 and 9 years of age; however, it *was* related in

interaction with the mothers' depression or bipolar (manic-depressive) disorder. Even more interesting, kinds of attachment could serve either as risk or protective factors depending on the kind of mother-child interaction. Thus, secure attachment in the context of severe maternal depression was linked to a child's developing a depressive disorder subsequently, while insecure attachment to a mother with a bipolar disorder was associated with an absence of problematic anxiety at 6 years of age. Thus, while in general security and insecurity can be regarded as protective and risk factors, respectively, under special circumstances their roles may be reversed (see Box 5.1).

Confirmatory Longitudinal Studies

One of the most impressive studies confirming a relation between infant attachment and subsequent psychopathology was conducted by Warren and colleagues (1997). They hypothesized that resistant attachment would be related to subsequent anxiety disorders since inconsistent caregiving would result in a chronic concern about whether needs would be met. In addition, this anxiety would be more overtly displayed than it would be in avoidant attachment. The data confirmed the hypothesis. Resistant attachment at 12 months of age was significantly related to anxiety disorders at 17.5 years of age. Moreover, the relation was a specific one. On the one hand, avoidant attachment did *not* predict later anxiety problems and, on the other hand, resistant attachment predicted anxiety disorders in particular rather than a variety of other disturbances.

In another longitudinal study of infants medically at risk, Goldberg (1997) found that, while there was no significant relation between general insecurity and subsequent behavior problems at 4 years of age, there was a significant relation between avoidant attachment in infancy and subsequent internalizing problems. However, there was also a tendency for avoidance to predict externalizing problems. (Recall our discussion of the overlap between internalizing and externalizing problems.) Disorganized/disoriented attachment did *not* represent a special risk for future disturbance.

Finally, Shaw and coworkers' (1996) longitudinal study found that only disorganized/disoriented attachment in infants predicted aggression at 5 years of age. However, this risk was not sufficient in itself but had to be potentiated by the mother's perception of the child as being particularly difficult to cope with in the second year of life. What is particularly interesting about this study is that the authors were able to address the issue of the *potency* of the risk of insecure attachment when compared with other risk factors. They found that disorganized/disoriented attachment, child-rearing disagreements between parents, maternal personality risk (aggression, depression, and suspiciousness), and child aggression at 3 years of age were *equally* predictive of aggression at 5 years of age. (Zeanah, Boris, and Scheeringa, 1997, summarize research on disorganized/disoriented attachment.)

We will return to the relation between insecure attachment and psychopathology when we discuss specific disturbances in subsequent chapters.

Summary and Comment

It is clear that the findings relating attachment to subsequent psychological disturbances are mixed. Moreover, it would be premature to attempt to integrate them at this point. The number of such studies and the number of children in the studies are both limited. Moreover, the studies differ in the kinds of children and the variables studied.

Even granting that insecure attachment might be a risk factor, we have little information concerning its potency. Recall that it must act in concert with other risk factors when it predicts the development of a disturbance. But this still does not answer the question of how much of a risk insecure attachment is when compared with other etiological variables such as temperament, family disharmony, or poverty.

The Toddler Period

The toddler period is a time of increased *expansiveness* on the child's part and increased *restrictions* on the part of the socializing adults. It is natural that these two should go hand in hand. Toddlers who are now physically able to explore vast new regions of the environment inadvertently damage valued household items and personal possessions, leave chaos in their wake, and occasionally endanger themselves. Such unfettered initiative must be limited by "No" and "Don't." Socializing parents want to teach their toddlers control of unacceptable behavior while the enterprising toddlers brazenly assert their autonomy. The ensuing battles are fought over the issue of who is going to control whom. The sometimes stormy confrontations are responsible for the entire period being humorously called the terrible twos.

However, confrontations do not originate in the toddler period. As we have seen (Chapter 2) infants have been observed clamping their jaws and lips tightly together in an effort to resist being fed before they are ready. Similar resistance to being weaned to a cup and, later, to being spoon-fed have been called the "battle of the cup" and the "battle of the spoon." There is some evidence that these battles are more severe in toddlers who have held the bottle themselves, thus literally taking feeding into their own hands (see Levy, 1955).

To return to the toddler period: If all goes well in the confrontations between expansive toddlers and the restricting parent, the toddlers will emerge as socialized preschoolers who can both *control themselves* and be assured of their *autonomy*. In short, they are both self-controlled and self-reliant.

However, there is also the possibility that this normal development will go awry, resulting in psychopathological deviations. The healthy need for self-assertion evidenced in negativism can be carried to an extreme of *oppositional-defiant* behavior, which disrupts relations with caregiving adults while blocking the child's own growth.

While the requirements for self-control affect many aspects of the toddler's life, they are keenly felt when they intrude upon bodily functions. The young child lives close to his or her body, and eating and elimination hold special pleasures and special fascinations. The socializing parents' demands can, therefore, trigger some of the most intense conflicts of early childhood. We will be exploring a major disturbance in regulating elimination—namely, enuresis.

Oppositional-Defiant Disorder

Definition and Characteristics

Definition

Oppositional-defiant behavior can range from focal opposition expressed in a single symptom to a generalized oppositional character disorder. It also spans the developmental periods from toddlerhood through adolescence. Levy (1955), for example, writes about therapy with oppositional 2-year-olds, while other clinicians describe it in middle childhood and especially in adolescence.

The terms "negativism," "noncompliance," and "oppositional behavior" can all be found in the literature, with no agreement as to when each should be used. For the sake of consistency in our presentation, we will use the terms **negativism** and *noncompliance* synonymously when discussing *normal behavior*, and *oppositional* or *oppositional-defiant* behavior when discussing a *clinical* entity.

According to DSM-IV, the manifestations of oppositional-defiant disorder (ODD) involve outbursts of temper; arguing; defying and deliberately annoying others and blaming others for their own mistakes; and being touchy, angry, and spiteful (see Table 5.2 and Box 5.2). However, unlike conduct disorder (CD), there are no violations of the basic rights of others or of major societal norms and rules, such as persistent lying, aggressiveness, and theft.

Characteristics

Prevalence   Data on the prevalence of ODD are sparse partly because the disorder was not added

to DSM until 1980 and partly because the United States has no national-scale, epidemiological database on childhood psychopathologies. Findings are apt to be spotty and inconsistent due to differences in the age, sex, and SES of the groups studied as well as to the use of different assessment methodologies.

Prevalence rates have been reported as low as 2 percent and as high as 16 percent in the general population. On the other hand, ODD is one of the most frequently reported problems of clinically referred children; for example, one-third of all clinically referred preadolescent and adolescent children are diagnosed as ODD (Rey, 1993).

Gender and Socioeconomic Status   ODD is more common in boys than in girls in early childhood, but this relationship is reversed in adolescence. Also, the single study of SES found that ODD was more prevalent in groups with lower socioeconomic status (Rey, 1993).

Comorbidity

ODD and Conduct Disorder (CD)

Both in the descriptive psychiatric literature and in objective studies there is a strong association between ODD and conduct disorder (CD). DSM-IV couples them under the more general rubric of *disruptive behavior disorders*. Similarly, factor analytic studies of specific problem behaviors classify both as externalizing disorders. In fact, a case has been made that the overlap is so extensive that ODD should be regarded as a mild form of CD rather than being a psychopathology in its own right.

However, there are a number of reasons why ODD is regarded as a separate disturbance. (For a detailed discussion see Hinshaw and Anderson, 1996.) As we have seen, the diagnostic description of DSM-IV separates the disorders on the basis that children with ODD do not violate the basic rights of others or major societal norms. Moreover, in ODD the deviant behaviors are more commonly, although not exclusively, limited to parents and the home environment, whereas in CD deviant behaviors frequently involve individuals

Table 5.2   DSM-IV Criteria for Oppositional-Defiant Disorder

A. A pattern of negativistic, hostile, and defiant behavior lasting at least six months, during which four (or more) of the following are present:
(1) often loses temper
(2) often argues with adults
(3) often actively defies or refuses to comply with adults' requests or rules
(4) often deliberately annoys people
(5) often blames others for his or her mistakes or misbehavior
(6) is often touchy or easily annoyed by others
(7) is often angry and resentful
(8) is often spiteful or vindictive
    NOTE: Consider a criterion met only if the behavior occurs more frequently than is typically observed in individuals of comparable age and developmental level.
B. The disturbance in behavior causes significant impairment in social, academic, or occupational functioning.

Reprinted with permission from the Diagnostic and Statistical Manual of Mental Disorders, Fourth Edition. Copyright 1994 American Psychiatric Association.

in extrafamilial settings. While both ODD and CD have similar correlates in terms of antisocial behavior and adverse events in the family, the severity of such problems is less in ODD children (Loeber, Lahey, & Thomas, 1991). In general, children with ODD are less disturbed than those with CD (Rey, 1993).

Developmental data provide additional reasons for regarding ODD as being independent of CD. ODD emerges in the preschool period, whereas CD typically does not appear until middle childhood. While it is true that in 90 percent of cases CD is preceded by ODD, the majority of ODD children do *not* go on to develop CD—approximately 50 percent continue to be diagnosed as ODD, while 25 percent "outgrow" the disturbance (Rey, 1993).

Turning now to objective studies, Frick and colleagues (1993) provide some of the best evidence of the independence of ODD and CD. In a meta-analysis of factor analytic studies of disruptive behaviors they found that items congruent with ODD belonged in a cluster of *overt nondestructive behaviors*, such as defies, annoys, argues, shows temper, and is stubborn. By contrast, items congruent

with CD belonged to three other clusters: overt destructive, such as assaults, fights, and bullies; covert destructive, such as steals, lies, and sets fires; and covert nondestructive, such as truants, uses controlled substances, and swears. The main overlap between ODD and CD was mildly aggressive behavior. (The comorbidity of ODD and CD will be discussed again in Chapter 9.)

ODD and Attention-Deficit Hyperactivity Disorder

There is also considerable overlap between ODD and attention-deficit hyperactivity disorder (ADHD), the percent of comorbidity ranging from 20 to 57 percent (Rey, 1993). ADHD increases the risk of early onset of ODD and, in children with *both* ADHD and CD, there is an increase in the severity of ODD symptoms (Biederman et al., 1996). This dual comorbidity is also clearly associated with substantial impairment in the personal, interpersonal, and family domains (Hinshaw & Anderson, 1996).

ODD and Learning Disabilities

ODD *by itself* is not associated with learning disabilities. When such a relationship is found it is due to the presence of ADHD as a comorbid disturbance (Hinshaw & Anderson, 1996).

Developmental Course

In spite of the prevalence of ODD the only issue that has generated a reasonable number of objective studies concerns the independence of ODD from CD. The issues we will consider now, which concern the developmental path and etiology of ODD, have received only sporadic attention. Moreover, most of the studies were done only on boys. Thus, we must rely on clinical observations and speculations more often than is desirable, and the findings presented are tentative for the most part.

Developmental Trends

As we have seen, ODD persists in half of the affected population, a quarter going on to develop CD while still retaining their ODD behaviors and a quarter "outgrowing" their disturbance. There is

Box 5.2   How Often Is Often?

All the DSM-IV criteria for ODD contain the word "often." Therefore, the clinical child psychologist is required to make a judgment as to whether a given behavior is occurring significantly more frequently than in the normal population. There is no assurance that one psychologist's judgment will be the same as another's, which introduces an element of unreliability into the diagnosis.

In order to put "often" on firmer empirical footing, Angold and Costello (1996) questioned 1,071 parents of 9-, 11-, and 13-year-olds with ODD concerning the frequency of the defining symptoms over the previous 3 months. They decided that occurrence at or above 90 percent frequency represented a reasonable way of operationalizing "often." Using this criterion they found that symptoms varied in frequency: "angry or resentful" and "deliberately annoying others" occurred at least four times a week; "touchy," "loses temper," "argues," and "refuses adults' requests" occurred at least twice a week; and "spiteful" and "blames others for own mistakes" did not occur at all. Thus, some symptoms can occur less frequently than others and still be regarded as happening "often." Moreover, clinicians are provided with a numerical standard for making judgments as to frequency. The gain in precision by substituting normative data for clinical judgment is obvious.

evidence that ODD declines in frequency during middle childhood but increases again in the adolescent period (Loeber, Lahey, & Thomas, 1991). Prognostically, ODD is one of the most stable diagnoses and one with the poorest rate of recovery (Rey, 1993). Nothing is available in the literature describing its fate in adulthood.

The symptom picture of ODD might change during different developmental periods, and the arena of confrontation might widen from family to school and teachers in middle childhood and to society and the law in adolescence. Thus, in the middle years children with ODD may fail to do their schoolwork, forget to bring home assignments, dawdle, and procrastinate.

Reasons for Change

There are some data on why certain ODD children develop the more serious psychopathology of CD while others "outgrow" their disturbance. In regard to the former, a high level of aggression seems to be the most important determinant of subsequent CD. However, family variables such as parental antisocial behavior, neglect, lack of parental monitoring, and father separation also play a role. In regard to recovery, aggression again plays a pivotal role but this time it is the nonaggressive child who is likely to return to the path of normal development. (See Loeber, Lahey, & Thomas, 1991.)

Etiology

There is general agreement that ODD is rooted in normal behavior. Thus, normal problem behaviors in toddlers include disobedience, defiance, tantrums, and negative mood (Campbell, 1995). The terrible twos are aptly named except that the behaviors can also extend into the preschool period. Psychopathology enters the picture when there is an increase in *frequency* and *intensity* of such behaviors or when they *persist* into later periods (Gabel, 1997). This conceptualization corresponds to our own model of the relation between normal and deviant development in Chapter 1.

However, the question of why development is diverted from its normal course has no satisfactory answer in terms of a conceptualization buttressed by a body of objective studies. We know that *genetic* factors play only a minor role, so our search for etiological factors must involve contexts other than the organic one. In our discussion of the intrapersonal context we will examine studies of both clinical and normal populations for leads concerning the transition from normal to problem behavior.

The Intrapersonal Context: Clinical Populations

Recently there has been some interest in relating attachment to ODD. DeKlyen (1996) found more *insecure attachment* in a group of 25 preschool boys

Oppositional-defiant behavior.

referred for disruptive behavior disorder than in normal controls. A prospective study by Erickson, Sroufe, and Egeland (1985) found that anxious-avoidant attachment predicted ODD problems in the preschool years. Speltz and coworkers (1995) also found that attachment classification discriminated clinically referred ODD preschoolers from normal controls better than measures of maternal behavior such as the number of commands and criticisms. The authors of all these studies are careful to point out that attachment should not be regarded as the sole cause of ODD but rather as a factor that interacts with other risk variables. (See Greenberg, Speltz, and DeKlyen, 1993.)

There is also some evidence that a *difficult temperament* in 7-year-olds predicts ODD in adolescence (Rey, 1993). However, as is the case with attachment, temperament should be regarded as one of many risk factors producing ODD.

The Intrapersonal Context: Normal Populations

If psychopathology can be understood as normal development gone awry, then it is reasonable to look to studies of normal development for clues to answering the etiological question of why it becomes diverted. The relevant literature concerns negativism, or noncompliant behavior.

Toddlers show great versatility in their techniques of noncompliance, according to Levy's (1955) observational study. Some are manifestly willful: "I should move my bowels, but I won't," as one toddler put it. But direct confrontations can be alloyed with passive maneuvers; for example, food refusals can become pickiness or dawdling. Finally, there are purely passive techniques, such as mutism or pretending not to hear or to understand parental directions.

In their objective longitudinal study of toddlers and preschoolers, Kuczynski and Kochanska (1990) conceptualize negativistic behavior in terms of *social strategies*. Direct defiance is the least skillful strategy because of its openness and aversiveness to parents. Passive noncompliance is also considered unskillful but not so aversive to parents. Negotiation, which attempts to persuade parents to modify their demands, is relatively indirect and nonaversive, so it is the most skillful. The investigators found that direct defiance and passive noncompliance decreased with age, while negotiation increased, reflecting a more active and adroit way of expressing resistance to parental requests. Of particular interest to us is the finding that only the least skillful forms of resistance were predictive of externalizing problem behaviors at 5 years of age.

Next there is evidence from Crockenberg and Litman's (1990) objective study that, as early as 2 years of age, defiance and self-assertion are independent of each other, the first behavior involving the adult ("No, I won't!"), the second involving the self ("I'll do it my way"). Self-assertion is associated with competence, while defiance is not. This study suggests that, within the general category of noncompliant behaviors, we can begin to distinguish those that are growth-promoting and those that place the child at risk for developing a behavior disorder.

Kuczynski and Kochanska (1990) also make a point concerning compliance which clinical child psychologists should note. Normatively, children's most frequent response to parental requests is compliance. If this were not so, socialization would not be possible. However, extremes of compliance are dangerous. A rigid and compulsive form of compliance develops among infants of abusive parents and, in the investigators' own study, overly compliant boys were perceived as having an increase in internalizing problems.

The Interpersonal Context: Parental Behavior

Research on the interpersonal context has primarily been concerned with the parental behavior, which has been viewed in three different ways. The first describes *global* characteristics of parents and of the interaction. Mothers of oppositional children have been described clinically as overcontrolling and aggressive, while fathers have been described as passive, peripheral, and distant. Objective studies show that these mothers are more negative toward and more critical of their children than are mothers of normal children and that they engage in more threatening, angry, and nagging behaviors. Both parents give their children significantly more commands and instructions while not allowing enough time for the child to comply. (See Gard and Berry, 1986, for a summary of the research.) As is always true of interactional studies, there is the "chicken and egg" problem of the direction of causation. Parents may either be contributing to or reacting to their children's behavior, and only additional studies can help distinguish which is happening.

Social learning theorists believe it is more fruitful to examine *specific parental behaviors* that elicit and maintain noncompliance than to deal with general characteristics of parents. An example of this approach is the work of Forehand (1977) and his colleagues. They found that noncompliant behavior is maintained by parental attention, which serves as a reinforcer even though such attention often takes the form of anger and punitiveness. In addition, they discovered the types of parental commands that are apt to elicit noncompliance. The so-called *alpha commands* are specific and clear and are less likely to produce noncompliance. They include commands that have a clearly designated, explicitly stated objective: for example, "Eat your peas or there will be no dessert" or "You can finish watching this program but then the TV goes off." The so-called *beta commands* are vague and interrupted. They are difficult or impossible to obey, either because of their ambiguity or because the parent issues a new command before the child has a chance to comply: "Do you think that you might want to do something not so noisy—or not?" or "Quit picking on your . . . Now help mommy find her pocketbook." Beta commands are more characteristic of parents of noncompliant children than are alpha commands.

Westerman (1990) regards the social learning approach as too static, preferring to study the *ongoing process* of interaction. In his research he videotaped and subsequently analyzed the behavior of mothers and their 3- to 4½-year-old sons doing various tasks. He found that mothers of the healthy group coordinated their behavior with that of their sons, becoming more specific in their directives when their children failed and less specific when they succeeded. By contrast, mothers of noncompliant problem children were less likely to regulate their directives according to their children's activities. Thus, the crucial variable was not so much the amount and kind of directives as the mother's sensitivity to ongoing behavior. One might infer that this sensitivity makes the difference between the children perceiving the mother as being "with" them or as imposing her directives upon them.

Summary

By way of summary let us review what we have presented about the etiology of ODD, framing our findings in terms of *risk* and *protective* factors while acknowledging the tentativeness of our integration. An insecure attachment in general and, perhaps an anxious-avoidant attachment in particular, along with a difficult temperament are risk factors for ODD. In the intrapersonal context, direct defiance is a risk factor in regard to developing ODD, while the ability to negotiate is protective. Moreover, within negativistic behaviors, unhealthy defiance should be distinguished from healthy self-assertion.

In the interpersonal context, a negative, critical attitude along with anger, threats, and nagging on the mother's part, and an increase in parental commands without allowing time for compliance, all increase the likelihood of ODD. Furthermore, vague intrusive commands and insensitivity to the child's ongoing needs are risk factors. On the other hand, clear, explicit commands and sensitivity to the child's changing needs are protective factors.

Intervention

Because there are few objective studies of intervention effectiveness and no studies of relative effectiveness of different intervention approaches, we will only touch upon some of them.

Psychodynamically oriented therapies explore the child's conscious and unconscious feelings toward family members, especially those feelings involved in the issue of autonomy and control. *Atheoretical* practitioners follow the commonsense technique of telling parents not to nag and coax and to avoid being dictatorial, overprotective, and overcorrecting and avoid putting the child into a "give in or lose" situation (Bakwin and Bakwin, 1972). *Medication* has not been effective with ODD alone, but it can be used to relieve some of the symptoms of ADHD in cases of comorbidity.

For the *social learning* camp Forehand (1977) instructs parents to replace their vague, interrupted beta commands with specific alpha ones; to shift from punishing noncompliant behavior to rewarding compliance with praise, approval, and positive physical attention; and to employ a "time-out" procedure of isolating the child for a brief period after noncompliance. It is also helpful to teach parents the general principles of operant learning rather than providing them solely with techniques for handling specific problems. While the successes in the home did not generalize to the school, they did affect other behaviors within the home; for example, one girl who was reinforced for picking up her toys spontaneously began to keep her clothes tidy. Moreover, there is evidence that the compliance of untreated siblings undergoes the same positive change, since the mother alters her behavior to them as well. Finally, there is evidence that gains made in middle childhood are sustained in adolescence. (For details of Forehand's parent-training technique, see Forehand and McMahon, 1981. For a review of studies of effectiveness, see McMahon and Wells, 1989.)

Enuresis

Definition and Characteristics

Definition

Enuresis has a distinguished lineage: it was mentioned in Egyptian medical texts as early as 1550 B.C. (Thompson & Rey, 1995). In current usage *enuresis* is defined as repeated involuntary or intentional discharge of urine into bed or clothes beyond the expected age for controlling urination. According to DSM-IV, this age is 5 years or a comparable developmental level. In regard to *frequency*, the behavior is clinically significant if it occurs twice a week for at least three consecutive months. However, it may also be regarded as significant if there is considerable *distress* or *impairment* in important areas of functioning. Another qualification is that enuresis is not due to a general medical condition or to drugs that affect urination. (See Table 5.3.)

There are three different types of enuresis. In *nocturnal* enuresis passing urine occurs only during nighttime sleep. In *diurnal* enuresis urine is passed during waking hours. In *mixed*, or nocturnal and diurnal enuresis, urine is passed during both waking and sleeping hours. These three distinctions are not always made in the research literature, however, resulting in a certain ambiguity in the findings.

There is another important classification. *Primary enuresis* refers to children who have never been successfully trained to control their urination. *Secondary enuresis* refers to children who have been successfully trained but revert back to wetting—for example, in response to a stressful situation in the family. In our developmental terminology, primary enuresis represents a *fixation*, whereas secondary enuresis represents a *regression*.

Characteristics

Prevalence and Developmental Course   Frequency of enuresis changes significantly with age. It is found in 20 percent of 5-year-olds, 5 percent of 10-year-olds, 2 percent of 12- to 14-year-olds, and 1 percent of adults. These figures are for nocturnal

Table 5.3   DSM-IV Criteria of Enuresis (Not Due to a General Medical Condition)

> A. Repeated voiding of urine into bed or clothes (whether involuntary or intentional)
> B. The behavior is clinically significant as manifested by either a frequency of twice a week for at least 3 consecutive months or the presence of clinically significant distress or impairment in social, academic (occupational), or other important areas of functioning
> C. Chronological age is at least 5 years (or equivalent developmental level)
> D. The behavior is not due exclusively to the direct physiological effect of a substance (e.g., diuretic) or a general medical condition (e.g., diabetes, spina bifida, a seizure disorder)
> Types:
>   Nocturnal Only: passage of urine only during nighttime sleep
>   Diurnal Only: passage of urine during waking hours
>   Nocturnal and Diurnal: a combination of the two subtypes above

Reprinted with permission from the Diagnostic and Statistical Manual of Mental Disorders, Fourth Edition. Copyright 1994 American Psychiatric Association.

enuresis. Diurnal enuresis is less prevalent, being present in only 3 percent of 6-year-olds (Harbeck-Weber & Peterson, 1996). However, both kinds of enuresis are self-limiting; that is children tend to "outgrow" them even without treatment. There is some evidence that remission rates for girls may be higher than those for boys, the ratio being 71 percent for girls and 44 percent for boys between the ages of 4 and 6 (Harbeck-Weber & Peterson, 1996). Since there are also effective treatments when needed, as we shall see, the prognosis is quite favorable for enuresis.

Gender   Between ages 4 and 6 years the number of boys and girls with enuresis is about equal. However, the ratio changes so that, by 11 years of age, there are twice as many boys as girls.

Socioeconomic Status   There is evidence that the incidence of enuresis varies from country to country and among racial and ethnic groups. In the United States it is more prevalent among lower socioeconomic groups (Walker, 1995).

Comorbidity   Research findings concerning comorbidity are often inconclusive and contradictory. There does seem to be an increase in behavior problems such as conduct problems, immaturity, and underachievement in school in children with enuresis. Whether there is also an increase in psychopathology is not clear. One can find statements in the literature that there is *no* relation between psychopathology and enuresis. On the other hand, enuresis has been implicated in studies of encopresis (fecal soiling), learning disabilities, and developmental delays in intelligence The evidence concerning the kind of enuresis is also inconclusive, with some studies finding a relation to primary enuresis and others finding no relation with either the primary or secondary type. (See Biederman et al., 1995, and Walsh and Menvielle, 1997.)

Etiology

The Interpersonal Context

The etiological picture in the interpersonal context is marked by conflicting findings. On one hand there is evidence that secondary enuresis may be a response to stress, especially in 4- to 6-year-olds (Walsh & Menvielle, 1997). On the other hand, recent studies have failed to find a relation between enuresis and a variety of psychosocial factors such as economic background, family intactness, and the quality of the family environment (Biederman, et al., 1995).

It may be that the negative findings regarding psychosocial variables were due to a failure to take intrapersonal variables into account along with the interaction between intra- and interpersonal ones. Also, none of the studies was developmental in nature. The research of Kaffman and Elizur (1977), while conducted a number of years ago, is unique in taking both interaction among contexts and development into account. It is worth describing in detail.

An Interactional Developmental Study

The setting for Kaffman and Elizur's (1977) study was a kibbutz in Israel. In the kibbutz, four to six infants are cared for by a trained caretaker, or *metapelet* (plural, *metaplot*), in a communal children's house. Each child spends four hours daily with his or her parents. Generally speaking, the children's development and the parent–child relationships are similar to those in traditional Western families. Toilet training in particular is benign and child-centered.

In Kaffman and Elizur's study, 153 children were assessed on a number of physiological, interpersonal, and intrapersonal variables from infancy to 8 years of age. The investigators regard enuresis as beginning at 4 rather than 5 years of age. While they found the usual genetic and physiological predisposing factors in the 4-year-olds with enuresis (siblings with enuresis, smaller functional bladder capacity, impaired motor coordination), the intrapersonal and interpersonal factors are of greater interest.

In the *intrapersonal context*, the children with enuresis had a significantly greater number of behavior symptoms than the nonenuretic ones, indicating that they were more disturbed. Within this general context, two high-risk personality patterns could be distinguished. Around 30 percent of the children were hyperactive, aggressive, and negativistic in response to discipline, had low frustration tolerance, and resisted adjusting to new situations. One can imagine how difficult it must have been for these children to sit or stand still when being potty-trained! A smaller group of children with enuresis were dependent and unassertive, had low achievement and mastery motivation, and masturbated frequently, perhaps to compensate for their lack of realistic pleasures. In contrast, the children who were *not* enuretic were self-reliant, independent, and adaptable, and they had a high level of achievement motivation.

In the *interpersonal context*, the clearest relation was between parental disinterest and enuresis. In addition, temporary separation from the parents was the only stress related to increased bed-wetting, for the kibbutz children took in stride the stresses of a sibling's birth, hospitalization, and even war. Interestingly, absence of the *metapelet* produced no such reaction, suggesting that the parent–child relationship was central. While not statistically significant, a relationship between bed-wetting and the *metapelet*'s behavior was

suggested. Permissiveness, low achievement demands, and insecurity on the part of the metapelet tended to be related to enuresis, whereas structured, goal-oriented, and directive toilet training in the context of a loving relationship enhanced early bladder control.

The authors draw some general conclusions from the data. For low-risk children the *timing* of toilet training does not matter. In the high-risk group, *delayed* training *increases* the likelihood of enuresis in the motorically active, resistive, and aggressive infant. Such an infant is difficult enough to socialize, but the difficulties are compounded during the terrible twos and threes. In the interpersonal realm, a *permissive* attitude, combined with noninvolvement or uncertainty, tends to perpetuate bed-wetting, since there is neither sufficient challenge nor sufficient support for the child to take this particular step toward maturity. Such a finding is congruent with studies of normal development that show that a child's competence is maximized when parental affection is combined with challenges and an expectation of achievement. Overall, the children's *personality characteristics* were more highly correlated with enuresis than were interpersonal variables.

In the longitudinal phase of their study Kaffman and Elizur (1977) found that 50 percent of the children with enuresis were identified as problem children when they were 6 to 8 years of age, in contrast to 12 percent in the nonenuretic group. Learning problems and scholastic underachievement were the most frequent symptoms, although some of the children also lacked self-confidence and felt ashamed, guilty, or depressed. Unfortunately, Kaffman and Elizur did not analyze their data further to determine *which* children were more apt to develop problems.

These longitudinal findings have important implications for developmental course. Looking at a graph showing the progressive decline of enuresis, one would opt for the prediction that children would "outgrow" their problem. Such graphs are based on cross-sectional data. But longitudinal studies that include intrapersonal and interpersonal variables alert the clinician to the possibility that enuresis in some 4-year-olds may be the first sign of other problems that will persist and perhaps escalate. In short, while most children may "grow out of" a psychopathology, a substantial subgroup might "grow into" other problems.

It is essential for the clinical child psychologist to have a good understanding of such longitudinal information when helping parents decide whether or not their child with enuresis is in need of intervention. After all, why "waste" time and money on a problem that is apt to disappear? Parents should be made aware that the prognosis is not so favorable when the focus shifts from enuresis alone (which is apt to be "outgrown") to problem behavior in general, so they can then make an informed decision about treatment by considering both sets of information.

The Organic Context

Enuresis can be caused by a number of purely organic factors such as anomalies of innervation of the bladder that result in an inability to empty it completely, illnesses such as diabetes insipidus or urinary tract infections, and drugs such as diuretics. The clinical child psychologist should make sure that these factors have been ruled out by a medical examination.

There is a definite genetic component to enuresis. For example, 70 percent of children with enuresis have two parents with a history of having been enuretic; furthermore, there is a 68 percent concordance rate for monozygotic twins and only a 36 percent concordance rate for dizygotic twins (Harbeck-Weber & Peterson, 1996).

Intervention

Behavioral Techniques

The *urine alarm*, or *pad-and-bell method*, has a proven record of effectiveness and of superiority to drug treatments. A urine-sensitive pad is placed in the child's bed. This pad activates a bell or buzzer when the child wets, thereby awakening the child, who then goes to the bathroom to finish voiding. Eventually the response of awakening becomes anticipatory, allowing the child to get up before urinating. Studies have shown the urine alarm to be effective in 70 to 95 percent of cases, although a

41 percent relapse rate within 6 months of treatment has been a problem. (See Christophersen and Edwards, 1992.)

There are two possible solutions to the problem of relapse. One is to initiate a second round of training identical to the first (Walsh & Menvielle, 1997). The other solution involves a different initial procedure that uses intermittent rather than continuous reinforcement; for example, the buzzer could be used only 70 percent rather than 100 percent of the time. According to operant learning principles, conditioning is more resistant to extinction with intermittent rather than with continuous reinforcement. While this method takes longer to achieve dryness, it significantly lowers the relapse rate.

Another procedure of proven effectiveness is *dry-bed training* (DBT), an omnibus approach involving, among other things, reinforcement for inhibiting urination, practice of appropriate voiding, retention-control training, nighttime awakening, mild punishment, family encouragement, and a urine alarm. Studies of the relative contribution of the various components of DBT indicate that the urine alarm is the single most effective element, with other procedures also making a unique contribution to overall effectiveness (Walsh & Menvielle, 1997).

Psychopharmacology

Various psychopharmacological agents have had qualified success in treating enuresis. Imipramine hydrochloride (IMI) has been studied extensively, although much of the research has been flawed. One of the better-designed studies was conducted by Fritz, Rockney, and Yeung (1994) on 18 children with nocturnal enuresis. At the end of a two-week period dryness was increased by 73% for the children on IMI as compared with 28 percent for the children on a placebo. The efficacy was moderately correlated with the strength of the dosage. While generally safe, IMI does have some side effects, such as toxicity on overdose. The principle problem with IMI is relapse when the drug is discontinued (Walsh & Menvielle, 1997).

Thompson and Rey (1995) reviewed studies of desmopressin, an antidiuretic agent administered intranasally. Using this agent one-quarter of the children were dry at the end of a two-week period.

Box 5.3	**The Best Versus the Prescribed Treatment**

In all of our presentations we will be raising the question, What is the treatment of choice? However, this is not the same as the practical question, Do children receive the treatment of choice? Enuresis is a case in point. Although the urine alarm is clearly superior, drugs are the preferred treatment of physicians; for example, one study found that IMI was the most frequently prescribed and the urine alarm the least frequently prescribed treatment (Thompson and Rey, 1995).

One reason for this discrepancy between effectiveness and utilization is that medically trained professionals, such as pediatricians and psychiatrists, are inclined to use medication. They are not alone in this because many families also may prefer medication to the typically more time-consuming behavioral treatment. Nor are medically trained professions alone in having strong preferences. Psychologists also may favor behavioral techniques or psychotherapy over medication. It is when such strongly held preferences fly in the face of evidence to the contrary that the child—as often is the case with biases among professionals—is the loser.

Side effects were mild, although more research needs to be done on this variable. Research is inconclusive concerning predictors of a positive response such as the age of the child, the frequency of wetting, and the type of enuresis. The main shortcoming is the high rate of relapse. The authors conclude that the overall efficacy of desmopressin appears to be comparable to that of IMI but lower than the efficacy of the urine alarm. They suggest that, because it is easy to administer, desmopressin might be most useful clinically on special occasions such as when a child with enuresis sleeps away from home. (See Box 5.3.) (A comprehensive account of treatment of enuresis can be found in Kronenberger and Meyer, 1996.)

Developmental Integration

Our discussions have served to illustrate two core features of our developmental model—interaction among variables and the crucial role development plays in conceptualizing psychopathology.

Interaction Among Variables

We have seen a number of illustrations of the importance of considering the interaction among variables rather than dealing with single variables in isolation.

Disturbances and Psychopathologies

Disturbances and psychopathologies are rarely the result of a single variable but rather arise as a result of the interaction among variables. The timing of toilet training, for example, does not matter for self-reliant, independent, and adaptable toddlers, while delayed training of hyperactive, aggressive, and negativistic toddlers is apt to result in enuresis. So when is the best time to start toilet training? The answer is, it all depends on the characteristics of the child in question.

Risk and Protective Factors

Recall that an insecure attachment becomes a risk factor only when other risks are present. Even more interesting is the finding that whether a variable is a risk or a protective factor may depend on its relation to other variables; for example, an avoidant attachment, which is usually a risk condition, can protect children against the erratic mood swings of a disturbed mother probably by enabling the children to distance themselves from her (Radke-Yarrow et al., 1995).

Unfinished Business

Granting the importance of interaction, what is needed now is more information concerning the relative potency of the etiological variables. For example, Warren and coworkers (1997) found that resistant attachment was more important than temperament in determining the development of anxiety disorders. On a practical level, information concerning relative potency can help clinical child psychologists prioritize remedial measures. To take a hypothetical example, if a parent's negative perception of their child contributes more to a disturbance than do parental arguments, then it should be the initial focus of treatment.

Conceptualizing the Psychopathology

All conceptualizations of psychopathology require a knowledge of normal development. (See Chapter 1.) Certain psychologies, like ODD, represent an *exaggeration* of normal development, which, in turn, requires normative information. Ideally, such information should be quantified, such as Angold and Costello's (1996) study of "How often is often?"

Then there are the psychopathologies of *timing*: *fixation*, or the continuation of normal behavior to the point that it becomes age-inappropriate, and *regression*, or the return of behavior that was once but is no longer age-appropriate. Primary enuresis is an example of fixation; secondary enuresis is an example of regression.

Our presentation of various psychopathologies will continue to examine initiative, but not the self-reliant expansiveness we have just discussed. Rather, the focus will shift to curiosity and exploration, which require the ability to pay attention and to work up to one's potential. As we will explore in Chapter 6, both of those can go awry, producing hyperactivity on the one hand and learning disabilities on the other.

The Preschool Period: Attention-Deficit Hyperactivity Disorder and Learning Disabilities

As we have just explored in Chapter 5, initiative can go awry in the toddler period by becoming excessive and producing an oppositional disorder. However, initiative involves not only self-reliance and autonomy but curiosity and exploration as well. As Piaget has taught us, even infants are problem solvers, implicitly asking, What is that? and How does it work? until, by the end of the first year, they are actively experimenting with the physical and social environment. In a like manner, toddlers have a remarkable ability to give their undivided attention to the tasks involved in exploration. Subsequently, school adds an element of requiredness to intrinsic curiosity which, in turn, is transformed into the work of learning specific subjects. (See Chapter 2.)

Yet this ability to concentrate on the task at hand in the toddler and preschool periods can be seriously curtailed by hyperactivity and an attention deficit, which prevent children from keeping their minds on a particular task. (See Taylor, 1995, for a general discussion of the development of attention and its dysfunctions.) When schooling begins, a different deviation can appear in intelligent, motivated children: the inability to achieve at an appropriate level in one or another academic subject such as reading or arithmetic. This deviation is called a learning disability (LD). In this chapter we will first discuss attention-deficit hyperactivity disorder and then consider learning disabilities and their consequences.

Attention-Deficit Hyperactivity Disorder

Definition and Characteristics

Definition

We will begin by presenting and discussing the DSM-IV criteria for attention-deficit hyperactivity disorder (ADHD) because they capture the restless history of the attempt to define this psychopathology. (See Table 6.1.)

Note that there are three major types of ADHD: one based on inattention, one based on hyperactivity-impulsivity, and one based on a combination of the two. Children with the *inattention* type are unable to sustain attention at an age-appropriate level. Parents and teachers might complain that the children cannot concentrate, are distractible, go from one activity to another, are disorganized, and are forgetful and prone to daydream. With *hyperactivity*, children are continually "on the go" as if "driven by a motor." This drive to move may be evidenced by climbing or running about, excessive talking, or continually and inappropriately leaving the seat during class. *Impulsivity* is "acting without thinking." Children may blurt out answers rather than taking time to think a problem through, they may interrupt or intrude on others by butting into conversations and games, or they may have difficulty waiting for their turn. All behavioral criteria are at an age-inappropriate level, since many of these behaviors can be found in normally developing younger children. (For a detailed presentation of ADHD, see Barkley, 1996. Cantwell, 1996, has a briefer summary of the disturbance.)

Historically, diagnoses have emphasized the most obvious manifestation of the disturbance, which is hyperactivity. For example, DSM-II (American Psychiatric Association, 1968) labeled the condition "hyperkinetic reactions of childhood," characterizing it by overactivity, distractibility, restlessness, and a short attention span. Subsequent research, particularly that conducted by Virginia Douglas, suggested that attention, rather than motor activity, was the crucial defect. (See Douglas, 1983, for a discussion of her research project.) This research lead to the primary diagnosis of attention deficit disorder (ADD) in DSM-III (American Psychiatric Association, 1980), which could be either with or without hyperactivity. More recent research questioned the centrality of the attention defect while showing that hyperactivity and impulsivity were so highly correlated that they should be combined into a single category. Thus we now have DSM-IV's tripartite diagnosis of ADHD Predominantly Inattentive Type, ADHD Predominantly Hyperactive-Impulsive type, and ADHD Combined type, which includes both behaviors.

Three other features of the DSM-IV classification deserve further comment: (1) the specific times defining age of onset, (2) duration of symptoms, and (3) the importance of setting.

Age of Onset   Age of onset of symptoms is set before 7 years in DSM-IV. However, an examination of a clinic sample of 380 youths 4 through 17 years of age showed that children who met this criterion were predominantly the hyperactive-impulsive type. The examination found that 43 percent of the inattentive type and 18 percent of the combined type did not manifest symptoms until after 7 years of age. Thus, DSM-IV's criteria reduces the accuracy of identifying these two subgroups. (See Applegate et al., 1997.) Also note that the period of origin affects the manifestations of the psychopathology, although why this is the case is not known.

Duration of Symptoms   In regard to duration of symptoms, there is evidence that the 6-month period outlined by DSM-IV is too short, particularly for preschoolers. Research data show that a 12-month period is more appropriate in regard to symptom duration for preschoolers. (See Barkley, 1996.)

Setting   The symptoms of ADHD may be present in only one setting, such as the home or at school, or they may be pervasive across settings. For example, a clinical child psychologist, after having read the referral on a hyperactive child, may be braced to deal with the "holy terror" the mother described, only to find the child to be a model of cooperativeness in the testing situation.

Prevalence

The prevalence of ADHD is frequently estimated as 3 to 5 percent of the school-age population. There is also evidence of a decline with age, especially for boys. However, it is not clear whether this is a true decline or an artifact due to the nature of the assessment instrument; for example, the criteria might not be as appropriate for adolescents as they are for those in middle childhood. (See Barkley, 1996.)

Gender Differences

Determining sex differences is complicated by referral bias. Since more boys than girls have the comorbid conditions of oppositional and conduct problems, they are more likely to be referred for ADHD. For example, the ratio of boys to girls in a clinical population is 6:1 to 9:1 in favor of boys,

Table 6.1   DSM-IV Criteria for Attention-Deficit/Hyperactivity Disorder

A. Either (1) or (2):
  (1) *Inattention*: Six (or more) of the following symptoms of inattention have persisted for at least 6 months to a degree that is maladaptive and inconsistent with developmental level:
  • Often fails to give close attention to details or makes careless mistakes in schoolwork, work, or other activities
  • Often has difficulty sustaining attention in tasks or play activities
  • Often does not seem to listen when spoken to directly
  • Often does not follow through on instructions and fails to finish schoolwork, chores, or duties in the workplace (not due to oppositional behavior or failure to understand instructions)
  • Often has difficulty organizing tasks and activities
  • Often avoids, dislikes, or is reluctant to engage in tasks that require sustained mental effort (such as schoolwork or homework)
  • Often loses things necessary for tasks or activities (e.g., toys, school assignments, pencils, books, or tools)
  • Is often easily distracted by extraneous stimuli
  • Is often forgetful in daily activities
  (2) *Hyperactivity-Impulsivity*: Six (or more) of the following symptoms of hyperactivity-impulsivity have persisted for at least 6 months to a degree that is maladaptive and inconsistent with developmental level.
  Hyperactivity
  • Often fidgets with hands or feet or squirms in seat
  • Often leaves seat in classroom or in other situations in which remaining seated is expected
  • Often runs about or climbs excessively in situations in which it is inappropriate (in adolescents and adults, may be limited to subjective feelings of restlessness)
  • Often has difficulty playing or engaging in leisure activities quietly
  • Is often "on the go" or often acts as if "driven by a motor"
  • Often talks excessively
  Impulsivity
  • Often blurts out answers to questions before the questions have been completed
  • Often has difficulty awaiting turn
  • Often interrupts or intrudes on others (e.g., butts into conversations or games)
B. Some hyperactive-impulsive or inattentive symptoms that caused impairment were present before 7 years
C. Some impairment from the symptoms is present in two or more settings (e.g., at school or work and at home).
Code based on type:
  Attention-Deficit/Hyperactivity Disorder, Combined Type: If both Criteria A1 and A2 are met for the past 6 months
  Attention Deficit/Hyperactivity Disorder, Predominantly Inattentive Type: If Criterion A1 is met but Criterion A2 is not met for the past 6 months
  Attention-Deficit/Hyperactivity Disorder, Predominantly Hyperactive-Impulsive Type: If Criterion A2 is met but Criterion A1 is not met for the past 6 months

Source: Adapted from DSM-IV. Copyright 1994 American Psychiatric Association.

while the ratio is 2:1 to 3:1 in a nonclinical sample. The literature is inconclusive on the question of whether further refinement of criteria would eliminate sex differences altogether. (See Arnold, 1996, for a detailed discussion of the issues involved in sex differences.)

Socioeconomic Status and Race

There is no clear evidence that either socioeconomic status (SES) or race affects prevalence of ADHD. While some studies show a greater percentage of ADHD in lower-SES children and in African-American children, this may be due to the increase in the comorbid conditions of aggression and conduct problems in these populations rather than to ADHD itself. (See Barkley, 1996.)

Comorbidity

Comorbidity affects many of the clinically relevant features of ADHD as well as its association with other disturbances. In the following summary we will combine studies of conduct disorder with those of aggression since the effects are similar. All comparisons are with children who have ADHD only. (Comorbidity of ADHD and learning disabilities will not be discussed here but will be addressed later, in the section of this chapter that discusses learning disabilities.) Our presentation follows Jensen, Martin, and Cantwell (1997) unless otherwise noted.

ADHD + Conduct Disorder   There is a strong association between ADHD and disruptive behavior disorders. By 7 years of age, 35 to 60 percent of clinically referred children with ADHD will also be diagnosed as having oppositional-defiant disorder (ODD), while 30 to 50 percent will have the additional diagnosis of CD in middle childhood and adolescence. ADHD + CD has an earlier onset than ADHD alone and a higher ratio of boys to girls. In general, it is a more severe disturbance, adversely affecting a wide array of variables in the children themselves, in their relations with parents, and in their performance at school. (See Kuhne, Schachar, and Tannock, 1997.)

ADHD + Anxiety Disorder   The overlap between ADHD and anxiety disorders (AX) is between 25 and 40 percent of the clinical population. The presence of an anxiety disorder, unlike that of a conduct disorder, tends to moderate rather than intensify the disturbance. Specifically, in ADHD + AX children there is a decrease in externalizing behaviors in general and in impulsivity in particular. This, in turn, is part of a picture of less severe symptoms of ADHD.

ADHD + Learning Disabilities (LD)   From 19 to 26 percent of children with ADHD are also apt to have learning disabilities.

Importance of Recognizing Comorbidity   The danger of failing to take comorbidity into account is that ADHD will be thought to be responsible for disturbances that, in effect, are due to the comorbid psychopathology. For example, Satterfield and Schnell (1997) found that the risk of hyperactive children becoming adult offenders was associated with the cooccurrence of problem behavior in childhood and serious antisocial behavior in adolescence. Hyperactivity alone does not increase the probability of later criminal behavior.

Associated Problems

Family Relations   DSM-IV characterizes ADHD as a "disruptive behavior disorder" because its symptoms of aggression, opposition, intrusion, and disorganization disrupt the normal give-and-take of social interaction. As might be expected, such symptoms have a negative impact on family relations. (Our presentation follows Barkley, 1996, unless otherwise noted.) Mothers are less responsive to their children with ADHD and are less rewarding, more negative, and more directive when they do respond. While the children are somewhat less problematic to their fathers, there is also an increase in father–child conflict.

There is also evidence that it is not the presence of ADHD per se but of the comorbid ODD and CD that is associated with most of the interpersonal conflicts in children and adolescence. This same comorbidity is associated with a greater degree of parental psychopathology, marital discord, and divorce than is found in ADHD alone. (See Anastopoulos et al., 1992.)

The perennial question in interactions concerns the direction of effect. Do negative parental behaviors cause the symptoms of ADHD, or are negative parental behaviors a *reaction* to such symptoms? Evidence suggests the latter—that parents are reacting to their children's behavior. Data come primarily from studies using stimulant medication to improve compliance and reduce children's negativism, talkativeness, and generally excessive behavior. Under such conditions parents also become less negative and directive. (See Barkley, 1996.)

Peer Relations   The annoying, intrusive, and insensitive behaviors of children with ADHD significantly increase the chances of peer rejection and social isolation. (See Hinshaw et al., 1997.) Moreover, the time required for peers to notice and react negatively to newly introduced children with ADHD is distressingly short, being measured in minutes and hours. Parental behavior also plays a role in the peer status of children with ADHD. Hinshaw et al. (1997) found that authoritative parenting, with its combination of firm limits, appropriate confrontations, reasoning, warmth, and support, significantly promoted social competence in children with ADHD.

Academic Problems   The majority of clinically referred children with ADHD have difficulty with school performance, while around a quarter of them have comorbid learning disabilities, as was mentioned earlier. Interestingly, the lower scores on standardized achievement tests are found even in the preschool period (Mariani & Barkley, 1997). Low academic achievement seems to be a natural consequence of children with the inattentive type of ADHD because of the difficulty in sustaining attention on tasks, distractibility, failure to follow through on instructions, and problems with organization. There is also a small but significant relation between lower IQ and the hyperactive-impulsive type of ADHD, which in turn plays a role in lower academic achievement. (See Barkley, 1996.)

Developmental Course

In keeping with our thesis that psychopathology is normal development gone awry, we will first present relevant material on normal development. This material, in turn, will serve as a point of departure for presenting the deviations evidenced by the symptoms of ADHD.

The Toddler/Preschool Period   Campbell (1990) makes the point that normal development shades imperceptibly into ADHD, especially in the first 6 years of life. One expects toddlers to be "all over the place and into everything," for example, and if they have a high energy level along with a determination to do what they want to do when they want to do it, it may not be easy to decide whether they are disturbed or not because these are age appropriate behaviors. In addition, the fluidity of early development makes it difficult to predict if a child will "outgrow" the behavior when it is deviant.

Normal preschoolers are expected to be sufficiently task-oriented to complete what they start and monitor the correctness of their behavior. They are

also sufficiently cooperative to accept tasks set by others and participate in peer activities. As in the toddler period, deviations from expectation may be part of normal development, perhaps because of temporary difficulties in adjustment or temperament or unrealistic adult requirements. The main clues to disturbance lie in the severity, frequency, pervasiveness, and chronicity of the problem behaviors (Campbell, 1990).

Now we consider ADHD itself. Before 3 years of age, toddlers evidence an undifferentiated cluster of behaviors that has been called an *undercontrolled pattern of conduct*. However, at around 3 years of age this pattern becomes differentiated, making it possible to distinguish hyperactive and impulsive behavior on the one hand from aggressive and defiant behavior on the other. Thus, 3 to 4 years of age is the lower limit for detecting ADHD (Barkley, 1996).

Hyperactive and impulsive preschoolers who continue to be difficult to control for a year or more are highly likely to have ADHD in middle childhood (Campbell, 1990). This persistence of ADHD, in turn, is more apt to occur if parent and child are locked into a pattern of negativism and directiveness on the mother's part and defiance on the child's. In fact, parental stress is at its highest during the preschool period (Campbell et al., 1991).

Middle Childhood   By middle childhood the standards for self-control, task orientation, self-monitoring of appropriate and inappropriate behavior, and cooperation in family and peer groups are sufficiently clear that the difference between normal variability of behavior and ADHD is more readily apparent. Thus a persistent constellation of disruptive behavior at home and in the classroom, along with disorganization and inability to follow routines, raises serious questions of psychopathology (Campbell, 1990).

Hyperactive-impulsive behavior is likely to persist throughout middle childhood. In addition, there are two new developments. One is the appearance of problems with **sustained attention**, or the ability to continue a task until completed. These problems appear at around 5 to 7 years of age (Loeber et al., 1992). Inattention, in turn, gives rise to difficulties with work completion, forgetfulness, poor organization, and distractibility, all of which may adversely affect the children's functioning at home and at school. (See Barkley, 1996.)

There is evidence that inattention remains stable through middle childhood whereas hyperactive-impulsive behavior declines (Hart et al., 1995). As has been noted, it is not clear whether the latter effect represents a true developmental phenomenon or whether it is an artifact of increasingly inappropriate behaviors used to define hyperactivity-impulsivity e.g., inappropriate running around and climbing (Barkley, 1996).

The second important development in middle childhood is the increased prevalence of comorbid conditions (Barkley, 1996). Early in the period ODD may develop in a significant number of children, and by 8 to 12 years of age such early forms of defiance and hostility are likely to evolve into symptoms of CD in up to half of the children (Hart et al., 1995). This development is particularly likely to occur among the older children who have pervasive rather than situational ADHD (McArdle, O'Brien, & Kolvin, 1995).

Adolescence   The previously held idea that ADHD is outgrown in adolescence has proved to be incorrect. From 50 to 80 percent of clinically referred children will continue to have ADHD into adolescence. While it is true that adolescence marks a decline in the symptoms of hyperactivity and inattention, the same decline is noted in normal controls. There may also be a change in the expression of symptoms; for example, driven motor activity may be replaced by an inner feeling of restlessness, or reckless behavior such as bike accidents may be replaced by automobile accidents (Cantwell, 1996).

In sum, adolescents with ADHD are significantly more disturbed than those without ADHD and must face the normal challenges of physiological changes, sexual adjustment, peer acceptance, and vocational choice burdened by the multiple problems arising from past developmental periods. A concomitant increase in problem behavior is therefore to be expected. Klein and Mannuzza (1991), in their review of longitudinal studies, found that a substantial subgroup (25 percent) of adolescents with ADHD engaged in antisocial activities

such as stealing and fire setting. Between 56 and 70 percent were likely to repeat grades, and the group as a whole was over eight times as likely to be expelled or drop out of school, as compared with normal controls (Barkley, 1990).

Adulthood   Cantwell (1996) estimates that around 30 percent of adolescents "outgrow" ADHD; 40 percent continue to have the symptoms of restlessness, inattention, and impulsivity; while 30 percent develop additional disturbances. For example, longitudinal studies of children with ADHD indicate that, as adults, they have more ADHD, conduct or antisocial disorders, and substance abuse than do normal control adults (Klein and Mannuzza, 1991). While the risk for criminal behavior increases in adulthood, this holds only for those who have both ADHD and CD or other antisocial behaviors; there is no direct connection between ADHD and criminality.

While no cognitive deficits have been documented in adults, academic achievement and educational history both suffer. Children with ADHD complete about two years less schooling than do controls. As can be expected, they subsequently have lower-ranking occupational positions. However, their rate of employment is not significantly different from that of controls (Mannuzza et al., 1997).

Summary of Developmental Course

In the preschool period hyperactive-impulsive behavior and aggressive and defiant behavior become differentiated out of a generalized pattern of uncontrolled behavior. Consequently, 3 to 4 years of age is the lower limit for diagnosing ADHD. Persistent ADHD in the preschool period is predictive of its continuation into middle childhood. Early middle childhood sees the addition of the inattentive type of ADHD. Moreover, comorbid ODD is added early in the period, while CD may be added later on. Whereas inattention remains constant throughout middle childhood, hyperactivity-impulsivity declines.

ADHD persists into adolescence and adulthood. While hyperactivity may decline in those with ADHD, it is still significantly greater than in non-ADHD controls, with motor behavior being replaced by feelings of restlessness. The adolescent with

ADHD may engage in antisocial behavior and do poorly academically. Adults may have problems with alcoholism and drug abuse, as well as with antisocial behavior. However, antisocial behavior is related to comorbid CD rather than to hyperactivity itself. While the rate of employment for ADHD adults is no different from that of non-ADHD adults, those with ADHD have lower-ranking occupational position.

Etiology

General Comments

In our presentation we will not be discussing the interpersonal context since genetic studies show that environmental factors, such as the parent–child relationship, account for only 10 to 15 percent of the variance in ADHD symptomatology. While this low percentage means that the interpersonal context plays only a minor role in etiology, it does not mean that the context can be dismissed as unimportant. As we have discussed, the parent–child relation plays a major role in the severity and persistence of ADHD and, as we shall see later on, is important in treatment. (Details of our presentation can be found in Barkley, 1996 and 1997a.)

The Organic Context

Unverified Hypotheses   We will note here a number of organic hypotheses that were once popular but have failed to stand up under the scrutiny of objective studies.

An influential etiological hypothesis around 50 years ago was that ADHD was due to *brain damage*. Subsequent research using more advanced technology for exploring the brain showed that fewer than 5 percent of the children with ADHD evidenced neurological damage (Barkley, 1990).

Some studies have targeted *diet* and *neurotoxins* as causes of ADHD. Sugar and food additives such as artificial coloring have been regarded as the culprits by some researchers, and special diets have been devised as treatment. However, subsequent objective studies indicated that the diets were largely ineffective in changing the symptoms of ADHD (Richters et al., 1995).

Elevated blood lead levels have been implicated as causing ADHD, but studies relating lead poisoning to the symptoms of ADHD have yielded conflicting results. While it is clear that lead blood level is not a primary etiological agent for ADHD, there is a small but significant relation between the two; for example, one estimate is that lead poisoning accounts for approximately 4 percent of the variance in the expression of symptoms (Fergusson et al., 1993).

Genetic Factors   There is compelling evidence that heredity plays a major role in causing ADHD. Results from studies of twins provide the most convincing evidence. In such studies the average heritability for symptoms is .80. For example, Levy and colleagues (1997), using a cohort of 1,938 families with twins and siblings ages 4 through 12, found heritability of .75 to .91. The finding was robust, holding across familial relations (between twins, between siblings, and between twins and other siblings) as well as across definitions of ADHD. However, the genetic mechanism responsible for this high heritability has yet to be discovered (Barkley, 1996).

Neurological Factors   A host of characteristics of ADHD implicate impairment within the brain: the early onset and persistence of symptoms, the dramatic improvement with medication, deficient performance on neuropsychological tests such as working memory and motor coordination, and the genetic risks just described. Such factors implicate but do not establish brain impairment, because they are all indirect indices. Data from direct examination of the brain have yielded suggestive but not definitive findings.

As already noted, there is no evidence of significant brain damage in children with ADHD. Moreover, data from computer-assisted tomography (CT scans) show no difference between children with ADHD and normal children in regard to the gross structure of the brain. However, while studies of the corpus callosum (the structure assisting interhemispheric transference of information) failed to show any difference in size or shape, magnetic resonance imaging (MRI) has revealed reduced brain size and density in the frontal lobes and striatum. Decreased blood flow within these regions, suggesting decreased activation, has also been documented. The frontal and frontal-limbic areas are of special interest because one of their functions is the inhibition of motor responses. (See Barkley, 1996, 1997a.)

Other Organic Factors   A number of different measures suggest physiological underresponsiveness to stimulation in children with ADHD. The measures include electroencephalogram (EEG), the galvanic skin response, and heart rate deceleration. Even when the findings are inconsistent they are frequently in the direction of diminished arousability. Underresponsiveness would also be congruent with the children's positive response to stimulant medication. A major problem is that diminished arousability is not specific to ADHD, being found also in children with LD and CD. (See Barkley, 1996.)

There also has been interest in investigating central nervous system neurotransmitters, particularly norepinephrine and dopamine. These two substances are thought to be important to the functioning of the frontal-limbic area of the brain (Taylor, 1994). However, research findings are not definitive. Even if they were, it would be difficult to decide on the direction of effect since ADHD could cause the dysfunctions in neurotransmitters as well as being caused by such disfunctions.

The Developmental Dimension   Seidman and associates (1997), who conducted one of the few studies yielding developmental data, were concerned with changes in neuropsychological functioning as assessed by tests of attention and executive functions. The 118 ADHD and control male participants, who were between 9 and 22 years of age, were divided into two age groups, one younger than 15, the other older. The investigators found both ADHD groups to be neuropsychologically impaired, attesting to the enduring nature of such deficits. In regard to development, older boys with ADHD performed better than younger ones did; however, this improvement was seen in normal controls as well. Consequently, while older boys with ADHD become less impaired, they still are not able to catch up with the normal group, which also has improved over time.

The Hyperactivity-Impulsive Type: An Integrative Model

Russell A. Barkley has developed a model that integrates research findings concerning ADHD. (See Figure 6.1.) The model is too complex to be discussed in its entirety, so we will present only the most salient features. (Barkley, 1997a, contains a brief exposition of the model, while a detailed account can be found in Barkley, 1997b.)

The keystone of the model is *behavior inhibition* or the delay of motor response. This delay, in turn, allows for the development of *executive functions*. There are four such functions: (1) working memory, which allows the child to hold ongoing information in mind while comparing it with relevant past events (hindsight) in order to plan future actions (foresight); (2) self-regulation of affect, which involves both the ability to moderate the expression of feelings so they do not get out of control and the ability to increase motivation as needed (for example, when doing a tedious task); (3) internalized speech, which facilitates the use of rules as guides to socially acceptable behavior and the use of strategies in problem solving; (4) reconstitution, which involves high-level thinking, particularly analysis, synthesis, and creativity.

The final resultant of executive functions is motor control, along with goal-directed behavior that becomes increasingly lengthy, complex, and adaptive. Barkley adds that each of the four components has it own developmental trajectory; for example, those involving speech develop later than those that do not.

Barkley claims that the primary deficit in ADHD is the weakened ability to inhibit behavior. All other deviations characteristic of ADHD are secondary to this reduced capacity since the four executive functions can only develop within a period of motor inhibition. Note that the delay *allows* executive functions to develop but does not *cause* them to develop; e.g., internalized speech develops as a result of its own set of causal factors not because of motor inhibition per se. Thus, the lines in Figure 6.1 from behavior inhibition to the four components of executive competence are blunted rather than having arrows.

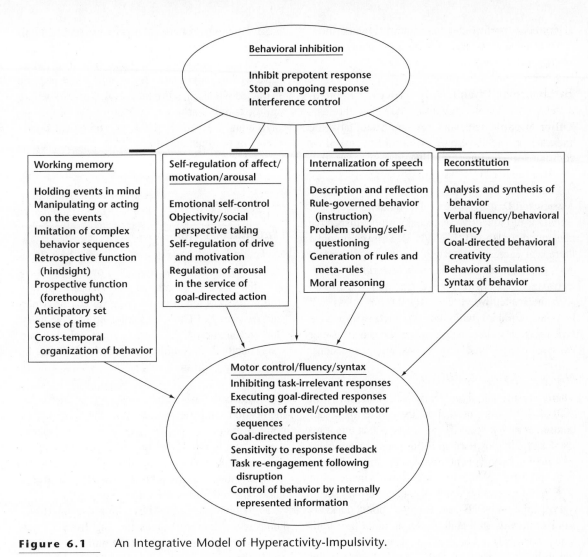

Figure 6.1   An Integrative Model of Hyperactivity-Impulsivity.

Source: Barkley, 1997b.

The Inattentive Type

Relatively little is known concerning the predominantly inattentive type of ADHD. The diagnosis itself was not established as a separate type until DSM-III, and the etiological research has yielded contradictory or inconclusive findings. In addition, the unobtrusiveness of the symptomatology has made the need for treatment seem less urgent than in the case of the obstreperous hyperactive-impulsive type.

Descriptive Characteristics

Children with the inattentive type of ADHD are described in terms such as dreamy, "in a fog", "spaced out," passive, or lethargic. However, their activity level is no different from that of normal children. With peers they are withdrawn, shy, and apprehensive rather than aggressive (Taylor, 1995). Compared with normal children they are more often "off task," are less likely to complete a task, are less persistent in correctly performing boring tasks, work more slowly, and are less likely to return to an interrupted task (Barkley, 1997a).

Prevalence and Gender Differences   Approximately 1 in 10 children with ADHD have the inattentive type, a much smaller number than have the hyperactive-impulsive type. Also, while marked by contradictory findings, the literature suggests that girls outnumber boys (Taylor, 1995).

Associated Disturbances   The inattentive type of ADHD is infrequently associated with the disruptive behavior disorders of ODD and CD. More commonly, there is an increase in anxiety and anxiety disorders and, possibly, in mood disorders (Barkley, 1996). Because of such introversive tendencies, children with the inattentive type of ADHD are at less risk than are children with the hyperactive-impulsive type for adolescent delinquency and substance use or abuse, as well as for school suspensions or expulsions.

Nature of the Deviation

There is substantial evidence that children with ADHD differ from normal children in terms of decreased *attention span*. The problem is that attention itself is a complex variable, and it is far from clear which of its components (or combination of components) is responsible for the children's inattention.

When Douglas (1983) was conducting her seminal research on ADHD, the evidence pointed to *sustained attention* (the ability to continue a task until it is completed) rather than selective attention (i.e., the ability to focus on relevant aspects of a task while ignoring others) as the basic component that was flawed in ADHD. However, further research revealed problems with the sustained attention hypothesis. If this were the crucial variable, then one would expect performance to worsen as the length of the task increased. This did not happen. Moreover, deficiencies in sustaining attention turned out to be dependent on both context and task; for example, sustained attention improved if the examiner was present rather than absent, if the child was penalized for errors, or if the task was interesting. Finally, inattention is not ADHD-specific since it is found in children with other disturbances (Halperin et al., 1992).

Selective attention as the primary flawed component causing ADHD has not fared better. Children with ADHD can resist the distraction from white noise while doing a task, for example, but become distracted when the stimulus is novel or compelling and the task is boring.

In sum, the nature of the psychological deviation(s) in the inattentive type of ADHD remains a mystery.

Intervention

Pharmacotherapy

Medication is the most powerful and best-documented intervention for ADHD. (For a comprehensive discussion of treatment, see AACAP Official Action, 1997, a report of a work group of the American Academy of Child and Adolescent Psychiatry. Our presentation follows this report unless otherwise specified. For another review, see Pelham, Jr., Wheeler, and Chronis, 1998.)

Stimulants   Stimulants are the first choice for medication, and the literature on them is voluminous. Stimulants are clearly effective, the onset of their action is rapid, and the side effects are either mild or easily managed The most popular stimulant is methylphenidate (Ritalin) followed by amphetamines (Dexedrine) and Pemoline (Cylert).

Most children with ADHD improve on stimulants, with the percentages ranging from 70 percent to as high as 96 percent. Stimulants not only affect the major symptoms of ADHD but also affect a host of social, cognitive, and academic problems. In regard to social problems, stimulants improve the mother–child and family interactions, reduce bossiness and aggression with peers, and increase the ability to work and play independently. Cognitively, short-term memory is improved along with the use of strategies already in the children's repertoire. Academically, classroom talking and disruptions decrease, while both the amount and accuracy of academic work completed increases. Incidentally, improvement is not specific to ADHD since normal children given these stimulants improve as well.

In regard to comorbid conditions, stimulants are as effective in children with ADHD and aggression as with those who have ADHD alone. Evidence concerning the effectiveness of stimulants in ADHD with comorbid anxiety is mixed. Finally, research on the comorbid conditions of ODD and CD is sparse.

In general, stimulants have an extremely high margin of safety, and there is little evidence of increased tolerance which would necessitate increased dosage. However, there are side effects. Mild appetite suppression is almost universal, while individual children might also respond with irritability, headaches, and abdominal pains. Concern about other side effects has been shown to be baseless. Children do not become "zombies" when medicated; on the contrary, they are alert and focused. Nor is there an increased risk of substance use or abuse. Adverse effects on height and weight are rarely large enough to be clinically significant. However, a general problem with all medications is that their positive effects are not sustained after they are withdrawn.

Tricyclic Antidepressants   While far less studied than stimulants, tricyclic antidepressants (TCSs) have demonstrated effectiveness in treating children and adolescents with ADHD. They are second-line drugs for children who do not respond to stimulants or who develop significant depressive or other side effects. Children with comorbid anxiety disorders, depression, or tics may respond better to TCSs than to stimulants.

However, there are drawbacks to TCSs. Efficiency in improving cognitive symptoms is not as great as for stimulants; there is a potential for cardiac side effects, especially in prepubertal children; and there is a possible decline in effectiveness over time.

Limitations to Medication

Scope of Research   While the quantity of research on medication is impressive, its scope is limited (Spencer et al, 1996). Most of the research consists of short-term studies of white boys in middle childhood. Relatively little is known about long-term effects or about possible gender and ethnic differences. Comorbidity has also been neglected, as was noted. The few studies of other age groups suggest that adolescents respond as well as do children in middle childhood but that preschoolers do not. (See Figure 6.2.)

Nonmedical Dangers   The twin dangers of pharmacotherapy for treating ADHD are the belief that drugs are a cure-all and that "one size (dosage) fits all." These dangers have little to do with the positive effects of the drugs themselves, but they can significantly obstruct progress in helping the children.

As we have seen, ADHD is accompanied by a wide variety of attendant problems. Medication, in spite of its effectiveness, does not solve them all. It can not magically produce the social and academic skills that the children have failed to acquire, it leaves learning disabilities untouched, and it does not resolve all the difficulties arising from the attempts of parents (who themselves often have ADHD) to deal with their disturbed children. Moreover, the illusion of the pill-as-cure-all provides an excuse for parents and professionals alike not to undertake the often arduous demands of other forms of treatment.

The "one size fits all" illusion ignores the fact that, while medication is generally effective, individual children vary widely in their response. For a particular child some symptoms and some attendant problems may improve while others in that same child are not helped at all. It is even possible that one academic subject may improve but not another, for reasons unknown.

There is also variability in compliance. Parents may be resistant to using medication, and adolescents in particular may fear stigmatization by peers. For physicians there is the danger of overprescribing medication and a subsequent failure to conduct the necessary but time-consuming monitoring of effectiveness of dosage.

Psychosocial Interventions

As we have seen, medication does not remedy all the problems that beset children with ADHD. Specifically, it may not affect comorbid conditions, parental psychopathology, academic and social skills, and peer popularity. Therefore, other remedial measures

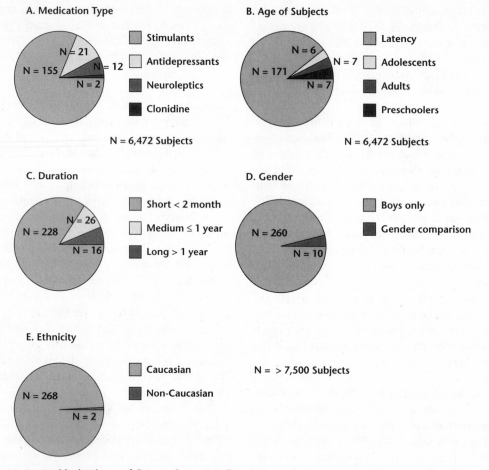

A. Medication Type

N = 21
N = 155
N = 12
N = 2

Stimulants
Antidepressants
Neuroleptics
Clonidine

N = 6,472 Subjects

B. Age of Subjects

N = 6
N = 171
N = 7
N = 7

Latency
Adolescents
Adults
Preschoolers

N = 6,472 Subjects

C. Duration

N = 26
N = 228
N = 16

Short < 2 month
Medium ≤ 1 year
Long > 1 year

D. Gender

N = 260
N = 10

Boys only
Gender comparison

E. Ethnicity

N = 268
N = 2

Caucasian
Non-Caucasian

N = > 7,500 Subjects

Figure 6.2   Limitations of Research on Medication.

Adapted from Spencer et al., 1996, pp. 409-430

are needed. We will describe some of these briefly. (A more detailed presentation can be found in AACAP Official Action, 1997.)

Behavior Modification   In the operant approach, environmental rewards and punishments along with modeling are used to decrease problem behaviors and increase adaptive ones. In the short term, behavioral interventions improve social skills and academic performance in a specific setting. There is evidence that the operant approach in the classroom setting significantly improves the behavior of children with ADHD (Pelham, Jr., Wheeler, & Chronis, 1998). The greatest weakness of behavior modifi-

cation is the lack of maintenance of improvement over time and the inability to generalize to other situations. However, techniques have been developed aimed at remedying these shortcomings.

In general, behavior modification alone is less effective than medication alone. Moreover, there is little research evidence of additional benefits when behavior modification is added to medication.

Cognitive Behavior Modification   Cognitive behavior modification (CBM) was developed to remedy the above-mentioned shortcomings of behavior modification. CBM teaches cognitive strategies, such as stepwise problem solving and self-monitoring. While initial studies of effectiveness were promising, subsequent results have been disappointing (Pelham, Jr., Wheeler, & Chronis, 1998). There is also no evidence that CBM improves outcome when added to stimulant medication.

Social Skills Training   Social skills training teaches children techniques for positive peer interactions while eliminating their unsuccessful "in your face" approaches. The training is most effective when conducted in groups where target behaviors emerge naturally and can be addressed through modeling, practice, feedback, and contingent reinforcement.

Parent Training   **Parent training** aims at substituting adaptive for maladaptive ways parents deal with their children. The parents are trained to focus on specific problematic behaviors and to devise strategies for changing them. Behavioral parent training has a well-documented record of effectiveness (Pelham, Jr., Wheeler, & Chronis, 1998). However, one problem is sustaining parental involvement, since parents also might have ADHD.

Academic Skills Training   Academic skills training involves specialized individual or group tutoring that teaches children to follow direction, become organized, use time efficiently, check their work, take notes, and, more generally, to study effectively. Remediation of comorbid learning disabilities may also be necessary. The effectiveness of academic skills training has received little systematic evaluation.

Multimodal Interventions

One would assume that multimodal intervention would be the approach of choice in remedying the multiple problems of children with ADHD. Surprisingly, research does not uniformly support such a logical inference. Instead, the approach has had some successes along with a number of failures. (Our presentation continues to follow AACAP Official Action, 1997.) On the positive side there is some evidence that, when behavioral techniques are combined with stimulant medication, peer relations improve to the point where they are on a par with those of nondisturbed children. In a like manner, the

addition of low-dose stimulants appears to help normalize the classroom behavior of children who are being treated by a behavioral program.

Against these isolated reports of success stand a number of reports of failures. As we have seen, behavior modification, cognitive behavior modification, and parent training add little to the effectiveness of medication alone. An ambitious study comparing a group receiving only stimulant medication with a group receiving an extensive range of treatments including all of those described above except medication, found that, at the two-year evaluation, there was no significant difference between groups (AACAP Official Action, 1997).

In sum, research findings do not support the idea that multimodal intervention is desirable for all children with ADHD. Rather, medication is the treatment of choice with other techniques being called into play to treat those problems that are resistant to stimulant or antidepressant medication.

Learning Disabilities

Definition and Characteristics

As we turn our attention to *learning disabilities* (LD) we must consider the two questions basic to understanding any psychopathology: How should it be defined? and How should the definition be operationalized? (See Shaw et al., 1995, for a detailed analysis of the problems of definition.)

Conceptualizing Learning Disabilities

In regard to conceptualizing LD, matters got off on the wrong foot in the widely adopted legal definition. In the Education for All Handicapped Children Act of 1977 (PL 94-142), LD was defined as a disorder in one or more of the *basic psychological processes* involved in understanding and using spoken or written language. It may manifest itself in a severe *discrepancy between age and ability levels* in one or more of the following areas of academic achievement: oral expression, listening comprehension, reading, writing, or arithmetic. According to this definition, LD does not include children who have learning problems that are primarily the result of visual, hearing, or motor handicaps, mental retardation, emotional disturbances, cultural or economic disadvantage, or limited educational opportunities.

A core problem with this definition is that the "basic psychological processes" are not specified, and, indeed, it is only now becoming clear what some of these processes might be. The exclusion of a number of other groups of disturbed and deprived children has been criticized on two counts: first, LD can co-occur with conditions excluded from the definition, such as physical handicaps or emotional disturbances, and second, it is not always possible to disentangle LD from these excluded conditions. (See Shaw et al., 1995.)

Definitions prepared subsequently by the National Joint Committee on Learning Disabilities (NJCLD) and DSM-IV come closer to hitting the mark, although they are not without problems. NJCLD (1988) defines LD as a heterogeneous group of disorders manifested by significant difficulty in the acquisition and use of listening, speaking, reading, writing, reasoning, or mathematical abilities. The specification of "underlying processes" has been deleted. NJCLD also states that the disorder can occur concomitantly with other handicapping conditions, such as sensory impairment, emotional disturbance, cultural differences, or insufficient instruction but that LD is not the result of these conditions. The disability is presumed to be due to a central nervous dysfunction.

DSM-IV does not have a general definition for LD, which it calls Learning Disorders; rather it lists the diagnostic criteria for three such disorders: reading, mathematical disorders and written expression. Since the criteria are essentially the same for all three, we will present only those for reading (see Table 6.2).

DSM-IV's definition is more precise in that it substitutes discrepancies between objective measures of achievement on the one hand and IQ, age, and grade on the other for NJCLD's somewhat nebulous "significant difficulty in acquisition and use" of an academic skill. DSM-IV is also more concerned with the effects of LD on the child's adjustment. However, NJCLD has a broader spectrum of concurrent conditions than does DSM-IV. (See Lyon, 1996a, for a more detailed account of the historical background and problems in conceptualizing LD.)

Table 6.2   DSM-IV Criteria for Reading Disorder

A. Reading achievement, as measured by individually administered standardized tests of reading accuracy or comprehension, is substantially below that expected given a person's chronological age, measured intelligence, and age-appropriate education.

B. The disturbance in Criterion A significantly interferes with academic achievement or activities of daily living that require reading skills.

C. If a sensory deficit is present, the reading difficulties are in excess of those usually associated with it.

Source: Adapted from DSM-IV. Copyright 1994 American Psychiatric Association.

Operationalizing Learning Disabilities

Satisfactorily operationalizing LD has proved to be an even more thorny undertaking than conceptualizing it. At the heart of the matter is the use of the **discrepancy model**—the difference between what students should achieve and what they actually are achieving. While discrepancy can be operationalized in terms of grades in a particular subject as compared with the child's age or grade placement, it is more desirable to use standardized tests of achievement and compare these with tests of general intelligence such as IQ tests.

A basic practical problem is that there is no general agreement as to how large a discrepancy should be in order to classify children as LD. Because legal criteria differ, a child can change from being LD to being non-LD simply by moving from one state to another. Moreover, professionals differ among themselves as to what scores on achievement and IQ tests constitute a significant discrepancy. (See Shaw et al., 1995.)

Another problem with the discrepancy model that particularly concerns clinicians is that it requires the children to fail academically before being diagnosed. This requirement impedes early detection. It is not unusual, for example, for children to be in the third grade before explanations other than LD are exhausted; for example, "He doesn't like the teacher" or "Girls just don't do well in math." The delay is important because the longer it persists, the less amenable the child is to remedial measures. (See Lyon, 1996b.)

A final limitation of the discrepancy model is that, at least in the case of reading, it does not serve the basic diagnostic function of differentiating a unique population of children. For example, there is evidence that children classified as LD in reading because their achievement is lower than their average or above IQ are no different from children who are classified as "slow readers" because their achievement in reading is congruent with their lower IQ level. This lack of differentiation of the two groups applies to a number of variables: information processing, response to instruction, genetic variability, and neurophysiological markers. (See Lyon, 1996b.)

Even with all its shortcomings and with the at-times heated controversies the concept of LD has spawned, it also has had a number of positive consequences. It has called attention to a population of children who are neither "stupid" nor "lazy" in regard to schoolwork, as they tended to be regarded in the past. In a like manner the concept of LD has relieved teachers of the accusation of being incompetent. The concept of LD has also stimulated research into cognitive skills and processes involved in learning specific subjects, the possible biological roots of such skills and processes, and the consequences of LD for general adjustment.

Prevalence and Gender Differences

Disagreements as how to define and operationalize a disturbance is bound to affect epidemiological data. Such is the case with LD, for which prevalence estimates have ranged from 1 to 40 percent of the population. The most frequently cited figure places prevalence between 4 and 5 percent of the population. (See Box 6.1.) While it was once believed that boys outnumbered girls in regard to LD, subsequent studies indicate there is no sex difference.

Associated Problems: Social Skills Deficits

The relation between LD and social skills deficits has been well established empirically. In a meta-analysis of 152 studies over the past 15 years, Kavale and Forness (1996) found that 75 percent of students with LD manifested significantly greater social skills deficits than did comparison groups. The finding was robust, being consistent across different evaluators (teachers, peers, and the students themselves) and across most of the major components of social skills.

In terms of peer evaluations, children with LD were considered less popular and cooperative, were selected less often as friends, and were avoided more than non-LD peers. These negative evaluations, in turn, were attributed to a perceived lack of communicative competence and reduced empathetic behavior. LD students themselves, like their peers, perceived their social functioning as adversely affected by a lack of competence in communication as well as deficient social problem-solving skills. There were two pervasive attitudes underlying their perceptions. The first was a general feeling of inferiority due to a poor self-concept and a lack of self-esteem. The second was an external locus of control that made them view success and failure as due to luck or chance rather than to their own effort. (See Kavale and Forness, 1996.)

Reading Disabilities

The recent trend in research is to study specific learning disabilities rather than the heterogeneous population that makes up LD as a whole. This approach is proving fruitful in uncovering core etiological variables and, in the case of reading disabilities, in forcing a rethinking of the nature of LD itself. We will concentrate on **reading disabilities** (RD) because it is the most frequent of the various disabilities and because the research findings are particularly substantial and revealing.

Definition and Characteristics

Definition   Most definitions of RD, which is also called *reading disorder* or *dyslexia*, conform to the discrepancy model. In the case of reading this means a significant discrepancy between reading accuracy, speed, or comprehension and chronological age or measured intelligence. (Our presentation follows Lyon, 1996a, unless otherwise noted. A briefer presentation can be found in Beitchman and

Box 6.1   **What Is the Real Prevalence of LD?**

Since 1977 there has been a steady rise in the number of students identified as LD. (See Figure 6.3.) That year also marked the full implementation of PL 94–142, the Education for All Handicapped Children Act of 1977 mandating services for the education of LD children. While a cynic might conclude that the number of children with LD depends on how many the federal, state, and local governments are willing to support, a more balanced evaluation of the data points to a variety of forces at work. (Our presentation follows Lyon, 1996b.)

Research findings have broadened the population identified as LD in three respects. It is now possible to identify LD earlier than it was in the past; for example, early identification in reading alone resulted in an increase in the percent of children identified as having LD

from 5 percent in 1976 to 17 percent in 1994. The finding that there are no appreciable gender differences has resulted in an increase in the number of girls diagnosed as LD. Finally, the recognition that mild cases may portend significant difficulties in academic learning has resulted in including them in the LD population rather than dismissing them as unimportant.

Extraneous factors both outside and within the profession are also at work. There are financial and political forces that seize upon the vagueness of the discrepancy model to manipulate prevalence either by increasing it in order to qualify for state funding or by decreasing it in order to cut back on remedial programs when they are perceived as too costly to the taxpayer. There are psychological forces as well. Note that the prevalence of LD increased after 1997 while

the prevalence of mental retardation declined (Figure 6.3). One explanation is that, for parents, the diagnosis of LD is both less prejudicial and more optimistic than that of mental retardation. Thus, prevalence rates might reflect parental diagnostic preference to a certain extent.

What can we conclude about the "real" prevalence of LD? Ideally, prevalence rates should only reflect changes due to the application of research findings and dissemination of information concerning criteria for diagnosis. But the ideal world is not the real world. Here, financial and political and parental pressures are at work. Moreover, such pressures will not go away just because they confound the data. The best we can do is to be aware of such confounding forces and, as much as possible, make allowances for their effects.

Young, 1997.) Children with RD are assumed to be different from children whose reading, while significantly below average, is in keeping with their lowered IQ. This latter group is sometimes called "garden variety reading disabled," and we will designate it as GRD.

RD is thought to be different from GRD for another reason. A number of years ago data showed that performance in reading, rather than being normally distributed, has a "hump" at the lower end of the curve. This hump was interpreted as being due to the addition of a special group of children with a special kind of reading problem. It was further assumed that these children with RD were qualitatively different from children with GRD.

Recent studies have cast doubt on the validity of the discrepancy model, as we have seen. For example, studies show that there is no difference between RD and GRD in the reading skills of word

recognition and knowledge, on nine cognitive variables such as vocabulary and memory that are related to reading proficiency, and on teachers' behavioral ratings. Moreover, subsequent population studies of school children have failed to find the hump at the lower end of the distribution of the reading curve. Rather than indicating a qualitatively different group, the data show that performance in reading is continuously distributed throughout the school population. On a practical level this means that trying to establish a cutoff point that will distinguish the RD population from other slow readers is doomed to fail.

Prevalence and Gender Differences   RD affects at least 10 million children, or approximately one child in five. While schools tend to identify more boys than girls, epidemiological and longitudinal studies show no sex differences. (See Lyon, 1996a.)

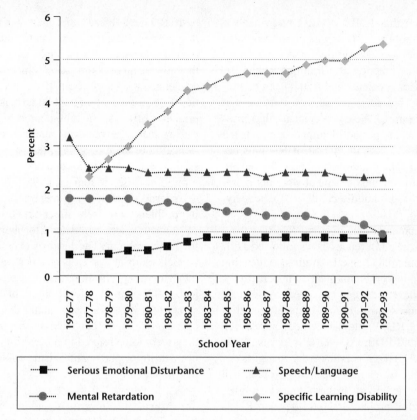

Figure 6.3   Percentage of Children Identified as Manifesting the Most Common Disabilities in the Years 1977 Through 1993.

Source: Lyon, 1996b

Comorbidity: RD and ADHD   Around 20 to 25 percent of students with RD also have ADHD. (Our presentation follows Beitchman & Young, 1997.) However, the reasons for this overlap are not known. There is evidence suggesting a shared genetic variation between the two conditions. One can also argue that problems with attention along with restlessness interfere with learning to read. It is equally plausible to argue that persistent academic failure can lead to restlessness and inattention in the classroom.

RD and Behavior Problems   Three longitudinal studies throw light on the relation between RD and behavior problems: Sanson, Prior, and Smart's (1996) study going from infancy to middle child-

hood; Smart, Sanson, and Prior's (1996) study of the middle childhood period; and Maughan and colleagues' (1996) study going from adolescence to early adulthood.

In general, the results indicate a lack of any direct causal relation between RD and behavior problems. For example, there was no evidence that RD in middle childhood was the precursor of behavior problems in general or externalizing problems in particular in adolescence and adulthood. In addition, adolescents who had RD had no higher rates of alcohol problems, antisocial personality disorders, or crime when they became adults. While there was an increase in delinquency in teenagers, this was due to poor school attendance (and, inferentially, increased opportunities for delinquent behavior) rather than to RD itself. Thus, whatever relation exists between RD and behavior problems is due to the comorbid condition of ADHD.

Reversing the direction of causation, we can ask whether behavior problems and ADHD can be precursors of RD. The longitudinal data indicate that they can. For example, there was evidence that problem behavior in the period of infancy through the preschool increased the likelihood of RD plus behavior problems in middle childhood. Moreover, while behavior problems in general were not a precursor of RD in the middle childhood period, hyperactivity in particular was.

The developmental data also indicate that there were important sex differences. Boys followed a different developmental course from girls, evidencing more externalizing problems such as hyperactivity, which, as we have seen, can be a precursor of RD. The finding raises an important issue in regard to explanations of RD. While the connection between hyperactivity and RD makes sense in terms of our discussion of ADHD, it is noteworthy that girls develop RD in the absence of behavior problems in general and hyperactivity in particular. Why girls with internalizing problems should develop RD is an unanswered question.

Developmental Course

A number of well-designed longitudinal studies attest to the continuity of RD from childhood into adulthood. (Our presentation follows Maughan, 1995, which is a more comprehensive review.) Not all aspects of reading are equally affected, however. Comprehension continues to improve well into adulthood, for example, while phonological processing (i.e., understanding the sound structure of words) is highly resistant to change.

A number of factors determine the developmental course of RD. As might be expected, initial severity of RD and general intelligence are the most potent predictors of progress; however, context factors also play an important role. Socially advantaged children who are given special attention at school and support at home can make good progress even though they take longer to achieve a given level of competence and they tend to avoid reading-intensive courses. The picture of the disadvantaged student

with RD is a bleak one characterized by early dropping-out along with a negative attitude toward formal schooling. For example, one study showed that 40 percent of poor readers remained without any academic or vocational qualifications in their twenties. Educational attainment, in turn, is the strongest predictor of occupational outcome, so it is not surprising that disadvantaged students with RD experience more unemployment, tend to work at semi-skilled or unskilled tasks, and have lower vocational aspirations. (See Maughan, 1995.)

In terms of adult self-perception, childhood reading problems adversely affect only the specific area of literacy, where adults tend to blame themselves for their problem. The level of overall self-esteem of such adults, however, is on a par with that of their more literate peers. In terms of general psychological well-being, the functioning of young adults shows little traces of the problems that had formerly characterized their behavior. Where problems exist they seem to be related to other difficulties, such as immaturity or personality disturbances, rather than to RD per se.

Summary   The severity of children's RD and their general intellectual level are the most powerful predictors of RD's developmental course. Advantaged children who receive support at home and special education at school and who, as adults, select vocations that maximize their strengths and minimize their limitations can have a positive view of their general self-worth (although still blaming themselves for their reading failure) and tend to "outgrow" their childhood problems. On the negative side, being disadvantaged increases the likelihood of dropping out of school at an early age which, in turn, limits vocational choice and increases the likelihood of unemployment.

Etiology: The Intrapersonal Context

Normal Development   Before discussing the etiology of RD it is essential to present the normal process by which children learn how to read. Reading is obviously a complex skill involving the entire gamut of psychological processes, from visual and auditory perception to the higher-order thinking

لما كنا في كندا قابلنا داوود في شلالات نياغرا.

Figure 6.4   Find the Name David.

processes of abstraction and conceptualization. Our discussion will concentrate on the very early stages of learning to read since these will be the most germane to our interest in the etiology of RD. (A more comprehensive presentation can be found in Lyon, 1996a.)

Consider this hypothetical situation: A friend shows you a sentence in Arabic and challenges you to find the name David, which is pronounced "Dah-oo-dah" in the Arabic language. (See Figure 6.4). Confronted with a swirl of graceful lines, dashes, dots, and curlicues, how would you go about it? One way is to assume that Arabic uses a phonetic alphabet as does English. Atomizing the sound of the word, you note that it begins and ends with the same sound, "dah." Next, you assume that the written Arabic reflects the sounds of the oral language on a one-to-one basis. Consequently, you look for a visual pattern that begins and ends with the same squiggle, with a different squiggle in between. Of course any or all of your assumptions may be wrong, but that is beside the point. What you are doing is proceeding from the known oral word to the unknown written representation of that word and trying to "break the code" of the latter. ("Dah-oo-dah" are the letters of the word on the far right.)

Many psychologists regard *breaking the code* as an essential first step in learning to read; specifically, the preschooler must find the relation between the *meaningless visual pattern* of the written language and the *meaningful auditory patterns* of words and sentences.

The major problem in breaking the written code is that spoken words are directly perceived as units; for example, "cat," when spoken, registers whole. The fact that "cat" is really made up of three separate sounds, or **phonemes**, does not occur to children. Written language is different. Written words do not register whole. Understanding that individual words are composed of units—the letters—and understanding that different letters represent differ-

ent phonemes is crucial to learning how to read. Awareness of and access to the sound structure of language is called **phonological awareness**, which, stated simply, is the awareness that words are made up of separate sounds, or phonemes.

Identification of the individual phonemes in words is called *phonological analysis*, while combining a sequence of isolated speech sounds in order to produce a recognizable word is *phonological synthesis*. One measure of phonological analysis involves orally presenting children with words containing two to five blended phonemes and asking them to tap out the number of phonemic segments. One measure of synthesizing skills is a word-blending task that consists of presenting individual phonemes at half-second intervals and asking the child to pronounce the word as a whole.

Phonemic awareness shows a developmental trend. At age 4 years few children can segment by phonemes, although half can segment by syllables. By 6 years of age 90 percent can segment by syllables and 70 percent can segment by phonemes. By 7 years of age 80 percent can segment syllables into their component phonemes, but between 15 and 20 percent still have difficulty understanding the alphabetic principle underlying the ability to segment words and syllables into phonemes—which is approximately the same percentage of children manifesting difficulties in learning to read.

Phonological Awareness and RD   According to Lyon (1996a) a deficit in phonological awareness is the major culprit that impedes learning how to read. Approximately 80 to 90 percent of children with RD have a defect in phonological processing, with the gender ratio being no different from that in the population as a whole. For example, studies show that children with RD have difficulty with segmenting phonemes, storing phonological codes in short-term memory, categorizing phonemes, and producing some speech sounds. Moreover, the research indicates that the relation is a causal one; that is, there is evidence that the deficit precedes the difficulty in learning to read.

There are two cautions in regard to the research findings. First, all of the studies used single words or word recognition as the measure of reading, and it remains to be seen whether differences exist on other measures of reading disability such as comprehension or response to instructions. Second, we are dealing with the weight of evidence rather than with universal findings since there are some contradictory data and some support for alternative etiological hypotheses.

Locating the origin of RD in the ability to decode and read single words runs counter to the idea that RD represents a defect in reading comprehension. However, comprehension itself is dependent upon the ability to decode single words rapidly and automatically. If words are not rapidly and accurately processed, children's ability to understand what they read is likewise hampered.

Rethinking LD

Let us review certain relevant findings concerning RD.

1. Children with RD do not form a distinct, qualitatively different group of readers. Rather, performance in reading is normally distributed with children with RD and children with GRD at the lower end of the continuum. Moreover, children with RD do not differ from children with GRD in regard to numerous cognitive dimensions.
2. Accurate, fluent reading, with appropriate comprehension, depends upon rapid and automatic recognition and decoding of the printed word—in short, on phonological processing. The basis of RD is a specific defect in this processing.
3. Phonological defects impede the normal progress of learning to read *regardless of the children's level of general intelligence*—that is, regardless of whether they have adequate intelligence and are labeled RD or whether their intelligence is below average and they are labeled GRD.

It is this last point that hides a demon. If the core difficulty in learning how to read exists regardless of IQ level, what happens to the concept of LD as a dis-

crepancy between achievement and ability? In regard to reading, at least, the disability has little to do with intellectual level and has everything to do with phonological defects. In short, the discrepancy model is invalid. At the very least, the conceptualization of LD must be broadened to recognize the fact that the discrepancy model is not universally applicable. Instead, there may be core deficiencies that impede academic progress regardless of children's general ability.

Conceptualizing the Psychopathology

Either fixation or a developmental delay seems the most appropriate conceptualization to account for learning disabilities in reading, although developmental data are too sparse to allow for a definitive statement concerning conceptualization. The finding that RD children fail to master the principle of the phonological nature of words implies that they continue to function at the level of preschoolers in middle childhood and beyond.

Etiology: The Organic Context

Genetic Influences   There is a strong genetic component in reading achievement. In their review of twin studies on reading achievement, Reynolds and associates (1996) found that the monozygotic correlations were uniformly greater than the dizygotic correlations. In their own study of oral reading performance, they found that 69 percent of the phenotypic variation was due to heritable influences and 13 percent was due to shared environmental effects. Thus, heritable influences were substantial, and environmental effects, while statistically significant, were small.

Next, heredity plays an important role both in RD in general and in phonological processing in particular (Lyon, 1996a). In regard to the latter, there is evidence that siblings of children with severe phonological disorder manifested significantly poorer performance than did siblings of nonimpaired children on several measures of phonological ability, such as rhyming and segmentation of words into phonemes. Twin studies have yielded similar results.

Brain Mechanisms   While it is generally hypothesized that the etiology of RD has a strong organic component, locating the responsible brain structures and functions has been hampered by a number of methodological shortcomings. (See Peterson, 1995.) Primary among these shortcomings is a failure to control for characteristics such as age, body and brain size, IQ, and handedness (an index of cerebral dominance).

One of the better-designed studies was conducted by Shaywitz and associates (1998). They used an imaging technique called functional magnetic resonance imaging (see Chapter 13) to find the location and extent of functional disruption in neural systems underlying the deficit in phonological awareness. Their subjects were 29 adults with dyslexia and 32 nonimpaired readers. The tasks presented to the subjects were graded in terms of the progressive demands they made on phonological analysis; that is, the tasks ranged from making no demands (e.g., matching visual patterns) to making greater demands (e.g., rhyming letters and nonsense words).

Brain activation patterns differed significantly between groups, with dyslexic readers showing relative underactivation in posterior regions (Wernicke's area, the angular gyrus, and striate cortex) and relative overactivation in an anterior region (inferior frontal gyrus). Even more interesting is the way in which the various components of reading were distributed among different regions of the brain. (See Figure 6.5.) In the nonimpaired group the visual cortex was activated on the simple perceptual task, and then the visual association or angular gyrus area took over and translated letters and words into language. The inferior frontal gyrus was engaged in letter-to-sound coding, while the Wernicke's area processed information in a more abstract phonological form, such as rhyming nonsense words. For the group with dyslexia, by contrast, the inferior frontal gyrus must carry the entire burden of reading from simple perceptual discrimination of letters to complex phonological processes.

For our purposes, the principle shortcoming of the research is that it was conducted on adults. The developmental antecedents of the pattern of relative underactivity in the posterior region and relative overactivity in the anterior region remains to be explored.

Intervention

Starting in the 1960s a number of approaches to treating LD have been tried, some based on etiological hypotheses, some on educational principles, some on techniques successful in treating other disturbances, and, most recently, some based on advances in technology. (See Hammill, 1993, for a review.) While all have met with some success, none has the kind of well-documented efficacy that would make it the treatment of choice.

Targeting Underlying Processes   In keeping with the federal government's PL 94-142, the Education for All Handicapped Children Act, a number of early treatments targeted processes assumed to underlie LD, such as motor, perceptual, and visual-motor processes. Other approaches tailored information to the children's preferred sensory modality, such as vision or hearing, or presented material in a multisensory manner that combined sight, touch, hearing, and kinesthetic cues. None of the approaches has a proven record of success.

Educational Approaches   In contrast to the "underlying processes" orientation, educational approaches emphasize pinpointing academic problems and remedying them by direct instruction; for example, providing a child with RD with exercises and practice with letters, words, and a variety of reading material. Another kind of educational approach involves policy making particularly in regard to the issue of whether the needs of children with LD are best served in special classrooms, in regular classrooms, or in a combination of the two. (See Hammill, 1993.)

The Behavioral Approach   The behavioral approach involves identifying the academic or social skills deficits and remedying them through contingent reinforcement, feedback, and modeling. The focus may be specifically academic, such as increasing the legibility of handwriting, or it may be a more general academic one such as increasing on-task behaviors.

Cognitive and Cognitive-Behavioral Approaches
In cognitive and cognitive-behavior therapy the goal is the broadly defined one of helping children with

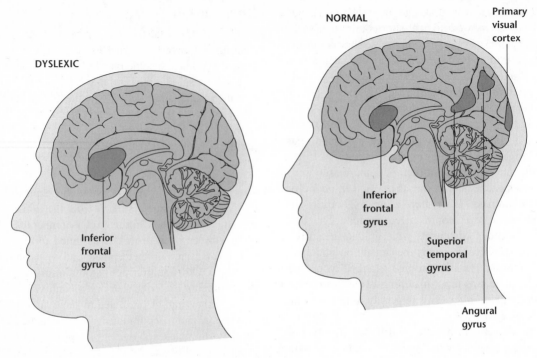

DYSLEXIC

NORMAL

Primary
visual
cortex

Inferior
frontal
gyrus

Inferior
frontal
gyrus

Superior
temporal
gyrus

Angural
gyrus

Figure 6.5   Brain Activity During Reading.

When people with dyslexia try to read, a front part of the brain is overstimulated while crucial portions in the center and back are understimulated. The diagrams show the areas of the brain that are stimulated during reading.

Source: Kolata, 1998.

LD understand what is required of them when confronting a specific learning task and how to go about meeting those requirements.

Medical Treatment   Direct medical treatment has played only a minor role among treatment approaches. Stimulant medication has been successful in decreasing the problems of inattention and noncompliance and improving classroom performance in children with LD both with and without ADHD. However, there is little sustained improvement in measures of achievement. Thus, the fact that the children are better behaved in class does not mean they are learning more. (See the discussion of medical treatment for ADHD in this chapter.)

Other Approaches   Other approaches have involved altering the children's diet, such as giving them massive doses of vitamins or reducing sugar

or food additives. While such measures may be successful with a small group of children—say, those with an allergy to additives—there is no evidence of their general effectiveness. (See Hammill, 1993.)

In general, treatments are most successful when they are directly related to academic content and rely on well-established components of learning, such as cognitive, behavioral, and linguistic principles. Treatment based on underlying physiological or psychological processes have yet to establish their effectiveness. However, no matter what treatment is used, the gains are modest (Kavale, 1990b).

The Use of Technology

In their introduction to the Special Series on Technology in the *Journal of Learning Disabilities*, Higgins and Boone (1996) note that the use of technology in schools is expanding at an astounding pace. Schools have added between 300,000 and 400,000 computers every year for the past ten years, while the expenditure for instructional technology was estimated at $2.13 billion in 1993 alone. Even with all this emphasis on technology, though, the studies of the effectiveness of technology for LD populations are still limited. (Our presentation is based on Higgins and Boone, 1996.)

The frequently mentioned advantages of technologies are those of making children active agents in the learning process and providing easy access to a vast quantity of information presented in a variety of forms (e.g., written, pictorial, and auditory). However, the assumption that computers are uniformly more effective instructors than teachers is unwarranted. For example, Wilson, Majsterek, and Simmons (1996) found that four elementary students mastered more multiplication facts in teacher-directed than in computer-assisted instruction.

Children with LD differ in the degree to which they profit by computer-assisted instruction. In Anderson-Inman, Knox-Quinn, and Horney's (1996) attempt to improve the study strategies of thirty secondary students with LD, seven of the students "bonded" with their laptops and were intrinsically motivated to use the computers to their fullest to help the students realize their academic potential. Sixteen of the students used their laptop to help them perform low-level tasks such as checking spelling but not to help them with higher-level tasks such as taking notes or developing outlines. Finally, seven students rarely used their acquired knowledge except under direct supervision of the teacher and developed a distaste for the laptop that corresponded to their distaste for school in general. Another important finding was that the three kinds of reactions to the program were positively correlated with IQ.

This means that the program was least effective for children with below-average intelligence who need help the most.

Wissick (1996) cites evidence that, while children with LD learn more math and science concepts through video-based courses than through traditional courses, they fail to generalize the information to related but nonvideo information. Children with LD need more structure than their non-LD peers; for example, they learn best when assigned tasks and can use menu-driven programs rather than when they must be self-directing and must deal with open searching. Children with LD also may need more guidance from teachers, for example, in such relatively simple matters as learning to use icons to depict the main menu selections.

In sum, the enthusiasm for technology is not matched, at present, by a solid body of research on its advantages, limitations, and cost-effectiveness in helping children with LD.

One consequence of various psychopathologies may be feelings of depression. Consider children with LD, who are forced to go to school every day and face failure in reading or math or spelling while being helpless to do anything about it, who are unpopular with peers, who must face parents or teachers who might regard them as "just lazy,"—all this is enough to make any child feel depressed. However, such natural reactions are different from the psychopathology of depression. Exploring depression and the related risk of adolescent suicide will be our concern in Chapter 7.

Note that this is the first psychopathology that is not located in any particular developmental age span. This is because depression can originate at any age span from infancy through adolescence.

Disorders in the Depressive Spectrum and Child and Adolescent Suicide

Depressive Spectrum Disorders

Most of us have times of experiencing something we call depression—being in low spirits, feeling "down," having "the blues." It is even appropriate to feel dejection or despair in response to loss of a loved one or other painful life events. Thus, depression as a *symptom* is relatively common, even normal. Depression as a **syndrome** is a constellation of symptoms that often co-occur, including feeling sadness and loneliness, as well as worry and nervousness. Depression as a *disorder* (often referred to as "clinical depression") refers to profound levels of these symptoms and has a specific etiology, course, and outcome (Petersen et al., 1993). As with all disorders defined by DSM, the key is that the combination of symptoms is significant enough to cause distress and/or to interfere with functioning. (See Box 7.1 for a case example.)

In times past, professionals did not believe that depression existed in childhood, partly because it was assumed that children did not have the cognitive complexity required for depression. This idea also had credibility because of the wide range of nondepressive responses children show in reaction to traumatic losses, such as rebelliousness, restlessness, and somatic symptoms. Such behaviors were thought to be "masking" an underlying depression. While the concept of **masked depression** was once widely accepted, investigators who have carefully studied depression in children confirm that it shares many of the same characteristics as adult depression and can be seen at all ages. Rather than *masking* depression in childhood, therefore, behavior problems actually *accompany* the symptoms of depression (Hammen & Compas, 1994).

Definitions and Characteristics

DSM-IV provides us with four major categories for diagnosing depression, which can be viewed as lying along a continuum of severity. The least severe form of

143

Box 7.1   **A Case Example of Depression**

Mary, a woman in her twenties, is currently experiencing her second major depressive episode. She recalls a childhood marked by tension and fighting between her parents, who were frequently critical of her or simply seemed disinterested. Her mother herself was depressed much of the time and was overwhelmed by the responsibilities of raising four children on her husband's limited income. As a consequence of her parents' unavailability and criticism, Mary perceived herself as less important and more incompetent than other children.

She did relatively well at school early on. However, her achievements rarely increased her confidence, instead making her think that the teacher felt sorry for her or causing her to worry that the other students might dislike her. With increasing family conflict, more demanding courses as she grew older, and increasing self-consciousness about whether she was popular or attractive enough, her concentration and motivation declined. She had friends, but

still felt like an outsider, dubious that she could really turn to them in need. If problems arose with her peers, she would typically acquiesce to their demands, keeping her anger and frustration to herself. In high school, her experience of misery grew more acute; she was more conscious of unhappiness and worried a great deal about her future and her looks, fearing that life didn't hold much for her. The one hope she held was to meet a man she could marry, who would make her feel happy and secure.

She met Jack in her first year of college. He was exciting, outgoing, and seemed capable of taking good care of her. He was also more handsome and popular than any man she thought she could attract and, out of fear of losing him, she accommodated to him when he insisted on sexual intimacy. When she became pregnant, the families pressured them to marry, and Mary dropped out of school to become a homemaker and mother. Soon afterward, Mary experienced a major depression

in the wake of discovering that Jack wouldn't provide financial or emotional support for her and that she was stuck at home with a small child and no job prospects.

The marriage limped along for several more years, while, with another child, the couple struggled to make ends meet. Jack began to complain that Mary was no fun to be with, owing to her depressed mood, lack of energy, and pessimism. He spent much of his free time with his friends and was verbally abusive to her if she complained. Mary devoted herself to being as good a parent as possible, although she often found the children a burden and couldn't bring herself to play with them or suppress her irritation. The older child suffered terrible separation anxiety upon starting school. Just recently—prior to her current depressive episode—she found out that Jack was having a serious affair with another woman, and she knew that their marriage had to end.

Source: Adapted from Hammen, 1992.

a depressive spectrum disorder is **adjustment disorder with depressed mood.** The essential feature of adjustment disorders (Chapter 3) is the development of short-term emotional or behavioral problems—in this case, sadness, tearfulness, and hopelessness—in reaction to a recent identified stressor.

Dysthymic disorder is characterized by the presence of depressed mood that has persisted for at least one year in children (as opposed to two years in adults). DSM-IV differentiates between child and adult dysthymic disorder in yet another way: in children and adolescents negative mood may take the form of *irritability* rather than depression. At least two specific symptoms must accompany the periods

of depression, such as loss of pleasure in activities, feelings of worthlessness, and fatigue. (See Table 7.1.) Dysthymia has an earlier onset than other forms of depression and also has a more protracted course.

Major depression is a more debilitating disorder. It requires the presence of five or more symptoms during a two-week period (see Table 7.1), one of which must be depressed mood, or irritability in children. Like adjustment disorder, major depression is an acute condition in that the onset is relatively sudden.

Bipolar disorder, commonly know as manic-depression, is a severe form of psychopathology characterized by depression alternating with states

Table 7.1   DSM-IV Criteria for Depression

Major Depression

Five (or more) of the following symptoms have been present during the same two-week period and represent a change from previous functioning; at least one of the symptoms is either (1) depressed mood or (2) loss of interest or pleasure.

1) Depressed mood most of the day, nearly every day, as indicated by either subjective report (e.g., feels sad or empty) or observation made by others (e.g., appears tearful). Note: in children and adolescents, can be irritable mood.
2) Markedly diminished interest or pleasure in all, or almost all, activities most of the day, nearly every day (as indicated either by subjective account or observation made by others).
3) Significant weight loss or weight gain when not dieting (e.g., more than 5 percent of body weight in a month), or decrease or increase in appetite nearly every day. Note: in children, consider failure to make expected weight gains.
4) Insomnia or hypersomnia nearly every day.
5) Psychomotor agitation or retardation nearly every day (observable by others, not merely subjective feelings of restlessness or being slowed down).
6) Fatigue or loss of energy nearly every day.
7) Feelings of worthlessness or excessive or inappropriate guilt (which may be delusional) nearly every day (not merely self-reproach or guilt about being sick).
8) Diminished ability to think or concentrate, or indecisiveness, nearly every day (either by subjective account or as observed by others).
9) Recurrent thoughts of death (not just fear of dying), recurrent suicidal ideation without a specific plan, or a suicide attempt or a specific plan for committing suicide.

Dysthymic Disorder

A. Depressed mood for most of the day, for more days than not, as indicated either by subjective account or observation by others, for at least 2 years. Note: In children and adolescents, mood can be irritable and duration must be at least 1 year.
B. Presence, while depressed, of two (or more) of the following:
1) Poor appetite or overeating
2) Insomnia or hypersomnia
3) Low energy or fatigue
4) Low self-esteem
5) Poor concentration or difficulty making decisions
6) Feelings of hopelessness

Reprinted with permission from the Diagnostic and Statistical Manual of Mental Disorders, Fourth Edition. Copyright 1994 American Psychiatric Association.

of euphoria or overactivity. The study of bipolar disorder in children has been relatively neglected, perhaps because it has been recognized only recently (Rapoport & Ismond, 1996).

Virtually none of the literature on the developmental psychopathology of depression addresses bipolar or adjustment disorders. Therefore, we will focus our discussion on dysthymic disorder and major depression.

Prevalence

Prevalence estimates vary widely, depending on the criteria and assessment instruments used. Many epidemiological studies only index whether children score above a certain point on a depression rating scale, failing to differentiate amongst the various diagnostic categories.

When viewed as a *symptom* (depressed mood), the prevalence is high in normative populations. (Here we follow Hammen and Rudolph, 1996, and Compas, 1997.) Large-scale studies in the United States and Canada have found that, according to parent reports, 10 to 20 percent of boys and 15 to 20 percent of girls in the general population go through periods of depressed mood. Among adolescents, from 20 to 46 percent of boys and 25 to 59 percent of girls report experiencing depressed mood. When depression is viewed as a *disorder*, prevalence rates are lower. Depressive disorders are rare in the preschool period, more frequent in middle childhood, and most prevalent in adolescence.

A distinction is made between *point prevalence* (how many children in the population are depressed) and *lifetime prevalence* (how many children will become depressed at some time in their lives). For major depression, point prevalence rates are less than 1 percent for preschool children, 2 to 3 percent for school-age children, and from 3 to 8 percent for adolescents (Brent et al., 1996; Cohen et al., 1993). Point prevalence of dysthymic disorder varies considerably from study to study, ranging from 1 to 3 percent for school-age children and from 1 to 5 percent for adolescents. Regarding lifetime prevalence, one large-scale longitudinal study of 386 nonreferred children found that over 9 percent had developed major depression by the time they reached age 18 (Reinhertz et al., 1993).

Lewinsohn and colleagues (1994), using diagnostic interviews, found that almost 3 percent of a sample of 1,710 adolescents fit criteria for dysthymia and/or major depression, with lifetime prevalence rates of 20 percent.

When clinical populations are studied, studies show 10 to 57 percent of disturbed children have a depressive disorder. School-age children referred to treatment have higher rates of major depression (about 13 percent) when compared to younger children (about 1 percent).

Ethnicity influences the likelihood of suicide, with the highest rates found for Caucasians. However, the suicide rate for African-Americans almost tripled between 1960 and 1987. Rates for Latinos and Native Americans showed a similar increase. As Cicchetti and Toth (1998) note, cross-cultural data suggest that suicide is a greater risk for those minority youth whose connections to traditional values and sources of support have been severed.

The Developmental Dimension

Developmental Differences in Depressive Symptoms

The question is often raised as to whether depression in children can be regarded as the same disorder as that in adults, or whether developmental differences necessitate modifications in our diagnostic criteria (Carlson & Garber, 1986). At one extreme are those who maintain that children's cognitive, linguistic, and affective functioning is so different from that of adults that the syndrome in children must be distinct. At the other extreme there are those who point to the similarities in the manifestations of depression in children and adults as evidence that depression is essentially the same in both. Kovacs and Beck (1977) find that a comparable set of symptoms are demonstrated in both depressed children and adults. They describe these as *emotional* (e.g., feels sad, cries, looks tearful), *cognitive* (e.g., anticipates failure, says "I'm no good"), *motivational* (e.g., achievement declines, shows no interest in pleasurable activities), and *physical* (e.g., loss of appetite, somatic complaints).

In general, developmental psychopathologists take a middle position, acknowledging that, while there is a significant correspondence between adult and childhood depression, children also have certain unique characteristics. Following Hammen and Rudolph (1996) and Shafii and Shafii (1992), we can summarize findings regarding developmental differences in the symptoms associated with depression.

Infancy and Toddlerhood   Signs of depression in very young children might include delays or losses of developmental accomplishments, such as toilet training, good sleeping habits, and intellectual growth. A sad facial expression and gaze aversion may be seen. Self-harming behavior such as head banging and self-biting occurs, as well as self-soothing behavior such as rocking or thumb sucking. Clinging and demanding behavior may alternate with apathy and listlessness.

Preschool   Depressed preschoolers are unlikely to verbalize feelings of dysphoria and hopelessness but instead tend to be characterized by a sad appearance. The depressed preschooler may experience a loss of interest in pleasurable activities or achievements. Developmental backsliding may be evident, such as loss of cognitive and language skills, social withdrawal, and excessive anxiety about separation from the caregiver. Vague somatic complaints, irritability, sleep problem and nightmares, and self-harming thoughts are also seen.

School-Age   As children approach school-age, their symptom picture is more similar to that of adults. Depressed mood becomes evident, as do expressions of self-criticism and guilt. Loss of motivation may affect the child's interest in participating in social or school-related activities. In addition, depressed school-age children may engage in disruptive and aggressive behavior that negatively affects their peer relationships and academic performance. Eating and sleep disturbances may be seen, as well as developmental delays. As children advance in age, symptoms become more severe, and there is a greater possibility of suicide and loss of interest or pleasure (anhedonia).

Adolescence   Adolescents are the most likely to directly verbalize their distress. Other symptoms of depression in adolescence include sharp mood swings and negativity, frequently accompanied by truancy, misbehavior, and a drop off in academic achievement.

To summarize, while developmental trends in depressive symptoms exist, age-related differences are not absolute. Studies generally find that depression can be reliably assessed in young children using criteria consistent with DSM-IV. Therefore, despite some age-related differences in symptoms, the existing criteria for depression appear to be valid for use with children.

Age and Gender Differences in Depression

Adolescence and Depression   Large-scale epidemiological studies show that the mean *age of onset* of the first major depressive episode is 15 years (Lewinsohn et al., 1994). In fact, the marked increase in prevalence that comes with *puberty* is probably the most significant developmental trend in the phenomenon of depression. There is a dramatic rise in depression between the ages of 13 and 15, a peak at ages 17 and 18, and a subsequent decline to adult levels.

Why the increase in depression in adolescence? Part of the explanation may lie with the *emotional* and *cognitive developmental* factors that come into play. Emotionally, adolescents are capable of experiencing intense sadness and of sustaining this experience over time. Cognitively, they can think in terms of generalizations and can project into the future. They can consciously evaluate the self and judge it as helpless or inept.

In addition, the *developmental context* of adolescence differs from that of childhood. Children have the basic security of knowing they are an integral part of the family unit. By contrast, adolescents are faced with the task of giving up their place within the family and developing a new status as an independent adult. Even in a healthy adolescent, therefore, one might expect to see some transitory depressive states when closeness to the family is taboo but mature sources of love have not yet been found. Thus, depression may be an exaggeration of normal developments in adolescence (Weiner, 1992). If moderate levels of depression appear as part of the expected turmoil of the adolescent period, the question has more to do with how we can tell normal from pathological symptoms.

Gender and Adolescent Depression   While prior to adolescence sex differences in depression are small and not reliably found, around age 12 there is an increase in both the prevalence and the severity of depression in girls, especially among those who are clinically referred (Compas et al., 1997). By the time they reach age 16, girls are twice as likely as boys to be diagnosed with depression (Hankin et al., 1998). (See Figure 7.1.)

Why are more girls depressed? While hormonal changes accompanying puberty are an obvious explanation, research disconfirms this (Angold & Rutter, 1992). A provocative set of findings suggests that there are different psychological predictors of depression in males and females. A prospective study by Block and Gjerde (1990; Gjerde & Block, 1991) found striking sex differences in the symptom picture leading up to depression in 18-year-olds. At 14 years of age, girls who later became depressed were described as vulnerable, anxious, worried, somatizing, and concerned with their adequacy—characteristics associated with *internalizing*. By contrast, at age 14 boys who became depressed were seen as antagonistic, aggressive, antisocial, self-indulgent, deceitful, and mistrustful of others—characteristics associated with *externalizing*. Further, depression was associated with low self-esteem only in girls; and, while female adolescents described themselves as aggressive and socially unskilled, observers found those traits only in males. These sex differences in precursors were in evidence as early as the preschool period. In subsequent work, Gjerde (1995) followed these same subjects to age 23. Consistent with previous findings, adult depression in males was predicted by preschool ratings of undercontrolled, aggressive behavior. For females, predictors of depression were not reliably identified until adolescence but included overcontrolled behavior and introspective self-concern.

How are we to understand these results? Gjerde (1995) and Nolen-Hoeksema and Girgus (1994) argue that adolescence is a developmentally sensitive period that may have different implications for males

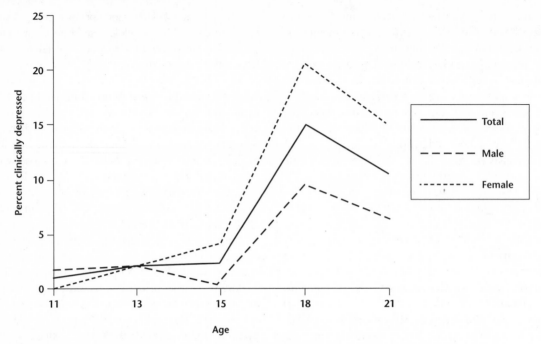

Figure 7.1   Prevalence Rates of Major Depressive Disorder by Gender.

Source: Hankin et al., 1998, p. 135

and females. While both boys and girls undergo significant biological changes, girls are more likely to evidence dissatisfaction with their bodies and dislike of the changes they are going through. Further, because they are more attuned to and sensitive to the opinions of others, girls may be more reactive to some of the stressors associated with adolescence, such as increasing peer pressures and sexual attention. In addition, gender roles and the expectation that one will conform to them increase in adolescence, and girls may believe that they will be disliked if they act in ways counter to their gender-role stereotype, such as by being assertive and independent-minded or by beating a boy in a competition. Girls are also more likely than boys to hide their competence in order to avoid others' negative opinions. Thus, both gender roles and developmental stage come into play.

Comorbidity

From 40 to 70 percent of depressed children and adolescents have at least one other disorder as well (Cicchetti & Toth, 1998). Symptoms of *anxiety* and

depression are highly correlated, with 60 to 70 percent of children identified as depressed having comorbid anxiety disorders. While some authors have used this to argue that the distinction between depression and anxiety be abandoned for children, the general consensus is that the two syndromes are sufficiently distinct to justify classifying children as having one disorder or the other, or a combination of the two (Cole, Truglio, & Peeke, 1997). Anxiety symptoms typically predate depression, suggesting a developmental relationship between these two forms of internalizing disorders (Kovacs & Devlin, 1998).

However, anger and aggression also play a significant role in childhood depression, especially among boys. One-third of depressed boys also have *conduct disorder*, and engage in aggressive antisocial acts such as setting fires, fighting, or stealing. Although this observation is compatible with the idea of masked depression described earlier, again, these misbehaviors are in addition to, rather than instead of, the symptoms of depression. Comorbid conduct disorder and aggression are also associated with a more negative outcome (Harrington et al., 1991).

Patterns of comorbidity also change with age. Depressed preschoolers are likely to demonstrate separation anxiety; depressed school-age children may also have conduct disorder; and depressed adolescents tend to show substance abuse or eating disorders (Hammen & Rudolph, 1996).

Developmental Course

While it was once believed that depression was a transitory phenomenon, certainly in contrast to the stability seen in externalizing behavior problems (see Chapter 9), evidence is accumulating regarding the *continuity* of depression. Studies of normative populations show that ratings of child depression taken at the beginning of the school years predict depressive symptoms three (Ialongo et al., 1993) and even six (Achenbach et al., 1995a) years later.

Studies of clinical samples offer some encouraging news. Evidence suggests fairly high rates of *recovery* from a given episode of depression. Kovacs and colleagues (1994) followed a group of children diagnosed with depression, assessing them every few years until late adolescence or early adulthood. Most children rebounded from their initial depressive episode. The highest probability of recovery was from major depressive episode; second highest, from adjustment disorder with depressed mood; and last, from dysthymia. It took longest to recover from dysthymia, while adjustment disorder required the shortest time for recovery.

However, the news is not as good as it looks at first glance. Although children were likely to recover from an episode of depression, *relapse* rates were also high. Within a period of five years, children with major depression or dysthymia had a high probability of suffering a new depressive episode. About two-thirds developed a new episode of depression while they were still in their teens. Early onset dysthymia was a particularly negative indicator, with 76 percent of the children in this category going on to develop a major depressive disorder.

Similar results concerning continuity have been reported in other longitudinal studies. For example, Harrington and his colleagues (1996) followed 80 children diagnosed with depression into adulthood and compared them to control subjects matched for age and sex. Those depressed as children were at significantly greater risk for developing affective disorder in adulthood: 84% of those depressed as children were depressed in adulthood, as opposed to 44% of those who had not had childhood depression.

Early *age of onset* is also a negative prognostic sign. Onset of depression prior to puberty is associated with more severe dysfunction and an even greater likelihood of continuity to adult depression (Harrington et al., 1996).

Some forms of depression might be precursors to others. Dysthymic disorder is an antecedent to major depression for many youth, with the course of dysthymia often punctuated by attacks of major depression. In addition, a significant number of depressed children and adolescents are later diagnosed with bipolar disorder (Akiskal, 1995).

Specificity   Is depression in childhood a *specific* predictor of later depression? As Harrington and colleagues (1996) point out, there are some limitations to the available evidence for the continuity of depression. *Looking backward* we find that, while childhood depression predicts adult depression, not all depressed adults were depressed as children; in fact, only a minority were. *Looking forward* we find that adult depression can be predicted by a number of different forms of childhood psychopathology, including externalizing disorders.

However, some recent work suggests that, at least in adolescence, depression is a risk factor specific to the development of adult depression. Bardone and colleagues (1996) compared a sample of well-adjusted 15-year-old girls with a group of same-age girls who had been diagnosed with either depression or conduct disorder. At age 21, while conduct-disordered girls generally demonstrated antisocial personality disorder, depressed girls tended to become depressed women. Further, depression in the earlier years specifically predicted symptoms of depression in adulthood.

Again, however, gender differences complicate the picture. Depression in childhood may have different consequences for males and females. For example, Achenbach and coworkers (1995a) found that depression in school-age girls predicted depression six years later, whereas depression in boys predicted diverse symptoms, including not only depression but also withdrawal, thought problems, and inattention. These results echo the findings reported earlier on gender differences in the factors that predict depression in males and females.

To summarize, the prognostic picture suggests that, while the recovery rate from depressive disorders is high, so is the relapse rate. Major depression and dysthymia tend to be chronic and recurring disorders and tend to put children at risk for a number of disorders later in development. Of those children with depression who go on to become disturbed, the great majority show depression as part of their adult disorder. Therefore, once on a depressed trajectory in development, a child is likely to stay on this course.

Etiology

The Intrapersonal Context

An Attachment Perspective   As Cicchetti and Toth (1998) note, evidence has accumulated regarding a link between *insecure attachment* and depression in infants, children, and adolescents. Children who internalize an image of themselves as unworthy and others as unloving are more vulnerable to the development of the cognitive, emotional, and biological processes that are associated with depression.

Blatt and Homann (1992) rely on attachment theory for their model, which distinguishes between two different kinds of depression. The first, *dependent depression*, is characterized by feelings of loneliness and helplessness as well as fear of abandonment and being left unprotected. Individuals with dependent depression cling to relationships with others and have unmet longings to be cared for and nurtured. Thus they have difficulty coping with separation and loss and are uncomfortable expressing anger for fear of driving others away. In contrast, *self-critical depression* is characterized by feelings of unworthiness, inferiority, failure, and guilt. Individuals with

self-critical depression have extremely high internal standards, resulting in harsh self-scrutiny and evaluation. They have a chronic fear of others' disapproval and criticism, and they worry about losing the regard of significant others. They are driven to achieve and attain perfection and thus make excessive demands on themselves. While they may even accomplish a great deal, they do so with little experience of lasting satisfaction or pleasure.

Blatt and Homann (1992) hypothesize that these different kinds of depression are due to particular kinds of attachment experiences affected individuals have in early childhood. The quality of their relationships with caregivers leads to the development of internal working models of self and other that leave these individuals vulnerable to depression. Inconsistent parental availability, associated with the *resistant/ambivalent* attachment pattern, may be more likely to result in depression related to issues of dependency, loss, and abandonment. In contrast, controlling and rejecting parenting associated with *avoidant* attachment would lead to self-criticism and low self-worth, as angry feelings about the caregiver are redirected against the self.

To date, the validation studies of this model have been based on retrospective research with adults. However, Blatt and associates (1996) were able to differentiate the two types of depression in a sample of adolescents. Further tentative support for the dual nature of depression in children comes from Harter's (1990) research, which revealed two groups of depressed children and adolescents. In the larger group depression was due to low self-esteem, while in the smaller group it was due to the loss of a significant person. However, the necessary developmental research—showing that dependent and self-critical depression in childhood are predicted from different kinds of attachment relationships in infancy—has not yet been conducted.

Cognitive Perspectives   Cognitive theories about childhood depression follow directly from those developed with adults. These theories center on the *cognitive triad*, consisting of appraisals of *worthlessness* ("I am no good"), *helplessness* ("There is nothing I can do about it"), and *hopelessness* ("It will always be this way").

First, there is good evidence of a relationship between childhood depression and feelings of *low self-worth* (Harter & Whitesell, 1996). Harter finds a strong relation between self-worth and mood, the correlations running between .67 and .82 in children 8 to 15 years of age. Longitudinal research has also demonstrated that low self-esteem is a specific predictor of depression (Lewinsohn, Gotlib, & Seeley, 1997). Moreover, children's negative view of the self leads to a biased interpretation of information in such a way that it "confirms" their belief in their inadequacy. For example, depressed children recall more negative adjectives describing themselves on a memory test, while nondepressed children recall more positive traits. This tendency is no longer evident when depression lifts (Zupan, Hammen, & Jaenicke, 1987).

Second, Seligman and Peterson's (1986) concept of **learned helplessness** has proven to be a fruitful behavioral translation of the *helplessness* dimension. The original data came from laboratory studies in which dogs who had had repeated experiences of being unable to escape a noxious stimulus failed to even attempt to do so when the opportunity was made available to them. This learned helplessness has cognitive and motivational components. Cognitively, the individual learns that responding is futile, and this knowledge concomitantly reduces the motivation to respond. In terms of self-conceptualization, the individual is no longer an active agent but rather the passive recipient of whatever unpleasantness happens to come along.

Third, Abramson, Seligman, and Teasdale (1978) contribute to our understanding of the *hopelessness* dimension by adding the variable of *causal attribution*, which is the cornerstone of **attribution theory**. Three dimensions are involved in the causal attributions leading to depression: they are *internal* ("It is because of me"), *stable* ("I will always be like this"), and *global* ("Everything about me is this way"). When uncontrollable events are attributed to characteristics of the individual, rather than to external agents, self-esteem diminishes as helplessness increases. When the uncontrollable events are attributed to factors that persist over time, then helplessness is stable. And when uncontrollability is attributed to causes present in a variety of situations,

helplessness is global. Stable and global attributions are clearly linked to the cognition of hopelessness, which has been shown to play a significant role in adolescent depression (Harter & Whitesell, 1996).

Where do these attributional styles come from? According to the cognitive model outlined by Rose and Abramson (1991), negative events during childhood—such as traumatic loss, maltreatment, and guilt-inducing parenting—set in motion a vicious cycle. As the individual attempts to interpret these events and find meaning in them, cognitions are generated related to their causes and solutions. When events are negative, uncontrollable, and repeated, hopelessness-inducing cognitions are likely. A number of other factors might facilitate or interfere with the development of negative cognitions, including the extent to which the negative events challenge the child's self-esteem, the child's own level of cognitive development, and the reactions and interpretations of events offered by parents (see Figure 7.2). For example, Stark and colleagues (1996) found that children with the cognitive triad of depression had parents who themselves evidenced depressive attributional styles and who communicated negative messages to the child about the self, the world, and the future. As parents disconfirm more hopeful-inducing cognitions, and negative events are repeated, a depressed mind-set is formed.

These negative cognitive *schemata* affect not only the present but also the child's future orientation toward the world. Schemata are stable mental structures that incorporate children's perceptions of self, their experiences in the past, and their expectations for the future (Dodge, 1993). Therefore, based on the lessons they draw from their past experiences, depressive schemata color children's perceptions of present and future events, drawing their attention to all that is negative and consistent with their pessimistic point of view. As they develop negative patterns of thinking and engaging with the world, and a stable negative cognitive style, the likelihood that children will develop depression increases.

There are some *limitations* to cognitive models of child depression. Some studies of children's attributional styles have produced mixed results; for instance, longitudinal research has found negative attributions to be *correlates* of youth depression

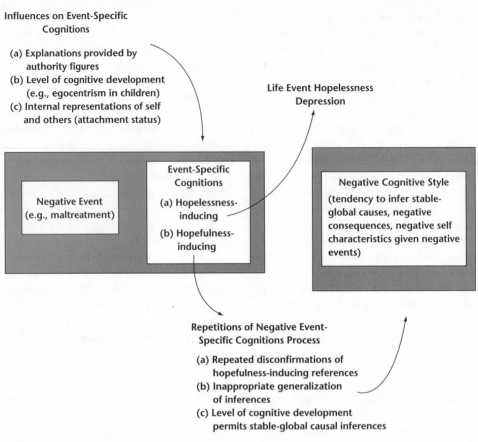

Influences on Event-Specific Cognitions

(a) Explanations provided by authority figures
(b) Level of cognitive development (e.g., egocentrism in children)
(c) Internal representations of self and others (attachment status)

Life Event Hopelessness Depression

Event-Specific Cognitions

(a) Hopelessness-inducing
(b) Hopefulness-inducing

Negative Event (e.g., maltreatment)

Negative Cognitive Style (tendency to infer stable-global causes, negative consequences, negative self characteristics given negative events)

Repetitions of Negative Event-Specific Cognitions Process

(a) Repeated disconfirmations of hopefulness-inducing references
(b) Inappropriate generalization of inferences
(c) Level of cognitive development permits stable-global causal inferences

Figure 7.2   A Model of the Development of Negative Cognitive Style.

Source: Rose and Abramson, 1991

rather than *predictors* of it (Bennett & Bates, 1995). There is also a question as to whether negative attributional styles are specific to depression rather than being characteristic of psychopathology in general (Lewinsohn, Gotlib, & Seeley, 1997). Hammen (1991) also cautions that depressive cognitions appear to be state-dependent, coming and going as depression waxes and wanes, rather than being an underlying trait that would serve as a "marker" of vulnerability. There is still much to be learned about the causal role of the cognitive triad in the etiology of depression.

Another question about the cognitive model is a *developmental* one. While depression can be detected in very young children, not all the cognitive markers theoretically associated with depression can be. (See Shirk, 1988.) The research methodology for assessing the cognitive triad requires children to use and understand complex language, which prevents us from investigating it prior to the late-preschool and middle childhood periods. Moreover, our understanding of cognitive development makes it difficult to picture the cognitive triad of worthlessness, helplessness, and hopelessness in infancy. In an attempt to resolve this dilemma, Rose and Abramson (1991) offer an intriguing speculation. While the onset of a depressive attributional style may indeed develop in early childhood, the cognitive components of depression may not become evident until years later. Negative experiences may only result in the cognitive triad of depression if they persist into the period of concrete operations, when the child is able to make causal inferences that are stable and global in nature.

The Interpersonal Context: Family Influences

Widening our scope to include the larger context of child development, we find abundant evidence that life stress and adversity have important roles in depression. Depressed children—and their parents— report experiencing more acute and chronic *life stress* than do others, and they have fewer supportive social relationships to act as a buffer to stress. *Family adversity*, including poverty and interparental conflict, also increases both parent and child depression (Hammen, 1991).

Depressed children describe their families as more *conflictual*, negative, and controlling, and less cohesive and supportive (Kaslow, Deering, & Racusin, 1994). Observations of the family interactions of depressed children and their parents confirm that they display high levels of negativity and disengagement, as well as harsh and controlling parenting (Messer & Gross, 1995) In addition, depression is linked to *maltreatment* of children (Toth, Manly, & Cicchetti, 1992; see Chapter 14), including emotional, physical, and sexual abuse (Lizardi et al., 1995). A poor family environment may undermine the child's self-esteem, which in turn contributes to a sense of failure and depression. Negative childhood events also interact with the other risk factors we have identified, such as by generating the attributional style of helplessness, hopelessness, and worthlessness that is characteristic of depression.

Further, the above-cited research has shown that children become depressed specifically in relation to *interpersonal stressors*, rather than to other kinds of negative events that might affect adults, such as achievement-related failures. Perhaps the single most traumatic interpersonal stressor for children is the loss of a parent, which we consider next.

Parental Loss   Our review of the concept of attachment in Chapter 5 demonstrated that adequate caregiving in infancy is not a sentimental luxury but an absolute necessity for optimal development. Although relatively rare, complete loss of a parent is an experience with dramatic effects on child functioning and clear links to depression.

The classic research on *maternal deprivation* was conducted by Spitz (1945) and Bowlby (1960), who studied infants in settings such as hospitals, orphanages, and foundling homes. Despite the fact that their physiological needs were met—they received adequate food, warmth, and hygiene—these infants lacked any kind of affectionate care. As a consequence, many wasted away, and even died—as many as 37 percent in one orphanage. Spitz filmed these children as they sobbed inconsolably or lay listlessly in their cribs, responding indifferently to the sporadic attentions of adults. While the title of his heartrending film is simply *Grief*, Spitz termed these infants' reaction **anaclitic depression** (meaning, essentially, loss of that upon which one depends) and believed that it represented a prototype of adult depression. Bowlby (1960) asserted that the loss of this important relationship—the infant's secure base—is so profound that it should be viewed on the same level as war and natural disaster.

The hypothesized link between maternal loss and depression has received empirical support (Weller et al., 1991). An important fact to keep in mind, however, is that Spitz's and Bowlby's research confounds loss of a parent with *institutionalization*. These variables were teased apart in a series of studies conducted by Joyce and James Robertson (1971). They observed young children who had been separated from their mothers, and found that the ill effects of parental loss were more severe for children who were placed in institutions as opposed to those who were placed in foster families. While large, impersonal orphanages provided children with minimal care and attention from an ever-changing series of nurses, children in loving foster families had available to them surrogate caregivers with whom they readily formed attachments. Children in foster care also demonstrated significantly less distress about the separation from their mothers, and they overcame their distress more readily when reunited with their own families. Therefore it is not separation per se that is so devastating, but rather the extended stay in a strange, bleak, or socially insensitive environment with little or no contact with the mother or other familiar figures.

Brown, Harris, and Bifulco (1986) examined other factors that can mediate the effect of loss of the mother. These investigators interviewed women who were bereaved as children and also those who underwent a significant period of separation from the mother. Loss of the mother before the age of 11, whether by death or separation, was associated with subsequent depression for most women. Thus, maternal deprivation acted as a *vulnerability factor*. However, loss of the mother had no effect in the absence of a *provoking event*, such as poverty or life stress.

Further research uncovered additional mediators. The rate of depression was twice as high in women who had experienced *traumatic* separations from their mothers, such as being neglected, abused, or abandoned, than it was in women separated by death or by socially accepted causes such as maternal illness or divorce (Brown, Bifulco, & Harris, 1987). And, in a subsequent study, Bifulco, Harris, and Brown (1992) found that the rate of adult depression was particularly high in women whose mother died before they were 6 years old and even greater if death occurred before they were 3 years old. However, it was not the early timing of the death per se that was important. Rather, it was the fact that the death came at the end of a long sickness, which, the authors infer, prevented the development of a secure *attachment*.

In sum, both in infancy and childhood, the idea that loss of a caregiver per se leads to depression is too simplistic to be accurate. Rather, depression is contingent upon the interaction of a host of factors, including the intrapersonal (e.g., helplessness), interpersonal (e.g., lack of social support), superordinate (e.g., socioeconomic level), and developmental (e.g., the child's level of cognitive sophistication). Therefore, the task of investigators is to tease out the interactions among variables and to examine the ways in which such interactions change as loss occurs at different points in development.

Children of Depressed Mothers   In a major review article in the *American Psychologist*, Peterson and colleagues (1993) state that "the need for services for children of depressed parents as closely approximates a prescriptive recommendation as can be found in the mental health professions" (p. 163). Approximately 40 percent of children of depressed mothers are themselves diagnosed with depression. Maternal depression more than doubles the risk of a child's developing depression across the life course, with episodes that are particularly severe and long-lasting. Further, longitudinal research by Hammen, Burge, and Stansbury (1990) showed that children of depressed mothers had a worse outcome than children of bipolar, medically ill, well, or even schizophrenic mothers. Perhaps, in contrast to the guilt-inducing qualities of parental depression, the overtly bizarre behavior associated with psychosis is more easily understood by children as being not under their control and not of their doing (Anderson & Hammen, 1993).

It is not clear how the intergenerational transmission of depression from parent to child takes place. Although the link may be a genetic one, another likely explanation is in terms of *parenting style*. Two dimensions of depressed parenting have been identified: *withdrawal* and *intrusiveness* (Malphurs et al., 1996). Depressed mothers are observed to be less psychologically available to their children: they offer less positive affect, warmth, praise, and positive feedback. They are also more likely to be controlling, impatient, and irritable; to use coercive discipline techniques; to make more negative attributions about child behavior; and to be less accurate in reading children's affect (Cicchetti & Toth, 1995a).

The clearest examples of the effects of maternal depression come from studies of young children. Maternal depression has even been experimentally manipulated, a rare thing in the literature on psychopathology. While playing with their toddlers, nondepressed mothers were asked to simulate depressed affect by keeping a "still face" and by exhibiting less positive affect, expressiveness, involvement, and responsiveness. Children reacted with clear distress, physically withdrawing from their mothers, making more negative bids for attention, and behaving in disorganized and oppositional ways (Seiner & Gelfand, 1995).

Field (1992) reports that infants of depressed mothers develop a depressive mood as early as 8 months of age. These depressive characteristics appear not only during interaction with the mothers but also with a nondepressed stranger, indicating the development of a stable interpersonal style. If maternal depression persists over a year, adverse effects on infant growth and intellectual development are seen, while in the toddler and preschool periods maternal depression is associated with the development of an insecure attachment (Teti et al., 1995).

What is the developmental process by which children of depressed mothers themselves become depressed? One proposal is that coping with a depressed parent prevents children from developing adequate strategies for *emotion regulation* (Cicchetti & Toth, 1995a). Emotion regulation, as we saw in Chapter 2, allows children to calm themselves in the face of upsetting circumstances. Healthy mothers aid the development of emotion regulation by soothing their children and helping to build their competency to soothe themselves. However, depressed mothers' inability to modulate their own negative feeling states interferes with the ability to modulate their children's moods. Thus, children of depressed mothers are exposed to chronically high levels of negative affect and fail to develop effective strategies for managing these distressing feelings (Garber, Braafladt, & Weiss, 1995).

Clinical observations of depressed mothers and toddlers also demonstrate *transactional* processes through which they influence each others' behavior (Cicchetti, Rogosch, & Toth, 1997). For example, infants of depressed mothers are more irritable and difficult to soothe and exhibit more negative affect, anger, sadness, and distress, thus taxing their mothers' parenting skills. Toddlers of depressed mothers are also highly attuned to their mother's negative affective, and sometimes even engage in role reversal as they try to mother or comfort the parent. In these ways, children's attempts to cope with and respond to their mothers' depression might counter or perpetuate problematic cycles of interaction. Over the long term, maternal and child depression have been shown to mutually affect one another, as research shows significant relationships between the onset and succession of depressive mood in at-risk mothers and their children (Hammen, Burge, & Adrian, 1991).

There is also research to indicate that the effects of maternal depression vary as a function of *gender*; the risk of developing depression appears to be higher for girls than boys. A seven-year longitudinal study by Hops (1992) shows stronger relationships between mother and daughter depressed mood than exists among other family members. Similarly, Davies and Windle (1997) report that maternal depression is associated with subsequent depression in female, but not male, adolescents. The emotional closeness of mother–daughter relationships (Chodorow, 1978) may place girls at particular risk for the effects of maternal depression.

However, many confounding factors conspire to prevent simplistic explanations about the intergenerational transmission of depression. First, depression is associated with a number of other forms of psychopathology in mothers, including anxiety and personality disorders, as well as family stressors such as marital conflict and adverse living conditions, many of which have similar affects on children's development (Cummings & Davies, 1994a). In addition, maternal depression is also associated with the development of other disorders in children, such as ADHD, anxiety, substance abuse, bulimia, and conduct disorder. Therefore, the concept of *multifinality* applies here, as maternal depression is a risk factor not specific to child depression but rather predictive of a variety of poor outcomes.

The Interpersonal Context: Peer Relations

Parents are not the only sources of negative evaluation that can result in depressed mood. Peers can be relentless in their taunting of the child who is "different" or socially awkward. Therefore, it is no surprise that low social support from peers, lack of perceived social competence, and loneliness are significant predictors of child and adolescent depression (Harter & Marold, 1994), particularly for females (Oldenburg & Kerns, 1997).

Evidence also suggests that depressed young people are less socially skilled than other children. Therefore, one proposal is that depression is a function of deficits in *interpersonal problem-solving* skills (Stark, 1990). While good problem-solving skills can act as a protective buffer against the impact of negative life events, depressed youth are less able to generate effective solutions to interpersonal problems. Consistent with this hypothesis, depressed children have poorer social skills (Bell-Dolan, Reaven, & Peterson, 1993) and they are less often chosen as playmates or workmates by other children (Rudolph, Hammen, & Burge, 1994).

Are depressed children the *victims* or the *initiators* of negative social relationships? An ingenious study by Altmann and Gotlib (1988) investigated the social behavior of depressed school-age children by observing them in a natural setting: at play during recess. The authors found that depressed children initiated play and made overtures for social contact at least as much as did nondepressed children, and were approached by other children just as often. Yet, depressed children ended up spending most of their time alone. By carefully observing the sequential exchanges between children, the researchers discovered the reason for this. Depressed children were more likely to respond to their peers with what was termed "negative/aggressive" behavior: hitting, name-calling, being verbally or physically abusive.

These observations fit well with the model developed by Patterson and Capaldi (1990), in which peer relations are posited to play the role of *mediators* of depression. According to this model, a negative family environment leads children prone to depression to enter school with low self-esteem, poor interpersonal skills, aggressiveness, and a negative cognitive style. They are less able to perceive constructive solutions to social problems and are more likely to be rejected by peers because of the way they behave. Peer rejection, in turn, increases their negative view of self and thus their depression.

In order to test this model, Capaldi (1991, 1992) differentiated four groups of boys depending on whether they demonstrated aggression, depressed mood, both aggression and depression, or neither. Boys were followed over a two-year period, from grades 6 to 8. While depression and adjustment problems tended to abate over time in the depressed group, no such improvement occurred in the two other disturbed groups. While, in general, aggressive behavior was more stable than depressed mood, conduct problems increased the risk of subsequently having a depressive mood. In fact, aggression in grade 6 predicted depressed mood in grade 8, while earlier depression did not predict later conduct problems.

Capaldi conceptualizes the process leading from aggression to depression as follows. (See Figure 7.3.) *Aggression* and noxious behavior alienates parents, peers, and teachers, resulting in more interpersonal conflict and *rejection*. Further, aggression leads to oppositional behavior in the classroom, which leads to *learning deficits* and poor skill development. Both of these factors result in profound *failure* experiences in the social and academic realms. Failure and rejection, in turn, produce *low self-esteem*. The impact of peer rejection, low academic skills, and low self-esteem is associated with increasingly serious deficits in adolescence, ultimately resulting in *depression*.

The Organic Context

Evidence that organic factors play an important etiological role in depression has emerged in studies of adult populations, while research evidence in regard to children is slight. (Our presentation follows Hammen and Rudolph, 1996, unless otherwise noted.)

Familial concordance rates provide evidence for a *genetic* component in depression. Children, adolescents, and adults who have close relatives with depression are at considerable risk for developing depression themselves. In fact, having a depressed parent is the single best predictor of whether a child will become depressed.

However, simply demonstrating a correlation between parent and child depression fails to disentangle the relative influence of heredity and environment. For this, twin and adoption studies are needed. One study of adolescents compared monozygotic and dizygotic twins, biological siblings, half-siblings, and biologically unrelated step-siblings and found significant genetic influences at lower levels of depression but significant environmental influences at high levels of depression (Rende et al., 1993). Another study investigated a large sample of monozygotic and dizygotic twin pairs aged 8 to 16 years (Thapar & McGuffin, 1996). While environmental factors seemed to best account for depression in childhood, evidence for a genetic component was strong in adolescence. In sum, while data support the

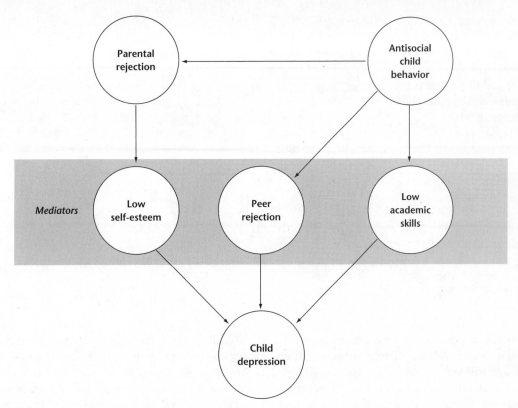

Figure 7.3   Mediators of the Effects of Child and Family Factors on Depression.

Source: Adapted from Patterson and Capaldi, 1990

theory of a genetic component to depression in adults and adolescents, other factors also play a major role in the etiology of depression in children.

Research with adults indicates a *neuroendocrine* imbalance as an etiological agent, particularly hypersecretion of the hormone *cortisol*. This is not surprising since hormone production regulates mood, appetite, and arousal, all of which are adversely affected by depression. However, little evidence exists for the role of cortisol in child depression.

Depression is also associated with low levels of the neurotransmitter *serotonin*. Antidepressant medications that act to increase serotonin availability, including tricyclics such as imipramine and the new generation of selective serotonin reuptake inhibitors (SSRIs), such as Prozac, have been proven effective in combating depression in adults. Again,

however, evidence in support of this mechanism in children is mixed at best. In many controlled studies, antidepressant medications have not been effective in combating child depression. Fisher and Fisher (1996) reviewed thirteen double-blind placebo-controlled studies published between 1965 and 1994 and found only two cases in which antidepressants relieved depression better than placebos. In fact, some studies seemed to show that the placebo was more effective! Similar null findings are reported in an exhaustive review by Sommers-Flanagan and Sommers-Flanagan (1996).

Much of the research these investigators reviewed was based on the older type of antidepressants rather than the new SSRIs, which may be both more effective and safer. Recent studies focusing on the efficacy of SSRIs in child and

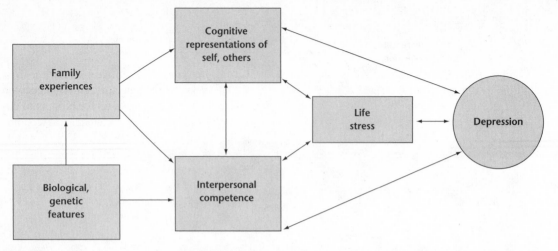

Figure 7.4   Hammen's Multifactorial Transactional Model of Child and Adolescent Depression.

Source: Hammen and Rudolph, 1996

adolescent depression are somewhat more promising (DeVane & Sallee, 1996). However, effect sizes are still small, and in some studies results emerged only for ratings of global improvement and not for symptoms of depression (Emslie, Kennard, & Kowatch, 1995).

In summary, research on child depression, while limited, suggests that organic theories of etiology derived from studies of adults cannot be applied as easily to children. Further, without prospective data demonstrating that biological indicators predate the onset of depression, there remains some question as to whether these are the cause or result of depression. Ultimately, the picture is likely to be a complex and transactional one. Experiences and mood act on biology, and, in turn, biology reciprocally affect cognitions, emotions, and memory (Post & Weiss, 1997).

Integrative Developmental Model

A comprehensive developmental psychopathology model of depression has been put forward by Hammen (1991, 1992; Hammen & Rudolph, 1996) and is presented in Figure 7.4. The case study that was presented in Box 7.1 also illustrates the elements of this model.

While acknowledging that there are many pathways to depression, Hammen's model places *dysfunctional cognitions* at the forefront. First, however, the stage for the development of these negative cognitions is set by *family factors*, such as a depressed parent, insecure attachment, and insensitive or rejecting caregiving. Adverse interpersonal experiences contribute to the child's development of negative *schemata*: of the self as unworthy, others as undependable and uncaring, and relationships as hurtful or unpredictable. The depressive cognitive style also involves the belief that others' judgments provide the basis for one's self-worth, as well as a tendency to selectively attend to only negative events and feedback about oneself.

Further, Hammen highlights the fact that the relationships among affect, cognition, and behavior are dynamic and transactional. For example, negative cognitive styles lead to problems in *interpersonal functioning*, which act both as vulnerabilities to depression and as stressors in their own right. The negative attributions of depressed children interfere with the development of adequate coping and social skills, and they respond to interpersonal problems through ineffective strategies such as withdrawal or acquiescence. These strategies not only fail to resolve interpersonal problems but even exacerbate them, increasing experiences of victimization, rejection, and isolation. Therefore, the negative cognitive styles and poor interpersonal problem-solving skills associated with depression further disrupt social relationships, undermine the child's competence, induce stress, and confirm the child's negative beliefs about the self and the world.

As development proceeds, these cognitive and interpersonal vulnerabilities increase the likelihood that individuals will respond with depression when faced with *stress* during development. Hammen's model describes three aspects to the role of stress in depression. First, as described above, individuals vulnerable to depression may actually generate some of their own stressors. In this way they contribute to the aversiveness of their social environments, as well as consolidating their negative perspectives on the world. An illustration of this kind of process later in development is "assortative mating," the tendency of individuals to choose partners who mirror or act on their vulnerabilities. For example, Hammen and colleagues find that depressed women are more likely than others to marry men with a diagnosable psychopathology, and, in turn, to experience marital problems and divorce which contribute further to their depression.

Second, the association between stress and depression is mediated by the individual's cognitive style and interpretation of the meaning of stressful events. While life stress increases the likelihood of psychopathology in general, it is the tendency to interpret negative events as disconfirmations of one's self-worth that leads to depression in particular. Third, certain groups of children are at high risk because they are exposed to the specific kinds of stressors that increase depression. These include maltreated children, those whose parents are emotionally disturbed, those in families with high levels of interparental conflict, or those who live in situations of chronic adversity that diminish the entire family's morale and sense of well-being.

Biological factors can come into play at any point in the cycle. For example, individual differences in temperament may contribute to problems in children's relationships with parents and others. Biological factors can affect children's ability to cope with stressful circumstances, as well as increasing their vulnerability to depression as a reaction to stress.

Developmental influences also enter into the picture in a number of ways. First, difficulties that occur earlier in development may have particularly deleterious effects, diverting children to a deviant pathway from which it is difficult to retrace their steps. Once on a deviant trajectory, children become increasingly less able to make up for failures to develop early stage-salient competencies. Accumulated stress may also alter the biological processes underlying depression, especially in young children, whose systems are not yet fully matured. Second, cognitive development can influence depression. As we have seen, young children's thinking tends to be undifferentiated and extreme, contributing to an "all or nothing" kind of reasoning. A negative cognitive style formed at an early age, therefore, may be particularly difficult to change once consolidated. Third, the organizational view of development argues that the connections among cognition, affect, behavior, and contextual factors strengthen over time. Thus, over the life course, depressive patterns are integrated into the self system, become increasingly stable, and require lower thresholds for activation.

Hammen's model is relatively new, and it is in the nature of research in developmental psychopathology that decades must pass before we have data available that fully test a given model by tracing pathways of development from infancy to adulthood. Therefore, it is too early to say whether this is an accurate account of the developmental psychopathology of depression. To date, parts of the model have held up to empirical scrutiny. Rudolph, Hammen, and Burge (1994) demonstrated links between child depression and negative cognitions about self and other, negative representations of family and peer relationships, biases in social information processing, and poor interpersonal skills. However, in a study of adults, Hammen and colleagues (1995) found that, while attachment-related negative cognitions and life stress predicted depression one year later, the results were not specific to symptoms of depression. Therefore, it may be that Hammen's model actually represents a general model for the development of psychopathology, one that can be applied to the understanding of depression but is not specific to it.

Intervention

Pharmacotherapy

As noted above, while some studies indicate that the new antidepressants (SSRIs) reduce depressive symptoms in children, results are mixed. Undesirable side effects also occur, including restlessness and irritability, insomnia, gastrointestinal discomfort, mania, and psychotic reactions (DeVane & Sallee, 1996). There are advocates for their continued use, who cite the low rates of serious side effects and the devastating consequences of untreated depression (Kye & Ryan, 1995). However, others are strongly opposed, arguing that their use is unethical given that their effectiveness is not supported by the existing research (Pellegrino, 1996).

Despite questions about the effectiveness of antidepressants with children, they are being prescribed at an increasing rate: in 1996, U.S. physicians wrote 735,000 prescriptions for SSRIs for children ages 6 to 18, a rise of 80 percent in only two years (Clay, 1997). Prozac now comes in peppermint flavor especially designed for children.

As with adult depression, for child depression the usual recommendation (if not the usual practice) is to use antidepressant medication only as an adjunct to other forms of treatment. Many factors that contribute to depression—stressful life circumstances, poor parent–child relationships, family conflict and dissolution, low self-esteem, and negative cognitive biases, for example—cannot be changed by psychopharmacology and can be better addressed by psychotherapy with the individual child or the family (Dujovne, Barnard, & Rapoff, 1995).

Psychodynamic Psychotherapy

Psychodynamic treatments for depression focus broadly on problems in underlying personality organization, tracing these back to the negative childhood experiences from which depression emerges. The goals of therapy are to decrease self-criticism and negative self-representations and to help the child to develop more adaptive defense mechanisms in order to be able to continue on a healthy course of emotional development. With younger children, the therapist may use play as a means of bringing

these issues into the therapy room, with the focus shifting to discussion as children become more cognitively mature (Speier et al., 1995).

Psychodynamic approaches rarely provide outcome studies beyond individual case reports. However, Fonagy and Target (1996) investigated the effectiveness of a developmentally oriented psychoanalytic approach with children. (This is described in more detail in Chapter 17.) Results showed that the treatment was effective, particularly for internalizing problems such as depression and anxiety. Younger children (i.e., under 11 years) responded best. However, the treatment was no quick cure; the best results were found when treatment sessions took place 4 to 5 times per week over a period of two years.

Cognitive Behavioral Therapy

An example of a cognitive-behavioral approach is the Coping with Depression Course for Adolescence (Lewinsohn et al., 1996), a downward extension of a treatment program originally designed for adults. This intervention includes role playing to teach interpersonal and problem-solving techniques, cognitive restructuring to decrease maladaptive cognitions such as "Nothing ever turns out right for me," and self-reinforcement techniques. Studies of the effectiveness of this approach show that, for the 80 percent of adolescents who improve, treatment gains are lasting. Cognitive behavioral therapies for child depression are the most extensively researched, and, overall, findings concerning their effectiveness are very positive (see Marcotte, 1997, and Southam-Gerow et al., 1997, for reviews).

Family Therapy

A comprehensive review by Dujovne, Barnard, & Rapoff (1995) examines the relative effectiveness of a number of different treatments for childhood depression. They conclude that family-focused treatments (family therapies) warrant primary consideration, given the roles of the family situation, parent–child relationships, and parent depression in the development of depressive spectrum disorders. Consistent with this, Lewinsohn's group (1996) found that the effectiveness of their cognitive-behavioral intervention for depressed children was enhanced by the addition of interventions with the parents. Group sessions are held in which parents are given the opportunity to discuss issues related to depression and to learn the same interpersonal communication and conflict resolution skills being taught to their children.

An effective multifaceted approach to treating child depression in the family context is described by Stark and associates (1996). Interventions with the child include the use of individual and group therapy in order to increase positive mood and expectations, restructure maladaptive schemata, and enhance social skills. Interventions aimed at the larger system include parent training and family therapy in order to reduce the environmental stresses that contribute to the development of depression. Further, consultation with teachers is provided to promote and reinforce children's use of adaptive coping strategies during the school day.

Prevention

Efforts to prevent the development of childhood depression have focused on those most at risk— namely, children of depressed mothers. For example, Gelfand and colleagues (1996) developed an intervention program for depressed mothers and their infants. Home visits were made by trained nurses whose goals were to increase depressed mothers' parenting efficacy as well as to foster more positive mother–infant interactions. Mothers who participated improved in reported depression and perceived stress, and both their own and their infants' overall adjustment improved. Children of mothers who participated were also less avoidant in their attachment than other children; however, they were also more resistant.

An intriguing study by Malphurs and colleagues (1996) targeted another at-risk sample, depressed teenage mothers. Mothers were observed interacting with their infants and were differentiated in terms of whether they demonstrated a withdrawn or an intrusive parenting style. Specific types of interventions were designed to help counter these problematic patterns. For example, intrusive mothers were coached to imitate their children's behavior, thus giving children more opportunities to initiate and influence the flow of the interaction. In contrast, withdrawn mothers were coached to keep their infant's attention, thus increasing the level of mutual interest and engagement. Results suggest that each specific coaching strategy improved the interactional behavior of the type of depressed mother for whom it was developed.

Child and Adolescent Suicide

Definitions and Prevalence

As we begin our discussion of suicide, we must immediately distinguish among three categories: suicidal thoughts, suicide attempts, and completed suicide. (Our review follows Garland and Zigler, 1993, except where noted.) *Suicidal thoughts*, once considered to be rare in childhood, are in fact disconcertingly prevalent. Studies of U.S. high school students have found that 63 percent experienced suicidal thoughts, while 54 percent of college students had considered suicide at least once in their lives.

Suicide attempts typically involve using a slow-acting method under circumstances in which discovery is possible. The act is most often in reaction to an interpersonal conflict or significant stressor. Although the attempt is unsuccessful, it may nevertheless be serious, serving as "practice" for a future lethal attempt. Approximately 7 percent of U.S. high school students attempt suicide in a given year (Centers for Disease Control, 1995), and there are reports of repeated and apparently serious attempts at suicide among preschoolers (Rosenthal & Rosenthal, 1984). Further, while as many as 10 percent of college students report having made a suicide attempt, only 2 percent of those had sought medical or psychological help. Therefore, our statistics on the prevalence of suicide attempts may be underestimates.

Completed suicide, while rare, is a significant problem among adolescents. Suicide is the third leading cause of death among 15- to 19-year-old adolescents in the United States, in line behind accidents and homicides (Garland & Zigler, 1993). Further, suicide among the young is increasing at an alarming rate, with rates rising much more dramatically than in the general population. While suicide in the general population has increased 17 percent

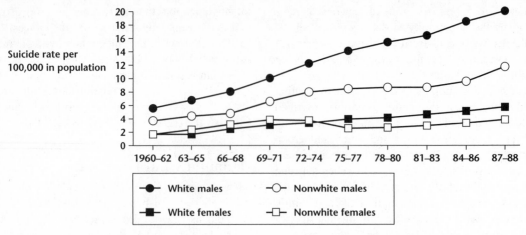

Figure 7.5   U.S. Youth Suicide Rates for 15- to 19-Year-Olds by Race and Gender.

Source: Garland and Zigler, 1993

since the 1960s, among adolescents it has increased 200 percent, to 11.3 per 100,000. (See Figure 7.5.) Rates for younger children are lower: In 1991, the suicide rate for children aged 5 to 14 was 0.5 per 100,000. A protective factor for younger children may be that they have more difficulty accessing lethal means; consequently, there are 14.4 attempts for every completed suicide in 10- to 11-year-olds (Pfeffer et al., 1994). Most suicides (70 percent) occur in the home. Firearms are the most frequent method used by both males and females (59 percent), followed by hanging for males and drug ingestion for females.

In all age groups, females are more likely than males to *attempt* suicide, while males are more likely to *succeed*. Females attempt suicide at least three times as often as males do, whereas males complete suicide about four times as often as females. The explanation for this appears to lie in the choice of method. In contrast to male suicides, two-thirds of whom die by self-inflicted gunshot wounds, the typical young female attempter ingests drugs at home. The latter case is called low-lethality behavior because of the length of time needed for the method to take effect and the likelihood that someone will find the attempter before it is too late to resuscitate. It should not be assumed, however, that young women are less serious about wanting to die. Females are

more likely to have an aversion to violent methods, and sometimes young people's understanding of how deadly a drug can be is simply inaccurate. Further, these statistics often come from mental health clinics and ignore one very important group incarcerated males. If we included males in juvenile detention facilities in these statistics, the gender differences in suicide attempts might not be so great.

Etiology

The Intrapersonal Context

Psychological characteristics distinguish some adolescent suicides, the majority of whom have a diagnosable psychopathology (Beautrais, Joyce, & Mulder, 1996). For example, 83 percent of youths with suicidal ideation show signs of *depression*. The relationship between suicide and depression is a significant but complex one. Most depressed youths are not suicidal. Further, while Harrington and colleagues' (1994) longitudinal research shows that childhood depression is a strong predictor of attempted suicide in adulthood, the key seems to be the association between childhood depression and adult depression. In other words, depressed children who grow up to be nondepressed adults are not at risk for suicide.

There are other significant predictors of youth suicide besides depression. Clues to these can be found in a study of 3,000 suicidal youths attending a free medical clinic (Adolinks, 1987). Feeling states preceding their suicide attempts were anger first, followed by loneliness, worry about the future, remorse or shame, and hopelessness. The reasons youths gave for attempting suicide were, in order, relief from an intolerable state of mind or escape from an impossible situation, making people understand how desperate they feel, making someone sorry or getting back at someone, trying to influence someone or change someone's mind, showing how much they loved someone or finding out whether someone really loved them, and seeking help. Many had been preoccupied with thoughts of death for an extended period of time, but only around half of the adolescents said they actually wanted the attempt to succeed. Typically, despite the long gestation period of suicidal thoughts, the actual attempt was made with little premeditation.

These data have two important implications. First, *impulsivity* is implicated in suicide. Impulsivity may be seen in many ways, including low frustration tolerance and lack of planning, poor self-control, disciplinary problems, poor academic performance, and risk-taking behavior. *Substance abuse* is found in 15 to 33 percent of suicide completers, with suicidal thoughts increasing after the onset of substance use. Substance abuse may play a role in increasing impulsivity, clouding judgment, and disinhibiting self-destructive behavior. Other disorders of impulse control, including eating disorders, are also related to an increased risk for suicide (Berman & Jobes, 1991).

Secondly, *anger and aggression* emerge as an important part of the suicide constellation. About 70 percent of suicidal youth exhibit conduct disorder and antisocial behavior (Berman & Jobes, 1991). Childhood conduct disorder also has been shown to predict adult suicidality independently of depression (Harrington et al., 1994). Achenbach and colleagues' (1995b) six-year longitudinal study also shows that suicidal ideation is predicted, not by depression, but by earlier signs of externalizing disorders: for boys, in the form of aggressiveness, and for girls, in the form of delinquent behavior.

The link between conduct disorder and suicide may also be strongest for boys, with the combination of depression and conduct problems particularly toxic. Capaldi (1992) found that, among boys who showed a combination of depression and aggression, school failure, poor relationships with parents and peers, and low self-esteem resulted in suicidal ideation two years later.

However, it is important to recognize that suicidal adolescents are a diverse group. Some may exhibit no apparent problems or disorders. They may appear to be "model" youth who keep their anxiety, perfectionism, and feelings of failure to themselves.

The Interpersonal Context: Family Influences

The family context is also important, although a significant weakness of many family studies is that they are *retrospective* rather than *prospective*. (Here we follow the review by Wagner, 1997, unless otherwise noted.) Assessing suicide only after it is attempted does not provide convincing evidence that family factors lead up to suicide.

A number of studies have confirmed the existence of a significant degree of *family dysfunction* and *adverse childhood experiences* among suicide attempters (Beautrais, Joyce, & Mulder, 1996). Prospective studies show that suicidal ideation and suicide attempts are predicted by low levels of parent warmth, communicativeness, support, and emotional responsiveness, and high levels of violence, disapproval, harsh discipline, abuse, and general family conflict. Retrospective studies show that attempters and their parents describe the family as having lower cohesion, less support, and poorer adaptability to change. Suicide attempters also are more likely to report feeling that they are unwanted or burdensome to their families. There is a significantly high level of *psychopathology* among family members, particularly suicide and depression.

Perceived *lack of support* from parents also has been implicated as a significant predictor of adolescent suicidal thinking (Harter & Marold, 1994). Further, Harter and Whitesell (1996) found that the depressed youths exhibiting the least suicidal ideation were those who perceived themselves to have more positive relationships with parents and more parent support. Thus supportive parent–child relationships may provide a buffer against suicidality in at-risk children.

Finally, exposure to the suicidal behavior of another person in the family or immediate social network is more common in suicidal adolescents than in controls. This has been referred to as a *contagion effect*: Children who are exposed to suicidal behavior, especially in family members or peers, are more likely to attempt it themselves. Such exposure should be regarded as accelerating the risk factors already present rather than being a sufficient cause of suicide.

The Interpersonal Context: Peer Relations

Perceived *lack of peer support* (Harter & Marold, 1994) and *poor social adjustment* (Pfeffer et al., 1994) have been identified as risk factors. Suicidal youth are more likely than others to feel ignored and rejected by peers. They also report having fewer friends and are concerned that their friendships are *contingent*—that they must behave a certain way in order to be accepted by agemates. Perceived social failures, rejection, humiliation, and romantic disappointments are common precipitants of youth suicide.

The Superordinate Context

Socioeconomic disadvantage has also been associated with suicide (Beautrais, Joyce, & Mulder, 1996), with children growing up in poverty being at greater risk for suicidal thoughts, attempts, and completions.

Developmental Course

The question often arises as to whether young children who attempt suicide are really trying to kill themselves, and therefore whether their attempts warrant serious concern or presage future suicidality. Doubt about whether they really intend to die is supported by cognitive-developmental research on children's limited understanding of the concept of death, as well as studies showing that suicidal children have a limited understanding of the permanency of death (Cuddy-Casey & Orvaschel, 1997). However, longitudinal research is consistent in

showing that childhood suicide attempts are a strong predictor of subsequent attempts and completions. For example, six to eight years after their first attempt, suicidal children were six times more likely than other children to have made another suicide attempt (Pfeffer et al., 1994). Most subsequent attempts occurred within two years of the initial attempt, and over half of those who continued to be suicidal made multiple attempts. Therefore, suicide attempts in children should not be dismissed as mere attention-getting behavior, since those who engage in them are at risk for more serious attempts and possible completions in the future.

Among adolescent suicide attempters, Adolinks (1987) found that the majority improved within one month. However, about one-third subsequently experienced major difficulties in the form of increased psychological and physical disorders, interpersonal problems, and increased criminal behavior. One in ten repeated the attempt, with boys succeeding more often than girls. The risk for future disturbances was particularly strong in teenage males.

Integrative Developmental Models

A classic reconstructive account is provided by Jacobs (1971), who investigated fifty 14- to 16-year-olds who attempted suicide. A control sample of thirty-one subjects, matched for age, race, sex, and level of mother's education was obtained from a local high school. Through an intensive, multi-technique investigation, Jacobs was able to reconstruct a five-step model of the factors leading up to suicidal attempts:

1. *Long-standing history of problems from early childhood.* Such problems included parental divorce, death of a family member, serious illness, parental alcoholism, and school failure. Subsequent research has shown that it is a high level of intrafamilial conflict along with a lack of support for the child that is the risk factor, not a particular family constellation such as divorce or single parenthood (Weiner, 1992).

2. *Acceleration of problems in adolescence.* Far more important than earlier childhood problems was the frequency of distressing events occurring within the last five years for the suicidal

youths; for example, 45 percent had dealt with divorce in the previous five years as compared to only 6 percent of the control group. Termination of a serious romance was also much higher among the suicidal group, as were arrests and jail sentences.

3. *Progressive failure to cope and isolation from meaningful social relationships.* The suicidal and control groups were equally rebellious in terms of becoming disobedient, sassy, and defiant. However, the coping strategies of suicidal adolescents were characterized much more by withdrawal behavior, such as avoiding others and engaging in long periods of silence (see also Spirito et al., 1996). The isolation in regard to parents was particularly striking. For example, while 70 percent of all suicide attempts took place in the home, only 20 percent of those who reported the attempt had informed their parents about it. In one instance an adolescent telephoned a friend who lived miles away, and he, in turn, telephoned the parents who were in the next room.

4. *Dissolution of social relationships.* In the days and weeks preceding the attempt, suicidal adolescents experienced the breaking off of social relationships, leading to the feeling of hopelessness.

5. *Justification of the suicidal act, giving the adolescent permission to make the attempt.* This justification was reconstructed from 112 suicide notes of adolescents and adults attempting and completing suicide. The notes contain certain recurring themes; for example, the problems are seen as long-standing and unsolvable, so death seems like the only solution. The authors of such notes also state that they know what they are doing, are sorry for their act, and beg indulgence. The motif of isolation and subsequent hopelessness is prevalent.

Another comprehensive account of the development of suicidal ideation is offered by Harter (Harter, Marold, & Whitesell, 1992; Harter & Marold, 1991, 1994), who integrates her own research with that of others. Her model reconstructs the successive steps that ultimately eventuate in suicidal ideation in a normative sample of 12- to 15-year-olds. (See Figure 7.6.)

Immediately preceding and highly related to suicidal ideation is what Harter calls the *depression composite*, which is made up of three interrelated variables: low global self-worth, negative affect, and hopelessness. The first two are highly correlated— the lower the perceived self-worth, the greater the feelings of negative mood.

Moreover, the depressive composite is rooted both in the adolescents' feelings of *incompetence* and in their *lack of support* from family and friends. These two variables of competence and support are, in turn, related in a special way. In regard to competence, physical appearance, peer likability, and athletic ability are related to peer support, while scholarly achievement and behavioral conduct are related to parental support. Finally, adolescents identify more strongly with peer-related competencies, with the others being regarded as more important to parents than to themselves.

Analyses of the data revealed that peer-related competencies and support were more strongly related to the depressive composite than were parental-related competencies and support, perhaps because the former are more closely connected with the adolescents' own self-concept. However, parental support was important in differentiating the adolescents who were only depressed from those who were depressed and had suicidal ideation. Further, the *quality* of support was crucial. Regardless of the level, if adolescents perceived they were acting only to please parents or peers, their self-esteem decreased and depression and hopelessness increased. On the other hand, unconditional support helped adolescents minimize the depressive composite.

In regard to the question of which came first, lowered self-worth or depression, the data indicate that causation can go in either direction. Some adolescents become depressed when they experience lowered self-worth, while others become depressed over other occurrences such as rejection or conflict, which in turn lower self-worth.

To answer the question, *Why adolescence?* Harter and colleagues (1997) marshal a number of findings concerning this period. In adolescence, self-awareness, self-consciousness, introspection, and

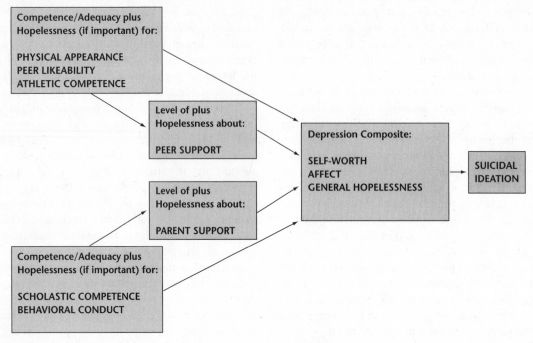

Figure 7.6   Risk Factors for Adolescent Suicidal Ideation.

Source: Harter, Marold, and Whitesell, 1992

preoccupation with self-image increase dramatically, while self-esteem becomes more vulnerable. Peer support becomes significantly more salient, although adolescents still struggle to remain connected with parents. For the first time, the adolescent can grasp the full cognitive meaning of hopelessness, while affectively there is an increase in depressive symptomatology. Suicidal ideation is viewed as an effort to cope with or escape from the painful cognitions and affects of the depressive composite.

Intervention

The vast majority of suicidal adolescents provide clues as to their imminent behavior; one study found that 83 percent of completers told others of their suicidal intentions in the week prior to their death. (Our presentation follows Berman and Jobes, 1991.) Most of the time such threats are made to family members or friends, who do not take them seriously,

try to deny them, or do not understand their importance. Friends, for example, might regard reporting the threats as a betrayal of trust. Thus, not only do adolescents themselves not seek professional help, but those in whom they confide tend to delay or resist getting help. Consequently, an important goal of prevention is to educate parents and peers concerning risk signs.

Once an adolescent comes for professional help, the immediate therapeutic task is to protect the youth from self-harm through *crisis intervention*. This might involve restricting access to the means of committing suicide, such as removing a gun from the house or pills from the medicine cabinet; a "no suicide contract" in which the adolescent agrees not to hurt himself or herself for an explicit time-limited period; decreasing isolation by having sympathetic family members or friends with the adolescent at all times; giving medication to reduce agitation or depression; or, in extreme cases, hospitalization.

Suicide Prevention

Turning again to Garland and Zigler's (1993) review, we find that two of the most commonly used suicide prevention efforts—suicide hot lines and media campaigns—are only minimally effective. Communities with suicide hot lines have slightly reduced suicide rates; however, hot lines tend to be utilized by only one segment of the population, Caucasian females. Even less helpful, well-meaning efforts to call media attention to the problem of suicide among teenagers may have the reverse effect. Several studies have shown increased suicide rates following television or newspaper coverage of suicide, particularly among teenagers.

School-based suicide prevention programs are extremely popular, with the number of schools implementing them increasing 200 percent in recent years. Goals of these programs are to raise awareness of the problem of adolescent suicide, train participants to identify those at risk, and educate youth about community resources available to them. However, a number of problems have been identified with school-based suicide prevention efforts. For one thing, they may never reach the populations most at risk because incarcerated youths, runaways, and school dropouts will never attend the classes. Even when students do attend the programs, there are questions as to their benefits. The programs tend to exaggerate the prevalence of teenage suicide, while at the same time de-emphasizing the fact that most adolescents who attempt suicide are emotionally disturbed. Thus, they ignore evidence for the contagion effect and encourage youth to identify with the case studies presented. By trying not to stigmatize suicide, these programs may inadvertently normalize suicidal behavior and reduce social taboos against it.

Large-scale, well-controlled studies provide some basis for these concerns. For example, one study of 300 teenagers showed that attending a suicide prevention program slightly increased knowledge about suicide but was not effective in changing attitudes about it. Boys in particular tended to change in the undesirable direction: more of them reported *increased* hopelessness and maladaptive coping after exposure to the suicide program (Overholser et al., 1989). Another study of 1,000 youths found no positive effects on attitudes toward suicide. In fact, participation in the program was associated with a small number of students responding that they now thought suicide was a plausible solution to their problems. The students most at risk for suicide to begin with (those who had made previous attempts) were the most likely to find the program distressing (Shaffer et al., 1991).

If suicide prevention programs are not the solution, what might be? While suicide is rare, Garland and Zigler (1993) point out, the stressors and life problems that may lead some youth to it are not. Therefore, successful prevention programs might be aimed toward such risk factors for suicide as substance abuse, impulsive behavior, depression, lack of social support, family discord, poor interpersonal problem-solving skills, social isolation, and low self-esteem.

Recall that in Chapter 5 we dealt with the issue of control in the toddler-preschool period—control of excessive negativism and control of the bodily functions of eating and urination. We will now return to this theme of control, exploring its manifestation in the middle childhood period. We will examine two extremes: excessive control, which is an important element in anxiety disorders, and inadequate self-control, which lies at the heart of conduct disorders.

Middle Childhood:
The Anxiety Disorders

In the course of being psycho-analyzed, a middle-aged man recalls, "When I acted up as a kid my grandmother would scold me, saying, 'You're too young to have nerves!' For a long time after that I kept wondering, 'Am I old enough now?' like having nerves was one of the signs of being grown up." Grandmother, unknowingly, was a good Freudian. According to psychoanalytic theory, psychoneurosis or neurosis is a developmental achievement. Not that infants and preschoolers cannot suffer—as we have seen, they can—but they are not sufficiently sophisticated psychologically to have a classical neurosis until middle childhood.

However, Freud's concept of neurosis has always been a controversial one. His ideas concerning unconscious motivation, infantile sexuality, and the relation between adult psychopathology and childhood trauma were greeted with incredulity, shock, and derision by members of the professional community. While many of his concepts are now regarded as plausible or obvious, the psychoanalytic formulation

of neurosis came under attack from two directions. As could be expected, behaviorally oriented psychologists regard the formulation as both incorrect and needlessly complex. In addition, DSM-III (1980) dropped the classification of neurosis completely, substituting the term "anxiety disorder," which is purely descriptive and bypasses the controversy between the psychoanalytic and behavioral theories of etiology.

In our own presentation we will proceed as follows. First we will deal with characteristics of the anxiety disorders as a whole. After that we will raise the question that lies at the heart of developmental psychopathology: Why does normal development go awry and produce anxiety disorders? We will discuss two theoretical answers to this question, the psychoanalytic and the behavioral, before turning to an empirical model that integrates the major research findings concerning etiology. We will then devote the remainder of our presentation to a discussion of five of the eight psychopathologies that are considered specific forms of anxiety disorders: specific phobias, school phobia, separation anxiety disorder, obsessive-compulsive disorder, and posttraumatic stress disorders. (See Spence, 1997, for a factor-analytic study for statistical verification of both a common element of anxiety and distinct subgroups of disturbances.) Because of limited developmental data we will not discuss three other disorders, namely, social phobia, generalized anxiety disorder, and panic disorder. (For a discussion of these disorders, see Albano, Chorpita and Barlow, 1996; see also Masia and Morris, 1998, for social anxiety and Mattis and Ollendick, 1997, for panic disorders.)

The Anxiety Disorders

Definition and Characteristics

Definition

As the name implies, **anxiety disorders** are a group of disturbances characterized by intense, chronic anxiety. They also have other characteristics in common: the unacceptable, alien nature of the symptoms to the individual; the relative intactness of reality contact; the enduring nature of the disturbance; and the fact that symptoms do not actively violate social norms. Descriptively, Freud was correct in locating the origins of anxiety disorders in middle childhood for the most part.

Individuals with anxiety disorders are **internalizers**; that is, their suffering is turned inward. This characteristic was demonstrated by various factor-analytic studies of psychopathological behavior in children. Typical of such studies was Achenbach's (Achenbach, 1966; Achenbach et al., 1989) factor analysis of a 91-item symptom checklist that yielded a first principal bipolar factor that he labeled "internalization–externalization." Among internalizing symptoms were phobias, worrying, stomachaches, withdrawal, nausea, compulsions, insomnia, seclusiveness, depression, crying—all indicating an inwardly suffering child. (See Figure 8.1.) (For a summary of objective studies of anxiety disorders, see Albano, Chorpita, and Barlow, 1996.)

Characteristics

Prevalence   Anxiety disorders are among the most common childhood and adolescent disorders. They are found in 7.3 percent of the population (Anderson, 1994). However, this overall figure masks a developmental trend of increased prevalence. For example, one prospective study found an increase from 7.5 percent of 11-year-olds to 20 percent of 21-year-olds (Kovacs & Devlin, 1998). To complicate the developmental picture even further, certain specific disorders increase while others decrease in prevalence, as we shall see. The reasons for these different developmental patterns are not clear.

Figure 8.1   An Internalizer: Worried, Depressed, Obsessing, and an Insomniac.

Gender Differences   In Lewinsohn and colleagues' (1998) study of 1,079 adolescents with anxiety disorders, there was a predominance of females. Moreover, while there was no sex difference in age of onset, by the age of 6 females were already twice as likely as males to have experienced an anxiety disorder.

Developmental Course   Until recently it was erroneously believed that anxiety disorders need not be taken too seriously because they were unstable and likely to be "outgrown." Data using diverse research designs and assessment approaches as well as geographically distinct populations show that, on the contrary, having an anxiety disorder increases the risk for future anxiety disorders or related disturbances. (See Kovacs and Devlin, 1998.) Moreover, anxiety disorders in childhood can be the beginning of a longtime pattern of disturbance, with 54 percent of adults with panic disorder, for example, reporting a history of childhood anxiety disorder (Pollock et al., 1996).

Comorbidity

Comorbidity is particularly high in anxiety disorders, with some studies showing rates between 65 and 95 percent of the population. For any given anxiety disorder another type of anxiety disorder is the most common comorbidity, followed by affective disorder (as we saw in Chapter 7 on depression). While externalizing disorders such as ADHD and conduct disorders can also be present, they are relatively infrequent. (See Kovacs and Devlin, 1998.) As might be expected, children and adolescents who are comorbid are also more generally disturbed than ones with only a single diagnosis. More important, comorbid conditions are sufficiently distinct to warrant being studied in their own right rather than assuming that what is known concerning the major diagnoses can be extrapolated to the comorbid condition (Ollendick & King, 1994). For example, in their genetic study of comorbidity, Thapar and McGuffin (1997) found that, while the contribution of anxiety can be totally explained in terms of a common set of genes, there must be an additional genetic factor specific to depression to account for the depressive symptoms.

Negative Affectivity   Because of the close relation between anxiety and depression, this comorbidity has been conceptualized in terms of a shared negative affectivity. **Negative affectivity** includes moods such as fear, sadness, anger, and guilt. Initially it was speculated that negative affectivity was an underlying unifying construct, so that anxiety and depression would be on a continuum rather than being independent entities. Subsequent research yielded a different picture. While negative affectivity was a common element in anxiety and depression, each disturbance also had distinctive features. Specifically, Lonigan, Carey, and Finch (1994) found that depressed children reported more problems related to loss of interest and low motivation and had a negative view of themselves, while anxious children reported more worry about the future, their well-being, and others' reactions to them. In addition, depressed children, unlike anxious ones, had low scores on measures of positive affect. Joiner, Catanzaro, and Laurent (1996), using a somewhat different procedure, added to the picture of anxiety disorders the characteristic of physiological hyperarousal, a characteristic that is not part of depression. In sum, both studies agree that anxiety and depression are distinct disturbances that share a common characteristic of negative affectivity.

From Normal Fears to Anxiety Disorders

Fear is usually defined as a normal reaction to an environmental threat. It is adaptive and even essential to survival because it warns the individual that a situation may be physically or psychologically harmful. Anxiety disorders are distinguished from fears on the basis of their *intensity*, which is out of proportion to the situation, their *maladaptiveness*, and their *persistence*. They are also *beyond voluntary control* and cannot be explained or reasoned away. Keeping to our theme of normal development gone awry, we want to examine why the development of normal fearfulness becomes diverted into various pathologies. We will first present the explanations offered by two major theories of anxiety and then proceed to examine the empirical evidence.

Etiology: Two Major Theories

Psychoanalytic Theory of Neurosis

Conflict lies at the heart of the psychoanalytic theory of neurosis—conflict between what infants, toddlers, and preschoolers want to do and what socializing adults require them to do. (Our presentation follows Nagera, 1966, and Shapiro, 1973.) The specific content of the conflict is determined by the psychosexual stages of development, described in Chapter 1.

The next central component of the theory of neurosis is *anxiety*. It is the threat of parental punishment and withdrawal of parental love that provides an affective charge sufficiently strong to lead to the inhibition of socially unacceptable behavior. Anxiety is not only a deterrent; if sufficiently strong, it is exceedingly painful and can set into motion a whole array of maneuvers designed to protect the child from experiencing the distress extreme anxiety produces. Examples of these maneuvers (defense mechanisms) are repression, projection, and reaction formation. (See Chapter 2.)

Finally, psychoanalytic theory states that neurotic symptoms have a *symbolic meaning* that differs from the manifest content of the behavior. Let us take the case of a 7-year-old girl who was terrified of spiders, which she feared would bite her. Psychoanalytically oriented play therapy revealed that the basic neurotic conflict was between a desire to express anger toward her mother and her primitive conscience's mandate that she be a good girl. Her self-condemnation as "bad" engendered anxiety, and, as is typical of phobias, a triple defense was set into play. First came repression, so that the girl could banish the angry thoughts and feelings from consciousness. Next came projection, in which the mother was seen as angry at the girl. Finally, came displacement, in which a relatively innocuous object (a spider) was invested with exaggerated destructive powers. Why a spider? There is never a pat answer to questions of symbolization, since the meaning is often highly idiosyncratic. In this instance the girl, having heard of the deadly bite of the black widow spider, equated both the quality of hostile attack and blackness with her mother, who made a great deal over the versatility of her basic black dress.

In dealing with the central question of developmental psychopathology—Why does normal development go awry?—psychoanalytic theory has two answers. Classical psychoanalytic theory states that too much or too little *libidinal gratification* tends to fixate a child at a particular stage and makes him or her vulnerable to regression. Subsequently, Anna Freud (1965) added the concept of the *balance of forces* making for progress or regression. The concept itself is similar to the now-familiar one stating that a developmental path is the result of the balance between vulnerabilities and protective factors. (See Chapter 2.)

Some sources of vulnerability are constitutional in that certain infants have more intense reactions of anxiety and rage than others and are persistently disrupted by their effects. Other vulnerabilities are experiential, with failure to receive sensitive care in infancy being particularly important.

As for protective factors, constitution and maturation can be aligned on the side of health as well as on the side of vulnerabilities. Certain infants are innately rugged and resilient, either experiencing less intense anxiety or readily taking it in stride. Growth-promoting experiences are legion: sensitive mothering in infancy; the development of friendships; achievement in school; positive relations with teachers, coaches, and other adult models. Even a neurotic conflict can itself become a constructive force in the child's developing personality: the boy who handles his hostility toward a younger sibling by the reaction formation of being especially concerned with the plight of relatively weak and helpless youngsters can eventually have a successful vocation in one of the helping professions. As Anna Freud (1965) puts it, one can never be sure whether a therapist is eliminating a neurosis or nipping a future physicist in the bud.

The Behavioral Theory

Behaviorists regard anxiety-flight as an adaptive response when it is a reaction to a realistic threat. When the response is inappropriate, however—that is, when no real danger exists—the behaviorists regard anxiety-flight as psychopathological.

Traditional *learning principles* can account for the various ways in which innocuous and inappropriate stimuli come to elicit aversive emotional responses. The most familiar principle is aversive classical conditioning, and the most familiar case is that of 11-month-old Albert who, after being exposed to a number of pairings of a white rat (conditioned stimulus—CS) with a loud, frightening noise (unconditioned stimulus—US), became frightened by the sight of the rat alone (conditioned response—CR). A variation in this same model is higher-order conditioning in which a stimulus, once conditioned, serves as the basis for further aversive conditioning when paired with neutral stimuli. Thus, a child who hears that sex is "dirty" may develop a disgust for sexual behavior even without engaging in it. A negative affective response may also be acquired by *observational learning* or *modeling*. Here the mere observing of another person responding with pain or anxiety to a previously innocuous stimulus can come to elicit anxiety in the observer. On this basis a girl whose parents are afraid of being burglarized can come to fear every creak of the stairs after bedtime, as her parents do.

Once established, inappropriate behavior can spread by *stimulus generalization*. The classical example is, once again, little Albert, who after being conditioned to fear a white rat, subsequently was afraid of a number of white, furry objects. However, stimulus generalization in an 11-year-old is bound to be more complex than in an 11-month-old. Semantically related cues enter the picture, and generalization can occur to categories of objects; for example, a subject who receives an electric shock when a rural word such as "barn" is presented will also have an aversive reaction to other rural words.

The final component in the behavioral explanation of anxiety disorders is the *reinforcement* of responses that enable the individual to avoid the conditioned aversive stimuli. Like psychoanalysts, behavioral theorists regard anxiety as an unusually potent motivator; any behavior that reduces or eliminates it will be reinforced. A wide array of such behaviors can be conceptualized as *avoidance responses*. One of the most important of these is response inhibition, in which the child avoids both doing and thinking about doing a forbidden act.

The behaviorist's etiologic account of phobias is the most convincing; the mechanisms of aversive and vicarious classical conditioning are well supported by laboratory studies on both animals and humans (Bandura, 1968). Behaviorists add that, once learned, the reaction of the social environment is a potent factor perpetuating the phobia. For example, while a child might originally develop a fear of insects by modeling a parent, the subsequent attention received from the parent, either positive or negative, may further reinforce the phobic response.

In order to enhance the explanatory potency of their point of view, certain behaviorists have added cognitive variables. Kendall and Ronan (1990) have proposed a *cognitive-behavioral model* of fears and phobias. Their conceptualization centers upon the cognitive representation of the self, or the self schema, and the cognitive representation of others, or the other schema. The self schema of anxious individuals contains a high level of content specific to anxiety; for example, anxious subjects recall more anxious-content adjectives in a list of words than do nonanxious subjects. In their other schema, anxious individuals focus on others' potentially hurtful judgments or harmful reactions. Another aspect of distorted thinking is an excessive self-focused attention and an inability to shift to a more external focus; for example, a girl who has to give a speech in class focuses on her own fears and her imagined critical attitudes of others to such a degree that she cannot concentrate on the speech itself and is overwhelmed by anxiety.

Etiology: An Integrative Empirical Model

Using the publications of Vasey (Vasey & Dadds, in press; Vasey & Ollendick, in press) as a guide, it is possible conceptually to integrate the etiological research on anxiety disorders. This integration involves three categories:

I. Predisposing factors
II. Pathways to acquisition including precipitating factors
III. Factors maintaining or intensifying anxiety

Table 8.1 presents this integration in outline form, and we will walk through it, point by point.

Table 8.1   Summary of Transition from Normal Fears to Anxiety Disorders

Variables Studied	Empirical Findings
I. Predisposing Factors	
A. The organic context	
1. Genetic risk	Anxiety disorders run in families
2. Temperament	Behavioral inhibition (BI) as a risk
B. The interpersonal context	
1. Attachment	Insecure attachment as a risk
C. The intrapersonal context	
1. Information processing	Attentional bias: sensitivity to threat; views world as dangerous and self as unable to cope
2. Emotion regulation	Believes cannot control anxiety
II. Pathways to Anxiety Acquisition	
A. The intrapersonal context	
1. Conditioning	Traumatic conditioning as cause
2. Dishabituation of fears	Return of mastered fear
3. Failure of mastery	Failure to master normal fears through exposure to them
3a. Habituation	Child is poor habituater to feared situation
B. The interpersonal context	
3b. Parent–child relation	Parents limit exposure to fearful stimuli, model anxious behavior, or reinforce child's anxiety
III. Factors Maintaining or Intensifying Anxiety	
A. The intrapersonal context	
1. Avoidance of anxiety-arousing situations	Avoidance produces social and cognitive incompetencies; e.g., social skills deficits and attentional biases
B. The interpersonal context	
1. Parents' and teachers' behavior	Overprotectiveness prevents exposure to anxiety-arousing situations
2. Parents	Parents reinforce avoidance and fail to provide emotional support

I. Predisposing Factors

The Organic Context   *Genetic risk.* There is good evidence that anxiety disorders run in families—that is, that there is *genetic risk.* The most convincing data come from twin studies, which show that the risk of developing the disorder is higher for twins than it is for ordinary siblings due to the greater similarity of genetic material. However, it is important to note that what is inherited is not an anxiety disorder per se but rather a predisposition to develop disorders associated with negative affectivity. As we have seen, these disorders include both anxiety and depression. (For specific studies, see Vasey and Ollendick, in press.)

Anxiety prone temperament. Currently, one of the most promising leads concerning the biological precursors of anxiety disorders is the temperament variable of **behavior inhibition**, or BI. While BI infants are characterized by high motor activity and irritability, BI children react to novelty with restraint, withdrawal, avoidance, or distress. In addition they are shy, withdrawn, and fearful, and they avoid challenges. Research suggests that around 20 percent of children inherit the inhibited or BI type. However, BI is stable from the early years into middle childhood only if two conditions are met: the inhibition is extreme, and the children have high and stable heart rates. Only 10 percent of the population meets these criteria. (See Turner, Beidel and Wolff, 1996.)

It is among stable BI children that the risk for developing anxiety disorders is heightened. There is a tendency for them to have two or more anxiety disorders when compared with uninhibited children; for example, they are more likely to have phobias such as the fear of being called on in class or the fear of strangers or crowds. The social and social evaluative nature of these phobias suggest an extreme version of the shy, avoidant behavior characteristic of BI.

Generally speaking, the evidence linking BI with anxiety disorders is preliminary rather than definitive and is not without methodological flaws and contradictory findings. Moreover, some uninhibited children can develop anxiety disorders, just as some inhibited children can develop other disturbances or none at all. Thus, BI is neither a necessary nor sufficient precursor of anxiety disorder; primarily, it increases the likelihood of occurrence. (A more detailed presentation can be found in Turner, Beidel and Wolff, 1996.)

The Interpersonal Context   *Attachment.* There are a number of reasons for hypothesizing that an *insecure attachment* increases the probability of developing an anxiety disorder. (Our presentation follows Cassidy, 1996, who deals specifically with generalized anxiety disorder.) Recall that insecure infants have caregivers who are either insensitive or nonresponsive to their needs. This, in turn, engenders a frightening view of the world as unreliable and unpredictable and a view of themselves as helpless to control the ensuing anxiety. While there is no research specifically connecting attachment with anxiety disorders, there is evidence that insecure infants are more fearful than secure ones in free-play situations and in exploring the environment and are also more shy and withdrawn with peers.

The Intrapersonal Context   *Information-processing biases.* Children with anxiety disorders have a number of *information-processing biases* (our presentation follows Vasey and Dadds, in press):

1. There is an attentional bias in that children with anxiety disorders are particularly sensitive to potentially threatening events; for example, they selectively attend to threatening versus non-threatening words in an experimental task, as compared with normal controls.
2. Children with anxiety disorders interpret ambiguous situations as threatening; for example, they are more apt to interpret a noise in the house as an intruder than as an unlatched window rattling.
3. Children with anxiety disorders show unrealistic cognitive beliefs so that they perceive the world as a dangerous place and perceive themselves as incompetent to deal with its threats. This latter quality of being either competent or incompetent in dealing with threats is one aspect of self-efficacy. (For a detailed discussion of information processing in childhood anxiety, see Daleiden and Vasey, 1997.)

Emotion regulation deficits. Not only do anxiety-prone children believe they cannot control threatening situations, they also believe they cannot control their own anxious responses. Thus, they have an *emotion regulation deficit.* In fact this "fear of fear" may be one source of their attentional bias with its hypersensitivity to threatening situations. Metaphorically speaking, it is as if every fire were viewed as a potential conflagration so that the slightest smell of smoke is cause for alarm.

II. Three Pathways to Anxiety Acquisition

Vasey and Ollendick (in press) speculate concerning the mechanisms by which anxiety disorders can be acquired: first, via respondent conditioning, second by disinhibition of previously mastered fears, and third, by a failure to master normal fears.

Respondent Conditioning   The simplest case of anxiety acquisition is traumatic conditioning, as in the case in which a child injured in a car accident subsequently becomes terrified of riding in cars. While traumatic condition does occur, it is also true that not every child who experiences a trauma becomes phobic nor has every phobic child experienced a trauma. Consequently, the classical conditioning model has undergone two modifications, one biological, the other cognitive.

The biological modification involves the concept of *preparedness*. Evolution has provided humans with a number of unlearned fear responses that, in prehistoric times, had survival value. Fear of separation and of strangers, for example, helped keep the infant close to the protecting parent, as did fear of animals and the dark. However, this biological variable cannot be regarded as a comprehensive account of fears—it is difficult to see the survival value of the fear of something such as spiders—and research support has been mixed (Menzies & Clarke, 1995).

The cognitive modification maintains that the relation between the CS and the US is not one of mindless association but rather that the CS sets up an *expectation* that the US will follow. Specifically in regard to phobias, whether a traumatic event will produce a phobic response depends on the child's past history of expectations in regard to the CS. For example, if a child has had many pleasurable experiences with dogs, so that dogs have become a CS to pleasure, a single noxious experience such as being bitten by a dog may not be sufficient to negate past expectancies. The child who is apt to become phobic is one who does not have such a history with dogs. The proposition that nonaversive experiences with the CS may inhibit fear conditioning is called *latent inhibition*. As is the case with preparedness, research on latent inhibition has produced mixed results (Menzies & Clarke, 1995).

In sum, neither the classical model of traumatic conditioning nor its two modifications can be regarded as comprehensive accounts of the development of all phobias, although they may account for the development of some.

Dishabituation of Mastered Fears   Fears are mastered in specific contexts. However, mastery generalizes poorly, and thus the fear can reappear in a context not associated with habituation. For example, separation anxiety that was mastered in the home when parents were in good health might reappear following illness or death in the family or following the move to a new home or school. (See Vasey and Ollendick, in press, and Menzies and Clark, 1995.)

Failure of Normal Fear Mastery Process   As we have seen, most normal fears are "outgrown." One mechanism for this mastery is the repeated, nontraumatic exposure to the feared object or situation. Thus a toddler might master his initial terror of the sound of a vacuum cleaner as he observes his mother using it or as she encourages him to "play horsey" on it or turn it off and on himself.

There are at least two specific conditions under which normal mastery is likely *not* to occur. The first is in the case of children who are exposed to the feared stimulus with normal frequency but are *poor habituaters*. This may be due to temperament; for example, some BI infants may be so highly reactive to such a wide range of stimuli that parents find it next to impossible to provide experiences that might extinguish their anxious responses.

The second condition is when various *parental behaviors* decrease children's chance of mastery. Anxious parents, because of their own unmastered anxiety, may be chary of exposing their child to fear-arousing situations, thus jeopardizing the child's chances for learning constructive ways of dealing with such situations. In addition, children can learn to be anxious by imitating or modeling their behavior on that of their anxious parents. Finally, anxious parents, in an effort to relieve their own distress when their child becomes anxious, may positively or negatively reinforce the child's response—for example, by offering all kinds of rewards in an effort to divert the child. (A more detailed presentation of this topic can be found in Vasey and Ollendick, in press, and in Menzies and Clarke, 1995.)

III. Factors Maintaining or Intensifying Anxiety

According to Vasey (Vasey & Dadds, in press; Vasey & Ollendick, in press), anxiety is maintained and intensified (1) by the child's own tendency to avoid anxiety-arousing situations and (2) by the impact of parents on the child's behavior. (Our presentation follows Vasey's unless otherwise noted.)

The Consequences of Avoidance   If mastery of anxiety typically involves facing a frightening situation and learning to cope with it constructively, *avoidance* prevents mastery and ensures perpetuation. Avoidance is a seductive trap because it reduces anxiety temporarily. A shy child may be relieved when she avoids participating in a feared group game during recess, but, at the same time, she is deprived not only of learning the social skills necessary for group participation but also of a chance to correct her unrealistic beliefs concerning what group activity really involves.

As the preceding example shows, avoidance can produce two kinds of *incompetencies*. First, habitual avoidance may result in skills deficits that can have an adverse effect on both academic achievement and social relations. For example, there is evidence that social anxiety and withdrawal lead to peer rejection and unpopularity in middle childhood and to loneliness and depression in adolescence (Rubin, 1993).

Avoidance can also produce cognitive incompetencies or distortions that serve to maintain anxiety. By their attentional bias to threatening cues and their interpreting of ambiguous information as threatening, anxious children construct a world in which anxiety is perpetuated. Thus a vicious cycle is set up in which increasing avoidance fosters increased incompetence and the likelihood of failure when the child faces challenges.

Parental Contributions   There is evidence that *overprotectiveness* on the part of parents or teachers contributes to the maintenance of anxiety by reducing the anxiety-provoking situations the child will encounter. There is also evidence that parents may actually reinforce avoidance on the child's part; for example, a mother might say her child does not have to go to a party if it upsets her so. Finally, parents may contribute to maintaining and intensifying anxiety by failing to provide adequate *emotional support*. The parent who demeans the shy child's behavior as "foolish nonsense" or who angrily forces the child into fear-inducing situations often is burdening the child with an additional

---

Box 8.1 | **The Developmental Dimension**

Looking back over our discussions of etiological theories and empirical findings, it seems that we are forced to choose between a developmental theory that is producing little objective data and theories that are beginning to generate an impressive body of research while paying scant attention to the developmental dimension. The psychoanalytic theory conforms to our model of psychopathology as normal development gone awry. The psychosexual stages describe normal development, while the balance of vulnerabilities and protective factors determine whether development will be normal or deviant. Yet the theory is currently producing little objective research. By contrast, behavioral and cognitive theories are spearheading a renewed interest in conducting objective studies of anxiety. Yet, as our presentation of etiological research shows, the developmental dimension is often neglected, particularly the relation between normal and deviant paths. For one thing, the variables are not systematically related to normal development; for example, what is the normal counterpart of attentional biases or unrealistic cognitive beliefs? Are they part of the expected cognitive distortions of the preschool period that are corrected by middle childhood in nondisturbed children, or is their appearance suspect at any age? Next, there is little information concerning how normal processes, such as emotion regulation or avoidance, become deviant and produce anxiety disorders.

Finally, there are few clues to answering the overarching developmental question of why anxiety disorders appear in middle childhood rather than at any other phase. Put another way, what do we know about normal development in middle childhood that would make the appearance of anxiety disorders possible at this time rather than earlier? Not only is there no answer but the question itself is rarely asked.

source of distress. (See Vasey and Ollendick, in press.) (Table 8.1 summarizes Vasey's integrative empirical model.)

Specific Phobias

Definition and Characteristics

Definition

According to DSM-IV, the defining feature of specific **phobias** is a marked and persistent fear that is excessive or unreasonable, cued by the presence or anticipation of a specific object or situation. Table 8.2 provides a comprehensive listing of the major symptoms.

There is evidence that the various types of phobias make up a diverse rather than a homogeneous group. (Our presentation follows Merckelbach, de Jong, Muris, and van den Hout, 1996.) To begin

Table 8.2   DSM-IV Criteria for Specific Phobia

> A. Marked and persistent fear that is excessive or unreasonable, cued by the presence or anticipation of a specific object or situation (e.g., flying, heights, animals, receiving an injection, seeing blood).
> B. Exposure to the phobic stimulus almost invariably provokes an immediate anxiety response which may take the form of a situationally bound or situationally predisposed Panic Attack. Note: In children, the anxiety may be expressed by crying, tantrums, freezing, or clinging.
> C. The person recognizes that the fear is excessive or unreasonable. Note: In children, this feature may be absent.
> D. The phobic situation(s) is avoided or else is endured with intense anxiety or distress.
> E. In individuals under age 18 years, the duration is at least 6 months.
> Specific type: Animal Type; Natural Environment Type, cued by objects such as storms, heights, or water; Blood-Injection-Injury Type; Situation Type cued by situations such as public transportation, tunnels, elevators, flying, driving, or enclosed places.

Reprinted with permission from the Diagnostic and Statistical Manual of Mental Disorders, Fourth Edition. Copyright 1994 American Psychiatric Association.

with, the phobias have different mixes of the three components of anxiety: behavioral, subjective, and physiological. In the subjective realm, for example, animal phobia takes the form of fear, while blood-injection-injury phobia is marked by strong feelings of disgust. Or again, in the physiological realm, animal phobia is accompanied by heightened arousal whereas blood-injection-injury phobia is accompanied by lowered arousal, which may result in fainting.

There are also differences in the cognitive components of various phobias. In the fear of enclosed places, anxiety involves not only danger (e.g., the fear of suffocation) but expectancies (e.g., the fear of going crazy) and bodily sensations as well, while animal phobias primarily involve only danger. There may also be different mechanisms involved in producing the various types of phobias: for example, conditioning is more pronounced in the fear of enclosures, whereas modeling and negative information is more pronounced in animal and blood-injection-injury phobias. Finally, as we shall see, there is a developmental difference among types, with some appearing earlier than others.

Characteristics

Since research on the descriptive aspects of specific phobias is typically meager or methodologically flawed, it will only be summarized rather than discussed. (Our presentation follows King and Ollendick, 1997, unless otherwise noted.)

In regard to *prevalence* of phobias, estimates range from 2.4 to 9.1 percent and average around 5 percent of the population across studies. In regard to *gender differences*, girls tend to outnumber boys. Little is known concerning the effects of *socioeconomic status* or *ethnicity*. *Comorbidity* with both internalizing and externalizing disturbances is high, as is the comorbidity among specific types of phobias.

Specific phobias have different *ages of onset*. Evidence suggests that animal phobia begins around 7 years of age, blood phobia round 9, and dental phobia around 12. Fear of enclosures and social phobias begin in adolescence or early adulthood (Silverman & Rabian, 1994). In regard to *developmental course*, specific phobias show a modest level of continuity across intervals varying from

2 to 5 years. This finding contradicts a previously held view that they were "outgrown" for the most part. (The issue of etiology of specific phobias was covered in the preceding section.)

Intervention

In their review of research on treating specific phobias, Silverman and Rabian (1994) list a number of methodological limitations: a predominance of single-case studies, research conducted on children with situational fears such as dental fears rather than on clinical populations of phobic children, lack of formal diagnosis, lack of adequate assessment, and lack of follow-up data. Such inadequacies make it impossible to determine which is the treatment of choice or even to judge the merits of a given treatment beyond saying that it shows promise. However, the authors also conclude that *exposure* to the fear stimulus is essential for a successful fear-reduction program. There are a number of ways in which this exposure can be achieved:

Systematic Desensitization   **Systematic desensitization** involves substituting the incompatible response of relaxation for the response of anxiety. (See Chapter 17 for details.) The therapist obtains a gradient of anxiety from the most intense (e.g., riding on a bus) to the least (e.g., walking along the street where the bus stop is). After being trained to relax, the children are instructed to relax after they imagine each successive step in the gradient until they eventually can do so at the point of highest anxiety. When practical considerations allow, the procedure can also be done using the actual feared object or situation, such as a dog or a dark room. In such cases, the procedure is called in vivo ("real life") desensitization.

Prolonged Exposure   Prolonged exposure takes the opposite tack from progressive desensitization by exposing children to the full intensity of the feared stimulus and reinforcing them for remaining in its presence for a prolonged period of time. This "flooding" with anxiety prevents children from being reinforced by escape and also triggers a physiological reaction involving a return to normal functioning. The exposure itself can be imaginary or in vivo.

Modeling   In modeling, the child observes another person interacting adaptively with the feared object. More effective is participatory modeling in which the child, after the observation period, joins the model in gradually approaching the feared object.

Cognitive Self-Management   Cognitive self-management strategies emphasize "self-talk" to counteract the effects of phobic ideation. There is some evidence that self-statements emphasizing competence (e.g., "I'm brave and can take care of myself") are more effective than those countering the fear-producing properties of the stimulus (e.g., "Riding on the bus is lots of fun"). This finding raises the more general question as to whether the effective mechanism in treatment is reduction of anxiety or an increase in feelings of mastery or both. (For a comprehensive review of behavioral treatment of simple phobias, see King and Ollendick, 1997.)

Effectiveness   After reviewing studies of effectiveness, Ollendick and King (1998) conclude that both imaginal and in vivo desensitization, filmed and live modeling, and cognitive-behavioral interventions are probably efficacious. However, most of the evidence comes from analogue studies conducted in research laboratory or school settings with nonclinically referred children. The effectiveness of the techniques with clinically referred children remains to be determined.

Separation Anxiety Disorder

As we have seen, the development of the bond of love to the caregiver and the fear of loss of the loved one go hand in hand in normal infant development. While a number of factors are responsible for the mastery of this separation anxiety in the toddler period, for unknown reasons the panic over separation can return from the preschool period through adolescence, producing two kinds of disturbance: separation anxiety and the special form of school phobia that is motivated by fear of being away from the caregiver. In both instances the psychopathologies can be conceptualized in terms of *regression*.

Table 8.3   DSM-IV Criteria for Separation Anxiety Disorder

A. Developmentally inappropriate and excessive anxiety concerning separation from home or from those to whom the individual is attached, as evidenced by three (or more) of the following:

(1) recurrent excessive distress when separation from home or major attachment figures occurs or is anticipated

(2) persistent and excessive worry about losing, or about possible harm befalling, major attachment figures

(3) persistent and excessive worry that an untoward event will lead to separation from a major attachment figure (e.g., getting lost or being kidnapped)

(4) persistent reluctance or refusal to go to school or elsewhere because of fear of separation

(5) persistently and excessively fearful or reluctant to be alone or without major attachment figures at home or without significant adults in other setting

(6) persistent reluctance or refusal to go to sleep without being near a major attachment figure or to sleep away from home

(7) repeated nightmares involving the theme of separation

(8) repeated complaints of physical symptoms (such as headaches, nausea, or vomiting) when separation from major attachment figures occurs or is anticipated

B. The duration of the disturbance is at least 4 weeks.

C. The onset is before the age of 18 years.

Specify if Early Onset: if onset occurs before age 6 years

Reprinted with permission from the Diagnostic and Statistical Manual of Mental Disorders, Fourth Edition. Copyright 1994 American Psychiatric Association.

Definition and Characteristics

Definition

The core characteristic of separation anxiety disorder (SAD) is excessive anxiety over separation from people to whom the child is attached, typically the parents. The DSM-IV criteria provide a comprehensive listing of symptoms. (See Table 8.3.)

Age of onset is before 18 years of age, and onset before 6 years receives a special designation of "early onset." Certain symptoms show a developmental progression. Symptoms characteristic of 5- to 8-year-olds are excessive worry about harm befalling an attachment figure, nightmares involving separation

themes, and school refusals because of separation anxiety; 9- to 12-year-olds are distressed at separation itself; and somatic complaints such as headaches and stomachaches and school refusals are characteristic of 13- to 16-year-olds. (See Albano, Chorpita, and Barlow, 1996.)

Characteristics

Prevalence   SAD is found in 2 to 3.5 percent of the general population and in 10 percent of the clinical population. It is the most prevalent of all the anxiety disorders and ranks third among childhood disorders in general (Tonge, 1994). There is also a developmental dimension in that there is more SAD in the preschool period than in adolescence (as one would expect).

Gender Differences   The evidence is conflicting in regard to gender differences, with some studies finding no evidence of difference and others finding that girls outnumber boys.

Socioeconomic Status and Race   Children with SAD tend to come from the lower class, and their parents have lower-than-average education. The families tend to be caring and close, and the incidence of SAD in children seems to be higher in mothers who have a panic disorder (Crowell & Waters, 1990). The data show a preponderance of Caucasian children, but the data should be considered preliminary.

Comorbidity   One-third of the children with SAD have a secondary diagnosis of overanxious disorder, while another third will subsequently develop depression.

Developmental Course   There are few studies of the developmental course of SAD, although there is some evidence that the course is a variable one, with remissions followed by recurrences either in response to stressors or "out of the blue." Finally, there is evidence that SAD increases the risk of anxiety or depressive disorders in adulthood and, for girls, increases the risk of panic disorder or agoraphobia in adulthood. (See Albano, Chorpita, and Barlow, 1996.)

Etiology   The specific etiology of SAD is largely unknown. What theories there are concern anxiety proneness in general rather than being specific to SAD. For example, children with BI show symptoms of SAD on the first day of school, but, as we have seen (Vasey and Dadds, in press), BI is an important predisposing factor to anxiety in general. The same can be said concerning other leads such as insecure attachment or parental behavior such as high levels of anxiety or overprotectiveness.

School Phobia

A youngster with a school phobia is a pitiful sight. On a school morning, a boy might sit at the breakfast table pale and silent, his eyes tearful, listlessly pushing a spoon around his bowl of oatmeal. If he forces himself to eat a spoonful and take a gulp of milk in response to parental coaxing, it is with great effort. Soon he says he has to go to the bathroom either to throw up or to have a bowel movement, which he might or might not do. As the time approaches for him to catch the school bus, he becomes increasingly agitated, pleading, crying, or shouting accusations at his mother. In no way can such distress be mistaken for malingering or attention-getting; rather, it has all the behavioral and physiological characteristics of intense fear. However, if the child is allowed to stay at home, he is relieved and may resume his usual activities.

Definition and Characteristics

Definition

School phobia is defined as an irrational dread of some aspect of the school situation accompanied by physiological symptoms of anxiety or panic when attendance is imminent and resulting in a partial or total inability to go to school.

Problems with Labeling   There is evidence that so-called school phobia may be due to a fear of separation from the caregiver in a number of instances rather than to any feature of the school itself. Thus, it seems to be a special form of separation anxiety. In an attempt to clarify the situation it has been suggested that the term *school refusal* be substituted for school phobia. Whether the new label is a real solution or creates its own problems is an open question. For example, school refusal can be due to a number of disturbances that have little to do with anxiety, such as oppositional-defiant disorder or depression. To complicate matters, Kearney, Eisen, and Silverman (1995) cite evidence that, except for the youngest children, the term "phobia" may be a misnomer. The affect lacks the intensity necessary to be a truly phobic response and is mixed with other negative affects such as depression and low self-esteem. They therefore conclude that "negative affectivity" is a more appropriate term than "phobia."

Characteristics

The *prevalence* of school phobia is estimated to be 1 percent of the general population and 5 to 7 percent of clinically referred children (Blagg & Yule, 1994). The mean *age of onset* of school phobia in which separation is the primary feature is below 10 years; where refusal is the primary feature, the mean age is above 10 years. Common precipitating events are change in schools, parental illness or death, and a stay at home because of accidents or illness; however, in many cases there is no obvious reason for onset. In regard to *gender* differences, boys outnumber girls, and the children belong to the higher socioeconomic status. In regard to *developmental course*, school phobia in childhood increases the risk of anxiety and depressive disorders in adulthood; for example, approximately a third of such children will need additional treatment for these disorders as adults (Blagg & Yule, 1994).

Comorbidity   The most common comorbid disturbances are simple phobias and separation anxiety disorder (SAD) (Albano, Chorpita, and Barlow, 1996). While there can be some overlap between school phobia and separation anxiety disorder, the two are distinct disturbances. Children who fear separation are generally female (when gender differences are found), prepubertal, and from families of low socioeconomic status, whereas children with a school phobia tend to be male, postpubertal, and of a high socioeconomic status. Children with SAD are more severely disturbed in that they have more additional psychopathologies and symptoms. Children with SAD always remain at home with an attachment figure when not in school, whereas children with a school phobia are comfortable in many settings, as long as it is not the school. Finally, there is evidence that mothers of children with SAD are more disturbed, particularly exhibiting an increase in depression (Last & Francis, 1988).

Intervention

Psychopharmacology   The data on the effectiveness of pharmacological treatment are either preliminary or inconclusive. (Allen, Leonard, and Swedo, 1995, summarize the literature.) For example, four controlled studies of the efficacy of tricyclic antidepressants involving 140 children found that they may be helpful in some cases of school phobia, but definitive proof is lacking.

Psychotherapy   The literature on psychotherapy is replete with reports of successful outcomes using a wide range of techniques from psychoanalysis to behavior modification. (Blagg and Yule, 1994, discuss the various issues and techniques.) However, few reports meet criteria for methodological soundness, and only two are both well-designed and compare the relative effectiveness of different approaches. In 1972 Miller and associates compared behavioral and psychoanalytically oriented play therapy, finding no difference in the effectiveness of the two. Whether the treated children improved more than the control group depended on who evaluated them: parents said they improved whereas a noninvolved clinician found they did not. Age was an important consideration, with younger children (6 to 10 years of age) improving more than older ones (11 to 15 years of age).

Last, Hansen, and Franco (1998) found no difference between cognitive-behavioral treatment of school phobias and educational support therapy. The latter consisted primarily of discussing phobias in general and the child's own phobic experiences in a supportive atmosphere. Unlike cognitive-behavioral treatment, there was no requirement that the child face phobic situations or substitute positive self-talk for phobic ideation. While there was no treatment of choice, both groups showed significant improvement.

A controversial issue cutting across specific psychotherapies concerns the amount of pressure that should be placed on a child to return to school. Some therapists regard an immediate return as essential, even if some force must be applied, while others recommend timing the return in keeping with therapeutic progress. There is some evidence that, while both procedures are successful, a graduated approach in conjunction with behavioral techniques circumvents the dropout problem that frequently occurs when the child is immediately returned to school (Klein & Last, 1989). However, there is general agreement that the child should return as soon as possible, even if only for a brief period.

Obsessive-Compulsive Disorder

Definition and Characteristics

Definition

Obsessive-compulsive disorder (OCD) is marked by intrusive ideas (**obsessions**) and impulses (**compulsions**) that (1) arise from sources over which the child has no control, (2) are irresistible, and (3) are often recognized as irrational. (The DSM-IV criteria are presented in Table 8.4). While hand washing is the most familiar example of a compulsion, other behaviors concern safety (such as continually checking the doors to make sure they are locked), a preoccupation with orderliness, and repeatedly counting to a particular number or touching objects a given number of times. The most frequent obsessions involve fear of contamination and the thought of harm to the self or familiar figures.

It is not unusual for a child to combine a number of rituals. An 11-year-old boy who was terrified of germs used his magic number 4 for protection in a variety of ways: he touched his fork four times before eating, counted to four when entering the locker room in the school gym, got in and out of bed four times before going to sleep, lined up his perfectly sharpened pencils in groups of four. When he became worried that a ritual might not have worked,

Table 8.4   DSM-IV Criteria for
Obsessive-Compulsive Disorder

A. Either obsessions or compulsions:
  Obsessions as defined by (1), (2), (3), and (4):
  (1) recurrent and persistent thoughts, impulses, or
      images that are experienced, at some time during
      the disturbance, as intrusive and inappropriate and
      that cause marked anxiety or distress
  (2) the thoughts, impulses, or images are not simply
      excessive worries about real-life problems
  (3) the person attempts to ignore or suppress the
      thoughts, impulses, or images, or to neutralize
      them with some other thought or action
  (4) the person recognizes that the obsessional
      thoughts, impulses, or images are a product of his
      or her own mind (not imposed from without as in
      thought insertion)
  Compulsions as defined by (1) and (2):
  (1) repetitive behaviors (e.g., hand washing, ordering,
      checking) or mental acts (e.g., praying, counting,
      repeating words silently) that the person feels
      driven to perform in response to an obsession,
      or according to rules that must be applied rigidly
  (2) the behaviors or mental acts are aimed at
      preventing or reducing distress or preventing
      some dreaded event or situation; however, these
      behaviors or mental acts either are not connected
      in a realistic way with what they are designed to
      neutralize or prevent or are clearly excessive
B. At some point during the course of the disorder, the
  person has recognized that the obsessions or
  compulsions are excessive or unreasonable. Note: This
  does not apply to children.

---

he repeated it four times. It is easy to see how crippling OCD can become; in fact, in 50 to 60 percent of such children the disorder interferes with their personal, social, and academic life, as well as becoming burdensome to the family. (Unless otherwise specified, our presentation follows Mash and Barkley, 1996.)

Developmental Dimension   In 6- to 8-year-olds, compulsive rituals occur in the absence of obsessions, whereas later on the two typically go together. The specific rituals and obsessions however are apt to change over time.

While the symptom picture for children and adults is the same, Geller and colleagues (1998) found that there are a number of differences. There is a gender difference, with males predominating among children but with no difference among adults. Child OCD is comorbid for disruptive disorders such as ADHD, which is not true for adults. Finally, children with OCD perform more poorly on intelligence tests than do adults, and there is a stronger genetic loading. The authors conclude that juvenile OCD be considered as a developmental subtype rather than being essentially the same as the adult disturbance. Here we have another example of the error of assuming that phenomenologically similar behavior (i.e., ones that look the same) in children and adults are, in fact, the same.

Characteristics

Prevalence   In regard to prevalence, rates of 1.9 percent in the general population of adolescents and of 3 to 4 percent in the clinical population of adolescents have been reported. (Our presentation continues to follow Mash and Barkley, 1996.)

Age of Onset   The age of onset can be as early as 7 years, although the mean age is 10 years.

Gender Differences   There is a gender difference in childhood, with boys starting earlier than girls and outnumbering girls. However, by adolescence this difference has all but disappeared.

Comorbidity   The comorbidity rate of OCD is high. In community samples around 84 percent of the children with OCD have comorbid conditions, while in clinic samples the figure is around 41 percent. Common comorbid conditions are depression and other anxiety disorders, although ADHD can also co-occur. (See Kovacs and Devlin, 1998.)

Socioeconomic Status and Race   Research data do not permit any firm conclusion concerning the relation of OCD to socioeconomic status and race.

Developmental Course   There is no doubt concerning the chronicity of OCD. One follow-up study found that 68 percent of 25 patients continued to have OCD 2 to 7 years later, while 32 percent had some other comorbid condition. Another follow-up study of treated individuals found that 43 percent still had OCD, while 30 percent had some other anxiety disorder (Kovacs & Devlin, 1998).

Etiology

The Intraindividual Context

The etiology of OCD remains a mystery. At a speculative level, compulsions are viewed as exaggerations of ritualistic behavior that is part of normal development, such as avoiding lines and cracks on the sidewalk or making sure special toys are lined up in a prescribed order before bedtime.

Leonard and coworkers (1994) explored this speculation by comparing a group of teenagers with obsessive-compulsive disorder with a normal control group. The similarities included the need to have things just so; counting (such as is done in jump rope and games like "one-potato, two-potato"); the use of lucky numbers; and the occurrence of rituals at bedtime, before leave-taking, and in periods of stress. But obsessive-compulsive rituals differ in that they come later in development. For example, there is evidence that normal compulsive behavior peaks at 2 to 4 years of age and declines steadily between 8 to 14 years of age; OCD, by contrast, not only becomes more frequent with age but also is accompanied by a greater degree of anxiety than is found in the normal population. (See Zohar and Bruno, 1997.) Other differences are that psychopathological obsessions and compulsions are viewed as unwanted but beyond the child's control, and they interfere with socialization and healthy mastery of anxiety.

A number of etiological hypotheses failed to be supported by data from a longitudinal study of 930 18-year-old adolescents who had been evaluated every two years (Douglass et al., 1995). Specifically, there was no evidence that OCD was related to perinatal problems or abnormal birth events, to poor performance on neuropsychological tests, to eating disorders, or to tics. However, the researchers did find that, when they were 11 years old, 18-year-old adolescents with OCD were significantly more depressed than the healthy group; and when these OCD adolescents were 15 years old they were significantly more anxious than the healthy group and had a higher level of substance abuse. While this study is valuable in refocusing attention to more promising etiological leads, it still leaves unanswered the question of how depression, anxiety, and substance abuse produce OCD rather than any other disturbance.

The Organic Context

Recently, interest in etiology has shifted to the organic context. To begin with, there is evidence of a *genetic* component in that there is a notable increase in risk of OCD in first-degree relations of individuals who have this disturbance (Kovacs & Devlin, 1998).

Next, a number of different lines of research suggest that OCD is due to a *neurological deficit*. (Our presentation follows Bolton, 1996.) This evidence includes OCD's relation to certain cerebral diseases and head injuries, the frequency of neurological soft (i.e., subtle) signs, the poor performance on certain neuropsychological tasks such as shifting attention, and the relation to tics, which also are assumed to be signs of cerebral disorder. The speculative conclusion is that compulsions should be regarded as a motor disorder caused by a neurological lesion. Obsessions appear only subsequently in order to justify the irrational motor behavior. (Recall that, developmentally, compulsions come before obsessions.) Admittedly, there is much that is speculative about this etiological reconstruction and, as we have just seen in our review of Douglass and coworkers' (1995) study, there are conflicting data. (Also see Bolton, 1996, for an attempt to integrate the organic and psychological explanations of the origins of OCD. A more detailed presentation of the organic context can be found in Henin and Kendall, 1997.)

Intervention

Pharmacotherapy

OCD is the best-studied of all pediatric anxiety disorders and the one most amenable to drug therapy. (Our presentation follows Allen, Leonard, and

Swedo, 1995.) A number of studies are models of well-controlled research—for example, comparing the effects of the drug with those of placebos, and doing double-blind and follow-up evaluations of the results.

Among drugs, selective serotonin reuptake inhibitors in particular have been found to be effective. One study, for example, found that 75 percent of OCD adolescents showed moderate to marked improvement. This improvement was sustained over time only if the adolescents continued to take the drug, however, indicating that they were helped but not cured. (A more detailed presentation of pharmacological treatment can be found in Henin and Kendall, 1997.)

Cognitive-Behavioral Treatment

Because of its success with OCD adults, cognitive-behavioral treatment has become a popular technique for treating OCD children. We will only describe its more disturbance-specific aspects. (For a more comprehensive account, see March, 1995, and Henin and Kendall, 1997.)

Exposure, as the term implies, involves exposing the child to the feared stimulus, sometimes gradually, sometimes abruptly. Thus, a child who fears contamination may be required to remain in contact with "contaminated" objects until the anxiety decreases. In response prevention, the compulsive ritual is blocked so that, for example, this same child would be prevented from washing his or her hands. (For an example of cognitive-behavioral treatment, see Franklin and associates, 1998.)

March (1995), who examined 32 reports of cognitive-behavioral treatment, found that most of the studies were flawed. Inclusion criteria were not adequately defined and assessed, reliable and valid measures of outcome were not applied, follow-up evaluations were not conducted, and control groups were not used. The fact that a variety of behavioral and nonbehavioral techniques were used made it difficult or impossible to determine the specific contribution of cognitive-behavioral treatment to the outcome. Therefore, it seems best to conclude that cognitive-behavioral therapy is a promising treatment whose effectiveness still

needs to be tested by more rigorous research. At preset its track record is not as impressive as that of psychopharmacology.

Posttraumatic Stress Disorder

In 1976 a busload of 26 children was kidnapped from their Chowchilla, California, school. The children and their driver were first driven around in a darkened van and then moved to a buried tractor-trailer, where they remained until some of the children dug themselves out. The imprisonment lasted 27 hours. In 1987 a sniper fired repeatedly into a school playground for a period of several hours, killing one child and one passerby and wounding 13 children. In 1998 a high school student who had been expelled for carrying a gun returned the following day and ran through the cafeteria firing his rifle from the hip, killing two students and wounding several others.

In one important respect **posttraumatic stress disorder** (PTSD) differs from other anxiety disorders—it lacks the element of irrationality. If a boy is terrified of riding the school bus when nothing out of the ordinary has happened, we are puzzled; however, if a boy is terrified of riding a school bus after being in one that has skidded off the road and turned over, we might say, "Of course!"

Until recently, the literature on PTSD in children consisted primarily of anecdotal reports. However, considerable progress has been made (1) in delineating the specific variables involved in the disorder and (2) in devising objective measures to quantify children's reactions. We will concentrate on the first area of progress. We shall attempt to discover what determines whether children will or will not develop PTSD after exposure to a traumatic situation. (The literature on PTSD is reviewed by Fletcher, 1996, and Pfefferbaum, 1997.)

Definition and Characteristics

Definition

DSM-IV describes a traumatic event a one involving actual or threatened death or serious injury, or a threat to the physical integrity of self or others. (See Table 8.5.) The three categories of behaviors defining the disorder are:

Table 8.5   DSM-IV Criteria for Posttraumatic Stress Disorder

A. The person has been exposed to a traumatic event in which both of the following were present:
  (1) The person experienced, witnessed, or was confronted with an event or events that involved actual or threatened death or serious injury, or a threat to the physical integrity of self or others.
  (2) The person's response involved intense fear, helplessness, or horror. Note: In children, this may be expressed instead by disorganized or agitated behavior.
B. The traumatic event is persistently reexperienced in one (or more) of the following ways:
  (1) Recurrent and intrusive distressing recollections of the event, including images, thoughts, or perceptions. Note: In young children, repetitive play may occur in which themes or aspects of the trauma are expressed.
  (2) Recurrent distressing dreams of the event. Note: In children, there may be frightening dreams without recognizable content.
  (3) Acting or feeling as if the traumatic event were recurring (includes a sense of reliving the experience, illusions, hallu-cinations, and dissociative flashback episodes, including those that occur on awakening or when intoxicated). Note: In young children, trauma-specific reenactment may occur.
  (4) Intense psychological distress at exposure to internal or external cues that symbolize or resemble an aspect of the traumatic event.
  (5) Psychological reactivity on exposure to internal or external cues that symbolize or resemble an aspect of the trau-matic event.
C. Persistent avoidance of stimuli associated with the trauma and numbing of general responsiveness (not present before the trauma) as indicated by three (or more) of the following:
  (1) Efforts to avoid thoughts, feelings, or conversations associated with the trauma
  (2) Efforts to avoid activities, places, or people that arouse recollections of the trauma
  (3) Inability to recall an important aspect of the trauma
  (4) Markedly diminished interest or participation in significant activities
  (5) Feeling of detachment or estrangement from others
  (6) Restricted range of affect (e.g., unable to have loving feelings)
  (7) Sense of a foreshortened future (e.g., does not expect to have a career, marriage, children, or a normal life span)
D. Persistent symptoms of increased arousal (not present before the trauma) as indicated by two (or more) of the following:
  (1) Difficulty falling or staying asleep
  (2) Irritability or outbursts of anger
  (3) Difficulty concentrating
  (4) Hypervigilance
  (5) Exaggerated startle response
E. Duration of the disturbance (symptoms in Criteria B, C, and D) is more than 1 month.

1. Persistent reexperiencing of the event, such as intrusive, distressing recollections of the event or, in young children, repetitive play in which aspects of the trauma are expressed
2. Persistent avoidance of stimuli associated with the trauma or numbing of general responsiveness, such as efforts to avoid thoughts or activities and people that arouse recollections of the trauma, or markedly diminished interest and participation in activities
3. Persistent symptoms of increased arousal such as irritability, outbursts of anger, difficulty concen-trating, and hypervigilance

Lonigan, Anthony, and Shannon (1998) found that, among the symptoms, those of numbing and avoidance were most predictive of the severity of the posttraumatic reaction. Other symptoms, such as anxiety, were not predictive of severity of reaction.

Developmental Dimension   The kinds of symp-toms children manifest after being exposed to trau-matic events vary with age.

Young children may regress to a previous level of functioning, such as losing bowel and bladder control, becoming irritable and crying frequently, sucking their thumbs, and developing fears and eating problems. Separation anxiety is apt to reappear. Young children also reenact the traumatic event though play, such behavior being unique to children. The play itself has a compulsive, repetitive quality that fails to relieve the accompanying anxiety. For example, a 5-year-old girl who was attacked and bitten by a monkey at the zoo would repeatedly return to this theme, although the play did nothing to help her master her fright.

For school-age children fears and anxieties are the predominant symptoms. The children also complain of headaches and visual and hearing problems, are inattentive at school, fight with or withdraw from peers, and have sleep disturbances such as nightmares and bed-wetting. Like younger children, they engage in elaborate reenactments of the traumatic event.

Preadolescents and adolescents, like school-age children, may develop various physical complaints, become withdrawn, suffer from loss of appetite and sleep, and become disruptive or fail at school. Unlike younger children, they do not reenact the traumatic event (Davidson & Baum, 1990).

Characteristics

Prevalence   From 6 to 7 percent of the population is exposed annually to extreme stressors, ranging from natural disasters to auto accidents to murders and gang warfare. For example, as many as 100,000 children may be kidnapped annually (Fletcher, 1996). An estimated 6 percent of children meet the criteria for PTSD by the age of 18 years (Pfefferbaum, 1997).

Gender Differences   The data in regard to gender differences are contradictory. A number of studies with large samples have found girls to be more symptomatic than boys, but other studies have found the opposite (Pfefferbaum, 1997).

Comorbidity   Comorbid conditions are common, with PTSD significantly increasing the risk of depression, anxiety, and alcohol and drug dependence (Pfefferbaum, 1997).

Racial and Cultural Factors   Data on racial differences have yielded contradictory results. However, studies of refugee populations who commonly suffer the stresses of political violence, displacement, and immigration show the importance of cultural factors. Cambodian refugees, for example, while suffering from PTSD and comorbid anxiety and depression, do not show an increase in conduct disorders or substance abuse. They are respectful of authority, have a positive view of school, and function at a high level (Pfefferbaum, 1997).

Developmental Course   The meager prospective data suggest that the developmental course depends on the frequency of trauma. Children tend to outgrow their reactions to single-occurrence stressors but (not surprisingly) continue to be disturbed by exposure to repeated, multiple stressors.

Variables Involved

Before answering the question of who will and who will not develop a PTSD after exposure to a traumatic event, we must first explore the variables involved in this reaction. These variables can be grouped into three categories: the nature of the traumatic event, the intrapersonal context, and the interpersonal context. (A more comprehensive presentation can be found in Fletcher, 1996.)

The Traumatic Event   Traumatic events can be categorized in terms of whether they are acute, such as a natural disaster or an auto accident, or chronic, such as living in a violent inner-city neighborhood or a war zone. A victim of an acute traumatic event has difficulty putting the experience out of his or her mind. In this case traumatization results in intrusive memories, hypervigilance, anxiety, and somatic complaints. Victims of chronic trauma are forced to make some kind of accommodation, which they do through avoiding reminders of the event, numbing of affect, and denial.

Degree of exposure to the traumatic event is another important dimension; for example, children on the playground during a sniper attack had more PTSD than did those in the school building, who in turn had more than those who stayed at home that day.

The Intrapersonal Context   Surprisingly little research has been done on children's emotional reactions to the traumatic event, such as being distressed, scared, or angry. However, one study found that such reactions were more strongly associated with PTSD than the actual physical damage done by the natural disaster such as a hurricane.

There is only tentative support for a biological predisposition to PTSD, but, on the positive side, a resilient temperament, marked by being outgoing, positive in mood, and adaptable to change in infancy, may mitigate some of the negative effects of traumatic stress. By the same token, a prior history of anxiety and psychopathological disturbances may increase vulnerability to traumatic stress. A history of stressful experiences may have two opposite effects. On the one hand it may increase vulnerability to PTSD (as do psychopathological disturbances). On the other hand, mastery of such events in the past may help steel the child against the noxious effects of exposure to the current traumatic event.

The Interpersonal Context   The reactions of children to traumatic events are often related to the reactions of their parents and other significant adults. This is particularly true of young children. Thus social support is an important variable; for example, parental support is associated with resilience in the face of stress, while separation from parents immediately after a natural disaster, ongoing maternal preoccupation with the event, and family conflict are associated with more severe symptoms of PTSD.

Summary   By way of summary, let us return to the question of who will and will not develop PTSD after exposure to a traumatic event. Children who are apt not to develop PTSD are not directly involved in the traumatic event. The event itself is an acute one which increases the likelihood that the children will outgrow its effects. The children have a resilient temperament with no history of prior psychopathological disturbances but with a history of learning how to cope with and master stressful events. They have parental support and are members of a family that has no severe problems. The opposite is true of children who are apt to develop PTSD.

Intervention

We will only discuss *crisis intervention*, a technique specifically directed at individuals who have recently been exposed to a traumatic situation. (For a more comprehensive coverage of treatment, see Pfefferbaum, 1997, and Yule, 1994.)

Within a few days of the traumatic event survivors are brought together in a group with an outside leader. The leader explains that the purpose of the session is to share feelings and help one another. The leader presents the facts concerning the event in order to correct any false rumors and proceeds to ask the participants to talk about their feelings. Children are often relieved to find that others felt what they did and that their feelings are normal reactions. Finally, the leader suggests ways of handling reactions and describes other sources of help.

In our discussions of depression and anxiety we have been dealing with children who are internalizers in the sense that their disturbances are marked by various degrees of internal distress and suffering. We now turn to children who are externalizers in the sense that they act out their problems via antisocial behavior. We have already discussed externalizers in earlier chapters in conjunction with oppositional-defiant disorder and attention-deficit hyperactive disorder; in the next chapter we will focus on conduct disorder and the development of antisocial behavior.

Conduct Disorder and the Development of Antisocial Behavior

Conduct disorder has a unique place among the psychopathologies. Not only is the development of the individual with this disorder disrupted, but along the way enormous costs are borne by society and the victims of antisocial acts. Therefore, it is not surprising that more attention has been paid to understanding the development of conduct disorder than any other childhood psychopathology.

Definition and Characteristics

DSM-IV defines **conduct disorder** (CD) as "a repetitive and persistent pattern of behavior in which either the basic rights of others or major age-appropriate societal norms or rules are violated." (See Table 9.1.) Conduct problems may occur in four categories: *aggression toward others, destruction of property, deceitfulness or theft,* and serious *rule violations*.

Severity is specified as *mild* (few conduct problems beyond those necessary to make the diagnosis, and those present cause

only minor harm to others); *moderate* (an intermediate number and severity of problems); and *severe* (many conduct problems *or* their effect causes considerable harm to others). DSM-IV further differentiates between conduct problems with a *childhood onset* (prior to age 10) or *adolescent onset* (absence of criteria characteristic of CD prior to age 10), which is an important distinction, as we shall see.

Problem Behavior versus Conduct Disorder   Misbehavior is part of normal development, as we know. Therefore, our first task is to determine when behavior problems warrant a diagnosis of CD. DSM-IV specifies that the category should be used only in cases in which the behavior is symptomatic of an *underlying dysfunction in the person* rather than being a reaction to the immediate social environment. DSM-IV suggests that in order to make this judgment the clinician should consider the *social and economic context* in which problem behavior occurs. For example, aggressive behavior may

Table 9.1   DSM-IV Criteria for Conduct Disorder

A repetitive and persistent pattern of behavior in which either the basic rights of others or major age-appropriate societal norms or rules are violated, during which at least three of the following are present in the past 12 months:

Aggression to people and animals
 (1) Often bullies, threatens, or intimidates others
 (2) Often initiates physical fights
 (3) Has used a weapon that can cause serious physical harm to others (e.g., a bat, brick, broken bottle, knife, gun)
 (4) Has stolen while confronting a victim (e.g., mugging, purse snatching, extortion, armed robbery)
 (5) Has been physically cruel to people
 (6) Has been physically cruel to animals
 (7) Has forced someone into sexual activity

Destruction of property
 (8) Has deliberately engaged in fire setting with the intention of causing serious damage
 (9) Has deliberately destroyed others' property (other than by fire setting)

Deceitfulness or theft
 (10) Has broken into someone else's house, building, or car
 (11) Often lies or breaks promises to obtain goods or favors or to avoid obligations (i.e., "cons" others)
 (12) Has stolen items of nontrivial value without confronting a victim (e.g., shoplifting, but without breaking and entering; forgery)

Serious violations of rules
 (13) Often stays out at night despite parental prohibitions, beginning before 13 years of age
 (14) Has run away from home overnight at least twice while living in parental or parental surrogate home (or once without returning for a lengthy period)
 (15) Is often truant from school, beginning before 13 years of age

Reprinted with permission from the Diagnostic and Statistical Manual of Mental Disorders, Fourth Edition. Copyright 1994 American Psychiatric Association.

have arisen out of a need for survival in immigrant youth from war-torn countries. Therefore, some youths' misbehavior might represent an adaptation to a deviant environment, rather than a mental disorder. Some concern has been expressed, however, about whether this guideline is sufficient to prevent misdiagnosis of behaviorally troublesome but otherwise normal youth (Richters & Cicchetti, 1993). (See Box 9.1.)

Prevalence   *Prevalence* rates are difficult to pinpoint. (Our review follows Hinshaw and Anderson, 1996, except where noted.) Reported prevalence rates for normative children and adolescents range widely from study to study, from as low as 1 percent to as high as 10 percent. A well-conducted large-scale study in Canada (Offord, Boyle, & Racine, 1991) used DSM criteria to define the disorder. For children ages 4 to 11, the investigators found rates of 6.5 percent for boys and 1.8 percent for girls. For youth 12 to 16 years old, percent rates were 10.4 for boys and 4.1 for girls.

CD is even more prevalent in *clinical samples*: referrals for conduct problems, aggressiveness, and antisocial behavior make up about one-third to one-half of all child and adolescent cases. Because they are observable and are disturbing to others, as Weisz and Weiss (1991) note, conduct problems are among the most "referable" forms of childhood disorder.

Gender Differences   Gender differences are significant. The diagnosis of CD is about four times more common in boys than in girls.

Typologies of Conduct Disorder

Childhood Onset versus Adolescent Onset

As noted above, DSM-IV distinguishes between two types of CD. *Childhood-onset* CD, also termed "life-course persistent" CD (Moffitt, 1993) or "aggressive-versatile" CD (Loeber, 1988), is associated with overt aggression and physical violence and tends to be accompanied by multiple problems, such as neuropsychological deficits, inattention, impulsivity, and poor school performance. It occurs most often in males and is predicted by antisocial behavior in parents and disturbed parent–child relationships. The childhood-onset type is the one most likely to show persistence across the life span.

Adolescent-onset CD, also termed "adolescence-limited" CD (Moffitt, 1993) or "nonaggressive-antisocial" CD (Loeber, 1988), is characterized by

Box 9.1 | "Mark Twain Meets DSM-IV"

Consider a school-age boy who is habitually truant from school, defies authority, runs away from home, consorts with criminals, and engages in smoking, drinking, and using foul language. Is this a conduct-disordered child, a future criminal, a fledgling psychopath? Not in this case, according to Richters and Cicchetti (1993), for this is a description of a boy named Huckleberry Finn, one of Mark Twain's most well-known creations.

Although developmental psychopathology emphasizes the continuum between normative and pathological development, diagnostic labels require that we place some boundary

between them. Nowhere is there more controversy over where the line should be drawn than in the diagnosis of conduct disorder. The behavioral criteria for the CD diagnosis are extremely wide-ranging, from shoplifting and truancy to murder and rape. While some forms of antisocial activity are in the behavioral repertoire of many of us (even if we have sufficient moxie to avoid being caught), others are outside the normal pale and suggest a psychopathological disturbance.

Richters and Cicchetti are concerned about the ease with which the CD criteria can be applied to children. They point out that some of the best-

loved characters in fiction, such as Huckleberry Finn—and even such real-life characters as Huck's creator, Mark Twain—could be considered deserving of the CD label. Clearly it is important to identify those youths who are emotionally disturbed and whose behavior presages more trouble to come. However, Richters and Cicchetti argue that it is equally important not to pathologize youth who might get into trouble because of characteristics—such as nonconformity, independent-mindedness, and "mischeevousness"—that represent potential sources of resiliency in the long term.

---

normal early development and less severe behavior problems in adolescence, particularly in the form of violence against others. In contrast to the higher prevalence of childhood-onset CD in males, adolescent-onset youth are just as likely to be female (Fergusson, Lynskey, & Horwood, 1996). Fewer comorbid problems and family dysfunctions are seen in comparison to the childhood-onset type.

Moffitt and colleagues (1996) have demonstrated that there are different developmental predictors and consequences of these two subtypes. Longitudinal data were obtained in New Zealand from a representative sample of males who were assessed every two years from ages 3 to 18. The investigators were able to establish a number of ways in which youth with childhood-onset CD could be distinguished from their "late-blooming" peers. A *difficult temperament* at age 3 was a predictor of childhood-onset CD, as was an early history of *aggressiveness* and antisocial behavior. In adolescence, in contrast to other youth, the early starters were more likely to describe themselves as *self-seeking, alienated, callous* toward others, and *unattached* to families. They were also more likely to have committed a *violent crime*: early starters were disproportionately

convicted of such offenses as assault, rape, and use of a deadly weapon. Further, few of those on the childhood-onset pathway evidenced recovery—less than 6 percent avoided developing conduct problems in adolescence.

Troubled youth may seek a sense of belonging and acceptance in an antisocial peer group.

Box 9.2

Case Examples of Conduct Disorder: Social Mimicry versus Psychopathy

Eleven-year-old Angelo was required by the judge to get psychological help or be confined in the juvenile correctional center. The judge was lenient because Angelo was the only member of his gang to get caught breaking into and robbing a corner grocery store. He was caught because he was obviously a not-too-bright follower who was doing what he was told. Yet his loyalty to the gang far outweighs any sense of wrongdoing. And for good reason. School has been an endless series of humiliations and failures. He was passed from grade to grade primarily because he was not a troublemaker, and his teachers became tired of calling him on the carpet for making mistakes and handing in sloppy homework.

His family is large and poor, and while they fight a good deal, they also have a sense of cohesion. The father is a laborer who is hired and fired according to the state of the economy. He is a bitter man who demands respect from his children but sees no reason for them to be good citizens in a society which has treated him so shabbily. His mother—a stressed, careworn woman—prays to the Virgin every night to help her children and wonders where she will get the strength to get through another day. So it is the gang that gives Angelo a sense of belonging, of sharing, of being valued. While his slowness makes him the goat, the leader has taken a liking to him, and Angelo's fondest dream is to one day become a leader himself.

Mark, another 11-year-old, is a lively, assured, nice-looking, all-American-type boy. Except that, for the past two years, he has been breaking into and robbing houses in the wealthy suburb where he lives. After a robbery was discovered, Mark would show up and offer to help put the house back in order. His manner was one of sincere concern, and he asked for no favors in return. He was

Moffitt (1993) argues that in contrast to their early developing peers, the majority of those with adolescent-onset CD do not deserve a diagnosis at all. Their behavior is best explained as a product of "*social mimicry*," in that they imitate the antisocial actions of others in order to gain status in the peer group. As they reach adulthood, as they have more opportunities to gain status in legitimate ways, their conduct problems generally desist. (Consider the case of Angelo in Box 9.2.)

Destructive/Nondestructive and Overt/Covert

More recent empirical research has pointed to another important distinction, this one based not on age of onset but on the kinds of acts perpetrated by the youth. Frick and colleagues (1993) conducted a meta-analysis of data from 60 factor-analytic studies involving more than 28,000 children. They identified two dimensions on which children's behavior could be distinguished. One dimension concerned whether misbehavior was *destructive* (cruelty to others, assault) or *nondestructive* (swearing,

breaking rules). The second dimension concerned whether behavior problems were *overt* (hitting, fighting, bullying) or *covert* (lying, stealing, destroying property), a distinction that has reliably been made in a number of studies.

Taking these two dimensions into account, the investigators were able to identify four subtypes of conduct-disordered youth, depending on the kind of misbehavior in which they engaged (see Figure 9.1, pg. 194). These were labeled *oppositional* (overt and nondestructive), *aggressive* (overt and destructive), *property violations* (covert and destructive), or *status violations* (covert and nondestructive).

Frick and colleagues (1993) also found that these types could be differentiated in terms of *age of onset*. Those who were primarily oppositional were identified by parents by as early as 4 years of age. Aggressive children, in contrast, demonstrated problems after their sixth year. Those who engaged in property violations showed an average age of onset of about 7½ while those whose misbehavior took the form of status violations had an average age of onset of about 9.

finally caught because a careless remark revealed that he knew an item had been stolen before the owner had mentioned it to anyone outside her family.

Mark is bright, enterprising, and capable beyond his years. But he is also a daredevil in the extreme. He was the youngest boy in his class to smoke marijuana and drink alcohol. He charmed his way into being taught how to drive a car and then bribed the gardener into letting him drive at breakneck speed on the back roads. He enjoys luring younger boys into joining him in venturing into forbidden places—a liquor store, an adult bookstore, an abandoned building—because he likes being in command. While other boys are sporadically attracted to Mark's daring and charm, his friendships are short-lived. In school he is restless and inattentive, except in shop, where his interests and skills make him the top student. He is a master of the sincere lie—looking the teacher straight in the face. One of his teachers said, "I just can't reach him. I could beat him or plead with him or cuddle him, and it just wouldn't matter."

Mark's father, a successful surgeon, has little time for his family during the week but enjoys being with his son on weekends. In his eyes, Mark can do no wrong. Even the robberies were extenuated: "Wild colts make good horses." Mark's mother is a kind and loving woman but lacking in resources. Early on she perceived Mark's disregard for her prohibitions concerning dangerous objects and activities, and she did not know what to do about his constant lying. Affection and reasoning gave way to angry shouts and finally to whippings. Mark was determined not to cry; he sensed that if she could not hurt him, she would be powerless. He was right, and the whippings gave way to resignation and withdrawal.

Psychopathy

An additional category has been necessitated by recent research on **psychopaths** (sometimes referred to as sociopaths). Hare (1996) has found that, among those with antisocial behavior, there is a subset who exhibit psychopathic personality traits. These include *callousness* (a lack of remorse, empathy, or guilt), *egocentricity, superficial charm, impulsivity, shallow emotions, manipulativeness*, and an *absence of meaningful relationships*. Psychopaths are individuals who commit antisocial acts against others not out of necessity—they do not rob because they are poor or strike out at others to defend themselves—but because they derive pleasure from hurting or manipulating other people. They exhibit a lack of awareness of other people as fellow human beings deserving of consideration or compassion. They are, in short, "without conscience" (Hare, 1993). (Consider the case of Mark in Box 9.2.)

Hare believes that ordinary antisocial behavior and psychopathy have different developmental origins. For example, while antisocial behavior *without* psychopathy is predicted by childhood adversity, psychopathy *alone* is not. This has led Hare to suspect that psychopathy derives from an innate predisposition. For example, brain scan imagery shows that psychopaths process information about emotions differently than do nonpsychopaths. Ordinarily, when people process information about emotionally meaningful words such as "love," the frontal cortex is activated, showing that the information is being processed at a deep level and many complex associations are being made. In contrast, the processing of a word with little emotional significance, such as "lamp," will not be associated with frontal activity. However, psychopaths process words having to do with feelings and relationships at the same shallow level that they do words about inanimate objects (Williamson, Harpur, & Hare, 1991). Consequently, Hare hypothesizes, psychopathy may have its origins in the "hard wiring" of the brain.

Can children be psychopaths? Evidence is accumulating that psychopathic youth can be identified (Lynam, 1997). For example, Frick and associates (1994) developed a child version of Hare's device for detecting psychopathic traits, the Psychopathy

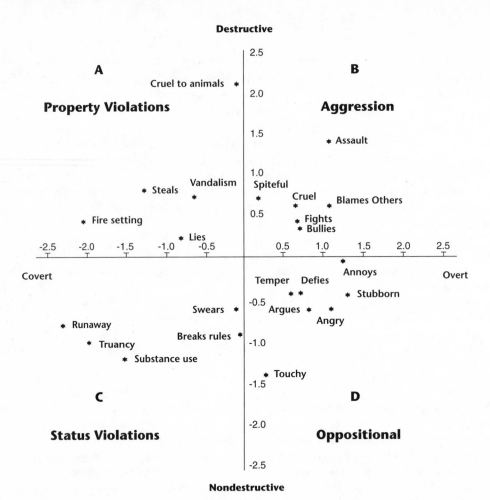

Figure 9.1   Meta-Analytic Factor Analysis of Child Conduct Problems.

Source: Frick et al., 1993

Checklist. Just as with Hare's studies of adults, they found two separate dimensions of behavior, one concerned with antisocial behavior, termed *impulsivity/conduct problems* and the other reflecting *callousness/unemotionality*. Consistent with the adult research, psychopathic traits in children and adolescents are related to the violence of their offenses and are predictive of the likelihood that they will reoffend (Forth, Hart, & Hare, 1990). Further, consistent with Hare's hypothesis about the distinct etiology of psychopathy, Wootton and colleagues (1997) found that ordinary conduct problems in children were predicted by ineffective parenting whereas psychopathic callousness/unemotionality was not.

Comorbidity

CD frequently co-occurs with other disturbances. (Here we follow Hinshaw and Anderson, 1996, excepted where noted.) *Attention-deficit hyperactivity disorder* (ADHD) and *oppositional-defiant disorder* (ODD) are the diagnostic categories most commonly associated with CD. Youths with comorbid ADHD and CD also are among the most disturbed. They display higher rates of physical aggression, more persistent behavior problems, poorer school achievement, and more rejection from peers than the "pure" CD type.

Learning disorders are associated with CD, particularly reading disorder. In some youth, learning problems may lead to frustration, oppositional attitudes, and misbehavior in school, and thus to a diagnosis of CD. However, as we saw in Chapter 6, the weight of the evidence argues that learning disorders do not lead to CD, but rather that a third variable accounts for the relationship between them. *ADHD* youth are overrepresented amongst those who have both conduct and learning disorders, and it may be the overlap of these disorders with ADHD that accounts for their co-occurrence.

Depression is highly correlated with CD. As we saw in Chapter 7, Capaldi's (1992) longitudinal research suggests that antisocial behavior in boys leads to academic failures and peer rejection, which lead, in turn, to depression. Comorbid depression and CD is of particular concern in that it is disproportionately associated with suicide. Finally, CD also co-occurs with *substance abuse* and may be a precursor to it, as we discuss in Chapter 11.

There is a *gender difference* in that comorbidity is most common in girls. Although girls develop CD less often than boys overall, when they do it is more likely to take a comorbid form (Loeber & Keenan, 1994). In particular, while *depression and anxiety* frequently occur in conduct-disordered youth, girls demonstrate higher rates of comorbidity with these internalizing problems. As we saw in our discussion of depression (Chapter 7), these different comorbidities might in fact represent different subtypes of CD.

Developmental Course

There is a high degree of *continuity* in conduct-disordered behavior. Large-scale epidemiological studies in the United States and other countries have established stability from preschool age to middle childhood (Campbell, 1997), from childhood to adolescence (Lahey et al., 1995), from adolescence to adulthood (Farrington, 1995), and, most impressively, from infancy to adulthood (Newman et al., 1997). Thus, the developmental course is a persistent one, and the prognosis poor. For example, Fergusson, Horwood, and Lynskey (1995) found that, over a two-year period, only 14 percent of children diagnosed with CD evidenced remission.

Researchers also have looked more closely at the developmental unfolding of problem behavior. Generally, a sequential progression is found such that one form of problem behavior virtually always occurs before the emergence of another. Relying on reconstructive data, Loeber and colleagues (1992) found an *"invariant sequence"* across development: from *hyperactivity-inattention* to *oppositional* behavior, and then to *conduct problems*. Combining Loeber's research with other work on the precursors

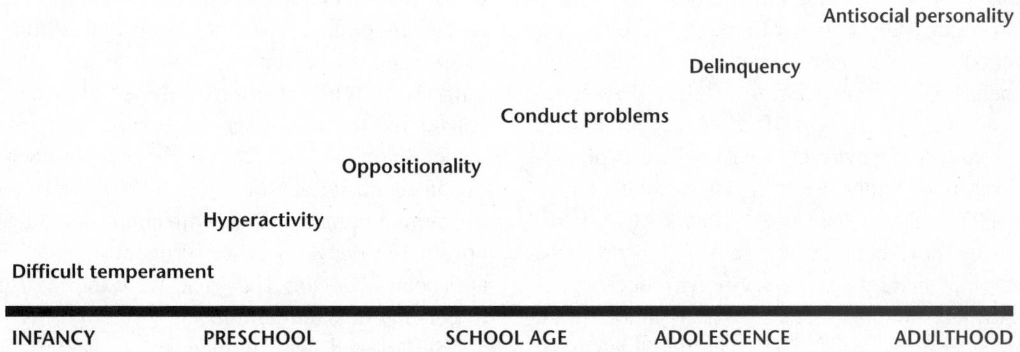

Antisocial personality

Delinquency

Conduct problems

Oppositionality

Hyperactivity

Difficult temperament

| INFANCY | PRESCHOOL | SCHOOL AGE | ADOLESCENCE | ADULTHOOD |

Figure 9.2   Developmental Transformations in Antisocial Behavior from Infancy to Adulthood.

and sequelae of conduct problems, we can construct a developmental model tracing the sequencing of behavior problems from difficult temperament in the early years to antisocial personality in adulthood. (See Figure 9.2.)

As youth progress through this sequence, they tend to maintain their prior antisocial behaviors; therefore, because behaviors are retained rather than replaced, the developmental progression is better described as one of *accretion* rather than succession. However, the fact that this sequence exists does not mean that all individuals are fated to go through all the steps. On the contrary, while most individuals progress to different stages of increasing seriousness of antisocial behavior, few progress through all of them.

On the other hand, as Loeber and Stouthamer-Loeber (1998) note, *discontinuity* in CD also can be found. For example, some studies show desistance rates from preschool to schoolage of about 25 percent. Although it appears that these are youth with less serious behavior problems, little is known about the factors that account for their ceasing their antisocial behavior. However, as longitudinal research on the precursors and consequences of CD has emerged, distinct developmental pathways have been identified over the life span, which we describe next.

Early Childhood: Pathways from ADHD to Conduct Disorder

As noted above, a number of studies have confirmed the link between CD and ADHD (Lahey et al., 1995). Symptoms of ADHD appear to increase the risk for childhood-onset CD, to be associated with more severe behavior problems, and to result in greater resistance to change. Thus, ADHD propels youth to an earlier onset of behavior problems, which is predictive, in turn, of a longer-lasting antisocial career.

ADHD does not lead irrevocably to CD, however. Only those children whose ADHD symptoms are accompanied by *antisocial behavior* such as aggression and noncompliance are at risk for future CD (Loeber & Keenan, 1994). Thus, in this case it appears that ADHD potentiates early conduct problems, hastening them on the way to full-blown CD.

Middle Childhood: Pathways from Oppositionality to Conduct Disorder

ODD, as described in Chapter 5, is characterized by persistent age-inappropriate displays of anger and defiance. While ODD and CD share some similar behavioral features and risk factors, the two syndromes can be distinguished from one another. As Figure 9.1 shows, large-scale meta-analyses of children's problem behavior reveal a unique factor comprising the kind of overt, nondestructive behaviors that define ODD. ODD also emerges earlier in development than CD, with an average age of onset of 6 years for oppositionality as compared to 9 years for conduct problems (Loeber et al., 1992).

Loeber and colleagues (1993) found that CD was almost universally preceded by ODD. In addition, the most severely disturbed children were likely to retain features of oppositionality in addition to acquiring CD symptoms (Lahey et al., 1995). Therefore, there is convincing evidence for a developmental progression from ODD to CD.

Late Childhood and Adolescence: Divergent Pathways

Loeber and colleagues (1993) used prospective data from a longitudinal study of high-risk boys in order to investigate the *developmental pathways* predictive of later problem behavior. Basing their thinking on previous research differentiating CD along the dimensions of overt/covert and destructive/nondestructive, they derived three distinct types (see Figure 9.3).

The first identified was the *authority conflict* pathway. The behavior of these youths was characterized by defiance, stubborn and oppositional behavior, and rule violations such as truancy and running away. While disruptive, these behaviors were considered to be less serious because they did not inflict direct harm on others. Those whose behavior escalated in the authority conflict pathway tended to have continual conflicts with adults, but they were not likely to develop other forms of aggressive and antisocial behavior. They also were the least likely to become labeled delinquent.

The second was termed the *covert* pathway. These youths engaged in minor and nonviolent acts such as shoplifting, joyriding, and vandalism. Esca-

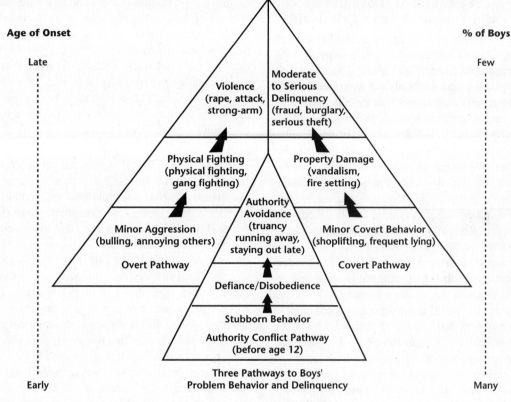

Age of Onset   **% of Boys**

Late   Few

Violence
(rape, attack,
strong-arm)

Moderate
to Serious
Delinquency
(fraud, burglary,
serious theft)

Physical Fighting
(physical fighting,
gang fighting)

Property Damage
(vandalism,
fire setting)

Authority
Avoidance
(truancy
running away,
staying out late)

Minor Aggression
(bulling, annoying others)

Minor Covert Behavior
(shoplifting, frequent lying)

Overt Pathway   Covert Pathway

Defiance/Disobedience

Stubborn Behavior

Authority Conflict Pathway
(before age 12)

Three Pathways to Boys'
Problem Behavior and Delinquency

Early   Many

Figure 9.3   Developmental Pathways to Conduct Disorder.

Source: Loeber and Keenan, 1994

lation in this pathway involved progressing to more serious forms of property crime and theft in later adolescence but was rarely associated with violence or more severe kinds of antisocial behavior.

The third, the *overt* pathway, was composed of children who exhibited aggression early in childhood. Escalation in this pathway was associated with progression from aggression to fighting to more serious assaults and violence against others. The overt pathway was linked to high rates of criminal offenses in adolescence. In addition, these youths were likely to add covert forms of aggression to their repertoire as their careers proceeded. *Dual overt/covert* pathway youth were more likely to become delinquents; however, the worst outcomes were seen in *triple-pathway* youth—those who showed a combination of overt and covert aggression, as well as authority conflict.

Loeber and Stouthamer-Loeber (1998) point out that not all youth who demonstrate conduct problems have a childhood history of aggression and antisocial behavior. Thus, in this developmental period arises the *adolescent-onset*, or late-onset, type. These youths have been neglected in previous studies of developmental psychopathology, perhaps because their numbers are fewer, but also perhaps because, by the time they have begun acting out in adolescence, they are not distinguishable from their early-onset peers. Therefore, attention to the youth's early developmental history is imperative to accurate identification of these subtypes. In contrast to the undercontrolled, early onset conduct-disordered child, these may be "overcontrolled offenders" in whom problem behavior is sparked by emotional distress.

Late Adolescence: Pathways to Antisocial Personality and Criminality

Two conclusions can be drawn from the research linking CD to adult *antisocial personality disorder* and criminal behavior. First, *looking backward*, we find that antisocial adults almost without exception met the criteria for CD earlier in their development. However, one of the criteria for the diagnosis of antisocial personality disorder is onset of problem behavior before age 15, so this is a link that is structured into the diagnostic criteria. Secondly, *looking forward*, we find that only a minority of conduct-disordered youths go on to develop the chronic and disabling patterns characteristic of the adult diagnosis.

The characteristics predictive of those who do go on to develop antisocial personality disorder include early age of onset and diverse, persistent conduct problems in childhood, including aggression and antisocial behavior. As we have seen previously, *age of onset* is one of the most significant predictors of the subsequent seriousness of antisocial behavior. Children with early onset have both a higher level of disruptive behavior and progress more rapidly to more serious problems (Loeber et al., 1992). There is clear evidence that those who begin their antisocial activities before the teenage years will continue to commit a large number of offenses at a high rate over a long period of time.

A landmark study by Magnusson and Bergman (1990) provides a unique glimpse into the sequences leading up to the development of CD in late adolescence. They utilized a remarkable longitudinal data set—3,244 male children drawn from a Swedish community and followed from childhood to adulthood. Some of the findings were to be expected: boys with no problems at 13 years of age had few problems as adults, while aggression and hyperactivity predicted later criminality. It was the *multiple-problem boys* who became disturbed adults: about half those with four to five problems became criminals, for example. The unexpected finding was that none of the variables—even aggression—predicted adult antisocial behavior by themselves. It was only when aggression was accompanied by *hyperactivity* that it predicted criminality, and only as poor peer relations were accompanied by several other problem behaviors that it also became predictive.

In sum, aggression is a risk factor for the development of antisocial personality disorder in adulthood. However, while aggression may be stable, Magnusson and Bergman found that aggression predicts criminal behavior in adulthood when it is accompanied by hyperactivity or is part of multiple problems. The further an individual has progressed along a path of antisocial behavior, the more likely continuity will be demonstrated.

Discontinuity   Not all aggressive youth go on to become antisocial adults. While most adult antisocial behavior is rooted in childhood, only half of the at-risk children grow up to be antisocial adults (Loeber & Hay, 1997). It is also important to understand the factors that account for this discontinuity. With this in mind, Kolvin and coworkers (1989) conducted a longitudinal study of the *protective factors* shielding high-risk boys from adult delinquency. They found that a number of factors were important and that they played different roles in different developmental periods. For the first five years, good parental care, positive social circumstances, and few adverse experiences (e.g., accidents) were protective. Protective factors in the preadolescent period included parental supervision, absence of developmental delays, relatively good intelligence and academic achievement, easy temperament, good peer relations and prosocial activities. More recently, Hoge, Andrews, and Leschied (1996) compiled a virtually identical list of protective factors in adolescence.

Gender Differences in Developmental Pathways

It is notable that almost all of the longitudinal studies cited have been based exclusively on males. What about *female* developmental trajectories? Because most CD appears in boys, the greater attention focused on males is justified to some extent. However, only by including girls in the research can we determine whether or not they are at reduced risk or have a different developmental course.

Of interest is the fact that girls are underrepresented amongst virtually all of the disorders that co-occur with—or are precursors to—CD, including oppositional defiance, ADHD, and learning dis-

Relational aggression.

orders. Various theoretical perspectives have been offered to explain this gender difference, summarized by Eme and Kavanaugh (1995). Some have argued that males are more biologically vulnerable to neuropsychological deficits that might underlie all these disorders. Others point to socialization factors, including parental reinforcement of aggressive behavior in boys and nurturance in girls, same-sex role modeling of aggression, and the peer group, which enforces sex-role stereotypic behavior such as an assertive-dominant style in males. Others hypothesize that girls misbehave in less overt ways. For example, while boys are more likely than girls to engage in physical aggression, girls engage in *relational aggression*: attempting to hurt others by ridiculing them, excluding them from the peer group, withdrawing friendship, and spreading rumors (Crick & Grotpeter, 1995).

Conduct-disordered girls and boys also tend to be identified on the basis of different kinds of behavior problems. Fighting and theft are the most frequent reasons for referring boys, while *covert antisocial activities* such as truancy are more often the cause for concern about girls (Zahn-Waxler, 1993).

Gender also appears to be a factor in *age of onset*. While boys and girls tend to go through the same sequence of behavior problems in the progression toward CD, these misbehaviors have a later onset in girls than in boys. Antisocial behavior usually starts at age 8 to 10 for boys, while for girls it generally does not appear until age 14 to 16 (Kazdin, 1997a).

Developmental factors also come into play in other gender-differentiated ways. For example, *sex-*

ual maturation is a powerful predictor of antisocial behavior for girls. Girls who develop early tend to engage in more norm-violating behavior, such as staying out late without parental permission, cheating on exams, being truant, taking drugs, and having unprotected sex (Simmons & Blyth, 1987). The reason for this appears to be that early maturing girls spend more time with older peers who involve them precociously in risk-taking behavior, as we will explore further when we discuss peer influences.

Despite these gender differences in prevalence, there is also evidence that, for those girls who do develop CD, the *continuity* is equivalent to that seen in boys. Bardone and colleagues (1996) found that among girls, CD at age 15 predicted antisocial behavior, substance dependence, and poor achievement in young adulthood.

Etiology

The Intrapersonal Context

As we have seen, there is a continuum between normalcy and psychopathology, and deviations in fundamental developmental processes underlie many disorders. Therefore, to better understand what has gone awry in the development of those children who come to be labeled "conduct-disordered," it will be helpful to review what is known about some of the major developmental variables underlying problem behavior: aggression, self-control, perspective taking, and interpersonal problem solving.

Aggression   CD is a syndrome or complex of behaviors; therefore, aggression does not define it any more than a sad mood defines depression. Indeed, aggression is part of normal development, and there is no reason for assuming that a "hothead" or a "scrapper" has CD if other aspects of his or her personality are proceeding apace. However, aggression is a major part of the picture of CD and accounts for the symptoms that raise the most concern in those who attempt to intervene with antisocial youth. Therefore, it is important to consider the natural course of aggression and its role in normative and pathological development.

Olweus's (1979) landmark review of sixteen longitudinal studies of aggression in boys sets the stage. Olweus concludes that there is a substantial degree of *continuity* in aggression over time; indeed, it seems to be as stable as intelligence. He summarizes the findings with a simple formula: the younger the subject and the longer the interval of time between evaluations, the less the stability. Thus, over the same interval of time, a 2-year-old's aggressiveness will vary more than that of a 10-year-old; and at any given age, predictability decreases with the passage of time. By the time a boy is 8 or 9, there is a substantial correlation with aggressive patterns ten to fourteen years later; by 12 to 13 years of age, the stability is even higher for the next 10 years and is a powerful predictor of later aggression.

The stability of aggressive behavior in the face of development and environmental variation leads Olweus to conclude that it arises from an inherent tendency or motivational system within the individual. In other words, rather than reacting to environmental provocation, highly aggressive children may actively seek out conflicts in order to express their impulses.

Loeber (1991) summarizes research on the factors associated with the *persistence* of aggression. In general, these are early onset; extremely high rates of such behavior; occurrence in more than one setting, such as home, school, and community; and multiple problem behaviors.

What about *discontinuity*—is aggression "outgrown"? Data to answer this question come from Kohn's (1977) five-year longitudinal study of 1,232 preschoolers. Kohn asked teachers to rate aggressive traits in children, including open defiance with teachers, hostility, and aggression with other children. While aggressiveness was highly consistent over the five-year period, the correlation of .36 was sufficiently low to indicate that a good deal of change was also taking place. Analysis of the data revealed that 59 percent of those high in aggressiveness during preschool were no longer disturbed in the fourth grade; moreover, 14 percent of the highest-scoring aggressive children were subsequently among the most well-functioning fourth graders. In contrast, 13 percent of the children whose behavior was positively rated during preschool were now extremely aggressive.

Self-Control   Self-control is essential to normative functioning, and the expectations placed on children to control their impulses increase with age. While we might not be surprised to see a 4-year-old have a temper tantrum on the floor of the grocery store when denied an ice cream cone, such behavior in a 14-year-old would raise a few eyebrows. However, the 4-year-old is still expected to refrain from attacking a sibling in a rage, masturbating in a restaurant, or trying out a new toy hammer on the stereo set. Early socialization of self-control is particularly important because toddlers and preschoolers have a strong desire for immediate gratification of their aggressive, sexual, and exploratory urges, and they tend to be egocentric and self-seeking. However, objective studies confirm that conduct-disordered children evidence a limited ability to delay impulses and tolerate frustration (see Hinshaw and Anderson, 1996).

Kochanska and Aksan (1995) have conducted studies devoted to uncovering the roots of self-control in young children, which they view as an outgrowth of the internalization of parental values (see Chapter 2). The researchers placed young children in a laboratory situation in which they were given time alone in a room with an attractive toy that their mothers had forbidden them to touch; self-control was indicated by their ability to resist the temptation. Those children who showed "committed compliance"—an eager and wholehearted endorsement of their mother's values, as opposed to mere obedience—were those who had experienced the most *mutually positive* affect in the parent–child relationship.

Further, Kochanska's (1997) research has shown that specific parenting styles are optimal for promoting self-control in children with different temperaments. Using longitudinal data, she found that for children assessed as fearful in toddlerhood, a gentle maternal discipline style was most effective. However, for children assessed as fearless, gentleness was not sufficient. Instead, mothers needed to heighten their emotional bond with children in order to foster the motivation to accept and internalize parental values. Therefore, conscience development in temperamentally difficult children, who are at risk for CD, may require the most *intensely involved* and *emotionally available* parenting—the kind they are least likely to receive.

Emotion Regulation   *Emotion regulation* is a specific aspect of self-control that has been implicated in the development of CD (Cole et al., 1996). Children chronically exposed to family adversity, poor parenting, and high levels of conflict, as we saw in Chapter 7, are overwhelmed by strong emotions and receive little help in managing them from stressed and unskilled parents. Therefore, they are at risk for failing to develop adequate strategies for coping with their negative emotions and regulating their expression. Consistent with this idea, research has shown that conduct-disordered children have difficulty managing strong affects, particularly anger, and that children with poor emotion regulation skills are more likely to respond aggressively to interpersonal problems (Eisenberg et al., 1997).

As was pointed out in Chapter 2, however, emotion regulation may involve not only underregulation but also overregulation. A good example of this can be found in Cole, Zahn-Waxler, and Smith's (1994) study. In order to obtain a sample of preschoolers at risk for developing CD, they specifically recruited children who were noncompliant, aggressive, and hard to manage. As expected, at-risk boys were more likely to respond to frustration by directing displays of negative affect to the experimenters, and they had more difficulty managing their anger. Poor emotion regulation, in turn, was related to symptoms of disruptive behavior and oppositionality. For girls, however, *overcontrol* of negative emotions predicted CD symptoms. Attempting to put too tight a lid on anger may cause it simply to spill over at a later time.

Perspective Taking, Moral Development, and Empathy   Piaget (1967) observed that one of the pivotal developments in the transition to middle childhood is decentering; that is, shifting from cognitive egocentrism—in which the world is viewed primarily from the child's own vantage point—to cognitive perspectivism—in which a situation can be seen from the diverse views of the individuals involved and their rights and feelings taken into account. **Perspective taking**, the ability to see things from others' point of view, is fundamental to the development of moral reasoning and empathy, both of which can counter the tendency to behave in antisocial and aggressive ways.

Research attests to the fact that aggressive and conduct-disordered youth are delayed in the development of these cognitive and affective variables. In contrast to their nondelinquent peers, juvenile delinquents are more cognitively immature in their *moral reasoning* (Smetana, 1990). In addition, conduct-disordered youth are less *empathic*, as well as being less accurate in reading the emotions of others when compared to their nondisturbed peers (Cohen & Strayer, 1996). Happe and Frith (1996) go so far as to propose that a conduct-disordered youth's lack of social insight and understanding of other people's mental states is akin to the deficits in *theory of mind* seen in autistic children. Accordingly, conduct-disordered youth tend to misperceive the motives of others and to exhibit distortions in their reasoning about social situations, both of which increase the likelihood that they will respond in an aggressive manner. We next turn to these social cognitive dimensions underlying problem behavior.

Social Cognition   Eron and Huesmann (1990), in musing about the stability of aggression across time and generations, state: "The frightening implication of this intractable consistency is that aggression is not situation specific or determined solely by the contingencies. The individual carries around something inside that impels him or her to act in a characteristically aggressive or nonaggressive way" (pp. 152–153). They conclude that underlying aggression are *cognitive schemata*: scripts for interpreting and responding to events that are derived from past experiences and are used to guide future behavior.

Some evidence suggests that children with CD have distinctive *social-information processing* styles (Crick and Dodge, 1994). For example, aggressive children misattribute aggressive intent to others when in an ambiguous situation, are insensitive to social cues that might help them more correctly interpret others' intentions, and respond impulsively on the basis of their faulty assumptions. In addition, these children are able to generate few alternatives for solving interpersonal problems, and they have positive expectations of the outcomes of aggression.

These social-information processing patterns have also been shown to account for the relationship between early experiences of maltreatment and later childhood aggression (Dodge et al., 1995). Harsh and abusive parenting appears to instill in children a generalized belief that others are hostile and have malicious intent toward them, an assumption that is verified each time they engage in negative exchanges with parents, peers, and others. Therefore, children come to internalize their experiences of family violence in ways that are deeply ingrained in their personalities and behavioral repertoires, replete with complex cognitive rationales that insure consistency in their behavior.

Selman and Schultz (1988) have proposed a model of the cognitive developmental processes underlying the ability to resolve interpersonal problems without resorting to aggression. Parallel to Kohlberg's stages of morality, the development of *interpersonal negotiation strategies* (INS) proceeds from lower to higher levels of cognitive complexity and comprehensiveness. Selman and Schultz delineate four stages of INS, which have both a thinking (cognitive) and a doing (action) component. (See Table 9.2.) The stages progress from physical aggression or withdrawal at Stage 0, to assertive ordering or submissive obedience at Stage 1, to persuasion and deference at Stage 2, and, finally, to collaboration at Stage 3.

Another contribution to understanding the cognitive basis for children's aggression and behavior problems has been made by Shure and Spivack (1988). They delineate the following cognitive components to *interpersonal problem solving* (IPS): a sensitivity to human problems, an ability to imagine alternative courses of action, an ability to conceptualize the means to achieve a given end, consideration of consequences, and an understanding of cause and effect in human relations.

There is a developmental unfolding of the components related to IPS. In the preschool period, *generating alternative solutions* to problems such as, "What could you do if your sister were playing with a toy you wanted?" is the single most significant predictor of interpersonal behavior in a classroom setting. Children who generate fewer alternatives are rated by their teachers as disruptive, disrespectful, and defiant, and unable to wait to take turns. In middle childhood, alternative thinking is still related to classroom adjustment, while *means–end thinking*

Table 9.2   Selman and Schultz's INS

Stage 0: Impulsive. The strategies are primitive—for example, based on fight or flight—and show no evidence of perspective taking. Either extremes of aggressiveness (e.g., "Tell him to screw off!") or passivity (e.g., "Just do what he says!") would be at this level.

Stage 1: Unilateral. Strategies here show an awareness of the other person's point of view and of the conflict that exists, but strategies are based on assertions of the child's needs or wants (e.g., "Tell him you are not going to show up") or simple accommodation (e.g., "He's the boss, so you've got to do what he says").

Stage 2: Self-reflective and reciprocal. Strategies are now based on reciprocal exchanges, with an awareness of the other party's point of view. However, negotiations are designed to protect the interests of the child: for example, "He'll help the boss out this time, and then the boss will owe him one."

Stage 3: Collaborative. The child or adolescent is now able to view the situation objectively, taking his or her own and the other person's perspective into account and recognizing that negotiations are necessary for the continuity of the relationship: for example, "The boss and he have to work it out together, so they might as well talk out their differences."

Source: Selman and Schultz, 1988.

emerges as an equally important correlate. For instance, when presented with the problem of a boy's feeling lonely after moving to a new neighborhood, the well-adjusted child can think not only of different solutions but also of ways to implement the solutions and overcome the obstacles involved, such as saying, "Maybe he could find someone who liked to play Nintendo like he does, but he'd better not go to a kid's house at suppertime or his mother might get mad!" Again, impulsive and inhibited children are deficient in these cognitive skills.

The data on adolescence are meager but suggest that means–end thinking and alternative thinking continue to be correlated with good adjustment. The new component to IPS involves *considering consequences* or weighing the pros and cons of potential action: "If I do X, then someone else will do Y and that will be good (or bad)." Thus the developing child is able to utilize progressively advanced cognitive skills to solve interpersonal problems.

The Interpersonal Context: Family Influences

Attachment   Insecure attachments with parents in infancy have been linked prospectively to preschool behavior problems such as hostility, oppositionality, and defiance. However, insecure attachment relationships predict elementary school aggression in girls but not boys, and these predictions are influenced by a number of other factors related to family adversity and environmental stress. As Greenberg, Speltz, and Deklyen (1993) conclude, the research to date has not established a direct effect of attachment on antisocial behavior, although a poor parent–child relationship is a clear risk factor for the development of psychopathology in general.

Family Discord   First, looking at whole-family processes, we find that family discord is fertile soil for producing antisocial acting out, especially in boys (Shaw et al., 1994). In particular, children exposed to *family violence* are more likely to develop behavior problems (Jouriles et al., 1996). Children exposed to violence in the home also start delinquent careers at an earlier age and perpetrate more serious offenses (Kruttschnitt & Dornfeld, 1993). Further, the children are often the targets of their parents' aggression; e.g., youths with CD are more likely to have been victims of *child maltreatment* (Dodge et al., 1994).

CD is also associated with nonviolent forms of *interparental conflict* (Cummings & Davies, 1994b) and *divorce* (Emery & Kitzmann, 1995). However, it is not coming from a "broken home" per se that leads to child behavior problems, but rather the turmoil and disruptions in parent–child relationships surrounding marital dissolution that increase the likelihood of antisocial acting out, as we explore in more detail in Chapter 14.

Boys growing up in *single-parent* households are also at risk. Vaden-Kiernan and colleagues (1995) found that, once family income, neighborhood, and earlier aggressive behavior were taken into account, boys with a father or father-figure in the home were less likely to be rated as aggressive than boys in mother-only families. No such relationship between family type and aggression was found for girls. On the other hand, there is evidence that boys are rarely juvenile delinquents in mother-alone families if the mother has good parenting skills and the parent–child relationship is a supportive one (McCord, 1990). Again, it is not the family structure that matters so much as the emotional quality of relationships within the family.

Family stress also increases the likelihood of CD. Children who develop behavior problems are more likely to come from families that have experienced more negative life events, daily hassles, unemployment, financial hardship, moves, and other disruptions. In addition, the family members of disruptive children have few sources of social support and engage in chronic conflict with others in the community (McMahon & Estes, 1997). However, it may be that family stress is not a direct cause of antisocial behavior but rather that it acts as an amplifier of other problematic parent–child relationship processes (Dishion, French, & Patterson, 1995).

Parent Psychopathology   Parental *substance abuse*, especially in fathers, is predictive of CD in children. *Maternal depression* has also been linked to child conduct problems, as well as a number of other kinds of maladjustment (Cummings & Davies, 1994a).

The most powerful parent-related predictor of CD in children is parent *antisocial personality disorder*, which increases both the incidence and the persistence of the CD. For example, Lahey and colleagues (1995) conducted a four-year prospective study of 171 children diagnosed with CD. Parental antisocial personality disorder was correlated with CD at the first assessment and, in combination with boys' verbal intelligence, predicted the continuation of conduct problems in later development. How does parent personality translate into child behavior problems? This question concerns us next.

Harsh Parenting and the Intergenerational Transmission of Aggression   There is strong evidence for the *intergenerational transmission* of aggression. Aggression is not only stable within a single generation but across generations as well. Eron and Huesmann (1990) conducted a 22-year prospective study, compiling data on 82 participants when they were 8 and 30 years of age, as well as collecting information from their parents and 8-year-old children. Strong associations were seen between grandparents', parents', and children's aggressiveness. The correlation between the aggression parents had shown at age 8 and that displayed by their children was remarkably high (.65), higher even than the consistency in parents' own behavior across the lifespan.

While the mechanisms responsible for the continuity of this behavior are not clear, Eron and Huesmann believe it is learned through *modeling*. As noted above, children who have antisocial parents are exposed to models of aggressive behavior, including interparental violence and child maltreatment. However, the aggression need not be so extreme in order to provide a model. For example, adult antisocial behavior is predicted by *harsh punishment* received as a child (Eron & Huesmann, 1990). In adulthood, those punished harshly as children were more likely endorse using severe discipline in child rearing—in fact, their responses to parenting style questionnaires were strikingly similar to the ones given by their own parents 22 years earlier.

Corresponding results have been obtained regarding the relationship between *spanking* and child aggression. Straus, Sugarman, and Gile-Sims (1997) followed a nationally representative sample of over 800 children ages 6 to 9 over a two-year period and found that spanking was associated with increased aggression and antisocial behavior. Childhood corporal punishment also increases the risk that men will become spousal batterers in adulthood (Straus & Yodanis, 1996). In sum, through their observations of their own parents, children learn that the rule governing interpersonal relationships is "might makes right."

Parenting Inconsistency Other research indicates that it is not only the severity of parental discipline but also a pattern of *parental inconsistency*—an inconsistent mix of harshness and laxness—that is related to antisocial acting out. Laxness may be evidenced in a number of ways: lack of supervision, parents being unconcerned with the children's whereabouts, absence of rules concerning where the children can go and whom they can be with. These are parents who, when phoned by researchers and asked, "It is 9 P.M.; do you know where your child is right now?" do not know the answer (Forgatch, 1994).

Coercion Theory Patterson, Reid, and Dishion (1992) have carried out an important program of research on the family origins of conduct disorder. Based on social learning theory, they set out to investigate the factors that might train antisocial behavior in children. They found that parents of antisocial children were more likely than others to *positively reinforce* aggressive behavior—for example, by regarding it as amusing. They also observed that these parents exhibited inconsistent outbursts of anger and punitiveness, and made harsh threats with no follow-through, both of which were ineffectual in curbing negative behavior. On the other side of the coin, children's prosocial behavior was either ignored or reinforced noncontingently. Therefore, the investigators conclude that CD is initiated and sustained in the home by maladaptive parent–child interactions.

Patterson's most important contribution was to analyze the interactions of antisocial children and their parents in terms of what he calls coercive family processes. By **coercion**, Patterson means negative behavior on the part of one person that is supported or directly reinforced by another person. These interactions are transactional and reciprocal; they involve both parent and child, whose responses to one another influence each other's behavior. For example, Patterson notes that the families of normal and CD children have different ways of responding to each other. When punished by parents, CD children are twice as likely as normal children to persist in negative behavior. This is because their family members tend to interact through the use of *negative reinforcement*. Unlike punishment, in which an unpleasant stimulus is applied in order to decrease a behavior, negative reinforcement increases the likelihood of a behavior by removing an unpleasant stimulus as the reward.

To illustrate this concept, consider the scenario presented in Figure 9.4. Who is reinforcing whom? Calvin has learned that if he behaves aversively

Figure 9.4   Coercion.

when his father says no, he can get his way—his father has inadvertently *positively reinforced* him for misbehaving. His father, in turn, has been *negatively reinforced* for giving Calvin what he wants when he misbehaves—he is rewarded by the fact that the child ceases his misbehavior.

Calvin's father has fallen into what Patterson calls the *"reinforcement trap"*: he obtains a short-term benefit at the expense of negative long-term consequences. The trap is that by giving in, he has ended Calvin's immediate negative behavior but has inadvertently increased the likelihood that he will behave the same way in the future. Through the reinforcement trap, children are inadvertently rewarded for aggressiveness and the escalation of coercive behavior, and parents are rewarded for giving in by the relief they experience when children cease their obstreperousness. However, the parents pay a heavy price. Not only are their socializing efforts negated, but their children's behavior will become increasingly coercive over time.

Transactional Processes   Another significant aspect to Patterson's observations is that they involve *transactional* processes between parents and children, such that they affect and shape one another's behavior. A number of investigators agree. For example, Campbell (1997) has observed the relationship between parenting stress and preschool children's aggressiveness and noncompliance. She infers

a bidirectional process whereby the stressed mother becomes more restrictive and negative when trying to cope with her impulsive, noncompliant child; this, in turn, makes the child more difficult to handle.

On a similar note, Dumas, LaFreniere, and Serketich (1995) studied the interactions between mothers and their children, who were categorized as being socially competent, anxious, or aggressive. Surprisingly, they found that aggressive children and their mothers overall shared a positive emotional tone. However, in comparison to other dyads, aggressive children were more likely to use *aversive control techniques*, and their mothers were more likely to *respond indiscriminately* and to *fail to set limits* on their children's more extreme forms of coercion. Thus, they conclude, both parents and young children are active agents in the interaction and reciprocally influence one another.

Others take a different view of who is in the driver's seat. Lytton (1990) describes a provocative experiment that tested the hypothesis that problematic parenting is a functioning of children's behavior. The investigators observed mothers of conduct-disordered and normative boys interacting with their own sons, an unrelated conduct-disordered boy, or an unrelated well-behaved child. As hypothesized, all mothers were more negative and demanding with conduct-disordered boys, with the highest rates of negativity displayed by mothers of antisocial children when interacting with their own sons.

However, when interacting with a normative child, mothers of conduct-disordered children behaved like any other mother. Lytton points to this study, as well as to evidence indicating that some children have a constitutional bias to be aggressive, difficult to manage, and underresponsive to rewards and punishments, in order to argue that we should not underestimate the child's contribution to aversive parent–child relationships.

In general, while attending to the child's contribution is a healthy antidote to parent-blaming, the prevailing opinion seems to be that transactional parent–child processes are more likely to provide an accurate explanation than is either a child-only focus or a parent-only focus (Dodge, 1990).

A Developmental Perspective on Parenting and Conduct Disorder

Shaw and Bell (1993) reviewed the available evidence in support of various parenting contributions to the development of antisocial behavior and constructed a speculative transactional account of how they might each come into play over the course of development.

During the first stage of life, from birth to 2 years of age, Shaw and Bell propose that the most important factor is likely to be *maternal responsiveness*. Through inconsistent and neglectful caregiving, nonresponsive mothers may contribute to the development of irritable, impulsive, and difficult infants, as well as to an insecure attachment. In the second stage, from 2 to 4 years, *parental demandingness* is hypothesized to take on greater importance. Rather than forming a "goal-directed partnership" based on mutual negotiation and compromise, the mothers of future antisocial children are more likely to initiate coercive and punitive patterns of exchange, which, in turn, contribute to children's further noncompliance and negativism. In the third stage, from 4 to 5 years, the most important factor is *parental inconsistency* or laxness in discipline. At this stage, as children begin to transfer the oppositional and coercive patterns of exchange learned at home to their peer relationships and school behavior, conduct problems intensify and the consequences become more severe, requiring increasing parental firmness and consistency. Instead, however, the parents of conduct-disordered children are likely to vacillate between ignoring misbehavior and employing—or merely threatening—harsh punishment.

Shaw and colleagues (1996) have just begun to test this developmental model. To date, they have followed a sample of children from infancy to age 5. Consistent with the model, they found that disorganized attachment was a predictor of disruptive behavior during the first year, while from the second year onward, maternal personality problems and parent–child conflicts also contributed.

The Interpersonal Context: Peer Relations

Children with CD are readily identified by peers. They are argumentative, easily angered, resentful, and deliberately annoying to others (Kazdin, 1997a). As early as the preschool period, habitual child aggression is associated with subsequent *peer rejection*, which leads, in turn, to further aggressive behavior (Capaldi & Patterson, 1994; Coie et al., 1995). Aggressive children also gain a *negative reputation* with peers that continues to follow them even when their behavior improves. Therefore, transactions between conduct-disordered children and their peers can contribute to further aggression and problem behavior.

There is another side to the coin, however. By middle childhood, while aggressive children may be avoided by their prosocial agemates, they are apt to be accepted into *antisocial peer groups* that tolerate or even value problem behavior. Antisocial youths spend most of their time in peer groups with no adult supervision, staying out after curfew, "hanging out" on the streets, and engaging in risky behavior. Thus, antisocial youth tend to gravitate toward one another and reinforce one another's behavior.

Consistent with this, Dishion, French, and Patterson (1995) found that peer rejection at age 10 (along with academic failure) predicted involvement with antisocial peers at age 12, more so than did parental discipline or monitoring practices. Involvement with antisocial peers, in turn, predicts escalating misbehavior (Kupersmidt, Burchinal, & Patterson, 1995). Similarly, Fergusson and Horwood's (1996) longitudinal research showed that association with antisocial peers had a reinforcing and sustaining effect on youth misbehavior from childhood to adolescence. Notably, one of the characteristics that accounted for the 12 percent of their sample of disruptive children who did not go on to develop adolescent CD was their lower rates of affiliation with delinquent peers.

Peer factors can be seen clearly in the development of CD during late childhood and adolescence in girls. As noted previously, *early sexual maturation* is a powerful predictor of antisocial behavior for females. Although at first blush sexual maturation might be assumed to be a strictly biological factor, the onset of menarche has important social implications. Puberty results in noticeable secondary sexual characteristics, such as breast development, which, for the first girl in her class to need a bra, can be a source of teasing from same-sex peers and unwanted sexual attention from males. In fact, evidence suggests that peer relations mediate the link between sexual maturation and norm violation. Early maturing girls attract the attention of older males who engage in norm-violating behavior and, in turn, involve the girls precociously in risk-taking behaviors and sexual activity (Simmons & Blyth, 1987). Late maturers evidence similar behavioral problems after they biologically "catch up" with their early maturing peers.

The mediating role of *heterosexual peer relationships* was made explicit by Caspi and coworkers (1993), who followed 297 girls from childhood to adolescence. They found that early maturation was only a risk factor for girls who attended mixed-sex schools. Those who attended all-female schools were not exposed to the social influences that made early maturation a predictor of conduct problems for other girls. In turn, CD in girls is related to a high risk for *teenage pregnancy* (Zoccolillo, 1997). Thus, it appears that peer modeling of antisocial behavior and increased pressure for sexual relations from males account for the effects of biological maturation on girls' behavior.

Not all children and youth are equally susceptible to peer influences, however. Vitaro and colleagues (1997) followed a sample of almost 900 boys from age 11 to age 13. Based on teacher reports, they typologized boys and their friends as moderately dis-

ruptive, highly disruptive, or conforming. Moderately disruptive boys who associated with disruptive peers engaged in more delinquent behavior as time went on. However, friends appeared to have no impact on the development of behavior problems in highly disruptive or conforming boys. For these latter two groups of youth, *intrapersonal characteristics* seem to be steering their development—in a positive direction when associated with prosocial skills but in a negative direction when associated with antisocial traits.

In sum, research on the influence of peers indicates that they are a contributing factor but not a determining one. Two different processes seem to be at work, which we might term "pushing" versus "pulling." While early aggression may cause a child to be pushed away by prosocial peers, positive attachments to antisocial peers may pull a youth in the direction of engaging in escalating misbehavior. This latter influence may be particularly important for understanding adolescent-onset CD. In fact, association with *antisocial peers* has a direct effect on delinquency only in the *adolescent-onset type*, while *parent socialization* is a more significant causal factor in the *child-onset* form of the disorder. For adolescent-onset conduct-disordered youth, then, antisocial peer influences appear to be essential, while for early onset youth the picture is more complicated.

The Superordinate Context

A number of superordinate factors are associated with the risk of CD. In particular, children growing up in communities marked by *poverty* and *violence* are more likely to develop antisocial behavior and CD (Osofsky, 1995). Impoverished inner-city children in the United States are routinely exposed to shocking degrees of violence: by age 5 most have seen a shooting, and by adolescence one-third have witnessed a murder (Bell & Jenkins, 1993). Chronic exposure to violence may desensitize children to these experiences. For example, Lorion and Satzman (1993) found that fifth- and sixth-grade children living in high-crime neighborhoods described the shootings, police raids, and dead bodies they had seen in blasé terms, as "nothing special." Further, the gang and drug culture of the inner cities offer few alternatives to youths, who feel they must join in, in order to survive.

Additionally, Kasen, Johnson, and Cohen (1990) found that a *school environment* characterized by a high degree of conflict (fighting, vandalism, defiant students, and teachers unable to maintain order) was related to an increase in CD over a two-year period.

At a larger social level, the *media* may also play a role in promoting—and even glamorizing—antisocial behavior. Violence has become a mainstay of American television and movies, is perpetrated by heroes as much as by villains, and is seldom met with negative consequences (Eron & Huesmann, 1990). Instead, the lesson is largely communicated that violence is an effective method of solving problems and will be rewarded. Research bears out the relationship between television violence and children's behavior. Children with strong preferences for viewing violent television programs are more aggressive than their peers, and laboratory studies also show that increased viewing of aggressive material leads to subsequent increases in aggressive behavior. Further, longitudinal studies also show that children who prefer violent television programs during elementary school engage in more violent and criminal activity as adults (Eron et al., 1996).

Further insights into specific cultural influences have also been offered, particularly regarding the role of *masculine socialization* in the development of male aggression. For instance, Cohen and colleagues (1996) describe the masculine ethic of the American South as a "culture of honor," which requires that males use physical force in order to defend against perceived insults to their own or their family's reputation. The investigators demonstrated this empirically by instructing a confederate to purposely bump into male research participants and to make a profane and personally disparaging comment. While Northerners were relatively unaffected by the insult, those participants who originated from the South were more likely to feel that their masculinity was threatened, to show heightened physiological arousal and signs of distress, to be more cognitively primed for aggression, and to be more likely to retaliate with violent behavior. The investigators interpret this response as a product of social learning, such that their cultural upbringing leads Southern men to experience interpersonal problems as threats to masculine honor that must be defended through physical aggression.

In sum, opportunities for learning antisocial behavior—and reinforcements for engaging in it—abound in the school, neighborhood, and the culture at large.

The Organic Context

Recent attention has been drawn to the possibility of uncovering organic factors underlying the development of CD. While much of this research is still in progress, and little of it is definitive, a number of suggestive leads have been identified.

One of the best predictors of conduct problems in children is parental criminality or antisocial behavior, especially when research focuses on fathers and sons. This may well be due to a *genetic* factor; however, environmental explanations cannot be ruled out. In general, there is evidence for both (Pike et al., 1996). For example, Ge and colleagues (1996) collected data on biological and adoptive parents of adolescents adopted at birth. Antisocial behavior in biological parents was significantly related to the aggressiveness of children adopted out of the home, providing evidence for a genetic influence. However, the adoptive parents' parenting practices also predicted children's aggression, suggesting that environmental influences also exist.

A shortcoming of the genetic research is that most of it has not attended to the subtypes of CD that have emerged as so important in our review of the literature. While adolescent-onset conduct problems show little evidence for continuity across the generations, evidence for heritability has been demonstrated for the childhood-onset version of the disorder (Frick & Jackson, 1993). On a similar note, Edelbrock and associates (1995) found a significant heritability quotient for overt aggression in twins, but not for covert, nonaggressive behavior problems.

Psychophysiological indicators also set early onset, aggressive, and undersocialized youth apart from their peers. These children demonstrate lower overall autonomic arousal, demonstrated by low heart rate and galvanic skin response. Youth with low heart rates are likely to fight and bully others at school, and are more likely to become violent adults. Low autonomic arousal leads to stimulation-seeking and behavioral undercontrol on the one hand, and diminished reactivity to punishment on the other. Quay (1993) hypothesizes that these children have an *underactive behavioral inhibition system*, leading to impulsive responding, heightened reactivity to reward, and an insensitivity to aversive stimuli.

A number of *biochemical* correlates have also been investigated (Hinshaw & Anderson, 1996). Testosterone is a likely candidate because of its relation to aggression in animals. However, research on humans indicates that such hormonal differences are not sufficient to account for aggressive and antisocial behavior, although they may serve a mediating role in individual responses to environmental circumstances. Low levels of serotonin and cortisol also have been linked to aggression in children, although it is worth noting that these deficits have also been identified as factors in the development of a quite different disorder, depression.

Moffit and Lynam (1994) propose that underlying the development of both CD and ADHD are neuropsychological dysfunctions associated with a *difficult temperament*, which predisposes children to impulsivity, irritability, and overactivity. Consistent with this, Newman and colleagues (1997) found that children who showed a difficult, undercontrolled temperamental type at age 3 were more likely to be rated as antisocial in adulthood. However, other longitudinal research indicates that the link between aggression and difficult temperament is not a direct one; instead, it is mediated by family factors (see McMahon and Estes, 1997).

Those pursuing research in the organic domain argue that the existence of biological factors in no way rules out or discounts the importance of social and psychological influences. In fact, there is a general appreciation of the complex *interplay* between psychology and biology. For example, Moffit and Lynam (1994) posit that neuropsychological dysfunctions may have a complex indirect relationship with conduct problems, such as through increasing children's vulnerability to stress. In contrast, Lahey and coworkers (1993) argue that stressful childhood experiences may become transformed into conduct problems through the changes they cause in neuropsychological activity. In a similar vein, Richters and Cicchetti (1993) propose that chronically violent environments might act on the autonomic nervous system in ways that promote underreactivity and the propensity toward disordered behavior. As with the other psychopathologies we have studied, there has been a progression from the "either/or" debates of the past to a new perspective of "yes, and . . ." regarding the relationship between nature and nurture.

Integrative Developmental Model

Patterson and his colleagues have been studying and theorizing about the origins of child conduct problems for over two decades. They provide an integrative developmental model based partly on research and partly on their own observations and experience. (Our presentation is based on Dishion, French, and Patterson, 1995; Patterson, DeBaryshe, and Ramsey, 1989; Patterson, Reid, and Dishion, 1992; and Capaldi and Patterson, 1994.)

The process of "growing" a conduct-disordered youth takes place in a series of hierarchical stages that build upon and elaborate one another, consistent with the organizational hypothesis of developmental psychopathology. (See Figure 9.5). The process begins with a host of risk factors, some of which are in place before the birth of the child. These include low socioeconomic status, living in a high-crime neighborhood, family stress, antisocial parents, and the parents' own history of being reared by unskilled caregivers. However, these risk factors do not directly lead to antisocial behavior. Rather, their effect is mediated by family variables: the basic training camp for antisocial behavior is the home.

The first stage begins in early childhood and involves *poor parental discipline strategies*, with initial coercive interactions escalating into increasingly punitive exchanges. Other poor parent management skills include little involvement and monitoring of children, inconsistency, lack of contingent positive reinforcement, and an absence of effective strategies for solving problems. The products of these dysfunctional family interactions are antisocial, socially incompetent children with low self-esteem.

The next stage occurs in middle childhood when children enter school, where their antisocial behavior and social incompetence result in *peer rejection*

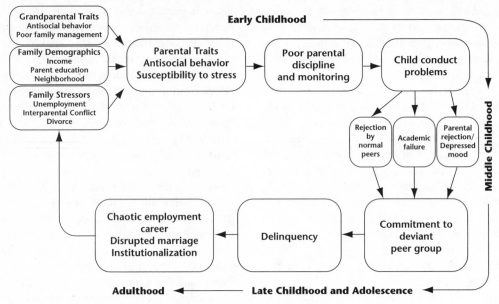

Figure 9.5   Patterson's Model of Conduct Disorder.

Source: Adapted from Patterson, DeBaryshe, and Ramsey, 1989; Patterson, Reid, and Dishion, 1992; and Capaldi and Patterson, 1994

and *poor academic performance*. Failures in these important developmental tasks also contribute to a *depressed mood*. Further, children who chronically bring home negative reports from teachers are more likely to experience *conflicts with parents*, and to be rejected by them.

In adolescence, these youths are drawn to a *deviant peer group* that has a negative attitude toward school and authority and is involved in *delinquency* and substance abuse. These delinquent peers support further problem behavior. As development proceeds, adolescents with an antisocial lifestyle are more likely to have similar difficulties in adulthood, including a *chaotic employment career*, a *disrupted marriage*, and *institutionalization* for crimes or mental disorder. In late adolescence and adulthood, the "assortative mating" process increases the likelihood that antisocial individuals will form relationships with partners with similar personalities and conduct problems. As stressed, unskilled, and antisocial individuals form families and have children of their own, the *intergenerational cycle* is complete.

Intervention

The continuity of CD from childhood to adulthood indicates that this is a psychopathology that becomes entrenched in early development and has long-lasting consequences. Further, other individuals and society pay a high price, in terms of both personal suffering and the dollars-and-cents costs of violence, property destruction, theft, and incarceration. Thus, there is an urgent need for prevention and treatment. Yet the multiple roots of CD—cognitive and affective dysfunctions within the child, psychopathology and discord within the family, encouragement from similarly disordered peers and society at large—present major obstacles to success in both undertakings. As Eron and Huesmann (1990) state, intervention with CD "will take all the knowledge, ingenuity, talent, and persistence we can muster" (p. 154).

In a recent review of the empirical literature, Kazdin (1997b) identified four treatments that seem to be the most promising for CD: parent management training, interpersonal problem-solving skills training, functional family therapy, and multisystemic therapy. We describe these next.

Behavioral Therapy: Parent Management Training

Parent management training (**PMT**) is one of the most successful and best-documented behavioral programs. PMT was developed by Patterson (see Forgatch and Patterson, 1998) based on his model of maladaptive parent–child relationships as central to the etiology of CD. PMT focuses on altering the interactions between parent and child so that prosocial rather than coercive behavior is reinforced. As the name implies, this is accomplished by training the parents to interact more effectively with the child, based on the principles of social learning theory. Parents learn to implement a number of behavior modification techniques, including the use of *positive reinforcement* for prosocial behavior and the use *mild punishment* such as the use of a "time-out" chair. This is a technique with a large body of empirical research behind it, and we will describe it in more detail when we discuss intervention in Chapter 17.

Cognitive-Behavioral Therapy: Social Problem-Solving Skills Training

As noted above, Shure and Spivack (1988) found that conduct-disordered children show poor problem-solving skills when faced with interpersonal problems. Consequently, their focus in intervention is on helping children to develop *interpersonal problem-solving skills* such as *generating alternative solutions* to problems, *anticipating the consequences* of their behavior, and *planning* and approaching problems in a step-by-step fashion. Structured games and stories are used to practice these skills, and they are progressively applied to more real-life situations. This technique is also described in more detail in Chapter 17.

Systemic Family Therapy

Functional family therapy (FFT) integrates behavioral, cognitive, and systemic perspectives (Alexander & Parsons, 1982). As the name implies,

behavior problems are viewed in the context of the functions they serve in the family. For example, misbehaving may be the only way that children can get needs for structure or intimacy met, or may be the only way that children can de-triangulate themselves from a troubled family system. (See Chapter 1.) Consistent with Minuchin's family systems approach, the goal of therapy is to help family members communicate and problem-solve in ways that allow them to meet these needs more satisfactorily. Although relatively few studies have been carried out to assess the effectiveness of FFT, those that do exist demonstrate a consistent positive outcome (Alexander, Holtzworth-Munroe, & Jameson, 1994).

Multisystemic Therapy

Multisystemic therapy (MST) is the fourth treatment recommended by Kazdin for intervention with CD, and it is certainly the most comprehensive (Henggeler & Bourdin, 1990). MST takes to heart the lesson learned by previous investigators—namely, that there are multiple roots of antisocial behavior. While focused on the family system and grounded in family systems theory, the treatment is individualized and flexible, offering a variety of interventions depending on the special needs of the particular child. Thus, treatment may focus on family disharmony and school underachievement in one case, and lack of social skills and parental unemployment in another. The therapist models an active, practical, and solution-focused approach: "You say you didn't understand the teacher's feedback on Casey's school report? Let's give him a call right now and ask for more information."

Empirical studies show the efficacy of the multisystemic approach with severely conduct-disordered youth (Bourdin et al., 1995). Family communication is improved, with a reduction in family patterns of triangulation and lower levels of conflict between parents and children and between parents themselves. Follow-up studies have shown that, for as long as 5 years following treatment, youths who receive MST have lower arrest rates than those who receive other forms of treatment.

Prevention

As Kazdin (1997b) notes, prevention efforts need to be as multifaceted and broad-based as are the risk factors for CD. A combination of family management training for parents and interpersonal problem-solving skills training for children has been used to good effect in prevention programs for kindergarteners and at-risk school-age children (McCord et al., 1994; Tremblay et al., 1995). Five, and even ten years later, those who had undergone these programs were achieving better in school and demonstrating less antisocial behavior than untreated youth.

In the previous five chapters, we have been concerned with disorders whose symptoms lie somewhere along the continuum between normal and abnormal. Depressed feelings, misconduct, anxiety, oppositionality, and inattentiveness all can be seen in well-functioning individuals across the life span. Our next chapter concerns a disorder which, like autism, lies at the extreme end of the continuum. The pervasive and erratic symptoms of schizophrenia lie far beyond the pale of normal development and thus present a major challenge to our ability to understand and treat the disorder.

Schizophrenia—A Severe Deviation of Middle Childhood and Adolescence

Like autism, schizophrenia is a severe, pervasive psychopathology that, in its extreme form, is incapacitating; however, in many other ways it differs significantly from autism. In this chapter we first present schizoprenia's descriptive characteristics and then spend a good deal of time reconstructing its developmental pathway, including both risk and protective factors. Regrettably, this pathway has none of the cohesiveness and richness of empirical data that marked our discussion of conduct disorder in Chapter 9. On the contrary, data are often sparse and fragmented. Attempted integrations are self-contained rather than enriching one another. Behavioral data are limited, in part because research interest has shifted to the organic context—although, even here, findings are more preliminary than definitive. In sum, in regard to schizophrenia a satisfactory answer to the question, Why does normal development go awry? is not yet available.

Definition and Characteristics

Definition

The relevant DSM-IV criteria for schizophrenia are presented in Table 10.1. In this section we will define and further elaborate on the major diagnostic features.

Hallucinations are sensory perceptions occurring in the absence of any appropriate external stimuli. Auditory hallucinations, such as hearing a voice saying "You are evil and should die" are more frequent than visual hallucinations, such as seeing a ghost with a burned and scarred face. The structure of hallucinations increases in complexity with age, while the content reflects age-appropriate concerns; for example, younger children have hallucinations about monsters and pets, while older children's hallucinations may involve sex. (See Russell, Bott, and Sammons, 1989.)

Hallucinations are not peculiar to schizophrenia, being also found in a number of psychiatric

Table 10.1 DSM-IV Criteria
for Schizophrenia

A. *Characteristic symptoms* Two (or more) of the
following, each present for a significant portion
of time during a 1-month period:
(1) delusions
(2) hallucinations
(3) disorganized speech (e.g., frequent derailment
or incoherence)
(4) grossly disorganized or catatonic behavior
(5) negative symptoms (i.e., affective flattening,
alogia, or avolition)
B. *Social/occupational dysfunction* When the onset is in
childhood, failure to achieve expected level of interpersonal, academic, or occupational achievement.
C. *Duration* Continuous signs of disturbance persist
for at least 6 months.

Reprinted with permission from the Diagnostic and Statistical Manual of Mental Disorders, Fourth Edition. Copyright 1994 American Psychiatric Association.

disorders and medical conditions as well as being a
response to drugs. For example, Altman, Collins, and
Mundy (1997) found that 33 percent of disturbed but
nonschizophrenic individuals reported hallucinations. They were particularly frequent in individuals
with posttraumatic stress disorder. Hallucinations are
also found in normal populations. Normal preschoolers, for example, can have transient hallucinations,
again in response to acute situational stress; for example, they may feel bugs crawling over their skin
or see bugs in their beds (Volkmar et al., 1995).

Delusions are firmly held, irrational beliefs that
run counter to reality. As with hallucinations, delusions become more complex with time, while their
content reflects age-appropriate concerns; for example, a younger boy might believe his stepfather wants
to kill him, while an older girl might think children
at school are plotting to kidnap and sexually molest
her. These two examples illustrate delusions of *per-
secution*. There are *somatic* delusions, such as believing the body is emitting a foul odor or feces will
come out of the mouth if the child speaks, and there
are also delusions of *grandeur*, as in the example of
a boy flipping through the pages of a book he has
never seen before and claiming he knows everything
the books says. Like hallucinations, delusions can
also be found in disturbed but nonschizophrenic pop-

ulations. For example, Altman, Collins, and Mundy
(1997) found that 24 percent of disturbed, nonschizophrenic individuals had delusional ideas.

Disorganized speech often involves loose associations and illogical reasoning in which the child's
language may be fragmented, dissociated, and
bizarre. For example:

> It's open in front but closed behind. I'm open in
> front but closed behind. Did you see me today? I
> think I was here, but Mommy wasn't. They don't
> take it away from Mommy. My dolly won't mind.
> I won't mind. [Enumerates all the family mem-
> bers who won't mind.] I was here yesterday. Was
> I here today?

There is evidence that the primary speech disorders
involve pragmatics, or the social use of language;
prosody, or the melody of speech; auditory processing, or attending to what others say while ignoring irrelevant information; and abstract language. However, these disorders do not distinguish
children with schizophrenia from those with autism.
(See Baltaxe and Simmons III, 1995.)

Grossly disorganized or catatonic behavior may
be expressed by facial grimaces; odd postures and
movements, such as persistent rocking while standing
or sitting; long periods of immobility; or bizarre repetitive actions such as incessantly rubbing the forehead
or angrily slapping the wrist or scratching the skin to
the point of producing open, bleeding sores. (For a
more detailed account, see Weiner, 1992.)

Social dysfunction may take a number of forms.
Withdrawal is common, with children with schizophrenia often being oblivious to others, excessively
preoccupied with their own thoughts, or puzzled by
things happening around them. Lack of social skills
may contribute to social isolation, particularly in regard to peers.

Subtypes of Schizophrenia Schizophrenia has
been divided into a number of subtypes. However,
only two will be relevant to our presentation of the
childhood version of the disorder.

First, the symptoms of schizophrenia have been
subsumed under the two broader categories of *positive*
and *negative*. Positive symptoms are characterized by
"the presence of . . ." and include thought disorders,

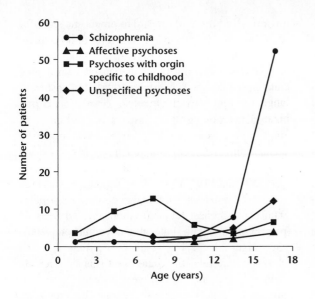

Source: Remschmidt et al., 1994

Figure 10.1
Increase in Schizophrenia in Adolescence.

delusions, and hallucinations. Negative symptoms are characterized by "an absence of . . ." and include sociability, pleasure, energy, and affect.

Another division is into the categories of process and reactive schizophrenia. In *process schizophrenia* there is a long history of deviance marked by chronic withdrawal, blunted affect, and below-average intelligence. The schizophrenic episode itself is not triggered by any specific stressful event. In *reactive schizophrenia*, children enjoy reasonably good physical and psychological health and make an adequate social and school adjustment. The schizophrenic reaction comes on suddenly, often in reaction to a stressful event, and is marked by volatile behavior such as excitement, agitation, and delusions. The prognosis for process schizophrenia is poor, whereas for reactive schizophrenia it is good. (For a more detailed presentation of subtypes, see Gooding and Iacono, 1995.)

Characteristics

Age of Onset   For our purposes the most important descriptive characteristic of schizophrenia is that it has two ages of onset: early onset (or childhood onset), which means it occurs prior to 14 to 15 years of age, and adolescent onset, which occurs between 14 to 15 years and young adulthood.

Prevalence   Childhood-onset schizophrenia is very rare. It is estimated that only 1 child in 10,000 will become schizophrenic (Asarnow & Asarnow, 1996). Because this type is so rare, it is also difficult to study, which in turn results in a certain tentativeness in conclusions drawn from research. After childhood the number of cases of schizophrenia rises dramatically, with one study showing an approximately tenfold increase in children between 12 and 15 years of age. This dramatic increase seems specific to schizophrenia, since it is not found in the affective psychoses such as depression or in other childhood psychoses (Häfner & Nowotny, 1995). (See Figure 10.1.)

Gender Differences   There is an interesting gender shift with age: males predominate in early-onset cases, but the male–female ratio becomes more even in adolescence. The reasons for this shift are not known.

Comorbidity   Taking child- and adolescent-onset schizophrenia together, there is evidence of a high rate of comorbidity. Russell, Bott, and Sammons (1989), for example, found that 68 percent of cases had another diagnosis, with depression being the most frequent (37 percent) followed closely by conduct/oppositional behavior.

Socioeconomic Status and Cultural Differences
While studies of adults with schizophrenia show an excess of cases from lower socioeconomic status groups, studies of children and adolescents have yielded equivocal findings. In a like manner, studies of adults show that the symptoms and incidence of schizophrenia in adults are highly similar across countries and cultures, but comparable data on children are not available (Asarnow & Asarnow, 1996).

Developmental Course   The limited data suggest a poor prognosis for child-onset schizophrenia. Remission rates range from 3 to 27 percent depending on the particular study, while 61 to 90 percent of the population become chronic schizophrenic with recurring episodes. In Eggers and Bunk's (1997) 42-year follow-up study, only 25 percent of those studied were completely remitted, while 25 percent were partially remitted and 50 percent were poorly remitted. These percentages show a somewhat poorer prognosis than in the case of adult-onset schizophrenia, in which 22 percent have no impairment, 35 percent have minimal impairment, and 35 percent have severe impairment (Barlow & Durand, 1995).

Prognostic Signs   In regard to prognostic signs for child-onset schizophrenia, a poor level of adjustment prior to the onset of schizophrenia and a high level of impairment following it are associated with a poor outcome (Asarnow & Asarnow, 1996). Prognostic criteria are similar for adult schizophrenia: good premorbid functioning, later onset, and rapid development of the psychopathology are favorable prognostic signs, while poor premorbid function, early onset, and an insidious course are unfavorable. For example, Eggers and Bunk (1997), in their 42-year follow-up study mentioned previously, found that none of the patients with chronic onset remitted completely whereas 33 percent of those with acute onset did remit completely. (See Figure 10.2) The results concerning age and chronicity are related—acute onset was significantly more frequent only after 12 years of age. These findings are congruent with those regarding the prognoses for the subtypes of chronic and reactive schizophrenia discussed above where the prognosis for the former was worse than the latter.

In addition to data on remission of symptoms there is also information concerning general adjustment of adults with schizophrenia. Again, age of onset plays a major role. For example, a study of adult schizo-

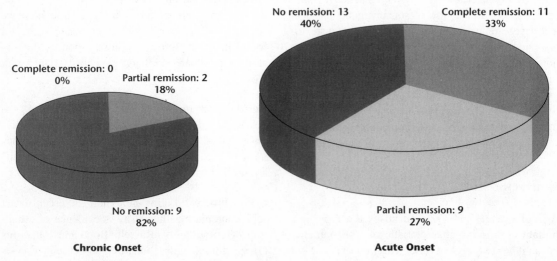

Complete remission: 0
0%
Partial remission: 2
18%
No remission: 9
82%
Chronic Onset

No remission: 13
40%
Complete remission: 11
33%
Partial remission: 9
27%
Acute Onset

Figure 10.2   Distribution of Outcome Categories of Chronic- and Acute-Onset Psychotic Patients.

Source: Eggers and Bunk, 1997

phrenics showed that 17 percent were in school or employed full-time. On the other hand, there is evidence that both child- and adolescent-onset schizophrenia adversely affect employment, independent living, and sexual partnership, with the only area spared being schooling (Häfner & Nowotny, 1995). The reason for the greater disruption in the younger group may be that, during this period, social roles in regard to independent living and sexual partnership are in the process of being formed. Consequently, these roles are more vulnerable to disruption than they will be after they have been more solidified in adulthood.

Is All Schizophrenia One?

DSM-IV states that the diagnostic criteria for schizophrenia apply to children as well as adults. While defensible, such a stand runs the risk of excluding symptoms that might be peculiar to middle childhood and adolescence. (Our presentation follows Gooding and Iacono, 1995.)

Evidence to date suggests that adolescent-onset and adult schizophrenia can be considered as essentially the same psychopathology, with some exceptions. The similarity concerns not only symptom manifestations but findings concerning genetic transmission, autonomic functioning, and brain morphology as well (Jacobsen and Rapoport, 1998). The situation in regard to child-onset schizophrenia is not so clear, partly because data are meager.

In regard to clinical manifestations, there are certain differences between child-onset and adult schizophrenia. Delusions and hallucinations do not appear until around 9 years of age, the former being less frequent than in adult schizophrenia. The symptoms and social impairment are also more severe in children than they are in adults, while the outcome is less favorable. In regard to sex differences, the shift to a comparable number of males and females in adolescence is not typical of adults, for which males outnumber females.

The above differences may not be sufficiently important to justify regarding childhood schizophrenia as a separate disturbance. At the very least, the reasons for the differences should be addressed; however, the door should be left open for discovering other ones.

Are schizophrenia and autism one? In the past a case was made that both schizophrenia and autism should be regarded as two manifestations of the same underlying psychopathology. The case is no longer regarded as defensible. While it is true that some children with autism later become schizophrenic, the percentage of those who do is no different from the percentage of children in the general population who develop schizophrenia (Klinger & Dawson, 1996). The clinical picture of the two is different also in that autism lacks the delusions and hallucinations, the loose associations, and the mood disturbances that characterize schizophrenia. The age of onset and developmental course are also different. Autism appears in the first 30 months of life whereas schizophrenia begins in childhood. Schizophrenia is also marked by progressions and regressions, but autism is highly stable.

Developmental Pathway

Except for the cases of acute onset, which are rare in childhood, schizophrenia does not appear all at once. Rather, it is proceeded by a long period of behavioral deviations. Discovering these precursors is important both to understanding the nature of the psychopathology when it appears and to developing programs aimed at preventing its occurrence. In addition, there is evidence that not all children who will become schizophrenic travel the same path; on the contrary, they may take distinctly different routes. Therefore, we will also need to examine these differences among pathways. Before turning to the data on precursors, however, we need to discuss the many methodological problems in obtaining valid data.

Methodological Issues

Disentangling precursors from consequences is a perennial problem in the study of psychopathologies. For example, if a delinquent adolescent has hostile parents, is the parental hostility a cause of or a reaction to having such a child? Solving the problem is particularly important in the case of schizophrenia, since the treatment of choice is medication, which has its own psychological and physiological repercussions. The same can be said of hospitalization, which is often required in severe cases.

While longitudinal data provide the best evidence for isolating causal factors, gathering such data is a daunting undertaking in the case of schizophrenia. We will review some of the difficulties.

Locating Cases   Schizophrenia is a rare disturbance, occurring in less than 1 percent of the population. This means that one would have to follow 10,000 randomly selected infants in order to obtain somewhere around 10 adolescents with schizophrenia. Such a procedure is possible, but it is so costly that it is rarely used.

The most popular solution to the problem of locating cases is to study children at risk for developing schizophrenia because their mother is schizophrenic. Since there is a genetic component to schizophrenia, this strategy significantly increases the chance that the children studied will become schizophrenic. The problem is that, even with this increased chance, the majority of the children selected for study will *not* become schizophrenic, because the genetic component is not strong enough to produce many cases.

Another strategy designed to capture more cases is to broaden the criteria to include disturbances related to schizophrenia, such as schizoid and paranoid personality disorders. This cluster of related disturbances is called *schizophrenia spectrum disorder*.

The Nature of Schizophrenia Itself   Schizophrenia is not a single entity but rather is a family of disturbances that can be divided into a number of subtypes. This complexity gives rise to a research dilemma: either study subtypes, thereby reducing the typically small number of cases even further, or combine the data from the entire group and risk obscuring findings concerning subtypes.

Next, the etiological variables may wax and wane rather than being stable over time. IQ, for example, which is a highly stable measure from middle childhood on in normal populations, is highly unstable in children of mothers with schizophrenia. The correlation of IQ over time is around .59 in at-risk groups rather than the .80 seen with other groups, including children of mothers who are psychotically depressed (Lewine, 1984). Instability, in turn, undermines long-range predictability. Added to this picture of instability is the fact that the definition of schizophrenia itself changes over time, requiring reclassification of the original sample and reanalysis of the data (Watt, 1984).

Sample Biases   There are numerous sources of sample bias. Women who are schizophrenic are apt to marry disturbed men, such as criminals, who in turn may significantly affect the children's behavior by their own psychopathology (Rutter & Garmezy, 1983). Moreover, mothers who are schizophrenic also might be older, unmarried, anxious, socially incompetent women from the lower class who have difficult pregnancies and deliveries and are likely to give their babies up for adoption or foster home placement (Watt, 1984). This constellation of risk factors would be apt to produce disturbances in the infant even if the mother were not schizophrenic.

Attrition   The problem of attrition is common to all longitudinal studies. The most severely disturbed subjects are the most likely to drop out of the research with time, either because of uncooperativeness or because they have drifted on to other locations without leaving a way to be reached.

A Model Study   In spite of the difficulties involved, data are now available from a number of follow-back and follow-up studies that provide important clues as to precursors of schizophrenia. We will describe the methodology of one such study in detail to illustrate how longitudinal data may be gathered. (For further details of the study, see Crow, Done, and Sacker, 1995.)

The Perinatal Mortality Survey included 98 percent of all births in England, Scotland, and Wales registered from March 3 to March 9, 1958. Four subsequent evaluations were made when the population was 7, 11, 16, and 23 years of age, and the project itself became known as the National Child Development Study (NCDS). There were 16,980 individuals in the initial group and 12,537 in the final one. Using a register of admissions to psychiatric hospitals, the investigators were able to identify all NCDS individuals who had been treated as inpatients for psychiatric reasons. In this way they located 57 individuals with schizophrenia, 35 with affective psychosis, and 79 with neurosis. These individuals were compared with a randomly selected sample from the entire population.

Data were gathered on a number of physiological and psychological variables. Physiological data included exposure of the women to an influenza epidemic during pregnancy, birth complications, the children's head circumference, their height and weight at 7, 11, and 16 years, and the timing of the onset of puberty. As for psychological variables, tests of visual and motor development were administered and information was collected concerning enuresis and incontinence during the preschool years. During middle childhood, teachers administered the Bristol Social Adjustment Guide in order to gather information about a variety of internalizing and externalizing behaviors. Both general intelligence and academic achievement were evaluated at 7, 11, and 16 years.

The design of the study is noteworthy because it allowed the investigators to determine what findings were specific to schizophrenia rather than being shared with other psychotic or neurotic populations. Designs that include only a schizophrenic and a normal control group do not allow for such a determination. In addition, the scope of the investigation is impressive, covering a variety of potentially important variables.

Other Sources of Data   Although follow-up studies are the methodology of choice, we will also be citing data from retrospective and follow-back studies. For example, Cantor (1988) obtained retrospective data using a standard series of interview questions administered to 29 mothers of children with schizophrenia who were 10 years of age or younger. Watkins, Asarnow, and Tanguay (1988) did a follow-back study of 18 children who had become schizophrenic at 10 years of age or younger, obtaining data from records of pediatricians, clinics, hospitals, schools, and mental health and other public agencies. In an interesting variation on the follow-back design, Walker and colleagues (1991) analyzed the home movies of the early years of children who had become schizophrenic.

Findings from Developmental Studies

The Prenatal Period

There is evidence that mothers who contract influenza during pregnancy have children who are at risk for becoming schizophrenic (Olin & Mednick, 1996). The evidence concerning obstetrical complications is mixed. While some studies show evidence of an increase in obstetrical complications in mothers whose children become schizophrenic (Olin & Mednick, 1996), Crow, Done, and Sacker (1995) failed to find such an increase. One reason for this discrepancy may be that the relation holds only for infants already at risk because their mothers also are schizophrenic.

Infancy

The Intrapersonal Context   Deviations in motor and sensory development along with passivity and deviant speech characterize infants at risk for becoming schizophrenic (Gooding & Iaocono, 1995). More specifically, there is a lag in motor and sensory development and deficiencies in gross and fine motor coordination. Walker, Savole, and Davis (1994) also found in at-risk children limb position and movement abnormalities, including choreoathetoid movements (i.e., involuntary twisting and slow, irregular, snakelike movements). All of these motor abnormalities are at their height in the first two years of life and subsequently diminish. Passivity is evidenced by the at-risk infant's being underaroused and unresponsive to external stimuli, by poor alertness and orientation, and by poor muscle tonus. There is some evidence that passivity may be predictive of adult schizophrenia (Gooding & Iacono, 1995). Finally, there is deviant speech development evidenced by the paucity of babbling and slowness in imitating sounds (Cantor, 1988, and Watkins, Asarnow, & Tanguay, 1988).

The Interpersonal Context   Only two studies concern attachment, and their findings are inconclusive. A special subgroup of at-risk neonates were found to be less cuddly and consolable, but this did not characterize the group as a whole (Watt et al., 1984). However, there is evidence that separation from the caregiver in the first year increases the risk for schizophrenia but only in infants already at genetic risk (i.e., their mothers are also schizophrenic) (Olin & Mednick, 1996).

The Toddler Through Preschool Periods

The Intrapersonal Context   Many of the deviations in infancy continue into the toddler-preschool period: the abnormality in gross and fine motor coordination, the passivity and low energy level, seriously delayed speech, and poor communication. Four studies of temperament yielded divergent and inconclusive findings (Watts et al., 1988). Next, there is evidence from a single study that children in the schizophrenic group show more psychological disturbance by the end of the preschool period than do children in comparison or control groups.

The Interpersonal Context   Cantor (1988) and Watkins, Asarnow, and Tanguay (1988) found social deviations consisting of a preference for being alone, perseverative play, and being "hyper" with peers, along with bizarre responses to the social environment. The children may be anxious and hostile with others and yet be affectively flat, withdrawn, and isolated in their relationship with their mothers. The meager data on parenting by mothers who are schizophrenic suggest that they are less affectionately involved, more hostile, and less stimulating than mothers in control groups.

Middle Childhood

The Intrapersonal Context   While deviant motor development continues to characterize the at-risk group in middle childhood, it is neither specific to this group nor predictive of future schizophrenia. On the other hand, attention deficits are both temporally stable and predictive of future development of schizophrenia. These deficits are evidenced on a number of tasks: the ability to repeat numbers forward and backward, letter cancellation, and the ability to detect a given letter in an array of other letters presented at a very brief interval (Gooding and Iacono, 1995).

In regard to personality variables, Crow, Done, and Sacker's (1995) NCDS, mentioned earlier, found that preschizophrenic boys were significantly more disturbed than the comparison groups at ages 7 and 11. Preschizophrenic girls, on the other hand, did not differ from those in the pre-affective and pre-neurotic groups at 7 years of age; by age 11 they were significantly more disturbed than they were at 7 years but not more so than the preneurotic group, which also had become more disturbed.

There is also information concerning the subtype of schizophrenia that will develop. The clearest relation is between basic withdrawal and passivity in childhood and the negative schizophrenic symptoms of social withdrawal, affective flattening, and poverty of speech. The evidence concerning positive symptoms of schizophrenia is inconsistent, with one study finding schizophrenia to be related to excitability, aggression, and disruptive behaviors in childhood and two other studies finding no relation. Thus, negative symptoms may reflect enduring predispositions and have roots in the premorbid phase of the disturbance, while positive symptoms may not have such roots (Walker et al., 1996).

In regard to general intelligence and academic achievement, Crow, Done, and Sacker's (1995) NCDS found widespread impairment. Not only was a measure of general intelligence below that of the other groups, including the normal control group, but reading and arithmetic achievement also significantly lagged.

While studies of language and communication are sparse, there is some evidence that the speech of high-risk subjects is vaguer than that of normal subjects, as well as having lower overall information content. The result is speech that is confusing, unclear, and poorly elaborated, although not sufficiently deviant to qualify as a formal thought disorder (Watts et al., 1984).

Adolescence

The Intrapersonal Context   Distractibility, or a deficit in selective attention, emerges in adolescence. It also may be prognostically important (Harvey, 1991). In regard to motor development, Crow, Done, and Sacker's (1995) NCDS found that prior signs of deviant development were no longer present, and motor coordination was age-appropriate. However, the at-risk group was rated as clumsy when compared with the other groups. Finally, there is a decline in IQ scores that is greater than the decline found in the scores of children whose mothers are depressed.

In light of the dramatic increase in schizophrenia during the adolescent period, it is worth noting that Crow, Done, and Sacker's (1995) NCDS found no significant difference in the time of onset of puberty for boys and girls when the at-risk group was compared with the normal controls. Thus, whatever organic factors are at work to produce schizophrenia, they do not affect the timing of puberty.

The Interpersonal Context   Since the interpersonal context is almost completely neglected in studies of precursors, we will report the results of a follow-up study of 50 children whose mothers were schizophrenic, some of whom were reared in an Israeli kibbutz, where they spent most of the day in a group setting but returned to their families at the end of the day, and some of whom were reared totally in the family (Mirsky, et al., 1995). At the first follow-up evaluation when the children were 25 to 26 years of age, there were more cases of schizophrenia in the kibbutz-reared than in the family-reared children. However, five years later, when the group was 31 years of age, there was no difference between the two groups in regard to developing schizophrenia. This phenomenon of *age-dependent findings*—that is, what you find depends on when you evaluate a given population—characterizes other findings concerning precursors. (See Box 10.1.)

Box 10.1	**Age-Dependent Variables**

The data in Table 10.2 illustrate the point that certain precursors are age-dependent. Motor impairment, which is an important differentiating characteristic of the at-risk children early in development, subsequently declines in importance until only a general clumsiness remains in adolescence. In the area of language development, Asarnow, Brown, and Strandburg (1995) found that the expressive language that was impaired during infancy and early childhood was the least impaired function by 9 years of age. Finally, in Mirsky's (1995) research just cited, there were more schizophrenics in the kibbutz-reared than in the family-reared groups when the children were 25 to 26 years old but not when they were 31 years of age.

What are we to make of a precursor that appears and then subsequently is no longer differentiating? Is it "outgrown" and therefore unimportant? Possibly, but not necessarily. Let us consider motor deviations as an example. They reach their height in the first two years of life when mastery of motor skills such as crawling and walking are at the center of the developmental stage. It is possible that the difficulties experienced at this age add to the general reservoir of stress that is accumulating as the child develops. Furthermore, it may be that it is the cumulative effects of stresses from many sources that ultimately causes the schizophrenic breakdown.

However, it is also possible that some age-dependent precursors have a specific effect subsequently. Continuing with our example of motor behavior, motor dysfunctions are associated with schizophrenia across the life span, and movement abnormalities are associated with greater symptom severity, cognitive defects, and poor prognosis (Walker et al., 1996). Instead of being "outgrown," therefore, age-dependent precursors may leave behind a specific vulnerability, which will be incorporated into the schizophrenic picture once the psychopathology appears.

At present all three interpretations of age-dependent precursors are tenable: that they are "outgrown" and have no effect on producing the psychopathology; that they represent stressors that, as they accumulate, increase the probability that schizophrenia will appear; and that they reappear as elements in the schizophrenic picture.

Summary   A summary of findings concerning precursors of schizophrenia is presented in Table 10.2. In light of the incompleteness of data, all conclusions concerning precursors are tentative, however. Motor deviations are present from infancy on but tend to be "outgrown" by adolescence, while deviations in speech and communication seem to be important throughout the entire developmental period. Passivity (a possible precursor of the negative subtype of schizophrenia) has been documented in the infancy through preschool period, but its subsequent fate has not been charted. Problems in social and general adjustment are present as early as the toddler period and continue through middle childhood, although only for boys. Deviations in attention, which are predictive of schizophrenia, have been found from middle childhood on, although there are no data on whether or not they appear earlier.

Different Pathways to Schizophrenia

So far we have raised the question, What are the precursors of child- and adolescent-onset schizophrenia? The best answers come from research designed to compare populations at risk for schizophrenia with populations at risk for affective psychosis, as well as with a normal control group. But there is a further question: Do all at risk children follow the same path to the ultimate psychopathology, or are there different ways of arriving at the same end point? Answering this question requires a *within-group* analysis of data obtained on at-risk children.

Walker and colleagues (1996) provide such a within-group analysis using a statistical technique called cluster analysis. They found that their follow-back data clustered in two groups. Cluster I children showed more behavioral and attentional problems and more rapid escalation of problems than did Cluster II children. For example, Cluster I children were both more withdrawn and delinquent and had more social problems than children in Cluster II. Moreover, Cluster I children were significantly different from their healthy siblings on all behavioral and attentional problems whereas Cluster II children were not.

Cluster I children had more motor abnormalities and a higher rate of obstetrical complications. This latter finding helps explain why some investigators, like Crow, Done, and Sacker (1995), found no difference in obstetrical complications while others did—namely, the data depend on what proportion of Cluster I and Cluster II children one happens to capture in the population.

Walker and colleagues (1996) conclude that there are two premorbid subtypes, one showing early, persistent, and escalating deviations and the other showing no difference from healthy children. These groups correspond to two different kinds of anecdotal information from parents, some saying that the child with schizophrenia was "different from the beginning" and others saying they were particularly dismayed by the onset because their child had been "perfectly normal." Both may be right. Incidentally, this finding is important for clinical child psychologists to know so they will not suspect parents of covering up deviations when they paint a picture of a well-adjusted childhood for a child who has been diagnosed with schizophrenia.

Next Walker and colleagues (1996) analyzed their data on precursors in terms of gender differences, with equally important findings. As have other investigators, they found that males had a predominance of both externalizing problems (i.e., acting out, disruptive behavior) *and* internalizing problems (i.e., social isolation), while the females had predominately internalizing problems (i.e., anxiety and depression). Thus, only girls conform to the stereotype of the preschizophrenic as being withdrawn; boys are more apt to be described as being emotionally unstable and having a "stormy" time.

Summary   In sum, there is no single path to schizophrenia; rather, there are different routes to the same outcome. Some children will be disturbed in many areas of functioning from an early age and become increasingly so, while others will be essentially normal before schizophrenia makes its appearance. In a like manner, the route will be different for males than for females, the former having both externalizing and internalizing

Table 10.2   Summary of Developmental Pathway to Schizophrenia*

Developmental Deviations	Developmental Periods			
	Infancy	Toddler-Preschool	Middle Childhood	Adolescence
Motor	Lags in gross and fine coordination; movement abnormalities	Lags in gross and fine coordination	Deviant but not specific to or predictive of schizophrenia	Clumsy but no longer deviant
Sensory	Lags			
Passivity	Underaroused and unresponsive; poor muscle tone (?P)	Low energy level		
Speech	Little babbling and imitation	Delayed; poor communication	Vague, confused, unclear (?)	
Social Adjustment		"Loner," "hyper"; anxious and hostile with peers Disturbed at end of period (?)	Increased disturbance in boys only	
Attention			Attention deficits (P)	Distractible (P)
IQ			Below normal	Declines
Miscellaneous	Increased obstetrical complications; separation from caregiver		Lags in reading and math	

*P = predictive of schizophrenia; ? = meager data

problems, the latter having primarily internalizing ones. The finding that different disturbances can lead to the same outcome is an example of *equifinality*.

Protective Factors

As we have seen, relatively few children whose mothers are schizophrenic become schizophrenic themselves. Moreover, 35 to 50 percent of them make a good adjustment. This finding has sparked an interest in studying high-risk children who cope well with life's demands in spite of an environment that would seem incompatible with normal functioning. Such an environment might include severely disturbed parents, poverty, and a dysfunctional family life. One well-functioning 8-year-old girl, for example, had a father who was in jail, a mother who was so depressed that she could not see even to the children's basic needs, and four siblings who were either retarded or predelinquent school dropouts.

Much of the research concerning protective factors involves parents who are psychotic and is not limited to those with schizophrenia. However, in light of the paucity of data concerning children at risk for schizophrenia, the literature is worth reviewing. In this literature the well-functioning children are called the **invulnerables**.

Preliminary studies suggest that these so-called invulnerable children have certain characteristics in common. (Our presentation follows Cohler, 1987, unless otherwise noted.) Rather than being engulfed by their parents' psychopathology, the invulnerable children have the ability to distance themselves psychologically, showing a detached curiosity about and understanding of what is troubling their parents while being compassionate toward them. They also have a high level of initiative. In the interpersonal realm this is evidenced by their taking advantage of the well parent's support or, lacking that, seeking adults outside the family. In fact, the presence of a single caring and concerned adult can do much to offset the impact of misfortune in the children's lives (Cohler, Stott, & Musick, 1995). Their capacity for making friends further enlarges their circle of growth-promoting social relations. The children's initiative is also evidenced by their engaging in diverse activities outside the home, holding down jobs, and having hobbies, all or which serve as buffers against the noxious influences of the home environment.

While the invulnerable children are intelligent, more important than that characteristic is their ability to try to understand the events in their lives and figure out ways of coping with them. They also tend to be physically and personally attractive. Finally, the ability to cope is enhanced if the disturbed parent is hospitalized later in the children's lives rather than early, and if the parent has some ability to relate positively to the child.

Subsequently, however, invulnerable children pay the price for their ability to cope effectively with adversity. As adults they have a diminished capacity to form sustained intimate relationships. They are concerned about their own needs but reluctant to explore their feelings. They gravitate toward impersonal pursuits and vocations such as science and technology and are most comfortable in tasks requiring group cooperation rather than close relations. Such a life pattern results from their defenses of distancing, suppression of affect, and intellectualization.

The studies on this population suggest that "invulnerable" might not be the most appropriate adjective for describing the children because it implies that they have developed an immunity to all of life's stresses and distresses. On the contrary, they, like most people, have their periods of setback marked by discouragement, uncertainty, and fear. However, they also have a basic strength that enables them to overcome such periods and to resume the positive course of their lives. Thus, it is not immunity that marks them but *resilience*.

Etiology

We now turn to research on children and adolescents who have become schizophrenic. Currently such etiological studies concentrate on the organic context, with some investigators going so far as to define schizophrenia in terms of a *central nervous system* (*CNS*) dysfunction. In this strong tilt toward the organic context, investigators are following the lead of those studying adults, although studies of children are still few in number. In the intrapersonal context

interest has centered on psychological variables that are purported to reflect central nervous system dysfunctions such as motor incoordination and inattention. We have looked at some of these variables already in charting the precursors of schizophrenia. However they are now relabeled *neuropsychological* variables and are regarded as organic warning signs of the psychopathology to come. Aside from neuropsychological variables, the intrapersonal context has been relatively neglected. The same is true of the interpersonal context, which is primarily represented by studies of family interaction.

Etiological variables are currently conceptualized in terms of the **diathesis/stress** model. "Diathesis" is another term for a vulnerability or a predisposition to develop schizophrenia. Stressors increase the likelihood that schizophrenia will actually appear.

The Organic Context

There are three sources of evidence concerning the organic etiology of schizophrenia: genetic studies, neurobiological studies (including studies of the brain and autonomic system), and studies of neuropsychological variables such as inattention and incoordination that purport to be indices of brain dysfunction.

Genetic Factors

Familial Transmission   There is no doubt that genetic factors play an etiologic role in schizophrenia. More than forty family studies spanning several decades of research show that risk to different relatives of individuals who are schizophrenic is considerably greater than the normal population risk. Moreover, risk varies as a function of the degree of genetic relatedness to the affected individual. Thus, the highest concordance is between monozygotic twins, who have 100 percent of their genes in common. The specific risk in this case is 48 percent, which is approximately three times the 14 percent concordance rate for dizygotic twins. (See Moldin and Gottesman, 1997.)

Mechanism of Transmission   Exactly which genes are involved in the transmission of schizophrenia is not known at present. While the strongest current evidence implicates chromosomes 6 and 8, these linkages have not yet been confirmed. Moreover, the challenge of detecting and isolating a disease gene is considerable; for example, the time between establishment of linkage to identification of the precise disease gene for Huntington's disease was 10 years (Moldin & Gottesman, 1997).

As for the mechanism of transmission, Rende and Plomin (1995) conclude that genetic influences reflect the impact of "many genes of small probabilistic effect rather than the sledge hammer effect of single deterministic genes" (p. 302). They also caution that symptoms influenced by genes do not necessarily coincide with symptoms used to define a disorder. Genetic influences can cut across different disorders, such as depression and anxiety, or can influence areas of functioning not considered as core symptoms, such as attention. This lack of a nice correspondence between genes that transmit the psychopathology and the defining clinical manifestations of the psychopathology itself adds just one more complication to research on genetic etiology.

Gene–Environment Interaction   The genetic loading still allows for environmental factors to play a major role in the final production of schizophrenia. One example of the interaction of genetic and environmental factors is the Finnish study (Tienari et al., 1983) in which ninety-two children of mothers who were schizophrenic and mothers who were normal were adopted into healthy and disturbed family environments. All the children who subsequently became schizophrenic were in the schizophrenic-mother, disturbed-family group. Schizophrenia did not develop when children of mothers who were not schizophrenic were adopted into disturbed families. Thus, the psychopathology was the result of the combination of a genetically vulnerable child being raised in a disturbed family environment. Equally important, the nondisturbed family protected the at-risk child from becoming schizophrenic.

Another example of gene–environment interaction is the finding that the incidence of schizophrenia increased sevenfold in African-Caribbean children whose parents had immigrated to London (Hutchinson et al., 1996). Possible environmental risks include prenatal rubella infection, drug abuse,

and factors associated with assimilation. However, pinpointing which variables in the environment are critical stressors for schizophrenia is as daunting a task as discovering which genes are crucial for its production. (For a list of common misconceptions concerning the genetics of schizophrenia, see Moldin and Gottesman, 1997.)

Central Nervous System Dysfunction

The lion's share of research on central nervous system dysfunctions has been conducted on adults with schizophrenia. (See Benes, 1995, for a review of this research. Buchanan, Stevens, and Carpenter, 1997, have edited a series of papers on the neuroanatomy of schizophrenia, again primarily addressed to the research on adults.) Pennington and Welsh (1995) summarize the research as follows: As can be expected, a number of areas of the brain have been implicated, particularly the hippocampus, frontal cortex, and selected left hemisphere structures. Current theories regarding the developmental timing of insults to the brain usually converge on the prenatal or early postnatal periods. In spite of vigorous research efforts, Benes concludes that a specific pathogenetic brain mechanism, whether structural or neurochemical, has not yet been clearly established. Stevens (1997) adds that no morphological or microscopic abnormality has been found that is either necessary or sufficient to account for the clinical picture of schizophrenia. Moreover, more refined typologies, such as positive/negative categories, have not lead to separating the disorder into pathologically similar subgroups.

In contrast to the research on adults, that on children with schizophrenia is meager, consisting at times of the study of a single individual. (Our presentation follows Jacobsen and Rapoport, 1998.) Studies of brain morphology reveal a significant decrease in total cerebral volume. This reduction is greater than that found in adults, and the reduction is strongly correlated with negative symptoms in the children. When corrected for the overall decrease in total cerebral volume, there is still a significant *increase* in lateral ventricles, while the midsagittal thalamic area is significantly *decreased* in patients with childhood-onset schizophrenia. A two-year follow-up revealed that the ventricular volume increased more rapidly in children with schizophrenia than in healthy children whereas the midsagittal thalamic area decreased significantly.

Jacobsen and Rapoport (1998) conclude that the progressive enlargement of ventricular volume after the onset of schizophrenia, coupled with the evidence of continued intellectual deterioration both before and after the appearance of schizophrenia, suggest that the pathological underpinnings of childhood schizophrenia consist of not a single static lesion or event but rather a continuous or multievent process.

Chemical Studies   Because of its proven efficacy in treatment, dopamine, a monoamine neurotransmitter ("chemical messenger") essential to normal nerve activity, plays a prominent role in chemical research and in etiological speculation concerning schizophrenia. Specifically, drugs that block dopaminergic transmission control psychotic symptoms, while those that produce excessive release of dopamine are associated with the intensification of psychotic symptoms. However the effect is not specific to schizophrenia but applies to a number of psychoses. Moreover, therapeutic effectiveness in controlling symptoms cannot be taken as proof of an etiological hypothesis since cures have no necessary relation to causes. Finally, the dopamine hypothesis is not completely secure as far as the empirical evidence is concerned (Häfner, 1995).

Autonomic Dysfunctions

In the research that concerns us, autonomic functions are measured by skin conductance and heart rate. The meager evidence indicates that children with schizophrenia, like their adult counterparts, have an abnormal pattern of reactivity. In the resting state their autonomic reactivity is higher than normal. However, their reactions to novel stimuli are lower but do not habituate or decline with successive presentations of the stimuli as is the case with normal children (Jacobsen & Rapoport, 1998).

Neuropsychological Dysfunctions

Neuropsychological dysfunctions represent an indirect way of locating central nervous system dysfunctions in schizophrenia, in contrast with the direct studies of the brain described in the previous section. (Our presentation follows Asarnow and Asarnow, 1996, unless otherwise noted.)

Attention   The most robust research finding on schizophrenia in children, adolescents, and adults is that they share a dysfunction in attention. This dysfunction is evidenced by studies of span of apprehension in which subjects have to identify a target letter (a T or an F) embedded in an array of other letters and displayed for 50 milliseconds. When the number of letters to be identified is large—specifically 5 to 10 rather than 1 to 3—the performance of schizophrenics is worse than that of normal individuals or ones with ADHD. Thus, the dysfunction is evidenced in those with schizophrenia when the task involves a significant burden for processing information. Finally, direct evaluation of the subjects' brain activity while performing the task showed a comparable deviation in event-related potential, a measure of the brain's electrical activity.

The above research nicely illustrates the advantage of using a basic psychological variable—namely, attention—as a bridge between schizophrenia and brain functioning. While other neuropsychological variables have been employed, their relation to brain functioning is more speculative and the studies of children are limited in number (Häfner, 1995). We will now briefly review this research, noting when the neuropsychological variables are and are not impaired.

Vision and Audition   There is no basic impairment in the reception and comprehension of visual and auditory stimuli. However, performance is impaired when memory is added to a visual task so that a child must hold the stimulus in mind before responding to it, or, in audition, when the child has to remember and respond to a series of verbal stimuli. The usual interpretation of these results is that the dysfunction is due to the greater demand for processing information, as was the case in the span of apprehension task.

In line with the idea of a dysfunction in processing complex information, there is the paradoxical finding that providing strategies for or information about performing a task can interfere with its performance at times. Instead of being helpful, the added information is too much to be assimilated. In regard to relating this finding to brain functioning, it suggests that children and adolescents with schizophrenia have difficulty with processing complex information regardless of the hemisphere subserving the function assessed by the task. In other words, the dysfunction is not localized in one hemisphere or the other.

Visual-Motor and Motor Functions   Both visual-motor coordination and fine motor speed are impaired in individuals with schizophrenia. There is also evidence that, while performance in these areas improves in controls, it does not improve in children with schizophrenia. This lack of improvement suggests either a delay in or failure of normal brain maturation (Jacobsen & Rapoport, 1998).

Eye Tracking   In eye-tracking tasks eye movement is recorded as individuals visually follow a moving target. Both children and adults with schizophrenia show greater eye-tracking impairment than do either normal individuals or ones with ADHD; for example, the eye is ahead of the target or less time is spent tracking the target. While eye-tracking abnormalities could be produced by lesions in a number of brain regions, they are not specific to any particular site (Jacobsen & Rapoport, 1998).

Executive Functions   As with adults with schizophrenia, executive functions (those responsible for flexible, goal-directed behavior) are impaired in children and adolescents with schizophrenia. (See Chapter 4 for a more detailed presentation of executive functions.) Schizophrenics are perseverative in their thinking and have a defective working memory. These two defects have been related to frontal lobe damage. More specifically, it is hypothesized that the impairment is due to a reduced ability to increase prefrontal cortex metabolism when the situation requires it. While there is evidence supporting this hypothesis, it is not conclusive. (See Pennington and Welsh, 1995.)

The Intrapersonal Context

Thought Disorders   The disorganized speech that characterizes schizophrenia is a reflection of disorders in thinking. Thought disorders are not only

diagnostic indices of schizophrenia but they have ominous implications for prognosis as well. However, certain of these disorders can be found in the normal population of younger children. Loose associations, for example, can be observed up to the age of 7 years, after which time they are infrequent. Illogical thinking also decreases markedly after that time. Therefore, the appearance of loose associations and illogical thinking in schizophrenia may be due a developmental delay, fixation, or regression, although this possible etiology is only speculation. (See Volkmar et al., 1996, which also contains a detailed summary of the literature on delusions, hallucinations, and other thought disorders.)

Controlled studies have been conducted on loose and illogical thinking underlying disorganized speech. Loose thinking is defined as an unpredictable change of topics, such as answering "Why do you like Tim?" with "I call my mother Sweetie." Illogical thinking is defined as contradictions or inappropriate causal relations, such as "I left my hat at home because her name is Mary." These thinking disorders may be specific to schizophrenia since they are not found in children diagnosed with ADHD, conduct disorder, or oppositional disorder.

The two kinds of thought disturbances are not correlated. Loose thinking is related to distractibility, while illogical thinking is related to a short attention span (Caplan et al., 1990). This latter attention deficit may underlie schizophrenic children's digressive speech, since they are deficient in the short-term attentional processes required for coherent conversation. In sum, we have two hypotheses concerning the etiology of loose and illogical thinking: fixation or regression on the one hand and an attentional deficit on the other. (For a more detailed presentation of thought disorders in childhood schizophrenia, see Caplan and Sherman, 1990.)

The Interpersonal Context: Family Interactions

While family dysfunction is sometimes regarded as a vulnerability or diathesis for schizophrenia, the evidence clearly shows that family dysfunction is in fact a stressor that increases the probability of schizophrenia in an already vulnerable individual, since there is no evidence that a dysfunctional family can produce schizophrenia in a nonvulnerable child. We will first review the clinical and observational studies of families that have a member with schizophrenia before going on to objective studies. (Our presentation follows Mishler and Waxler, 1965.)

Clinical and Observational Studies   Lyman Wynne (1984) regards schizophrenia as the result of a *diffuse* or *fragmented family structure*. Diffuse patterns of interaction are marked by vague ideas, by blurring of meaning, and by irrelevancies. Thus, the drifting or scattered thinking of individuals who are schizophrenic represents the internalization of such a family structure. As an example of amorphous thinking, note the following responses of a mother being interviewed for the developmental history of her child who has schizophrenia:

> Psychologist: Was it a difficult delivery or did everything go OK?
> Mother: I know just what you mean. And I can say for certain that I'm not one of those women you read about where they are so brave and natural childbirth is just the greatest thing in their life (laughs). Believe me, when the time comes, I want the works when it comes to pain.
> Psychologist: But did everything go OK?
> Mother: Well, there was this Dr. Wisekoff that I never liked and he said all kinds of doom and gloom things, but I told my husband I was the one that had the baby and I was the one that ought to know, so my husband got into this big fight and didn't pay the bill for a whole year and the doctor threatened to hire one of these collection agencies, and what that was all about don't ask me—just don't ask me.
> Psychologist: I see, but I'm still not sure . . .
> Mother (interrupting): That's just what I mean.

Later the psychologist, who was just beginning his clinical internship, told his supervisor that he wanted to shake the mother and yell at the top of his lungs, "But was the delivery difficult or easy?" One can only imagine how difficult it would be for a child to grow up surrounded by such diffuseness, accompanied by an obliviousness to the diffuseness itself.

Like amorphous thinking, fragmented thinking can be traced to parental communication. In this case communication is marked by digression from topic to topic, non sequitur reasoning, and extraneous, illogical, or contradictory comments. While attention can be focused for brief moments, bits and pieces of memories become intermixed with the current train of thought. The technical term for this abrupt shift from one topic to another is overinclusive thinking, or **overinclusiveness**.

Wynne delineates other faults in the family structure. The family members cannot maintain appropriate psychological *boundaries*, and thus detached impersonality unpredictably alternates with highly personal remarks and confrontations. However, there is a concerted effort to act as if there were a strong sense of unity, resulting in what Wynne calls **pseudo-mutuality**. There is a great pressure to maintain a facade of harmony, and the child is not allowed to deviate from or question his or her prescribed role. Beneath this facade lies pervasive feelings of futility and meaninglessness.

Theodore Lidz (1973), another family theorist, posits less in terms of family structure and more in terms of *roles and functions*. In the healthy family maternal and paternal roles are clearly delineated, as are generational or parent–child roles, while parents transmit to their children useful ways of adapting to the demands of society. There is also role reciprocity that requires the acceptance of each member's role, values, and goals.

In the family with a child who is schizophrenic, roles are blurred and parents use children to serve their own egocentric needs. Lidz describes two kinds of distorted patterns. In the **skewed family**, more commonly found with boys than girls, the mother is overprotective, intrusive, dominating, and seductive, while the father is passive and weak. Because of her tenuous emotional equilibrium, the mother perceives events according to her own needs and insists that her son do likewise. In adolescence the boy becomes increasingly fearful of being engulfed by his mother, but moves toward autonomy produce unbearable guilt.

In the **schismatic family**, more characteristic of girls than boys, there is a continuing overt conflict between the parents, each depreciating the other to their children and often competing for the children's loyalty. The mother has little self-esteem or security because she is constantly being undermined by her husband's contempt. The father is insecure in his masculinity, is in constant need of admiration, and uses domination as a substitute for strength of character. Disappointed in his wife, the father turns to his daughter to fill his emotional needs. His behavior may be highly inconsistent, alternating between tyrannical tempers and seductiveness or even maternal tenderness. The daughter is caught in a bind since pleasing one parent alienates the other. The self-disparaging mother is a poor model of mature femininity, while the women-disparaging father is an equally poor model of adult masculinity.

Objective Studies   Objective studies are more congruent with Wynne's observations concerning communication deviance than with Lidz's concerning role deviance. While none clearly establishes family interaction as an etiological agent in schizophrenia, they do find that such interactions play an important role in recurrence, precipitation, and severity of schizophrenic episodes. (Our presentation follows the more extensive review of Miklowitz, 1994, unless otherwise indicated.)

Three aspects of family interaction have been studied extensively. *Expressed emotion* (EE) involves attitudes of criticism, hostility, or overinvolvement held by key relatives toward a child or adolescent with schizophrenia. There is evidence that, in observed interactions, parents of children with schizophrenia spectrum disorders are more likely to express harsh criticism toward their child and to respond to the child's negative verbal behavior with a reciprocal negative response. Neither of these behaviors characterize parents of individuals with depression (Asarnow, 1994).

Affective style (AS) is concerned with emotional behavior, as measured by the number of critical, guilt-inducing, or intrusive statements made during a 10-minute discussion session between family members. Finally, *communication deviance* (CD) evaluates the degree to which relatives' communication lacks clarity as measured by the number of unclear, amorphous, disruptive, or fragmented statements they make in response to projective tests.

As for findings, both EE and AS are good predictors of relapse after a schizophrenic episode; for example, for hospitalized individuals with schizophrenia who return to a high-EE family, relapse within 9 months to a year is two to three times higher than for those who return to a low EE family.

Communication deviance reliably differentiates parents of individuals with schizophrenia from parents of persons without schizophrenia but not from those with bipolar (manic-depressive) disorders. Along with AS, CD also predicts the onset in adulthood of schizophrenia spectrum disorders. For example, a fifteen-year follow-up study of sixty-four families with mild to moderately disturbed adolescents found that the incidence of schizophrenia or schizophrenia spectrum disorders was highest in families initially classified as having high communication deviance, that there were no cases of schizophrenia in families with low communication deviance, and that adding measures of AS increased the predictive power (Goldstein, 1990). These results suggest that, for vulnerable children, disturbance in the family climate in the form of unclear or affectively negative communication presages the appearance of schizophrenia and related disorders in adulthood.

Next, there is evidence supporting Wynne's observation that CD in parents interferes with the development of attention and logical thinking in their children. Mothers with high CD and their offspring with schizophrenia perform poorly on measures of attention and vigilance, as well as on tasks evaluating the ability to integrate and organize complex social information into a coherent whole. Finally, there is evidence that CD in parents is associated with the severity of the psychopathology. While CD is also found in some parents of children with depression, it is not associated either with attentional problems or severity of disturbance in depression, suggesting that it is particularly important for the development of schizophrenic disorders (Asarnow & Asarnow, 1996).

However, there is a problem bedeviling all interactional research—namely, disentangling precursors from consequences. There is evidence, for example, that in observed family interactions, children with schizophrenia or schizotypical disorders evidence a higher level of thought disorders and attentional drift (difficulty in maintaining attention to a task) than do children with major depression (Asarnow, 1994). This finding raises the question, Are the harsh critical comments of high EE parents one of the factors *responsible* for their children's disturbance or do they arise in *response to* the frustration of having such a child? The question can best be answered by the kind of longitudinal data that are not presently available.

Comparative Study   In one of the few comparative studies of thought disorder and communication problems among family members, Thompson and associates (1990) found that children with schizophrenia spectrum disorders showed significantly more thought disorder than their normal peers. The level of thought disorder among children with depression fell between those of the schizophrenic spectrum and normal groups but did not differ significantly from either. Similarly, mothers of children with schizophrenic spectrum disorder showed more thought disorder than did mothers in the normal group but did not differ significantly from mothers of children with depression. These limited data raise but do not answer the question of how specific to schizophrenia are the thought and communication disorders among family members.

Integrative Models

To maintain that many kinds of deviations are involved in a disturbance as severe as schizophrenia is too general. The challenge is to integrate the specific findings and to narrow down possible etiologies to necessary and sufficient ones. At present it is impossible to meet this challenge with childhood and adolescent schizophrenia because of meager and incomplete data. However, there are models from diverse sources—longitudinal data, statistical analyses, and conceptualizations of research findings—that represent different approaches to integration.

Mednick's Developmental-Interactional Integration   Mednick, who pioneered at-risk prospective research with his so-called Danish study, has integrated the various factors in the organic, intrapersonal,

and interpersonal contexts that increase the chances of developing schizophrenia spectrum disorders. (Our presentation follows Cannon, Barr, and Mednick, 1991.) First, the genetic predisposition to schizophrenia disrupts fetal brain development. CT scans of high-risk subjects' brains revealed two separate neurological conditions: multisite neural developmental deficits and periventricular damage reflected in enlargement of the third and lateral ventricles. Environmental events such as the mother's contracting influenza in the second trimester of gestation can similarly disrupt fetal neurological development. Next, delivery complications can produce ventricular damage, which increases the risk for schizophrenia spectrum disorders in infants with an especially high genetic risk (both parents are schizophrenic). In sum, there is a genetic-perinatal determination of ventricular damage with various genetic and perinatal factors acting singly or in concert to produce the damage.

Among subsequent environmental variables, separation from parents and institutionalization increase the likelihood of schizophrenia in high-risk but not low-risk groups. Furthermore, while negative affective style and communication deviance in families predict schizophrenia spectrum disorders in general, Mednick claims that the more severe forms of family instability represented by separation and institutionalization are unique to producing schizophrenia itself.

Cannon, Barr, and Mednick have further analyzed their data in terms of schizophrenics with positive and negative symptoms. Enlarged third ventricles damage diencephalic and limbic structures involved in excitatory autonomic functioning. The resulting reduction in autonomic responsiveness contributes to schizophrenia characterized by negative symptoms. High-risk subjects who have normal births but have unstable families early in life, and who also have genetically determined high levels of autonomic responsiveness in adolescence, tend to develop schizophrenia with positive symptoms.

Mednick's synthesis is not without its problems. The number of subjects in the active and passive groups is 7 and 8, respectively, which is small, and other studies have failed to find a relation between autonomic nervous system arousal and schizophrenia. However, the synthesis does serve as a model for integrating variables in terms of their predictive power and for differentiating crucial from peripheral ones.

Statistical Integrations   Statistical techniques also can integrate variables, although such analyses are few and have been done only on psychosocial variables. In descending order of predictive importance the variables are lack of goal-directedness and poor identity; anxiety; interpersonal difficulties evidenced by undependability, isolation, and few or no peer relations; self-directed anger or inexplicable outbursts; low competence evidenced by developmental delays, poor schoolwork, and a poor sense of competence; and, finally, distractibility, daydreaming, and tangential thinking. (See Watt and Saiz, 1991.)

A second use of statistics is to uncover constellations or patterns of risk variables. As we have seen, a number of research findings apply to psychotic individuals in general rather than being specific to schizophrenia. One reason for this failure to find differences may be that only single variables have typically been studied. When constellations of variables are used—such as poor motor development, high intraindividual variability on cognitive tasks, social withdrawal, emotional flatness, irritability, and emotional instability—children of schizophrenics can more readily be distinguished from both normal and other disturbed populations. (See Ledingham, 1990, for more examples.) Thus, specificity to schizophrenia may be a matter of the *patterning* of risk variables.

Finally, statistical analyses can be used as the basis for conceptualizations concerning etiology. To return to the statistical analysis of psychosocial variables, note how many concern lacks or deficiencies. Extrapolating the notion of lacks and deficiencies to the cognitive sphere, Watt and Saiz (1991) epitomize the findings concerning schizophrenic thinking in terms of *passivising* which is evidenced in many ways. There is the weakness of sustained effort and attention, as if the schizophrenic could not summon the mental energy necessary for organized thought; there is helplessness and a sense of being the passive object of environmental events; there is the failure to sustain the more demanding kinds of cognition such as abstract thinking and complex learning.

Ironically, there is evidence that flatness of affect, which seems congruent with the notion of passivity, is more potent in differentiating schizophrenia from other severe disturbances and is more stable and predictive of schizophrenia than are thinking disorders (Knight and Roff, 1985). Yet it is rarely studied, perhaps because of assessment difficulties or perhaps because of the strong cognitive bias in current research. If Watt and Saiz are correct in their conceptualization, then the basic defect in schizophrenia is a motivational one. In terms of our variables, passivizing represents an extreme deficiency in initiative.

The Case for Discontinuity   The overarching assumption in all the research so far is that adolescent schizophrenia has its roots in earlier developmental periods. Certain investigators have challenged this assumption on empirical and conceptual grounds.

Hanson, Gottesman, and Heston (1990), after reviewing the results of follow-up, follow-back, and high-risk studies, conclude that none of them establish a causal relation between the resulting variables and schizophrenia. They also maintain that the majority of variables are related to disturbance in general, while genetic data are schizophrenia-specific.

Conceptually, according to Hanson, Gottesman, and Heston (1990), researchers make the mistake of thinking linearly ("puppies become dogs") instead of nonlinearly ("caterpillars become moths" but one will search in vain for embryonic wings on them). Specifically, genetic events happen in adolescence that have little or no relation to prior development. The authors state that schizophrenia is a "qualitatively different" disorder, using the term to denote developmental discontinuity rather than to denote behavior that has little or no counterpart in normal development (as the term was used to describe autism in Chapter 4).

In a similar vein, Pogue-Geile (1991), drawing upon developmental behavior genetics, postulates that a defect in genes controlling postpubital brain development plays the crucial role in causing schizophrenia. Thus, abnormalities in genetically controlled brain development during adolescence is the key etiological agent. In Pogue-Geile's theory, the early obstetrical complications and insults to the organism that experts like Mednick regard as causal do nothing more than increase the probability that the genetic abnormalities will produce the clinical symptoms of schizophrenia. Such variables are basically ancillary and nonspecific. Thus the relation between early and late, specific and nonspecific causes is reversed. One major shortcoming of this genetic hypothesis is that it is not clear how a genetically defective program in adolescence would account for childhood-onset schizophrenia.

As we noted in the introduction, attempts at integrating the data are self-contained and have little to say to one another. While each is helpful, taken together they show how far we are from an overall integration.

Conceptualizing the Psychopathology

In general, investigators of child and adolescent schizophrenia have not been concerned with answering the question of how normal development has gone awry. Some data indicate a developmental fixation or delay. For example, the performance of children with schizophrenia on span-of-attention tasks is like that of younger children, while loose and illogical thinking in middle childhood may represent a failure to develop beyond the thinking of the preschool period. Hallucinations in late childhood and adolescence might represent a regression to the preschool period when they occur in response to extreme stress. Negative symptoms in general and passivising in particular fit the behavioral definition of psychopathology as a deficit.

However, the data have presented us with two new phenomena. Deviant motor development as evidenced by awkwardness is found from infancy through adolescence, which means it is a *nondevelopmental* variable. It also means that the developmental approach does not require that all variables change over time; rather, both changing and unchanging ones must be discovered and considered.

The next new model of psychopathology is developmental *discontinuity*, in which the present clinical picture bears little or no relation to the past. According to some investigators a genetic malfunctioning in adolescence deflects the developmental trajectory and sends it off in a new direction. While

this is a radical view, it is not incompatible with a developmental approach, which involves discontinuities as well as continuities.

Intervention

The lack of well-designed objective studies that has hampered our understanding of the nature and origins of childhood and adolescent schizophrenia continues to characterize the literature on intervention. In spite of the widespread use of neuroleptics (dopamine receptor blockers) in the treatment of children, for example, and in spite of the serious and sometimes toxic side effects that can develop, there are few controlled studies of drug treatment. The literature on psychosocial interventions consists solely of clinical reports, with no controlled studies reported (Asarnow & Asarnow, 1996).

Psychopharmacological Therapy   Psychopharmacology is the therapy of choice, and there is some evidence concerning the effectiveness of various neuroleptics. (Our presentation follows Asarnow and Asarnow, 1996, and Remschmidt et al., 1994.) Reduction in psychotic symptoms was found in a double-blind, crossover design study (i.e., alternating the drug with a placebo) investigating the effects of the neuroleptic haloperidol (Haldol) on 16 children between 5 and 12 years of age. In another study 75 percent of 41 adolescents with schizophrenia showed improvement in symptoms after being treated with clozapine, another neuroleptic. Preliminary results suggest that clozapine may be more effective than haloperidol while being safer in terms of avoiding its side effects, such as seizures (Jacobsen & Rapoport, 1998).

Other Remedial Approaches   Because schizophrenia may have such widespread effects on the individual as well as on the family, pharmacological treatment must be supplemented by various other kinds of remedial and rehabilitative measures. Weiner (1992) describes a program of individual psychotherapy aimed at countering the social isolation and impaired reality contact found in schizophrenia through relationship building and reality testing. The former involves a combination of warmth and nurturance for those who have been deprived of love, and firmness without anger or punitiveness for those who cannot control their aggressive acting out. To correct delusions and hallucinations, the therapist must point out that, while they are real to the patient, they are not real to the therapist. The next step involves identifying the needs giving rise to the cognitive distortions and dealing constructively with them. At a more practical level, the therapist helps the patient develop more effective social skills so as to counter social isolation.

It is often essential to involve the family in the treatment process in order to help family members correct any of the communication and affective patterns that can precipitate a relapse. There is suggestive evidence that family treatment aimed at increasing communication and problem-solving skills can lower the levels of EE and AS and that such treatment is more effective than individual treatment or medication alone. Finally, support from individuals outside the family, such as teachers or coaches, may be enlisted.

Behavior therapy stresses the reinforcement of adaptive responses, such as realistic thinking, and the weakening of maladaptive ones, such as delusions, by not reinforcing them. It also utilizes social skills training to help the individual with schizophrenia overcome social isolation. Finally, educational and vocational rehabilitation programs help the child or adolescent adjust to the demands of school or work.

As we have noted, research on child and adolescent schizophrenia is sparse, and investigators, aside from those studying precursors, have paid scant attention to the developmental dimension. By contrast, the psychopathologies we will discuss next—substance abuse and eating disorders—have been well researched and are closely tied in to the developments characterizing the adolescent period.

Psychopathologies of the Adolescent Transition: Eating Disorders and Substance Abuse

Normative Adolescent Development

Adolescence marks a major life change. The shift from childhood to adulthood is accompanied by changes in every aspect of individual development and every social context. In addition, adolescence is unique in that it involves two transitions: into the stage as one moves from childhood to adolescence, and out of the stage as the adolescent enters adulthood (Ebata, Peterson, & Conger, 1990). Thus the developmental picture is a complex one.

The *body* itself sets the stage with physical changes more rapid than those of any other developmental period except infancy, including the attainment of a mature size and body shape, hormonal changes associated with puberty, and the advent of adult sexuality. *Society* follows suit by requiring the youth to master more complex tasks, relinquish dependence on the family, and assume responsibility for making decisions regarding the two major tasks of adulthood, love and work. This transition is facilitated by the increasingly important role *peer relations* play

and by the newfound cognitive sophistication that enables the adolescent both to think abstractly and envision future possibilities, expanding the situation-specific self-perception of childhood into the overarching question, Who am I?

Adolescence gives special meaning to many of the personality variables we have been discussing. *Initiative* propels the forward momentum toward adulthood, and *self-control* allows for experimenting with new experiences while avoiding the extremes of inhibition and impulsivity. The intimacy of *attachment* merges with the *sexual* drive, and social relations with *peers* take on a new importance. In the realm of *work*, vocational choice becomes a realistic concern. Because of physiological changes, the psychological representation of the body, or the *body image*, is more salient than it has been since the early years. Increased *cognitive* complexity allows the adolescent both to entertain hypothetical possibilities and to ask abstract questions concerning the self and the future.

Cognitive development also allows the adolescent a more sophisticated level of self-exploration and a more realistic grasp of the options that society offers. Finally, the *family context* is also changing, since parents are often going through their own developmental transitions in the spheres of work, marriage, and personal growth.

Psychopathology in Adolescence

Western society has traditionally viewed the adolescent transition as one of turmoil, the inherent instability of the period being epitomized by the phrase "storm and stress." Psychoanalysts characterize the period as marking the return of primitive impulses and unresolved conflicts from the early stages of psychosexual development while, according to Erikson, a weakened ego struggles to master an identity crisis and role diffusion. However, it is becoming increasingly clear that the image of adolescence as a time of turmoil is applicable primarily to a minority of troubled teens. Most adolescents make the transition without significant emotional problems. Parent–adolescent relationships are generally harmonious, and for most adolescents the search for identity goes on unaccompanied by crises.

The revised picture should not be taken to mean that adolescence is uniformly serene. Moodiness, self-depreciation, and depression reach a peak in adolescence, and other psychopathologies also show a sharp rise, including suicide, schizophrenia, alcohol and drug abuse, and eating disorders. Although the overall rate of psychopathology increases only slightly, since other disturbances are on the decline, the new disturbances are far more serious than the ones they replace, making the picture an ominous one.

As Ebata, Peterson, and Conger (1990) point out, a developmental psychopathology perspective on adolescence needs to attend to (1) the *normative developmental capacities* that can serve as either risk or protective mechanisms for the individual, (2) the *social context* in which individual development takes place, and (3) the dynamic and *transactional processes* that characterize the relationship between

the individual and the social context. For example, while peer relations and academic expectations might become more challenging in adolescence, adding sources of stress than can undermine adjustment, adolescents are increasingly able to choose and influence their social contexts and in this way to have more control over their own development. In addition, they have an expanded ability to draw on their own resources, as well as those in the environment, in order to adapt and cope. (See Zahn-Waxler, 1996.)

Erikson's concept of **identity** integrates many of the diverse strands of adolescent development as well as providing leads as to potential sources of protection and vulnerability. Identity involves both inner continuity and interpersonal mutuality; it is a process of coming to terms with oneself and finding one's place in society. Adolescence is marked by an identity crisis because it is a "turning point, a crucial moment" (Erikson, 1968, p. 16), in which the adolescent must master the challenges of finding a fulfilling vocation, sexual role, and ideology, in order to avoid stagnation and regression. Youths approach the task of achieving an identity in ways that are influenced by how they have resolved previous stages of psychosocial development. Trust, autonomy, initiative, and industry act as protective factors, while mistrust, shame, doubt, guilt, and inferiority act as vulnerabilities.

The two psychopathologies we will discuss represent different ways in which developmental processes can go awry. In the relentless pursuit of thinness associated with eating disorders, the body image becomes a destructive tyrant, while the self-defeating need for autonomy is reminiscent of the oppositional behavior of the toddler period. In substance abuse, initiative propels the adolescent into assuming adult roles and freedoms for which he or she is ill prepared.

Eating Disorders: Anorexia Nervosa

Definition and Characteristics

Anorexia nervosa involves at least a 15 percent loss of body weight through purging and/or voluntary restriction, as well as an active pursuit of thinness.

Table 11.1   DSM-IV Criteria for Eating Disorders

Anorexia Nervosa

A. Refusal to maintain body weight at or above a minimally normal weight for age and height (e.g., weight loss leading to maintenance of body weight less than 85% of that expected; or failure to make expected weight gain during period of growth, leading to body weight less than 85% of that expected).

B. Intense fear of gaining weight or becoming fat, even though underweight.

C. Disturbance in the way in which one's body weight or shape is experienced, undue influence of body weight or shape on self-evaluation, or denial of the seriousness of the current low body weight.

D. In postmenarcheal females, amenorrhea (i.e., the absence of at least three consecutive menstrual cycles).

Specify type:

Restricting Type: During the current episode of Anorexia Nervosa, the person has not regularly engaged in binge-eating or purging behavior (i.e., self-induced vomiting or the misuse of laxatives, diuretics, or enemas).

Binge-Eating/Purging Type: During the current episode of Anorexia Nervosa, the person has regularly engaged in binge-eating or purging behavior.

Bulimia Nervosa

A. Recurrent episodes of binge eating, characterized by both of the following:

   (1) Eating, in a discrete period of time (e.g., within any 2-hour period), an amount of food that is definitely larger than most people would eat during a similar period of time and under similar circumstances.

   (2) A sense of lack of control over eating during the episode (e.g., a feeling that one cannot stop eating or control what or how much one is eating).

B. Recurrent inappropriate compensatory behavior in order to prevent weight gain, such as self-induced vomiting; misuse of laxatives, diuretics, enemas; fasting; or excessive exercise.

C. The binge-eating and inappropriate compensatory behaviors both occur, on average, at least twice a week for 3 months.

D. Self-evaluation is unduly influenced by body shape and weight.

E. The disturbance does not occur exclusively during episodes of Anorexia Nervosa.

Specify type:

Purging Type: During the current episode of Bulimia Nervosa, the person has regularly engaged in self-induced vomiting or the misuse of laxatives, diuretics, or enemas

Nonpurging Type: During the current episode of Bulimia Nervosa, the person has used other inappropriate compensatory behaviors, such as fasting or excessive exercise, but has not regularly engaged in self-induced vomiting or the misuse of laxatives, diuretics, or enemas.

Source: American Psychiatric Association, 1994.

DSM-IV differentiates two types based on the different means used to achieve thinness. The first relies solely on strict dieting and is called the **restricting type**. The second, the **binge-eating/purging type**, alternates between dieting and binge eating, followed by self-induced vomiting or purging. (See Table 11.1.)

Youths with anorexia have a normal awareness of hunger but are terrified of giving in to the impulse to eat. Unlike an ordinary dieter, the individual wastes away to a dangerous state of emaciation in pursuit of some ideal image of thinness. As the condition advances, diets become increasingly restrictive. For example, one girl would eat only two chicken livers a day, while another ate only celery sticks and chewing gum for a year before her death (Bruch, 1973). People who have anorexia often take extreme pride in the control they demonstrate over their food intake.

Among the secondary symptoms of anorexia, *excessive activity* is one of the most common. (Our review follows Foreyt and Mikhail, 1997, and Wilson, Heffernan, and Black, 1996, except where noted.) At times the intensity of the activity is masked by its socially acceptable form, such as participation in sports. *Amenorrhea* is another common secondary symptom, with menstruation often ceasing prior to weight loss.

Anorexia is one of the few psychopathologies that can lead to death. Studies have reported a *fatality rate* of as high as 10 percent due to suicide or medical complications secondary to the disorder. Semi-starvation can affect most major organ systems, resulting in anemia, renal system impairments, and cardiovascular problems; imbalances in the electrolyte system crucial to heart functioning, which can lead to sudden death; and osteoporosis and an irreversible shortness of stature.

Anorexia is predominantly a disorder of *females*, with an estimated *prevalence* of 1 in 100. Only 4 to 8 percent of those diagnosed with anorexia are male. Anorexia is most prevalent in middle-and upper-class Caucasian adolescents, but it is increasingly found among all social classes and ethnicities (Pate et al., 1992). The peak periods of onset are ages 14 and 18.

Anorexia involves a distortion of the body image.

Etiology

The Organic Context

There is evidence of a *genetic* component in anorexia: the concordance for dizygotic twins is 5 percent, while for monozygotic twins it is 56 percent. The exact mechanism of transmission is not known. Speculation has implicated deficits impairing the release of particular hormones (gonadotropins) from the pituitary gland, or else imbalances in certain neurotransmitters, such as dopamine or norepinephrine (Herzog & Beresin, 1991). However, many of the biological correlates of anorexia appear to be secondary to weight loss and are reversible with weight gain.

The Intrapersonal Context

The Body Image   Along with menarche and breast development, during puberty females undergo a "fat spurt," an accumulation of large quantities of subcutaneous fat that adds an average of 24 pounds of weight. The physical changes associated with puberty force the adolescent to make a fundamental reorganization of her body image, which—coupled with her increased capacity for self-reflection—may result in a preoccupation with her body and with the responses of others to it. There is evidence that these pubertal changes are linked to preoccupation with weight and dieting in normative populations. In ad-

dition, *early maturing* girls are more likely to develop eating disorders than those who begin to physically develop later (Swarr & Richards, 1996).

Studies of individuals with anorexia have suggested a developmental sequence in which body dissatisfaction leads to typical dieting attempts, which give way to preoccupation with food and weight and the use of increasingly more maladaptive methods of weight control. Therefore *ordinary dieting*, in the context of other psychological risk factors, may be the first step in a trajectory toward psychopathology.

Bruch's (1973) clinical observations also suggest that girls with anorexia often have *inaccurate perceptions* of their bodies. They literally do not perceive how thin their bodies have become. One patient had difficulty discriminating between two photographs of herself even though there was a 70-pound difference in her weight. Another said she could see how emaciated her body was when looking in a mirror, but when she looked away she reverted to her belief that she was larger. Thus the image of the body, which is a reasonably accurate psychological construction in normal development, borders on a somatic delusion in the anorexic. Perception is determined not by reality but by emotional conflicts. According to Bruch's (1973) classic theory, the anorexic's pursuit of self-respect through food refusal is expressed in the vain pursuit of a body that literally is never perceived as sufficiently thin. More recent research confirms the relationship between eating disorder symptomatology and distortions in body image (Foreyt & Mikhail, 1997).

Bruch (1973) also suggests that anorexic girls are unable to accurately identify and discriminate between *proprioceptive* (internal body) states, such as hunger, satiety, anger, and sadness. Therefore, they are likely to mislabel their feelings, or to confuse emotions such as anger with the desire to eat. Measurement of poor proprioceptive awareness is included in screening assessments for anorexia and has been found to be associated with increased risk for the development of the disorder (Lyon et al., 1997).

Personality Characteristics   While both types of anorexia are characterized by their pursuit of thinness, those who restrict tend to be more *rigid* and *conforming, socially insecure, obsessional*, and *lacking in insight*. Those who binge-purge, which make up about half the population of those with anorexia, are more *extroverted* and *sociable* but are more emotionally *unstable* and *feel hunger* more intensely. They also tend to have problems with *impulse control*. In their study of fifty women hospitalized for anorexia, for example, Casper, Hedeker, and McClough (1992) found that restricters were higher in self-control, inhibition of emotionality, and conscientiousness. By contrast, binge-purgers were more impulsive (although still in the average range), and while they shared the restricters' belief in moral family values, they were emotionally more adventurous and had more characterological problems.

Cognition   As Foreyt and Mikhail (1997) note, there are no satisfactory theories about the role of cognitions in the origins of anorexia. However, *cognitive distortions*, such as "catastrophizing," overgeneralizing, and personalizing, have been found in anorexics to a much greater degree than in controls. Other dysfunctional cognitive styles, such as *obsessional thinking* and *negative self-judgments*, are also commonly seen in those diagnosed with anorexia.

Cognitive factors are also important in regulating eating behavior, as has been learned from studying normative dieters. Adherence to a diet is cognitively controlled, often in terms of quotas on food

intake. Moreover, chronic dieters are vulnerable to *"counterregulatory" eating*, or binge eating on high-calorie food; for example, the mere belief that one has transgressed one's diet can break the dieter's resolve and trigger increased food consumption. Such findings on normal populations are relevant to understanding the binge-purge cycle.

The Interpersonal Context: Family Influences

Minuchin, Rosman, and Baker's (1978) observation of "anorexic families" provided the basis for much of the theorizing about the influence of the family system on psychopathology. They describe four characteristic patterns of interaction in families of adolescents with anorexia:

1. *Enmeshment.* Members of the pathologically enmeshed family are highly involved and responsive to one another but in an intrusive way. As we saw in Chapter 1, enmeshed families have poorly differentiated perceptions of each other, and roles and lines of authority are diffuse (for example, children may assume parental roles).
2. *Overprotectiveness.* Family members of psychosomatically ill children are overly concerned for each other's welfare. A sneeze can set off "a flurry of handkerchief offers," and criticism must be cushioned by pacifying behavior. The family's **overprotectiveness** and exaggerated concern for the child retards the development of autonomy, and the child, in turn, feels responsible for protecting the family from distress.
3. *Rigidity.* Pathological families resist change. Particularly in periods of normal growth, such as adolescence, they intensify their efforts to retain their customary patterns. One consequence of **rigidity** is that the child's illness is used as an excuse for avoiding problems accompanying change.
4. *Lack of conflict resolution.* Some families deny conflict; others bicker in a diffuse, scattered, ineffectual way; and yet others have a parent who is conflict-avoidant, such as a father who leaves the house every time a confrontation threatens.

Minuchin, Rosman, and Baker (1978) describe the family of the future anorexic as overly concerned with diet, appearance, and control. The family's intrusiveness undermines the child's autonomy, and both her psychological and bodily functions are continually subject to scrutiny. Adolescence is a particularly stressful time for the enmeshed family, which is unable to cope with the developmental task of separation. The youth, sensing the stress, responds with troubled behavior such as self-starvation. Perhaps even more important, being symptomatic helps to maintain the youth in an ostensibly dependent role in relation to her parents, while at the same time her refusal to eat allows her a covert form of rebellion.

Empirical support can be found for the family model. For example, Fosson and coworkers (1987) found that the families of girls with anorexia evidenced overinvolvement, failure to resolve conflicts, and poor communication. Further, Humphrey (1989) observed the families of normal female adolescents and compared their interactions to those of girls with restricting-type anorexia, binge-purging anorexia, and bulimia. In support of Minuchin's ideas, parents of daughters with anorexia tended to communicate a double message of nurturance and affection combined with discounting the daughter's expressions of her own thoughts and feelings. The daughters, in turn, vacillated between asserting their feelings and yielding to their parents.

On the other hand, there is evidence that these family dynamics are not unique to the development of anorexia, as they are found in families of children with other psychosomatic illnesses such as asthma. A similar case can be made for many of the other family factors associated with anorexia. For example, a family history of depression—especially maternal depression—has been linked not only to an increased risk of anorexia (Lyon et al., 1997), but to several other disorders as well (see Chapter 7). A number of authors have refuted the idea that there is one "anorexogenic" family type (e.g., Rastam and Gillberg, 1991).

The Interpersonal Context: Peer Relations

Anorexics often report that they were *excessively shy*, or even friendless, as children. In adolescence they are also reluctant to form close relationships outside the family, thereby isolating themselves

from the important growth-promoting functions of peer relations in the adolescent period. *Sexual relations*, in particular, are avoided. For example, Leon and associates (1985) found that both restricters and binge-purgers had a markedly negative evaluation of sex and lacked interest in developing sexual relationships; and Carlat, Camargo, and Herzog (1997) report that 58 percent of males with anorexia describe themselves as "asexual."

A recent study has indicated that there may actually be a *developmental shift* in the sexual behavior of eating-disordered girls. Cauffman and Sternberg (1996) found that girls with disordered eating matured sooner and were involved in sexual activity earlier than other girls. Although they appear more mature than their years, these girls may be emotionally unprepared for the social pressures associated with sexuality. Over time, anxiety about their appearance, lack of pleasure derived from sex, and the withdrawal associated with self-starvation lead them to withdraw from the sexual activities that contributed to the disorder in the first place.

Research on anorexia is complicated by the fact that starvation per se significantly affects behavior, producing depression, irritability, social isolation, and decreased sexual interest. Starvation can also alter relationships with family members and friends, who are helpless to intervene in eating patterns that produce striking emaciation and might eventuate in death. Thus the problem of distinguishing causes from consequences is a knotty one.

The Superordinate Context

In our society the ideal of feminine beauty has changed from the curvaceous figure epitomized by such icons as Marilyn Monroe to the lean and svelte look admired today. For example, contestants in Miss America pageants have steadily decreased in weight over the past decades. Currently the average weight is 13 to 19 percent below normal—the "ideal" woman, in other words, meets the first criterion for an eating disorder diagnosis (Attie & Brooks-Gunn, 1995).

Few young women are able to achieve the exaggeratedly tall and thin proportions exemplified by pageant contestants and high fashion models. But cultural norms dictate that "fat" is ugly and what is ugly is bad, while thin is beautiful and what is beautiful is good. Moreover, the message is more powerful in certain settings: colleges and boarding schools, where beauty and dating are emphasized, and professions such as dancing and modeling, which dictate certain body weights, are breeding grounds for anorexia. Further, there is evidence that *physical attractiveness* is central to the female sex-role stereotype (but is peripheral to the masculine sex role stereotype, which may be why far fewer men become anorexic).

Comorbidity

Depression is often present in adolescents with anorexia, and one study found a comorbidity rate of 73 percent (Herzog et al., 1992). Such high comorbidity led to the speculation that anorexia and depression share a common etiology. However, subsequent research indicated that, while they occur together, they are independent disturbances: for example, improvement in the eating disorder does not necessarily relieve the depression. Also, the onset of depressive disorders is secondary to the development of anorexia (Rastam, 1992). This is understandable, as depressed mood accompanies any form of starvation.

Personality disorders co-occur in as many as 74 percent of those with anorexia (Skodol et al., 1993), particularly borderline and avoidant personality (Piran et al., 1988). *Obsessive-compulsive* traits are often found, with both restricting and binge-purging types being chronically preoccupied with counting calories and with images of food. Some longitudinal research suggests that obsessive traits predate the development of anorexic symptoms (Rastam, 1992). Comorbidity with *anxiety disorders* is also seen.

Developmental Course

Follow-up studies show that only about 10 percent of those with anorexia fully recover. While almost half may show *partial recovery*, many continue to be seriously impaired by depression, social phobias, or recurrent symptoms (Herzog et al., 1993). Even in treated populations, *avoidance of sexual activity* remains in over half of the sample, and *social problems* also tend to persist. In adulthood, women with anorexia are less likely to be married or heterosex-

ually involved than others. *Early onset* (i.e., before 16 years of age) may be associated with a less negative prognosis, although a far from favorable one (Theander, 1996). Anorexia may also be a precursor to *bulimia* for some females; more than half of females with anorexia are diagnosed with bulimia at a later stage (Clinton & Glant, 1992).

Eating Disorders: Bulimia Nervosa

Definition and Characteristics

Bulimia is characterized by recurrent episodes of binge eating, or the rapid consumption of large quantities of food in a brief period of time. Binge eating is followed by attempts to prevent weight gain, such as through self-induced vomiting and the misuse of laxatives or diuretics (the *purging type*) or by fasting and excessive exercise (the *nonpurging type*). Although individuals with bulimia may be either under- or overweight, their weight is usually within the average range. (See Table 11.1.)

A binge should be distinguished from normal overeating. True bingeing involves ingestion of massive amounts of food irrespective of actual hunger, consuming to the point of discomfort or even pain, and subsequent feelings of self-disgust or depression. Further, individuals with bulimia are terrified of losing control over their eating, and it is this feeling of loss of control, rather than the amount of food consumed, that differentiates a binge from ordinary overindulgence. In their "all or none" way of thinking, young women with bulimia fear that even eating a small amount of a favorite food could result in catastrophic intake. In a less extreme form, they also share the anorexic's fear of becoming obese and perceive themselves as fat even when their body weight is normal. Thus the·uncontrolled desire to gorge traps the adolescent with bulimia between anxiety over anticipated loss of control and obesity on the one hand, and guilt, shame, and self-contempt following a binge on the other hand.

Although less often associated with death than self-starvation, purging also represents a serious risk to *physical health*. Gorging and vomiting can

Binge eating.

harm the stomach and esophagus, and the repeated wash of stomach acids can erode the enamel of the teeth, causing permanent damage. Frequent purging causes electrolyte and fluid imbalances, leading to weakness, lethargy, and depression, as well as irregular heartbeat, kidney problems, and sudden death. Habitual vomiting is also associated with broken blood vessels in the face, blotchy skin, excessive water retention, and enlargement of the salivary glands, producing a "chipmunk cheek" appearance; also, the odor of vomitus may linger on the purger. Thus, the goal of being physically attractive is defeated by the maladaptive strategies used to pursue it.

Prevalence   The prevalence of bulimia in female adolescents and young adults overall is about 1 percent, but this rises to an estimated 4 percent in college females. (Here we follow Wilson, Heffernan, and Black, 1996.) Larger percentages are found when studies inquire about binge-purging without reference to DSM criteria. For example, almost 20 percent of one sample of college students admitted to engaging in such behavior.

While most bulimia is seen in females, the disorder is not as rare among males as is anorexia. It is estimated that 10 to 15 percent of those with bulimia are *male*. Evidence suggests that, in comparison to females, males show a later onset (between ages 18 and 26), a higher prevalence of childhood obesity, and less involvement with dieting (Carlat, Camargo, & Herzog, 1997).

Etiology

The Organic Context

There is likely to be a history of *maternal obesity* in the families of adolescents diagnosed with bulimia. Therefore, there is speculation that a constitutional predisposition makes weight loss difficult for these individuals. The tendency toward being overweight increases the likelihood that they will be dissatisfied with their body shape and that they will attempt excessive weight loss strategies such as purging (Wilson et al., 1996).

A number of studies have reported deficient levels of the neurotransmitter *serotonin* in those with bulimia, although Jimerson and colleagues (1997) note that serotonin levels were related to the number of binge episodes participants reported engaging in prior to their study, thus leaving open the question of cause and effect. It has been supposed that low serotonin might interfere with the brain's ability to register carbohydrate intake, thus causing an abnormal craving for the kinds of carbohydrate-rich food that is often involved in binging. However, the evidence supporting the idea of binge eating as driven by "carbohydrate craving" is not strong. It is also important to note that *dieting* has both psychological and physiological effects that increase the likelihood of food cravings and binge eating (Leon et al., 1995). Restricting food intake thus contributes to both further weight gain and disordered eating. Indeed, most adolescents report that the onset of the disorder followed a period of dieting.

The Intrapersonal Context

Although there is no clear bulimic "personality," among the intrapersonal factors associated with bulimia are *perfectionism* and *self-criticism*, a *need for approval*, and *low self-esteem*. Feelings of inadequacy and low self-worth are associated with disordered eating as early as in the sixth and seventh grades (Killen et al., 1994). The self-esteem of youth with bulimia is dependent on the opinions of others. They seem to be willing to neglect their own needs and feelings in order to devote themselves to winning others' approval. *Anxiety* is also a common feature of bulimia, and some studies have shown that anxiety precedes the onset of bulimia and may precipitate eating problems (Schwalberg et al., 1992).

Further, adolescents with bulimia are described as being *sensitive to rejection* and being *high achievers*, with their strivings channeled into their dogged pursuit of thinness. They are likely to have a history of *childhood maladjustment* and to be alienated from their families. In addition, their behavior is more extroverted, and they are more likely to abuse alcohol, to steal, to attempt suicide, and to be affectively unstable rather than depressed (Rodin, Striegel-Moore, & Silberstein, 1990). Thus their behavior, like their eating pattern, suggests a basic difficulty in *self-regulation*.

In order to study the psychological processes associated with binge-purging, Johnson and Larson (1982) came up with an ingenious strategy. They asked women with bulimia to carry a pager so that the investigators could cue them to write down their thoughts, feelings, and behavior at random intervals throughout the day. Two hours before an episode of binge-eating, women with bulimia reported feeling anger and guilt, while their perceptions of self-control and adequacy were low. During the binge, feelings of anger, guilt, and loss of control intensified. After the binge, feelings of depression, disgust, and self-deprecation dominated. Purges were associated with a reestablishment of a sense of calm, self-control, and adequacy—described in terms such as being "clean," "empty," "spaced out," and "ready to sleep." See Box 11.1 for an illustration of this in author Evelyn Lau's description of her own eight-year battle with bulimia.

Purging, therefore, seems to have certain reinforcing properties in itself. In fact, some researchers have speculated that individuals with bulimia binge so they will be able to purge (Heatherton & Baumeister, 1991). Purging seems to act as a form of *self-sedation*, allowing the adolescent to escape from negative affects and regulate her mood (Stice et al., 1996).

The Interpersonal Context: Peer Relations

One way in which peer influences play a role is in terms of *initiating* the adolescent into bulimic behavior. Many adolescents are introduced to vomiting or use of laxatives as a weight-control technique by friends. (One young woman stopped giving inspirational talks about her own recovery from bulimia when she found that the high school girls who attended were only interested in learning the techniques she'd used for purging herself of food!) While most young women ultimately abstain from these maladaptive techniques, others become caught in the repetitive cycle of binge-purging.

Qualities of peer relationships also differentiate anorexia and bulimia. Adolescents with bulimia are more *outgoing* and are thus more likely than those with anorexia to appear on the surface to be functioning adequately in their academic and social worlds. Further, adolescents with bulimia tend to be more *sexually active* than those with anorexia, and some are even promiscuous (Garfinkel & Garner, 1986). However, there is also evidence that they enjoy sex less than do other youth. Rather than seeking out sex for self-gratification, adolescents with bulimia are overly compliant with pressure to engage in sexual activities because of their strong need for social approval and difficulty identifying and asserting their own needs.

On the other hand, when the binge-purge cycle is well-established, the shame associated with these activities tends to *isolate* adolescents from their peers. The adolescent with advanced bulimia is preoccupied with thoughts of food, eating, and purging to the point that all other matters fall by the wayside. Such adolescents spend less time socializing and more time alone than normal controls. Many describe spending most of their time and energy planning and amassing food for their binges, as well as seeking seclusion in order to purge. As one remarked, "Food has become my closest companion" (Johnson & Larson, 1982).

The Interpersonal Context: Family Influences

In contrast to the family of the adolescent diagnosed with anorexia, whose family members may present themselves as untroubled except for the problems

Box 11.1   **A Case of Bulimia: Evelyn Lau**

"I no longer clearly remember the first time I forced myself to throw up. What I do remember is how inexpert I was and how long it took before I succeeded in actually vomiting instead of just gagging and retching. . . . In my mid-teens I was too young to believe I was anything but immortal. It didn't occur to me that what I was doing was dangerous—instead, it seemed a smart and practical way of coping with things. I went through months of throwing up once or twice a day, then brief periods when I did not throw up at all, when I seemed to have broken the pattern. Surely this meant I was in control. But by the time I turned 18, the months of not throwing up had diminished to weeks, and when I was vomiting I was doing it four, five, six times a day. I had become addicted to the sensation. It was no longer a penance I had to perform after eating, but the reward at the end of a binge. I loved the feeling I had after purging, of being clean and shiny inside like a scrubbed machine, superhuman. I would rise from the bathroom floor, splash my face with cold water, vigorously brush the acid from my mouth. I would take a wet cloth, wipe off the vomit that had spattered my arms, and feel as energized as someone who had just woken from a nap or returned from an invigorating jog around the block. I felt as if everything inside me had been displaced so that it was now outside myself. Not only all the food I had eaten, but my entire past. No one could tell me to stop, not even my friends, who eventually knew what I was doing. They could not control this part of my life or any other. This was mine alone. . . .

"I finally stopped being bulimic nearly two years ago, when I was 22. It ended not because of willpower or therapy. . . . It ended because the pain from throwing up rendered the pleasure slight by comparison. It ended when my softened teeth cringed at every mouthful and when I woke several times each night with cramps wracking my stomach. . . . It ended when I arrived at the point where I could no longer feel my feet. Months later, when I went to the doctor, he would diagnose it as an electrolyte imbalance caused by the vomiting up of so many vitamins and minerals. . . . By then I had also developed a hiatal hernia—a portion of my stomach protruded through my esophagus—and my teeth became so compromised that one day one of them simply disintegrated under pressure. . . .

"The last time I forced myself to throw up, it felt like internal surgery. Grief, love, rage, pain—it all came pouring out, yet afterwards it was still there inside me. I had been bulimic off and on for eight years, and in all that vomiting I had not purged myself of any of the things that were making me sick."

Source: Lau, 1995.

of the "identified patient," the family members of youth with bulimia are more likely to be overtly disturbed. *Parental psychopathology* is often observed, particularly *depression* and *substance abuse* (Fairburn et al., 1997).

As with anorexia, in cases of bulimia family relationships have been described as *enmeshed* and *rigid* (Leon et al., 1994). However, more characteristic of bulimia is *family discord*, including *parent–child conflict* and overt *hostility* (Fairburn et al., 1997). Humphrey's (1989) observations indicated that, in contrast to those of normal female adolescents or those with anorexia, families of bulimics showed less affection in their interactions. They were also "hostilely enmeshed," with family members blaming or controlling each other. When mothers thwarted their efforts to assert their individuality, daughters submitted in a petulant and passive-aggressive way.

The Superordinate Context

The same societal influences that contribute to the development of anorexia have been implicated in the development of bulimia, including Western culture's emphasis on slenderness, and the tendency to judge females on the basis of their physical appearance. Striegel-Moore (1993) emphasizes two aspects of Western feminine sex-role socialization that contribute to the risk of bulimia: the emphasis placed on *beauty* as an essential component of femininity, and the *interpersonal, communal orientation* that leads girls to base their self-evaluations on the opinions and perceptions of others.

Empirical evidence in support of these ideas is available. In contrast to males, the self-esteem of female children and adults is based on body image and is influenced by the opinions of others. Dissatisfaction with body weight and maladaptive eating are endemic among young females in North America, even in the preadolescent years. Dieting, fear of fatness, and binge eating have been found in 31 to 46 percent of 9-year-old girls and in 46 to 81 percent of 10-year-old girls (Mellin, Irwin, & Scully, 1992). This is, Rodin, Striegel-Moore, and Silberstein (1990) claim, "the age of eating disorders" (p. 361), and dissatisfaction with their appearance is women's "normative discontent" (p. 362).

Further, individuals with bulimia report greater perceived pressure from their peers and parents to be thin, and they are particularly more likely to believe that society in general requires them to be slender (Stice et al., 1996). In this way, they seem to have internalized these larger social dictates more than other girls.

Comorbidity

Anxiety disorders are found in as many as 80 percent of females with bulimia (see Foreyt and Mikhail, 1997). Symptoms of *depression* are frequently seen: between 35 and 78 percent meet criteria for an affective disorder at some point in their illness. In addition, *obsessive-compulsive* disorder often co-occurs. *Substance abuse* occurs in about one-third of individuals with bulimia, frequently involving the misuse of stimulants to reduce weight. These two disorders also share in common particular predisposing personality factors, including the inability to regulate negative feelings, the need for immediate gratification, and a fragile sense of self. It is estimated that between one-third and one-half of those with bulimia also meet criteria for one or more *personality disorders*.

Developmental Course

When compared to anorexia, rates of *recovery* from an episode of bulimia are relatively high; Herzog and colleagues (1993) found that 56 percent of young women treated for bulimia were without symptoms after a period of one year. Unfortunately, over the long term, periods of recovery are punctuated by episodes of *relapse*. So, like anorexia, bulimia tends to be a chronic disorder (Keller et al., 1992).

A Comparison of Eating Disorders

Table 11.2 compares the diagnostic criteria and empirical findings concerning anorexia and bulimia. When compared with those who restrict their food intake, those with anorexia who binge and purge experience more emotional insecurity, impulsivity, and substance abuse, characteristics that are also descriptive of bulimia. However, while families of adolescents with anorexia are characterized by rigidity and enmeshment, families of those with bulimia are more openly hostile, noncohesive, and non-nurturing (see Attie and Brooks-Gunn, 1995).

In general, bulimia and the binge-purger type of anorexia may have more in common with each other than either does with restricting-type anorexia. In fact, it has been suggested that it might be preferable to regard binge-purging anorexia as a special subgroup of bulimia rather than as a special subgroup of anorexia. However, more comparative studies must be done before the issue of classification can be resolved.

Integrative Developmental Models

Two of the more comprehensive accounts of the developmental psychopathology of eating disorders are those offered by Rodin, Striegel-Moore, and Silberstein (1990) and Attie and Brooks-Gunn, (1995). As noted above, Rodin, Striegel-Moore, and Silberstein emphasize *superordinate* factors, including society's emphasis on thinness as a mark of beauty, and beauty as essential to the feminine ideal. However, clearly not all females exposed to these pressures develop eating disorders. Therefore, a number of other *predisposing, precipitating*, and *sustaining* factors come into play in the various domains of development.

In the *family* domain, the parents are likely to be conflicted and insecure. In the case of anorexia, they are perfectionistic and judgmental, while, in the case of bulimia, they are emotionally disturbed and

Table 11.2   Comparison of Eating Disorders

Anorexia: Restricting Type	Anorexia: Binge-Purging Type	Bulimia
Typical onset age 14		Typical onset age 18
Excessive thinness		Normal or overweight
Intense fear of gaining weight		Fear of losing control over eating
Disturbance of body image (self-perception as fat)		Self-evaluation unduly influenced by weight
Amenorrhea		Normal menstruation
Voluntary food restrictions	Binge-eating and purging	
Family enmeshed, overprotective, rigid, poor conflict resolution		Family history of psychological problems, substance abuse; family discord and overt hostility
Socially isolated	Socially insecure	Low self-esteem; rejection-sensitive
Disinterested in sex		Sexually active with little enjoyment
Overcontrolled	Emotionally labile, poor impulse control	
Comorbid with depression, anxiety, personality disorder	Comorbid with depression, obsessive-compulsiveness, substance abuse	
Maternal history of anorexia	Family history and predisposition to obesity	

impulsive. Their care of the infant, therefore, while on the surface devoted and attentive, is marred by insensitivity, taking the form of intrusive overprotectiveness or excessive control. The result is a hostile-dependent relationship in which the exploited child cannot express her rage because of the fear that the mother will leave her alone and helpless. Because feeling states are given the labels acceptable to parents—rather than those accurate for the child—poor recognition of feelings, and difficulty regulating and expressing them, develops.

Strober and Humphrey (1987) propose that these family interactions undermine the daughter's development of a sense of *self-efficacy* and interfere with her development of strategies for coping with negative emotions. Thus, the parents overcontrol their daughter and ignore and negate her self-expression, which undermines her efforts to individuate and keeps her in a dependent state. When the normal development of healthy initiative and self-assertiveness (see Chapter 5) is blocked, the only alternative is self-destructive opposition.

Included in the *intrapersonal domain* are factors such as lack of a sense of mastery and autonomy, maturational fears, conscientiousness and confor-

mity, and rigid thinking. Other personality characteristics may include a strong need for social approval and immediate need for gratification, poor impulse control, obsessionality, depression, and a fragile sense of self.

Organic factors also come into play. A temperamental tendency toward obsessional thinking, rigidity, and poor adaptability to change may, in turn, leave the young woman poorly equipped to cope with the challenges of adolescence (Strober, 1995). In addition, particularly in the case of bulimia, these girls may be genetically programmed to be heavier than the svelte ideal. They may begin puberty earlier, making them particularly unhappy with their weight because of the weight gain that naturally occurs at that time. Thus, the young woman predisposed to eating disorders is more vulnerable because she finds it physically difficult to achieve the slender ideal. However, she is also more likely to have internalized the belief that her appearance will determine how successful she will be in life, and so her natural shape is unacceptable to her.

Development comes into play in specific ways. Attie and Brooks-Gunn (1995) emphasize the significance of the fact that eating disorders tend to occur at two developmental transitions: at entry into adolescence and at the borderline between adolescence and young adulthood. The *stage-salient tasks* of adolescence, then, present a number of challenges. Tasks of early adolescence involve establishing a stable self-structure and regulating emotions, impulses, and self-esteem; resolving identity issues; developing sexual relationships and coping with the implications of reproductive capacity; renegotiating relationships with parents so as to develop autonomy while still remaining connected; and establishing achievement goals and a meaningful life trajectory. During the transition to adulthood, tasks include establishing intimate relationships, determining and pursuing one's own values and goals, and developing an independent identity.

However, for *females* especially, a number of factors conspire against the easy resolution of issues related to sexuality, identity, and achievement. By middle childhood, a girl's self-esteem begins to depend on others' opinions of her. In addition, a girl's perception of her own attractiveness, popularity, and success is often related to a thin body image. However, the pubertal fat spurt, coupled with increasing social sensitivity and the equating of self-worth with physical appearance image, may well cause distress and lead to preoccupation with weight and dieting.

Because of her prior history and psychological makeup, the young woman vulnerable to eating disorders is particularly ill-equipped to cope with the normative demands of adolescence. Although she cannot halt the changes occurring in her body or in her interpersonal world, food becomes one realm in which she can exert some control. Anorexia is thus a distorted attempt to resolve the conflict between the uncontrollable and rapid changes associated with the onset of puberty on the one hand, and the need for order and predictability on the other (Strober, 1995).

Intervention

Adolescents with eating disorders are difficult to treat successfully. Half of those treated continue to have eating difficulties and psychological problems. Even recovered patients continue to have distorted attitudes toward eating and weight, along with de-

pression and unsatisfactory social relations. Thus there is a tendency toward chronicity even with long and intensive treatment. (Our review follows Johnson, Tsoh, and Varnado, 1996, except where noted.)

Pharmacological Intervention   Many different psychopharmacological interventions have been tried with anorexia, without great success. While medications may be helpful in alleviating associated psychopathologies such as anxiety or depression, they have little effect on eating behavior or weight gain. Some promising results in the treatment of bulimia have been found with *antidepressants*, particularly the newer type of SSRIs (see Chapter 7). However, comparative studies find that antidepressant medications have weaker effects than psychotherapy. Further, dropout rates are higher among those treated with medications, usually due to unwanted side effects, and relapse rates are also higher once treatment ends. Other forms of therapy, therefore, appear to be more effective than medication.

Psychodynamic Psychotherapy   The goals of psychodynamic psychotherapy are to help the adolescent adopt a more realistic approach to eating, to counter her feelings of inadequacy and need for perfection, and to help her achieve self-esteem and autonomy. Because of the many ways in which the adolescent tries to undermine these treatment goals, therapists are usually advised to be sympathetic but firm in their approach. However, for these very reasons, nondirective approaches and classical psychoanalytic procedures for exploring unconscious motivations meet with limited success.

Behavior Modification   Behavior modification is often the treatment of choice for the adolescent hospitalized with anorexia, because the urgent need is to save her life by restoring her body weight. *Operant conditioning* techniques include rewarding eating through such individualized reinforcers as television viewing or visits from friends, and withholding rewards when there is noncompliance. For bulimia, *behavior modification* focuses on discontinuing the dieting behavior that contributes to food cravings and disordered eating, as well as encouraging more adaptive strategies for mood regulation, such as physical exercise. However, there is evidence that the behavioral approach, while effective in achieving the goal of immediate weight gain in anorexia, does not have long-lasting effects. It does not address faulty notions concerning eating, nor does it help the adolescent improve personality and interpersonal problems. These may be addressed by cognitive therapy.

Cognitive Therapy   Cognitive therapy aims at changing cognitive distortions, overgeneralizations, negative self-perceptions, and irrational beliefs about eating and about the self, such as "If only I were thin I would be perfect" (Stice et al., 1996). Techniques include *self-monitoring* to increase awareness of the situations, thoughts, and emotions that trigger disordered eating. Cognitive approaches for bulimia have been generally proven to be successful (Lewandowski et al., 1997), with full recovery reported in 50 to 90 percent of cases and low rates of relapse over a year. And, while other approaches may reduce binge eating and enhance general psychological well-being, the cognitive approach is more effective in changing attitudes about the body and also maladaptive dieting behavior (Fairburn et al., 1995).

Family Therapies   Family therapies aim at restructuring family interactions in order to break the patterns of enmeshment and rigidity. A classic technique used is the "*family lunch session*," in which the therapist involves the entire family in sharing a meal together in order to observe their interactions (Minuchin, 1974). In one example, when an overprotective mother and father immediately began the session by nagging their daughter to eat—which she, in response, steadfastly refused to do—the therapist distracted their attention by engaging the parents in a lively discussion of their religion's dietary laws and cuisine. While they were busy feeding the therapist this interesting information, he pointed out, their daughter had begun to eat her lunch.

Behavioral Family Systems Therapy   Behavioral family systems therapy integrates social learning and systemic family approaches (Robin et al., 1996). By engaging the parents in implementing a food-related *behavior modification* program, the therapist helps them to be effective in changing their daughter's problematic eating and to develop better *parent management skills*. In addition, parent–child interactions related to the behavior program provide many opportunities to work on *family systemic* issues, as maladaptive strategies of conflict avoidance, overprotectiveness, and enmeshment come into high relief.

Substance Abuse

We turn next to a very different psychopathology that emerges during adolescence; however, there are some parallels between this and our previous topic. While eating disorders represent problems with the regulation of food intake, substance abuse involves problems with controlling the craving for alcohol and illicit drugs.

Viewed in a historical context, we see that substance use has been a part of human society throughout time. Most cultures have used alcohol: mead was possibly used around 8000 B.C., the biblical Noah became drunk, and the Indians who met Columbus had their own "home brew." Drugs have been used in religious ceremonies, to medicate, to counteract fatigue, to increase fierceness in battle, as well as for recreation. Cultures have applied different sanctions to drugs; one drug may have multiple uses, while another is strongly prohibited.

In modern times, there were more opiate addicts in the United States at the turn of the century than there are now, many being women using opiate-based patent medicines to treat various physical complaints. Some physicians considered opium as a cure for alcoholism, while heroin was regarded as less harmful still, with medical journals stressing its nonaddictive properties. After the Harrison Narcotics Act of 1914 banned opiates, the number of women addicts decreased, while male addicts turned to crime in order to obtain the now-illegal drugs.

In the late 1960s and 1970s use of illicit drugs burgeoned into what some described as a drug epidemic, as marijuana along with other stimulants, sedatives, and analgesics joined the traditional drugs of nicotine, alcohol, and caffeine (Johnston, 1985). By the early 1970s the majority of adolescents had experimented with one or more of these illicit drugs by the end of high school. The fact that the so-called epidemic spread primarily among adolescents and young adults suggests that the teens and early twenties are particularly important developmental stages for the establishment of drug behavior.

Overall use of most drugs increased from the mid-1970s to 1981, while from 1981 through 1992 adolescent use of drugs declined steadily. However, this positive trend has turned around, with adolescent drug use rising in recent years (Johnston, O'Malley, and Bachman, 1995, 1996). The level of drug use in the United States is the highest of any industrialized nation. From 1992 to 1995, the number of high school seniors reporting the use of marijuana in the past 30 days increased 78 percent (from 11.9 to 21 percent), while among tenth graders it more than doubled (from 8.1 to 17.2 percent). Upward trends have also been noted in the use of other drugs, including LSD and cocaine. Multiple use has also increased, so that regular use of a variety of psychoactive substances has become typical.

Definitions and Characteristics

DSM-IV defines **substance abuse** (also called drug abuse) by the presence of one or more symptoms indicating the excessive use of a substance to the extent that it interferes with work or school and interpersonal relationships (see Table 11.3).

Recent data revealing the *prevalence* of *substance use* are reported by Johnston, O'Malley, and Bachman (1995, 1996). Among twelfth graders, 50 percent admitted using alcohol in the past month. Almost 30 percent of high school seniors reported incidents of heavy drinking (five or more drinks in a row) in the past two weeks, while over 14 percent of eighth graders and 24 percent of tenth graders did so. Studies reporting specific prevalence rates for the diagnosis of *substance abuse* in adolescents are harder to find. However, Cohen and associates (1993) conducted diagnostic interviews with a sample of approximately 500 youth. Virtu-

Table 11.3   DSM-IV Criteria for Substance Abuse

A maladaptive pattern of substance use leading to clinically significant impairment or distress, as manifested by one (or more) of the following, occurring within a 12-month period:

(1) Recurrent substance use resulting in a failure to fulfill major role obligations at work, school, or home (e.g., repeated absences or poor work performance related to substance use; substance-related absences, suspensions, or expulsions from school; neglect of children or household)

(2) Recurrent substance use in situations in which it is physically hazardous (e.g., driving an automobile or operating a machine when impaired by substance use)

(3) Recurrent substance-related legal problems (e.g., arrests for substance-related disorderly conduct)

(4) Continued substance use despite having persistent or recurrent social or interpersonal problems caused or exacerbated by the effects of the substance (e.g., arguments with spouse about consequences of intoxication, physical fights)

Source: American Psychiatric Association, 1994.

ally no substance abuse was found among children 10 to 13 years of age. Among 14- to 16-year-olds, approximately 4 percent of boys and 3 percent of girls met criteria for alcohol abuse, while less than 2 percent met criteria for drug abuse. In contrast, among 17- to 20-year-olds, rates for alcohol abuse were 20 percent for boys and 9 percent for girls, while rates for drug abuse were over 5 percent for boys, and less than 3 percent for girls.

These data reveal another consistent finding, that substance abuse is more commonly found in *males* than females. Girls start drinking at a later age than boys and consume less alcohol when they do drink. *Ethnic differences* are also seen. Caucasian adolescents have the highest rates of barbituate, amphetamine, hallucinogen, and alcohol abuse (with Native Americans a close second in the abuse of alcohol), while Hispanic youth use more heroin, cocaine, and crack (Vik, Brown, & Myers, 1997).

Age of onset appears to be steadily decreasing. First initiation into drug use now occurs at about age 12, and there seems to be a shrinking time span between first use and the onset of substance abuse (Fitzgerald et al., 1994).

Etiology

By the age of 18 almost all adolescents have had some exposure to substance use. Since substance use is normative, our first questions about etiology are, What sets some adolescents on the pathway from use to abuse? and, Why does it occur in adolescence? In seeking answers we will reintroduce the psychopathology conduct disorder (see Chapter 9), which can occur with substance use and can play a determining role in escalation. We will then round out our developmental picture by describing the effect of adolescent drug abuse on adjustment in early adulthood.

The Organic Context

Although environmental factors play a dominant role in substance abuse, *genetics* may be a contributing factor in some individuals. Large-scale studies have found higher rates of alcoholism and drug use in the families of narcotic addicts, which may be associated with an inherited vulnerability (Rounsaville et al., 1991). However, the family members of drug addicts also are more likely to demonstrate other kinds of psychopathology, including depression and antisocial personality disorder. Therefore, it is not clear whether the family link is *specific* to substance abuse. In the field of alcohol problems, both twin and adoption studies support a genetic component for alcoholism, at least for males (McGue, 1995). The precise genetic mechanism has not been identified. Current thinking is that there may be several genetic vulnerability factors at work rather than just one (Stone & Gottesman, 1993).

One hypothesis is that what is inherited is a predisposition to general *biobehavioral dysregulation*, which, under particular environmental circumstances, will move an individual along the pathway to substance abuse (Tarter, Moss, & Banukov, 1995). The likely culprit is *difficult temperament*, which involves poor adaptation to change, negative mood, social withdrawal, and high intensity of emotional reactions (see Chapter 2). For example, adult cocaine abuse is predicted by ratings of difficult temperament in adolescence (Kagan, Reznick, & Snidman, 1988). Thus, biobehavioral dysregulation might underlie individuals' likelihood to develop a drug habit, or even their attraction to trying drugs in the first place.

The Intrapersonal Context

With the majority of drug use beginning in junior high school, we must seek its precursors during the elementary school period. Among intraindividual variables, *aggressiveness* is a strong predictor of subsequent drug use. For example, aggression in first-grade boys predicts drug use ten years later, while, conversely, a strong investment in prosocial behavior can prevent both antisocial behavior and drug use. Block, Block, and Keyes' (1988) longitudinal sample identified predictors of teenage substance abuse that were present as early as 3 years of age. These personality attributes included antisocial behavior, rebelliousness, poor frustration tolerance, lack of motivation and goal-directedness, lack of concern for others, and unconventionality.

A classic longitudinal study by Jessor and Jessor (1977) focused on personality correlates of drug use in high school and college students over a period of four years. Adolescents who did not use drugs were likely to value academic achievement, to be unconcerned with independence from their families, to be accepting of the social status quo and involved in a religion, and to regard transgressions as having more negative than positive consequences. Those with high proneness to drug use had the opposite characteristics, including tolerance of deviance, nonreligiousness, the valuing of independence over achievement, and a critical attitude toward society. The Jessors characterized the personality dimension underlying their findings in terms of *conventionality versus unconventionality*.

However, unconventionality may not always be associated with negative outcomes. Shedler and Block's (1990) longitudinal study examined substance use among 101 eighteen-year-olds who had been extensively evaluated since preschool. The adolescents fell into three groups. Abstainers had never tried marijuana or any other drug, experimenters had used marijuana a few times and no more than one drug other than marijuana, and frequent users had used marijuana at least once a week and had tried a drug other than marijuana.

The personality picture of the *frequent user* was one of a troubled, manifestly unhappy adolescent who was interpersonally alienated and emotionally withdrawn and who expressed his or her disturbance through overly antisocial behavior. In terms of our variables, these adolescents were deficient in peer relations, being mistrustful, hostile, and withdrawn; in the realm of work, they were neither invested in school nor in channeling their energies toward meaningful vocational goals; finally, their self-control was weak, resulting in antisocial acting out.

The picture of *abstainers* was a surprising one. Far from being well-adjusted, they were relatively tense, emotionally constricted individuals who were prone to delay gratification unnecessarily. They avoided close interpersonal relationships and were not liked and accepted by others. While not as disturbed as the frequent users, they shared the quality of social alienation, while being overcontrolled rather than impulsive.

It was the *experimenters* who were the most well-adapted, in that they were sociable and warm, evidenced the least distress, and had stable self-control. They also felt the freedom to experiment with values, beliefs, and roles as part of the process of forging a new identity. Thus, the authors conclude that, in adolescence, a certain amount of behavior that society judges as being a problem may be part of the normal growth process. They also show that in this period abstainers should not be regarded as the "normal" group, either statistically or psychologically.

Shedler and Block's (1990) analysis of their longitudinal data showed that the personality characteristics of the three groups were present in early childhood. Thus, as early as 7 years of age, frequent users were insecure, emotionally distressed, and unable to form good relationships. Abstainers were relatively overcontrolled, timid, fearful, and morose. The mothers of both groups of children were cold and unresponsive, giving their children little encouragement while pressuring them to perform. The authors conclude that abstinence, experimentation, and frequent use represent three relatively distinct personality constellations that are established early in life.

A cautionary note is needed, however. Luthar, Cushing, and McMahon (1997) point out that Shelder and Block's data were derived from normative youths, and focused on the use of marijuana, a relatively socially acceptable drug in the teen culture of the time. In contrast, studies of opiate addicts demonstrate that youthful experimentation with drugs is a strong predictor of later substance abuse disorder.

The Interpersonal Context: Family Influences

Among family predictors, parental drug use, family conflict, low income, and family unsociability are related to increased drug use in teens. Parental *modeling* of drug use and children's direct involvement in their parents' drug use are particularly important in the early years. Thus, the more adult family members use alcohol or marijuana, the more likely it is that children will use them. This is particularly the case when the parent–child relationship is a close one: youths are less likely to model their parents' substance abuse when their relationships with parents are poor (Andrews, Hops, & Duncan, 1997).

However, a number of negative indicators co-occur in families in which parents use drugs and alcohol, the effects of which are difficult to untangle. Substance-abusing parents not only model maladaptive drug use but also engage in more *antisocial activity* in general, are more physically and emotionally *abusive* to their partners and children,

Parental modeling of substance use.

have more *economic problems*, and are more likely to *divorce*. Thus, children exposed to substance abuse are being raised in environments that are stressful in a variety of ways.

Luthar, Cushing, and McMahon (1997) have demonstrated that *maternal depression*, but not maternal alcoholism, is predictive of youth substance abuse. Because mothers are often the primary caregivers, the negative effects associated with emotionally unavailable and negative parenting may play an important role in the development of problem behavior. In contrast, *paternal alcoholism*, but not depression, predicts substance use specifically for African-African youth. More research will be needed to explain these gender and ethnic differences.

On the encouraging side, a number of studies have indicated that positive parent–child relationships can decrease the risk of substance abuse in young people. For example, Baumrind (1991) found that *authoritative* parenting (see Chapter 2)—characterized by high warmth *and* structure—was associated with a lower likelihood of drug use. Similarly, lower drug use is found when parent–youth relationships are emotionally supportive, warm, and allow children to participate in decision making—and when parents themselves are abstainers (Hundleby & Mercer, 1987).

It is important to note, however, that family variables were weaker predictors of teenage drug use than were peer influences in the above studies. The same finding is reported in O'Donnell, Hawkins, and Abbott's (1995) longitudinal study of substance-abusing boys. Therefore, it behooves us to turn next to the important variable of peer relations.

The Interpersonal Context: Peer Relations

Peer relationships have emerged as one of the most powerful predictors of adolescent drug use in both longitudinal and cross-sectional studies (Catalano & Hawkins, 1995). Heavy drinkers, for example, are more likely to have friends—especially best friends—who also drink. In addition, peer relations may interact with the other variables and risk factors we reviewed above. Adolescents with low self-esteem may be more attracted to drug use as a means of boosting self-image and gaining status in the peer group (Maggs & Galambos, 1993). In addition,

adolescents are more vulnerable to peer pressure to use drugs when they live in single-parent homes and their relationships with their mothers are conflictual (Farrell & White, 1998).

Another interpersonal variable linked to substance use in girls is *sexual maturation*. As with the data we reviewed related to conduct disorder (see Chapter 9), drinking and substance abuse are two forms of problem behavior seen more often in early maturing girls than in late-maturing girls (Simmons & Blyth, 1987). Early maturers spend more time with older peers, who introduce them to norm-violating behaviors such as drug use.

The Superordinate Context

The highest rate of drug involvement occurs in settings where economically disadvantaged young people live in crime-ridden inner-city neighborhoods and ghettoized enclaves. Here social isolation compounds the problems of poverty, prejudice, unemployment, deviant role models, and gang influence to produce heavy drug involvement. In addition, participation in drug dealing may appear to disadvantaged youth to be the easiest—and perhaps the only—way out of poverty (Feigelman, Stanton, & Ricardo, 1993).

Comorbidity

Depression is one of the most common correlates of substance abuse, and it appears to predate the onset of drug taking (Wilens et al., 1997). Further, Windle and Windle (1997) followed a group of 975 adolescents and found that the combination of substance abuse and depression leads to an increased risk for suicide over time.

By far the highest level of comorbidity is between substance abuse and *conduct disorder*, especially among boys, and some studies report comorbidity as high as 95 percent (Brown et al., 1996). Such a link is inevitable, given that use of illicit substances is the very kind of norm-violating and illegal behavior required for the diagnosis of conduct disorder. Substance use and delinquency may also have reciprocal influences on one another, each increasing the risk for the other disorder. Loeber and Keenan (1994) review the available longitudinal research in order to determine whether substance use leads to antisocial behavior or vice versa. While the direction of effect is far from clear, the preponderance of evidence suggests that the onset of conduct disorder precedes substance use and abuse.

Of particular concern are *multiple-problem youth*, who abuse various substances and engage in a number of delinquent behaviors (Elliot, Huizinga, & Menard, 1989). Such youth have longer criminal and drug careers, are less likely to "outgrow" their problem behavior, and are less responsive to treatment.

Many other comorbidities are also frequently observed, including *obsessive-compulsive* disorder, *bipolar disorder*, *panic disorder*, and *schizophrenia*. It may be that, like purging in bulimia, substance use is an attempt to "self-medicate" against other sources of emotional distress.

Developmental Course

Developmental Pathways in Early Adolescence: Risk and Protection

Jessor and colleagues (1995) tested a multidimensional model of the factors predictive of drug and alcohol abuse in youth. The investigators followed almost 2,000 students in grades 7, 8, and 9 over a period of three years. Risk and protective factors were identified in three systems of development: personality, environment, and behavior.

Risk Factors   In the *personality* domain, risk factors included low expectations of success, poor self-esteem, hopelessness, and alienation. In the *environmental* realm, risk factors included peer models for problem behavior, and orientation toward peers rather than parents as guides for behavior and life choices. Risks in the *behavioral* realm included poor school performance.

Protective Factors   In regard to protective factors, those in the *personality* domain included a positive orientation toward school, concern about personal health, and intolerance toward deviance. In the *environmental* domain, protective factors included positive relationships with adults, regulatory controls imposed by adults on youth behavior, and peer mod-

els for prosocial behavior. Protection in the *behavioral* domain was represented by engagement in prosocial activities.

Results of Jessor and colleagues' study showed that the single most powerful *predictor* of substance use was the presence of antisocial peer models, followed by the personality variables of low expectations of success, poor self-esteem, and hopelessness. The *protective factors* that had the greatest impact on reducing youth substance abuse were an attitude of intolerance toward deviance and a positive orientation toward school. Further, over the three-year period, those whose problem behavior diminished over time were not those whose exposure to risk factors decreased but rather were those who had available to them more protective factors at early stages in development. Thus, the authors conclude, "antecedent protection has a stronger relation to change . . . than antecedent risk" (p. 931). This suggests that prevention efforts directed at bolstering resistance to the temptations of drug use may be the most effective, a thread we will pick up later when we discuss intervention.

Developmental Pathways in Late Adolescence: From Use to Abuse

Studies of older youth reveal that two of the most important determinants of the transition from substance use to abuse are *timing*, or the age when use began, and the presence of a *conduct disorder*. Robins and McEvoy's (1990) research using retrospective accounts of drug users and abusers depicts the interplay of these two variables.

To begin with, the *earlier* substance use began (i.e., before the age of 15), the more likely the progression to subsequent abuse. In regard to conduct problems, it was the sheer *quantity* of such problems—five or more—that predicted subsequent abuse rather than any specific problem or groups of problems. In fact, number of conduct problems was a better predictor of substance abuse than age of onset; of those beginning substance use before age 15 with seven or more problems, more than half developed serious substance abuse. While there was an interaction between the two variables, the number of problems remained a powerful predictor of substance abuse even when age and exposure were controlled.

Newcomb and Bentler's (1988) nine-year prospective study of 654 adolescents provides information about the transition from adolescence to early adulthood. The authors summarize the results in terms of the following developmental tasks faced in the transition to adulthood:

1. *Social integration.* (This corresponds to our variable of social relations.) Drug use interferes with this development by reducing social support and increasing loneliness.
2. *Occupation.* (This corresponds to our variable of work.) Teenage drug use accelerates involvement in the job market, while impeding successful functioning at work. Traditional educational pursuits are abandoned, thereby limiting the range of career opportunities.
3. *Family and heterosexual relations.* (This corresponds to our variables of attachment and sex.) Drug use has both an accelerating and detrimental impact, leading to early marriage and child bearing on the one hand, and divorce on the other.
4. *Criminal behavior.* Youthful drug use is differentially related to criminal behavior. Multiple substance use is predictive of increased stealing and drug law violation, such as driving while intoxicated or selling drugs, but also of a decrease in violent crimes.
5. *Mental health.* Multiple drug use is related to a small but significant increase in psychosis and a decreased ability to plan, organize, and direct behavior. Hard-drug use increases suicidal ideation in young adulthood, while alcohol increases depression.

Newcomb and Bentler (1988) conceptualize their findings in terms of *precocious development.* This involves a significant discrepancy between developmental level and competence. Teenage drug users push themselves toward a maturity that they are incapable of assuming effectively because they have not given themselves time to accumulate the needed skills and experience. Premature involvement in adult roles prior to acquiring adequate competence to handle such challenges leads to a likelihood of failure. The use of drugs also directly interferes with social integration and acceptance of adult civic and societal responsibilities while at the same time in-

creasing feelings of social isolation from peers. Finally, drug use can affect cognition by making thinking more disorganized and bizarre, sometimes resulting in increased suicidal ideation. In short, substance use diverts the adolescent from mastering developmental tasks that are critical to healthy adjustment in adulthood.

On the positive side, Eliott, Huizinga, and Menard's (1989) prospective study of drug use in 1,725 youths found that the pull to *desistence* was stronger than the pull to escalation. Substance use generally levels off in young adulthood, and delinquency usually declines after mid-adolescence. Only cautious optimism is warranted, however, since alcohol use often increases in adulthood.

Integrative Developmental Model

Illustrating the complexity of the factors involved in predicting substance abuse, Fitzgerald and colleagues (1994) have compiled a list of risks derived from various studies. (See Figure 11.1.) As these authors note, substance abuse is best conceptualized as a life-span problem, with origins at least as far back as the preschool years. They conceptualize the risks as falling within five domains, which map nicely onto our own dimensions: *intraindividual* (intrapersonal), *interindividual* (interpersonal), *family*, *peer*, and those in the larger context such as *school* and *culture* (superordinate). Thus drug use is not due to any single cause but to a number of variables. In addition, many of these factors interact with one another, thus contributing in complex ways to the development of substance-related problems.

An important question that remains is one we posed at the beginning of these chapter: *Why adolescence?* Jessor and Jessor (1977) provide a developmental framework that addresses this issue. Their model regards behavior as a result of interactions between personality and the perceived environment. According to the Jessors, the transition to adolescence takes place in a societal context that affects individuals differently. While prized roles and rewards come with age in our society, the adolescent, especially the early adolescent, has limited access to the valued goals of adulthood, such as autonomy, prestige, sex, and mobility. In addition, societal expectations and rules are based on chronological age alone, which ignores individual differences in adolescents' desire or readiness to pursue adult goals. While some "late bloomers" may feel pushed to take on responsibilities for which they are not ready, other adolescents who are ready to make the transition may feel frustrated and tantalized by the unattainable attractiveness of mature status. The result is *precocious* engagement in adult-oriented activities—a constellation including alcohol use, cigarette smoking, substance use, sexual intercourse, and delinquency.

The transition from a less mature to a more mature adult status, the Jessors state, is often marked by problem behavior. Adolescence is just such a time of transition in which stage-salient issues related to identity formation and the assumption of adult roles come to the fore. Adolescence is also a time of increasing experimentation, exploration, and risk taking. Some experimentation with drugs, therefore, is relatively normative for the majority of adolescents.

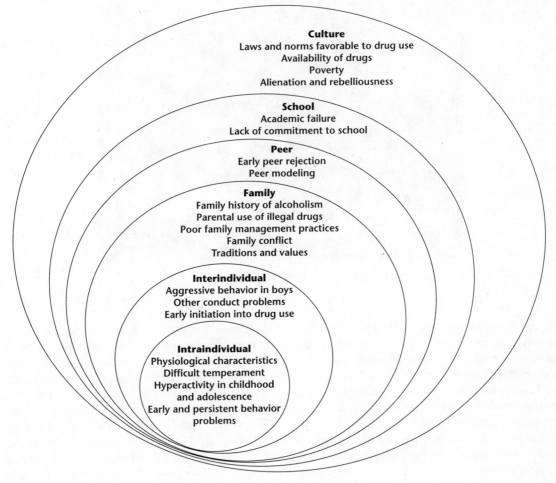

Figure 11.1   Antecedents of Adolescent Substance Abuse.

Source: Adapted from Fitzgerald et al., 1994

Peer and societal factors are risks for substance use.

In general, Jessor, Donovan, and Costa (1991) argue, as development proceeds from adolescence into early adulthood, these kinds of problem activities will decline in most young people.

Thus, when viewed within a developmental context, problem behavior is not necessarily deviant or psychopathological. Many problem behaviors, such as drinking and sex, are regarded as acceptable and will even be encouraged by society when the adolescent is old enough to be considered an adult. In essence, the Jessors regard adolescence as a period in which departure from accepted norms is not only to be expected but also may be a sign of healthy development. "Problem behavior may be viewed, at least in part, as an aspect of growing up" (p. 238).

What about those for whom drug abuse and dependence result? Recall that, in discussing *negativism* (Chapter 5) we saw that an exaggeration of normal problem behavior that threatens to jeopardize future growth can be regarded as psychopathological. The same principle can be applied here. When rebellion, defiance, and antisocial behaviors become ends in themselves rather than means for promoting autonomy, adolescents may be in a state not of transition but of stagnation. Or again, if problem behaviors seem primarily directed against the parents—if adolescents seem to be going out of their way to defy and upset parents, if unconsciously they are behaving like "bad children" in order to prolong their status as children—then we begin to suspect that fixation rather than transition is calling the tune.

Erikson's (1968) writings on *identity* are useful at this point. He states that youths often go to extremes in order to test the "rock bottom of some truth" before committing themselves to a particular way of life (p. 236). These extremes may include not only rebelliousness but also deviant, delinquent, and self-destructive behaviors. It is only when such tendencies defeat the purpose of experimentation by fixating the adolescent in this behavior that they become psychopathological. Take, for example, a *negative identity*, which in many ways is the adolescent counterpart of the toddler's negativism. Here the adolescent perversely identifies with all the roles that have been presented as undesirable or dangerous by others. Despairing of ever realizing the unattainable positive roles, the adolescents become "the last thing in the world" the parents would want them to be. Thus the psychopathology underlying substance abuse represents not only a more extreme form of adolescent rebellion but a retreat from the struggle to establish an identity rather than a progression along the way toward reaching that goal.

Finally, the fact that substance use and abuse is largely associated with the *male gender* is worth considering. Just as adolescent females may feel pressure to become the epitome of femininity, thus increasing their concern with body shape and dieting, males may feel pressure to fulfill a masculine archetype by being audacious, risk-taking, and fearless. The cachet attached to illicit substance use—in its extreme, the image of the hypermasculine "gansta," who is both feared and admired—may be attractive to those thwarted in their attempts to find more prosocial ways of achieving a masculine identity.

Conceptualization of Psychopathology   The literature on substance abuse also offers the concept of *precocity* as a conceptualization of psychopathology. While precocity is generally viewed posi-

tively—in a child with musical talents, athletic abilities, or intellectual capabilities beyond his or her age level, for example—pathogenic precocity jeopardizes normal development. Clinicians will see children who are old before their time, who have been burdened by adult responsibilities and have paid the price in terms of being robbed of their childhood. Adolescent drug abusers run a similar risk by taking on adult functions for which they are poorly prepared. The outcome is often failure or, in extreme cases, social isolation and despair.

Intervention

Although much of the research is focused on intervention for adult substance abusers rather than adolescents, a general conclusion is that *psychodynamic* treatment for substance abuse is relatively unsuccessful. This approach often requires a willingness to change and the formation of a positive relationship between youth and therapist, neither of which may be present or workable for the drug abuser (Copans & Kinney, 1996). *Behavioral* therapies, which often involve pairing the drug with a noxious stimulus (such as a nausea-inducing chemical or a painful electric shock), have not proven effective either.

Intervention with adolescents also needs to take into account the family context in which substance abuse develops (Thomas & Schandler, 1996). Indeed, *family therapy* has been recommended as a treatment of choice for adolescence substance abuse. Empirical research bears this out: In seven out of eight studies comparing family treatment to other forms of intervention, family therapy was found to be the most effective in reducing substance use (Waldron, 1997). Participants are also more likely to engage in family therapy, and to remain in treatment longer, than those assigned to other interventions (Stanton & Shadish, 1997).

Another form of intervention is the *self-help group*. "Twelve-step programs" such as Alcoholics Anonymous, Cocaine Anonymous, and Narcotics Anonymous are widely accepted by adolescents. In fact, Brown (1993) found that these groups are the method most widely used by those adolescents who find a pathway out of substance abuse.

Prevention

Prevention is generally less costly than treatment and may be particularly important in the case of substance abuse. As our review of the research has shown, providing protective factors early in development is more effective than reducing risk factors later. Further, if there is a stepwise progression from less to more serious involvement in drugs, efforts at preventing substance use are well worthwhile. (Our presentation follows Durlak, 1997.)

While earlier approaches to substance use prevention showed disappointing results, recent prevention programs have been more successful. Earlier programs were based on erroneous assumptions, such as that increases in self-esteem alone would prevent substance use or that scare tactics would be effective in deterring youth from using drugs. Newer approaches, in contrast, are informed by empirical research regarding the multiple factors that influence substance use and abuse and use well-tested intervention techniques.

Resistance skills programs take their cue from the fact that peers are one of the most powerful influences on initiating substance use. Therefore, they teach students how to recognize, handle, and avoid situations in which they experience peer pressure to smoke, drink, or use drugs. Students role-play and practice ways of delivering specific refusal messages effectively. Many programs use peer leaders, who often have higher credibility with adolescents than do adults. Evaluation studies show that resistance skills training is effective in reducing smoking, alcohol, and marijuana use by 35 to 45 percent.

Life skills training teaches a broad range of general skills for coping with challenging situations. Among the components are problem-solving and decision-making skills, self-control and self-esteem enhancement, general interpersonal skills, and assertiveness training. These skills are taught by a combination of instruction, demonstration, feedback, reinforcement, and practice. Studies show the effectiveness of these programs in reducing tobacco, alcohol, and marijuana use in fifth and sixth graders (Botvin et al., 1995).

Comprehensive prevention programs are informed by the research implicating multiple risk factors in the etiology of substance abuse and consequently target a number of different domains for intervention. A prime example is Project Success (Richards-Colocino et al., 1996), in which interventions take place at the level of the individual, school, community, and family. Targeted goals include reducing antisocial behavior and addressing personality risk factors; changing norm perceptions about substance use; increasing positive bonding between children and their schools and between families and the community; and enhancing parenting effectiveness. While evaluation studies indicate that such programs have a positive effect in terms of "holding the line" against increased substance use, they are not successful in eradicating alcohol and substance abuse in youths who are already involved in drugs. Once established, substance use may be difficult to reverse even as early as in the sixth grade (Perry et al., 1996).

Prevention programs that are *specific* to substance use may also be more effective than those that are more broadly directed toward promoting a healthy lifestyle in general. Further, Johnson, MacKinnon, and Pentz (1996) propose a prevention regime sensitive to *stage-salient issues* of development, targeting diet and exercise in middle childhood, smoking in late childhood, alcohol and marijuana use in middle adolescence, and cocaine and hard-drug use in later adolescence. (Hall and Zigler, 1997, review prevention efforts with preschoolers.)

Discussions of psychopathology usually assume that the developing child is not deviant either intellectually or physiologically. The assumption has not always proved correct; in the instance of autism, for example, both mental retardation and organic brain pathology are present. However, the etiological significance of intellectual and organic deviation has had to be demonstrated. This procedure will be reversed with our next two topics. Mental retardation or a lack of organic intactness will be assumed, so that we may ask, What developmental deviations— if any—ensue?

The Developmental Consequences of Mental Retardation

Why include *mental retardation* (MR) in a discussion of psychopathology? Just because a child has a low score on an IQ test, should he or she be placed in the company of children who have a conduct disorder or a phobia or an attention-deficit hyperactive disorder? On the surface of it, such a child does not seem to "have problems" in the way those other children do—he or she is just intellectually slower than normal. On the other hand, it does not seem right to exclude from our discussions the entire population of children whose degree of retardation might place them at risk for developing psychological disturbances. As we shall soon see, the question that troubles us also troubles the experts who have made the definition of MR increasingly contingent upon factors other than IQ scores alone. It is this literature on defining MR that we will turn to first.

Definition

Changing Definitions

Mental retardation is not something you have, like blue eyes or a bad heart. Nor is it something you are, like being short or thin. It is not a medical disorder . . . nor is it a mental disorder. . . . Mental retardation is present when specific intellectual limitations affect the person's ability to cope with the ordinary challenges of everyday living in the community. If the intellectual limitations have no real effect on functioning, then the person does not have mental retardation. (Association on Mental Retardation, 1992, pp. 9, 13.)

These are startling statements for those who believe that MR is defined in terms of a low IQ and that once retarded, always retarded. These statements represent the latest in a series of definitions and conceptualizations by the American Association on Mental Retardation (AAMR). We will briefly trace the changes in definition of MR, present its agreed-upon characteristics, and then return to an examination the AAMR revisions in detail.

Historical Background

The original definition of MR was in terms of *subnormal intelligence*, but in 1959 the AAMR added **adaptive behavior** as a criterion. If a person were adapting adequately to the environment, why regard him or her as psychopathologically disturbed or deviant or abnormal just because the IQ score was below a given cutoff point? For example, there is a group called "six-hour retardates" who do poorly in school (which is approximately six hours per day) but function well, say, in a rural or inner-city environment. Thus the key to MR is not an IQ score but the way an individual *functions*.

Current Criteria

All current definitions of MR have three criteria in common: (1) subnormal intelligence defined as IQ scores below a certain level; (2) deficits in adaptive behavior; and (3) early onset typically defined as below 18 years of age. (See DSM-IV criteria in Table 12.1.)

Intellectual Deficits　The first criterion for MR involves significantly subaverage general intellectual functioning, typically as measured by a standardized **intelligence test**, such as the Stanford-Binet or the Wechsler Intelligence Scale for Children. Numerically, an IQ (**intelligence quotient**) score that is more than two standard deviations below the mean is regarded as a significant deviation from average intelligence. Traditionally, a cutoff score of 70 has been used.

IQ scores are also used to make finer classifications according to levels of retardation:

1. *Mild* mental retardation: IQ 55 to 70. This level comprises as many as 85 percent of all persons with retardation. These individuals acquire academic skills up to approximately the sixth-grade level by their late teens and can live successfully

Table 12.1　DSM-IV Criteria for Mental Retardation

A. Significant subaverage intellectual functioning: an IQ of approximately 70 or below on an individually administered IQ test (for infants, a clinical judgment of significantly subaverage intellectual functioning).

B. Concurrent deficits or impairments in present adaptive functioning (i.e., the person's effectiveness in meeting the standards expected for his or her age by his or her cultural group) in at least two of the following areas: communication, self-care, home living, social/interpersonal skills, use of community resources, self-direction, functional academic skills, work, leisure, health, and safety.

C. Onset is before age 18 years.

Code degree of severity reflecting level of intellectual impairment:

Mild Mental Retardation
IQ level 50–55 to approximately 70
Moderate Mental Retardation
IQ level 35–40 to 50–55
Severe Mental Retardation
IQ level 20–25 to 35–40
Profound Mental Retardation
IQ level below 20 to 25

Source: Adapted from DSM-IV, copyright 1994, American Psychiatric Association.

in the community either independently or in supervised settings.

2. *Moderate* mental retardation: IQ 40 to 54. While some of these individuals require few supportive services, most require some help throughout life. They adapt well to community life in supervised settings.

3. *Severe* mental retardation: IQ 25 to 39. These individuals have limited ability to master academic skills, although they can learn to read certain "survival" words. As adults they may perform simple tasks under supervision and adapt to the community by living with their family or in group homes.

4. *Profound* mental retardation: IQ below 25. These individuals require lifelong care and assistance, and intensive training is needed to teach basic eating, toileting, and dressing skills. Almost all show organic causes for their retardation. (For a more detailed description of levels, see DSM-IV, American Psychiatric Association, 1994.)

Adaptive Behavior   Intellectual level and adaptation are undoubtedly related; however, the correlation is not so high that the latter can accurately be inferred from the former. In certain instances the correlation may be low.

We will discuss the AAMR Adaptive Behavior Scale (Nihira et al., 1974) as an example of an instrument that assesses adaptive behavior. Factor analyses showed that the scale contains three factors: personal self-sufficiency, community self-sufficiency, and personal-social responsibility (Nihira, 1976).

Personal self-sufficiency is found at all ages and involves the ability to satisfy immediate personal needs such as eating, toileting, and dressing. *Community self-sufficiency* involves independence beyond immediate needs, along with self-sufficiency in relation to others; for example, using money, traveling, shopping, and communicating adequately. *Personal-social responsibility* involves initiative and perseverance—the ability to undertake a task on one's own and see it through to completion. These last two factors emerge at around 10 years of age and are either weak or nonexistent in younger children. They also represent higher-level behavior than the mere satisfaction of immediate needs. (See Widaman and McGrew, 1996, for a more detailed presentation of adaptive behavior and its structure.)

The Current Revision

We now return to the AAMR's 1992 revision. This revision takes the concept of adaptation further than had been done in the past. Adaptation itself is not some kind of trait or absolute quality individuals possess. Rather, adaptation is always *in relation to an environment.* Therefore the environment must be scrutinized before one calls an individual mentally retarded.

The new conceptualization of MR is represented in Figure 12.1. Note that the variable *functioning* is at the base of the triangle, signifying that it is the basic, or fundament, term. Thus, how well or how poorly a child can function in a given environment now supersedes intellectual level. Functioning, in turn, is equally contributed to by *capabilities* and *environments*, the other two variables in the conceptualization.

Capabilities (or competencies) is an intrapersonal variable. There are two kinds of capabilities:

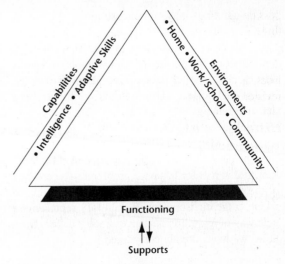

Figure 12.1   General Structure of the Definition of Mental Retardation.

Source: American Association on Mental Retardation, 1992

1. *Intelligence*, which encompasses cognition and learning
2. *Adaptive skills*, which are made up of *practical* and *social* intelligence

Adaptive difficulties derive from limitations in practical and social intelligence. The former limits the ability to maintain oneself as an independent person in managing the ordinary activities of daily living. The latter limits the ability to comprehend social behavior (e.g., via perspective taking), to develop social skills, and to show good ethical judgment in interpersonal situations.

Environments are conceptualized as the *specific settings* in which the person lives, learns, plays, works, socializes, and interacts. The environment must be typical of the child's same-age peers and appropriate to the child's socioeconomic background. MR quite literally does not exist when the individual is able to function well in the community without special support services. However, if the individual requires special supports or services, such as a sheltered workshop or institutional care, that person can be considered to be mentally retarded.

According to the AAMR revision, duration of MR need not be lifelong. If the environment becomes less demanding—say, in the case of a child's leaving school—and the child adapts to it, then MR is "outgrown." It is important to note that intellectual functioning as measured by an IQ score is fairly stable from childhood on; however, it is the impact of intellectual limitations on functioning that may change.

Finally, the AAMR conceptualization explicitly states that MR is *not* a psychopathology. In addition, the definition in no way implies that MR places the child at risk for behavior problems. The essence of the definition is the child's adapting or failing to adapt to the environment. It therefore represents a new way of regarding deviance, since it differs from those we have already considered.

Controversial Issues   The AAMR's 1992 revisionist approach to defining MR was controversial from the start and was not universally accepted by other organizations or by practitioners and researchers.

The first controversy concerned a feature we have not mentioned, namely, raising the MR-defining IQ score from 70 to 75. While this may seem to be a slight adjustment it would, in effect, actually double the number of individuals in the MR category (because IQ scores form a bell curve).

Even more radical was the elimination of the classifications in terms of levels of retardation (mild, moderate, etc.) and substituting *levels of impairment* defined in terms of *need for support services*. There are four such levels: intermittent, limited, extensive, and pervasive. For example, one child might only need special tutoring in academic courses, while another might need 24-hour custodial care.

While there are specific criteria for defining these levels, there are no objective assessment instruments like there are for intelligence and adaptive behavior. Since assigning levels depends on clinical judgment, the chances of unreliability and misdiagnosis are increased. Moreover, there is evidence that levels of retardation and need for supportive services *cannot* be equated, especially for mildly retarded children who vary in their need for support. One consequence of this lack of equivalence is that the findings from a vast amount of research utilizing levels of retardation to define the MR population are

left in limbo. (See Hodapp and Dykens, 1996, for a more detailed presentation of controversies concerning the current definition.)

Is MR a Psychopathology?   Returning to the question that opened our discussion, the AAMR answer is clearly no; MR is neither a psychopathology nor a risk condition. In light of its controversial status, however, it would not be prudent to use the AAMD's stance to exclude MR at this point. It seems better to use the AAMR revision to reorient our own thinking about children with MR. Instead of assuming that they will be disturbed (like the other children we have discussed), it is better to assume that they are adjusting adequately, as indeed many of them are. Then we can ask, How can we understand and help those who *are* disturbed and failing to live up to their potential?

The "Two Cultures" of Mental Retardation

Investigators have tended to focus on two different aspects of MR. The first group has been concerned with exploring different *degrees* of retardation. This group is primarily composed of psychologists, educators, and social workers. The second group has been concerned with *etiology* or, more specifically, with the *organic* causes of different kinds of MR. Within this organic context *genetic* factors play a prominent role, although it also includes retardation due to perinatal factors, such as prematurity and anoxia, and to postnatal factors, such as head injury and disease. This group of investigators is primarily composed of geneticists, pediatricians, and psychiatrists. The two approaches have been informally labeled as the "two cultures" of MR because they have proceeded more or less independently of one another. Psychologists, for example, are relatively unconcerned about etiology, and pediatricians are relatively unconcerned about degree of retardation. (See Hodapp and Dykens, 1996.)

Although there is no basic incompatibility between the "two cultures" since they are exploring different facets of the same disturbance, there is at present no major attempt being made for integration. However, there are some preliminary data suggesting the dis-

Table 12.2   The "Two Cultures" of Behavioral Research in Mental Retardation

Level of Impairment-Based	Etiology-Based
Main characteristics	
Group by degree of disability	Group by etiology
Less regard for genetic etiology	De-emphasize degree of disability
Professions (with some overlap)	
Behavioral psychologists	Geneticists
Special educators	Genetic counselors
Clinical psychologists	Child psychiatrists
Social workers	Pediatricians
	Psychiatrists
Strengths	
Advances in behavioral measurement	Advances in molecular genetics
Weaknesses	
Often less aware of advances in genetics and molecular genetics	Often less sophisticated in behavioral measurement
Often less appreciation for impact of genetic etiology on research or intervention	Often less application of findings to pertinent issues in larger mental retardation field

Source: Hodapp & Dykens, 1996.

advantages of isolation. In evaluating severely retarded individuals with two different kinds of genetically caused MR (fragile X and Down syndrome), Simon and colleagues (1995) found that there was *no* evidence of syndrome-specific cognitive profiles of strengths and weaknesses; however, when the same children were divided in terms of high or low IQs, unique profiles of intellectual strengths and weaknesses were found; for example, the high-IQ group was weak on visual-spatial construction, while the low-IQ group was weak on personal information. The authors conclude that ignoring degrees of retardation might well obscure important differences within each kind of MR. It also runs the risk of jeopardizing the effectiveness of intervention programs that are typically tailored to the pattern of strengths and weaknesses of a particular population. (See Table 12.2)

Since we will be dealing with etiologically based mental retardation in future discussions, we will now briefly describe three of the disorders we will encounter. All are due to genetic abnormalities. (A more detailed presentation can be found in State, King, and Dykens, 1997.)

Genetically Determined Mental Retardation

Down Syndrome   Children with **Down syndrome** have three number 21 chromosomes instead of the normal two; hence, the condition is also called "trisomy 21." (Other genetic abnormalities will be discussed later.) The children have a decelerating rate of mental growth, and the mean IQ of the group as a whole is around 50. Their social intelligence tends to be high, but their speech and comprehension of grammar are low. The typical picture is one of a friendly, sociable child, although some studies suggest that this picture becomes more negative with age. Finally, the children tend to have a low level of behavioral disturbance.

Fragile X Syndrome   This condition is due to a fragile site on the X chromosome and occurs more often in males than females. There is a moderate degree of retardation with development slowing from puberty on. The children do well on tasks requiring simultaneous processing of information

A child with Down syndrome can be an enjoyable playmate.

but do poorly on those requiring sequential processing such as auditory short-term memory. The children tend to be hyperactive or to show autistic-like behavior.

Prader-Willi Syndrome   This condition is due to deletions on chromosome 15 in the majority of cases. There is a mild degree of retardation. The children tend to be obese and preoccupied with eating. There is evidence that this eating problem may be due to an impaired satiety mechanism in that the children report feeling "full" only after eating a significantly greater amount of food than normal controls, and the hungry feeling returns to a pre-meal level sooner (Holland et al., 1995). Finally, the children tend to have a large number of behavior problems (Einfeld & Aman, 1995). (For a comparison of behavior problems in children with Prader-Willi syndrome and Down syndrome, see Dykens and Kasari, 1997.)

These brief descriptions illustrate how different the consequences of different genetic disorders can be in terms of intellectual level and strengths and weaknesses as well as in terms of personality

variables and adjustment. The etiology-based "culture" is particularly exciting these days since it is part of the burgeoning research relating genes to behavior.

Familial Mental Retardation

Familial mental retardation illustrates the other "culture," which focuses on level of retardation. Approximately half of all cases of MR have no clear organic cause and are called **familial** or **familial-cultural retardation**.

The descriptive characteristics of this kind of retardation are well-established. The level of retardation is usually mild, with IQs rarely lower than 45 to 50. Individuals are likely to blend into the general population before and after school ages. Familial retardation is more prevalent among minorities and individuals of low socioeconomic status. One or both parents is likely to be retarded.

However, the causes of familial retardation remain a mystery. It is claimed that environmental and genetic factors may be involved, the contribution of each being about equal (Plomin, 1989). On the organic side it is also hypothesized that the retarded individuals have minor, difficult-to-detect neurological problems. For their part, environmentalists emphasize the features of low socioeconomic status that place intellectual growth in jeopardy—prenatal and postnatal risk, inadequate health care, large families, a disorganized home environment lacking in personal attention and growth-promoting objects such as books and "readiness" games. Finally, statisticians claim that familial retardation represents the lower end of the bell-shaped curve of intelligence. (For a more detailed discussion of familial retardation, see Hodapp, 1994.)

In sum, the mental retardation of children in the organic category has a clear organic etiology whereas for children in the familial-cultural category both organic and environmental factors are involved. Children in the organic category tend to be moderately to severely retarded and come from all ethnic groups and socioeconomic levels, while those in the familial-cultural category tend to be mildly retarded and come from minority groups and low socioeconomic levels.

Environmental Risks   While the causes of familial retardation are not known, there are data concerning environmental variables that place children at risk for becoming retarded. Sameroff (1990) hypothesized that it was not the kind but the number of risks that determined intellectual functioning in children of comparable biological status. He extracted ten such risk factors from previous research, including maternal mental illness, rigid values in regard to child development, large family, and minimal education. Using longitudinal data, he found that, when they were 4 years old, children with no risks scored more than 30 IQ points higher than children with eight or nine risks. In general, IQ declined as risk factors increased; for example, in multiple-risk families, 24 percent of the children had IQ scores below 85, while none of the children in the low-risk families did.

Further analysis of Sameroff's (1990) data revealed that no single risk variable and no one pattern of variables reduced intellectual performance; rather, different families had different constellations of risk factors. While the low socioeconomic status group had more high-risk families, high-risk

middle- and upper-class families were equally damaging to their children's intellectual growth. Finally, Sameroff found that the same lack of environmental support that undermined the children's competence at an early age would continue to do so when they were 13 years old.

The picture was not totally pessimistic, however, since 20 percent of the high-risk children escaped the fate of the group at large. The variables responsible for a more favorable outcome were parental restrictiveness, little democracy, clarity of rules, and emotional warmth. This pattern of "tough love" was sufficiently potent to counteract environmental risks.

Characteristics

Prevalence

The problems involved in defining MR clearly impinge directly on the issue of prevalence. Using IQ scores alone as the criterion, prevalence changes significantly if one raises the cutoff score from 70 to 75, as we have seen. Using the more traditional score of 70 and below, 3 percent of the population can be classified as mentally retarded.

However, IQ scores ignore other factors affecting MR, the most obvious one being adaptive behavior. Particularly at the level of mild retardation, IQ and adaptive behavior are not highly correlated, so IQ scores alone would overestimate the retarded population. Overestimation can also be due to the instability of IQ scores since, with time, a number of children who are mildly retarded will fall in the lower reaches of normal intelligence.

Finally, children with mild mental retardation are most likely to be diagnosed during the school years, when academic performance serves to highlight their limitations. Therefore, the prevalence rate tends to be low in the preschool years, then gradually rises and peaks in early adolescence and declines subsequently.

Taking all of the above factors into account would lower the estimated prevalence of MR from 3 percent to between 1 and 2 percent for the population (Hodapp and Dykens, 1996).

Gender, Socioeconomic Status, and Ethnicity

In regard to gender, more boys than girls are mentally retarded due largely to the fact that genetically linked disorders affect males more than females. The relation of MR to social class and ethnic factors depends on the degree of retardation. Mild MR is more prevalent among children of low socioeconomic status and minority groups. The more severe levels of MR occur about equally in various economic and racial groups. (A more detailed discussion of economic level and race as they relate to MR can be found in Hodapp and Dykens, 1996.)

Developmental Course

While MR is relatively stable from childhood to adulthood, its course is affected both by the level and the type of retardation.

The Effects of Level of Retardation   First we will look at the effect of initial level of MR on the developmental trajectory. IQ is most likely to change either in an upward or downward direction in individuals with mild retardation whereas it tends to be stable for those with more severe degrees of retardation. (See Hodapp and Dykens, 1996.) However, this generalization concerning the severely retarded can mask some important variability within the group. An eight-year longitudinal study of eighty-two severely retarded 3-year-olds found that, while the majority of children's IQs remained constant over time, in a third of the population the scores declined. This group was characterized as having severe and pervasive delays across several major developmental areas such as motor, language, and adaptive behavior. An unexpected finding was that children with difficult temperaments had a slower rate of decline than those with easy temperaments, perhaps because these difficult children energized their families to attend to and stimulate them more than did their placid counterparts. (See Keogh, Bernheimer, and Guthrie, 1997.)

Type of Retardation   Developmental course is also affected by the type of MR. In regard to intelligence, the IQ of children with Down syndrome continues to develop but at a decelerating rate, making smaller and smaller gains over time. Children with fragile X syndrome, on the other hand, show a steady or near-steady gain in IQ until they are 10 to 15 years old, at which point the development slows considerably. (See Hodapp and Dykens, 1996.)

Type of retardation also affects the developmental trajectory of adaptive behavior. Children with Down syndrome reach a plateau during middle childhood, making few advances between 7 and 11 years of age. A longitudinal, cross-sectional study of boys with fragile X syndrome, on the other hand, showed the most striking gains in the toddler and preschool periods, less marked but still significant gains up until 11 years of age, and no age-related gains into early adulthood (Dykens et al., 1996).

Comorbidity

While the AAMR's 1992 definition states that MR is not a psychopathology, there is good evidence that it increases the risk of developing psychological disturbances. For example, Einfeld and Tonge's (1996) epidemiological study of 454 MR-diagnosed children between 4 and 18 years of age found that 41 percent could be classified as having a severe emotional or behavioral disorder, including aggression, withdrawal, hyperactivity, and anxiety. In general, studies find the rate of disturbance to be two to four times that in the nonretarded population.

Einfeld and Tonge (1996) also found that, unlike the nonretarded population, prevalence of disturbance in the retarded population was not affected by age or sex. However, degree of retardation was important, with the profoundly retarded group having a considerably lower prevalence, probably because their behavioral repertoire was more limited as was their capacity to communicate emotional problems. Level of retardation also affected the kind of disturbance seen, with the mildly retarded group having a predominance of disruptive and antisocial behavior and the severely retarded group being characterized by self-absorbed and autistic-like behavior.

Einfeld and Aman's (1995) summary of factor-analytic studies of problem behaviors in children with MR is instructive in regard to the overlap with nonretarded populations. While there is overlap in regard to withdrawal, aggression, and hyperactivity, anxiety is rare in children with MR. In addition, stereotypic and self-injurious behaviors are common in children with MR but are rare in those who are not retarded. Consequently, withdrawn children with MR are not anxious, as are their nonretarded counterparts, and their aggression is more often accompanied by self-injurious behavior. In short, there seems to be a different mix of problems in children with MR.

The Interpersonal Context

Parents

Recent studies of parental reactions to having a child with MR have shifted from a pathology orientation to a *stress and coping approach*. For example, parental reactions used to be described in terms of depression and various stages of mourning. Currently researchers regard retardation as an added stressor on the family system and explore the coping techniques used by parents. This new approach allows for positive as well as negative consequences, such as parents being brought closer together or siblings developing an empathy with and concern for children with handicapping conditions. (See Hodapp and Dykens, 1996.)

A popular model for conceptualizing the new approach is called the *Double ABCX* (Minnes, 1988). *X* represents the *stress* of having a child with MR, and that stress is a function of the *specific characteristics* of the child, or *A*; the family's internal and external *resources*, or *B*; and the family's *perception* of the child, or *C*. "*Double*" refers to the *developmental* dimension that takes account of the fact that all the components may change with time. It will be worthwhile to examine this model in greater detail. (Unless otherwise noted our presentation is based on Hodapp and Dykens, 1996.)

Characteristics of the Child   As we have seen, children with different *types* of MR can behave differently and these differences can affect parental behavior. In families of children with Prader-Willi

syndrome, for example, stress was found to be related to such syndrome-specific behaviors as overeating, skin-picking, sleeping more than usual, and hoarding objects (Hodapp, Dykens, & Masino, 1997). Until recently, research findings indicated that families of children with Down syndrome were more cohesive and harmonious than families of children with other kinds of MR, with the mother experiencing less stress and having a more satisfactory social network. However, there is now evidence that, when methodological flaws in previous studies are eliminated, ease of rearing children with Down syndrome is no different from that of rearing children with other disabilities (Cahill & Glidden, 1996; see also Scott et al., 1997, for parental reactions to infants with Down syndrome). Moreover, this study also found that the average adjustment of all families was quite good, being at or near the norm for families with children who were not retarded.

Turning to research on children with MR as a whole, there is evidence that parents have to put more effort into accommodating to those children who are less competent, who have more problem behavior, and who create greater hassle by having a disruptive impact on daily routine (Gallimore, et al., 1996). The authors caution against focusing exclusively on level of cognitive development in studying the impact of children on family life and in planning interventions, as sometimes has been done in the past.

Internal and External Resources   Some of the factors enabling parents to cope are obvious: affluent parents cope better than do poor ones, two-parent families cope better than single-parent families, and mothers in harmonious marriages cope better than those in conflicted marriages. More interesting are the findings that parents differ in the kinds of support they find helpful. Mothers require more social-emotional support along with more information about the child's condition and help in child care, while fathers are more concerned with the financial cost of rearing the child. Mothers are helped by a close, supportive social network, while fathers cope better when they have an extended, noncritical social network.

Perception of the Child   Our example here comes from research on communication between mother and child. (See Hodapp and Zigler, 1995.) Both mothers of children who are retarded and mothers of children who are not retarded shorten their sentences and emphasize and repeat key words when the children are learning to speak. However, unlike their counterparts, mothers of children who are retarded are more didactic and directive, initiating bids more often and more often speaking at the same time as their children. By contrast, the interaction between mothers and children who are not retarded is more playful and spontaneous and is less goal-oriented. The behavior of mothers of children who are retarded is motivated by their perception of the child as needing to be taught, along with their fear concerning the child's ability to learn to speak. Ironically, the mother's intrusiveness runs the risk of further increasing the child's communicative difficulties. In fact, certain remedial programs aim at helping the mothers to relax and to imitate the child more, thus allowing the child to take a more active role in learning to speak.

The Developmental Dimension   Instead of parents having a single initial depressive response to having a child who is retarded, there is evidence that depression may occur at a number of points in the child's life. For example, it may appear in a mother of a child with Down syndrome when the child is about 4 months old, at which time the child's inconsistent smiles and dampened affect set them apart from the vigorous and gleeful responses of infants who are not retarded (Hodapp and Zigler, 1995). A depressive reaction may appear again in the parent when the child is 11 to 15 years of age (entering puberty) or at 21 years of age (entering adulthood). Parents may also begin to distance themselves both emotionally and physically from the child from middle childhood on in order to prepare the child for becoming independent.

Peers

There is evidence that children with MR often are not accepted by their nonretarded peers, although they tend to be ignored rather than actively rejected (Nabors, 1997; Siperstein & Leffert, 1997). Their friendship patterns in preadolescence also differ. Friendships among preadolescents who are not retarded are marked by a high level of engagement, evidenced by frequent verbal communication, shared decision making, and mutual responsiveness at a high affective level such as laughing together. Friendships between a preadolescent who is nonretarded and one who is mildly retarded have a low level of engagement, with the children often working independently and rarely laughing together. In short, the children look more like acquaintances than friends (Siperstein, Leffert, & Wenz-Gross, 1997).

Social Cognition   The lack of peer acceptance is usually attributed to a low level of social competence in children with MR. While social competence has been conceptualized in a variety of ways and involves a number of variables, research has primarily been concerned with the variable of social cognition, which lies at the juncture between intelligence on the one hand and adaptive behavior on the other.

There is evidence that children with MR, as compared with those who are not retarded, have less developed perspective taking, are less skilled in interpreting social cues, and have less advanced social strategies for dealing with problem situations (e.g., joining a group or responding to provocative behavior). (For a summary of the literature, see Leffert and Siperstein, 1996.)

Siperstein and Leffert (1997) also studied the difference between mildly retarded fourth and sixth graders who were socially accepted and those who were socially rejected. The findings concerning social behavior and social cognition seem paradoxical. Accepted children favored submissive goals and generated few positive, outgoing strategies. In contrast, it was the rejected children who favored assertive goals and positive, outgoing strategies. One explanation for this unexpected finding is that low-key, deferential, and accommodating goals and strategies protect children against being rejected by making them "blend in" with the others whereas socially assertive and intrusive goals and strategies do not. Since peer rejection and indifference are more likely than acceptance in children with MR, they have more to lose if assertiveness goes wrong than do children who are not retarded.

Mainstreaming   Since social interaction is facilitated when normal children of different chronological ages are grouped together, one might expect a similar facilitation when children with MR are **mainstreamed**, or placed in educational settings with normally developing children. However, the limited data available suggest that involvement with children who are not retarded produces only modest improvement in social and play interactions among preschoolers, perhaps because the tendency to form socially separate subgroups is a powerful one during this period (Guralnick, 1986). Thus, while children who are mildly retarded and those who are not interact frequently and in similar ways, children who are moderately and severely retarded receive only infrequent attention from their nonretarded classmates. Interestingly, the interactions that do occur are not aversive, nor is there a failure in communication; on the contrary, the speech of children who are not retarded is simpler and more repetitive when they address cognitively less advanced children, and they are extremely persistent, creative, and successful in achieving their interpersonal goals. Even with children who are mildly retarded, however, the pattern of communication shows subtle differences, with the children who are not retarded assuming an instructional mode, thereby being more "adultlike" than "peerlike" in their communication style (Guralnick, 1986).

A Developmental Study

Carr (1975) conducted one of the few studies asking the question, How does mental retardation affect the *socialization* of children in the first few years of life? The children she studied had Down syndrome. (In our presentation we will supplement Carr's research with other studies that enrich her findings.)

Infancy

Carr (1975) found that, in regard to *feeding*, infants with Down syndrome were less alert and eager for food, had weaker sucking reflexes, and were sleepier

than the normal controls. The mothers did not feed on demand simply because the infants were so undemanding, rarely crying and having to be awakened in certain instances. Moreover, fewer infants were breast-fed because of the difficulty involved in getting them to suck. Understandably, the mothers were more anxious over feeding than were mothers of infants who were not retarded.

Not only was bottle-feeding the rule, but children with Down syndrome also remained dependent on the bottle longer owing to their lag in motor development. At 12 months they were like 8-month-olds, lacking the control of grasping necessary for self-feeding. More mothers of infants with Down syndrome reacted with concern over feeding, forcing or encouraging the toddler or saving the food until later. While the 4-year-old preschoolers with Down syndrome still lagged behind the controls in self-feeding, two-thirds were capable of eating ordinary family meals, and feeding was no longer a problem to most of the mothers. Here, we see the infant "outgrowing" a problem and maternal concern diminishing.

Progression in the development of *attachment* was broadly the same in infants who had Down syndrome as in infants who did not, although one did not exactly mirror the other. In the preattachment months eye contact was delayed, the social smile was less frequent and intense, and, while the infant vocalized more than the control group after the first two to three months of life, there was less coordinated vocal turn-taking and more vocal clashes between mother and infant. Yet mothers were able to accommodate to these deviations and mother and infant were able to enter into reciprocal interactions, which are the prelude to attachment (Berger, 1991).

The complex behaviors making up attachment itself (proximity seeking, separation protest, wariness of strangers) were organized in the same manner as they are in infants who are not retarded, and in the majority of cases a secure attachment was formed. However, there were differences in the quality of certain component behaviors: affect was dampened, the latency of crying at separation was increased, and soothability was decreased (Cicchetti and Beeghly, 1991).

The period following attachment (ages 9 to 36 months) had its own special problems. In normal development, the mother and child at this stage begin to do things together, and their interaction increasingly incorporates objects such as toys and pictures. The child with Down syndrome both had less interest in exploring objects and greater difficulty in maintaining joint attention to objects and caregiver, tending instead to withdraw from playing. Unfortunately, perhaps out of their own concern or because of literature stressing the importance of stimulation to cognitive growth, mothers may begin to make too great demands on their child's ability to understand and perform. Consequently, the interaction becomes frustrating to both partners (Berger, 1991).

The Toddler Period

Carr (1975) found that *toilet training* showed the opposite development from feeding in that the children with Down syndrome "grew into" deviant behavior. At 15 months there was no difference between groups in terms of the age at which training was started and in terms of maternal attitudes. However, by 4 years of age the children with Down syndrome were significantly retarded in all aspects of toileting; they wet their beds and wet or soiled their pants more and were less adept at self-care. Unlike early feeding which caused maternal concern, differences in toilet training did *not* differentially affect the mother's attitudes.

As to *initiative*, toddlers with Down syndrome were reactive to the environment but had neither the intensity of investment nor the attraction to novelty that characterized their nonretarded peers. Thus, they were described as high in approach, low in intensity of response, positive in mood, and perseverative (Ganiban, Wagner, and Cicchetti, 1991). They also initiated fewer behaviors with caregivers (Beeghly, Weiss-Perry, and Cicchetti, 1991). The adjective "passive" often crops up in the literature describing the quality of initiative.

The Preschool Period

Carr's (1975) longitudinal data present a fluctuating picture in the first four years of life, with children growing into and out of *behavior problems*. How-

ever, by 4 years of age, there was no difference between children with Down syndrome and the control group in terms of kinds or amount of problems, such as temper tantrums, aggressiveness, distress, and oppositional behavior, although the children with Down syndrome got into mischief more frequently (for example, fiddling with light switches or putting things in the toilet).

Summary

Infants with Down syndrome tend to "outgrow" their feeding problems by 4 years of age, and maternal concern about it diminishes concomitantly. The children go through the expected progression in forming an attachment, although there are qualitative differences such as their having less-intense positive affective responses to caregivers both before and after an attachment is formed. There is less joint attention to objects with the mother, who may begin to become more demanding and thus initiate a pattern of frustrating interaction. In regard to toileting, children with Down syndrome are significantly retarded at 4 years so they "grow into" problems in this area, although this does not affect mothers' attitudes. There is diminishing initiative in the toddler period, with the children being more passive in exploring objects and relating to the caregiver. Behavior problems fluctuate in the toddler period but by age 4 they are the same as in the control group, even though children with Down syndrome do get into mischief more frequently.

Etiology: The Intrapersonal Context

Answering the question, What has gone awry with normal development in the case of mental retardation? has resulted in an impressive body of research addressing both the cognitive and the personality-motivational factors involved.

Cognitive Factors

Two different questions have been raised concerning the cognitive factors involved in MR. One is a general question: Is the *development* of intelligence in children with MR the same as or different from

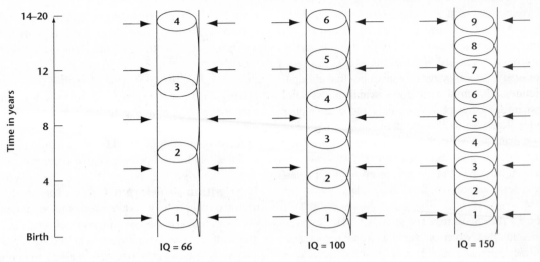

Figure 12.2   Developmental Model of Cognitive Growth.

The single vertical arrow represents the passage of time. The horizontal arrows represent environmental events impinging on the individual, who is represented as a pair of vertical lines. The individual's cognitive development appears as an internal ascending spiral, in which the numbered loops represent successive stages of cognitive growth.

Source: Hodapp and Zigler, 1990

its development in children with normal intelligence? This is known as the *difference versus development* issue. The second question is a specific one: What *particular deviations* underlie the subnormal intellectual functioning of individuals who are retarded?

The Difference Versus Development Issue

Historically, there have been two points of view concerning the nature of MR. One is that MR is due to a *basic cognitive deficit* that results in thinking that is *fundamentally different* from that found in non-retarded populations. The term "mental *deficiency*" epitomizes this view. The second point of view is that thinking in mental retardation is the same as it is in normal intelligence, the only difference being a *developmental* one, which results in *slower progress* and a *lower level of final achievement*. (See Figure 12.2.) There are data supporting both sides of the controversy.

Zigler has been the principle advocate of the developmental approach, proposing two hypotheses to test it. One is concerned with similar sequencing of

cognitive development, the other with similar structure. (A detailed account of these hypotheses and the research testing them can be found in Hodapp and Zigler, 1995.)

The Similar Sequencing Hypothesis   This hypothesis states that children with MR will proceed through the same *stages* of cognitive development and in the same *order* as do children who are not retarded. For example, children with MR will go through the same Piagetian stages in the same invariant order from sensorimotor to preoperational to concrete operational thought. (They rarely reach the final level of formal operational thinking.) Retardation is the result of slower progress and a lower level of achievement.

A considerable body of research supports the similar sequence hypothesis, which holds for retardation due to both organic and nonorganic (or familial) causes. Thus the same sequential development has been found in Piagetian tasks, moral reasoning, symbolic play, geometric concepts, and language, to name some of the specific areas.

Moreover, when strict sequencing does not hold for the retarded population, as in the more advanced stages of moral reasoning, it tends not to hold for nonretarded populations as well.

Finally, there is suggestive evidence that children with some kinds of retardation exhibit a less solid grasp of the kinds of thinking involved at the higher levels. Thus they are more apt to show a mixture of higher and lower levels of thinking than are their nonretarded counterparts. This variability can be evidenced from month to month or even within a single testing session (Hodapp and Zigler, 1995).

The Similar Structure Hypothesis   This hypothesis states that, when matched for overall mental age, children who are retarded will be at the same level of functioning on a variety of intellectual tasks (other than those used to measure intelligence) as are children who are not retarded. Thus, this hypothesis is concerned with *intertask* functioning. It runs counter to the idea that there are specific areas of deficit in thinking in MR.

The support for the similar structure hypothesis is more qualified than that for the similar sequencing hypothesis. When doing Piagetian-based tasks, the performance of children with familial (i.e., nonorganically determined) retardation is comparable to mental-age-matched nonretarded children. However, in performance on information-processing tasks of learning, memory, learning set formation, distractibility, and selective attention, the MR group tends to be inferior. The reason for this puzzling finding is not clear.

The performance of children whose retardation is due to organic factors does *not* support the similar structure hypothesis. Not only is such performance worse than matched mental-age controls, but there are also specific areas of deficit. For example, children with Down syndrome have deficits in grammar relative to other abilities, while boys with fragile X syndrome are particularly weak in sequential thinking such as remembering a sequence of digits. (See Hodapp and Zigler, 1995, for details.)

In sum, there is good support for the similar sequencing hypothesis, but the support for the similar structure hypothesis is limited to Piagetian tasks in children with nonorganically determined retarda-

tion. The similar structure hypothesis is not supported when information-processing tasks are used and retardation is due to organic factors.

Specific Deviations in Thinking

Having discussed the general developmental question concerning cognitive factors involved in MR, we now turn to the research on specific deviations underlying subnormal intellectual functioning. The findings can be grouped under five categories.

1. Attention to Relevant Cues   The basic research paradigm here is called *discrimination learning*. The child is presented with a succession of stimuli, such as objects differing in color, shape, and size, two or three at a time and is asked to choose one. On the basis of being told that a choice is either right or wrong, the child must learn what dimension—color, shape, or size in this instance—is the key to making a correct choice. To illustrate: A girl is presented with a red circle and a blue square. Guessing that "circle" is the correct response, she chooses the first figure and is told she made a correct choice. Next time a green circle and a blue triangle are presented and she is told her choice of the circle is incorrect. She must now change her hypothesis. If she remembers that the original circle was also red, she strongly suspects "red" to be the solution, which she verifies when another red object is shown. If she does not remember, she must adopt another hypothesis such as "triangle" or "green".

In discrimination learning situations the learning curve for children of normal intelligence rises quickly at first and then levels off. For children who are retarded, choices are no better than chance for a number of trials, but then there is rapid improvement.

Further investigation reveals that children with MR often do not attend to relevant aspects of the situation; for example, they are not asking themselves, Is it color or shape or size? On the contrary, they have a strong initial preference for position, such as the first object, which they persist in using despite being told that their choice is frequently incorrect. Once they can break this irrelevant set, they learn rapidly. Given a task in which position is the relevant cue they learn as fast as or faster than children with normal intelligence. Thus, in a special sense they are not slow learners but they are slow to catch on to the relevant question. (See Hale and Borkowski, 1991.)

The preference for position responses seen in children who are retarded has its counterpart in normal development, since position habits have been observed to interfere with discrimination learning in one-year-olds. Such habits no longer seem to affect discrimination learning in the toddler and preschooler, although the evidence is not conclusive on this point. If the preference in children who are retarded does in fact represent a fixation, it is one that goes back to earliest childhood and may significantly interfere with subsequent learning.

However, investigators have not been satisfied with the general explanation of failure to attend to relevant cues and, using the information-processing model, have set out to pinpoint the source or sources of malfunctioning. Most of the studies have been done on children with mild to moderate retardation who are organically intact. (Unless otherwise specified, our presentation follows Borkowski, Peck, and Damberg, 1983, and Hale and Borkowski, 1991.)

2. Attention Children who are mentally retarded may have a basic attentional deficit. For example, they have slower reaction times in simple reaction-time experiments. These experiments involve a preparatory signal, such as a buzzer, followed by a stimulus, such as a light, to which the subject must respond as quickly as possible (for example, by pressing a button). Another kind of evidence of a decreased ability to maintain adequate attentional levels is the increase in off-task glancing both in simple and complex tasks.

3. Memory There is no evidence that children who are retarded have a deficit in short-term memory, as tested in tasks involving repeating back digits. The findings concerning a possible deficit in long-term memory are contradictory and inconclusive because it is exceedingly difficult to control all the prior processes in order to obtain an unconfounded evaluation of this one alone. The situation is also complicated by the fact that long-term memory depends on the use of a number of *strategies*

designed to aid retention and organize the incoming information. Such strategies include rehearsal, mediation, and clustering.

3a. Rehearsal *Rehearsal* typically consists of repeating each new item along with all the prior ones; for example, in remembering a series of numbers a child may think, "six, six-three, six-three-eight," and so forth. Rehearsal is clearly evidenced by the third grade in children who are not retarded. Research indicates that children who are retarded are deficient in rehearsal. If they are trained, their performance improves, but in most cases they will not spontaneously use such aids. As with discrimination learning, they fail to do what they are capable of doing. And again, as with discrimination learning, this failure has its counterpart in normal development, since first-graders also make no use of their ability to rehearse.

3b. Clustering Remembering improves if incoming information is organized in a meaningful manner, a strategy called *clustering*. Present the average child with, say, a list comprised of three categories of words arranged in random order, and the child will tend to recall them by categories; for example, the words the child remembers and says following "dog" will tend to be other animal words in the list, and those following "apple" will be the other food words. Both children who are retarded and young children of normal intelligence show little evidence of using the strategy of clustering. While children who are retarded can be taught to do so, once again they fail to use this aid spontaneously.

3c. Mediation Memory is also facilitated by mediation strategies. The research paradigm here is paired-associate learning. Initially, two stimuli are presented, and subsequently, only the first is shown, and the child is asked to recall the second. Paired-associate learning can be facilitated if the child ties the two stimuli together in a meaningful manner; for example, "sun" and "bird" are more readily associated if related by something like "the sun shines on the bird." While 5- to 6-year-olds can produce and use mediational strategies, younger children and those who are retarded do not use them. If the latter children are provided with mediators or even instructed to generate them, their learning is significantly improved. However, if the experimenter no longer instructs the children, they may fail to continue using mediators on their own. Training them to get into the habit has met with only limited success, being effective primarily with the mildly retarded. Thus it is not that children with MR are deficient in the sense that they are incapable of grasping higher-level strategies; rather, for some unknown reason, they fail to use spontaneously the abilities they possess.

3d. Retrieval   There is evidence that the same deviation in categorization which hampers memory also adversely affects the retrieval of information that has been learned. It makes sense to assume that items stored singly in memory would be more difficult to retrieve than items stored by categories that represent superordinate organizations of the individual items. As was the case in regard to rehearsal and clustering, the deficit seems to be one of lack of *use* of category knowledge rather than lack of category knowledge itself.

3e. Metamemory   *Metamemory* refers to children's understanding of how memory works, such as knowing it takes more time and effort to memorize a long list of words than a short one. While metamemory improves dramatically with age in children of normal intelligence, the rate of improvement is variable in populations with MR. For example, their understanding of the relation between amount of study time and remembering or the effect of delay of recall on performance is commensurate with mental-age-matched peers; however, even children with higher levels of intellectual functioning lack awareness of the fact that it is easier to relearn old material than to learn new material.

4. Problem Solving   Problem solving typically requires attention, abstraction, planning, and logical thinking. The same failure to generate relevant hypotheses that mars discrimination learning in children with MR also affects the more complex task of solving problems. For example, even when the classic "twenty questions" task has been modified so that, in the simplest case, only one question is sufficient to supply the information necessary to make a correct choice, children who are retarded ask noncritical questions as frequently as critical ones. Once the information is supplied, they can use it effectively, however.

5. Generalization   Finally, while children with MR can be trained to do a specific problem successfully, they characteristically do not generalize to similar problems. It is as if each task is a new one that must be mastered in its own right. The impediment to learning is obvious.

Summary   Children with MR perform poorly on discrimination learning tasks, although, once their position set is broken, they learn as fast as children who are not retarded. The same failure to generate relevant hypotheses that hampers discrimination learning also adversely affects problem solving. Children with MR have a basic deficiency in attention and generalization, but their short-term memory is intact. While they are not incapable of grasping the strategies of rehearsal, mediation, and clustering that facilitate long-term memory, they neither spontaneously generate such strategies nor assimilate them to the point of habitually using them after being instructed or taught to do so. In a similar manner, children with MR do not use their categorizing ability to facilitate the retrieval of information. For unknown reasons, their performance in regard to metamemory tasks is variable, being a mixture of adequate and low-level functioning.

Personality-Motivational Factors

The Similar Reaction Hypothesis   Zigler's third hypothesis, called the *similar reaction hypothesis*, states that there is no basic difference between children who are and are not retarded in their reactions to life experiences. However, since these experiences might well be different for children who are retarded, such as repeated failure or institutionalization, the children with MR may have special motivational and personality characteristics. A number of these characteristics have been investigated. (Our presentation follows Hodapp and Zigler, 1995.)

Dependency and Outerdirectedness   Children with MR are more attentive to and dependent upon adults. For example, because of their need to gain positive reinforcement from adults, institutionalized children will play a boring, repetitive game longer than will noninstitutionalized children matched for mental and chronological age. Zigler calls this need for positive reinforcement the *positive reaction tendency*. Along with this tendency goes outerdirectedness, or *an exaggerated need to look to others* for clues as to how to solve problems. Such clues will subsequently be used even when they are extraneous or misleading. Outerdirectedness contrasts with the behavior of children who are not retarded, who are more self-reliant and use their own judgment more.

Lower Expectancy of Success   Because of repeated experiences with failure, children who are retarded have a lower expectancy of success that makes them give up more readily than children who are not retarded. In certain instances this can lead to a vicious cycle, with the self-protective need to avoid yet another failure experience resulting in a premature abandoning of the attempt to solve problems—which in turn further reduces the likelihood of success.

Lower Effectance Motivation   Finally, there is a decrease in effectance motivation, or what we call initiative, in children who are retarded. There is less interest and pleasure in tackling new tasks or meeting new challenges, less intrinsic reward in achievement for its own sake.

The Self   In regard to personality, the self of a child who is retarded is less differentiated than it is for children in the nonretarded population. Recall that, while there is a generalized view of the self, it is also divided into various domains such as intellectual, social and athletic. Thus a child might say, "I don't do well in school but I have lots of friends." Compared with children matched for chronological age, those who are retarded have fewer specific domains and a more impoverished concept of the self.

Individuals also have an ideal self and a real self—a "me as I would like to be" and a "me as I am." Compared with nonretarded children, those

with MR have a lower ideal self, perhaps due to their greater number of failures and to their being treated as incompetent. (See Hodapp and Zigler, 1995.)

We now see that the child with MR has two handicaps, one intellectual, the other motivational. The problem may further be compounded in institutional settings where docility and conformity to a drab routine are rewarded, while assertiveness and initiative are punished. The challenge to researchers is to disentangle basic intellectual handicaps from those that result from motivational and environmental influences. The therapeutic challenge is to find ways our society can accommodate the realistic limitations while maximizing the assets of the child who is retarded. Meeting this challenge will result in a more balanced mixture of successes and failures for those with MR than presently exists. It is helpful to remind ourselves that in certain societies MR is not stigmatized or even viewed as a problem that need to be corrected. Our achievement-oriented society might profit from such examples of acceptance.

Etiology: The Organic Context

It is estimated that there are over 1,000 different organic causes of mental retardation. Although there are exceptions, such as children with Prader-Willi syndrome, who are only mildly retarded, most children with organically based retardation are severely impaired; for example, 77 percent of cases in the moderate-to-profound range are due to organic factors. (See Hodapp and Dykens, 1996.)

Selected Organic Etiologies

Prenatal and Postnatal Factors   A host of prenatal and postnatal factors can damage the central nervous system and result in MR. Rubella (German measles) contracted by the mother during the first trimester of pregnancy can cause a number of impairments, MR being one. Syphilis is another cause of MR. Exposure to massive doses of radiation in the first few months of pregnancy, chronic alcoholism, age (35 years or older), and severe emotional stress throughout pregnancy are among the numerous maternal factors that increase the risk of MR in the infant.

Prematurity and prenatal asphyxia (oxygen deprivation during or immediately after delivery) are hazards of birth. Postnatal sources of mental subnormality are head injuries (most commonly resulting from automobile accidents and child abuse), encephalitis and meningitis (inflammations of the brain resulting from infections by bacteria, viruses, or tuberculosis organisms), particularly if they occur during infancy.

Clinical Disorders   Clinical disorders associated with MR include cerebral palsy, seizure disorders (epilepsy), and lead and mercury poisoning from chemical pollutants ingested by the child (for example, by eating lead-based paint or shellfish that have absorbed methyl mercury from industrial waste).

The foregoing list is intended solely to provide an overview of selected organic etiologies. In each instance the relation to MR, the degree of retardation, and the percent of affected children vary widely. It would be erroneous to conclude, for example, that all children with cerebral palsy or with seizures are also retarded, since a considerable portion are not. (For a more detailed discussion of organic factors see Bregman and Hodapp, 1991, and Deitz and Repp, 1989.)

AIDS   Because of the widespread concern with AIDS, the relation of MR to this condition needs to be discussed in some detail. As of 1995 there were 6,817 documented cases of HIV infants and children from birth to 13 years of age, 5,432 of whom were 5 years old or younger. Of the infected children, 90 percent had mothers who were also HIV-positive. Early studies indicated that 80 to 90 percent of these infected children had neurodevelopmental conditions, including MR, which occurred in 25 to 40 percent of the population. However, the problem with the finding concerning MR is that, unless placed with caring foster or adoptive parents, the children were apt to be from impoverished homes, to have one or two drug abusing parents whose child-rearing practices were questionable, and to have inadequate medical attention. (See Cohen et al., 1997.) Such a constellation of adverse environmental conditions could produce MR independent of infection with the HIV virus.

Research by Mayes and associates (1996) controlled for the above adverse social conditions by studying school-age boys with hemophilia, a medical condition not associated with MR. Of these children, eighteen were HIV-positive but asymptomatic and forty-eight were HIV-negative. The mean IQ of the group was 113.5. There was *no significant difference* between IQ scores of HIV-positive and HIV-negative boys, nor was there a significant difference in achievement test scores, grade point average, or the need for educational interventions. It is important to emphasize that the HIV-positive boys were asymptomatic; when the disease progresses and there is an increase in neuropsychological involvement, intelligence is apt to deteriorate.

Genetic Factors

There are more than 500 genetic causes of intellectual disability (King et al., 1997). State, King, and Dykens (1997) summarize the current research situation as follows:

> New genetic technologies have played a key part in elucidating causes of mental retardation, and the study of intellectual disability has played a seminal role in advancing the understanding of the genetics of disease more broadly. (p. 1664)

With this advance has come a rethinking of classical Mendelian principles. We will sample some of the findings. (A more complete presentation can be found in State, King, and Dykens, 1997.)

As we have seen, in Down syndrome there are three number 21 chromosomes instead of the normal two (recall that the condition is also called "trisomy 21"). Recently, however, a critical region on chromosome 21 has been described and the available markers for this and flanking regions have enabled clinicians to confirm cases of Down syndrome in the context of subtle translocations and chromosomal abnormalities other than trisomy (King et al., 1997). Thus, the genetic basis for the syndrome has been expanded.

Equally impressive is the finding that the Prader-Willi syndrome is caused by a deletion in a region of chromosome 15 (15q11-13). In addition, 60 to 80 percent of those with the syndrome have a microscopic or submicroscopic deletion, always found on the paternal chromosome 15, while the remaining individuals have been found to have two copies of the maternal chromosome and no paternal contribution.

Neurological Factors

We will concentrate on data from neuroimaging studies of children and adolescents with Down syndrome. (See Peterson, 1995, for a more comprehensive coverage.) In this syndrome there is a significant reduction in overall brain volume, with a disproportionately large reduction in frontal gray-matter volume. There is also a reduction in size of the anterior regions of the corpus callosum, the portion through which the interhemispheric fibers of the prefrontal cortex pass. Whether this reduction represents a failure to develop or a degenerative process is not clear at this point, but data suggest that both might be involved.

Metabolic patterns involving the frontal and parietal regions appear to be abnormal. This abnormality is thought to underlie the language disability commonly seen in Down syndrome. On the other hand, the volumes of the ventricular nucleus and diencephalon (thalamus and hypothalamus) do not differ from those of normal controls. These findings suggest a relative sparing of subcortical motor and sensory systems.

Intervention

The Overall Need

Because severe and profound levels of retardation tend to persist into adulthood rather than being outgrown, it is clear that special preventive and remedial measures need to be taken. However, the situation is somewhat deceptive in regard to children at less retarded levels who make up the vast majority of the MR population. Most of them live in the homes of parents or other relatives or with foster parents, and most of them function well, going to school during middle childhood, moving reasonably freely about the community, and participating in family life. Many of them subsequently hold jobs. However, while many of these mildly to moderately retarded adults are absorbed into society and it may

seem that their difficulties are solely in connection with having to attend school, members of this group do tend to turn up in a disproportionate number both on the welfare rolls and on police blotters (Haywood, Meyers, and Switzky, 1982). While they do not need the kind of extensive care that severely retarded children do, they are clearly at risk in regard to making an adequate adjustment to society.

Government Regulations

One aspect of programs for the mentally retarded that is of special interest is the involvement of the federal government. Legislative activity was climaxed by PL 94-142, known as the Education for All Handicapped Children Act of 1975. Its purpose was to assure that all handicapped children have a free public education tailored to their unique needs, to assure the rights of handicapped children and their parents or guardians, to assist states in providing education, and to assess and assure the effectiveness of efforts toward education.

Two specific requirements have had far-reaching effects. The first is that an *individualized education program (IEP)* be devised for each child with special needs. Implementing an IEP involves assessing the child's present level of functioning, setting goals, and providing educational services and procedures for evaluating educational progress. Parents as well as various professionals participate in the decision-making process.

The second requirement is that handicapped children be educated in the *least restrictive environment*. This requirement reversed the 75-year-old tradition of placing children who are retarded in self-contained special settings, such as special classrooms for the educable mentally retarded (EMR). The contention was that such classes were ineffective in helping many EMR children learn basic academic and occupational skills, that minorities were overrepresented, and that advances in education have made individualized instruction in regular classes feasible (Beyer, 1991).

Special Education

Children classified as *educable mentally retarded (EMR)* have IQ scores between 55 and 80 and are expected to perform at least at a third-grade level and occasionally as high as a sixth-grade level by the time they finish school. The *trainable mentally retarded* (*TMR*), who have IQ scores between 25 and 55, are taught to function in a restricted environment and are not expected to master traditional academic skills.

In special education classes, EMR pupils are taught academic subjects as tools to enhance social competence and occupational skills. Small classes with individualized attention are recommended. Between 6 and 10 years of age, the EMR child, whose mental age is between 3 and 6 years, is given the kind of readiness programs usually found in kindergarten: the emphasis is on language enrichment and self-confidence, along with good health, work, and play habits. EMR children between 9 and 13 years of age, whose mental age is about 6 to 9 years, can master the basic academic skills involved in the three R's. At the junior and senior high school levels the applied emphasis continues; for example, the children are trained to read the newspaper and job application forms and to make correct change. Occupational education stresses appropriate work habits such as punctuality and following directions, since most vocational failures are due to poor adjustment rather than low mental ability. After formal schooling, sheltered workshops and vocational rehabilitation centers help the mildly retarded adjust to our complex society.

The curriculum for TMRs emphasizes self-care and communication skills, work habits, following directions, and rudimentary social participation. Reading instruction, for example, is likely to include recognizing signs such as "Stop," " Men," and "Women," while arithmetic is limited to making change. The majority of these children do not achieve social or economic independence as adults, although they can engage in useful work and adjust well in the protective setting of the family.

Mainstreaming   Educating children with MR in regular classrooms is called mainstreaming. In keeping with the social fervor of the civil rights movement in the 1960s and 1970s, special classes were labeled another form of discrimination and segregation. The claim was buttressed by poorly designed studies showing that children with MR in special classes fare worse than those in regular classes. Such studies ignored the fact that children were often placed in spe-

cial classes because they were doing poorly or were so disruptive that it was impossible for the teacher to handle them in the regular classroom.

While mainstreaming still has its passionate advocates, empirical evidence has failed to support the contention that all mentally retarded (as well as emotionally disturbed) children should be mainstreamed. Gottlieb, Alter, and Gottlieb (1991), for example, found that mainstreaming did not affect the academic achievement of EMR children. In addition, mainstreaming does not increase social acceptance, nor does it uniformly result in a more positive self-concept. (A critical evaluation of mainstreaming can be found in MacMillan, Gresham, and Forness, 1996.)

Treatment

Behavior Modification   By far the most successful and widely used therapeutic technique for children with MR is behavior modification. This technique involves the operant principles of changing undesirable behaviors by altering the specific consequences that reinforce them and by reinforcing new, more socially acceptable responses (Huguenin, Weidenman, and Mulick, 1991). It has been used to increase a wide array of behaviors: self-help behaviors (toileting, feeding, dressing), work-oriented behaviors (productivity, task completion), social behaviors (cooperation, group activities), nonacademic classroom behaviors (attending, taking turns, talking at appropriate times), academic learning (arithmetic, sight vocabulary), as well as decreasing undesirable behaviors such as attention-getting and aggressive or self-injurious behaviors. An important benefit is that parents can actively participate in the therapeutic program in the home setting. Most important of all, behavior modification, more than any other single therapeutic technique, has been responsible for changing the prevailing attitude of hopelessness among professional and nonprofessional caregivers. (A detailed description of behavioral techniques can be found in Singh, Osborne, and Huguenin, 1996. For a discussion of psychotherapy, see Hurley et al., 1996.)

Treatment Effectiveness   Didden, Duker, and Korzilius's (1997) meta-analysis of 482 published studies covering a period of 26 years provides some specific details in regard to treatment outcomes. As to overall effectiveness, 26.5% of all behaviors can be treated quite effectively, 47.1% can be treated fairly effectively while treatment effectiveness of the remaining 26% is questionable or poor. In regard to the kinds of problems treated, internally maladaptive ones such as self-injurious or stereotypic behaviors along with socially disruptive ones such as public disrobing or inappropriate vocalization are most amenable to change while externally destructive problems such as destruction of property are least amenable. In regard to kinds of treatment, response contingent procedures (i.e. those based on the operant principle of immediate reinforcement) are significantly more effective than are other techniques, such as various forms of psychotherapy.

Our discussion would not be complete without brief mention of *psychopharmotherapy*. This treatment modality has been used not for mental retardation itself but for some of its accompanying disturbances. In their review, Aman and Singh (1991) conclude that, after 35 years of research, most studies are so poorly designed that findings cannot be accepted with any degree of confidence. More recently, Didden, Duker, and Korzilius's (1997) meta-analysis of 482 studies on treatment of problem behaviors in individuals with mental retardation found pharmacological procedures to be the least effective of all treatment modalities reported.

Prevention

The diversity of preventive programs reflects the diverse etiologies of MR itself. A number of programs are medically oriented, such as genetic counseling, therapeutic abortions, elimination of defect-producing illnesses, and compulsory tests for phenylketonuria. (See Pueschel and Goldstein, 1991, for a discussion of genetic counseling.) More relevant are the compensatory educational programs, especially those involving preschool children, of which Head Start is probably the best known.

Programs Targeting Parenting Skills

The most challenging population to involve in prevention consists of mothers who are mentally retarded, 40 percent of whose children will be re-

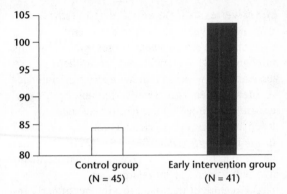

Figure 12.3   Mean Stanford-Binet IQs at Age 3 Years for Groups from Abecedarian Project.

Source: Ramey & Ramey, 1992

tarded themselves. (Our presentation is based on Feldman, 1997. Spiker and Hopmann, 1997, discuss intervention for children with Down syndrome.) While most of these mothers come from low socioeconomic status, the basic problem is not so much poverty itself but impaired parenting skills. The children of mothers in this group are the target of preventive programs such as parent education, placing the child in a more stimulating environment, or both.

Some of the more successful and better-designed programs were conducted by Ramey and Ramey (1992). One such program is called the Abecedarian Project. Evidence shows that, without early intervention, infants of mothers with low IQs are particularly at risk for poor intellectual outcomes. The lower the mother's IQ, the greater the risk. The Rameys' programs were designed to counter the early decline in infant IQ. The programs themselves were intensive, involving a full day, 5 days a week, for 50 weeks a year for the first 5 years. By the time the children were 3 years old, those receiving educational intervention scored 20 IQ points higher than children in the control group, putting 95 percent of them in the normal range as compared with 49 percent of the control children. Moreover, the programs had a particularly powerful preventive effect on children whose mothers had the lowest IQs—the group most at risk for becoming retarded. (See Figure 12.3.)

Effectiveness of Preventive Programs

Guralnick (1998) summarizes the overall findings concerning the effectiveness of preventive programs on cognitive development, indicating there is now "unequivocal evidence that the declines in intellectual development that occur in the absence of systematic early intervention can be substantially reduced by intervention implemented and evaluated *during the first 5 years of life*" (p. 321). This statement holds for both biologically and environmentally determined mental retardation.

The picture of the long-term impact of early intervention is not so optimistic. Particularly in terms of cognitive development, gains diminish over time in many instances for children both at biological and environment risk. In the noncognitive realm the findings are more positive. Children at environment risk who participate in early intervention programs have less grade retention, fewer special education placements, and better school attendance. There is also suggestive evidence that the rate of juvenile delinquency is reduced. (Ramey and Ramey, 1992, present guidelines for effective intervention.)

From this point on, we will be concerned with children at risk for developing behavior problems. Some have to cope with stress arising from chronic illness and brain damage, some with stress arising from parents or other caregivers, and some with stress from a prejudicial society. While they may become psychopathologically disturbed, typically they do not. In fact, many adjust remarkably well, as we shall see in the next several chapters.

Risks of Physical Illness and Brain Damage

Throughout life, but particularly during childhood, the body is the stage on which some of the most significant developmental dramas are enacted. We have already explored the importance of eating and elimination in the normal and psychopathological development of children who are physically healthy. If children are chronically ill or brain-damaged, we might rightly suspect that they must contend with special stresses and problems. Some children may be able to take such stresses in stride and even be stronger because of them; however, some may be taxed beyond their ability to cope successfully.

Pediatric Psychology

The basic assumption of **pediatric psychology** (which is also known as *behavioral medicine*) is that both sickness and health result from the interplay between organic factors on the one hand and psychological, social, and cultural factors on the other. Thus, pediatric psychology conforms to our now familiar *interactional model*. This interplay among factors is present at every stage of the disease process, from etiology to course to treatment, although at different points one or another factor may predominate. In addition, the field includes the psychological and social variables involved in *prevention* and *health maintenance*. Finally, pediatric psychology is primarily concerned with chronically ill children, as life-threatening illnesses are increasingly being eliminated or controlled. (For a general reference, see Roberts, 1995.)

The Effects of Chronic Illness on Adjustment

It is estimated that 10 to 20 percent of children have chronic illnesses, although only 1 to 2 percent of such illnesses are severe (Wallander & Thompson, 1995). The sources of stress in severely ill children are numerous: the pain of the illness and of medical procedures; hospitalization; and the disruption of family life, peer relations, and schooling, to name only a few. In the past the focus of enquiry was on such negative aspects and the toll they were expected to take on the child's psychological well-being. The fact that such expectations were often not realized forced researchers to turn attention to protective factors such as the resilience of children, the resources and adaptability of family members, and the support of health care professionals.

Overview of Findings

The major findings concerning the effects of chronic illness on adjustment are listed below:

1. Chronically ill children are more disturbed than physically healthy ones but are *not* as disturbed as children making up a clinical population.
2. Among kinds of chronic illnesses those involving central nervous system damage have the highest rate of psychological disturbance.
3. Psychological factors are a more important influence on adjustment than are the characteristics of the illness itself. Specifically, (a) children's perception of their illness as stressful is more important than the kind and severity of the illness, and (b) family characteristics of cohesion and support and maternal disturbance such as anxiety and depression play a prominent role in determining the child's adjustment. (For a more detailed presentation of research on adjustment, see Wallander and Thompson, 1995.)

With these points in mind we will examine research findings in greater detail. Unless otherwise noted, our presentation is based on the review chapter of Wallander and Thompson, 1995, and on the comprehensive coverage of the topic by Thompson and Gustafson, 1996.

The Intrapersonal Context

There is no simple or direct relation between chronic illness and adjustment. Rather, a wide range of responses from no disturbance to psychopathology is to be expected. Children with chronic physical illness are more likely to exhibit an increased incidence of internalizing problems, particularly anxiety, although anxiety can be combined with milder forms of externalizing problems such as opposition behaviors.

Chronically ill children may also have an increased incidence of psychopathological disturbances, but the increase tends to be small. For example, Bennett's (1994) meta-analysis of 60 studies of depressive symptoms among children and adolescents with chronic medical problems found only a slightly elevated risk for depressive symptoms and depressive disorders—for example, 9 percent in the illness population compared with 1 to 5 percent in the healthy population.

In sum, major psychopathological disorders are not common among children with chronic illness; however, there is an increased risk for adjustment problems, particularly internalizing ones.

Children's *perception* of illness is more strongly related to adjustment than are the characteristics of the illnesses themselves. Perceived stress is positively related to increased anxiety and depression, as well as to lower self-esteem. Self-esteem itself is also related to adjustment, low esteem increasing depression and behavior problems.

The Interpersonal Context: The Family

Chronic illness confronts families with a host of challenges and problems. Parents, particularly the mother, are responsible for relating to medical personnel, understanding information concerning the nature and treatment of the illness, and implementing the medical regimens. Family routines must accommodate to changes ranging from such minor ones as providing special diets to major ones such as having the child at home rather than in school or being with the child during lengthy hospital stays. Parents must strike the proper balance between sympathizing with the child's distress and encouraging healthy coping mechanisms and age-appropriate behavior. They must also find ways of dealing with added financial burdens as well as with their own anxieties, frustrations, and heartaches.

Most families, like most children, do meet such challenges successfully. Some even find the experience brings a new sense of closeness. Yet, again as with children, families do not emerge unscathed. (A detailed discussion of family characteristics as they relate to chronic illness can be found in Kazak, Segal-Andrews, and Johnson, 1995.)

Children's Adjustment   Studies of family functioning provide evidence for its importance to the children's adjustment in that children in poorly functioning families have a high incidence of psychological problems. By the same token, cohesion and support are particularly important in protecting the child against psychological disturbances.

However, Drotar's (1997) review of the research cautions against overestimating the importance of the family. Not only are there inconsistent findings but also the amount of variance in children's psychological adjustment accounted for by parental or familial variables is only between 10 and 15 percent.

Marital Relationships   There is no difference in marital satisfaction between families with children who are chronically ill and those with children who are healthy. Neither the severity nor the visibility of a handicap is related to this aspect of family functioning (Kazak, Segal-Andrews, and Johnson, 1995).

Parental Functioning   There are few differences between families with a child who is chronically ill and comparison families in regard to a number of dimensions of parental functioning (Kazak, 1992). One exception is maternal adjustment. Perhaps because she has the major responsibility for the care of the child, the mother experiences a high degree of stress and is prone to feelings of depression and has more emotional and practical needs (Kazak, Segal-Andrews, and Johnson, 1995). However, the mother is *not* more apt to be a single parent, to be socially isolated, or to have alcohol problems (Wallander and Varni, 1998).

In regard to risk factors, maternal adjustment is adversely affected by disability-related stresses such as hospitalization and by daily hassles but is not related to major life stresses apart from the child's illness. Thus, a depressive reaction seems to be illness-specific. As for protective factors, these include the mothers' perception of herself as competent in solving problems, social support from family and friends, and hope. (See Wallander and Varni, 1998.)

Social Support   There is evidence that, in general, social isolation increases the risk of psychological disturbance in families of children with chronic illnesses. Social support, on the other hand, functions as a protective factor (Kazak, 1992). Thus, a large social network protects against disturbances, while

isolation increases the chances of disturbance. For example, Barakat and Linney (1992) found that a large network that included a number of family members along with satisfactory relations among members was related to higher maternal and child adjustment. The results are interesting in their own right while suggesting one means of protecting mothers of chronically ill children from the danger of becoming depressed.

The Interpersonal Context: Peer Relations

Chronic illness may adversely affect peer relations. Severe illness may disrupt the child's life and limit opportunities for social interaction; for example, frequent hospitalizations may be associated with loneliness, sensitivity, and isolation. Boys may be at greater risk than girls in regard to negative effects on peer relations. On the positive side, family cohesiveness, support, and expressiveness serve as protective factors.

The Organic Context

Type of Illness   Generally speaking, there is no consistent relation between type of illness and adjustment. The single exception is conditions involving central nervous system disorders or brain damage, in which case there is an increase in behavior problems along with an increase in poor peer relations and school problems. (Nassau and Drotar, 1997, review the research on the social adjustment of children with central nervous system disorders.)

Severity and Duration of Illness   Severity of illness is not usually associated with an increase in behavior problems; however, there are exceptions. Severity of central nervous system disorders does adversely affect peer relations regardless of how severity is operationalized—in terms of degree of medical intervention required, functional impairment such as being ambulatory versus nonambulatory, neuropsychological impairment, or school placement in a regular or mainstreamed classroom. Moreover, adolescents with three or more severe impairments are likely to have very restricted social lives, with the combination of an IQ below 85, walking problems, and obesity being particularly detrimental. (See Nassau and Drotar, 1997.) In addition, there is some evidence of a positive relation between duration of illness and adjustment in that the longer children are ill the more adjustment problems they are apt to have.

The Developmental Dimension

The few longitudinal studies that have been done suggest that overall rate of poor psychological adjustment is reasonably stable in children with chronic illnesses. However, the illnesses themselves tend to change over time. The exception to this generalization is disturbances involving the central nervous system, which tend to be stable over time.

One reason why more developmental studies are desirable is that their data will provide a clearer idea of which specific subpopulations of children are at risk for becoming increasingly disturbed and which are apt to go on to more benign disturbances. With such information, preventive measures, which are often in short supply, could be concentrated on the former group.

A Developmental Psychology of Illness

It is natural initially to view the unknown in terms of the known. At times the strategy is successful. At times it misses the mark. A case in point is pediatric psychology. Clinical child psychologists who became interested in understanding and helping pediatric patients tended to ask the clinician's questions: How is physical illness related to traditional disturbances such as anxiety disorder, depression, and conduct disorders? What traditional treatments would benefit such children? While these are legitimate questions, they are too narrow to capture essential features of physical illness in children. Our own preference is to ask the developmental psychopathologist's questions: What is the child's experience and understanding of illness at various developmental levels? How do these affect the intrapersonal and interpersonal variables (particularly the family) that have concerned us all along? In short, what we are searching for is a *developmental psychology of illness*.

The Ideal   First let us start with the ideal of a developmental psychology of illness. As an initial step, go back to Figure 1.2 and, instead of visualizing a healthy child in the center, substitute a physically ill one. How would physical illness reverberate throughout all of the contexts? In the intrapersonal context, how would it be understood and coped with, and how would it affect the child's personality and adjustment? In the interpersonal context, in what ways would illness alter parental and peer relations? At the superordinate level, how would the ill child fare in school and in occupations, and how would cultural values shape the perception of illness and its management? To the familiar list of interpersonal variables we must add *health care professionals*, such as pediatricians, nurses, and therapists, just as we must add the *hospital* to the list of social institutions.

Finally, and most important of all, we must ask, How do all of these variables change with time? In addition we should know what risk factors are pressing to divert development from its normal course and what protective factors can counter such a diversion.

This ideal of a developmental psychology of illness is nowhere in sight. However, there are fragments of the total picture that have generated a body of observational and objective data. We will present three such fragments: children's understanding of illness, their understanding of pain, and the effects of hospitalization.

Children's Understanding of Illness

The Piagetian Framework

With some exceptions, research shows that the understanding and explanation of illness follows the Piagetian stages of cognitive development. (Our presentation is based on Harbeck-Weber and Peterson, 1993, and on Thompson and Gustafson, 1996, unless otherwise noted.)

The Preoperational Period   Recall that, in this period, thinking is based on naive perception—in a literal sense, seeing is believing. Thus, the perceived cause of illness tends to be *external* events, objects, or persons that the preschooler has associated with the illness through experience. These causes may be remote from the child ("A cold is caused by trees") or in physical proximity ("You get a cold when somebody stands near you"). As seen in the latter instance, preschoolers may begin to grasp the idea of *contagion*, but their thinking is still at an unsophisticated level since they do not understand the reasons why proximity is related to illness.

Finally, in this period of concrete associations *causes* can be confused with *consequences*; for example, preschoolers may think that a bowel movement is caused by going to the toilet or you get a stomachache through vomiting. Incidentally, these examples nicely illustrate the logical fallacy of post hoc reasoning: because B follows A, B causes A.

The Concrete Operations Period   While children in middle childhood still focus on external events, they now can grasp the idea of *contamination* in that there is something harmful that causes the illness; for example, you get a cold from playing with a dirty toy. Later in this period children explain illness in terms of *internalization* such as swallowing or breathing. In addition, internalization directly affects the *internal organs*.

In sum, the children can now make inferences: it is not the perceived object per se but an inferred quality of the object (its harmfulness) that causes illness. Moreover, invisible objects (internal organs) play a role in sickness. While causes now consist of sequences of events, they tend to be limited to a single sequence.

The Formal Operations Period   Adolescents can grasp *internal* causes at two levels. First, they can understand *physiological* causation in terms of the functioning of body organs. Next, they can also understand *psychological* states such as fearfulness as causes. Thus, illness is now *multidetermined*, with a number of external and internal factors playing a role. Finally, adolescents can grasp *abstract* causes such as "poor nutrition."

The Relation Between Stage and Age

One of the dangers of Piaget's stage approach is that of assuming a one-to-one relation between stage and age. This is not an assumption of Piaget's

actual theory, nor does it correspond to reality. In terms of our present discussion, it would be a mistake to assume that, because formal operations tends to appear in adolescence, all adolescents have a sophisticated, abstract concept of the causes of illness. Such is not the case. Crisp, Ungerer, and Goodnow (1996), for example, were interested in the effect of experience on the level of understanding the causes of illness. They called children with little experience with illness "Novices" and those with a good deal of experience "Experts." They then compared a younger group (ages 7 to 10) of "Novices" and "Experts" with an older group (ages 10.7 to 14) of "Novices" and "Experts" in terms of whether their explanations of causation fell in the preoperational, concrete operations, or formal operations stage of development. Their results are presented in Figure 13.1.

Analysis of their data showed that experience did affect level of understanding. However, what interests us is that there is *not* a total shift from concrete to formal operations in adolescence. While there is a statistically significant increase in such thinking, concrete operations thinking still predominates. When we discuss compliance with medical treatment we will examine the danger of assuming that adolescents are more sophisticated about illness than they really are.

Illness as Punishment

Until recently it was generally accepted that young children regard illness as punishment for wrongdoing. Such a view of causation derives from Piaget's concept of *imminent justice*. This is the erroneous belief that noxious consequences such as punishment *automatically* result from wrongdoing. A corollary of this belief is that noxious happenings, such as punishment or illness, are proof that the child has done wrong; for example, "If I am punished or become ill, I must have done something wrong." A considerable body of observational and objective studies of both healthy and ill children seemed to confirm the idea that they view illness as punishment.

However, the evidence has been criticized as being methodologically flawed in that the child's becoming ill is presented first and the misdeed (e.g., stealing) second. The child is then asked whether

Younger

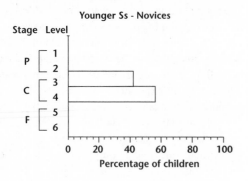

Younger Ss - Novices

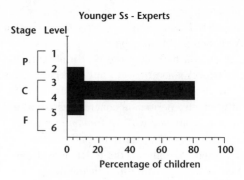

Younger Ss - Experts

Older

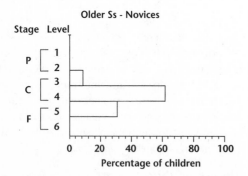

Older Ss - Novices

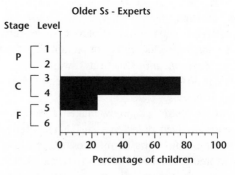

Older Ss - Experts

Figure 13.1   Understanding Illness Causation. (P=Preoperational; C=Concrete Operations; F=Formal Operations)

Source: Crisp, Ungerer, & Goodnow, 1996, p.68

the latter could cause the former. Such sequencing may bias the child to answer in the affirmative (Springer, 1994). The revised methodology reverses the sequences in that the misdeed is presented first and is followed by the causative question. For example: A boy stole an apple; do you think he could get sick from eating it?

In Springer's (1994) study, seventeen 4- and 5-year-olds diagnosed as having acute lymphoblastic leukemia (cancer) and a comparable group of healthy children were asked questions about causality using the revised order. Some questions were sit-

uation-specific, such as the above example of the stolen apples; others concerned misbehavior over a long period of time, such as a girl being "mean" to her parents and playmates. The question in this case was, Do you think she'll get sick from being a bad little girl? Finally there were situations involving possible contamination rather than misbehavior, such as eating cheese after dropping it in the dirt or eating very old corn.

The results showed that most preschoolers in both groups believed contamination was the cause of illness and rejected the possibility of misbehavior as being causative. Moreover, half of the children who seemed to endorse imminent justice, reasoned in terms of contamination on further questioning; for example, the boy who stole the apples got sick because the apples had poison on them.

Springer's (1994) results do not show that imminent justice plays no part in preschooler's thinking. A few preschoolers do associate illness with punishment, and, if they are also chronically ill, this association may add to their distress. However, the research findings do suggest that, for the majority of preschoolers, contamination rather than misbehavior is regarded as the cause of illness.

Children's Understanding of Pain

The Infant and Toddler Periods

At one time a widely held view among pediatricians was that neonates could not experience pain. The view is erroneous. The healthy neonate responds to painful stimuli with loud crying, dramatic facial grimaces, tightly clenched fists, limb thrashing, and torso rigidity. One consequence of the erroneous view was that pediatricians withheld analgesics, resulting in needless suffering on the part of neonates. (Our presentation follows Craig and Grunau, 1991, unless otherwise indicated.)

For our purposes it is more correct to speak of the neonates' response to painful stimuli rather than of their understanding of pain. These initial responses— for example, to a hypodermic injection—are global, diffuse, and prolonged. Moreover, the neonate neither localizes the region of distress nor engages in self-protective behavior. However, cognitive elements soon enter the picture, as we shall see.

Between 6 and 8 months the infant begins to display anticipatory fear—for example, at the sight of a hypodermic needle. Thus learning and memory add anticipation to the painful response itself. In addition, the infant engages in rudimentary behavior designed to ward off the threatening stimulus.

During the second year of life, toddlers become more competent in their response to an injection. They scream for a shorter period, orient toward the site of the injection, attempt to protect themselves or pull away, and use language to communicate their feelings. They also visually scan their mothers' face, indicating an integration of the pain experience into the social environment. As the period progresses the response to pain becomes more localized to the painful body region, and efforts to relieve pain become more purposeful and versatile, while verbal demands for aid and expressions of anger increase.

In sum, the developmental trends in the first two years of life are:

1. From global, diffuse, prolonged reactions to specific, shorter ones
2. From immediate reactions to anticipatory anxiety
3. From unlocalized to localized sources of pain
4. From no self-protective behavior to efforts to fend off or avoid the painful stimulus
5. From nonsocial, nonverbal responses to increasingly social and verbal responses

The Preschool and Middle Childhood Periods

As was the case with the understanding of illness, research on children's understanding of pain has been heavily influenced by Piaget's theory of cognitive development. (Our presentation follows Peterson et al., 1991, and Thompson and Gustafson, 1996, unless otherwise noted.)

In the preschool period pain is viewed more as an unpleasant physical entity, a *thing* that hurts or is sore. Pain is caused by external events such as having an accident. In coping with pain children are passive in that they rely on concrete methods of relief such as medicine or food, or they turn to parents to care for them.

In middle childhood pain is viewed as a feeling rather than as a thing one has. Children's understanding is more differentiated in two respects. First, pain itself is differentiated in terms of intensity, quality, and duration. Second, localization of pain within the body is more differentiated. Physical and psychological causes are now recognized, although the children refer to one or the other, rather than to both. Finally, children take more initiative in coping with pain, such as diverting themselves by exercising or talking with friends. Level of understanding,

| Box 13.1 | The Use and Misuse of Pain |

Pain can be effectively relieved in 90 percent of patients; however, 80 percent of patients do not receive the medication needed to relieve their pain. (Our presentation follows Walco, 1994.) The tendency toward undermedication is even more pronounced in children than in adults.

The justification for undermedication in infants is that infants do not feel pain—or, if they do, they do not remember it. As we have discussed, there is evidence that infants do perceive pain. There is also evidence that the experience of pain can endure; for example, circumcision results in subsequent disturbances in feeding, sleeping, and the stability of the state of arousal. Other defenses of undermedication are also not valid. While fear of the needle can be distressing to children, there are now techniques to minimize the pain. In a like manner, averse side effects of analgesic medication can be controlled by monitoring or can be reversed when they occur. The fear of addiction is particularly unjustified as there is no evidence it is a danger.

However, pain *is* useful in diagnosis and as an index of the effectiveness of treatment. In weighing the benefits against the harm of pain, the physician should ask whether the pain is useful and necessary to effective medical management. If so, pain should be kept at the lowest possible level.

however, is dependent upon the kind of pain; for example, children have the least understanding of the cause of headaches and the most advanced and precise understanding of pain caused by injections.

Adolescence

Cognitively, adolescents are capable of giving sophisticated descriptions of pain and of its causes. (Our presentation of the adolescent period follows McGrath and Pisterman, 1991.) Descriptions can involve the use of physical analogies, such as "It's like a sharp knife slicing my insides." Causation includes both physiological and psychological factors, and adolescents are aware that psychological factors such as anxiety may intensify the purely physical reaction. Finally, adolescents are capable of understanding the value of pain, such as its signaling the presence of disease.

Summary

The *concept of pain* goes from its being a physical entity in the preschool period to its being a feeling differentiated as to components and localization in middle childhood to sophisticated descriptions in adolescence. The *understanding of the cause of pain* goes from external events in the preschool period to either physical or psychological causes in middle childhood to both physical and psychological causes in adolescence. *Coping with pain* goes from passive reliance on pills or parents in the preschool period to taking initiative, such as diverting the self in middle childhood. The value of pain is not grasped until adolescence. (See Box 13.1.)

The Effects of Hospitalization

Up to this point the emphasis has been on cognitive development and its influence on understanding illness. Studies of the effects of hospitalization illustrate the effects of illness on socioemotional development. (See Garrison and McQuiston, 1989.)

Infancy

Two pivotal developments of infancy are achieving physiological integration and forming an attachment. Hospitalization may interfere with both. The hospitalized, chronically ill infant may experience highly intrusive, often painful medical procedures and intense and often noncontingent stimulation such as the continuous noise of monitors, ventilators, and staff conversations in the intensive care unit. All this painful, noncontingent stimulation interferes with the integration of autonomic and motor systems such as digestion, respiration, posture, and movement.

Separation anxiety does not appear in infants hospitalized during the first few months of life because an attachment to parents has not been formed. The continual change of caregivers in the hospital itself is a major impediment to the development of an attachment. However, in the latter part of the first year, separation anxiety is expected to appear and may be a major source of distress.

The Toddler Period

Initiative is the major development in this period. Along with separation anxiety and the stresses of a painful illness and medical procedures, the toddler may experience the frustrations due to physical restraint or restriction of movement. Parental worry or possible overprotectiveness also may frustrate the desire to explore and master the environment. The realistic increased dependence on parents for health care, particularly when compounded by parental overconcern in regard to the toddler's vulnerability, makes the struggle for autonomy more difficult and may tempt some toddlers to regress to the infantile stage.

Middle Childhood

Very little is known about hospitalization during this period since there have been relatively few clinical and objective studies done on this specific topic. There is some evidence that concern centers on the anticipation of pain, children being particularly upset by their fantasy that some kind of mutilation of their bodies will occur in the hospital.

Adolescence

Just at the time when peer relations take on increased importance, chronic illness may diminish such contacts by limiting participation in social events and school. Delayed physical development or physical disfigurement—such as the small stature, chronic cough, barrel chest, and low exercise tolerance that may accompany cystic fibrosis (a disease of the mucous glands)—can be particularly distressing for the body-conscious adolescent. For its part, the medical community tends to perceive the adolescent as a chronic noncomplier; therapeutic procedures, even those essential to health, may fall victim to the adolescent's general need to assert independence.

Recent Improvements   The past few decades have witnessed significant changes in hospital policies aimed at reducing the children's distress; for example, instead of restricting parental visits, almost all hospitals now allow unlimited visitation and

rooming-in. Most hospitals also offer prehospital preparation for both the children and their parents. For example, Christiano and Tarbell (1998) found that children as young as 1 year old to children 5½ years old had less postoperative pain after a hernia repair when their parents provided surgery-relevant information to the children during the preoperative period. In spite of improvement, however, there is still more that can be done to minimize children's distress. (See Harbeck-Weber and McKee, 1995.)

While the developmental literature is of most interest to us, much of the research on illness in children has not been specifically concerned with development. It is this literature that we will turn to now, organizing our presentation around three topics and using three chronic illnesses to illustrate them. We have chosen asthma to illustrate the complex interaction between organic and psychological factors, diabetes mellitus to introduce the problem of noncompliance with medical regimens, and cancer to explore the topic of pain management.

The Interaction of Contexts: Asthma

Until recently, illness was thought of either as basically physiological with some psychological components or as basically psychological with some physiological components (the so-called *psychosomatic* approach to etiology). However, the psychosomatic model could not accommodate the constant interplay of biological, intrapersonal, interpersonal, and superordinate contexts that characterize all phases of illness from etiology to maintenance to treatment. Asthma nicely illustrates this *interactional* approach to understanding illness, and the approach itself is applicable to all chronic illnesses. (Unless otherwise noted, our presentation is based on a comprehensive account of asthma by Creer and Bender, 1995.)

Definition and Characteristics

Asthma is a disorder of the *respiratory system*. Hyperresponsiveness or hypersensitivity of the trachea, bronchi, and bronchiole produces a narrowing of air passages. The result may be intermittent episodes of wheezing and shortness of breath called *dyspnea*.

Severe attacks, known as *status asmaticus*, can be life-threatening and require emergency medical treatment. While asthma can be fatal, the fatality rate is low.

The Organic Context

As we have seen, asthma involves airway hyperresponsiveness. Etiological research has concentrated on bronchial inflammation as an important mecha-

nism responsible for this condition. However, how inflammation occurs in the airways and how it produces hyperactivity are unknown. In short, the organic cause of asthma has yet to be discovered.

Once established, hyperresponsivity makes children sensitive to a number of irritants. These irritants are regarded as *trigger mechanisms* that produce an attack rather than being regarded as etiological agents. At the organic level, viral in-

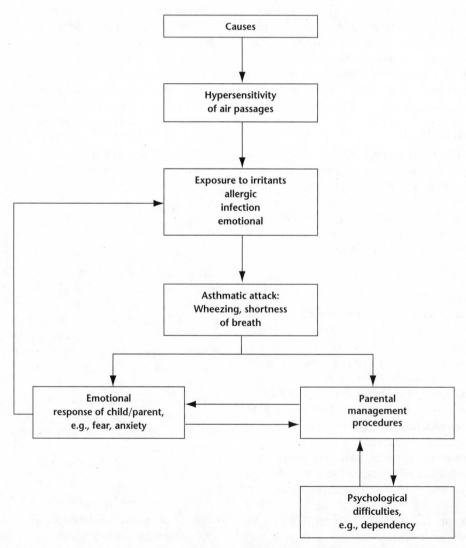

Figure 13.2   Schematic Diagram for the Development of Asthma.

Source: Wicks-Nelson and Israel, 1997

fections can set off or worsen the severity of an attack. Allergies may also be related to the development and occurrence of attacks; for example, the child may be allergic to inhaled substances, such as dust, the dander of pets, or pollen, or to ingested substances, such as milk, wheat, or chocolate. Finally, physical factors such as cold temperature, tobacco smoke, pungent odors, exercise, and rapid breathing may serve as trigger mechanisms for an attack.

The Intrapersonal and Interpersonal Contexts

In the intrapersonal context, anxiety may occur in anticipation of or during attacks. This anxiety can increase the probability of the occurrence or the intensity of the asthmatic attacks. In the interpersonal context, the natural concern of parents may become exaggerated anxiety and overprotection. These parental behaviors may in turn lead to age-inappropriate dependency on the parents, isolation from peers, and an increase in behavior problems. The causal loop is completed when the child's emotional upset resulting from overdependence or social isolation or behavior problems becomes yet another trigger mechanism for an asthmatic attack.

Figure 13.2 depicts the complex interaction of the organic, intrapersonal, and interpersonal contexts in asthma. (For a discussion of management and treatment, see Creer and Bender, 1995.)

Adherence to Medical Regimens: Diabetes Mellitus

The concern with illness per se has been expanded to include a host of health-related issues. We will discuss two such issues, the first being adherence to medical regimens. (The second is pain management, which we will discuss later in the chapter.) We use diabetes mellitus as an example of adherence, although it is important to note that the issue applies to all illnesses.

It has been estimated that the overall rate of adherence to prescribed medical procedures is only 50 percent for the pediatric population in general.

Not surprisingly, compliance is greatest in cases in which *acute*, *painful* symptoms can be relieved by some *simple measure*, such as taking a pill. Again not surprisingly, the treatment for diabetes mellitus, which meets none of those basic conditions, presents major problems in regard to adherence. (A detailed presentation of the issue of adherence can be found in La Greca and Schuman, 1995. Johnson, 1995, covers the topic of diabetes mellitus. Our presentation is based on these sources unless otherwise mentioned.)

Definition and Characteristics

Diabetes mellitus is a chronic, lifelong disorder that results when the pancreas does not *produce sufficient insulin*. Research suggests that the destruction of insulin-producing cells within the pancreas is an autoimmune process; however, the mechanism that triggers this autoimmune process is unknown. Diabetes mellitus is a common chronic illness that affects about 1 in every 600 children in the United States. While it can appear at any age, the peak incidence occurs around puberty.

The overt symptoms of diabetes mellitus are fatigue, weight loss, increased urination, and excessive thirst. The long-term consequences of uncontrolled diabetes include blindness, renal (kidney) failure, nerve damage, and heart disease. Diabetes can also lead to coma and death. Thus the stakes are high in regard to compliance with medical regimens.

Medical Regimen

The treatment regimen for diabetes mellitus is complex. Blood glucose must be monitored daily to prevent hypoglycemia (too little blood sugar) or hyperglycemia (too much blood sugar). Insulin dosages must be adjusted accordingly. Monitoring is accomplished by obtaining a small sample of blood from a finger stick, placing it on a strip that changes color, and comparing the color with those of a chart showing the glucose levels. Because of the critical role of insulin, the illness is often referred to as insulin-dependent diabetes mellitus (IDDM).

Blood glucose variability is to be expected, because diet, exercise, illness, and emotional state all affect it. Consequently, the regimen involves two additional components. A special diet is necessary to prevent excessively high or low blood sugar, and frequent small meals throughout the day are recommended. Exercise also improves insulin action; however, it may also result in hypoglycemia and thus must be closely monitored.

Problems with Adherence

Complexity and Lifestyle Changes   The first problem in regard to adherence is complexity. Generally speaking, prescriptions of more than one medication have lower adherence rates than do single prescriptions. In addition, activity limitations or changes in personal habits or lifestyles are more difficult to adhere to than medication. Diabetes involves both a complex monitoring procedure and a lifestyle change, especially in regard to eating.

Furthermore, the complexity of treating diabetes requires greater knowledge and skill on the part of the parent and child than does simple medication. For example, the skill of glucose testing is not mastered by the child until around 12 years of age. Ironically, adolescents, who are old enough to have the requisite knowledge and skill, are *less* apt to adhere to the regimen than are younger children. For example, Thomas, Peterson, and Goldstein (1997) evaluated children's and adolescent's ability to solve problems in which regimen adherence was pitted against peer acceptability. Adolescents were significantly more versatile in generating solutions to these dilemmas than were younger children; however, they were also more likely to choose behaviors that were less regimen adherent than those chosen by the children. It may well be that their increased cognitive sophistication is no match for their strong social need for peer acceptance and the obstacles their illness presents to this acceptance. These obstacles include feeling different from peers because of disease-associated delayed sexual maturation, the unusual behaviors of injections and glucose testing, and dietary restrictions that forbid them to eat the very sweets and junk food that their peers favor.

Chronicity   The next problem in regard to adherence is chronicity, which is associated with poorer compliance regardless of the particular illness. Once symptoms have abated, there is also a tendency to discontinue some or all medication.

Relief from Pain and Long-Range Consequences Finally, there is the problem that, since diabetes is an asymptomatic disease, adherence does not involve relief from pain. Consequently, one of the major motivations for compliance is lacking. In addition, the possible long-range consequences of IDMM, while ominous, lack potency. Prevention is a difficult idea to grasp, even in middle childhood, since it requires children to project themselves into the future and realistically grasp what that future might hold for them. While adolescents are cognitively capable of understanding prevention, they must weigh it against the present unhappiness of dietary and activity restrictions and being different from their peers. Thus, projections into the future must have a strong affective charge to counter the risk of peer rejection inherent in regimen compliance.

Other factors figure significantly in compliance, not only in IDDM but in chronic illnesses in general. We will deal with both the general case and with studies of diabetes mellitus.

Level of Cognitive Development   The concrete, rule-oriented thinking of middle childhood fosters a belief that recovery results from strict adherence to medical regimens, and this belief promotes compliance. By contrast adherence declines in the cognitively more sophisticated adolescent, as we have seen. Thus, one cannot assume that level of cognitive development and compliance are positively correlated.

Moreover, Berry and colleagues' (1993) study of children between 6 and 17 years of age with diabetes mellitus found that the older ones, in spite of being at the stage of formal operations, continued to think at the concrete level in regard to their illness; for example, they attributed it to such concrete events as an accident or overdoing it in sports. The finding is even more striking in light of the fact that the nature of the disease had been explained to them at the time of diagnosis and also when a modification of treatment was deemed necessary. Thus the older children were both capable of understanding and had had the information necessary to understand.

Personal Adjustment   Adherence is greatest among children who are well-adjusted and declines among those with serious emotional difficulties. In regard to IDDM in particular, Murphy, Thompson, and Morris (1997) found that poor compliance among adolescents was related to (1) a negative perception of their bodies, (2) a perception that what they did would not alter their health status, and (3) the belief that negative events were due to external forces rather than being of their own making.

Family Adjustment   As we have seen, the family, and the mother in particular, play a crucial role in the child's adjustment to illness. It follows that dysfunctional families show increased problems with treatment adherence, while family support decreases such problems. In regard to IDDM, families play a similar role, with variables such as cohesion, organization, and support facilitating better adherence.

Medical Factors   Adherence assumes that the responsible medical professionals know the best regimen for a given child and communicate the information clearly, and that the involved parents understand and remember what they have been told. Any or all of these assumptions may be unwarranted. Studies show that physicians may not follow published clinical recommendations, that staff nurses overestimate their own knowledge of diabetes, that families remember less than a quarter of the information they receive, and that almost half of the families "remember" recommendations that were not made!

Increasing Adherence

In this section we discuss ways to increase adherence in illnesses in general rather than in IDDM specifically. Providing verbal and written instructions, visual cues or reminders (such as a clock with times for medication in red pasted on the prescription label), and increased medical supervision (such as

phone calls from nurses) result in some success in the cases of acute illnesses with short-term regimens. For chronic illnesses, multicomponent intervention programs combining intensive education with behavioral techniques such as self-monitoring and reinforcement procedures have had some limited success in promoting adherence, although the evidence is preliminary. In spite of some encouraging initial attempts, the challenge of significantly improving treatment adherence for chronic illnesses with complex regimens has yet to be successfully met.

Pain Management: Cancer

Definition and Characteristics

Cancer in children, rather than being a single entity, includes a heterogeneous group of conditions, the common characteristic being a *proliferation of malignant cells*. Hematological malignancies involving the blood-forming tissues (i.e., leukemia and lymphoma) account for approximately half of the cancer diagnoses; tumors of the brain and central nervous system make up the second-largest group; and tumors affecting specific tissues and organ systems, such as bone or kidney, come in third (Dolgin & Jay, 1989.)

Our discussion concentrates on acute lymphoblastic leukemia. (A summary of cancer in children can be found in Harbeck-Weber and Peterson, 1996, and a more extended presentation is given in Powers et al., 1995. For a discussion of the general topic of pain management, see Varni et al., 1995.)

While comparatively rare, cancer accounts for a large number of disease-related deaths in persons under 16 years of age. However, there has been a heartening increase in survival rate. The introduction of chemotherapy in the 1970s, for example, reduced the relapse rate from 80 to 90 percent to just 10 percent. Moreover, this downward trend in mortality is expected to continue (Powers, et al., 1995).

Treatment

Treatment of acute lymphoblastic leukemia is a heroic undertaking involving four phases. The first phase is designed to eliminate all evidence of

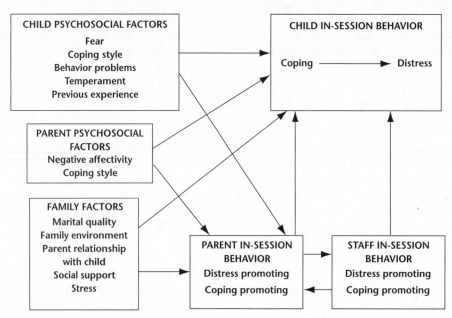

Figure 13.3   Factors Influencing Child Coping and Distress During Painful Medical Procedures.

Source: Varni et al., 1995

leukemic cells. This phase is followed by central nervous system prophylaxis such as brain radiation therapy. Next comes a consolidation phase designed to eliminate leukemic cells that may have developed drug resistance, and, finally, a maintenance phase lasting 2 to 3 years. Many of these procedures are painful, involving finger sticks, intramuscular intravenous (IV) injections, lumbar punctures (spinal tap), and bone marrow aspirations (removal by suction). Moreover, the side effects of treatment are themselves noxious (e.g., vomiting, diarrhea, pain) or socially embarrassing (e.g., loss of hair, weight gains).

Coping with Procedural Pain

How well the child copes with the pain involved in treatment depends on a number of factors in the child, in the family, and in the medical staff. Some of these factors are proximal in that they come into play in connection with the procedures themselves. Others are distal in that they serve as general background factors. (See Figure 13.3.) Note that Figure 3.3 is primarily a teaching aid. There is very little

research on a number of the variables and their relationships. (In the following presentation we follow Varni et al., 1995, unless otherwise noted.)

Intrapersonal Factors   Children's reactions to painful medical procedures depend on their ability to cope with the distress involved. An encouraging finding is that 25 to 30 percent of children cope well with the pain. Coping does *not* mean an absence of distress; rather, the children see the anxiety and pain as manageable even though unpleasant.

This ability to cope with stress is, in turn, a function of a number of distal factors. These include the children's general level of fearfulness and counterbalancing coping mechanisms, such as the ability to divert their thoughts away from the pain or to tell themselves that they can "take it." Some children are *sensitizers* ("approachers"), who cope by actively seeking information as a means of preparing to experience pain. Others are *repressors* ("avoiders"), who avoid information and deal with threat by not thinking about it, either rationalizing or denying its potential stressfulness. Information helps the sensitizers master stress; the repressors, however, become more distressed, as in the case of the girl being given information before a procedure who wanted to shut her eyes and scream, "Just do it!"

More general distal factors involved in coping with pain include behavior problems, since well-adjusted children deal with pain better than those with adjustment problems. Temperament, such as being sensitive or robust, is another relevant distal factor, as is previous experience with pain and how well the children fared.

Interpersonal Factors   Children's reactions to procedural pain are significantly influenced by parental behavior. Negative affectivity such as anxiety can undermine the children's confidence. Parents also may not know how to cope with the situation. There is evidence, for example, that empathy, reassurance, and apologies, even though done with the best of intentions, are of little help to the child. On the other hand, providing specific coping mechanisms, such as helping the child concentrate on breathing or providing distracting conversation, are effective.

Distal family factors serve as a background to parental behavior in the medical situation. In general, a positive marital and parent–child relation, good social support, and no undue stress increase the chances of helpful parental behavior. By the same token a negative family environment increases the possibility that parental behavior will aggravate the child's experience of distress.

Staff Behavior   Medical staff may be more or less competent in performing procedures, have different degrees of confidence or anxiety, and have different levels of interpersonal skills as well as different personalities. All these factors will serve either to make the situation more tolerable or more difficult to bear for the child. However, it should be noted that medical personnel have few guides as to ways of promoting coping in children.

Aids to Pain Management

While it is generally true that both parents and medical personnel lack clear guides as to how to help children cope with procedural pain, there have been a number of techniques that have been designed for this purpose. We will discuss those used in bone marrow aspiration (BMA). (We follow Jay's 1988 summary of the research. A more general discussion of management of pain can be found in Varni et al., 1995.)

BMAs involve inserting a needle into the child's hip bone and suctioning marrow out with a syringe. The marrow is then examined to determine whether prior treatment has successfully destroyed the cancer cells. While lasting only a few minutes, BMA is a painful and anxiety-provoking procedure. Anticipatory anxiety can cause nausea, vomiting, insomnia, and crying days before the procedures are scheduled. Young children in particular often kick, scream, and physically resist to the point of having to be carried into the treatment room. Because of the traumatic nature of the procedure, it may take as long as two to three years for some children to learn to cope with it.

A number of procedures have been devised to help children cope with the pain and anxiety of BMAs.

Hypnosis   Hypnosis is one of the most frequently reported interventions. Patients are given suggestions for progressive muscle relaxation, slow rhythmic breathing, and an increasing sense of well-being. After having achieved deep relaxation, posthypnotic suggestions for reduced discomfort and greater mastery during the procedure are given.

In regard to effectiveness there are documented reports of success. Hypnosis has also been shown to be more effective than distraction or play techniques. The technique does have two limitations, however: not all people are susceptible to hypnosis, and its effectiveness tends to dissipate with repeated sessions.

Cognitive-Behavioral Techniques   There are a number of cognitive-behavioral techniques available that can help children cope with the pain of BMA. We will describe the multiprocedure one developed by Jay (Jay et al., 1987) that has served as a prototype for the others.

Children are first shown a film of another child receiving a BMA, in which the model describes her thoughts and feelings at each step of the procedure. The child in the film also models positive coping behaviors and positive self-statements such as "I can do it." Thus, the film portrays the reality of the pain children will experience but provides them with ways of dealing with it. This is called the *coping model* and is distinct from the *mastery model*, which aims to reduce or eliminate the pain and anxiety themselves. The film also provides information concerning the procedures and why they are being done.

Following the film, children are taught a simple breathing exercise, which serves as an attention distraction and gives them something active to do. Ever since Freud's day, clinicians have recognized that being an active agent in the sense of having something to do reduces anxiety, while having passively to endure pain increases anxiety. Next, the children are shown a small trophy that serves as positive reinforcement for courage and doing their very best. The purpose is to change the meaning of pain from an aversive, punitive event to a challenge to be mastered.

Emotive imagery, the next component, involves weaving the child's image of a superhero into the present medical situation—for example, Wonderwoman testing her superpowers by withstanding the pain of BMAs. The purpose is again to transform the meaning of pain while providing another distraction. The final component is behavior rehearsal in which the child plays doctor and gives a doll the BMA.

At the end of training, the psychologist has the children practice undergoing the procedure by lying still, doing the breathing exercises, and so forth. The intervention package is administered in the hour before the BMA.

Studies show that children exposed to Jay's cognitive-behavioral technique have lower distress during the BMA procedure than do a no-treatment control group and a group receiving a tranquilizer. Such findings are encouraging, although more studies of effectiveness need to be done.

Brain Damage and Brain Injury

Brain Damage

Because brain damage can be defined in various ways and assessed by a variety of techniques, we must pay more than the usual attention to the issues of definition and assessment. This discussion, in turn, will help us understand research findings.

Definition

Brain damage can be defined in three different ways. A strictly *neurological* definition concerns itself with the nature, site, and size of damage to the brain. A *behavioral* definition is concerned with the functions impaired by the damage: motor and communication disorders, sensory and perceptual deficits, intellectual impairment, and so on. Brain damage can also be conceptualized in terms of a wide array of *etiological factors*, such as traumatic injury, anoxia, encephalitis, epilepsy, cerebral palsy, and lead poisoning, to name a few. Each approach is valid, but the complex interrelations among them have yet to be worked out. Therefore, it is important for us to realize at the outset that "the brain-damaged child" is an abstraction that glosses over crucial distinctions among children. (For a more detailed discussion of the issue of definition, see Werry, 1986.)

Assessment

While *autopsy* is the surest technique for establishing brain damage, it is, of course, no help in diagnosing a living child. Diagnosis of brain damage frequently relies on the child's *history*, covering factors such as pregnancy and delivery complications; developmental milestones such as sitting up, walking, and speaking; and illnesses. Not only is there evidence that such information is often unreliable, but there is also no direct relation between the information and brain damage. Paradoxically, developmental histories are the least useful yet most frequently used of all diagnostic procedures.

The *neurological* examination covers such classic signs as failure of the patellar (knee-jerk) reflex and presence of a Babinski reflex, restriction of the visual field, and loss of sensation and function in any part of the body. The examination is most accurate when there are lesions in nonsilent areas of the brain. In other kinds of brain damage the findings may be ambiguous, or they may even be normal in children with head injuries and encephalitis. While *psychological tests* are invaluable in assessing specific cognitive deficiencies in children with brain damage, in and of themselves they are insufficient for making a diagnosis of brain damage. (See Werry, 1986.)

Brain Imaging   Remarkable progress has recently been made in techniques for *visualizing* brain structure and functioning. The traditional **electroencephalogram** (EEG), which measures electrical activity of the brain, can detect gross damage, but most of the records fall in a no-man's-land between normality and pathology (Werry, 1986). In fact, 10 to 20 percent of normal children also display abnormal records.

However, there have been two advances in electroencephalographic techniques that have resulted in increased sensitivity to brain damage. The first is the **event-related potential**, or **ERP**. When a stimulus such as a light or sound is presented, the brain produces a characteristic response, or ERP. Knowing the ERP in the intact brain allows diagnosticians to detect malfunctions such as visual disorders and deafness in very young or mentally retarded children who cannot be tested by the usual techniques.

Next, developments in *computer analysis* and *computer graphics* have made it possible to use many recording leads simultaneously rather than using just the few recording leads of traditional EEGs. Consequently, a detailed computer-drawn picture of the brain is now available.

There have also been advances in imaging techniques for visualizing brain structure deriving from the *x-ray* technique. Traditional X rays were limited by the fact that they could detect only gross abnormalities. **Computerized axial tomography (CAT) scans**—also called computer-assisted tomography (CT) scans—using computer-driven X-ray machines, produces exceptionally detailed images both of the brain's surface and of the levels below, making it possible to localize lesions at any level of the brain. An imaging method called **magnetic resonance imaging (MRI)** produces even clearer images. Using images from successive layers of the brain, it is possible to generate an MRI-based three-dimensional image of various brain structures. (See Figure 13.4.)

Functional magnetic resonance imaging (fMRI) is one of the most rapidly growing methods for imaging the living brain. It tracks subtle increases and decreases in oxygen on a moment-to-moment basis as a person performs a given task, such as attending to a visual stimulus. Then, by taking consecutive slices of the brain in various orientations, the MRI scanner reconstructs where in the

Figure 13.4   Three-Dimensional Representation of Corpus Callosum (light grey) and Ventricle (dark gray) using MR-Based 3-D Imaging. (Computer graphic work done by Tracy Abildskov.)

brain the greatest areas of activation occur. For example, fMRI has been used to map areas of the brain used for the visual system, working memory, learning, and problem solving. (For a summary and critiques of neuroimaging techniques, see Nelson and Bloom, 1997. For a more detailed presentation, see Bigler et al., 1997.)

Positron emission tomography (**PET scans**), unlike imaging techniques, which produce static pictures of the brain and reveal only structural or anatomical deficits, can detect abnormal functioning in brains that might look structurally intact. Because brain cells metabolize glucose, radioactive glucose is introduced into the cerebral artery and the rate at which it is metabolized in various parts of the brain is recorded. The resulting PET images can then be compared with those of a normally functioning brain.

Psychological Disturbances

There is evidence that brain damage increases the risk for psychological disturbances. In his two classical studies, Rutter (1977, 1981) compared 99 children ages 5 to 14 who had cerebral palsy, epilepsy, or other clearly established brain disorders with 189 children from the general population of 10- and 11-year-olds and with 139 children ages 10 to 12 who had physical disorders not involving the brain, such as asthma, diabetes, heart disease, and orthopedic injuries. The rate of psychological disturbance in the brain-damaged group was 34.3 percent of the population, while the rate of psychological disturbance in the group with other physical handicaps was 11.5 percent—which still was almost twice that of the normal population.

Rutter's findings do not mean that all children with brain damage are at risk, however; on the contrary, only when biological factors result in major brain disorders is the risk of psychopathology significantly increased, although, even in this case, it is not inevitable. Aside from this special group, the risk of psychopathology is minimal and difficult to detect. The functions most powerfully affected by brain damage are cognition, sensory and motor functions, and seizure thresholds. (For a more recent confirmatory study, see Max, Sharma, and Qurashi, 1997.)

In light of the importance of the brain, many of the above findings may seem unexpectedly benign. However, it is important to remember the remarkable recuperative powers of the brain—for example, from injuries, strokes, or infections. Two mechanisms aiding recuperation are *sprouting* and *vicarious functioning*. In the former an undamaged neuron makes synaptic contact with neurons beyond the lesion, while in the latter another area of the brain takes over the functions subserved by the damaged area (such as the transfer of speech from the left to the right hemisphere). Also, as we will soon see, the ameliorating potential of the social environment has been underestimated until relatively recently.

It is important to note that there is no evidence that brain damage leads to a characteristic clinical picture that can be labeled "the brain-damaged child." Effects tend to be nonspecific, with deviant behavior the same as that found in other disturbed populations.

We will now turn to the specific kind of brain damage called pediatric brain injury. (Our presentation will follow Boll and Stanford, 1997, unless otherwise specified.)

Brain Injury

Definition and Characteristics

There are two kinds of brain injury: *penetrating head injury* and *closed head injury*. In the former there is penetration of the skull, dura, and actual brain tissue.

Penetration can be produced by a small object moving rapidly, such as a bullet, or a large, dull object such as a baseball bat. Closed head injury occurs when a blow to the head does not penetrate the dura— for example, when a child is propelled violently forward in an automobile accident and the head strikes a solid object. Closed head injury is the more common of the two injuries. (A comprehensive discussion of closed head injuries can be found in Gerring, 1997.) The two kinds of injuries have different effects on the brain. Penetrating head injuries produce specific and focal deficits whereas closed head injuries of equal severity produce general neurologic disruption and consequently are more serious.

Prevalence   Injuries of all kinds are the leading cause of death for children over one year of age. The annual brain injury rate per 100,000 children is 185. The fatality rate is 2 to 3 per 100 cases (Kraus, 1995).

Gender, Race, and Socioeconomic Status   Males outnumber females more than two to one in regard to head injuries. There is little information concerning the role of race, and the meager data that exist suggest a predominance of children from the lower socioeconomic status.

Developmental Pathway   The incidence of head injuries increases between 3 and 8 years of age, with another increase at 15 to 16 years of age (probably because at this age children are allowed to drive or ride with other young drivers). Falls are the predominant injury for younger children, with motor vehicle accidents being more prominent in adolescents over the age of 16.

The Effect on Contexts

The Organic Context   Because of its complexity, understanding the effects of traumatic injury on the brain is exceedingly difficult. To illustrate this difficulty we will describe some of the mechanisms involved. (Our presentation follows Bigler, 1996.)

The simplest explanation of the effects of traumatic injury is a mechanism called the *shear/strain effect* on the axon (the nerve fiber responsible for conducting impulses). Any structure can withstand only so much tensile strain when stretched length-wise. During trauma, stretching may exceed the boundaries of normal tissue extension of the axon resulting in its being torn or ruptured.

However, the effects of traumatic injury cannot be explained by the shear/strain mechanism alone. To begin with, certain areas of the brain appear to be more sensitive to damage regardless of the point of impact or severity of injury. Thus there is a *selective vulnerability* among areas of the brain. One such sensitive area is the hippocampal formation, the most critical limbic system structure for memory functions. This would help explain why one of the most common symptoms of traumatic brain injury is a disturbance of memory functions.

Trauma also may bring about *biochemical changes* such as an excessive release of potassium (an ion critical for neural transmission) in the intracellular fluid. Excessive release, in turn, may lead to prolonged overexcitation that impairs metabolic cell functions and may eventuate in cell death.

Finally, *secondary brain-damaging* effects may be added to the basic damage. These secondary effects include edema (swelling), brain hemorrhages, infection, and anoxia due to brain stem injury.

The Intrapersonal Context   Severe brain injury can have widespread effects. Its effects on intrapersonal variables can be summarized as follows:

1. *Cognition.* Higher-level functions are more vulnerable to disruption than are lower-level ones. Thus, the child with severe brain injury may have difficulty with reasoning, problem solving, mental flexibility, and adaptability to tasks.
2. *Physical effects.* Severely brain-injured children may experience problems related to endurance and fatigue, the regulation of bodily functions, and motor deficits.
3. *Personality.* Irritability, lowered frustration tolerance, lowered impulse control, and increased aggression may characterize children with severe brain injury.

The Interpersonal Context: Family and Peers
The family may experience increased stress as it struggles to respond to the new and difficult challenges of coping with the child's deviant behavior. It may have to alter its previous lifestyle—for example, by devoting financial resources to medical treatments rather than to vacations or by turning part of the home into a rehabilitation environment rather than a recreation room. Families that are adaptable and loving can take these stresses in stride. Those that are rigid and resentful are at risk for becoming increasingly dysfunctional while at the same time impeding the child's recovery and rehabilitation. (The literature on the importance of the family in recovery is reviewed by Taylor et al., 1995.)

The children's increased impulsivity, irritability, and aggressiveness may jeopardize peer relations. Old friends may become impatient, while new friendships may be difficult to make. Thus, there is an increased risk of social isolation.

The Superordinate Context: The School   Both the cognitive and personality changes we have just described may adversely affect schooling. Impaired ability to learn new information, concrete thinking, and language disturbances all impede academic progress, while the increased distractibility may make the child more of a behavior problem. (See Boll and Stanford, 1997.)

Developmental Consequences

The psychological difficulties enumerated above may have long-term effects. Patients with severe head injury may become more sensitive to the effects of alcohol. This sensitivity, in turn, is substantially related to additional head injuries, accidents, and aggression. There is some evidence of increased risk for partner abuse and violent criminal behavior. Finally, the cognitive effects may increase the likelihood of occupational difficulties. (See Boll and Stanford, 1997.)

Variability of Effects

There are no distinct or unitary patterns of deviation following injury to the brain. In fact, head injuries have the effect of increasing variability of behavior among children rather than forcing them into one mold.

Sources of Variability   There are many sources of variability of behavior in brain injury. We have already discussed two of them: type and severity of injury. Thus, penetrating injuries have effects different from closed head injuries, and mild injuries have different effects from severe ones. However, there are a number of other sources of variability, some organic and others psychological. To give a few examples:

1. *Duration of reaction.* The duration of coma is one of the most important determiners of recovery; the shorter the duration, the more complete the recovery.
2. *Phase of recovery.* Mutism, for example, is common in the acute phase of recovery but not in the long run.
3. *Status of affected skills.* Skills that are in the process of being acquired are more vulnerable to damage than are fully developed ones.
4. *Intra- and interpersonal variables.* The individual characteristics of the children and their interpersonal relations with family and peers serve to individualize the effects of brain injury. Thus, the adjustment of the child and the family before the injury has a significant impact on the effectiveness of coping with the effects of the injury. (See Boll and Stanford, 1997.)

Reliability of Research Data   In light of the remarkable technological advances in assessing brain structure and function, one might expect studies of brain injury to be highly reliable. Such is not the case. Our examination of the many organic and psychological sources of variability helps us understand one reason for the low replicability of studies. It stands to reason that the more factors influencing the variable being investigated the more difficult it is to achieve the kind of control that is essential to replication. (Shaywitz, 1995, has a more detailed presentation of reasons for the nonreplicablity of research findings.)

Another potential source of nonreplicability is that the effects of brain injury are not static; on the contrary, the effects depend on when they are measured. For example, measurements taken in the emergency room may well differ from those taken 24 hours or weeks or months later. Moreover, in order to evaluate the effects of injury on intra- and interpersonal variables it is essential to have information on the premorbid functioning of the children and their families. Some of this information may be nonexistent or difficult to obtain, and retrospective accounts from parents may be biased by the occurrence of the injury itself.

Yet another source of unreliability is poorly designed studies. For example, age, sex, handedness, and severity of injury all influence morphological measurement but are not uniformly controlled in most studies despite the fact that information concerning these variables is readily obtained. On the positive side, there are a number of studies that can serve as models of both awareness and control of the variables that might influence the data obtained. (See Broman and Michel, 1995.)

How Basic Is the Brain?

It is tempting to assign the brain a uniquely important status among etiological variables. As one neuropsychologist picturesquely put it, "Every twisted thought is due to a twisted neuron." This *reductionism* is a valid rationale for psychophysiological research; however, it ignores the fact that the "twisted thought" can cause the neuron to become "twisted" as well as the other away around. In the present instance, reductionism should not be used to justify the assumption that, in every case in which brain damage is involved, the brain damage is the basic etiological variable.

One reason for not regarding brain damage as the basic etiological variable is the epidemiological finding that brain injury does not happen at random. Rather, the population with brain injury is predominantly male and tends to be from the lower socioeconomic status. The child tends to be action-oriented (hyperactive), is a risk taker, and has academic difficulties along with many other life stresses. Severe head injuries happen when the children are not being observed by caregivers either because the caregivers have absented themselves or are negligent. Finally, the parents are apt to have psychiatric and marital problems. (See Boll and Stanford, 1997.)

Box 13.2	**An Illustrative Developmental Study**

A classic longitudinal study evaluated anoxic infants (i.e., those having **anoxia**, a pathological oxygen deficiency) when they were 3 and 7 years of age (Corah et al., 1965; Graham et al., 1962). In the first phase, 116 anoxic and 159 normal 3-year-olds were assessed in terms of their cognitive and personality development. Anoxic children did significantly poorer than the controls on all tests of cognitive functioning, including the Stanford-Binet, a vocabulary test, and a concept test. In general, the differences in personality were not as striking as those in cognitive development.

By 7 years of age, when 134 of the normal and 101 of the anoxic children from the study were located, the pattern was reversed. The overall difference in intelligence was no longer significant, while the most striking differences between groups were in the area of social competence. However, such differences between groups, even when significant, were minimal. In some of the discriminating measures, the differences were smaller than sex or socioeconomic status.

We can draw two conclusions from this study. The first is a variation on a theme we have presented several times since the beginning of

Chapter 1: behavioral correlates of brain damage are a function of *when* one evaluates the children, since they are apt to "grow out of" certain deficits (such as a lower IQ score) and "grow into" others (such as a deficit in social competence). The second conclusion is that, while anoxia increases the risk for subsequent deviant behavior, most infants with anoxia will be developing normally by the time they enter school. The prognosis is ominous primarily in those cases in which anoxia is *severe*, producing deep brain damage that can result in mental retardation, cerebral palsy, epilepsy, or even death.

Knowing what we do about psychopathology, we could infer that such children are at risk for developing some kind of externalizing psychiatric disorder *regardless* of whether there was brain injury. In fact, research has shown a high correlation between children's preinjury behavior and their subsequent psychiatric difficulties. Had the children been making an adequate adjustment prior to the injury or had brain injury affected a random sample of children, then we might well regard the damage as the prepotent etiological agent. As things stand, the etiological question becomes, What role and how much of a role did the injury play? Instead of being assumed to be the basic variable, the brain is just one among many variables whose potency is contingent upon its interaction with the other etiological agents. In short, there is no reason for abandoning our multiple-context, interactive approach to etiology because we are dealing with the brain rather than with the lungs or the joints or any other part of the damaged body.

Incidentally, this interactional approach helps explain another finding. Except in severe cases, there is no simple relation between degree or extent of brain involvement and the degree of behavioral disorder among children with brain pathology (Fennell & Bauer, 1997). For example, we can understand how the effects of a moderate brain injury could precipitate a severe disturbance in a child already making a marginal adjustment and beset by problems at home and at school. Or, turning to the area of recovery, we can understand how a severely damaged child could recover surprisingly rapidly if he were well adjusted prior to the injury and had parents who were both supportive beforehand and cooperative with the remedial program.

The Developmental Dimension

If the developmental dimension has been relatively neglected in our discussion of brain damage it is because there is little to discuss. Aside from the prospective research described in Box 13.2 there are few longitudinal studies of the effects of brain injury on development. Ironically, there is an impressive body of research on the organic side concerning normal and deviant development of the brain per se. But few studies bridge the gap between the injured brain at given points in time and its concomitant effects on intra- and interpersonal variables. There are even fewer studies that raise the subsequent developmental question: How does brain injury at a given point in time affect the trajectory of these same intra- and interpersonal variables? While there is some evidence that children are more affected by brain injury than are adults, this finding does scant justice to the potentially rich harvest of data that awaits those who raise the developmental question, How does normal development go awry?

We will now shift our focus from the body to the interpersonal context and examine two risk conditions arising from family interactions—child maltreatment and divorce.

Risks in the Family Context: Child Maltreatment and Divorce

Child Maltreatment

According to the United Nations Convention on the Rights of the Child (1989; Limber & Wilcox, 1996), each child the world over is entitled to "a standard of living adequate for the child's physical, mental, spiritual, moral, and social development" (p. 6). In the developmental psychopathology literature, these basic necessities for well-being are referred to as the *average expectable environment* (Cicchetti & Lynch, 1995). Perhaps the most profound failure of the interpersonal environment to provide these growth-promoting opportunities occurs when the child's home is a source of fear rather than a place of solace. While others may maltreat a child, it is abuse that takes place at the hands of parents—the very people that children turn to for comfort and protection—that has the most pervasive and long-lasting effects on development. Therefore, we will focus on maltreatment in the family context.

The "discovery" of child **maltreatment** (also called child abuse) also represents one of the most sensational chapters in the history of child psychology. The very existence of physical and sexual abuse of children was largely denied until early in the 1960s when C. Henry Kempe and colleagues brought the problem of the "battered child syndrome" to the nation's attention (Helfer, Kempe, & Krugman, 1997). Kempe found that, while most physicians and mental health professionals honestly believed that they had never encountered a case of child abuse, this was simply because they could not bring themselves to acknowledge that such a thing took place.

However, maltreatment is highly prevalent in the United States, and rates are rising. The number of *substantiated* cases of all forms of abuse was over 1 million in 1993, with an incidence of 16 cases for every 1,000 children in the United States. The number of *reported* cases has risen even more dramatically, to a rate of 43 reports per 1,000 children. This represents an increase in reports of 331 percent over the rates established in 1976 (National Center on Child Abuse and Neglect, 1995).

The gradual uncovering of the prevalence of child maltreatment sent shock waves throughout the nation. Professionals were galvanized into seeking ways of protecting the child from further abuse, as well as searching for causes that could serve as the basis for intervention and prevention. The search has proved difficult. The initial assumption that abusing parents must be psychologically deviant was overly simplistic and ultimately erroneous. Child maltreatment came to be viewed as multidetermined, involving the interaction among variables from all of the contexts with which we have been concerned.

As our understanding of the determinants of child maltreatment has become more complex and multidimensional, so has our view of what constitutes maltreatment. Maltreatment occurs in a variety of forms, not all of which leave signs as blatant as bruises or broken bones. Along with this broader definition has come a growing recognition of the importance of developmental, interpersonal, and superordinate variables that determine the effects of a particular abusive act on a child.

Recently, perspectives on child abuse have diverged again, with some questioning the extent to which the phenomenon truly exists. These questions have been spurred by sensational cases of false allegations and spurious "recovered memories" of abuse. However, while repressed memories of childhood abuse do not lurk underneath every problem in living, it is equally remiss to think that all reports of child maltreatment are fabricated. Our review will navigate this territory with the help of empirical research, which offers us signposts for assessing the authenticity and implications of the various forms of maltreatment that do, unfortunately, occur in the lives of some children.

Defining Maltreatment

One of the first hurdles we have to overcome is the problem of defining maltreatment. Unfortunately, no universally accepted definition exists. In actual practice, most professionals base their definitions on the laws governing mandated reporting of child abuse in their locality. However, since local laws vary significantly from place to place, such laws do not provide a satisfactory definition. Next, while some forms of maltreatment may be overt, with immediately detectable effects (e.g., a physical blow resulting in a red, angry welt), other forms are more subtle, with effects emerging only after some time (e.g., chronic parental indifference resulting in a lack of self-esteem). Additionally, cultural differences in child-rearing attitudes and norms make it possible for one parent's "tough love" to be another's "abuse."

One definition designed to address some of these issues arose from a conference held by the National Institute of Child Health and Human Development (Christoffel et al., 1992). The conference defined maltreatment as follows:

> Behavior toward another person, which (a) is outside the norms of conduct *and* (b) entails a substantial risk of causing physical or emotional harm. The behavior included will consist of actions and omissions, ones that are intentional and ones that are unintentional. They will have severe, mild, or no immediate adverse consequences (p. 1033).

Types of Maltreatment

Another complication with defining maltreatment is that there are various kinds of abuse that may have different effects on children's development (Cicchetti & Olsen, 1990). It is unlikely that the child who is emotionally rejected by a parent is affected in exactly the same way as the one who is habitually beaten. Therefore, much attention has been paid to the need to distinguish among types of maltreatment.

A comprehensive typology of maltreatment is proposed by Barnett, Manly, and Cicchetti (1993). These authors distinguish between **physical abuse** (e.g., beating, scalding, slapping, punching, kicking) and **sexual abuse** (e.g., fondling, intercourse, exposure to sexual acts, involvement in pornography). Another category is **neglect**, which may take such form as failure to provide basic necessities (e.g., not ensuring that adequate food, medical care, or shelter is available) or lack of supervision (e.g., leaving a young child unattended or in the care of an unreliable person). The fourth category is **psychological** or **emotional abuse** (e.g., failing to meet a child's needs for emotional security, acceptance, or autonomy, such as by ridiculing, terrorizing, or excessively controlling the child). Psychological maltreatment is the most recently proposed category and is the one about which there is the least agreement (see Cicchetti, 1991).

However, the task of identifying the kind of maltreatment children have experienced—for example, physical versus sexual abuse—is complicated by the fact that these different forms of abuse often co-occur. This is known as *multiple victimization* (Rossman & Rosenberg, 1997). For example, Barnett, Manly, and Cicchetti (1993) found that three-quarters of their sample evidenced multiple forms of maltreatment, particularly the combination of physical abuse, neglect, and psychological abuse. In sum, multiple victimization may be the norm for maltreated children.

The Developmental Dimension

Cicchetti and Toth (1995b) argue that in order to define maltreatment, it is necessary to place it in a developmental context. A developmental psychopathology perspective focuses our attention on the needs children have at each stage of development, as well as the potential for harm inherent in a parent's failure to meet those needs. As Barnett, Manly, and Cicchetti (1993) state:

> The parental acts that are judged to be unacceptable by society change as a function of the child's age. Moreover, the types of parental acts that can enhance development, or that can result in psychological harm to children, also change over the course of development. Thus, acts that might be maltreatment for a toddler would not be for an adolescent, and acts that are maltreatment for an adolescent might not be for a preschooler. (p. 24)

For example, because young children are utterly dependent on caregivers for their physical and emotional well-being, inattentive, lax, or indifferent parenting might have the most severe consequences in infancy. In contrast, the opposite—overprotective, intrusive, or controlling parenting—would be more

disruptive for adolescent development. Therefore, a developmental perspective alerts us to the need to define maltreatment in terms of the potential impact of parental behavior on the adjustment of a child at a particular age and stage.

Further, perhaps the most significant aspect of child maltreatment is that it often takes place in the context of the family, perpetrated by the very adults on whom children rely for protection (Trickett & McBride-Chang, 1995). Consequently, the literature focuses on the major developmental capacities that emerge in the context of the parent–child relationship—emotion regulation, interpersonal trust, and self-esteem—that might interfere with the child's ability to master stage-salient issues and move forward in development.

Physical Maltreatment

Definition and Characteristics

Definition   **Physical maltreatment** involves the presence of *injuries resulting from acts of commission or omission in which the child's life, health, or safety are endangered*. (Our review follows Kolko, 1996; Wekerle and Wolfe, 1996; and Wolfe and McEachran, 1997.) Physical abuse can range widely in terms of severity and potential to cause lasting physical harm. Injuries may be relatively minor, such as bruises or cuts, or major, such as brain damage, internal injuries, burns, and lacerations. A rare form of physical abuse is called *Munchausen by proxy syndrome*, in which a parent fabricates or creates physical illness in a child, causing psychological or physical harm through subjecting the child to repeated and unnecessary medical procedures. (See Box 14.1.)

Prevalence   The prevalence rate of *substantiated* physical abuse in the United States is 3.5 per 1,000. Physical abuse accounts for 23 percent of all cases of *reported* maltreatment, with rates increasing 58 percent over the past two decades. However, the *actual* rates are probably much higher. A nationwide telephone survey of 1,000 U.S. parents found that the number who admitted to physically abusing their

| Box 14.1 | **Munchausen by Proxy Syndrome** |

Baron von Munchausen was a seventeenth-century nobleman famous for concocting wild tales. His name was given to a syndrome in which adults repeatedly seek medical attention for fictitious illnesses. Munchausen by proxy syndrome involves a parent's simulating illness in a child in order to attract the attention of medical professionals (Meadow, 1993). The effects of this are far from benign. The child may undergo painful and invasive medical procedures and suffer the emotional stress of repeated hospitalizations. Also, in the most extreme form, the parent may intentionally subject the child to injury in order to bring about an illness.

One case involved an 8-year-old girl whose mother repeatedly sought help for a string of vague physical problems. While the physicians sought in vain to find a cause, the girl's health rapidly deteriorated. Although previously a slender and vivacious child, she became enormously obese and apathetic. Examination showed that her bones were under such severe stress that hairline fractures were developing throughout her body. Clearly, something was terribly wrong, and she was brought into the hospital. With more opportunity to observe mother and child, the staff began to notice other peculiarities. While previous reports indicated that this child had been progressing well in development, she now behaved immaturely and had no interest in school or peer relationships. She and her mother were inseparable, spending long periods gazing adoringly into one another's eyes in a way that the staff found unnerving. The mother was initially unwilling to cooperate with the clinical psychologists brought in to consult on the case, but slowly her trust was won. As she began to reveal more information about herself, the psychologists learned a number of peculiar facts. For example, the mother believed that her milk was the only proper sustenance for her child, and therefore years ago, when breast-feeding her younger child, she froze a large supply of breast milk "popsicles." These were now a part of her school-age child's regular diet. Curious about the younger child, the psychologists inquired further about him and learned that he had died of undiagnosed causes two years before, following prolonged treatment at the very same hospital.

The solution to the mystery came when a staff member observed the mother giving the child some tablets during visiting hours. Her purse was searched, and steroids were found. Through administering massive doses of steroids to her child, this mother had created a severe and debilitating illness.

What could cause a parent to mistreat a child in such a way? Very little research has been done in this area. This is unfortunate, since the syndrome might not be as rare as originally thought. A survey of 316 pediatricians uncovered 273 confirmed cases, with 192 more suspected (Schreier & Libow, 1993). While the perpetrating parent is in almost all cases the mother, fathers are sometimes seen to play a passively enabling role. The marital relationship is generally a distant one, and the mothers are characterized by severe psychopathology, particularly borderline, histrionic, and dependent personality disorders (Bools, Neale, & Meadow, 1994).

children was 16 times higher than officially reported (Gallup Poll Report, 1995). Similarly, while over 1,200 abuse-related *fatalities* occur in the United States each year, this is believed to be an underestimate, since many child deaths are misattributed to "accidents" or "sudden infant death syndrome."

Child Characteristics The incidence of abuse varies by *age*. The majority of abused children are young: 51 percent are 7 years of age or younger, while 26 percent are 3 or younger. Adolescents account for 20 percent of the sample, the third largest group (National Center on Child Abuse and Neglect, 1995). Serious injuries are more common among the older children, but most child fatalities occur in those under the age of 2. A small *gender difference* exists in that female children account for 51 percent of victims of child abuse, while males account for 45 percent (the remainder were not identified by gender). In addition, age interacts with gender. Among children under the age of 12, boys are more likely to be physically abused, while among children older than 12, girls are more likely to be abused.

Children at greater risk for abuse are those who are *difficult* or have special needs, including those who are premature or mentally retarded. Westat (1993) found that *disabled* children were almost twice as likely as other children to be maltreated and that the disability played a role in the abuse in almost half the cases. Behaviorally challenging children may overtax the resources of the parent, who then parents poorly, thus increasing child difficulty—which in turn further stresses the parent, with the downward spiral ultimately leading to violence.

Developmental Course

Our review integrates information from exhaustive reviews by Trickett and McBride-Chang, 1995; Wekerle and Wolfe, 1996; and Wolfe and McEachran, 1997, unless otherwise noted.

Cognitive Development   Young maltreated children show significant delays in *cognitive* and *language* development, particularly expressive language. As they enter middle childhood, physically abused children continue to demonstrate cognitive delays in all areas, scoring 20 points lower than nonabused children on standardized IQ points. Similarly, school achievement tests show that physically abused children perform two years below grade level in verbal and math abilities, with one-third of them requiring special education. They are also overrepresented among those with *learning disorders*. In adolescence, *lower achievement* and more *grade retention* is seen.

Emotional Development   The intrapersonal and interpersonal contexts intersect in the major stage-salient task of infancy—the formation of a secure attachment relationship—which is necessary for providing the child with a sense of security, mutuality, and self-esteem. Significantly, from 70 to 100 percent of maltreated infants demonstrate insecure attachments with their caregivers. Physically abused children are most likely to show a pattern of *avoidant attachment*, in which they refrain from seeking attention or contact when under stress (Crittenden, 1992). This behavior may be adaptive in that it reduces the likelihood of maternal anger by keeping bids for attention minimal and low-key. However, because avoidant children's needs for security and comforting are not met, their future development is negatively affected.

There is also evidence that physical abuse interferes with the normal development of the *self* in the early years. One of the tests of the early development of the self as an independent entity is toddlers' ability to recognize their reflection in a mirror. Such visual self-recognition is delayed in maltreated toddlers. Moreover, they react with neutral or negative affect when they do inspect their faces in the mirror, rather than with the positive affect that nonabused children show.

In the early preschool period, the development of the self and the recognition of the selfhood of others is manifested by the ability to talk about emotions and internal states. Beeghly and Cicchetti (1994) found that maltreated toddlers had a poor *internal state lexicon*—that is, that they had fewer words for describing emotional states, particularly regarding negative emotions. The long-term consequences are lack of access to emotions and the ability to regulate them. In the school years, physically abused children continue to be deficient in the ability to detect and respond to emotions in others. In addition, they demonstrate poor *emotion regulation*, resulting in either overcontrol or undercontrol of emotions.

Problems of *externalizing*, such as aggression, noncompliance, and conduct disorder, are frequently seen in abused boys. *Internalizing* problems such as depression and low self-esteem also emerge during the school-age years, especially, but not exclusively, in girls. Toth, Manly, and Cicchetti (1992) found that 22 percent of a sample of physically abused children evidenced clinical levels of *depression*, in contrast to 3 percent of those who had been neglected and 6 percent of the nonmaltreated group. A depressive cognitive style is particularly likely to develop if maltreatment begins prior to age 11, when young children depend on their parents to provide them with a sense of interpersonal trust and personal efficacy.

While deficits in self-esteem most often take the form of the maltreated children underestimating their capacities, some maltreated children also demonstrate unrealistically *inflated self-esteem.* This emphatic assertion that "I am the best at everything!" may serve as a primitive defense against deeper feelings of powerlessness and inadequacy (Vondra, Barnett, & Cicchetti, 1989). However, because it is not based on actual competence, this defensive overestimation of self is brittle and easily shattered. Thus, overestimation of self serves not as a protective mechanism but rather as a new source of vulnerability (Cicchetti & Howes, 1991).

Far from abating, the emotional and behavioral problems of abused children intensify in adolescence. Childhood abuse is a significant predictor of adolescent *depression, low self-esteem, conduct disorder,* and *antisocial behavior.*

Interpersonal Development Abused toddlers respond to peers in ways that parallel the behavior of their own parents. For example, when exposed to a peer in distress, abused toddlers are less likely to respond with sympathy or concern than are other toddlers and are more likely to react with *fear,* and *physical aggression.* Similarly, Egeland's (1991) longitudinal research showed that physically abused children were more aggressive in the preschool when compared to neglected, psychologically abused, and nonabused children.

Peer relationships become of increasing importance in the school-age years; therefore, it is significant that one of the most consistent consequences of physical abuse is increased *hostility* and *aggression* against others. Maltreated children are reactive to the slightest provocation and are more likely than other children to retaliate against perceived slights with aggression. Like conduct-disordered children (see Chapter 9) they have poor *interpersonal problem-solving skills* and demonstrate a *hostile attribution bias.* Abused children assume that others harbor negative intentions toward them and thus "deserve" the same in kind. The problem behavior of abused children contributes to the development of a negative reputation in the peer group. They are more likely to experience *peer rejection,* are least often nominated as a choice of playmate, and receive less social support from their classmates (Salzinger et al., 1993). And, as we saw in Chapter 9, peer rejection fuels further aggression.

Adolescence is a time when young people begin to develop significant love relationships, and often their family provides them with the blueprint. Wolfe and colleagues (1998) investigated the effects of childhood abuse on adolescents' dating relationships. They found that youths who experienced abuse at the hands of their own parents were more likely to be verbally and physically *abusive toward dating partners.* The imitation of their parents' behavior occurred despite the fact that those who were physically abused held negative attitudes about their parents and blamed them for the abuse. Victimization in childhood, therefore, appears to set the stage for violence in later intimate relationships and thus for the intergenerational transmission of abuse.

Summary Recasting the findings concerning abuse in terms of the personality variables we have been using in this text, we have found that attachment, aggression, self-control, cognition, affect, sociability, and initiative are all adversely affected. Avoidant *attachment* sets the stage by denying the child the opportunity to have needs for security met and to develop a positive working model of self and other. Physical abuse is a particular risk factor for the development of *aggression* with family members and peers. This decreased *self-control* is due in part to *cognitive* and *affective* deficiencies, including a depressive cognitive style, hostile attribution bias, and lack of emotional sensitivity. In terms of *sociability,* abused children have poor interpersonal skills and fewer friends. There is also an increase in internalizing problems evidenced by their being more withdrawn and depressed. *Initiative* also suffers, since abused children are more dependent than nonabused children and less ambitious in regard to occupational goals.

Etiology: The Physically Abusive Parent

Parents perpetrate 77 percent of child maltreatment, while other family members account for another 12 percent. (In this discussion we follow Wolfe and McEachran, 1997.) Approximately equal numbers of males and females perpetrate physical abuse; however, fathers and male caregivers are responsible for the majority of child fatalities (Levine, Compaan, & Freeman, 1995). These deaths are caused by extreme forms of assault, such as beating children about the head or violently shaking, suffocating, or scalding them.

The Intrapersonal Context   Who would abuse a child? A simple explanation might be that these parents are mentally ill; however, this is not the case. Almost nothing is known about male abusers; however, what can be said about the typical abusing mother is that she is *young* having usually had her first child while still in her teens. Her *life stress* is high: she often has *many young children* in the home and lives in *poverty*.

While poverty is a risk factor and stressful life events increase that risk, most poor, stressed mothers do not abuse their children. Instead, there are individual differences in parents' vulnerability to stress. For example, Pianta, Egeland, and Sroufe (1990) found that the amount of stress did not predict maternal abusiveness, but certain personality characteristics and competencies did. The abusing mothers were highly *anxious*, *angry*, and *defensive*, while the nonabusing ones were better able to take stress in stride. The mothers' emotional instability was the most important factor contributing to maltreatment in the early preschool period, while stress and social support were of secondary importance.

There are many ways in which abusing mothers appear to be ill-equipped for the parenting role. Dukewich, Borkowski, and Whitman (1996) found that lack of *preparation for parenting*—knowledge about child development, child-centeredness, and appropriate expectations for the parenting role— was the strongest predictor of abusiveness in adolescent mothers. These effects were partially explained by the mothers' predisposition to use *aggressive coping strategies* when under stress. Physical abusers also tend to have low *impulse control* and *frustration tolerance*. These mothers may be unable to tolerate even the run-of-the-mill demands of child rearing; for example, they respond to films of a screaming infant and a noncompliant child with heightened psychophysiological arousal, as indexed by heart rate and galvanic skin response.

The abusive parents' cognitive processing of child behavior also appears to be aberrant. For example, abusive parents engage in *cognitive distortions* regarding their children. These might take the form of misattributing behavior problems to the child's intentionality (e.g., "He *knew* it would get to me") or to internal and stable negative traits (e.g., "She's a sneak"), or of discrimination failures when the parent allows negative feelings toward others to color perceptions of the child (e.g., "He's just like his father—no good!") (Azar, 1997). The parent who perceives child misbehavior as willful and wicked is more distressed by it, as well as having a self-justification for responding in a highly punitive way. Parental *depression* may play a role in these distorted attributions by reducing the parent's tolerance for stress and increasing the tendency to appraise events in negative ways.

Much has been made of the statement that abusing parents were themselves abused as children. While it is true that abusers often were abused, those maltreated as children are not "doomed to repeat." An estimate of the *intergenerational transmission* of abuse is that around 30 percent of children will go on to repeat the cycle of maltreatment in adulthood (Kaufman & Zigler, 1989). *Protective factors* have been identified. Parents who do not become abusers are likely to have had a supportive relation with the nonabusing parent while growing up. They also are apt to have a supportive adult relationship currently and to be experiencing fewer stressful events. Additionally, they are more openly angry about the abuse they received and more explicit in recounting their past and their determination not to repeat it (Egeland, 1988).

Interpersonal Context   While found at all socioeconomic levels, abusive families on average are considerably below national norms on several socioeconomic indicators such as income and employment. *Poverty*, *family disorganization*, *crowded housing*, and frequent *disruptions* in living arrangements increase the likelihood of parent-to-child violence, with the risk increasing as the number of indicators increases (Peterson & Brown, 1994). Abuse also tends to co-occur with many sources of *family dysfunction*, including parental alcoholism, divorce and separation, frequent moves, and marital violence. The fact that there are so many negative influences operating at the same time in these families makes it difficult to isolate the specific effects associated with abuse.

Stage	Destabilizing (risk) factors	Compensatory (protective) factors
I. Reduced tolerance for stress and disinhibition of aggression	Poor preparation for parenting Low control and lack of coping strategies Stressful life events	Social support Economic stability, success in work or school Exposure to models of successful coping
II. Poor management of acute crises and provocations	Conditioned emotional arousal Appraisals of threat, harm, or loss Attributing intentionality to child	Improved child behavior Relief from stress Better coping responses
III. Habitual patterns of arousal and aggression	Short term: Parent reinforced for abusiveness by child compliance Long term: Child habituates to punishment; child misbehavior increases due to parents' punitiveness	Parent gains insight into own role in pattern Child responds to noncoercive measures Crisis intervention

Figure 14.1   Wolfe's Model of the Development of Child Abuse.

Source: Wolfe, 1987

The Superordinate Context   The United States has the highest level of *violence* of any Western society, as evidenced by statistics on crime and murder. Moreover, the rate of violence is higher among family members than among any other social group. As shocking as physical abuse of children is, it is even more disturbing to realize that it is just one manifestation of family violence in a society marked by violence.

Integrative Model

Wolfe (1987) has conceptualized the research findings on physically abusing parents in terms of deviations from the normal pattern of authoritarian child rearing. Physical abuse itself is not viewed as an inexplicable outburst but as the result of forces that tip the delicate balance between anger and control. Though conceptualized in terms of a series of stages, the transitions are not inevitable and the parents can move back and forth among them. (See Figure 14.1.)

The *first stage* is marked by a *reduced tolerance for stress* and a *disinhibition of aggression*. There are three *destabilizing* or risk factors contributing to this state of affairs. The first is *poor preparation for parenting*. This may be due to the mother's own family, which relied upon punitive authoritarian discipline and was deficient in empathy, reasoning, and the cultivation of problem-solving and social skills. Thus the mother has learned that the principal way to cope with frustration is attack. The next component is *low control*, which may be viewed as another untoward consequence of punitive, authoritarian rearing. An impoverished repertoire of coping strategies is accompanied by a feeling of vulnerability to losing control: If saying "no" does not work, what can I do then? The final component is *stressful life events*, usually an accumulation of the common, everyday problems of parenting, marriage, and work.

Counterbalancing the three destabilizing factors are *compensatory*, or protective factors: a supportive spouse, friends or organizations, socioeconomic stability, success at work or school, or people who can serve as models of effective coping.

The *second stage* is characterized by *poor management of acute crises and provocations*. The punitive, authoritarian parent uses short-term and possibly self-defeating solutions to problems, such as excessive alcohol or drug use, relocation to escape from debtors, or, in the case of children, harsh punishment.

There are three *destabilizing factors* that turn punishment into abuse. The first is *conditioned emotional arousal*. The potentially abusive parent has had many experiences of being angry with the child. By a process of classical conditioning, specific aspects of the child's behavior or appearance, such as a facial expression or whining, can come to be associated with irritation or rage. In the future, similar behaviors on the child's part will arouse similar affects in the parent. The second destabilizing factor involves *attribution*. In this case a person who is unaware of the source of anger misattributes it to a current event, which provokes aggression. This is akin to the defense mechanism of displacement: a man who feels irritable after a hard day at work spanks his son for leaving the tricycle in the driveway. The third destabilizing factor is an intensification of aggression by the attribution of *intentionality*. The parent views the child's acts as purposely defiant or provocative, thereby justifying excessive punishment.

Compensatory factors in the second stage include *improvements in the child's behavior*, say, through maturation or a positive experience in school or with peers. There may be *community resources* that can offer relief from the home situation, such as day-care facilities. Finally, *parental coping resources* can be increased through the intervention of concerned individuals or professionals, so that stress is perceived as less overwhelming.

The *third stage* is characterized by *habitual patterns of arousal and aggression*. Here the preceding pattern of increased stress, arousal, and overgeneralized response to the child becomes habitual. In part the change comes about because some children

easily *habituate* to existing levels of intensity of punishment so that harsher measures are required to maintain a given level of compliance. In part, parents are immediately *reinforced* by venting their anger and making the child comply. However, in the long run they are paving the way for further escalation of punishment while concomitantly failing to help the child find alternative modes of behaving that would decrease or eliminate the necessity of punishment. Thus the parents' complaint, "No matter what I do he won't listen" and "He only listens if I get really mad" are justified to a certain extent. What the parents have failed to grasp is their own role in this impasse.

Compensatory factors in this final stage, unfortunately, are minimal. Parents, either on their own or through help from others, may come to *realize* the self-defeating nature of their behavior. The child in turn may *respond positively* to noncoercive measures. Finally, *community services* such as crisis intervention centers may help change the pattern of parental behavior.

Neglect

Definition and Characteristics

Definition   The definition of **neglect** includes *deficiencies in provision of caregiving, such as nourishment, shelter, health care, supervision, and education, that compromise the child's physical and/or psychological health* (National Research Council, 1993). Neglect is an act of *omission* rather than *commission* and thus may be difficult to detect. For example, many "accidental" deaths and injuries occur because children were left unsupervised, which may constitute neglect. The most frequently detected form of neglect in children age 2 and younger is called *failure to thrive*, which is characterized by a significant delay in growth resulting from inadequate caloric intake. (See Wren and Tarbell, 1998.)

Prevalence and Child Characteristics   Neglect is the most prevalent form of maltreatment, accounting for 49 percent of all reported cases (7.6 per 1,000 children). *Age differences* are significant.

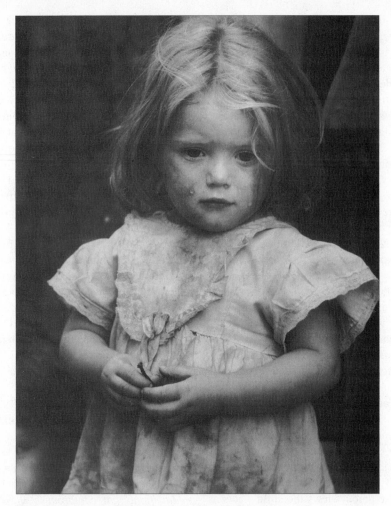

Neglect may be more devastating than physical abuse.

Neglect is most prevalent in the infant and toddler period and decreases substantially as children get older. No gender differences have been found (Erickson & Egeland, 1996; Wekerle & Wolfe, 1996).

Developmental Course

For this discussion we integrate information from exhaustive reviews by Trickett and McBride-Chang, 1995; Wekerle and Wolfe, 1996; and Wolfe and McEachran, 1997, unless otherwise noted.

Cognitive Development   *Cognitive* and *language* development are more severely affected by neglect than by other forms of maltreatment. This is not surprising, as neglect generally occurs in an environment that is low in stimulation and responsiveness from the earliest years, with parents who show little interest in the child's achievements. Deficits in cognitive ability persist from early childhood to school age, with neglected children demonstrating the most deleterious effects when compared to other abused children or controls. Neglected children have fewer basic skills at school entry and perform as much as two years below grade level on measures of language, reading, and math throughout their school years. Similarly, neglected adolescents achieve the *lowest school grades* of all abused children and are the most likely to *repeat a grade*.

Emotional Development   *Insecure attachment* is a major consequence of neglect, occurring in 90 percent of children with failure to thrive. Neglected infants relate to their mothers in ways that articulate clearly their sense of insecurity and their view of their mothers as unreliable and unavailable. They are less able to tolerate the stress of separation, to modulate their own affect and distress, and to cope with new situations. While their *passivity* toward their mother differentiates neglected children from those who have been physically abused, increasing *anger and resistance* are seen through the toddler years. Consequently, the *ambivalent attachment* pattern has been specifically associated with neglect, characterized by an ambivalent mixture of longing for contact and anger that such longings are frustrated.

Compared to other maltreated children, neglected preschoolers and school-age children are more *distractible*, have *low self-esteem*, and are the least skillful in *coping* with stress. In adolescence, children from neglectful families demonstrate both *internalizing* and *externalizing* problems, as well as adverse effects in the realm of *initiative*. For example, Steinberg and colleagues (1994) found that, over the period of a year, neglected 14- to 18-year-olds evidenced decreasing interest in work and school, and increasing delinquency and substance abuse.

Interpersonal Development   Neglected children's *passivity* with mothers extends to their peer relationships in the preschool years. They are generally described as avoidant, withdrawn, unassertive, lacking in social competence, and unable to cope with challenging interpersonal situations. Observations of neglected preschoolers show that they *lack persistence* and enthusiasm, demonstrate *negative affect*, and are highly *dependent* on caregivers and teachers for support and nurturance. As with preschoolers, neglected school-age children are more likely than either nonmaltreated or physically abused children to remain *isolated* and passive with peers, to withdraw from social interactions, and to make fewer initiations for play.

Summary   The domains of development affected by neglect parallel those affected by physical abuse in many ways. However, *attachment* takes an ambivalent form, and *aggression* is blended with *passivity* and *avoidance*. Moreover, *cognitive development* is more negatively affected by neglect than by any other form of maltreatment. Significantly, the effects of neglect do not appear to be moderated by the presence or absence of physical abuse; neglect derails children's development regardless. While the drama of violence receives the most attention, the corrosive effects of fitful, unpredictable, inept parenting are more insidious.

Etiology: The Neglecting Parent

In contrast to the equal numbers of mothers and fathers who physically abuse children, the majority of perpetrators of neglect are *female* (69 percent). This is to be expected, since women are usually the primary caregivers for young children. Neglecting mothers tend to be *young* and *single* and to live in *poverty*.

The Intrapersonal Context   There are a number of ways in which parents who neglect their children differ from those who are physically abusive. Neglecting parents tend to have a greater degree of *global distress*, as indicated by the presence of multiple psychiatric symptoms. Also, in contrast to the impulsive and intermittent nature of physical abuse, neglect occurs in the context of *chronic inadequacy*. Neglecting mothers experience more stress, failure, unmet needs, loneliness, and discontent in all aspects of their lives. They tend to have few friends and to lack *social support* (DePanfilis, 1996). In addition, neglecting mothers may have a general coping style that relies on such unhelpful strategies as *withdrawal*, *passivity*, and *mental disengagement* to cope with life problems.

Neglecting mothers are likely to have *negative views about relationships* and to dismiss the importance of them. Thus, they see little significance in their parenting behavior and have little motivation to change it. Further, these mothers are also more likely to have personality characteristics—such as *low self-efficacy*, *self-preoccupation*, *depression*, and developmentally *inappropriate expectations* regarding children—that interfere with their sensitivity to the child's signals or emotional distress (Crittenden, 1993). One explanation for this may lie in the histories of these parents, many of whom were maltreated in childhood. Those who were powerless to elicit care from others may be ill-equipped to provide it. They may even defensively block awareness of the child's distress just as they had to inure themselves to their own childhood unhappiness.

The Superordinate Context   Although *poverty* is associated with increased risk for all forms of maltreatment, neglect is the most strongly predicted by economic distress (Drake & Pandey, 1996). Families with incomes less than $15,000 are seven times more likely to be reported for child neglect than those at higher income levels.

Psychological Maltreatment

Definition and Characteristics

Definition   A widely cited definition of **psychological maltreatment** is the one proposed by Hart, Germain, and Brassard (1987):

> Acts of commission and omission which are judged on a basis of a combination of community standards and professional expertise to be psychologically damaging. Such acts are committed by individuals . . . in a position of differential power that renders a child vulnerable. Such acts damage immediately or ultimately the behavioral, cognitive, affective, or physical functioning of the child. (p. 6)

Psychologically damaging acts are those that convey the message that the child is worthless, inadequate, unloved, endangered, or only valuable in so far as he or she meets someone else's needs (Hart, Binggeli, & Brassard, 1998). Such acts might include *rejecting* (e.g., rejection, criticism, and hostility); *degrading* (e.g., publicly insulting or humiliating a child); *terrorizing* (e.g., threatening violence against a child or the child's loved ones, placing a child in dangerous situations); *isolating* (e.g., confining a child to the home, refusing to allow a child to interact with others outside the family); *missocializing or corrupting* (e.g., modeling or encouraging criminal or developmentally inappropriate behavior); *exploiting* (e.g., treating a child as a servant, involving a child in pornography or prostitution, coercing a

child into playing a parentified role and meeting parent's emotional needs); and *denying emotional responsiveness* (e.g., interacting with a child only when necessary and failing to express affection, caring, and love).

Prevalence and Characteristics   Because psychological maltreatment is the most difficult to substantiate, rates of confirmed cases are relatively rare, accounting for only 5 percent of all *substantiated* cases of child abuse. (See Hart, Binggeli, and Brassard, 1998; Wekerle and Wolfe, 1996; and Wolfe and McEachran, 1997.)

It has been argued that psychological maltreatment is intrinsic to all forms of abuse. Physical abuse, neglect, and sexual molestation all constitute major disruptions in the parent–child relationship that deprive the child of emotional security and thus involve psychological harm. However, despite the fact that psychological maltreatment *co-occurs* with other forms of abuse, evidence suggests that it has *specific* and *independent consequences* (Hart, Binggeli, and Brassard, 1998). For example, Claussen and Crittenden (1991) found that psychological maltreatment was almost always accompanied by physical abuse. Their most important finding, however, was that physical injury did not predict detrimental outcome, whereas the severity of psychological maltreatment did.

Developmental Course

Our review integrates information from Vondra, Kolar, and Radigan, 1992; Wekerle and Wolfe, 1996; and Wolfe and McEachran, 1997, unless otherwise noted.

Cognitive Development   There is a correlation between psychological maltreatment and *cognitive delays* in young children. For example, Egeland and colleagues (1990) found that cognitive skills declined from ages 9 to 24 months for children of psychologically unavailable mothers. In addition, just as with children maltreated in other ways, psychologically abused school-age children demonstrate lower scores on achievement and intelligence tests and poorer school performance when compared to nonabused children.

Emotional Development   Egeland and colleagues' (1990) longitudinal study assessed two parenting styles that fall under the heading of psychological maltreatment: *verbal abuse* and *psychological unavailability*. These forms of psychological maltreatment in the toddler and preschool period had different effects from physical abuse and neglect. While all maltreated children were noncompliant, had low self-control, and lacked persistence and enthusiasm for tasks, psychologically unavailable mothering was associated with the most devastating developmental consequences throughout the early years. These included declines in *competence* and increases in *self-abusive behavior* and serious *psychopathology*.

A number of studies have suggested that psychological abuse is related to the development of the cognitive style associated with *depression* in middle childhood, including low self-esteem, hopelessness, external locus of control, and a pessimistic view of life. Further, Stone (1993) found that depression was more strongly associated with psychological abuse than with other forms of maltreatment. Externalizing problems may also result, however. Herrenkohl, Egolf, and Herrenkohl (1997) found that children subjected to parental criticism, rejection, and terrorization demonstrated both *low self-esteem* and heightened *aggressiveness* during the school-age period.

Similarly, in adolescence, psychologically maltreated youth are at risk for *externalizing problems* such as conduct disorder, aggression, and juvenile delinquency, as well as *internalizing problems* such as depression, learned helplessness, and low self-esteem. In addition, *emotional instability* has emerged as a consequence of psychological maltreatment. Thus, it is not surprising that other disorders of impulse control and emotion regulation, such as substance abuse and eating disorders, are seen in psychologically maltreated adolescents.

In late adolescence, psychologically abused females report frequent hospitalizations, somatic complaints, and poor overall sense of well-being.

Interpersonal Development   Psychologically maltreated children demonstrate *poor social competence*. They are likely to respond with *hostility* toward others as well as to *withdraw* from social interaction.

Summary

Psychological maltreatment is embedded in the experience of all other forms of abuse and may even account for many of their effects (Hart, Binggeli, & Brassard, 1998). In addition, however, psychological maltreatment has *discrete effects*, with pervasive and insidious consequences for development. While aggression is seen increasingly over the course of development, *depression* and *internalizing disorders* appear to be most strongly related to psychological maltreatment. The resulting negative views of self and others—feelings of worthlessness, self-loathing, and insecurity—compromise the ability to get emotional needs met in current or future relationships.

Sexual Maltreatment

Definition and Characteristics

Definition   **Sexual maltreatment** includes *incest, sexual assault, fondling, exposure to sexual acts*, and *involvement in pornography* (National Research Council, 1993). The sexual act itself may range from actual penetration to acts that involve no physical contact with the child. The context may be sudden and violent, as in the case of rape, or may involve a long period of seduction and "grooming." The perpetrator may be a family member or a stranger, and the abuse may be acute or chronic over a period of years. (See Berliner and Elliott, 1996; Wolfe and McEachran, 1997.)

Prevalence and Child Characteristics   Sexual abuse accounts for 14 percent of *substantiated* child maltreatment cases (2.3 cases per 1,000 children). *Reported* cases of sexual abuse rose more dramatically than any other category of maltreatment in the period between 1976 and 1993, with an increase of 300 percent (National Center on Child Abuse and Neglect, 1995). However, there is some indication that the numbers of reported and substantiated cases have leveled off in recent years.

Once again, evidence is strong that these rates underestimate the *actual* prevalence rates. In a national survey of 2,626 American men and women, Finkelhor and colleagues (1990) found that 27 percent of the women and 16 percent of the men reported at least one of four kinds of childhood sexual abuse—sexual intercourse, touching or kissing their body, taking nude photographs or exhibitionism, and oral sex or sodomy. Sixty-two percent of male victims and 49 percent of female victims experienced actual or attempted intercourse. The majority of encounters were one-time events for both sexes; however, a significant minority had experiences lasting more than a year. Most of the abusers were men, who comprised 98 percent of those who abused girls and 83 percent of those who abused boys, although boys were more likely to be abused by older adolescents. Strikingly, 42 percent of males and 33 percent of females never disclosed the abuse to anyone, again pointing to the unreliability of official prevalence data.

There are clear *gender differences* in sexual abuse, as Finkelhor's data indicate. In general, girls are overwhelmingly more likely to be victims, and the ratio of girls to boys also increases with age: 2:1 for infants, 3:1 for school-age children, and 6:1 for adolescents.

Developmental Course

For our discussion we integrate information from Berliner and Elliott, 1996; Trickett and McBride-Chang, 1995; Wekerle and Wolfe, 1996; and Wolfe and McEachran, 1997, unless otherwise noted.

Cognitive Development   In contrast to physically abused and neglected school-age children, those who have been sexually abused do not show poorer school performance on such markers as grades and grade retention. However, they are rated by teachers as having poor overall *academic competence*, including low task orientation, school avoidance, and distractibility. However, sexually abused teenagers demonstrate lower academic performance as well as more *learning disorders.*

The *cognitive attributions* children make about the sexual abuse have important implications for development. The abused children face the difficult task of processing the experience in such a way that they can make sense of it and integrate it into their developing schemata about themselves and others. Reaching an adequate understanding of the experi-

ence can be further complicated by the distorted rationales given by the abuser: sexual violation is "love," abuse is "normal," a painful and degrading act is "pleasurable," betraying the secret makes the child "bad." The resulting attributions of *powerlessness*, *external locus of control*, and *self-blame* predict the severity of symptoms in sexually abused girls (Mannarino & Cohen, 1996).

Emotional Development   Between 20 and 52 percent of sexually abused children have *internalizing* problems, including fears, anxiety, low self-esteem, and excessive shyness. In the preschool years, the most frequent symptoms are *anxiety* and *withdrawal*. By middle childhood, from 28 percent to 67 percent of sexually abused girls meet criteria for a diagnosis of *depression*. Studies of adolescents confirm that childhood sexual abuse is a strong predictor of depression. Almost half evidence *suicidal ideation*, and suicide attempts and self-harming are more prevalent in this group than in nonabused controls.

Further, 50 to 100 percent of sexually abused children meet the criteria for *posttraumatic stress disorder* (Chapter 8). (See Foy et al., 1996.). Many of the acute symptoms of sexual abuse resemble general *stress reactions*. Signs include headaches, stomachaches, loss of appetite, enuresis, vomiting, sensitivity to touch, and hypersecretion of cortisol (see Chapter 7).

In young children, other emotional problems may include *regression* and loss of developmental achievements (e.g., bedwetting, clinging, tantrums, fearfulness), *insomnia* and *nightmares*. In adolescence, signs of severe disturbance linked to sexual abuse include *eating disorders* and *substance abuse* (see Chapter 11), *self-injury*, and *running away*.

Interpersonal Development   A behavioral sign highly specific to sexual abuse is *inappropriate sexual behavior*, including excessive masturbation, compulsive sexual play, seductive behavior toward adults, and victimization of other children. McClellan and colleagues (1996) found that over 70 percent of sexually abused preschoolers demonstrated such behavior, while the prevalence was also related to the age of onset of the abuse. Inappropriate sexual behavior was most common in the *preschool period* and declined somewhat in middle childhood. Sexually inappropriate behavior reemerges in adolescence in the form of *promiscuity* and increased likelihood to engage in unprotected and risky sex.

One of the dynamics of a sexually abusive relationship is that it is a *psychologically controlling* one in which the child is coerced to participate through manipulation or fear. Thus, sexually abused children are likely to develop an *internal working model* of others as untrustworthy and the self as shameful and bad. For example, victims of sexual abuse tend to believe that such abuse is pervasive and that adults are generally exploitative of children. This has negative implications for their self-esteem and capacity for forming satisfying relationships.

In addition, the sense that they "deserved" the abuse increases the likelihood that sexually abused children will not be able to correctly identify or respond to risky situations in the future and that they will feel that they have no right to defend themselves against unwanted sexual attention. This is borne out by the fact that sexually abused children are highly likely to be *revictimized* by peers and other adults (Boney-McCoy & Finkelhor, 1995).

Long-Term Course

No one symptom characterizes the entire population and there is no pattern of symptoms that can define a "sexual abuse syndrome." In general, approximately one-third of child victims are *asymptomatic* over the long term. The number of children who either show no symptoms or recover may seem surprisingly high in light of the inferred traumatic nature of the experience. Remarkably, Rind, Tromovitch, and Bauserman (1998) conducted a meta-analysis that showed that, once all other variables were accounted for, those sexually abused in childhood looked little different from other adults.

Much of the variation in outcome may be related to the variation in the kinds of experiences that fall under the heading of sexual abuse, ranging from a one-time experience of fondling to repeated violent sexual assaults. As might be expected, the factors that lead to the greatest number of symptoms are a *high frequency* and *long duration* of sexual contacts, the use of *force*, a close

relationship *to the perpetrator*, and oral, anal, or vaginal *penetration* (Kendall-Tackett, Williams, & Finkelhor, 1993).

In addition, there is a phenomenon called the *"sleeper effect"* in which the impact of an event occurs sometime later rather than immediately after an experience. For example, the effects of childhood sexual abuse in early childhood may emerge in adolescence when the youth attempts to cope with the stage-salient issues of sexuality and intimate relationships.

On the other hand, 10 to 24 percent of children get worse with time. Retrospective studies of adult women sexually abused as children show significantly higher lifetime and current episodes of *suicide*, *anxiety*, and *conduct disorders* (Fergusson & Horwood, 1996), as well as *depression*, *substance abuse*, and *posttraumatic stress disorder* (Duncan et al., 1996). Strikingly, Rodriguez and colleagues (1997) found that 87 percent of adult female survivors of childhood sexual abuse met criteria for a diagnosis of posttraumatic stress disorder in comparison to 19 percent of those seeking treatment for other problems. Similarly, sexually abused boys are at risk for adult *substance abuse*, *conduct problems*, and *suicidal behavior* (Garnefski & Arends, 1998).

Integrative Model

Finkelhor and Browne (1988) conceptualize the effects of sexual abuse in terms of four trauma-causing or *traumagenic dynamics*.

1. *Traumatic sexualization.* Sexual abuse shapes the child's sexuality in a developmentally inappropriate and interpersonally dysfunctional manner. The child may be repeatedly rewarded by affection, privileges, and gifts for sexual behavior and may also learn that sex is a means of manipulating others into meeting inappropriate needs. Traumatic sexualization may occur when certain parts of the child's body are given distorted importance and when the offender transmits misconceptions about sexual behavior and sexual morality to the child.

   The psychological impact of traumatic sexualization includes an increased salience of sexual issues, a confusion of sex with care, and negative associations concerning sex or intimacy.

The behavioral consequences might include sexual preoccupations, precocious or aggressive sexual behavior, or promiscuity, on the one hand, and sexual dysfunctions and avoidance of sexual intimacy on the other.

2. *Betrayal.* Betrayal concerns the children's discovery that a trusted person on whom they depend has done them harm. During or after abuse, for example, children can come to realize that they have been manipulated through lies or misrepresentations about proper standards of behavior, or they can realize that a loved adult treated them with callous disregard. Children can also feel betrayed by other family members who are unwilling to protect or believe them or who withdraw support after the disclosure. Betrayal can lead to a number of diverse affective reactions, such as depression and grief or anger and hostility. Young children in particular can become clinging because of an intense need to regain a sense of trust and security. Betrayal can produce a mistrust of others and subsequently can impair the adult's ability to judge the trustworthiness of others.

3. *Powerlessness.* When a child's will, desires, and initiative are constantly opposed, disregarded, or undermined, the result is a feeling of powerlessness. In sexual abuse, this can result when a child's body is repeatedly invaded against the child's will and when the process of abuse involves coercion and manipulation on the part of the offender. Powerlessness is strongly reinforced when the child's attempts to halt the abuse are frustrated and when efforts to make adults understand what is happening are ignored. Finally, a child's inevitable dependence on the very adults who abuse and ignore them produces a feeling of being trapped.

Powerlessness can have two opposite effects. Children may feel anxious or helpless and perceive themselves as victims. As a protection against such terrifying feelings they may go to the opposite extreme of identifying with the aggressive abuser or, less dramatically, may have an exaggerated need to dominate and be in control of every situation. The behavioral manifestations of powerlessness may be a number of neurotic symptoms such as nightmares, phobias,

and eating disorders, along with running away from home and truancy. There may also be learning and employment difficulties as victims feel unable to cope with the usual demands of life. At the other extreme, children might attempt to manage anxiety by "turning passive into active," taking on the role of abuser themselves through aggressive and antisocial behavior and even the perpetration of sexual abuse on other children.

4. *Stigmatization.* Stigmatization refers to the negative connotations such as badness, shame, and guilt that are communicated to the child and then become incorporated into the child's self-image. Such negative meanings can come directly from the abuser, who may blame or denigrate the victim, or they may be implicit in the pressure for secrecy with its implication of having done something shameful. Positive feelings attached to the abuse (enjoyment of special attention and rewards, sexual stimulation) may further contribute to the child's feelings of being bad and blameworthy. Stigmatization may result from the child's prior knowledge that the sexual activity is deviant and taboo, and it may result from the reaction of others who hold the child responsible or regard the child as "damaged goods" because of the molestation.

The psychological impact on the child consists of guilt, shame, and lowered self-esteem. Behaviorally, stigmatization may be manifested by isolation, and, in extreme cases, suicide. The child may gravitate to various stigmatized levels of society and become involved in drug abuse, criminal activity, or prostitution. Stigmatization may result in a sense of being different from everyone else and a constant concern over being rejected if the truth were discovered.

Protective Factors   The most consistently identified protective factor for sexually abused children is a *supportive relationship with the mother* (Kendall-Tackett, Williams, & Finkelhor, 1993). Contrast the experience of a child whose revelation is greeted with empathy and concern to the child who is disbelieved, held responsible, or criticized for getting the family in trouble. Accordingly, perceived support from the mother is found to be the most important mediator of the effects of sexual abuse on children's adjustment over time.

Controversies in the Study of Sexual Abuse

False Allegations   As awareness of the prevalence of sexual abuse has grown, the legal system has responded in a number of ways to give children their "day in court." (Our review follows Bruck, Ceci, and Hembrooke, 1998.) In the past couple of decades, courts have begun to allow children to provide uncorroborated testimony about sexual abuse, since often the only available evidence is the child's own report. With this increase in the availability of children's testimony, however, has come increasing concern about its reliability and validity.

Of the greatest concern are *false allegations*— fabricated reports of sexual abuse. Overall, estimates of the prevalence of false reports vary from 5 percent to 35 percent. They are more common in such situations as a conflictual divorce, during which a parent might coach a child to make false allegations in order to wrest custody away from the other parent. In other cases, false reports may arise from suggestive questions, including those made by child abuse investigators.

Researchers investigating the *suggestibility* of children's testimony typically have children witness an event and, on subsequent questioning, suggest that they witnessed something different. The results of this research can be summarized as follows. (See Ceci and Bruck, 1995.) As one would predict from studies of memory, children are more apt to accept an interviewer's suggestions the longer the delay between event and interview. Children between 3 and 5 years of age are more vulnerable to suggestion than are older ones. Suggestions tend to be accepted when children feel intimidated by the interviewer, when the interviewer's suggestions are strongly stated and frequently repeated, and when more than one interviewer makes the same suggestion.

Many of the early studies on children's suggestibility had limited ecological validity. They were carried out in the artificial conditions of the labora-

tory and often involved questions—such as whether or not a cabinet door was open—that had little relationship to the experience of sexual abuse. Recently, investigators have improved on this methodology by conducting more naturalistic investigations. For example, Saywitz and colleagues (1991) interviewed 72 five- to seven-year-old girls who underwent a medical checkup, half of whom had an external genital examination. First, regarding errors of omission, or *false negatives*, only 40 percent of the children who had been touched in the genital area mentioned it when asked the open-ended question, "Tell me everything that happened." However, they were more likely to do so when asked specific questions. Secondly, regarding errors of commission, or *false positives*, only three girls who had not had a genital exam gave a false positive response when asked a leading question. Ornstein and colleagues (1995) conducted a similar study by assessing 3- to 5-year-olds about their visits to the pediatrician. In general, preschool children could provide fairly accurate information about bodily touching. However, preschoolers were more likely than the older children to report events that did not happen when asked leading questions (e.g., "Did the doctor lick your knee?" "Did the nurse sit on top of you?").

In sum, the research presents the clinician with a dilemma. While specific questions may increase the likelihood of false positives, interviewing that is limited to open-ended questions may allow a preponderance of sexual abuse to go undetected. Therefore, it is important to navigate between two types of error: that of manufacturing abuse reports and that of dismissing all child abuse as fabrication.

Repressed Memories   On the other side of the coin, it has been argued that, rather than fabricating memories of sexual abuse, many children may be unable to access their memories of it. The rationale for the existence of such *repressed memories* comes from trauma theory, which suggests that strong emotions interfere with the consolidation of information in memory (Ceci & Bruck, 1995). The question of whether such memories can be recovered in psychotherapy is even more controversial. (See Pope, 1996, and Crews, 1997, for both sides of the debate.)

Research evidence for the existence of repressed memories is mixed. On the one hand is the finding that, in general, upsetting events are all the more vividly retained in memory (Saywitz & Goodman, 1996). On the other hand, retrospective studies show that 40 to 50 percent of sexually abused adults report having experienced a period of time during which they could not remember all or part of the abuse (Briere & Conte, 1993). Williams (1994) conducted a prospective study of women who as children had undergone physical examinations for suspected sexual abuse at a hospital emergency room. Approximately 38 percent of the women had no memory of the examination, nor of the substantiated sexual abuse. Memories were most likely to be absent in women who were age 7 or younger at the time of the event. In sum, while some support for the idea of repressed memories can be mustered, little of it is conclusive, and the controversy continues to rage.

Etiology: The Sexual Abuser

As noted previously, the overwhelming majority of sexual abusers are *male* (82 percent of substantiated cases). However, as was true of physical abuse, there is no specific "type" of person who sexually abuses children, nor is there a simple cause. To begin with, child sexual abuse may be just one manifestation of a more general state of being sexually aroused by children, or **pedophilia**. Pedophiles may experience sexual excitement only in relationship to children; some become sexual predators, while others may confine themselves to masturbating to magazine advertisements of children. Other sexual abusers also engage in relations with adult women.

A general guideline used to distinguish sexual abuse from normal childhood sexual exploration among peers is an age difference of five years between the perpetrator and the victim. However, this criterion ignores the fact that a significant proportion of the perpetrators of sexual abuse are other *youth*. Vizard, Monch, and Misch (1995) cite studies showing that 27 to 36 percent of the perpetrators of sexual assault against children are themselves under 18 years of age. In many cases—in some studies more than half—the victim is a sibling. The ratio of male to female adolescent sex offenders is about 20 to 1.

The Intrapersonal Context   Although *antisocial personality disorder* is frequently seen among sexual abusers, no psychiatric profile has been reliably established. Some abusers are described as timid and unassertive, while others demonstrate an authoritarian interpersonal style and poor impulse control. *Alcohol abuse*, however, is frequently found among sexually abusive fathers (Fleming, Mullen, & Bammer, 1997).

A clearer picture is provided of juvenile sex offenders. They are described as *socially isolated*, and *alienated* from their families, with *few female friends* and *poor social skills. Language and learning problems* are common, perhaps contributing to their social isolation. Many evidence significant *depression*, often related to their own histories of *sexual or physical abuse*: family violence and early sexual victimization are strong predictors of sexual aggression (Vizard, Monch, & Misch, 1995).

The Interpersonal Context: Family Characteristics   Madonna, Van Scoyk, and Jones (1991) conducted an observational study of families in which father–daughter incest had taken place. Family characteristics included a *weak parental coalition*, *enmeshment* and the discouragement of autonomy, and a *rigid* family belief system. Parents were described as showing an inability to appreciate the child's needs and as being *emotionally unavailable*.

Integrative Model

Finkelhor (1984) identifies four predictors that increase the potential for an adult to sexually assault a child, integrating the intrapersonal, interpersonal, and superordinate contexts:

1. *Motivation to sexually abuse.* Adults more likely to offend are those who are sexually aroused by children and are blocked from other, more appropriate sexual outlets. In addition, their emotional needs are sexualized, such that they seek love, care, and attention solely through sexual gratification. Other emotional needs may include the need for power and control over another person, as well as the need to reenact their own experiences of abuse and trauma. At the superordi-

nate level, the availability of erotic portrayals of children in advertising and pornography can foster these impulses.

2. *Disinhibition of internal constraints.* Characteristics of perpetrators that can overcome internal constraints include mental retardation, impulsivity, lack of empathy, use of alcohol, and a family belief system that legitimizes incest or the use of children for sexual purposes. Further, the abuser may cognitively distort cause-and-effect in order to self-servingly rationalize the abuse as a response to the child's initiation. Superordinate factors might include weak legal sanctions against sex offenders, and an ideology that supports adults' absolute rights over children.

3. *Disinhibition of external constraints.* The major factor here is the accessibility of a child to the abuser. Children most vulnerable to sexual assault are those who receive inadequate supervision, whether through parental stress, illness, or intentional indifference. Living situations that provide opportunities for the abuser to be alone with the child contribute (e.g., children left unattended, sleeping arrangements that place an adult in a child's room). Superordinate contributions include the erosion of social support networks for single mothers.

4. *Overcoming the child's resistance.* Although an adult is physically capable of forcing a child to engage in sexual activity, many abusers avoid physical force, instead using patience and sophisticated psychological strategies to overcome the child's will to resist. Often the abuse takes place only after a prolonged period of "grooming" and gradual indoctrination (Conte, 1992). The abuser's power over the victim is enhanced when he is in a position of trust and responsibility over children—for example, as a coach, babysitter, or stepparent—with which the child has been socialized to comply.

Comparison of Maltreatment Types

Two kinds of data are available to allow us to distinguish the effects of different types of maltreatment. Most of the studies cited so far are *noncomparative*—that is, they are based on samples of children who

experienced one or another form of abuse. As the summary of this research presented in Table 14.1 suggests, some trends can be found indicating unique effects of specific forms of maltreatment. While *physical abuse* is associated with *aggression*, *neglect* is more likely to be linked to *social withdrawal*. Neglected children also show the most serious *developmental* and *cognitive delays*. *Sexual abuse*, in turn, is associated with *sexualized behavior* and *internalizing disorders*, particularly depression. In general, the symptoms linked to sexual abuse center around trauma-related emotional and behavioral problems rather than the cognitive and interpersonal problems that follow from physical abuse and neglect. Lastly, *psychological maltreatment* is associated with the most significant levels of *depression*, as well as increasing *aggression* over the course of development.

Comparative studies, which directly assess the degree to which children have been exposed to different forms of maltreatment, are more rare. Moreover, such research is often based on small samples; therefore, it is not surprising that the findings are not always consistent. For example, McGee, Wolfe, and Wilson (1997) found that *psychological maltreatment* had the most pernicious effects on adolescents' mental health and exacerbated the effects of all other forms of abuse. In contrast, Manly, Cicchetti, and Barnett (1994) found child *neglect* to have the most detrimental consequences. Kaufman and colleagues (1994) conducted one of the rare studies that directly compared different forms of maltreatment, although they did not include sexual abuse. The authors summarize the results as follows: (1) *neglect* was associated with the greatest deficits in *intellectual functioning*, (2) *physical abuse* was associated with *aggressive behavior*, and (3) *psychological maltreatment* was the best predictor of *depression*.

Intervention

Physical Abuse, Neglect, and Psychological Abuse

Interventions for Children   Friedrich (1996) has developed an integrative model for intervention with maltreated children, focusing on three developmental

Table 14.1   Developmental Summary of the Effects of Different Forms of Maltreatment

	Physical Abuse	Neglect	Psychological Abuse	Sexual Abuse
Infancy and Early Childhood				
Cognitive	Cognitive delays	Most severe cognitive and language delays	Cognitive delays	Cognitive delays
Emotional	Avoidant attachment; limited understanding of emotions	Ambivalent attachment	Anger and avoidance; serious psychopathology	Anxiety, withdrawal
Interpersonal	Fearfulness, aggression	Withdrawal, dependence		Inappropriate sexual behavior
Middle Childhood				
Cognitive	Cognitive and language delays; learning disorder	Most severe cognitive deficits	Low achievement and IQ; poor school performance	School avoidance, poor academic competence
Emotional	Poor affect recognition; externalizing (boys), internalizing (especially girls)	Dependence, lowest self-esteem	Depression most likely; aggression	Posttraumatic stress disorder, fears, low self-esteem, depression, regression
Interpersonal	Aggression, peer rejection	Isolation, passivity	Poor social competence, aggression, withdrawal	Inappropriate sexual behavior; revictimization
Adolescence				
Cognitive	Low academic achievement	Lowest grades, most likely to be retained		Poor academic performance
Emotional	Depression, low self-esteem, conduct disorder, violence	Internalizing, externalizing, low initiative	Conduct disorder, delinquency, depression, poor emotion regulation	Depression, suicide, substance abuse, running away
Interpersonal	Dating violence		Pessimism	Promiscuity

domains affected by abuse: attachment, emotion regulation, and self-perception. In the domain of *attachment*, targets for intervention include poor differentiation of self and other, the tendency to recapitulate the role of victim or victimizer, distrust, and distorted perceptions of others. These issues can be addressed in therapy through establishing clear and appropriate boundaries between the child and therapist, as well as the therapist's consistent kindness and trustworthiness.

Emotion regulation is hampered by the experience of overwhelming negative emotions without the benefit of a soothing caregiver. Consequently, children who cannot tolerate strong emotions are likely to veer away from uncovering thoughts and feelings related to their abuse—just what is required of them in therapy. Techniques for addressing this problem include giving children control over the process, such as scheduling when and for how long they will talk about the abuse, or utilizing anxiety-reduction strategies such as relaxation training.

Lastly, abuse is a threat to the child's development of an accurate *self-perception*. Strategies for addressing this include fostering the child's understanding of his or her own world. This may require refraining from rushing to offer blanket reassurances that may ring false to a child who does not experience himself or herself as good-looking, smart, or fun to be with. At the same time, the child can be encouraged to take progressive steps away from an "all bad" view of self and to develop authentic realms of competence and mastery.

Studies of the *effectiveness* of interventions with abused children are sparse. Many of the approaches tried have a catch-as-catch-can quality and have not been adequately evaluated. However, improvement in a number of areas of functioning has resulted from placing preschoolers in a day treatment program, as well as from counseling school-age children and enhancing their problem-solving skills and self-esteem (Mannarino & Cohen, 1990).

Interventions for Parents   Most intervention efforts involve abusing parents rather than the abused child. Various strategies have been utilized, including parenting education, problem-solving skills training, stress reduction, group discussion and support, and individual psychodynamic therapy. Azar (1997) describes a promising *cognitive-behavioral* approach aimed at restructuring the distorted cognitions that lead parents to abuse. The intervention was highly successful. At a one-year follow-up, not one of the parents in the cognitive-behavioral group had abused their children, while 21 percent of those treated with insight-oriented therapy had done so.

Sexual Abuse

Interventions with Children   The very nature of the problem of sexual abuse challenges our ability to treat it. While sexual abuse may lead to psychopathology, it is not a disorder in and of itself. Sexually abused children may have undergone different kinds of experiences, and they may be brought to treatment for different kinds of problems. Also, some may evidence no symptoms at all. Although the majority of sexually abused children are female, there are significant number of males, who may need treatment sensitive to their particular symptoms and experiences. (Friedrich, 1997, describes treatment of sexually abused boys.) This diversity makes it difficult to define one correct approach to intervention. However, Finkelhor and Berliner (1995) outline the common elements to interventions designed for sexually abused children.

These include: (1) *encouraging expression of feelings about the experience*; (2) *altering erroneous beliefs and negative attributions*, such as self-blame; (3) *teaching abuse-prevention skills*; and (4) *diminishing a sense of isolation and stigmatization*.

Meta-analytic studies confirm that treatments for sexually abused children are helpful in reducing symptoms, with group, individual, and family therapies showing similar levels of effectiveness (Reeker, Ensing, and Elliott, 1997). However, most of the research has compared children's symptoms pre-and post-therapy rather than comparing them to an untreated control group (Finkelhor & Berliner, 1995). Therefore, it is not known whether improvement is due to the intervention or simply due to the passage of time.

By the same token, most studies fail to show gains related to the specific goals of the treatment. A notable exception is Celano and colleagues (1996), who developed an intervention designed to reduce "*traumagenic beliefs*"—self-blame and powerlessness—in girls who had been sexually abused. A sample of 32 primarily low-income, African-American girls aged 8 to 13 were randomly assigned to the experimental treatment or an unstructured comparison program. While both interventions were successful in reducing symptoms of posttraumatic stress disorder, the experimental treatment was more effective in reducing traumagenic beliefs and increasing overall adjustment. Another unique aspect to this study is that mothers underwent a parallel intervention. Following treatment, mothers were more supportive of their child, were less likely to engage in self-blame, and exhibited fewer exaggerated fears about the effects of the abuse.

Interventions with Perpetrators of Sexual Abuse Vizard, Monch, & Misch (1995) review the available research on interventions with youth who are sexual abuse perpetrators. Many different types of intervention have been implemented: one survey revealed that 338 different therapies were being used in various correctional institutions throughout the United States. Some unifying themes in the goals of treatment can be identified: (1) *confronting denial*, (2) *identifying risk factors*, (3) *decreasing cognitive distortions*, (4) *increasing empathy for the victim*, (5) *increasing social* *competence*, (6) *decreasing deviant arousal*, and, when appropriate, (7) *addressing the perpetrator's own history of victimization*. Most use a group format to take advantage of the fact that confrontations are more powerful when voiced by a chorus of peers.

Overall, evidence for treatment *efficacy* is not encouraging. For example, Kahn and Chambers (1991) evaluated the effectiveness of a number of sex-offender treatment programs. Fewer than 25 percent of the participants were discharged from treatment because they had significantly improved. Those in outpatient programs were slightly less likely to re-offend than those who were institutionalized, but the difference was not a significant one.

Prevention

Physical and Psychological Abuse and Neglect
Prevention programs are the most promising of all in that their goal is to keep abuse from ever occurring. *Primary prevention* strives to alter maladaptive patterns of parent–child interactions, as well as addressing the larger family and community context within which abusive parenting arises (Guterman, 1997). At-risk parents are targeted either during the mother's pregnancy or at the time of birth. The prevention programs provide them with assistance at a number of levels: meeting concrete needs such as obtaining food, diapers, child care, or job skills training; enhancing parenting skills and efficacy through parenting education and support; increasing the quality of parent–child interaction through relationship-oriented interventions; and, in some cases, providing cognitive stimulation for the infant or individual therapy for the mother.

The most successful programs are those that offer *home-based interventions* (Emery & Laumann-Billings, 1998). A premier example is the Prenatal and Infancy Home Visitors Program (Olds, 1997). Four hundred low income, adolescent and single mothers were contacted when pregnant with their first child. Home-based support was carried out by a nurse practitioner, who provided parent education regarding child development, involved the family and friends of the mother in providing an extended network of help and support, and linked the family to other medical and social services. Follow-up 2 years and even 10 to 15 years later showed that, in comparison to control group mothers, those who received home visits were less likely to be reported to child protection agencies, had fewer subsequent children, spent less time on welfare, and were less likely to be arrested or engage in substance abuse. Inspired by the success of this work, the National Committee to Prevent Child Abuse initiated a program called Healthy Families America, the goal of which is to create a universal system of home visitation for *all* new parents. As of 1998, the program was in place in over 240 communities across the United States.

Sexual Abuse
Most preventive programs involve children and are aimed at teaching certain key concepts and skills. Among these are that children own their bodies and can control access to them; there is a continuum from good to bad touching; and trusted adults should be informed if someone makes a child feel uncomfortable or strange. Children are also informed that potential abusers are apt to be familiar individuals rather than strangers and are taught ways of coping with attempted molestation such as saying no or running away (Wurtele, 1997).

Prevention programs are effective in increasing children's knowledge of sexual abuse concepts and self-protection skills (Rispens, Aleman, & Goudena, 1997). Younger children, such as those under age 5, are particularly likely to benefit. However, evidence that such knowledge is effective in preventing sexual abuse or increasing its reporting is still lacking. Additional criticisms have been levied against these prevention efforts (see Melton, 1992). For example, some children who participate in these programs become more worried and fearful about the possibility of abuse. On the other hand, those children appear to gain the most from the programs; thus, their worry may have a useful function (Finkelhor & Dziuba-Leatherman, 1995). On the positive side, there is evidence that sexual abusers are deterred by children who indicate that they would tell a specific adult about an assault. Thus, there may be significant benefits to teaching children, especially those who are passive, lonely, or troubled, the simple strategy of telling an adult about sexual abuse.

Divorce

In this section we briefly touch upon one of the other risks in the family context, that of interparental conflict and divorce. Like child maltreatment, divorce has been increasing at a rapid pace, and the United States has the highest rates in the world (Emery & Kitzmann, 1995). Almost one-half of marriages end in divorce, and approximately 1 million children experience their parents' divorce each year. These high prevalence rates indicate that divorce is no longer an unusual or even a socially stigmatized event. However, the fact that divorce is so common does not mean that its effects are benign. Both immediate and long-lasting consequences are documented.

Developmental Course

Overall, findings from various studies suggest that children of divorce show a twofold increase in emotional and behavioral problems as compared to children from intact families. (Our review follows Hetherington, Bridges, and Insabella, 1998, except where noted.) Risks for academic problems, school drop out, antisocial behavior, depression, and anxiety are increased. However, the *age of the child* at the time of divorce is an important moderator of these effects, as emerged in Wallerstein's (1991) ten-year follow-up of children of divorce, the results of which we review here.

Preschoolers   In the initial evaluation, preschoolers were significantly more disturbed than older children. The general picture was one of severe distress, particularly *separation anxiety*. The children were clinging, demanding of attention, and needy. There were a number of *regressive behaviors* such as enuresis and soiling, thumb sucking, and masturbation. Eighteen months later half the children looked even more disturbed than initially, *boys* more so than girls.

The picture ten years later was quite different. Those who were preschoolers at the time of divorce were less disturbed than those who were older at the time of divorce. To begin with, the preschool group had *no pre-divorce memories*, and they remembered only fragments of the conflicts during and after the divorce. Their relation with the *custodial mother* was close, open, and trusting. The *father* remained psychologically important; even those children who had been abandoned or neglected by their fathers still maintained a positive image, sometimes an idealized one. The importance of the father increased during adolescence, especially for girls. Significantly, these adolescents looked forward to the future with *optimism*.

School-Age Children   School-age children were less overtly symptomatic than preschoolers immediately after the divorce; however, negative effects were seen in terms of *declining school performance* and *social withdrawal. Gender differences* also emerged, with more negative effects found for boys, particularly in the form of increased anger and *aggression*.

Over time, school-age children showed dramatic reactions to the divorce. Lacking the preschoolers' protective forgetting or repression, they retained vivid *painful memories* of their parents' marital conflicts and experienced *longings* for return to an idealized pre-divorce family life. Ten years later, more than half described the divorce as the central experience of their lives. Feelings *of loss regarding the father* were intense, even though many of them lived nearby and visited regularly. Now late adolescents, their current intimate relationships were shadowed by *negative expectations* and *fear of disappointment*. In addition, while boys had seemed more affected by the divorce earlier, a sleeper effect seemed to emerge for *girls*, for whom rates of *promiscuity* and *teenage pregnancy* were high.

Adolescents   The adolescents were also disturbed by the divorce initially, but less so than younger children. They experienced a painful sense of *betrayal*, feelings of *loss* and *anger*, and *conflicting loyalties*. They were concerned about their own future marriages and about financial security. However, they were able to *distance themselves* from the family by increasing social activities and avoiding home. At the same time, however, almost all of them were able to be supportive of and empathetic with their parents.

Ten years later, the picture of the adolescent group had changed. The effects of the divorce exerted a major influence on their lives. Now young adults, they continued to be burdened by *vivid memories* of the marital rupture. Feelings of *sadness, resentment*, and a sense of *deprivation* were strong. The women especially were apprehensive about repeating their parents' unhappy marriage.

Summary   Wallerstein's findings point out the importance of longitudinal data and alert us to the spurious conclusions that might be reached by extrapolating from data obtained at one period of time. However, it is important to keep in mind that Wallerstein's was a clinical study relying heavily on intensive interview of the subjects. It is therefore open to the potential biases of such an approach; for example, the subjects may not be a representative sample and the data were not objective. (For a review of other long-term studies, see Grych and Fincham, 1997.)

Long-Term Effects

Subsequent long-term follow-up studies have overcome many of the methodological limitations of Wallerstein's study. Chase-Lansdale, Cherlin, and Kiernan (1995) examined the effects of divorce on young adult development by using data from a nationally representative longitudinal sample gathered in Great Britain. Almost 8,000 individuals born in 1958 were followed until age 23. Of these, 382 experienced their parents' divorce prior to age 16. Results showed significant long-term effects of parental divorce, with a 20 percent increase in ratings of general *psychological distress*, and a 39 percent increase in the likelihood of reaching clinical levels of *psychopathology*. However, the investigators hasten to add, the effects are modest in absolute terms: 82 percent of the women and 94 percent of the men were functioning adequately.

An even more long-term picture is offered by Tucker and colleagues (1997) from a study of 1,261 children followed until age 40. *Men* who had experienced their parents' divorce during childhood were more likely to be *divorced* themselves, to have obtained *less education*, and to be *less ac-*tive in their communities. *Women* with the same childhood experience of divorce were also more likely to be *divorced*; in addition, they *smoked more* and had *shorter life spans*. Clearly, divorce can cast a long shadow.

Risk Factors for Children's Post-Divorce Adjustment

Interparental Conflict   Divorce is not a single event; it is the culmination of a long process. The majority of couples report years of marital acrimony leading up to the decision to divorce. The children, therefore, are exposed to chronic *interparental conflict*, and sometimes even violence. Evidence is clear that children are already affected by the acrimony between their parents long before the divorce occurs and that it is the interparental conflict rather than the divorce per se that accounts for the deleterious effects on children. (See Grych and Fincham, in press.)

Further, divorce does not necessarily mean an end to interparental conflict. The divorce process itself brings up many heated and divisive issues, many of which directly concern the children (e.g., custody, visitation, and child support). In addition, many children feel "caught in the middle" (Buchanan, Maccoby, & Dornbusch, 1991), particularly when they are asked to take sides with one parent against the other, to inform parents of one another's activities, or to carry messages back and forth between their parents. As we saw in Chapter 1, this kind of *triangulation* is highly stressful for children.

Life Stress and Socioeconomic Disadvantage   Divorce is accompanied by a number of *life stresses* and disruptions: children may have to move, change schools, separate from friends, and cope with many losses. Additionally, for most children divorce is associated with a significant decline in economic circumstances (Guidubaldi, Perry, & Nastasi, 1987). However, claims that the effects of divorce are completely accounted for by economic distress do not hold up to scrutiny. Even when income is controlled, children of divorce show more problems than do children of intact families (Amato, 1994).

Parental Distress and Unavailability For many parents, the divorce represents a painful failure at one of life's most important accomplishments, that of sustaining a love relationship. All of the life changes and stresses that affect children are felt keenly by parents, who may also face unpleasant interpersonal repercussions should friends and in-laws take sides against them. Consequently, divorce is associated with a number of signs of *emotional distress* in parents, including depression, anxiety, irritability, and alcohol abuse (Hines, 1997).

The parents' distress may also spill over to the parent–child relationship, with negative consequences for children's development. Mothers may become *emotionally unavailable* to children, and their *parenting skills* may be disrupted. Fathers are likely to become more *distant* and *unaffectionate* toward their children after divorce (Amato & Booth, 1996).

Protective Factors for Children of Divorce

The majority of children of divorce do not show significant levels of psychopathology; by and large, they are characterized by *resiliency*. This is not to say that divorce is not painful for children; however, a significant percent are able to adapt successfully within two to three years. What protective factors account for this?

Exposure to interparental conflict.

Intrapersonal Characteristics Many of the child characteristics related to resilience in other contexts also emerge as protective factors in studies of divorce: *intelligence, easy temperament, self-esteem,* and an *internal locus of control* (Hetherington, 1991). As we have seen, *young age* may have a protective function for children. Over time, young children have less vivid memories of the divorce and of the pre-divorce family, which may shield them from the feelings of loss and longings for reunification that characterize older children. In addition, while older children do not adapt easily to remarriage, younger children benefit from the return to an intact family structure (Chase-Lansdale, Cherlin, and Kiernan, 1995).

Evidence for *gender differences* is less clear. While some earlier studies reported that girls were less affected by divorce than boys, this pattern of results has not been found consistently in more recent studies. However, there is a small but statistically significant and often-replicated finding that parents of sons are less likely to divorce than parents of daughters (Katzev, Warner, & Acock, 1994). The investment that fathers have in raising a son and the perception by both parents that "a boy needs a father" may shield boys from divorce. Many fathers maintain closer contact with sons than daughters after divorce, further softening the blow.

Coparenting Cooperation between ex-spouses regarding parenting and child rearing—termed *coparenting* (McHale & Cowan, 1996)—can also buffer children from the negative effects of divorce. This is an important factor to consider in determining custody arrangements. While children may indeed benefit from continued contact with both parents, the benefits are eroded when joint custody takes place in an atmosphere of acrimony and antagonism.

Coping Strategies As we saw in Chapter 1, the strategies that children use to cope with stress can help to buffer them from its effects. Sandler, Tein, and West (1995) found that school-age children who used *active coping* strategies—problem solving and constructive actions—demonstrated fewer conduct problems and depression five months after divorce. Coping involving *distraction* (distracting

oneself by engaging in other activities) was also protective, while *avoidance* (passive withdrawal) was not. Most important is that children use coping strategies that do not involve them directly in their parents' disputes (Kerig, in press). This is a difficult task when parents engage in what sometimes is quite literally a tug-of-war over the child. (See Johnston, Campbell, and Mayes, 1985, for vivid examples.)

Parental Support As Rutter (1990) proposes, a close, *supportive relationship with one parent* can help to buffer children from the effects of stress. This holds true in the case of divorce as well (Hines, 1997). The key, however, is a warm and supportive relationship that is oriented toward meeting the child's needs rather than the parents' (Brown & Kerig, 1998).

Authoritative Parenting Positive parenting comprises more than warmth and support, it also requires structure. This we know as authoritativeness. *Authoritative parenting* is associated with better adjustment in children of divorce, especially preschoolers (Hetherington, 1993). The parenting style of the custodial parent has the greatest influence on child development, and, in the majority of cases, this is the mother.

Social Support As children approach adolescence, they increasingly look outside the family to peers and other adults as sources of *social support*. Many adolescents affected by divorce intensify this process, disengaging from their families and seeking independence earlier than their peers (Hetherington, 1993). When young people find prosocial individuals to turn to, this can be beneficial; however, as we saw in Chapter 11, precocious autonomy support from antisocial peers can also have pernicious effects.

Integrative Developmental Model

As Hetherington, Bridges, and Insabella (1998) note, divorce sets off a whole chain of events in a child's life. Changes in residences and schools, increasing stress, and changes in family roles and responsibilities may ensue. However, it is also possible that

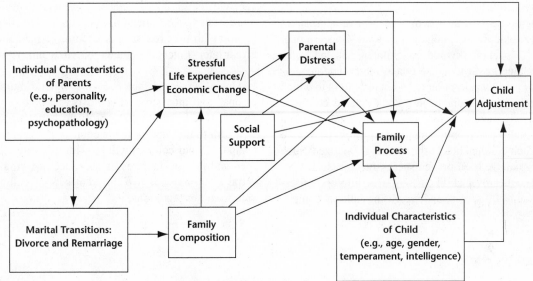

Figure 14.2   Transactional Model of the Effects of Divorce on Children's Adjustment.

divorce will bring an increase in harmony in the home and will provide opportunities for growth. The effects on the individual child will depend on a host of factors, including the quality of relationships in the family preceding the divorce; the uncertainty, disruption, and conflict that accompanies it; and the developmental stage in which it occurs.

Consequently, these authors propose a multi-dimensional and transactional model of the risks and protective factors that predict children's post-divorce adjustment. (See Figure 14.2.) The *stresses* associated with the divorce process affect all family members in different ways, ranging from loss of the father and the economic resources he provides to increased psychological distress and poor parenting. These effects may be buffered by *protective factors* such as social support or intensified by individual characteristics of children that increase *vulnerability*. Further, the risk and protective factors *transact* with one another in complex ways. For example, while parental stress (e.g., maternal depression) affects children's development, it does so indirectly, through its effects on the parent–child relationship. On the other hand, an easy child tem-

perament can help to moderate the impact of family disruption on development. Further, Hetherington and colleagues point out that these transactional processes emerge only after time; the static snapshots provided by cross-sectional data are unable to reveal the true picture of children's development following divorce.

Intervention

Grych and Fincham (1992, 1997) review the literature on interventions with children of divorce. The majority involve *group therapies* for children, designed to reduce self-blame for marital dissolution and to remove the stigma associated with parental divorce. Other interventions focus attention on *parents* in an attempt to prevent some of the risks associated with child maladjustment, such as parent unavailability, poor parenting practices, and interparental conflict. Yet other interventions are *systemic*, including both children and their custodial parents. Although some data in support of the effectiveness of each of these interventions have been offered, few have been assessed in a methodologically satisfactory way.

Prevention

One of the most far-reaching *preventive* approaches takes place at the public policy level. Concern over the impact of divorce on children has led some jurisdictions to mandate that parents undergo *custody mediation* in order to lessen the extent to which children are inveigled in divorce-related conflicts. Custody mediation requires that parents come to a mutually acceptable agreement regarding the care of their children before the divorce is finalized. Such efforts have been proven successful in reducing legal battles over child custody, speeding up the resolution of disputes, and increasing fathers' compliance with child support orders. However, effects are more positive for fathers; mothers report less satisfaction with the process and outcome of mediation a year later (Emery, Matthews, & Kitzmann, 1994).

Having explored factors in the organic, intrapersonal, and interpersonal contexts that place children at risk for developing problem behavior, we now turn to the superordinate context of society. In Chapter 15 our concern will be with minority children and the special stresses they face in trying to come to terms with two different sets of cultural values and expectations.

The Risks of Ethnic Minority Children

Introduction

Scope of the Problem

Approximately one out of four Americans belongs to an ethnic minority: 11.7 percent of the population is African American, 9.9 percent Hispanic, 2.8 percent Asian or Pacific Islander, and 0.7 percent Native American or Eskimo. By the year 2000 it is estimated that nearly 40 percent of clients in the mental health delivery system will come from one of these ethnic minority groups. (See Johnson-Powell, 1997b.)

These major ethnic groups are far from homogenous; on the contrary, there is considerable variability within each. For example, in the category of Pacific Asian Americans there are an estimated twenty-nine distinct cultural groups ranging from preliterate to technologically advanced societies. A middle-class African-American family may have little in common with an African-American family from the slums, just as a third-generation Japanese family may have little in common with a first-generation one.

Ethnic labels are another source of intragroup variability. Individuals of Mexican origin can be called Mexican, Chicano, Latino, Hispanic, and Mexican American. Such labels are not equivalent, since they have different psychological meanings. The shift from "colored-negro-darkie" to "black," epitomized by the slogan "Black is beautiful," reflected a significant shift away from a depreciated image and toward self-respect. Subsequently, "black" and "African American" came to have different connotations. In their study of 232 African Americans, Speight, Vera, and Derrickson (1996) found that those who identified themselves as black had no particular ideology ("That's what I am"). They were indifferent to, avoided, or even were disdainful of their ethnic identity. By contrast, those who called themselves African Americans did so because of its symbolic, political, and cultural meaning. They were actively grappling with issues of identity, pride, and heritage, were politically conscious, and regarded the designation as a sign of empowerment.

Finally, individuals can change their ethnic label for practical reasons. For example, Pavel, Sanchez, and Machamer (1994) found that of 259 university students claiming to be American Indian or Alaska Native in order to receive the benefits of a minority status, only 52 were able to verify their membership in one of the groups. At the opposite extreme are people who try to hide their minority status in an attempt to avoid discrimination and prejudice.

Counteracting Ethnocentrism

Aside from its importance to effective clinical practice, the study of ethnic minorities helps dispel the ethnocentric belief that "our way" (i.e., the way of the majority group) is both the only and the best way. In reality, there are many ways of rearing children, many sets of values, and each has its assets and liabilities. Clinical child psychologists have learned this lesson in regard to individuals. Children differ, and because of this there are numerous fulfilling lifestyles. Both the sensitive scholar and the popular extrovert can be developing normally although each has a different mix of the variables we regard as essential to growth, such as attachment, initiative, and self-control.

The same is true of culture. The Anglo-American culture is only one of many cultures, and perspective on it can best be gained by a knowledge of diversity. In this way an ethnocentric view of what is good for children can be replaced by an understanding that our society, like all others, involves its special combination of factors that tend to promote and impede development. For example, the United States has the highest rate of crime of any industrialized country, while the crime rate in mainland China is low. Among the many variables contributing to the low crime rate are the closeness of the Chinese family, the constant surveillance of the children, and the deep sense of shame if a child commits an antisocial act. On the other hand, the Anglo-American emphasis on autonomy and independence opens up avenues of individual initiative that would not readily be available to the traditional Chinese adolescent.

Our presentation first defines relevant terms and then considers a number of general issues, such as changing societies, minority and socioeconomic status, minority-majority relations, and ethnic patterns. All of these issues involve the superordinate context. After that we discuss the intra- and interpersonal contexts of ethnic identity and then finally the clinical implications of our presentation for the assessment and treatment of ethnic minorities.

Since it would be impossible to do justice to the richness of the field of ethnic minority children, we have chosen to concentrate on three themes, using a single minority group as an exemplar of each. The themes (and the selected groups) are as follows: *ethnic identity* in African-American adolescents, *cultural diversity* among Japanese-American children, and *clinical practice* with Mexican-American children. (For a detailed discussion of ethnic minority children see Johnson-Powell et al., 1997. Diagnosis and treatment are discussed by Canino and Spurlock, 1994, and by Ho, 1992.)

Definitions

Both "ethnic" and "minority" belong in the superordinate context and take us into the province of sociology and anthropology rather than psychology. In fact, this is the first time in our discussions that the superordinate context has served as a point of departure. Because the realm is alien to psychology, we will not try to master its concepts and methodologies; rather, we will stay only long enough to become acquainted with some basic definitions and with some essential background data.

There is no general agreement on the definition of ethnic groups. (Our discussion of definitions follows Foster and Martinez, 1995, unless otherwise noted.) The definition we will use states that an **ethnic group** shares certain *practices, values, and beliefs based on exposure to a common culture*. Its members regard themselves as distinct from others in some significant way and transmit their culture from generation to generation.

For the purpose of federal surveys, the Office of Management and Budget has established five ethnic groups in the United States: American Indian or

Native Alaskan, Asian or Pacific Islander, black, Hispanic, and white. In the literature, blacks may be referred to as African Americans, American Indians as Native Americans, and whites as Anglo-Americans.

Race can be defined as a grouping based on *genetic inheritance and/or physical characteristics*. Race often overlaps with ethnicity and may be confused with it. However, the two are not the same. Hispanics, for example, trace their origin to Spain and identify their race as white; blacks can include individuals from Haiti and Brazil as well as African Americans.

Culture can be defined as a *shared set of learning experiences, situations, beliefs, and behavioral norms*, as well as *physical objects* unique to the group such as tools, art, and buildings. While used interchangeably with ethnicity, the two are not the same since culture is more broadly based.

The simplest definition of a **minority group** is one having *fewer members than the majority group*. Obviously, not all ethnic groups are minorities (for example, whites are not a minority in the United States—although they are a minority group worldwide), and not all minority groups are ethnic (consider minority groups such as the physically handicapped or the Quakers). M. E. Bernal (1989) adds two more characteristics that, while not generally agreed upon, are relevant to our concern with psychological adjustment. She regards an ethnic minority as being *powerless or subordinate* and the *object of discrimination*. Native Americans and African Americans, for example, experience powerlessness and discrimination along with conflict with the dominant group; Polish or Irish Americans by contrast are not relegated to a subordinate role and are not in conflict with the dominant group. While some patterns of subordination and discrimination are relatively fixed (as in the case of Native Americans) others can change over time (such as the prejudice against the Irish at a previous time in our country's history).

Ethnic identity refers to *knowledge about one's ethnic group* and a *sense of belonging* to that group. Ethnic identity is an important part of an individual's total identity but should not be equated with it. **Ethnic socialization** refers to the *developmental processes* by which children acquire the behaviors, perceptions, values, and attitudes of an ethnic group and come to see themselves and others as members of such a group (Rotheram & Phinney, 1987).

General Issues

Minority Status and Socioeconomic Status

Poverty, in and of itself, can have a number of risks and untoward consequences for children—for example, poor maternal health and nutrition prenatally and a greater number of obstetrical complications and child illnesses, along with a lack of proper medical care, increased family stress and discord, ADHD, violence, and substance abuse (Yamamoto, 1997). (See Figure 15.1 for the effects of poverty on schooling and employment.) Therefore, it is unfortunate that both minority status and race have been confounded with poverty not only in popular thinking but in the research literature as well; for example, only 10 percent of articles on race published between 1970 and 1990 controlled for socioeconomic status (Graham, 1992). This perpetuates negative stereotypes while making it impossible to know the relative contribution of each factor to disturbed behavior.

There are a few studies, however, that have untangled race from socioeconomic status. Patterson, Kupersmidt, and Vaden (1990) found that, overall, income level and gender rather than race were the strongest predictors of conduct problems, peer relations, and academic achievement in African-American and white elementary school children. In a similar vein, Stevenson, Chen, and Uttal (1990) found that children of poorly educated mothers, whether African American, white, or Hispanic, did less well in grade school math than did children of better-educated mothers. Finally, in Achenbach and Edelbrock's (1981) standardization of their Child Behavior Checklist, neither socioeconomic status nor race made a statistically significant contribution to problem behavior, although socioeconomic status was nearer to being significant than was race. Thus, while not irrelevant, race contributes less to children's school and general adjustment than does poverty.

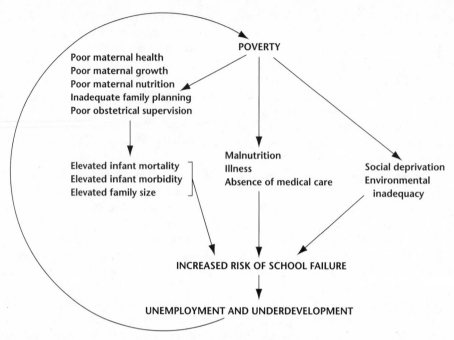

Figure 15.1   Environmental Relationships Between Poverty and Educational Failure.

Source: Birch and Gussow, 1970.

Resilience   Recall that our developmental model states that normal or deviant development depends on the balance between risk and resilience. While the ravages of poverty, powerlessness, and prejudice have been amply documented, the variable of resilience has been neglected. For example, the majority of African-American children are doing well in terms of mental health, education, and subsequent employment, but research has primarily focused on delinquency, aggression, and social and academic maladjustment (Barbarin, 1993).

Because the study of resilience has been neglected, we know little of the resources that ethnic groups provide for their members or the various coping strategies that are available to them. (For a detailed discussion of the issue of resilience, see Cohler, Stott, and Musick, 1995.) However, we do have a few hints concerning protective mechanisms. There is some evidence that oppression and exploitation tend to make minority groups emphasize collective values over individualistic ones

(Gaines & Reed, 1995). There is a price, though. Gaining strength through unity can also make members of minority groups suspicious and rejecting of genuine efforts on the part of Anglo-Americans to help them.

Ethnic Patterns

After reviewing the literature, Rotheram and Phinney (1987) were able to delineate four dimensions that are central to differentiating the social behavior of ethnic groups. These dimensions are as follows:

1. An orientation toward *group affiliation* and interdependence versus *competition*
2. An active, *achievement-oriented* style versus a passive, *accepting* style
3. *Authoritarianism* and the acceptance of hierarchical relationships versus *egalitarianism*
4. An *expressive*, overt, personal style of communication versus a *restrained*, impersonal, and formal style (p. 22)

The Anglo-American pattern values independence and competition, achievement, egalitarianism, and an expressive style of communication. This picture contrasts with many other patterns that emphasize the primacy of the family and the group, deference to and respect for the father and other authority figures, and placing the good of the group over individual assertiveness and advancement. (See Phinney, 1996, for a discussion of the limitation of the concept of ethnicity as an explanation of normal and deviant behavior.)

Ethnic Identity

Ethnic identity, which will figure prominently in subsequent discussions, can be conceptualized as having five components. (Our presentation follows Bernal and others, 1993, and Rotheram and Phinney, 1987.)

1. *Ethnic knowledge or awareness* entails the acquisition of knowledge concerning the critical attributes of one's own ethnic group and how it differs from the ethnic groups of others. This includes physical characteristics and language along with roles, values, and customs.
2. In *ethnic self-identification* children categorize themselves as members of their ethnic group, adopting the labels used for that group.
3. *Ethnic constancy* consists of the understanding that ethnic characteristics are unchanging and permanent across time and setting.
4. *Ethnic attitudes, feelings, and preferences* involve children's attitudes and feelings about their own ethnic group members along with preferences for ethnic behaviors, values, traditions, and language.
5. *Ethnic behaviors* are behavior patterns characteristic of a given ethnic group. These may be specific, such as bowing versus shaking hands, or general, such as expressing feelings versus being self-contained.

Development of Ethnic Identity

Cognitive Variables   Ethnic identification may seem simple to adults, but it actually involves a number of high-level cognitive processes. In many ways it is akin to gender identity, to which it is closely related. (See Ocampo, Bernal, and Knight, 1993.)

Preschoolers very early learn that certain labels are applied to them, such as "girl" or "Chinese." Subsequently they can parrot these labels (e.g., "I am a Chinese") but are left on their own to figure out what the labels mean. Figuring out the meaning of labels involves three basic processes. First, children must determine what are the *essential elements* in the label so that, if the elements were not present, the label would not be applicable. Next, they must discover what characteristics *differentiate* this particular label from labels given other groups, such as "boy" or "African American." If there were no such differentiating features, then labels would not be necessary. Finally, they must learn that the label is *constant* across situations and over time, so that one is always a girl or Chinese wherever one is throughout one's lifetime (Aboud, 1987).

While children eventually master these three cognitive challenges, the process takes a number of years and may involve many errors along the way. In our discussion of gender identity (in Chapter 2), we found that the preschooler thinks in concrete terms, such as, "A girl is a person who is small and wears dresses," or "I am someone who plays ball." Only in middle childhood does thinking become abstract and accurate. A similar progression from concrete to abstract and from perceptual to conceptual takes place with ethnic identification, as outlined below:

1. *Recognition of different ethnic groups.* Recognition of different ethnic groups in the preschool period is based on the salience of *perceptual cues*, with skin color and hair type being particularly important. Thus, children can recognize African Americans and whites by 3 to 4 years of age but cannot recognize Chinese, Hispanics, or Native Americans until around 8 years of age. Even adults show a similar lack of differentiation concerning ethnic groups when they say that "All Asians look alike." In both instances, perception is not sufficiently detailed to permit fine discriminations. By middle childhood, perception has become sufficiently detailed to allow the differentiation of a number of ethnic groups. (See Bernal and Knight, 1997.)
2. *Self-identification.* Self-identification is typically measured by presenting the child with dolls or pictures of children from different ethnic groups and

asking, Which one looks most like you? African-American and white children can perform the task reasonably well by 5 years of age, although accuracy continues to improve until 9 years of age. On the other hand, only 37 percent of Mexican-American preschoolers can self-identify by ethnic labels and even when correct cannot explain why. By middle childhood 96 percent of the children are correct (Foster & Martinez, 1995).

3. *Ethnic differences.* Ethnic differences are studied by a technique similar to that used in self-identification except the child is asked which group is *not* like him or her. Children from various ethnic groups perform this task correctly more than 80 percent of the time by 4 or 5 years of age. Research also shows that children from different ethnic groups use different criteria for recognizing members of their own group and differentiating them from others. French Canadians use language; Chinese use eyes, food, and language; Native Americans use possessions and activities; and African Americans rely on skin color and hair type (Aboud, 1987). This diversity of criteria shows the limitations of research techniques using appearance alone, such as dolls or drawings of different ethnic groups.

4. *Conceptualizing ethnic groups.* Conceptualizing the essential features of ethnic groups is a more difficult task than the previous ones since it requires the ability to think abstractly. One technique for measuring this conceptual ability involves presenting children with pictures of a number of people belonging to different ethnic groups and asking them to put all the members of the same group in separate piles. The categorization task becomes accurate only at around 7 years of age.

5. *Ethnic constancy.* Ethnic constancy can be measured by asking children if they would be the same if they were dressed like another ethnic group—for example, asking a white child, If you dressed like an Eskimo, would you be white or an Eskimo? Temporal constancy can also be measured. For example, a Native American child can be asked, How long have you been a Native American? and Will you be a Native American ten years from now? While achievement of constancy is not well-documented, the evidence indicates that it happens at around 8 years of age. (See Figure 15.2 for a summary of the development of ethnic identity.)

While developmental data are limited, Bernal and associates' (1993) study of 45 Mexican-American children between the ages of 6 and 10 and found that ethnic self-identification, constancy, knowledge, and preference scores (e.g., preference for typically Mexican over non-Mexican activities) all increased with age. Only ethnic roles did not change, perhaps because those roles tapped by the assessment technique, like speaking Spanish at home, are fairly constant in this age span. (For more details concerning the research on ethnic identity along with a critique of the limitations of the techniques used, see Aboud, 1987.)

Summary   Bernal and Knight (1997) summarize the major trends in the early development of ethnic identity as follows:

1. *The preschool period.* For the preschooler, ethnic identity consists of simple, concrete descriptions of physical attributes, appearance, and behaviors. Ethnic labels have little meaning at this age. In addition, the children engage in the customs and behaviors of their culture by aping what their families do and may not even associate these customs with ethnicity.
2. *The early school-age period.* At the early school-age level children's ethnic identity is more complex and traitlike. Ethnic labels have meaning, and the constancy of ethnicity is grasped. Children engage in more ethnic role behaviors, know more about the ethnic relevance of these behaviors, and have feelings and preferences about their ethnic group.

We will complete the developmental picture of ethnic identity later, in the section that explores identity in African-American adolescents.

Impact on Assessment, Diagnosis, and Treatment

Only a small percent of mental health professionals come from minority groups. This means that, both literally and figuratively, they cannot speak

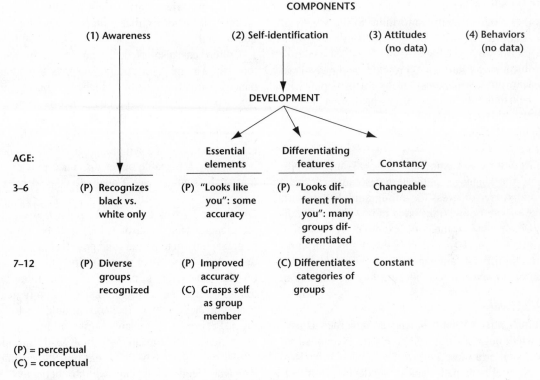

Figure 15.2   The Development of Ethnic Identity.

their clients' language. Consequently, the universal requirements of establishing rapport and understanding the client's point of view present special problems and require special training. (The training issue is addressed by Ricardo and Holden, 1994.) The problem of helping children from minority groups is compounded by the paucity of research on the topic and the meagerness of financial support for such studies (Vargas & Willis, 1994).

Assessment

The ethnic minority child is confronted with a special set of culturally mediated stressors that must be assessed for their potential of increasing the risk of the child's becoming mentally disturbed. Evaluating such stressors entails a broadening of tradi-

tional assessment procedures. (For a more detailed discussion of assessment, diagnosis, and treatment of ethnic minority children, see Canino and Spurlock, 1994, and Ho, 1992.)

There are special psychosocial stressors associated with being a member of an ethnic minority, over and above those of poverty. We will describe a few of the major ones.

Migration and Acculturation   Migration involves the disruption of one way of life and the necessity of accommodating to another. The process of migration can involve different kinds and degrees of stress, while acculturation varies in stressfulness depending on the congruence between the old and new cultures. Moreover, there can be intrafamilial stress when parents and grandparents disapprove of the new behaviors children display as the children begin conforming to the values of the majority.

Prejudice and Racism   Prejudice and racism can exist at the interpersonal level—for example, with peers. However, they can also be institutionalized in the school system, the police force, and the businesses community.

Language   Not being able to speak and comprehend the language of the larger society can be a major source of stress for immigrants. For its part, society wrestles with the issue of how far to accommodate to immigrants—for example, by providing bilingual education or, conversely, by making English the official language of the country, with no uniform provision for special bilingual education.

Diagnosis

Culture affects what behaviors are regarded as psychopathological or as symptoms of psychopathology and, at a more general level, what behaviors, while not psychopathological, are deviant from cultural norms and a potential source of considerable parental concern.

Culture-Bound Syndromes   There are disturbances that seem to be specific to particular cultures. For example, among Japanese, *taijin kyofusho* consists of an excessive concern that one's body, its parts, or functions are offensive to others in appearance, odor, expression (as in facial expression), or movement. Whether such culture-bound syndromes represent unique disturbances or variations of other diagnostic categories is a much debated and unresolved issue. (See Hughes, 1997, for a discussion of the issue.)

Symptoms   Culture can affect what behaviors are considered to be symptoms. Asian Americans, for example, are more apt to believe that answering back to parents, becoming angry over minor insults, and talking openly with others about personal problems and secrets are signs of psychological disturbance. It would be a mistake for the clinical child psychologist to trivialize such behaviors in an Asian-American child or dismiss them as being normal, because for that child's culture they are not normal.

Culture can also affect the prevalence of symptoms. In a number of cultures there is a predominance of somatic symptoms, such as stomach pains, headaches, and chronic fatigue. There is some evidence that somatization flourishes in societies that place a premium on self-control and concern for others. Theoretically, the symptoms serve as a disguised but socially acceptable outlet for unacceptable feelings such as anger. (See Yamamoto et al., 1997.)

Deviations from Cultural Expectations   An intergenerational clash of values may be a source of great concern to parents and grandparents as children adopt the ways of the majority. Thus, a desire on the adolescent's part to become more autonomous may be deeply offensive to family members who believe that decisions should be left to them. Peers can also champion the traditional ethnic values. For example, Canino and Spurlock (1994) cite the case of a 17-year-old Native American who received a special award for being a champion boxer along with a congratulatory address by the principal upon graduation. After the ceremony a group of Native American peers gave him a beating for betraying the value of putting the good of the group above personal gain (p. 52).

While deviations from ethnic values may be a source of distress among members of the minority group, as alluded to earlier it would also be a mistake for the clinical child psychologist to regard conformity to ethnic values as a sign of psychological disturbance. For example, many ethnic minority groups are family-oriented and authoritarian. The adolescent transition to independence, which plays such an important role in Anglo-American society, is *not* expected in cultures where adolescents continue to be part of the family. Thus, interpreting continued closeness to the family as "a failure to resolve adolescent dependency needs" may be in error because a resolution in terms of independence is not expected.

Ideas Concerning Etiology   Ethnicity can determine how the causes of mental illness are construed. A number of cultures hold the view that the spiritual world readily interacts with the material world, producing misfortunes and psychological disturbances. Some of the better-known examples of spiritual causality are hexes, "the evil eye," and voodoo. In fact, one-third of African-American patients treated in a Southern psychiatric center believed they were victims of witchcraft. The belief is found among whites as well (Hughes, 1996).

The implication for diagnosis is clear. An adolescent's belief that his or her psychological disturbance is due to malevolent external forces would be evaluated differently depending upon whether he did or did not come from an ethnic background with a strong belief in the intrusion of spirits into human affairs.

Utilization of Mental Health Facilities   Mental health facilities are underused by ethnic minorities. For example, while 18 percent of whites with mental disorders receive outpatient mental health services, only 9 percent of African Americans, 8 percent of Puerto Ricans, and 10 percent of all other minorities including Hispanics receive such help (Vargas, 1997). Turning first to the minorities themselves, there are many reasons for this underuse. Mental illness may be a source of great shame or evidence of punishment from God. Somaticizers may understandably turn to a physician for help, while those with problems in cultures with strong bonds within an extended family may seek out particular family members to provide help and guidance. Certain cultures prefer indigenous sources of help; for example, Native Americans may use medicine men, sweat lodges, or clan-based dances. (See Canino and Spurlock, 1994.) Another reason for the underuse of mental health facilities by minorities may be that the facilities themselves are not sensitive to cultural differences and do not adjust their personnel and procedures to such differences.

Treatment

Ethnic minority groups differ in their expectations of treatment, with some expecting medication, for example, and others expecting direct advice. We will discuss in detail both the issues of utilizing

mental health facilities and of treatment in the subsequent section on the treating of Mexican-American minorities. (For a general discussion of treatment of ethnic minority children, see Canino and Spurlock, 1994.)

Comment on Research

In light of the national concern with the status of minority groups in society, with discrimination and prejudice, and with the implications of a culturally diverse rather than a culturally homogeneous society, one would expect there to be an extensive body of data on ethnic minority children. Such is not the case. Objective studies tend to be limited in scope or poorly designed (the confounding of ethnicity with poverty has already been noted) or dated. As Vargas (1997) notes, there are no large population studies of mental disorders in ethnic minority children. At best we have a few studies of subpopulations within an ethnic group, with no way of telling whether the findings can be generalized to the group as a whole.

Identity in African-American Adolescents

Background Information

Before discussing the specific topic of ethnic identity in African-American adolescents, we present some helpful background information on African Americans in general.

Special Characteristics

African Americans have some special characteristics as an ethnic group. Primary among these is the fact that they were involuntarily incorporated into the existing society and permanently assigned an inferior status by legal, economic, and social forces (Spencer, 1991). In spite of this status, African Americans found ways of expressing their pride during the period of slavery and throughout the twentieth century (Stuckey, 1987). This determination to throw off the yoke of slavery reached a climax in the civil rights movement of the 1960s (Gibbs, 1990). For our purposes, the success of this movement meant that African-American children could now identify with a positive societal image of their ethnic group.

However, the process of change has been hampered by lingering prejudice and particularly by poverty. The economic situation is not as disheartening as it once was, since an increasing number of African Americans are moving into the upper-middle income bracket of $50,000 a year or more. However, in spite of impressive gains, the overall picture is still bleak: in 1990 the poverty rate for white families was 14.1 percent, while for African-American families it was 50 percent (Fuller, 1997. This chapter also contains a general summary of research on the African American child.)

Values and Kin Relationships

It is important to understand the ethnic values of African Americans, especially since they differ from those of the white majority. These values include affective expressiveness, energy, and verve; communalism or a social orientation emphasizing the interdependence of people; spirituality or a conviction that greater powers than man's are at play in life; and a special time orientation that constructs time fluidly in terms of events rather than rigidly in terms of the clock and calendar (Fuller, 1997).

Next, there is the centrality of kin relationships over marital relationships. This reliance on the extended family with its network of support has been disrupted for middle-class mothers who have gravitated toward the nuclear family as upward mobility necessitates frequent moves within and between cities. Thus, they are potentially subjected to the stress of living in relative isolation. (See Fuller, 1997.)

Coping Strategies and Protective Mechanisms

Phinney (1990) describes four ways of coping with the special problems created by poverty, prejudice, and powerlessness on the one hand and having a different set of cultural values on the other. One is to *accept society's negative image* and become an alienated member. This solution runs the risk of increasing personal problems and decreasing educational achievement. The next solution is to *identify with the dominant white culture* and assimilate into it. Anecdotal evidence attests to the strains of assimilation,

such as not being totally accepted by whites while being rejected by African Americans. Another coping strategy is *withdrawal*, which involves a retreat into the African-American culture and "being happy in the ghetto." There are advantages to this solution, with research showing that self-esteem of African Americans is higher in segregated schools than in integrated schools. However, maintaining a lifelong pattern of withdrawal is difficult in the modern world, and those who do so are poorly equipped for confrontations with a white-dominated society. Finally, there is *biculturalism*, in which minority individuals retain their own culture but also adapt to the dominant one by learning the necessary skills. There is research suggesting that this may be the best solution in terms of psychological adjustment, but it also has its special stresses both in terms of parental opposition and social discrimination. (LaFromboise, Coleman, and Gerton, 1993, has a detailed discussion of minority–majority relationships.)

The Process of Identity Formation

For this discussion we follow Phinney's (1993) integrative summary concerning the process by which African-American identity is formed. (See Helms, 1990, for an application of the model to other minorities.)

Stage 1: Unexamined Ethnic Identity   The first stage is characterized by a lack of exploration of ethnicity. Here there are two possibilities. The first is identity *diffusion,* or a lack of interest in or concern with ethnicity. For example, an adolescent girl said, "Why do I need to learn about who was the first black woman to do this or that? I'm just not interested." The second is identity *foreclosure,* or adopting the views of ethnicity based on the opinions of others. For example, an adolescent boy said, "I don't go looking for my culture. I just go by what my parents say and do, and what they tell me to do, the way they are."

Stage 2: Ethnic Identity Search/Moratorium   The next stage is ethnic identity search, characterized by an involvement in exploring and seeking to understand the meaning of ethnicity for oneself. This stage may be initiated by a growing awareness that not all cultural values of the dominant group are beneficial to ethnic minorities. The search itself involves an interest in learning about African-American culture through talking with friends and reading, and grappling with the issues of prejudice and the difficulties in attaining educational or career goals. Recall that the adolescent is now cognitively capable of weighing and balancing divergent viewpoints before arriving at a decision.

Stage 3: Ethnic Identity Achievement   The final stage is one of identity achievement, or a clear, confident sense of one's own ethnicity. Individuals differ in how this achievement is expressed. Some, for example, want to maintain ethnic language and customs, while others choose not to.

Ethnic Identity and Adjustment

While the data are preliminary, there is evidence from Phinney's various investigations that ethnic identity achievement is positively related to ego

identity, positive self-evaluation, a sense of mastery, and positive relations to peers and family (Phinney, 1993, Phinney & Kohatsu 1997). (See Figure 15.3.) The correlations with self-esteem, while positive, tend to be low because factors other than racial identity play an important role in determining the level of self-esteem.

Adolescents with a strong ethnic identity are less likely to commit crimes against other African Americans and against property. In addition, their cultural identity is a stronger predictor of psychosocial adjustment than is self-esteem (Whaley, 1993). While Speight, Vera, and Derrickson (1996) found a positive correlation between stages of ethnic identity and both education and income, other investigations have found the opposite.

Ethnic Identity and Intervention

The stages of ethnic identity development are related to treatment. (Here we follow Helms, 1990, which also describes the different kinds of relationships

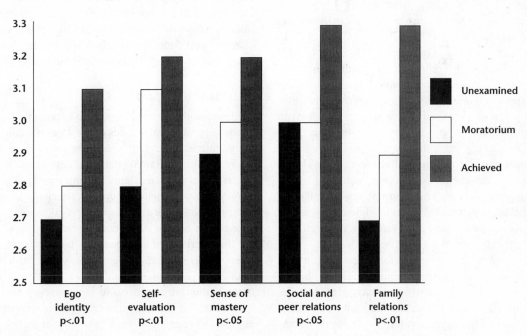

Figure 15.3   Ego Identity and Adjustment Scores by Stages of Ethnic Identity.

Source: Phinney, J.S., 1993

that are established when counselor and client are at different stages of identity development.) African-American adolescents in the early stage of identity development prefer white counselors, those in the middle stage prefer African Americans, and those in the final stage have no preferences or prefer African Americans. Clients in the initial stage will attend more sessions with white than with African-American therapists, while those in the second and third stages will be more satisfied with the sessions; thus attendance and satisfaction are relatively independent. There is also tentative evidence that racial issues will play a more prominent role in counseling if the client is in the exploratory phase rather than in the final phase.

Understanding the findings concerning stages can help the clinical child psychologist individualize the client at hand, rather than assuming that he or she has a fixed attitude such as being hostile toward white therapists. (For a discussion of assessment and treatment of African-American adolescents, see Gibbs, 1990, and Ho, 1992.)

Summary

Here we will highlight what we have presented about (1) the special stresses on African-American adolescents and the possible ways of coping with them, (2) the process of identity formation, and (3) its implications for adjustment and treatment.

Poverty, powerlessness, and prejudice increase the risk for psychopathology, perhaps more than ethnicity per se. Faced with these stresses, the African American can choose to accept society's negative image, identify with and try to assimilate into the dominant white culture, withdraw and try to "be happy in the ghetto," or become bicultural by retaining the African-American culture but adapting to the white-dominated society. While each solution has its advantages and disadvantages, research suggests that biculturalism may be the best.

African-American identity formation goes through three stages: unexamined identity marked either by diffusion (i.e., disinterest in ethnicity) or by foreclosure (i.e., blindly adopting the views of others); ethnic identity search/moratorium, or actively seeking to understand the meaning of ethnicity; and ethnic identity achievement. or gaining a clear, confident sense of one's ethnicity.

Stage of identity is positively correlated with a number of measures of adjustment: positive self-evaluation, a sense of mastery, and positive relations with family members and peers. It is also negatively correlated with the likelihood of committing crimes against other African Americans and against property. Stage of identity affects treatment, those in the first stage preferring white therapists, those in the second preferring African American, while those in the final stage have no preference or prefer African Americans. Race may also play a more prominent role in treatment of adolescents in the exploratory stage rather than in the final stage.

Finally, it should be noted that we have been considering various levels of adjustment, not psychopathology. The relation between identity formation and psychological disturbances is largely unknown.

Cultural Diversity in Japanese-American Children

As we have seen, minority groups differ not only among themselves but within themselves as well. One source of intragroup variability is intergenerational change. While many minority groups have changed over time, we will discuss Japanese Americans, whose history is particularly dramatic.

Traditional Japanese Culture

We begin with a reminder: while it is possible to describe general characteristics of the Japanese culture, the culture is undergoing change in Japan itself. After World War II both Western and democratic ideas began to play an increasingly important role in Japanese society, while national goals were changed from concerns with war to industrial productivity. Such changes are not our direct concern but they do affect the characteristics of immigrants to this country at different points in time. For example, while the initial immigrants were uneducated laborers, many of the current group are employees of Japanese corporations who spend 3 to 5 years representing their companies and plan to return to Japan (Yamamoto et al., 1997).

At the most general level American and Japanese cultures can be contrasted in the following manner. In America the emphasis is on change, individuality, self-assertion, and equality. The Japanese culture emphasizes tradition, vertical relationships, interdependence, and self-denial. Both cultures value diligence, education, and postponement of immediate pleasures for future gratifications (Ho, 1992; Yamamoto & Iga, 1983). We will discuss in detail two of the cultural differences—namely, vertical organization and interdependence.

Vertical Organization

The culture in the United States values equality and upward mobility: even rail splitters, peanut farmers, and actors can become president. The Japanese culture, by contrast, is highly stratified, making for keen status consciousness. Even language varies according to whether the person is of higher or lower rank, and a person of higher rank does not bow as deeply as one of lower rank (Yamamoto & Kubota, 1983).

While members of the lower strata are required to serve the people in the higher strata, the emphasis is on mutual obligation and loyalty. Thus the relation between classes is not like that of master and servant but one of interlocking responsibilities, with individuals in the higher strata being as bound by prescribed duties and behaviors as those in the lower. This image of social organization echoes the teachings of Confucius, who advocated loyalty between lord and subject, order between senior and junior, propriety between husband and wife, closeness between father and son, and trust between friends (Yamamoto et al., 1997).

Interdependence

Instead of Anglo-American individualism, the Japanese culture's pervasive emphasis is on interdependence. A person identifies himself or herself within a social group such as the family, the school, or the workplace. (See Box 15.1.) Group cooperation and participation are taken for granted in everyday activities. This cooperation in turn fosters a sense of togetherness and results in long-lasting relationships. Finally, not only subordinates but authority figures as well must conform to group objectives. Thus, a corporation must be as totally committed to the employee as the employee is to the corporation. In fact, executives and production line workers may dress alike and eat in the same

cafeteria, a custom that symbolizes interdependence and subordination of all individuals to group objectives. (See Yamamoto & Iga, 1983.)

Another aspect of interdependence is an emphasis on empathy, which is a highly valued virtue. It also is a far cry from the American idea of "looking out for number one." The cultivation of the ability to feel what another person is feeling goes along with the motivation to help others achieve their wishes and goals. Part of this emphasis on empathy is an attempt to maintain consensus or positive feelings of agreement between people. Confrontations are avoided; accommodations are essential. Self-restraint is another means by which problems are avoided.

Finally, at the national level, the strong sense of group membership is related to an equally strong sense of nationalism. Traditionally, Japanese people have perceived themselves as being unique and separate from other nationalities, and the Japanese emphasis on interdependence has referred primarily to relationships among those of Japanese heritage. (See Yamamoto and Iga, 1983.)

Generational Changes

The Issei Generation

The Issei, or first-generation Japanese, arrived shortly after the turn of the century when Japan was only beginning to be industrialized and the tradition of caste and class was strong. (We follow Yamamoto and Kubota, 1983, unless otherwise indicated.) The majority of immigrants were poorly educated, tended to be from rural areas, were disadvantaged educationally and culturally, and had been without employment in their native country. Most spoke only Japanese and were preoccupied with the problem of survival.

First regarded as a source of cheap labor in this country, they were subsequently subjected to blatant racism, violence, restrictive legislation, and antimiscegenational statutes. They coped with their strange and hostile environment by trying to be inconspicuous, adopting Western dress, and being polite, stoic, nonemotional, and self-effacing, as well as hardworking and conscientious. While adaptive, such mechanisms also perpetuated both a physical and psychological "ghetto-ization."

Box 15.1 | **"Who Are You?"**

One of the basic differences between Western and Asian cultures concerns the concept of the self. (Our presentation follows Landrine, 1992.) In Western cultures the self is independent of society. It is a unique entity, free to choose and responsible for its choices. Its ideal goal is often self-fulfillment. In Asian cultures, the self is interdependent. It is defined in terms of social context, relationships, and interactions. From the very beginning, for example, an infant is defined as its parents' child. Moreover, the social network includes ancestors who play an active role in decision making and in approving or disapproving of actions. In sum, there is no independent self that relates to others; relationships to others define what the self is. Ask the Anglo-American boy, "Who are you?" and he is apt to answer something like, "I'm a

good ball player" or "I'm smart." Ask the traditional Japanese-American boy the same question, and the answer is apt to be something like, "I'm the third son." (Markus and Kitayama, 1991, discuss the effects of the independent and interdependent self on cognition, emotion, and motivation.)

These differences in the self-concept have implications for clinical practice. In an unstructured interview the clinician often says, "Tell me something about yourself." The traditional Japanese American is likely to describe encounters with others rather than listing traits. The uninformed clinician may misinterpret such a response as evidence of evasive or tangential thinking. Such thinking, at times, may be erroneously regarded as evidence of a borderline or schizoid personality disorder.

Or again, in the interview situation, the clinician might say, "You have told me a good deal about how you get along with others; now what do you really want for yourself?" Such a question may only be baffling and upsetting to traditional Japanese Americans because they do not understand the idea of having a "real self." Again, their perplexity should not be interpreted as evidence of identity diffusion or of pathologically low self-esteem.

One final example. Since ancestors play an active role in traditional Japanese Americans' lives, hearing them speak should not, on the face of it, be regarded as hallucination. The failure to distinguish cultural differences from a genuine loss of reality contact may be one reason why Japanese Americans are frequently misdiagnosed as schizophrenic.

The Nisei

The Nisei are American-born children of the Issei immigrants and are considered second-generation Japanese Americans. They were raised before World War II and were bilingual, with Japanese as their primary language. They came to be called the model minority, although they did not view themselves in this manner. However, they were the most educated and successful ethnic group in the United States, even though the process by which they achieved this status was a painful one.

The hysteria following the bombing of Pearl Harbor was a turning point for Japanese Americans. The majority of their community leaders were arrested, separated from their families, and placed in a segregated facility in Crystal City, Texas, with the designation of dangerous aliens. West Coast families were uprooted and placed in concentration camps in the spring of 1942.

The people found they had to live in cramped quarters and use centralized eating, bathroom, and laundry facilities. The lack of privacy and the communal facilities disrupted traditional family life, depriving the Nisei of its stabilizing influence. But it emancipated them as well. The necessity of communicating in English with federal representatives escalated Nisei into roles of prominence overnight; however, it simultaneously contributed to the erosion of established roles and functions within the family unit since the younger family members took over leadership roles from the elders. Peer groups, organized around athletic competition between blocks, became primary socialization units. Older Nisei were selected as coaches and parent surrogates, while parental supervision itself gradually dissipated over time.

Because it was possible to leave the camps under special dispensation between 1942 and 1946, Nisei attended colleges and universities in unprecedented numbers, making them the most educated ethnic sub-group within the United States. They also formed an all-Nisei combat unit, which became the most decorated battle unit in World War II.

The post–World War II era had an air of starting over. Compared with the Issei, the Nisei were better educated and more worldly and were sufficiently flexible to abandon ghetto life in exchange for an assimilated form of living in mainstream America. Their diligence and education enhanced employment opportunities and facilitated acceptance by the majority culture.

The Sansei and the Gonsei

The Sansei, or third-generation Japanese Americans, and the Gonsei, or fourth-generation Japanese Americans, in many ways resemble middle-class white American children in attitudes, belief, and lifestyle. Most no longer speak Japanese. Sansei, like Nisei, tend to identify themselves not with Japan but with the camp in which the Nisei spent the four impressionable years between 1942 and 1946. Both Sansei and Gonsei continue to show some of their parents' characteristics in that they are less aggressive socially than Anglo-Americans and overachieve in school. The majority do well and have the reputation of being model children.

The Family Context

The Traditional Picture

The vertical organization of traditional Japanese culture defined the structure of the family as well. (Our presentation follows Yamamoto and Kubota, 1983, unless otherwise noted.) Primogeniture and lineage were an integral part of Japanese culture. The eldest son became head of the household and was responsible for both his parents in their old age and for his brothers and sisters. Consequently, males were preferred above females, with the first-born male being of special importance.

In the traditional family, rankings were related to seniority and gender, with the father having the most authority, followed by the mother in an unofficial capacity and then the eldest and then the next eldest sons. In fact, the Japanese language

contains no generic words for "brother" and "sister" but only words that designate whether they are older or younger.

Interdependence was expressed in a high degree of family togetherness. Families did everything together, including eating, bathing, sleeping, and participating in recreational activities. Characteristically, hierarchical relationships were preserved in all these activities, with the members with the highest status being served or bathed first, for example. Family members were restrained rather than autonomous and spontaneous as in the American culture. Other-directedness and externality were further consequences of interdependence, with children not only being concerned for the welfare of other family members but also feeling that their behavior was constantly monitored by them.

Future orientation was shown in two ways. First, parents were frugal in order to provide their children with the best educational advantages. Children, in turn, were expected to show filial piety and take care of their parents in old age. Consequently, there was no need for social security.

Evaluation   The American emphasis on equality and autonomy might give Japanese-American children opportunities for *maximizing their potential* which otherwise might not be available to Japanese children locked into specified roles and stratified classes (particularly those locked into the traditional role for Japanese girls). Yet emphasis on individuality may not provide sufficient protection against *isolation and alienation* on the one hand and *social irresponsibility* on the other. Such vulnerabilities are nearly absent in traditional Japanese child rearing with its emphasis on interdependence, group identity, and group monitoring. In sum, there is a balancing of assets and vulnerabilities between cultural patterns just as we see a balancing of assets and vulnerabilities in individual children.

The Current Picture

Three aspects of acculturation have diluted the traditional family relationships. The first is the dramatic increase in intermarriage. The percentage of marriages to non-Japanese is around 51 percent, with women outnumbering men. Next, the rate of divorce has also increased dramatically, although it is still lower than in the Anglo-American population. Finally, fair housing legislation has enabled Japanese Americans to move freely about rather than being confined to cultural enclaves. (See Yamamoto et al., 1997.)

As a result of acculturation, many but not all of the traditional Japanese values have been modified. Consequently, the current picture is a mixed one. (Our presentation is based on del Carmen's 1990 integrative summary of objective studies.) Both here and in Japan the extended family has been replaced by the nuclear family. Japanese families have a lower rate of divorce, a lower proportion of households headed by a woman, and a lower rate of fertility than non-Asian families. Ironically, this "nuclearization" occurred at the same time that the nuclear family in the United States was undermined by an increase in divorce and single-parent households.

Marital roles are shifting away from the strong paternalism of traditional Japanese culture to a more egalitarian arrangement between husband and wife. However, Japanese-American women have more readily adopted this perspective than have Japanese-American men, who are still more in the traditional mold. Decision making, which used to be unilateral, is being modified, with the more educated and Americanized women enjoying higher status within the family.

Yet the Americanization is not total. Japanese-American parents value having well-behaved children more highly than do Anglo-American parents. In their family communications, Japanese Americans are more cautious, indirect, and restrained and show less warmth and affection. Thus, it is important for the clinical child psychologist not to interpret such behavior as evidence of coldness or hostility or inhibition. One final example of the persistence of tradition: while ethnic group identity usually declines in successive generations, there are no differences among third- and fourth-generation Japanese Americans in this regard (Wooden, Leon, & Toshima, 1988). (Del Carmen, 1990, discusses the assessment and treatment implications of the changes in Japanese American family life. See also Ho, 1992.)

Psychopathology

Information on specific psychopathologies is meager. The incidence of suicide for Japanese Americans is low—9.4 per 100,000 as of 1980, compared with 13.5 per 100,000 for whites. However, suicide accounts for a larger *proportion* of deaths for Japanese Americans than it does for whites—19.0 percent versus 11.9 percent (see Liu et al., 1990). The rate of juvenile delinquency and alcohol consumption is lower than it is for white Americans, although it is increasing with successive generations (Fugita, 1990). Unfortunately, the true extent of psychopathology is unknown because of the lack of epidemiologic data.

Psychopathology in general tends to be viewed by Japanese Americans as inappropriate behavior or as malingering. There are a greater number of somatic complaints among Japanese-American college students than among their peers, perhaps because somatization is more acceptable than a direct expression of a psychological problem (Nagata, 1989).

The stereotype of the Japanese American as the ideal minority has a number of drawbacks, not the least of which is a trivialization of their problems. For example, among minorities, they have the lowest priorities for federal and state funding for physical and mental treatment and intervention, as well as for research and training (Liu et al., 1990). While it is true that Japanese Americans have the lowest poverty rate among minorities, it is also true that they are underemployed, with college-educated Japanese Americans earning several thousand dollars less per year than their college-educated non-Asian peers (Nagata, 1989).

Finally, the mental health picture is far from positive for Sansei who stop their education after high school or earlier. The blue-collar class tends to discriminate against them more openly than the middle class, while the options for work are more limited. In addition, these Sansei become progressively alienated from their college-bound peers. Consequently, they are at risk for drug abuse and narcotic addiction as well as for conflicts with family, peers, and police (Santa, 1983).

Helping Mexican-American Families and Children

The clinical goals of accurate evaluation and effective help for minorities can be achieved only by understanding ethnic backgrounds and modifying clinical procedures accordingly. We have arbitrarily chosen the Mexican American culture to illustrate this thesis. Before proceeding to clinical considerations, therefore, we will describe some general characteristics of the Mexican-American population, the traditional Mexican values, and how these values have been modified over successive generations of immigrants. (For a general reference, see Arroyo, 1997.)

General Characteristics

Descriptive data do not always differentiate Mexican Americans from Latinos, the category label that includes all people of Latin American descent. Whenever possible we will present information concerning Mexican Americans only.

Currently, Mexican Americans make up 5 percent of the total population of the United States and 60 percent of all Latinos in the United States (Garcia & Marotta, 1997). It is estimated that, by the year 2020, Latinos will be the largest ethnic minority in the United States, making up 15 percent of the total population, with 63 percent of this population being Mexican. Immigration accounts for the major portion of the increase because of the proximity of Mexico to the United States (Arroyo & Cervantes, 1997). The exact number of illegal immigrants is unknown, but it is estimated to be around one-third of the U.S. Mexican population (Garcia & Marotta, 1997). However, the fertility rate also plays a role in the increased number because Mexican Americans have the largest households of any Latino group; for example, 16 percent have a household with six or more persons (Garcia & Marotta, 1997).

Economically, 30 percent of Mexican Americans are below the poverty level as compared with 14 percent of the general population. In regard to education Latinos are significantly underrepresented at every school level, and only 53 percent complete high school as compared with 80 percent of the general population. (See Garcia and Marotta, 1997.) Since poverty is correlated with child psychopathology, it is reasonable to infer that a significant percent of Mexican-American children are in need of psychological help. However, the actual prevalence of mental disorders is unknown (Arroyo & Cervantes, 1997).

Family Structure and Values

The interdependence of Mexican Americans is nicely illustrated by the structure of the family, which is neither nuclear nor extended but rather a combination of the two. As in Mexico, the family unit is of prime importance to its members, with grandparents playing an important part in family life. This sharing of family functions is called *familism*. The functions themselves include caregiving and disciplining of children, companionship, financial responsibility, emotional support, and problem solving (Arroyo & Cervantes, 1997). Sex roles are clearly demarcated; males are granted independence at an earlier age than females and are expected to achieve in the outside world (Diaz-Guerrero & Szalay, 1991).

Family members also have ancillary relationships that serve as a support system as well as a way of transmitting information and providing access to resources such as jobs. There is a fictive kin system called *compadrazgo*, or coparents, whose members are usually selected from close friends and relatives. *Padrinos*, or godparents, are particularly important members of this group. They are responsible for the well-being of the child, thereby serving as a source of security for him or her and support for the parents (Arroyo & Cervantes, 1997).

There are neighborhood helpers (*servidores*) who further extend the social network in terms of assisting with chores and providing companionship. Friends and friendships are broader in scope, more enduring, and affectively deeper than they are in the dominant American culture (Diaz-Guerrero and Szalay, 1991). In short, Mexican Americans have an extensive support system that can help them cope with stress and can also be used as a resource by mental health workers.

A multigenerational Mexican family.

The prime values of Mexican-American families are religion, interdependence, honor, self-respect, and self-sufficiency. All members are expected to protect the family image, honor, and well-being. Respect within the family is hierarchically organized by age and sex, with older males being given the most respect (Ho, 1992).

Family Roles

The traditional male role is epitomized by *machismo*. However, the term means more than just masculine superiority and forcefulness. It encompasses a strong sense of personal honor, family loyalty, love of children, and respect for the aged, as well as status in the community (Arroyo & Cervantes, 1997). There is evidence that the more extreme emphasis on masculine dominance has moderated in the modern Mexican-American

family; for example, there is more joint decision making and greater equality of roles in regard to vocational opportunities. While the father is still the authority and disciplinarian for his children, he is also friend and companion (Diaz-Guerrero & Szalay, 1991).

The more narrowly defined aspects of machismo are present in the *palomillos*, or social groups, in which young males display their prowess through drinking and feats of daring. In addition, the groups offer social support, giving help and advice to members who are having marital, familial, or work problems.

The traditional female role is a family-centered and subservient one. The mother is expected to be nurturant and self-sacrificing, while the daughter's socialization stresses caring for the siblings and the home. The daughter is allowed to spend less time away from the house than the son, and her social activities are more limited and carefully monitored.

However, this situation is undergoing rapid change as women want more education and vocational opportunities and more freedom in their social and sexual life (Zea et al., 1997).

Child Rearing

The parent–child relationship is the central focus of family life rather than the husband–wife relationship, which is central in the dominant American culture (Diaz-Guerrero & Szalay, 1991). Parents express their family-centeredness not only with their children but also in their close relation with their own parents and the frequency of visiting relatives. Parents encourage their children to be more dependent on the family than do Anglo-Americans—for example, many Mexican-American parents believe that their child's best friend should be a sibling. They allow fewer small decisions such as what to wear, encourage the children to play near home, worry when a child is not at home, and do not encourage children to bring their friends home as much as do Anglo-American parents. Obedience to authority and loyalty to the family are essential (Diaz-Guerrero, 1990).

The model child is not viewed as one who is achievement-oriented and successful in the academic and economic spheres. Rather, model children are skilled in human understanding and interpersonal relationships. They are polite, socially adept, courteous, respectful of elders, and deserving of respect, as well as being mindful of the dignity and individuality of others. The name for these values is *respecto,* or respect (Arroyo & Cervantes, 1997).

Socioeconomic Status

As we have seen, a disproportionate number of Mexican Americans live in poverty. There is the *underclass* consisting of poor, uneducated transients who migrate in search of employment and a stable support system to tide them over until they can cope using their own resources. The families are large, Spanish-speaking households living in chronically overcrowded conditions. The *low-income families* resemble the underclass except that they have employment and residential stability. They have limited education, work at semiskilled

or service jobs, and have large, unacculturated families. The children are unlikely to be high achievers or to do well in school, thereby continuing the cycle of poverty.

The immigrant *working-class family* tends to be better educated than the previous two classes, with some members of this class having completed high school. They have stable employment in skilled or semiskilled occupations, their homes are ample (if overcrowded), and they have the resources to save money and take an occasional vacation. Their involvement in the community facilitates the social mobility of their children, who are aggressive, articulate, and independent, with some eventually acquiring a good deal of wealth.

The *middle class* is similar to the Anglo-American middle class. The parents are rarely immigrants unless they were also from the middle class in Mexico, the household is English-speaking, and education is stressed. However, adolescents, because they stand out as a distinct minority, may have a particularly difficult time with their ethnic identity. On the one hand, if they cling to their Mexican-American heritage they are apt to be regarded as outsiders by peers. If they renounce their heritage and model their behavior on peers they are apt to be in conflict with the conservative members of the older generation with whom they live. (The mental health needs of professional Latinos are discussed in detail by Comas-Diaz, 1997.)

It would be a mistake to equate increased acculturation with increased adjustment, however. On the contrary, research suggests that the optimal mix (as for African Americans) is a *bicultural* one marked by adaptation to the dominant culture while maintaining an identification with the traditional culture. The evidence is clearest in the area of academic achievement. In elementary school, there is little evidence that failure is due to the discrepancy between the two cultures (Ocampo et al., 1991). In high school, earlier-generation students obtain higher grades than their later-generation, more acculturated counterparts, while college-bound adolescents are more bicultural than non-college-bound ones. Finally, those who retain the traditional Mexican-American culture stay in college longer and receive higher grades than do later-generation students (Chavez and Rodney, 1990).

Helping the Child and the Family

Regardless of the nature of the problem or the source of risk, Mexican-American children and their families must be treated in a manner congruent with their ethnic values and customs if psychological services are to be maximally effective or, indeed, if such services are even to be accepted. We now examine the implications of this theme of cultural congruence in terms of providing mental health services, assessment, and treatment.

Mental Health Services

Despite the increased risk for psychological disturbances, mental health services are underused by Mexican Americans. A number of factors contribute to underuse. (Our presentation is based on Echeverry, 1997.)

Geography   Mental health facilities located in middle-class neighborhoods are apt to be perceived as foreign, unfriendly, and not really there to serve Mexican Americans. Ideally, then, such facilities should be located near the population they intend to serve.

Cost   A substantial segment of the population either has no health insurance or has insurance that does not cover mental health services. Consequently, cost can be a major barrier to using such services.

Procedural Barriers   Poor people in general are unaccustomed to forms and paperwork. Mexican Americans may be especially suspicious if they or their relatives and friends are illegal aliens. Ideally, then, forms should be in Spanish and should be kept to a minimum. In addition, some clients assume that there is a direct conduit between the clinic and the Immigration and Naturalization Service and that they would therefore be immediately deported if they used the clinic's services. They need to be assured that there are no grounds for such fears.

There are also scheduling problems since many Mexican Americans cannot take time off during the day to go to the clinic. Thus, they have to rely on agencies that are open in the evening.

The Language Barrier   An English-speaking staff can do little for families who speak only Spanish or whose understanding of English is limited. Bilingualism is important not only for communication and rapport but for diagnosis as well. For example, interviewing in English may result in an underestimation of the degree of psychopathology in general and an overestimation of the degree of disturbance in schizophrenics.

To solve the problem of lack of bilingual clinicians, innovative use has been made of paraprofessionals recruited from the community as interpreters. They also serve as cultural consultants to the English-speaking therapists and as a link between the community and the clinic. (A detailed account of linguistic barriers in mental health services can be found in Preciado and Henry, 1997.)

Cultural Barriers   Mental illness may be viewed as a sign of weakness by Mexican Americans, and thus family pride may lead to an attempt to conceal disturbances. The extended social network or the clergy may be the preferred source of help. Finally, belief in the supernatural can play a role both as an explanation for distress and as a source of comfort. Mexican Americans may seek supernatural intervention not only from religious figures but also from folk beliefs and healers. For example, natural healers bring relief from various health, mental health, and life crisis problems through a variety of healing modalities such as massage, herbs, and spiritual treatment.

Assessment

Since the diversity of the Mexican-American population makes generalization difficult, we will concentrate our discussion primarily on the immigrant group, which has the greatest number of culture-specific stresses. Such stresses begin with emigration itself, which might involve the disruption of the family and social support systems. For undocumented individuals, crossing the border may be a harrowing experience marked by robbery, rape, and murder. Once in this country, the immigrant faces the stress of unemployment or of an unsatisfactory job; of exploitation, discrimination, and powerlessness; and of adapting to an alien culture and language. In addition to assessing the nature and sources of stresses, sources of support should also be evaluated, including the family, the social network, organizations, religion, and folk beliefs and practices. (For a more detailed account of assessment, see Ho, 1992.)

Assessment Instruments   Assessment instruments such as psychological tests that have been standardized on Anglo Americans cannot be used uncritically with minorities. Such misuse of tests was frequently done in the past, not only in clinical practice but in research as well. Typically minority groups were found to be inferior, not necessarily because of any basic inferiority but because of biases in the tests themselves (Arroyo & Cervantes, 1997.)

E. M. Bernal (1990) lists a number of biases that might spuriously lower the scores of Mexican-American children on intelligence and achievement tests:

1. *Proficiency in English.* Many psychological tests require a degree of proficiency in English that Mexican-American children may not have. Clinicians may mistakenly assume that the ability to engage in a conversation is a sufficiently sensitive measure of mastery of English; however, it is not. Specifically designed tests of proficiency should be used instead. If proficiency is low, test results may reflect a limited ability to understand the task itself rather than an inability to do it well. To take just one example: a number of words used in a vocabulary test may have no exact equivalent in Spanish; consequently, a child's vague definition may represent a lack of familiarity with the word or an attempt to define it in terms of its nearest Spanish equivalent.
2. *Interpersonal variables.* An important interpersonal variable is the ability of the psychologist to speak Spanish. While acculturated children score highest with English-speaking examiners, less acculturated ones score highest with Spanish-speaking ones.
3. *Intrapersonal variables.* Some children lack test-taking skills, hurrying through as quickly as possible to escape an unpleasant situation. Merely having taken tests over the years does not necessarily remedy the situation. Personality

factors, particularly high anxiety and self-deprecation, may lower scores. Both of these personality variables may increase with age rather than dissipating, and children in transition from a lower to a higher socioeconomic status are particularly prone to having them.

Knowing the sources of bias suggests remedies: devising special tests for Mexican-American children or using English-proficiency measures in interpreting standard test results; having the test administered by a Spanish-speaking psychologist for certain groups of children; helping children develop useful test-taking attitudes and skills as well as reassuring them and relieving their anxiety.

Standardized test results can be useful to clinicians if properly interpreted, however. Achievement tests, for example, may be important measures of the level of a child's current functioning as compared with Anglo-American peers. In interpreting such tests, clinicians should say something like, "Juan is two years behind in reading and arithmetic" rather than "Juan is a slow learner." The first sentence leaves open the issues of etiology and ability; the second does not.

Intervention

Just as culturally sensitive assessment is attuned to the special values, stresses, and resources of Mexican Americans, so guidelines for treatment follow from what we have learned of their culture.

Clients' Expectations   Because many low-income clients view the clinician as they would a medical doctor, they tend to expect advice and direction. Thus they anticipate an active approach such as questions focused on the presenting problems followed by concrete solutions. Nondirective techniques, a probing into details of childhood history, or requests for introspection should be used sparingly (Ruiz & Padilla, 1983).

Establishing Rapport   Cultural values can serve as guides to establishing rapport and conducting the initial sessions. For example, the friendly impersonality and task orientation of the professional dealing with Anglo-American clients is not suited to Mexican Americans. Rather, the quality Mexican Americans

Box 15.2   **The Different Versus Deviant Issue**

In evaluating minority families and children there is no easy answer to the question, What is a cultural difference and what is detrimental to the child's development above and beyond cultural considerations? Nor, in planning remedial measures, is there a simple way of deciding when one is "imposing one's cultural values" on the child and when one is preventing normal development from going awry. However, it is possible to avoid the two pitfalls we have been discussing. By way of summary, these are (1) being ignorant of or insensitive to ethnic differences and the im-

plications of these differences for clinical practice, and (2) deciding that all ethnic minority clients are best served by helping them conform to the values and behaviors of the majority.

In addition, Martinez (1994) alerts us to another pitfall. This is being overly sensitive to cultural differences to the point that almost all behaviors are interpreted in terms of cultural stereotypes. The result is that most behaviors are no longer regarded as deviant; rather they are considered merely "different." Take the example of a Mexican father who continually beats his son as the sole method of

discipline. The overly sensitive clinical child psychologist might interpret such behavior as an instance of machismo and therefore diminish or even dismiss its importance. Or again, such a clinician might passively accept the father's saying, in effect, This is the way we treat children in our culture. What is lost is the fact that severely beating children places them at risk for developing psychopathology regardless of cultural considerations. In general, a respect for cultural differences does not entail excusing the kinds of child maltreatment discussed in Chapter 14.

value is *personalismo*, which is a combination of warmth, empathy, and equality between clinician and client (Arroyo & Cervantes, 1997). Since touching is more frequent in Mexican-American culture than in Anglo-American society, a clinician might extend her hand upon meeting a new client, introduce herself by including her first name rather than a formal title, and engage in small talk in order to establish an atmosphere of friendly give-and-take. The clinician may talk about her own past as she inquires into the past of the parent. Personalismo also includes an attitude of respect and tactfulness. Thus, sensitive clinical topics should be approached slowly and cautiously, and confrontations should be avoided (Ramirez, 1989).

The Importance of the Family   Because of the central importance of the family, treatment should be family-oriented. This orientation pervades a number of areas. (For a detailed discussion of family therapy with Latino families, see Szapocznik et al., 1997.) In families in which the traditional structure prevails, the father should be addressed first, then the mother, then the older children. Since Mexican-American families believe it is impolite to disagree, the therapist must watch for overt compliance that masks resistance to treatment. Respect for family

values also means that the therapist might postpone advice that could be readily given to Anglo-American parents; for example, to suggest that the mother needs more time for herself might imply that she is not putting the family's needs ahead of her own as a good mother should (Ramirez, 1989).

By knowing Mexican-American family values, the clinician can interpret behavior differently than would be appropriate for Anglo-American clients. For example, a mother who walks her children to and from school may just be expressing typical family closeness rather than being overprotective.

The clinician should constantly be mindful of the reverberations of remedial measures throughout the network of family relations. In one case intrusive grandparents were causing marital problems, and the therapist made the mistake of recommending that the grandparents stay out of the picture. This recommendation only intensified the problems. The therapist then changed tactics so as to increase the couple's self-confidence, only gradually focusing on the grandparents' involvement at a level the parents themselves determined. This tactful approach, in which change took place within the context of respect for traditional relationships, succeeded where the confrontational approach had failed.

Dealing with Gender Roles   One risk of machismo is that the young boy will identify only with its aggressive aspects or even that he will be encouraged by his father to be too aggressive. If acting-out behavior brings such a boy to a clinical child psychologist, the relation with the father must be handled with the utmost tact. The clinician might accommodate the father in scheduling visits after hours or meeting the father at home, rather than assuming the stance of the expert who knows best what the father should do. It also might be a good strategy to appeal to paternal values incompatible with aggressiveness, such as pride in the family whose reputation is being threatened by the boy's antisocial acting out. Whatever is done, the father cannot feel that his authority is being threatened by the clinician, but rather that the clinician needs his help in making important decisions about the family. (For a discussion of treating Mexican-American gang members, see Belitz and Valdez, 1997.)

Helping the daughter with problems regarding gender roles may present a different kind of challenge for the therapist. The authoritarian male and the dependent female are no longer the accepted images of gender roles for many Anglo-Americans. However, the clinical child psychologist must be sensitive to the intense family conflicts and individual anxieties and guilt that might be engendered in changing from traditional Mexican to current American values. In certain instances the clinician may even decide that masculine dominance or feminine dependence should be supported because the girl would be more fulfilled in the traditional model. Respect for ethnic culture entails this kind of respect for ethnic diversity. Also recall the research showing that individuals who are making the best adjustment are not the ones who are most thoroughly "Americanized" but those who can incorporate elements of Mexican and American culture. (See Box 15.2.) (For a discussion of specific treatment approaches, see Vargas and Koss-Chioino, 1992.)

In many of our discussions we have touched upon the issues of assessment and remediation. However, because these are the activities that concern practicing clinical child psychologists the most, they each deserve a full-dress presentation of their own, which we provide in Chapters 16 and 17.

Psychological Assessment

Up to this point our goal has been the scientific one of investigating the factors that help us to understand the development of psychopathology. Clinical assessment, while guided by scientific principles, has a practical focus somewhat different from that of empirical inquiry. The clinician's primary role is that of a help-giver. Therefore, the ultimate goal of child assessment is to develop an effective treatment plan.

We will take the point of view of a clinician who seeks a comprehensive understanding of the child's psychopathology, noting how different theoretical orientations, such as psychodynamic or behavioral, might influence the assessment process. In addition, in order to bring these concepts alive, we will follow a hypothetical assessment of a boy named Kenny. Coverage of specific techniques will be selective. We will assume that readers have an understanding of test construction, reliability, and validity commensurate with that gained in an introductory course in psychology.

(For more detailed coverage, see Sattler, 1992, and Kamphaus and Frick, 1996.)

Assessment from a Developmental Psychopathology Perspective

In conducting an assessment, the clinician looks for data that will confirm or rule out various hypotheses about the nature of the child's problems and the processes that account for their development. Therefore, assessment cannot be divorced from theory. The *theoretical perspective* of the clinician influences which hypotheses come most readily to mind and which kind of data will be useful for testing them. For example, *behaviorally* oriented clinicians believe that psychopathology can be understood in terms of social learning principles. Therefore, they tend to study the antecedents and consequences of children's problem behavior in order to determine what in the environment might be reinforcing it. *Cognitively* oriented clinicians are more interested in children's reasoning processes and the appraisals that lead them to respond maladaptively. *Psychoanalytically* oriented clinicians focus on the unconscious determinants of children's symptoms, which cannot be observed directly but must be inferred from children's projections and fantasies. Clinicians with a *systemic* orientation believe that children's problems arise within the context of the family system and thus want to assess the ways that all the members of the family interact with one another in the here and now. In contrast, *humanistic* clinicians do not want to interfere with self-discovery by imposing their interpretations on children, and therefore they reduce assessment to a bare minimum.

However, developmental psychopathologists argue that each of these clinicians is only obtaining a piece of the puzzle. The organizational perspective (see Chapter 1) suggests that a complete assessment of a child needs to *integrate* information from a number of domains, including the behavioral, cognitive, emotional, psychodynamic, interpersonal, and systemic (Achenbach, 1995). Moreover, developmental psychopathologists view children not as a sum of these separate parts, but as integrated, organized, and dynamic systems (Cicchetti & Wagner, 1990).

For example, even when children are working on what is ostensibly a cognitive task, such as solving a math problem, they are also engaged at the emotional, behavioral, and interpersonal level. For example, are they happy to be challenged, anxious to please the examiner, crushed by failure, irritated at the task's difficulty? Are they bright but oppositional, determined to fail as a way of "getting the goat" of the examiner? Are they striving to compete with peers, or, quite the reverse, to underachieve in order to be perceived as "one of the gang"? And there is a family context: are children worried about their parents' reaction should they fail, or about upsetting the balance in the family if they succeed too well?

Yet another way in which an assessment needs to be integrative is in terms of the need to obtain reports on children's behavior from a number of different perspectives. As we discussed in Chapter 3, multiple sources of information may help us obtain a more accurate picture of the child, "triangulating" perspectives much the way a surveyor does (Cowan, 1978). Teachers have unique knowledge of the child's classroom behavior, while parents have a long-span view of their child that is invaluable. And only children have access to their own innermost thoughts and feelings. Therefore, each perspective may have something to contribute. Parents and teachers might be particularly good informants in regard to observable behavior, such as hyperactivity and conduct problems, while children's reports may be more informative about subjective symptoms such as anxiety and depression (Cantwell, 1996).

Lastly, because our goal is to understand the child as a whole person, we must identify not only deficits, but also strengths and *competencies* that can be used to help the child overcome any areas of disadvantage. Therefore a comprehensive assessment of many different aspects of functioning is required.

The *developmental dimension* plays an important role in child assessment. First, there are the challenges to developing rapport and communicating clearly with children of different ages, which we will discuss below. Further, standardized tests incorporate development into the assessment technique itself. Such tests define the age of the population for which they are used, such as tests of infant cognition or high school achievement. Only age-appropriate items are included, and items progress in difficulty according to age. Consequently, the clinician can compare the developmental status of a given child with the norms established on a population of children his or her age. Even nonstandardized tests, such as projective techniques, are scored in terms of normative information about what is appropriate for children at different ages. In sum, results of any assessment measure always carry the implicit proviso, "for a child at this developmental level."

The Assessment Process

Assessment is like a hypothesis-testing enterprise. In attempting to assimilate, integrate, and interpret the massive amount of data they collect, clinicians implicitly proceed just like other scientists do (Johnson & Goldman, 1990). No single bit of behavior is definitive, but each is suggestive. As these bits accumulate, certain initial hunches are confirmed and others discarded. By the end of the assessment process, the clinician can make some statements concerning the child's problem with a reasonable degree of assurance; other statements will be tentative and qualified, and a number of questions will remain unanswered.

Clinicians never assume that within the space of a few hours they will be able to fully apprehend the nature and origin of the problems that bring a particular child to their attention. They realize they are viewing parent and child under special circumstances that both limit and bias the data they will obtain. The child who is frightened by a clinic waiting room may not be a generally fearful child, just as one who is hyperactive in school may be a model of cooperation when taking an intelligence test. Parents may have their own misperceptions and blind spots in regard to their child's behavior, along with varying degrees of willingness to reveal information about themselves. Standardized tests also have limitations in terms of reliability, validity, or appropriateness for different populations. Thus, as much as clinicians strive toward achieving an understanding of the child and family, they also must be duly mindful about the limitations of the assessment techniques they use (American Psychological Association, 1992).

Purposes of Assessment

The end product of assessment is the **case formulation**, a succinct description of the child that incorporates the clinician's interpretation of how the problem came about and how it might be remediated (Shirk & Russell, 1996). The case formulation helps to synthesize all of the information the clinician obtained and to put it into a form that will be useful to those who requested the assessment. An effective assessment report on a child helps its reader to understand the child and generates ideas about how to intervene effectively (Wertlieb, 1989). While the case formulation helps the clinician to find a path through the forest of information col-

lected during the assessment, it should not be a rigid one. Like all hypotheses, the case formulation is open to new information and can be revised in the face of disconfirming data.

Initial Sources of Data

Referrals

The first data concerning the child come from the *referring person*—teacher, parent, physician, and so on—who can provide information about the problem as perceived by concerned adults, its duration and onset, its effects on the child and on others, and what measures, if any, have been taken to remedy it. *Parents* and *teachers* are the major sources of referrals.

In contrast to adults, children rarely refer themselves to treatment, a fact that has important psychological implications. Seeking help is very different than being told one needs help. Children may not feel the need to change and may not understand why they are being brought for an evaluation. Sometimes parents give children reasons the children disagree with, or even fail to tell them why they are being brought to the clinic. Therefore, during the first telephone contact, it can be helpful to discuss with parents how they might introduce the topic of the assessment with their children.

> You are a clinical child psychologist who has been asked to assess Kenny, an 8-year-old boy. His teacher suggested an evaluation because of academic and behavioral problems in the classroom. Specifically, his mother tells you that Kenny is failing reading and arithmetic and that his teacher describes him as "lazy," withdrawn, and uncooperative in class. The first questions in the back of your mind concern the reasons for this referral, and the constructions being placed on this problem by the mother, the teacher, and Kenny himself. Is this a learning problem, a conduct problem, or the consequence of a negative interaction between this family and the school? Are the teacher and the parents going to be supportive of Kenny during the assessment process, or have they taken a blaming attitude that will complicate your work? Is Kenny willing to come to the clinic, or will he be angry and oppositional with you? As your consultants, we'll follow the evaluation of Kenny throughout this chapter in order to see how an assessment like this might play out.

Parent Interviews

Information concerning the child and the family usually comes first from an interview with the parents (Wachtel, 1994). Typically, the interview begins with an account of the presenting problem. Next, a detailed *developmental history* is obtained in order to explore the antecedent conditions that might have contributed to the child's present difficulties. Among the topics covered are the child's prenatal and birth history and early development. The subsequent adjustment of the child within the family and with peers is explored, along with social and academic adjustment. For teenagers, information is obtained concerning sexual development and work history, as well as possible drug and alcohol use and delinquent behavior. The clinician also inquires about major illnesses and injuries and stresses experienced by the child and family. To complete the picture, the parents may be asked about their own individual, marital, and occupational adjustment; their specific goals, satisfactions, and dissatisfactions; and the attempts they have made to deal with the problem in the past.

What about the studies showing the *unreliability* of retrospective reports? While parents may not always report accurate information concerning many aspects of the child and family, it is still important for the clinician to know the parents' perception of the facts. Whether the child was a "difficult" infant and a "bad" toddler may not be as important as the parents' perception or memory of the child as difficult and bad.

In the process of interviewing, the clinician is beginning to know the parents, while the parents are also beginning to know the clinician. Since there is no hard and fast line between assessment and therapy, skilled interviewers can use this initial contact to lay the groundwork for the trust and respect that will be so crucial in future. The establishment of *rapport* between the parent and the clinician is an important part of the process. Parents may feel shamed about bringing their child for an assessment and may have concerns either that their parenting is at fault or that the clinician will blame them for causing the problem. Thus, the interviewer wants to take care to put parents at ease, support them for their obvious concern for their children, and establish that the parents and the assessor are "rowing on the same team."

In addition, the parent interview provides the clinician the opportunity to gather information about the present family system of relationships, as well as the possible role that the parents' own family histories might play in their difficulties with their child. To accomplish this, McGoldrick and Gerson (1985) suggest asking parents to complete a family *genogram* as part of the assessment. The genogram is a pictorial representation of the relationships among the people in a family, usually spanning three generations to include the child, parents, and grandparents. First, demographic information is recorded, such as birth and death dates, places of origin, and career paths. Second, critical events are indicated, such as divorces, moves, or traumatic experiences. Third, interaction patterns are represented by special lines connecting various family members. For example, lines can indicate relationships that are close, enmeshed, distant, conflictual, or cut off. (See Figure 16.1.) The genogram can help the clinician to identify coalitions and triangles in the family, as well as intergenerational patterns of conflict, estrangement, role-reversal, and so forth that interfere with parents' ability to respond appropriately to their children's developmental needs. (See McGoldrick and Gerson, 1985, for a number of intriguing examples.)

Kenny's mother, Marta, is 20 minutes late for her first meeting with you, arriving flustered and disheveled. She explains that, as a single parent, she found it difficult to manage the complications of getting off work early and arranging day care for her youngest son, Langston. She divorced the boys' father, Kyle, two years ago, and they have rarely heard from him since. "Everything was fine with Kenny up until then," she says. "Sometimes I wonder if we should've stayed together for the boys. But Kyle is no good—nothing but a drunken brute. Kenny is nothing like him, thank goodness. He's a terrific kid—my little man." In contrast, she seems to have little to say about little Langston. He is described as a "handful," and she states she is glad to have Kenny's help with managing her younger son's behavior.

Marta's description of Kenny's early history includes nothing remarkable. She reports no major illnesses or deviations from expected development until the time of the divorce, which, you note, also

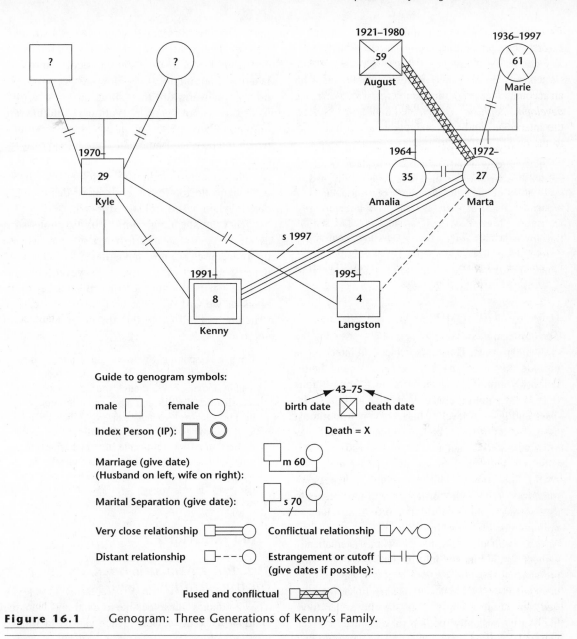

Figure 16.1   Genogram: Three Generations of Kenny's Family.

occurred the year that Kenny entered first grade. She doesn't believe that there is anything "wrong" with Kenny; she suspects that the teacher "just can't relate to him for some reason." She acknowledges that she and the teacher are not on particularly good terms. She explains that she herself had a lot of difficulty in school, and, with some humor, states that she looks back on her teachers as "torturers."

Marta is uncomfortable at first with the idea of completing a family genogram, commenting that she doesn't understand "what this has to do with anything." However, as your rapport improves, she agrees. What emerges is a history of broken relationships across the generations. (See Figure 16.1.) Kenny's father cut off contact with his own parents, and little is known about them. Marta also has nothing to do with her own family of origin. Her father, August, was a violent but charming man who died of cirrhosis of the liver when she was about Kenny's age. She was his "favorite" when drink made him affectionate, and the special target of his abuse when he was "mean drunk." She says, "I adored him and hated him in equal amounts." Following the father's death, Marta's mother abandoned the children, leaving Marta in the care of her older sister, Amalia. The two sisters, always rivals for the little affection there was in the family, had a falling-out about the disposition of their mother's will a couple of years ago and have not spoken since. When asked about current sources of support in her life, Marta pauses, and then confides that she attends AA meetings. This is your first intimation that, like her father and Kenny's father, she has a problem with alcohol.

Informal Observations

The clinician's assessment begins on first seeing the child and parents. Their appearance and interactions provide clues as to *family characteristics* and the relationships among its members. First impressions furnish information concerning the family's social class and general level of harmony or disharmony, as well as its stylistic characteristics—reserved, expressive, authoritarian, intellectual, and so on. As always, the clinical child psychologist evaluates behavior in terms of its age appropriateness or inappropriateness, the former providing clues as to assets and resources, the latter providing clues to possible disturbances.

Once with the child, the clinician systematically gathers certain kinds of information. The overall impression of the child's *personality* is always important: "an all-American boy"; "he already has the worried look of an old man"; "she has that sullen look, like she is constantly spoiling for a fight"; "a direct, honest, no-nonsense pre-adolescent girl, who doesn't want to be coddled." While it is important not to prejudge children on the basis of initial impressions, these first reactions might give the clinician clues as to the child's social-stimulus value, which may be a potent elicitor of positive or negative reactions from others.

The child's *manner of relating* to the clinician furnishes information concerning his or her perception of adults. It is natural for children to be

reserved initially, since the clinician is a stranger. As they discover that the clinician is an interested and friendly adult, they should become more relaxed and communicative. However, certain children never warm up; they sit as far back in their chair as possible, speak in an almost inaudible monotone, either rarely look at the examiner or else watch intently, as if he or she were a kind of monster who might strike out at any minute. Provocative children "test the limits," mischievously peeking when told to close their eyes or destroying a puzzle when asked to leave it intact.

Generally speaking, clinical observations such as these are nearer an art than a science because the procedures are not standardized and the target behaviors are so wide-ranging. However, observation per se is not unscientific. Behavioral clinicians, as we will see later, bring to assessment the structure and reliability that the more open-ended approach lacks.

> Upon first spotting Kenny in the waiting room, your impression is that he is a handsome and healthy-looking boy, although you are struck by the fact that he is neater and more carefully groomed than is usual for a youngster his age. When you enter the room he is disciplining his little brother, cautioning him not to handle the magazines too roughly. He greets you brightly but checks back with his mother before he goes with you, asking her if she will be "okay."

Child Interviews

Structured, Semistructured, and Unstructured Interviews

The clinician wants to be able to see things from the child's-eye point of view, which can be facilitated by conducting an interview. Interviews confer a number of advantages, such as giving children a chance to present their *own perspective* on the problem, allowing the interviewer to assess areas of functioning that might not be accessible through other means, enabling the interviewer to *observe* children's behavior and attitudes relevant to the problem, and providing an opportunity to establish the *rapport* that will be necessary if a therapeutic relationship is to develop (McConaughy & Achenbach, 1994). In addition, the interview gives the clinician the opportunity to clarify with children why they are there and to explain what the assessment process will be like.

Interviews can be conceptualized along a continuum based on how structured they are. In *unstructured interviews*, clinicians encourage children to put in their own words their views about the problem; the family, school, and peers; interests, hopes, and fears; self-concept; and, for adolescents, career aspirations, sexual relations, and drug or alcohol use.

In contrast to unstructured interviews, which allow the interviewer considerable leeway for improvising and following up unexpected leads, *semistructured interviews* consist of a series of open-ended questions followed by specific probes to help the interviewer determine the presence or absence of diagnostic symptoms. An example is the Semistructured Clinical Interview for Children and Adolescents (SCICA; McConaughy & Achenbach, 1994), which was developed for children ages 6 through 18. A series of open-ended questions is interspersed with nonverbal tasks, such as drawings and play activities, designed to set children at ease and to encourage them to reveal their thoughts, feelings, and behavior through their interaction with the examiner. The interviewer uses both child self-reports and his or her own observations of the child in order to rate psychopathology.

Structured interviews also consist of a series of specific questions or statements, but the child's response is structured as well, whether as a "yes-no" choice or as a point on a scale ranging from "strongly agree" to "disagree." Structured interviews devised for children include the Diagnostic Interview for Children and Adolescents (DICA-IV; Reich, Welner, & Herjanic, 1997); the Schedule for Affective Disorders and Schizophrenia for School-Age Children (K-SADS; Puig-Antich & Chambers, 1978), and the Diagnostic Interview Schedule for Children (DISC-2; Fisher et al., 1991). Each of these interviews has both a child and parent version, and all generate DSM diagnoses for most disorders seen in childhood. (See Hodges, 1993, and Kamphaus and Frick, 1996, for reviews). Figure 16.2 presents excerpts

from the K-SADS and DISC illustrating the questions used to elicit information about impulsive/inattentive behavior.

Rapport

In order for any assessment technique to be of use, the child must at least be minimally cooperative; ideally, the child should participate wholeheartedly. Therefore, essential to the assessment process is good *rapport*. The establishment of rapport requires clinical skills, sensitivity, and experience. Moreover, the clinician must be prepared to deal with a variety of obstacles at different ages—a crying infant; a toddler fearful of leaving the mother; a provocative, defiant school-age child; a sullen teenager who resents all questioning by adults. But aside from such dramatic challenges, there is always the question of how one goes about establishing oneself as an interested, friendly adult to children of different ages. For example, while a preschool child might be set at ease by meeting the clinician in a playroom and using puppets or drawings to express thoughts and feelings, an adolescent might feel insulted by being interviewed in such a setting. In addition, older youths may warm more readily to an examiner who is candid and direct, treating them as competent young persons whose active participation in the assessment process is invited.

Barker (1990) makes a number of helpful suggestions for enhancing rapport with children. He recommends that the interviewer adopt a *warm, interested*, and *respectful* attitude that engages the child, without being overly formal. He also suggests that the interviewer attempt to match the *pace* and *interpersonal style* of the child. A shy and reticent child may be more comfortable with an examiner who talks softly and slowly, while a rough-and-tumble or streetwise child may respond best to a lively and fast-paced interviewing style. Children can also be set at ease by some side conversations that establish common ground or mutual interests between themselves and the examiner, even if it is only to discuss the child's "cool" T-shirt or to satisfy the child's curiosity about how the tape recorder works. In addition, Barker suggests that interviewers be willing to adopt a *"one-down"* position with children, allowing them to play the experts with their special knowledge

K-SADS

Impulsivity: Refers to the child's characteristic pattern of acting before thinking about the consequences. It does not refer to "bad" actions only but to a behavioral characteristic spanning all types of behavior independent of moral significance.

Are you the kind of person who tends to get into trouble, or maybe even get hurt, because you rush into things without thinking what might happen?	0 No information 1 Not present 2 Slight: May occur on occasion when excited (party, etc.) but not typical and no bad consequences.
Are you often wrong in school because you answer with the first thing that comes to your mind instead of thinking it over first?	3 Mild: Definitely present. Acts impulsively at least 3 times a week in at least 2 settings.
Do you get into trouble in school because you often speak out when you're supposed to be quiet?	4 Moderate: Impulsive in all settings. 5 Severe: Impulsive in all settings and has gotten into dangerous situations for lack of foresight in a few
Does your teacher often have to tell you what you are supposed to do after the rest of the class has started doing it?	instances (more than 3 times in a year). 6 Extreme: Very impulsive; it is an almost constant characteristic of child's behavior. Gets into danger at
Do you have trouble organizing your work?	least once a week.
Do you often do things on a dare or just because the idea popped into your head or just for the heck of it?	

DISC

Impulsivity	No	Sometimes	Yes
Does your teacher often tell you that you don't listen?	0		2
(if yes) Does he/she say that to you more than to most kids?	0	1	2
(if yes) How long has that been happening?	Months:		
(if yes) Have you been like that since you started school?	0		2
Does your teacher often tell you that you're not keeping your mind on your work?	0		2
(if yes) Does he/she say that to you more than to most kids?	0		2
(if yes) How long has that been happening?	Months:		
(if yes) Have you been like that since you started school?	0		2
Sometimes kids rush into things without thinking about what may happen. Do you do that?	0	1	2
(if yes) Have you always been like that?	0		2
(if yes) How long have you been like that?	Months:		
Some kids have trouble organizing their schoolwork. They can't decide what they need. They can't plan what to do first, what to do second. Are you like that?	0	1	2
(if yes) How long have you been like that?	Months:		
Do you start your schoolwork and not finish it?	0	1	2
(if yes) How long has that been happening?	Months:		
(if yes) Have you always had trouble finishing it?	0		2
(if yes) Is that because you don't know how to do it?	0	1	2

Figure 16.2   Examples of Questions Used in Structured and Semi-Structured Interviews.

Source: K-SADS (Puig-Antich & Chambers, 1978); DISC (Costello et al., 1984).

regarding the latest video games, television shows, or music. (For further reading, see Garbarino et al., 1992, and Kanfer, Eyberg, and Krahn, 1992.)

Developmental Considerations

For any interview to be valid, it must be tailored to the child's level of understanding. At the very least, it is important for the interviewer to match the vocabulary level of the child in order to be understood and to help the interview go smoothly (Barker, 1990). However, the child's developmental level will affect many other aspects of the interview process.

During the *preschool* years, children's self-understanding is expressed primarily in terms of *physical characteristics* and *actions* ("I have brown hair," "I play ball," "I have a dog"). (Here we follow Harter, 1988; Steward et al., 1993; Stone and Lemanek, 1990.) Consequently, questions about the nature of the problem that brought them to see a psychologist are apt to elicit responses couched

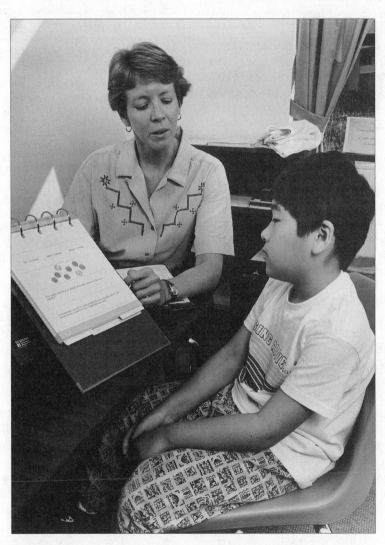

The importance of good rapport in assessment: Will this child give his best performance?

in terms of specific behaviors ("I hit my brother") rather than internal experiences. These, in turn, probably echo what parents or other adults have said to them about being "bad." Recall that young children are never self-referred and often do not see themselves as having problems. In a like manner, children's view of the cause of the problem is apt to be specific and external ("I hit my brother because he takes my things").

Preschoolers' evaluations of their own emotions and those of other people are also *concrete* and *situational*; for example, being happy is having a birthday party. Consequently, interview questions must be similarly concrete and action-oriented ("Do you cry?" rather than "Do you feel sad?"). The interviewer should also expect people to be described in terms of what they do rather than what they think or how they feel.

In middle childhood, children are able to express ideas about the self-concept that are "psychological" and more differentiated; for example, instead of being judged "smart" or "dumb," the child can be "smart" in some things and "dumb" in others. In this period children are able to provide accurate reports of their own emotions by using *internal*, *psychological* cues. They also begin to attribute psychological characteristics to others and realize other people have perspectives different from their own. Along with these cognitive advances goes the ability to recognize deviance. However, even in early adolescence there is still the tendency to attribute cause to external, typically social, events, such as family quarrels and conflicts.

Cognitive development determines how the child will understand the helping relationship, including the concept of the psychologist as helper as well as the concept of being helped. The *preschooler* is apt to view the former in terms of general traits, such as being "kind" or "nice," along with the psychologist's specific behaviors, such as "playing games." In *middle childhood* references to competence begin to appear, such as "She knows what she is doing," while the early *adolescent* recognizes the role of inner qualities of empathy and a desire to help. Being helped itself changes from denoting some form of direct action in the preschool period (for example, "Buy me a new game to play and tell my brother to quit picking on me") to a recognition of the importance of support, validation, regard, and other kinds of indirect help in early adolescence.

Because Kenny is in middle childhood, you decide to equip the interview room with colored pens and paper, clay, checkers, and a few other games that might help to set him at ease. Your first observation is that Kenny ignores all of the toys and attends carefully to you, eager to answer all your questions. While most children are cautious initially, and rightly so, from the beginning of the interview Kenny is unusually open and communicative. As the interview progresses, he continues to impress you as a bright, alert, open youngster. You mentally note Kenny's behavior and wonder what it might represent. Perhaps this is a basically well-functioning boy whose problems have been exaggerated; perhaps he has been too close to adults at the cost of developing appropriate peer relationships; perhaps he is a charming psychopath; perhaps his social skills are a defense against some unknown fear.

Kenny offers his own perspective on the problem. "I don't like school," he says, and when asked what he doesn't like about it, replies with a downcast face, "Schoolwork is boring. And the other kids are jerks. I don't like any of them." He spends most of his time after school helping his mother around the house and taking care of his little brother. "I like to help out," he says. He states that if he could have three wishes they would be "to stay home instead of going to school," "to buy a big house for us to live in," and "to have a billion dollars so that my mom wouldn't have to go to work anymore."

Psychological Tests

Of all professionals dealing with disturbed children, clinical psychologists have been the most concerned with developing assessment techniques that can be objectively administered and scored, that have norms based on clearly defined populations, and that have established reliability and validity. While many different tests have been developed, our coverage here will focus only on a few of the more widely used tests. (For more extensive and detailed reviews of a variety of psychological tests for children, refer to Sattler, 1992.)

Cognitive Testing from Infancy to Adolescence

Infant Cognitive Testing

Infant testing requires that the examiner have special skills in *accommodation* so as to elicit the child's optimal performance. The examiner must know how to intrigue the infant with the test material, allow for distractions, temporarily become a comforting caretaker in response to fretting, postpone testing when distress becomes too great—in short, the good examiner must have the sensitivity, flexibility, and warmth of a good parent.

One of the best constructed standardized infant tests is the *Bayley Scales of Infant Development—Second Edition* (Bayley, 1993), which evaluates cognitive, language, motor, and social functioning of children 1 to 42 months of age. The Mental Scale evaluates the infant's perceptual acuity, object constancy, memory, learning, problem solving, and verbal communication and yields a normalized standard score, the Mental Development Index. The Motor Scale evaluates fine and gross motor coordination and body control and also yields a standard score, the Psychomotor Development Index. The Behavior Rating Scale assesses the infant's attention and arousal, social engagement with others, and emotional regulation.

The Bayley can help to identify areas of development in which there are delays or impairments and can be used to design interventions to address those problems. However, while scores on the Bayley are associated with children's current developmental status, unless the scores are extremely low they are not strong predictors of future intelligence (Nellis & Gridley, 1994). Therefore, unless there are concerns that emerge very early in a child's life, such as the possibility of mental retardation, autism, or developmental disability, it is more common for cognitive testing to occur in the preschool or school-age years. (For a more detailed presentation of infant assessment, see Wyly, 1997.)

The Wechsler Scales

The *Wechsler Intelligence Scale for Children* (WISC-III; Wechsler, 1991) is the most widely used intelligence test for children aged 6 through 16. The Wechsler Preschool and Primary Scale of Intelligence—Revised (Wechsler, 1989) is used for children aged 3 to 7.

The WISC-III consists of thirteen subtests, the items in each being arranged according to increasing difficulty. (See Figure 16.3.) The *Verbal Scale*, which requires facility in using verbal symbols, consists of five basic subtests (Information, Similarities, Arithmetic, Vocabulary, and Comprehension) and one supplementary test (Digit Span). The *Performance Scale*, which involves concrete material such as pictures, blocks, and jigsaw puzzles, also consists of five basic subtests (Picture Completion, Coding, Picture Arrangement, Block Design, and Object Assembly) and two supplementary subtests (Symbol Search and Mazes). Note that the terms "verbal" and "performance" refer to the form in which the task is presented, not the level of thinking required; certain performance subtests require higher-level thinking than certain verbal subtests. Scoring yields a *Verbal IQ* and *Performance IQ*, as well as a *Full-Scale IQ*. Each scale has a mean score of 100 and a standard deviation of 15. For example, a child with a total score of 115 will be one standard deviation above the mean or in approximately the 84th percentile.

While the IQ score is important, it is only one of many pieces of information gained from an intelligence test. The *discrepancy* between the Verbal and Performance IQs on the WISC-III furnishes clues as to the child's differential ability to handle the two kinds of tasks: the child who has a Full-Scale IQ of 100, a Verbal IQ of 130, and a Performance IQ of 70 is quite different from a child with the same overall IQ but with a Verbal IQ of 70 and a Performance IQ of 130. The second child may be particularly penalized in school, where the manipulation of verbal symbols becomes increasingly important, while being quite talented on tasks that require minimal verbal facility.

Analysis of successes and failures on individual items may provide further clues to intellectual strengths and weaknesses. A child may do well on problems involving rote learning and the accumulation of facts but do poorly on ones requiring reasoning and judgment. As another example, an otherwise bright child may be weak in visual-motor coordination, which might make learning to write difficult (Sattler, 1992).

Information (30 questions)

How many legs do you have?
What must you do to make water freeze?
Who discovered the North Pole?
What is the capital of France?

Similarities (17 questions)

In what way are pencil and crayon alike?
In what way are coffee and tea alike?
In what way are inch and mile alike?
In what way are binoculars and microscope alike?

Arithmetic (18 questions)

If I have one piece of candy and get another one, how
    many pieces will I have?
At 12 cents each, how much will 4 bars of soap cost?
If a suit sells for 1/2 the ticket price, what is the cost
    of a $120 suit?

Vocabulary (32 words)

What does _____ mean?
ball   poem
summer   obstreperous

Comprehension (17 questions)

Why do we wear shoes?
What is the thing to do if you see someone dropping his
    packages?
In what ways is a lamp better than a candle?
Why are we tried by a jury of our peers?

Digit Span

Digits Forward contains seven series of digits, 3 to 9
    digits in length (Example: 1-8-9).
Digits Backward contains seven series of digits, 2 to 8
    digits in length (Example: 5-8-1-9).

Picture Completion (26 items)

The task is to identify the essential missing part of the
    picture.
A picture of a car without a wheel.
A picture of a dog without a leg.
A picture of a telephone without numbers on the dial.
An example of a Picture Completion task is shown below.

Courtesy of The Psychological Corporation.

Picture Arrangement (12 items)

The task is to arrange a series of pictures into a
meaningful sequence.

Block Design (11 items)

The task is to reproduce stimulus designs using four or
nine blocks. An example of a Block Design item is shown
below.

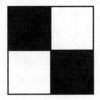

Object Assembly (4 items)

The task is to arrange pieces into a meaningful object.
An example of an Object Assembly item is shown below.

Courtesy of The Psychological Corporation.

Coding

The task is to copy symbols from a key (see below).

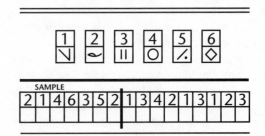

Courtesy of The Psychological Corporation.

Mazes

The task is to complete a series of mazes.

Note. The questions resemble those that appear on the
WISC-III but are not actually from the test.

Figure 16.3   WISC-III-Like Items.

Stanford-Binet: FE

The *Stanford-Binet Fourth Edition* (SB: FE) (Thorndike, Hagen, & Sattler, 1986) covers the age span of 2 to 23 years. It consists of fifteen tests, organized into four broad areas of cognitive abilities. In the *Verbal Reasoning* category are tests of vocabulary and comprehension (e.g., questions such as "What does envelope mean?" and "Why are there traffic signs?"). *Quantitative Reasoning* includes tests of quantitative ability (e.g., counting and knowledge of fractions) and number series (e.g., figuring out which numbers come next in a series of numbers that increases by 4). *Abstract/Visual Reasoning* includes tests of copying figures (e.g., copying a diamond or two intersecting circles) and pattern analysis (e.g., putting blocks together to make a pattern depicted on a card). *Short-Term Memory* tests include remembering a series of digits and remembering sentences. At a higher level of abstraction, Verbal Reasoning and Quantitative Reasoning are regarded as *crystallized abilities,* which are greatly influenced by schooling. Abstract/Visual Reasoning is regarded as a *fluid-analytic ability*, which requires the invention of new cognitive strategies and is more dependent on general experiences than on what is learned in school.

The items in each test are arranged according to difficulty; thus, the more items children successfully complete, the higher their abilities are when compared with children their own age. However, instead of an IQ, the results are expressed in terms of *Standard Age Scores* (SASs). For the total scale, the mean score is 100 and the standard deviation is 16. Since the same formula is used for IQs, the SASs and the IQ scores are comparable.

Observations During Cognitive Testing

The purpose of cognitive testing is not simply to derive an IQ score. The testing situation can also provide important clues as to the child's *style of thinking*. Note the responses of two equally bright 8-year-olds to the question, "What should you do when you lose a ball that belongs to someone else?" One child answered, "I'd get him another one." The other said, "I'd pay money for it. I'd look for it. I'd give him another ball. I'd try to find it, but if I couldn't, I'd give him money for it because I might not have the kind of ball he wants." Both answers receive the same high score, but one is clear, simple, and to the point, while the other is needlessly cluttered.

Styles of thinking are closely related to psychological health or *disturbance*. Intelligence is not some kind of disembodied skill existing apart from the rest of the child's personality. On the contrary, a psychologically well-functioning child tends to think clearly, a child with poor self-control tends to think impulsively, and an obsessive child (like the one just quoted) tends to think in terms of so many possible alternatives that it becomes difficult to decide on one and act on it. A schizophrenic child tends to think bizarrely, as is revealed in this rambling, fantasy-saturated answer to the simple question, "Why should one tell the truth?"

> If you don't tell the truth you get into trouble; you go to court; like teenagers who don't tell the truth; they're usually armed, guys who run around the forest and woods, the woods near the house. We go there to catch frogs, and we always have to have older people go with us because of the teenagers with guns and knives. A child drowned there not long ago. If you don't tell the truth they start a gang and drown you.

The intelligence test also allows the clinician to evaluate the child's *work habits*. Some children are task-oriented and self-motivated; they need almost no encouragement or help from the examiner. Others are uncertain and insecure, giving up readily unless encouraged or prodded, constantly seeking reassurance that they are doing well, or asking to know whether their response was right or wrong.

Finally, the tests yield information concerning the child's capacity for *self-monitoring*, which is the ability to evaluate the quality of the responses. Some children seem to be implicitly asking, "Is that really correct?" or "Is that the best I can do?" while others seem to have little ability to judge when they are right or wrong, an incorrect response being given with the same air of uncritical assurance as a correct one.

Strengths and Limitations of Cognitive Testing

Intelligence tests can play a useful role in child assessment. The IQ score itself is related to many aspects of the child's life—success in school, vocational choice, peer relations—and IQ is a better predictor of future adjustment than any score on a personality test. In addition, the test provides data concerning general areas of strength and weakness; the kind and degree of impairment of specific intellectual functions, such as immediate recall or abstract reasoning; the child's coping techniques, work habits, and motivation; stylistic characteristics of thinking that may well be related to personality variables; and the presence of distorted thinking that might indicate either organic brain pathology or psychosis (Sattler, 1992).

Yet care must be taken that an intelligence test is used *appropriately* and that results are properly understood. As IQ became a household term, so did the misconception that the score represents an unalterable intellectual potential existing independent of background and experience. In particular, concerns have been expressed that these tests might do more harm than good by underestimating the abilities of children from cultural groups other than the mainstream (see Bender et al., 1995, and Kaminer and Vig, 1995, for both sides of the issue).

These issues were influential in the abandonment of the term "IQ" in the most recent revision of the Stanford-Binet. In addition, the ethical guidelines of the American Psychological Association (1992) require that clinicians develop *cultural competence* and demonstrate the ability to interpret test data in the light of the unique cultural and environmental factors that affect the child (see also Dana, 1996).

> In contrast to his friendly and open manner during the interview, Kenny's behavior changes markedly during the intelligence test. His brow is furrowed, and he responds to the tasks as though they are stressful and even irritating to him. In addition, he tends to make self-derogatory remarks at the beginning of each new task. He says "I don't know" too readily when items become difficult, and he quickly destroys a puzzle he had put together incorrectly, as if trying to cover up his mistake. At times he seems to use his conversational skills to divert attention away from the test material. He is willing to try the first arithmetic problems, which are easy for him and allow him to be certain about the right answer. As they get more difficult, however, he refuses to even try. He states that he "hates" this test. When encouraged to respond to difficult items, it is clear that he does not know the correct answer.

The test scores add a significant bit of data: while he has high expectations for himself, Kenny has only average intelligence. You begin speculating, "If his sociability misled me into thinking he was intellectually bright, his mother and teachers might have also been misled into setting unrealistically high goals and pressuring him to achieve them." This hypothesis naturally would have to be checked by interviewing the parents and teacher. Clearly there is more to be learned about Kenny's abilities to achieve in school and how they mesh with expectations that others have of him and that he has for himself.

Tests of Achievement and Neurological Problems

Achievement Tests

An assessment of academic achievement is important in deciding whether a child has a learning disability and in evaluating the effectiveness of a remedial program. Low academic achievement may also contribute to the development of a behavior problem. As with intelligence tests, individually administered *achievement tests* allow the clinician to make behavioral observations of the child and to analyze the nature of the child's failures. These data may provide helpful clues as to motivational and academic problems; for example, a boy who gives up without trying is different from one who fails after trying his best, just as a girl who fails multiplication problems because of careless mistakes is different from another who fails because she has not grasped the basic process of multiplying. A comprehensive battery is provided by the *Woodcock-Johnson Psycho-Educational Battery—Revised* (WJ-R; Woodcock et al., 1989). The tests cover ten areas, including the child's mastery of grade-level reading, math, written language, and knowledge of social studies, science, and the humanities.

Neuropsychological Assessment

A neuropsychological assessment usually begins with tests of intelligence and achievement. These tests not only provide information as to the children's intellectual level and academic progress but, more important, they also provide clues as to what psychological functions might be affected by organic brain damage. As we have seen, the manifestations of brain damage may range from a slight deficit in sensorimotor abilities to a pervasive disruption of every aspect of a child's intellectual and personality functioning. It follows that there can be no single diagnostic test for organicity.

If brain damage potentially affects a variety of functions, then a battery of tests casting a wide psychological net would seem to provide a reasonable strategy for capturing the elusive diagnosis. Two of the most widely used are the *Reitan-Indiana Neuropsychological Test Battery* (1969) for children 5 to 8 years of age and the *Halstead Neuropsychological Test Battery for Children* (1969), which is applicable to children 9 to 14 years of age.

The diversity of the tests may be seen in the following sampling. In the Tactual Performance Test, the blindfolded child is required to fit variously shaped blocks into a form board with the preferred hand, the nonpreferred hand, and then both hands; then, with blindfold, blocks, and form board removed, the child is to draw a diagram of the board. This test evaluates memory and spatial location, both of which may be adversely affected by organicity. In Trailmaking B, the child is given a piece of paper on which twenty-five circles are scattered about; the circles are randomly numbered from 1 to 13 and randomly lettered from A through L. The child's task is to connect alternate numbers and letters, that is, to go from A to 1 to B to 2 and so on. The score is the time taken, and the child is penalized for errors. Among other things, Trailmaking B is a test of flexibility of thinking, a facility that may be impaired in certain kinds of organic brain damage.

Currently, specialized techniques are being developed on the basis of research concerning the effects of various kinds of brain damage on children of different ages. These techniques have two advantages. First, they are tailored to children of different ages rather than representing downward extensions of adult techniques. Next, they are specific to the various kinds of brain damage, such as seizures or head injuries. (For a general discussion of neuropsychological assessment, see Reynolds and Fletcher-Janzen, 1997).

In order to assess the possibility that Kenny has learning problems, you administer the WJ-R. Kenny's scores indicate that his achievement in most areas is about average, while his mathematics skills are far below what is expected of children at his age. Apparently, therefore, there are reasons for Kenny to report that he "hates" math. However, you note that his reading skills are at age level, and therefore the explanation for his failing reading grades does not seem to lie in the direction of a learning disorder. Taken together with the IQ tests results, these data also raise further questions, such as the effects of being regarded as "lazy" on the boy's self-image. There is more to learn about Kenny the person, and the ways his learning problems are affecting him emotionally.

Socioemotional Assessment

Parent and Teacher Report Scales

One of the most widely used adult-report inventories is the *Child Behavior Checklist* (CBCL; Achenbach, 1991), which was described in Chapter 3. There are different forms for parents (CBCL) and teachers (Teacher Report Form), and norms are provided for children from 4 to 16 years of age. Figure 16.4 presents a segment of the parent-report version of the CBCL. (A detailed presentation can be found in Achenbach & McConaughy, 1997.)

An alternative rating scale, which uses the same form for either teacher's or parent's reports, is the *Devereux Scales of Mental Disorders* (Naglieri, LeBuffe, & Pfeiffer, 1994). There are two versions, one for children ages 5 to 12 and one for ages 13 to 18; each version has 110 items. Three composite scales are derived: *Internalizing* (anxiety, depression), *Externalizing* (conduct problems, delinquency, attention problems), and *Critical Pathology* (autistic features such as self-harming, substance abuse, fire setting, hallucinations).

The *Personality Inventory for Children—Revised* (PIC-R; Wirt et al., 1990), designed for children ages 3 through 16, requires the parent to rate the presence or absence of 420 characteristics (shorter forms are also available, which include fewer items). Scales include depression and poor self-concept; worry and anxiety; reality distortion; peer

Below is a list of items that describe children. For each item that describes your child now or within the past 6 months, please circle the 2 if the item is very true or often true of your child. Circle the 1 if the item is somewhat or sometimes true of your child. If the item is not true of your child, circle the 0. Please answer all items as well as you can, even if some do not seem to apply to your child.

0 = Not True (as far as you know)   1 = Somewhat or Sometimes True   2 = Very True or Often True

0 1 2 1. Acts too young for his/her age	0 1 2 10. Can't sit still, restless, or hyperactive
0 1 2 2. Allergy (describe): _____	
_____	0 1 2 11. Clings to adults or too dependent
	0 1 2 12. Complains of loneliness
0 1 2 3. Argues a lot	
0 1 2 4. Asthma	0 1 2 13. Confused or seems to be in a fog
	0 1 2 14. Cries a lot
0 1 2 5. Behaves like opposite sex	
0 1 2 6. Bowel movements outside toilet	0 1 2 15. Cruel to animals
	0 1 2 16. Cruelty, bullying, or meanness to others
0 1 2 7. Bragging, boasting	
0 1 2 8. Can't concentrate, can't pay attention	0 1 2 17. Daydreams or gets lost in his/her thought
for long	0 1 2 18. Deliberately harms self or attempts suicide
0 1 2 9. Can't get his/her mind off certain	0 1 2 19. Demands a lot of attention
thoughts; obsessions (describe): _____	0 1 2 20. Destroys his/her own things
_____	

Figure 16.4   Excerpt from Parent Version of the Child Behavior Checklist.

relations; unsocialized aggression; conscience development; poor judgment; atypical development; distractibility, activity level, and coordination; speech and language; somatic complaints; school adjustment; and family discord. Factor analysis was used to derive four broad-band scales: *Undisciplined/Poor Self-Control*, *Social Incompetence*, *Internalization/Somatic Symptoms*, and *Cognitive Development*.

His mother's responses on the CBCL place Kenny well below the clinical cutoff for the disruptive behavior scales, consistent with her description of him as a "terrific kid." However, what emerges on the CBCL profile that was *not* revealed by your interview with her are a significant number of internalizing symptoms: she indicates that Kenny often worries, feels tense and anxious, has trouble sleeping, and complains of headaches and stomachaches. The fact that the mother is aware of these problems indicates that she has the capacity to be empathic and sensitive to her son, a source of strength that you note.

His teacher's responses on the Teacher Report Form paint a very different picture of Kenny. The teacher rates him high in oppositionality and describes him as having poor interpersonal skills. Clearly, either Kenny's behavior—or adults' perception of it—is markedly different in the classroom than at home.

Child Self-Report Scales

Commonly used child-report measures are those that assess specific kinds of symptoms. Particularly useful are measures of internalizing symptoms, about which children's reports may be the most informative. One of the most widely used of these, the *Children's Depression Inventory* (CDI; Kovacs, 1992), is a 27-item paper-and-pencil measure for children ages 6 through 17 that assesses sadness, cognitive symptoms of depression, somatic complaints, social problems, and acting out. The *Revised Children's Manifest Anxiety Scale* (RCMAS; Reynolds & Richmond, 1985), used for children 6 through 17, includes 37 items assessing physiological anxiety, social concerns, worry, and oversensitivity, as well as defensive responding.

An example of a multidimensional child self-report measure is the *Personality Inventory for Youth* (PIY; Lachar & Gruber, 1994). The PIY parallels the parent-report measure, the Personality Inventory for Children, and is designed to assess academic, emotional, behavioral, and interpersonal adjustment in children 9 through 19 years of age. Four broad factors are derived: *externalizing/internalizing, cognitive impairment, social withdrawal*, and *social skills deficit*. In addition, three scales were developed to assess the validity of children's responses, including inattentive or provocative responses, as well as inconsistent or defensive responding. While this measure is promising, it is new on the scene, and so its utility is still unknown.

The *Self-Report of Personality* (SRP) is part of the multifaceted Behavior Assessment System for Children (BASC; Reynolds & Kamphaus, 1992). The SRP is designed to assess children's perceptions of school, parents, peers, and self. Factor analysis was used to develop four scores. *Clinical Maladjustment* includes scales assessing anxiety, atypical feelings and behaviors, social stress, locus of control and somatization. *Personal Adjustment* includes scales assessing self-esteem, self-reliance, peer relations, and positive parent–child relationships. Another scale assesses *School Maladjustment*, which includes items tapping problems that might interfere with academic functioning, such as negative attitudes toward school and teachers, and sensation-seeking for adolescents. *Emotional Symptoms* is a composite score that gives an indication of general psychopathology. A lie scale detects "fake good" response sets by assessing whether children deny even the most ordinary, run-of-the-mill misbehavior (e.g., "I never get angry"). Forms are available for children 8 through 11, as well as adolescents 12 through 18. Norms are available for different age groups, as well as for clinical samples.

Strengths of the SRP include a large standardization sample matched demographically to 1990 U.S. Census figures, good reliabilities, and some evidence for validity derived from comparisons between the SRP and similar scales of more estab-

lished measures. Because fairly good reading ability is required, the measure might not be appropriate for mentally retarded or learning disabled youth at any age. Again, this measure has not been widely used to date.

Other measures have been developed specifically for adolescents. The *Minnesota Multiphasic Personality Inventory—Adolescent* (MMPI-A; Butcher et al., 1992) is a downward extension of the well-known adult measure, the MMPI-2. Scales assess such symptoms as depression, psychopathy, paranoia, schizophrenia, anxiety, obsessiveness, conduct problems, low self-esteem, alcohol and drug abuse proneness, and school and family problems, among others. Validity scales also assess attempts to present oneself in a good or bad light, as well as defensiveness and inconsistent responding. Like the original adult version, the MMPI-A requires English literacy, and it is extremely long, preventing some youths from completing it in one sitting.

The *Youth Self-Report* (YSR; Achenbach & Edelbrock, 1991) is used to obtain self-report ratings from adolescents ages 11 through 18 regarding *internalizing* and *externalizing* symptoms, paralleling parent's reports on the CBCL. Scales include Withdrawn, Somatic Complaints, Anxious/Depressed, Social Problems, Thought Problems, Attention Problems, Delinquent Behavior, and Aggressive Behavior. Social Competence scales also assess participation in social activities and peer relationships.

Projective Techniques

In all the assessment instruments discussed so far, the stimulus material is as clear and unambiguous as possible. **Projective techniques** take the opposite tack by using ambiguous or unstructured material; either the stimulus has no inherent meaning, such as an inkblot, or it has a number of potential meanings, such as a picture that is to be used as the basis of a story. Theoretically, the particular meaning attributed to the unstructured material is a reflection of the individual's particular personality. The disguised nature of the responses allows the individual to express ideas that would be too threatening to talk about directly; for example, a girl who is too frightened to talk about her anger toward her mother may feel free to tell a story about a daughter being angry with and defying a parental figure.

The Rorschach

The *Rorschach* is a series of ten inkblots, which are presented to the child one at a time with the question, "What could this be?" The child's responses are recorded verbatim, and after the cards have been viewed once, the examiner asks the child to look at each card again and to explain what part of the blot was used ("Where did you see it?") and what suggested each particular response ("What made it look like that?").

Although the validity of the Rorschach has been the subject of much debate, in recent years Exner (1993) made three important contributions to Rorschach analysis. First, he took the numerous scoring systems available and *integrated* them into a single comprehensive one. Second, he reviewed the available research and conducted a number of additional studies of the Rorschach in order to develop an *empirically based* interpretation scheme. Third, he provided separate *norms* for adults and for children 5 to 16 years of age, so that clinicians can evaluate the deviancy of a given child's responses in comparison to those of his or her peers.

Exner's system requires the examiner to code each response on seven different criteria. The first of these is *location*, or where on the blot the percept is seen. For example, it might be based on a small detail ("this little spot looks like a peephole"), or the whole blot might be used to create a complex and elaborated response ("this is an aquarium with lots of exotic plants and fish swimming around"). Second, each response is scored in terms of the *determinants*, or features that contribute to the percept described. These include such features as the form of the blot ("it is a bat because it is shaped like one") or its color or shading ("this gray part makes it look fuzzy and furry, like a bear skin rug"). Third, *form quality* is assessed, which concerns how well the percept actually fits the blot; for example, poor form quality would be indicated by a response that in no way follows the outline or features of the blot presented. The *content* of the percept is also recorded—that is, whether the percept involves humans, animals, or objects. *Popularity* is noted in terms of whether the percept is one that is commonly seen by others. *Organizational activity* concerns the degree of cognitive effort required to organize and integrate the parts of the blot into a coherent response; for example, the "aquarium" response quoted above would be rated as high in organization. Lastly, *special scores* are given to certain responses, such as those that include violent or morbid themes ("two cannibals eating the brains out of their victim's head").

After scoring the child's responses, the examiner first uses the norms obtained from other children of the same age in order to gauge the developmental appropriateness of the child's response. While some ways of responding to the Rorschach are indicative of psychopathology in adolescents and older children, they are normal for younger children. For example, young children are highly reactive to the color of the inkblots and thus tend to use color as a determinant of their responses rather than form. Because this reactivity to color is believed to represent emotional liability, this is a response style that, while perhaps a sign of immaturity in an adult, is not at all surprising to find in children. In fact, a young child who does *not* give many color-based responses might warrant concern, as this could suggest pseudomaturity and excessive control of emotions (Exner, 1994).

Exner has also constructed a number of scales that allow the assessor to gauge the likelihood that a child's Rorschach responses are indicative of a particular psychopathology, such as schizophrenia, anxiety, conduct disorder, or depression. For example, characteristics of depressed children's responses include a high number of morbid responses (sad or damaged images—for example, "an abandoned house that is falling apart because no one cares about it anymore"); responses based on white space in the inkblots rather than the shaded or colored portions; and a low ratio of responses based on color as opposed to black and white features. Characteristics of psychotic thought processes include poor form quality, incongruous combinations ("a bird holding a basketball" or "a man with three heads"), and bizarre or gruesome content.

It should be noted that, despite Exner's efforts, not all psychometricians are satisfied that the Rorschach has proven its validity and utility. While there have been a sufficient number of positive research findings to reassure its advocates (see Weiner, 1996), there have also been a sufficient number of negative ones to bolster the arguments of its detractors (see Dawes, 1994). The use of the Rorschach, therefore, is still subject to controversy.

> Kenny engages readily with the Rorschach, and his responses are well-elaborated and imaginative. However, he strives too hard to integrate every detail of each inkblot into his responses, sometimes at the expense of accuracy, and the themes of his percepts are not as highly sophisticated as the effort he puts into them warrants. His responses also include a significant use of white space and few responses based on color. In addition, morbid themes emerge in many of his responses, which tend to involve helpless victims that have been "blasted," "knocked down," and "squished" by sadistic monsters. You note that these responses suggest a child who is striving to accomplish beyond his abilities, and they also are consistent with the key indicators of depression.

Projective Drawings

The *Draw-A-Person* (DAP) is one of the most widely used of the projective drawing techniques. According to Machover's (1949) original procedure, the child is first asked to draw a person, then to draw a person of the other sex. Next, a series of questions follows, such as "What is the person doing?" "How old is he or she?" "What does the person like and dislike?" although the questions asked are not standard across clinicians.

Theoretically, the child's drawing is a projection of both the self-image and the body image. Various characteristics of the drawing are interpreted in terms of psychological variables—a small figure indicating inferiority, faint lines suggesting anxiety or an amorphous identity, an overly large head indicating excessive intellectualization—while the child's answers to the assessor's questions are interpreted thematically; for example, a figure who is "just standing there" suggests passivity, while one who is a cheerleader suggests energy and extroversion. The figure may represent either the "real" self or the idealized self.

The *House-Tree-Person* (HTP) drawing is a variation on this theme in which the child completes three drawings—of a person, a house, and a tree—in order to provide a richer source of data. In theory, the house represents the individual's home life and family situation, while the person represents the self-image and the tree represents aspects of the self-concept that are less consciously accessible (Hammer, 1958).

Yet another projective drawing task is the *Kinetic Family Drawing* (KFD; Burns, 1982). Children are instructed to draw their family "doing something— some kind of action." The active, or kinetic, aspect of the drawing is intended to elicit material related to the emotional quality of relationships among family members. Children's drawings are scored in terms of actions (e.g., cooperation, nurturance, tension, or sadism); positions (e.g., whether figures are facing one another); physical characteristics (e.g., sizes of figures, details, and facial expressions); styles (e.g., whether the figures are placed in separate "compartments," or lined up at the top or bottom of the page); and whether there are distances separating family members or barriers blocking their access to one another.

Validity of Drawing Interpretations While their popularity attests to their intuitive appeal, projective drawing tasks such as the DAP, HTP, and KFD only rarely withstand empirical scrutiny. In general, the scoring systems developed lack sufficient norms and have not been subjected to adequate tests of validity. In some cases the research simply has not been done; in other cases the research has been nonsupportive (Handler & Habenicht, 1994).

There is one point in particular on which considerable research converges. Studies of the DAP and KFD indicate that the *individual details* in children's drawings on which most scoring systems base their interpretations are *not* linked to specific kinds of psychopathology and are not predictive of behavior. Therefore, glossaries to drawing features that make such interpretations as "large eyes = suspiciousness," "a hole in the tree signifies abuse has taken place," or "family members placed higher on the page are more significant" have not been found to be valid.

However, scoring systems based on more *global* screenings of children's drawings have demonstrated some success in empirical research. For example, Naglieri and Pfeiffer (1992) established a screening procedure for human figure drawings that indexes a large array of possible indicators of psychopathology and successfully differentiates emotionally disturbed from normative children. Similar results were reported by Tharinger and Stark (1990), who found that a holistic scoring technique for children's drawings was better able to detect internalizing disorders than was a detailed 37-item scoring system. The holistic system was based on raters' clinical impressions of such attributes as engagement or conflict depicted among family members, as well as distortions and "inhuman" qualities in the figures drawn.

In sum, children's drawings are probably most useful as means of providing ideas for further exploration rather than as providing definitive data in and of themselves. As Knoff (1990) concludes, "Projective drawings are probably best used *to generate hypotheses* about the referral situation rather than *to validate those hypotheses*" (p. 101).

A better use of projective drawing tasks with children may be to focus on the *process* rather than the content of drawing. Drawing is an inherently enjoyable activity, which can help the clinician to establish rapport with children who might be shy or uncommunicative. In addition, through showing active interest in children's drawings (e.g., "Tell me about your family picture. What is everyone doing?"), the clinician encourages children to describe their private worlds in a less threatening way than by direct questioning.

> Kenny is reluctant to draw a picture of a person, complaining that he's "not a good drawer" and "it will look stupid." He first draws a boy, and although the quality of his drawing is age-appropriate, it is somewhat sparse and lacking in detail. In addition, his picture is small, and shows many erasures and hesitations. He frets over getting the boy's hands right, finally giving up and saying, "His hands are in his pockets. He doesn't care." His Kinetic Family Drawing is also sketchy and reluctantly drawn. Kenny depicts his little brother high on a Ferris wheel, while he and his mother stand on the ground waving at him. He wistfully describes this as representing a fun day when they went to the fair together "a long time ago."
>
> Many different observations might be made of these drawings. For instance, we might remark on Kenny's attitude toward the tasks themselves. His

reluctance to draw may derive from his harsh criticism of what he will produce. Moreover, both the process and the content of his drawings reflect an incapacity to play and to be the carefree boy he wishes he could be.

Apperception Tests

The *Thematic Apperception Test* (TAT) consists of a set of pictures about which the child is instructed to tell a story. Each of the pictures is intentionally ambiguous, with the assumption that in attempting to impose meaning or structure, the child will project onto the pictures his or her own needs, desires, and conflicts. For example, a sketchy figure depicted leaning against a couch may be male or female, exhausted or relaxed, suicidal, in a state of bliss, or merely resting. Because any of these responses is equally plausible, the only determinant of the child's own perception is his or her frame of mind. In this way, the technique is designed to allow unconscious aspects of personality to be expressed. About ten pictures are selected for a particular child. Specific cards are designed for males or females, children, adolescents, or adults. The child is instructed to make up a story about the picture, including a beginning, middle, and end, and to describe what the people in the story are thinking and feeling. The examiner records the story verbatim and asks questions concerning any elements that may have been omitted.

When interpreting the TAT, most clinicians report that in actual practice they do not use a standard procedure (Rossini & Moretti, 1997). The commonly accepted assumption underlying TAT interpretation is that the protagonists of the stories represent various aspects of the individual's *self-concept*, both conscious and unconscious. Thus special attention is paid to the protagonists' needs, interests, traits, strivings, and competencies. In the *interpersonal* sphere, themes concerning parent–child and family relationships are of special interest, with the stories analyzed for the extent to which others are represented as nurturing, trustworthy, hostile, or unreliable. Stories are also examined for their overall *emotional tone*, along with the effectiveness of *coping strategies* used to deal with the problems generated in the stories.

Westen (1990) has contributed an empirically validated system for TAT interpretation. The Social Cognition and Object Relations Scale (SCORS) integrates psychodynamic theory and knowledge of social-cognitive development to assess individuals' representations of interpersonal relationships. Four dimensions are rated. The first of these concerns the *complexity* of representations of people. A low score indicates a lack of differentiation between self and other, while a high score indicates that others are seen in complex and multidimensional ways. Second, the *affective tone* of relationships is rated. A low score indicates that the social world is perceived as hostile and depriving; while a high score is given to responses that include a range of affects but, on balance, present others as positive and trustworthy. Third, the capacity for *emotional investment* in relationships and *moral standards* is rated. A low score indicates that people are represented as being motivated solely by self-interest, with relationships as simply means to achieving self-serving ends; a high score indicates a reciprocity and valuing of relationships with others. The fourth dimension concerns the understanding of *social causality*. A low score indicates an absence of apparent interest in interpreting the internal motivations underlying others' behavior, while a high score indicates an understanding of the thoughts, feelings, and unconscious conflicts that underlie the behavior of people. The SCORS has fared well in reliability and validity studies and differentiates various psychopathological groups, including youths with psychosis, delinquency, borderline personality disorder, and a history of sexual abuse. (For further information, see Alvarado, 1994.)

An effort to adapt the apperception approach to children is the *Roberts Apperception Test for Children* (RATC; McArthur & Roberts, 1982). There are sixteen stimulus cards depicting common situations, conflicts, and stresses in children's lives—for example, interparental arguments, child misbehavior, sibling rivalry, and peer conflicts. The RATC provides criteria and examples for scoring the stories in terms of six *adaptive scales*, including such dimensions as reliance on others, support provided to others, self-sufficiency and maturity, limit setting by parents and authority figures, the ability to formu-

late concepts about the problem situation, and the child's ability to construct positive and realistic solutions to conflicts. Five *clinical scales* are rated, including anxiety, aggression, depression, rejection, and lack of resolution. Critical indicators are also assessed, including atypical responses, maladaptive outcomes, and card rejections. Advantages of the RATC include high agreement between assessors, and the existence of norms for children ages 6 to 15 that aid the clinician in evaluating an individual child's adjustment.

You ask Kenny to respond to a TAT card that depicts a boy looking at a violin on a table in front of him, an ambiguous expression on his face. The following is Kenny's story:

"Well, there is a little boy, and his teacher told him to practice the violin, and he doesn't want to practice the violin, so he just sits there staring at it. After a while he fell asleep, and he has a dream and—now I have to think up a dream. He dreamed he was the greatest violinist in the world, and fame and success brought him riches and happiness. He bought his mother beautiful things, and they like lived in luxury. Um . . . these are hard to figure out. He had a special violin, and he couldn't play no other violin because this was the only one that ever worked for him, because there was only one that could play the right tunes. It seemed like magic that it played all right. He kept it by his bedside because if he lost the violin he would lose his wealth and everything. It was almost like magic. Finally, there came a time when his worst rival realized he could only play that one violin, and he sent some bandits to break up his violin and ruin his career. Just as the bandits were going to break the violin in half, he woke up."

What can we make of Kenny's story? First, it is important to keep in mind that no one story is definitive in itself; it is merely suggestive. Only as themes occur repeatedly and can be fitted together does the clinician have confidence in the interpretation of the data. Keeping that caveat in mind, it is useful to know that this particular picture often elicits stories concerning achievement and initiative, which seem to be important themes in Kenny's life. Kenny's version contains the familiar theme of a child having to do something he does not want to do because an adult says he must. Kenny's method of coping with this conflict is to flee into a dream. Further, most striking is the contrast between the initial picture of the put-upon boy and the grandiose world-famous virtuoso in the dream. However, instead of bringing security, success is accompanied by a state of heightened vulnerability, since a competitive rival sets out to destroy him. These story themes fit with some of the formulations we have derived from other data. We might hypothesize that Kenny's strivings to meet unrealistic expectations—to meet impossible academic goals and to act as the "man of the house"—have generated feelings of inadequacy. In addition, Kenny seems to perceive aggression and hostile competitiveness to be an integral part of achievement. Perhaps because his actual abilities do not fit with his expectations of himself, and he fears hostility and rejection from his peers, Kenny withdraws from the whole enterprise. On the positive side, Kenny's assets include a lively imagination and an ability to express thoughts and feelings in a disguised form when they are too painful to face directly. These characteristics suggest that he might be a good candidate for psychotherapy.

Behavioral Assessment

As we have noted, a key purpose of clinical assessment is to understand the basis of the child's psychopathology sufficiently so that the clinician can design an effective intervention. A prime example of tailoring the inquiry to a therapeutic procedure is **behavioral assessment**. Since behavior therapy concerns the current situation, assessment aims at obtaining a specific account of a child's problem behaviors along with their immediate antecedents and consequences.

Behavioral assessment utilizes many traditional diagnostic procedures, but the emphasis differs. In obtaining referral information, the clinician focuses on the question of who has seen what behaviors in which situations. Similarly, the *behavioral interview* aims primarily at obtaining behavior-specific accounts of the problem and the environmental factors that may be eliciting and maintaining it. The behavioral clinician also inquires into attempts to change the troublesome behavior and the results obtained. Adults directly involved with the child's problem, such as parents, teachers, and relatives, are inter-

viewed. Generally speaking, obtaining historical information is minimized, since the clinician is only incidentally interested in reconstructing etiology.

Some of the main features of the behavioral interview deserve to be presented in detail. To begin with, the interviewer *operationalizes* general descriptions of the child, such as "uncooperative," "withdrawn," or "lazy," by translating them into concrete *behaviors*. Specificity is of the essence: "Kenny misbehaves in class" is not as helpful as "Kenny stares out the window, doesn't answer when he's called on, and gets into arguments with the other children." Next, the interviewer inquires concerning *antecedents* (a description of the situations in which the problem behavior occurs). Next, the clinician inquires as to events that occur immediately following the problem behavior—namely, its *consequences*. Here, as in every aspect of the interview, behavioral specificity is sought in terms of exactly who is present and what is done: "When Kenny doesn't answer me, I call him up to the front of the class and he always says something rude to the boy who sits in the second row."

Certain ancillary information is helpful. The clinician may obtain an initial inventory of potential reinforcers to be used in therapy by asking what the child enjoys, such as favorite foods, recreational activities, or pastimes. The parents or teachers may be asked what behavior they would wish to have as a replacement for the present objectionable ones. The clinician may assess the amount of time the parent has to participate in a therapeutic program if one were deemed desirable and may evaluate the parent's ability and willingness to do so. Finally, the child may be interviewed to obtain his or her perception of the problems as well as a list of likes and dislikes.

The interviewer's emphasis on specific behavior in no way eliminates the problems inherent in conducting any clinical interview. Parents and teachers are personally involved rather than objective reporters; for example, in the preceding illustration, the teacher may have cited only Kenny's behavior as an antecedent and omitted the other child's provocation out of prejudice or honest obliviousness. Thus the behavioral clinician must be as skilled as any other in establishing rapport, constructively handling negative feelings, judging the accuracy of the information and when it is suspect, finding ways of eliciting a realistic account without antagonizing or alienating the parent.

Behavior Rating Scales

A number of scales have been developed for rating observed child behavior. While they are reliable and robust, considerable time and effort is often required to train coders to use these systems.

One example is the *Behavioral Coding System* (BCS; Reid, 1978), which was designed to rate children's behavior both at home and at school. Specific positive and negative behaviors are rated, including verbalizations (such as laughing, whining, complying, and teasing) and nonverbal behaviors (such as destructiveness, ignoring, or touching another person). Good interrater reliabilities have been demonstrated, and the BCS successfully differentiates clinical and normative samples, such as aggressive and prosocial boys, as well as revealing significant changes in rates of negative behavior before and after behavioral treatment.

The Child Behavior Checklist *Direct Observation Form* (DOF; Achenbach, 1991) has the advantage of directly paralleling the parent and teacher versions of the CBCL. There are 96 behavior items that are rated, of which 86 overlap with the parent-report form and 73 overlap with the teacher-report form. The DOF requires the assessor to observe a child for six 10-minute sessions, during which a narrative description of the child's behavior is recorded, including the occurrence, duration, and intensity of any problem behaviors. At the end of each session, each behavior is rated on a 4-point scale. Good interrater reliabilities have been demonstrated, as well as correspondence between parents', and teachers', and other observers' reports.

Behavioral Observation

The behavioral approach has made a unique contribution by adapting the technique of naturalistic observation—previously used primarily for research purposes—to assessment goals and placing it at the heart of the process. It is easy to understand this emphasis on direct observation, since abnormal behavior is assumed to develop and to be maintained by environmental stimuli, while behavior modification corrects problem behaviors by altering the environmental conditions maintaining them.

To begin with, the clinician identifies the *target behaviors* to be observed. These are derived from the information obtained from the referral, checklist, and interview but also should be behaviors for which specific treatment goals can be specified. These behaviors are, in effect, the operational definition of the child's problem. "Uncooperative," for example, might be translated into "not answering the teacher when called upon." Other disruptive behaviors in the classroom might include the child's being out of his or her chair without permission; touching, grabbing, or destroying another child's property; vocalizing, speaking, or noisemaking without permission; hitting other children; and failing to do assignments.

The behavioral clinician's next task is to determine the frequency of the target behavior in order to establish a *baseline* for its natural occurrence against which to evaluate the effectiveness of the therapeutic intervention. Observations are scheduled for the specific periods in which the problem behavior is most likely to happen. Depending on the natural occurrence of the target behavior, the period may last half an hour to an entire day, while observations may be made daily or only on particular days. Kenny, for example, may need to be observed for only about thirty minutes in the classroom.

There are a number of different methods for quantifying behavioral observations. *Frequency* involves counting the number of times the target behavior occurs within a specific period. Frequency divided by time yields a measure called *response rate*; for example, a disruptive boy may leave his seat without permission five times in a fifty-minute class period, and his response rate would be recorded as 5/50, or .10. In *interval recording* an observer has a data sheet divided into small time units, such as twenty seconds. Aided by a timing device (such as a stopwatch) attached to a clipboard, the observer indicates whether the target behavior occurred in a given time unit. Frequently, a *time-sampling* method is used in which the observer observes the child's behavior for ten seconds, for example, and spends the next five seconds recording the target behaviors which occurred in that fifteen-second interval. This sequence is repeated for the duration of the observational period. Typically, only the presence or absence of target behavior is recorded. Some data are lost if a behavior occurs more than once during an interval, but such losses are often unimportant. Interval recording is usually more practicable than the frequency method when the observer wishes to record a number of behaviors. Finally, *duration* consists of measuring the interval of time between the onset and termination of the target behavior. This method is appropriate when decreasing the time spent in a particular behavior, such as head banging, is a therapeutic goal.

In addition, observation is used to carry out a *functional analysis* of the target behavior. A common strategy for accomplishing this is the A-B-C method, which requires attending to *antecedents*, *behavior*, and *consequences* that might perpetuate problem behavior (see Figure 16.5 for an example). These data are more qualitative than quantitative, with a description of the child's behavior provided in a narrative form. As always, the observer is aware of the situation-specific nature of the relationships observed and is alert to the possibility that the setting may significantly alter the functional meaning of behavior. For example, a teacher's reprimand may tend to decrease provocative behavior when teacher and child are alone, but it may increase such behavior when other children are present, particularly if they tease or egg on the target child.

Theoretically, the baseline phase should continue until the target behavior has become stable. Because of the variability of human behavior, such an ideal is often difficult to achieve. The general consensus is that there should be a minimal baseline period of one week of data collection. (For a more extended presentation, see La Greca and Stone, 1992.)

Reliability

In order to ensure reliability, researchers using naturalistic observation have found it necessary to train observers. Typically, two or more trainees observe, record, and score the behavior of the same child. Disagreements are discussed and reconciled. Additional observations are made and scored until agreement between observers is at least 80 to 85 percent.

Even after training is completed, it is highly desirable to "recalibrate" the observers periodically by repeating the training procedures. Such intensive training further attests to the fact that, the emperor's new clothes notwithstanding, the untrained eye is an inaccurate observational instrument.

Behavioral clinicians rarely have the time or the personnel to train for accurate observation. Consequently, they must rely on untrained adults such as parents and teachers, whose reliability, as might be expected, is significantly lower (Achenbach & McConaughy, 1997). In general, a given individual is consistent with himself or herself over a period of one week to one month; even after six months, consistency is marginal but adequate. Reliability between similar observers, such as between parents or between teachers, is satisfactory but not so high as to prevent disagreements between mother and father or between teachers. Reliability plunges precipitously between adults who view the same child in different situations, such as parents and teachers, teachers and mental health workers, or even teachers who see the child in different settings. This last finding suggests that many problem behaviors may be situation-specific. Thus reliability is affected both by the implicit definitions and biases of the observers, and by the different information input they have in terms of the situations in which they have observed the child.

The Developmental Dimension in Behavioral Assessment

Developmental considerations, while often neglected, need to be integrated into the behavioral assessment process (Ollendick & King, 1991). It is important to be able to compare the child's behavior to *normative information* about what can be expected of a child this age. For example, while a teacher may perceive a school-age child who does not stay in his seat as overly active and disruptive, knowledge of developmental norms will help the behavioral assessor to recognize whether it is the child's behavior that is deviant or the adult's expectations. A second way in which developmental norms for behavior need to be understood is in terms of *patterns of behavior*. Behaviors associated with the same disorder might differ across gender and age. For example, while depression in older boys is associated with "uncommunicativeness," depressed girls are more likely to exhibit "social withdrawal." Similarly, older children with separation anxiety are characterized by physical complaints and school refusal, while younger children show behaviors such as sleep disturbances and excessive anxiety about their attachment figures. Therefore, behavioral assessors must be sensitive to the fact that the signs and symptoms rated change with gender and development. Finally, establishing *rapport* with children is a universal feature of assessment that requires developmentally relevant knowledge and skills.

Kenny's teacher is eager to be of help to your assessment and agrees to allow you to conduct a behavioral assessment through the one-way mirror

Time/Setting	Antecedent	Behavior	Consequence
8:30/Math class – copying from board		B takes pencil from another child	Child ignores him
	Child ignores him	B tears paper on child's desk	Child tells teacher and teacher reprimands B
	Teacher reprimands B	B sulks	Teacher allows B to erase board
8:35/Math class – doing seatwork		B leaves seat to sharpen pencil	Teacher asks B to raise hand to leave seat
		B raises hand	Teacher continues to work with other student
	Teacher ignores B	B gets out of seat & pulls on teacher's shirt to get attention	Teacher scolds B for leaving seat and places name on board
	Teacher puts B's name on board	B starts to cry	Child teases B
	Child teases B	B tries to hit other child	B sent to office
8:55/Math class – completing seatwork	B returns to class	B sullen and refuses to work	Teacher allows B to collect assignments

Figure 16.5   A Hypothetical Example of Simple A-B-C Observational System of an 8-Year-Old Boy (B).

Source: Kamphaus & Frick, 1996.

that looks into the classroom. You make note of the antecedents and consequences of Kenny's behavior in four specific categories: on-task behavior (doing the work assigned, raising his hand to contribute to the class discussion, asking relevant questions about the material); off-task behavior (staring off into space, engaging in activities other than the one assigned by the teacher); oppositionality (refusing to answer the teacher when called upon); and peer conflicts (negative exchanges with other children, including verbal or physical aggression, and incidents in which Kenny is the initiator or the victim). During one half hour, you observe one brief moment of on-task behavior, six incidents of off-task behavior, three of oppositionality, and three peer conflicts. Each off-task incident seems to occur when other students are responding to the teacher's questions, something Kenny never volunteers to do. The episodes of oppositionality occur during arithmetic lessons, and the teacher's response each time is to call him to the front of the room. As he passes one particular boy near the front, you observe subtle provocative behaviors by this other youngster, such as murmured insults, attempts to trip Kenny, and so forth. Kenny's retorts to these provocations are neither subtle nor quiet—his attempts to strike back verbally catch the teacher's attention and land Kenny in even more trouble. The other children seem to watch these little dramas with glee and even to look forward to them.

Clinical Assessment: Art and Science

While differences in assessment procedures can best be understood in terms of clinicians' different theoretical and therapeutic allegiances, there is another, related source of disagreement. As scientists, psychologists strive for objectivity and precision, which require, among other things, clearly delineated procedures that are available to the scientific community. It is no accident that psychologists in the past championed the use of standardized assessment techniques over impressionistic evaluations. Nor is it by chance that behavioral assessment, with its explicit procedures for observation and avoidance of inferences about personality characteristics and motivations, is exercising a similar appeal. Concomitantly,

there is a mistrust of the hypothesis-testing clinician initially described in this discussion. While utilizing theoretical and experiential guides, the process by which the clinician generates, tests, accepts, and discards ideas is nearer to an art than a science. He or she may indeed come up with impressive insights but also may be seriously in error; more important— and this is what concerns the critical psychologist— there is no clearly established procedure for deciding in favor of one outcome over the other.

Certain clinicians might answer that scores are only one kind of information to be gained from a test, as we have seen in discussing intelligence tests. To limit assessment to such scores would be to eliminate the added behavioral data so vital to understanding an individual child. If such data have yet to be standardized and are of unknown reliability, their clinical utility justifies their use for the present. These clinicians rightly claim that there are a number of important areas for which no standardized, clinically useful instruments exists. Thus they can do no more than put the pieces of assessment data together as best they can. Moreover, it is just such efforts to understand complex, heretofore unsystematized data that can ultimately serve as the basis for objective assessment techniques.

While techniques and goals may vary, all clinical assessment requires a high degree of *professional competence*. Clinicians must be skillful and sensitive in handling the many interpersonal problems inherent in dealing with troubled parents and children; they must be knowledgeable concerning the procedures they use and the problems they are called upon to evaluate; they must be well acquainted with and abide by the ethical principles of their profession; and they must have received adequate academic and professional preparation, which for a clinical child psychologist typically involves a Ph.D. or Psy.D. from an accredited university and at least two years of supervised experience (American Psychological Association, 1985).

Another aspect of assessment that is more art than science is the *integration* of various discrete findings into a meaningful whole. To return to the case of Kenny, the data we gathered illustrate the fact that children's emotional and behavioral problems have multiple dimensions. Therefore, there is no simple statement that will capture all the richness of the data. There is a *cognitive* component, as evidenced by Kenny's learning difficulties in the area of arithmetic; an *emotional* or psychodynamic component, as seen in his tendency to internalize his distress as well as his conflicts over achievement and aggression; a *family system* component, suggested by the caregiving role he plays with his mother; and a *behavioral* component, seen in his difficulties interacting with teachers and peers.

Which of these provides the "right" hypothesis? Clinicians from different theoretical orientations will focus on the data that present them with the most plausible case formulation and treatment plan for a given child. However, the clinician operating from a developmental psychopathology perspective has an advantage in that no one theory dictates to him or her what evidence is to be gathered nor which data warrant attention. Instead, the developmental psychopathologist will evaluate each bit of evidence

and data—regardless of what theoretical orientation it derives from or supports—in order to construct a mosaic that best depicts this most interesting and complex young person. Further, each of these orientations suggests particular avenues for intervention—for example, with Kenny, his family, or the school—that might be integrated into an effective multidimensional treatment plan. Kenny's response to these different interventions, in turn, will provide the clinician with feedback as to the accuracy of his or her formulation of the problem and the possible need for further psychological testing. Therefore, just as assessment informs intervention, intervention can inform assessment.

The dovetailing of assessment and psychotherapy we have emphasized throughout this chapter will become even clearer after we explore the major intervention techniques themselves. This is the topic of our final chapter.

Intervention and Prevention

Conceptualizing and Evaluating Child Interventions

It is estimated that over 200 psychotherapies are currently in use with children and adolescents (Kazdin & Weisz, 1998). These interventions arise from different assumptions about the nature of psychopathology and about the means necessary to alleviate it. How is the clinician to choose the best course of action? Our consideration of the topic of intervention requires that we come full circle and return to the theme first introduced in Chapter 1: the various theories of psychopathology. Theory guides the clinician's understanding of what causes—and what might alleviate—children's mental health problems.

In the past, it was often the case that therapists adhered rigidly to a theoretical point of view, whether psychoanalytic, behavioral, or systemic. Adherence to their "brand" of psychotherapy led clinicians to see all cases through only one set of lenses and, in many instances, to recommend the same form of treatment for everyone (Matarazzo, 1990). Following this kind of thinking, clinical researchers set out to determine which was the overall best therapy by conducting studies in which they pitted various kinds of intervention against one another. Overall, the results of these "horse race" studies were not very discriminating. While treatment was consistently associated with improvement, and treated participants fared better than those in the no-treatment group, few differences among therapies were found. As the Dodo in Lewis Carroll's *Alice in Wonderland* declared, "*Everybody* has won and *all* must have prizes" (Luborsky, Singer, & Luborsky, 1975).

These earlier studies were predicated on an assumption—called the "*uniformity myth*"—that one form of therapy would be the treatment of choice for all psychopathologies. Increasingly, the movement is toward asking more complex and sophisticated questions, such as *which* therapy is most effective for *whom, when* (Roth & Fonagy, 1996). Therefore, a better approach is to find the "best fit" for a given child, depending on his or her developmental stage, psychopathology, and intrapersonal and family characteristics. In the same light, another current trend in psychotherapy practice is toward developing *integrative* models that take a multifaceted approach to solving child and family problems. Integration can take place by combining individual and family treatment or by utilizing a variety of techniques drawn from psychodynamic, cognitive, and behavioral theory (see Wachtel, 1994).

Finally, there is a movement afoot to promote the use of *empirically validated* or *evidence-based* treatments (Kazdin, 1997c). This is particularly the case in the field of clinical psychology, where the Ethical Principles of Psychologists (American Psychological Association, 1992) explicitly call for psychologists to use interventions for which there is some evidence of effectiveness.

In this chapter we discuss ways in which psychopathologies of childhood can be ameliorated or even prevented. Our presentation is selective, offering examples of only a few of the 200 treatment techniques available. (For more extensive overviews, see Hibbs and Jensen, 1996, and Mash and Barkley, 1998.) In the realm of *intervention* we present five of the major therapeutic approaches—psychoanalytic, humanistic, behavioral, cognitive, and systemic—along with the conceptualization of psychopathology that provides the rationale for the therapeutic techniques each employs. As we consider *prevention* we discuss programs that target at-risk populations in order to prevent psychopathology from developing. Following the movement for evidence-based treatments, we examine the available research regarding the major forms of intervention used with children and focus our attention on those that have received empirical support. First, however, we must consider *how* we can determine whether a given treatment is effective.

Empirical Validation: Methods and Challenges

While it might seem a simple matter to prove that an intervention "works," there are actually a number of challenges to this endeavor (Peterson & Bell-Dolan, 1995). For example, a large number of chil-

dren with the same diagnosis must be recruited. Children must be assigned to treatment and control groups on a random basis, and yet these groups should not differ significantly from one another in terms of such characteristics as severity of the disturbance, age, ethnicity, family constellation, and social class. A number of therapists expert in the intervention of choice must be available, and the treatment protocol must be laid out specifically so that all of the therapists carry out the prescribed treatment in the same way. The outcome must be operationalized clearly, reliably, and validly and should indicate that the treatment has made a difference that is lasting and of real-world significance.

Kazdin (1997c) illustrates the ways in which the majority of child therapy outcome studies have failed to hit the mark. Most of the research on child interventions consists of *analogue* studies that only approximate the way that psychotherapy is carried out in the real world. Generally, an analogue study involves the delivery of an intervention to nonclinical samples by inexperienced therapists, often graduate student research assistants. Thus, the therapies are a far cry from the actual practice of skilled professionals, and the children treated do not evidence the high *levels of disturbance* and *comorbidity* that are characteristic of real clinical samples. The levels of distress and disruption exhibited by children and their families are important determinants of the response to treatment and the willingness to remain in treatment; *attrition*, or treatment dropout, is a major problem with real clinical samples. In addition, most of the studies use *narrow outcome criteria* such as symptom relief that, while statistically significant, may lack clinical significance in terms of their impact on the child's life outside of therapy. *Follow-up* is generally only short-term, with a median length of five months after termination, so that little evidence is presented for therapy's effectiveness over the long haul.

Further, few studies have made an effort to demonstrate that the intervention *processes* themselves are what account for the change associated with therapy. Whether the intervention targets the acquisition of a skill, insight into an internal conflict, or change in maladaptive cognitions, research should establish that it is alterations in these processes that leads to improvement. Without such evidence, intervention studies are vulnerable to the challenge that *nonspecific effects*, such as attention from a caring adult—or unintended effects, such as inadvertent positive reinforcement provided by a psychoanalysts' smiles and nods—are what lead to the positive outcome. Finally, the majority of studies neglect to attend to the many *mediating factors*—for example, age, family constellation, quality of the therapeutic relationship—that might influence the impact of treatment on individual children.

Despite these limitations, the research on psychotherapy outcome in general paints an encouraging picture. Effective interventions for children have been developed, and increasing attention is being paid to the need to document their effectiveness with specific problems and across samples. In fact, Kazdin (1997c) makes the following bold assertion: "The basic question about whether psychotherapy 'works' has been answered affirmatively and can be put to rest" (p. 115). The most convincing evidence for the effectiveness of child interventions comes from *meta-analysis*, which aggregates data from a number of studies. The outcome of a meta-analysis is an estimation of *effect size*: overall, in all these different samples studied in all these different settings, how much difference did treatment make?

A recent broad-based meta-analysis of the child intervention research included 150 studies published between 1967 and 1993, involving children 2 to 18 years of age (Weisz et al., 1995). The effect size indicated that the average child who underwent treatment was less symptomatic at follow-up than 76 percent of the untreated children. This is considered to be a significant effect, in the medium to large range, comparable to that found in psychotherapy outcome studies conducted with adults.

On the one hand, Weisz and colleagues found that *behavior therapies* consistently were the most effective interventions for children, contradicting the "Dodo verdict" reached with adults. On the other hand, only 10 percent of the studies they reviewed involved nonbehavioral interventions. Given the dearth of empirical research conducted on other forms of therapy, therefore, the jury may still be out.

In general, *adolescents* tended to improve more than younger children. Curiously, *females*, especially female adolescents, gained the most from intervention. *Experienced* therapists were more effective than well-trained paraprofessionals in treating overcontrolled problems, such as anxiety and depression, but the *paraprofessionals* were equally as effective in treating undercontrolled problems such as conduct disorder. Further, effects were overwhelmingly stronger for *laboratory-based* interventions than for those conducted in "real-life" settings. Finally, effects were strongest for outcome measures that were *specifically matched* to the treatment technique, arguing against the idea that the effectiveness of child therapy can be accounted for by nonspecific effects.

The Developmental Psychopathology Approach

Developmental Psychopathology Concepts Applied to Intervention

A number of authors have suggested that an understanding of developmental psychopathology might inform our interventions with children (see Cicchetti and Toth, 1992). At the most fundamental level, knowledge of *normal development* is essential. First, familiarity with what is typical for children of a given age allows the clinician to *distinguish normal from pathological* behavior (Forehand & Wierson, 1993). Second, an understanding of the developmental tasks the child faces may help to put the behavior in *context* and explain its etiology. Further, the child's level of *cognitive and emotional development* must be taken into account when selecting an appropriate intervention technique (Shirk, 1988). While the need to adapt to the child's developmental level is obvious, few therapies have actually attended to the cognitive and linguistic differences between, for example, a preschooler or school-age child.

Other principles of developmental psychopathology also have implications for intervention. Attention to *stage-salient issues* may help tailor treatments so as to be maximally effective for children at particular developmental periods (Cicchetti et al., 1988). For example, individuals may be more amenable to change during times of *developmental transitions*, such as first entry into school, or when poised at the cusp of adolescence. Therefore, interventions might be more effective if timed to take such transitions into account. As Rutter (1990) states: "Particular attention needs to be paid to the mechanisms operating at key turning points in individual's lives, when a risk trajectory may be redirected onto a more adaptive path" (p. 210).

Finally, because problems emerge as a function of *transactional processes*, intervention in those processes provides a powerful way of inducing change (Rutter, 1990). Accordingly, interpersonal relationships are likely to provide a key to therapeutic change in the developmental psychopathology perspective.

An Integrative Approach

Shirk and Russell (1996) offer an intriguing new conceptualization of child psychotherapy. Influenced by the developmental psychopathology perspective, they argue for therapists to relinquish adherence to "brands" of psychotherapy and instead link intervention planning to an understanding of *pathogenic processes*. This term refers to the clinician's theoretical formulation of the developmental issues underlying the child's problems, which we encountered in Chapter 16 as the *case formulation*. The case formulation goes beyond simple diagnosis. Because there are divergent pathways to specific psychopathologies, children who share the same diagnosis may not have reached the therapist's doorway via the same road and thus may not share the same pathogenic processes.

Shirk and Russell focus on three major domains of development: cognitive, emotional, and interpersonal. Within the *cognitive* realm, pathogenic processes might take the form of deficits in knowledge or skills, such as in the understanding of how to solve interpersonal problems, cognitive distortions and maladaptive schema about the self or others, or simply lack of insight into one's own motivations and behavior. In the *emotional* realm, pathogenic processes might include blocked access

to feelings, lack of understanding of emotions, or an inability to regulate and cope with affective states. In the *interpersonal* realm, pathogenic processes might include caregivers who fail to validate the child's self-worth, deprive the child of support and structure, or contribute to the development of insecure models of attachment relationships.

A clear understanding of the pathological processes that brought the disorder about can help the clinician to develop a treatment plan. The strategy is to match the formulation of the pathological process to the most relevant *change process*. These change processes are derived from the major theoretical orientations, with which we are familiar (see Table 17.1). For example, the formulation that an aggressive child's difficulties are a product of inadequate attachments would suggest that the therapist strive to provide a "corrective emotional experience" via a psychodynamically nurturing relationship. In contrast, the formulation that the child's difficulties derive from a lack of social skills would suggest that the therapist play an educative function and help the child to learn those skills.

Shirk and Russell limit their discussion to *psycho*therapies, defined as therapies directed at changing internal factors that mediate between the environment and the child's behavior. Thus, they distinguish psychotherapies from *behavior* therapies and *family systemic* therapies, both of which are directed toward changing the environment itself. However, their scheme can easily be expanded to include behaviorally oriented and systemic interventions; therefore, we have added these two conceptualizations to Table 17.1. For example, the formulation that the child's aggression is being positively reinforced by poor parenting practices suggests that intervention should take a behavioral bent. In contrast, the formulation that the child's behavior is an attempt to distract the parents from their marital difficulties suggests a systemic orientation.

To illustrate their approach to treatment formulation, Shirk and Russell offer the case of "Jack." Jack was a 10-year-old boy brought to the clinician by his single mother, who was concerned about his short temper and inability to tolerate frustration.

Table 17.1   Integrating Theories, Case Formulations, and Change Processes in Child Psychotherapy

Theory	Pathological Process		Associated Change Process
Psychodynamic	Internal conflict	Symptoms are compromise between an unacceptable impulse and the defense against its expression	Insight/interpretation
	Ego deficit	Developmental deficits arise as a function of failure of the environment to meet child's emotional needs	Corrective emotional experience
Humanistic	Low self-esteem	Psychopathology arises as a function of feelings of inadequacy, low self-worth, lack of self-acceptance	Validation/support
	Emotional obstruction	Psychopathology arises as a function of feelings that are not expressed or not accepted	Encouragement of emotional expression
Behavioral	Maladaptive conditioning	Problem behavior occurs when a maladaptive link is made between a stimulus and a response	Re-conditioning to foster more adaptive responses
	Inappropriate contingencies	Problem behavior occurs through punishment, reinforcement, and modeling	Alteration of contingencies in the environment
Cognitive	Cognitive deficit	Psychopathology arises when child lacks necessary cognitive skills to cope with life problems	Skill development
	Cognitive distortion	Distorted, maladaptive interpretations give rise to psychopathology	Schema transformation
Systemic	Enmeshment-disengagement	Overly rigid or diffuse boundaries prevent family members from meeting developmental needs	Restructuring; strengthening or loosening boundaries
	Triangulation	Triangles and coalitions have formed that place family members in inappropriate roles	Restructuring; detriangulating

Source: Adapted from Shirk and Russell (1996), with additions.

Struggles at home revolved around Jack's refusal to complete his chores, and teachers complained that, despite Jack's good intelligence, he seldom completed school assignments. Increasingly, Jack was coming home with bruises and scrapes that testified to his aggressive behavior with peers. Jack showed all the signs of oppositional-defiant disorder and was in danger of sliding down the slope toward more serious conduct problems.

An empirically based approach to treatment planning suggested that Jack was a prime candidate for interpersonal problem-solving skills training (see Chapter 9), one of the most effective techniques for curbing child misbehavior. However, a trial of this kind of therapy made little headway. Jack quickly grasped the necessary concepts and demonstrated the ability to execute the requisite social problem-solving skills, but there was no apparent change in his behavior outside of the therapy room.

Going back to the drawing board, the therapist took into consideration Jack's developmental history, which suggested an alternative formulation regarding the pathogenic processes that led to his behavior problems. During his first two years, Jack's mother was the target of physical abuse by his father and was consequently an anxious, depressed, and preoccupied parent. Jack's early life, therefore, was marked by turmoil, unpredictability, and violence. Thus, he developed a set of negative expectations of others, viewing them as unreliable, self-centered, and uncaring. Sensitized to this issue, the therapist began to notice other evidence of Jack's cognitive distortions: his problems at school were due to his teachers' "unfairness," his mother's motivation to help Jack was to "look good to her boyfriends," the therapist met with the boy only because "he was paid to." A new formulation was developed that centered on the negative schemata that interfered with

Jack's ability to utilize adaptive social skills. Accordingly, the target of the treatment plan shifted to the need to change his maladaptive cognitions.

Shirk and Russell's perspective is a promising one. In the short term, they provide a useful guide to case formulation and treatment planning in child psychotherapy. For the future, their work promises to revitalize research on psychotherapy with children by contributing to the development of clear and testable hypotheses regarding the link between pathological processes and the interventions used to address them. Next, we take a closer look at how each of these formulations is put into action.

The Psychoanalytic Approach

Classical Psychoanalysis

The Conceptual Model

Psychoanalytic theory presents us with an inherently developmental model, with the *psychosexual stages* defining the pivotal conflicts to be mastered on the way to maturity. (Our presentation is based on the writings of Anna Freud, 1965.) Consequently, the focus of therapy is on the particular psychosexual stage or stages presumed to be responsible for the psychopathology (see Chapter 1).

Classical psychoanalysis grows directly out of the psychoanalytic theory of neurosis. According to this theory, psychopathology originates in the psychosexual stages, in which the child who is unable to master psychosexual anxieties defends himself or herself against them. The essence of psychoanalysis consists of reversing the *defensive process*, reconfronting the individual with the original trauma so that it can be mastered belatedly. Successful psychoanalysis is epitomized by Freud's aphorism, "*Where id was, there shall ego be.*" The once-overwhelming hates, jealousies, and fears of the Oedipal period, for example, can now be revived and viewed from a more mature perspective. The ensuing insight into the root of the problem exorcises it. The result is a "*widening of consciousness*" in two senses: the individual can face previously unacceptable aspects of his or her personality, and the energy used for defensive maneuvers can now be employed in growth-promoting activities.

The Therapeutic Process

A general feature of psychoanalysis is the maximizing of free expression during the psychoanalytic hour. With adult patients, this is accomplished through verbal **free association**, which involves speaking freely about whatever comes to mind. However, classical psychoanalysis with children requires major changes in procedures and techniques. In particular, because children cannot verbally free-associate, *play* is substituted.

The use of play presents special challenges to the therapist. Through verbal associations, adults provide the key to the idiosyncratic meaning of events or dreams; since children provide no such key, the analyst is left with the task of decoding the meaning of their fantasies. In order to ensure that the play is rich in the kind of material that will be useful to the analyst, the child is introduced to play material that is *projective*, such as a doll family, crayons, or clay. Such play materials tap into fantasies rather than skills. The analyst watches for signs that a theme is of special importance—signs such as repetition, excessive affect, regression in the form of more infantile play or speech, loss of control such as scattering the toys around, or a "they lived happily ever after" dismissal of a conflict situation.

As with adult psychoanalysis, a major goal of child psychoanalysis in the undoing of the *defense mechanisms* that inhibit self-awareness and emotional growth. One technique for overcoming defenses is to analyze the **transference**. This term refers to the patient's displacing, or transferring, to the therapist his or her feelings toward the parents. The analyst calls attention to transferences so that by exploring them patients can begin to gain access to the distressing relationships that played a decisive role in their neurosis. However, children's transferences, unlike those of adults, do not involve feelings toward shadowy parental figures dating back to the distant past. Instead, the child's current relationships with parents may be acted out with the analyst in a direct and immediate way.

A second technique for dealing with defenses is by analyzing the *resistance*. Since defenses protect the patient from anxiety, he or she will find numerous ways to retain them. The analyst gently and persistently makes **interpretations** that call attention to

A play therapy session.

such maneuvers and help the patient to focus on the threatening material that prompted them. Often this is done through the metaphor of the child's play rather than by confronting the child directly with his or her own feelings (e.g., "I bet that family was really scared when the hurricane started coming toward their house." "Being locked in a closet for two years after misbehaving does seem a long time." "The girl doll got angry at her mommy and then suddenly ran away. I wonder if it is scary for her to feel angry.") As therapy progresses, the analyst can build bridges from the safe disguise of make-believe to the child's own feelings; for example, "That hurricane sounds like what you told me about your mom and dad fighting." Through such interpretations the child is led back to the original traumatic situation and is helped to recognize, reevaluate, and master it.

Correctly timed, interpretations produce **insights**; prematurely timed, they are rejected and fuel the patient's resistance. A therapeutic cure does not come in one blinding flash of insight, however. Instead, the same material has to be approached again and again from many different directions and through many different experiences in order for the insight to be firmly established—a process called **working through**. Again, however, children differ from adults in terms of their tolerance for this process. Children often lack the capacity for self-observation or self-monitoring that enables adults to participate in an intense emotional experience while at the same time observing themselves reacting. Finally, during times of developmental stress such as adolescence, children are reluctant to add to their emotional burdens by confronting their anxieties. Thus, psychoanalysis with children is a challenging enterprise.

Ego Psychology

The next stage in the development of psychoanalytic theory is *ego psychology*, associated with the work of Erik Erikson (1950). Erikson's perspective emphasizes the ego and healthy, reality-oriented aspects of development, as opposed to Freud's emphasis on the primitive drives of sex and aggression. We offer only a brief presentation of ego psychology here.

The Conceptual Model

Erikson's theory of development is familiar to us (see Chapter 1). He delineates stages of *ego development* from infancy to late adulthood, as well the issues or crises that must be resolved at each step in order for development to proceed. (See Table 3.4.) Psychopathology results when the tasks of a given stage are not mastered and the individual cannot progress to the next stage in development, or when the individual resolves the conflict in a negative way. For example, as in the case of Jack presented above, a boy who experiences unreliable care in the early years may develop a sense of basic mistrust that colors his future relationships.

Erikson's model epitomizes the *stage-salient* approach recommended by developmental psychopathology. One of the implications of this approach is that children's behavior problems are not thought of in terms of diagnoses so much as in terms of the stage-salient issues that underlie them. Therefore, whether a school-age child is diagnosed with depression or conduct disorder, Erikson would hypothesize that underlying the behavioral problem is a struggle over feelings of inferiority and lack of industry, while an adolescent with the same diagnosis might be hypothesized to be struggling with identity confusion.

The Therapeutic Process

Consistent with his emphasis on ego functioning and adaptive strivings, Erikson sees the key to change in child therapy as the opportunity to gain *mastery* over conflicts, and the medium for this mastery is play. Play gives the child the opportunity to act out disturbing events and feelings in a safe environment, with objects that are under the child's control. As Erikson (1950) states, play allows the child "to deal with experience by creating model situations and to master reality by experiment and planning. . . . To 'play it out' is the most natural self-healing measure childhood affords" (p. 222).

The therapist's role is that of a facilitator of healthy ego functioning. Sometimes this role is played by being unobtrusive and *emotionally available*, allowing

the child's natural self-healing processes to unfold. The therapist's acceptance and understanding give the child the opportunity to play out secret fears or hates in order to gain internal peace. Ultimately, however, like the classical psychoanalyst, the ego psychologist strives to facilitate children's awareness of their repressed feelings through the means of *interpretation*.

Erikson made many significant contributions to the psychodynamic understanding of children through his observations of play behavior (Erikson, 1964a). For example, one of his insights had to do with the significance of *play disruptions*, those moments when children abruptly change the themes of their play or cease playing altogether (Erikson, 1964b). A therapist who attends carefully to the process of the session, noting what leads up to and follows after a play disruption, gains insight into the sources of conflict in the child's internal world.

Object Relations Theory

In its third wave, psychoanalytic theory supplemented its traditional concern with the intrapsychic variables (id, ego, and superego) with an emphasis on interpersonal relations. This is the realm of *object relations theory* (see Chapter 1), which we will describe briefly here.

The Conceptual Model

As we encountered in Chapter 1, the object relations model posits that psychopathology results from arrests in the separation-individuation process due to negative experiences with caregivers. (See Masterson, Tolpin, and Sifneos, 1991.) In more severe forms of psychopathology, inadequate parenting may interfere with the development of an autonomous *self*. The child without a secure and stable sense of his or her own individual selfhood is unable to move beyond the need to use primitive defense mechanisms such as *splitting*. Further along in the separation-individuation process, after children have learned to discriminate the boundary between self and other, threats to healthy development hinge on the valence, or emotional coloring, of *internal representations* of self and other. Affectionless, abusive, or inconsistent parenting may deprive the child of appropriate self-esteem as well as the capacity for interpersonal trust. The result is an internal model of others as unreliable and unloving and of the self as unlovable. The therapist's task, therefore, is to assess the point in development at which the child is arrested and to supply a *corrective emotional experience* that will help development return again to its normal course.

The Therapeutic Process

As with classical psychoanalysis, the therapist understands the children's internal world through the *transference*. Children's feelings and expectations about relationships come to life in the therapy session as they are reenacted with the therapist. However, just as the role of relationships is crucial in the etiology of psychopathology, the *therapeutic relationship* is critical to the effectiveness of object relations therapy. In contrast to the Freudian model, the psychoanalyst is more than a detached observer and interpreter. The therapist's real, human presence is an important part of object relations therapy's curative power: "psychoanalytic interpretation is not therapeutic *per se*, but only as it expresses a personal relationship of genuine understanding" (Guntrip, 1986, p. 448).

An object relations therapist who epitomizes this approach is D.W. Winnicott (1975). Although much of Winnicott's work was with children, a revealing portrait of his therapeutic style was presented by one of his adult analysands, Guntrip (1986), who contrasted Winnicott's warm and personable manner with the "blank screen" presentation of his previous, more classically styled psychoanalyst.

Winnicott's technique is difficult to summarize, and only a flavor of it can be given here. One of Winnicott's techniques to engage children in the therapy relationship is the "squiggle game," in which child and therapist take turns drawing a random squiggle and then asking the other to make something out of it. The squiggles and their transformations introduce playfulness into the interaction and supply the therapist with projective material regarding children's concerns. As part of the ongoing therapy process, the squiggle game allows the therapist to work with unconscious material at a non-

verbal level, more appropriate for children than the cognitively and linguistically demanding "talking cure" of classical psychoanalysis.

Again in contrast to classical psychoanalysis, the therapist's own emotional reactions are not considered to be sources of interference in the therapeutic process but rather to be meaningful sources of data. Here the concept of *projective identification* (Chapter 2) comes into play. (See Lieberman, 1992.) Children may evoke in the therapist feelings that they themselves are unable to tolerate as a way of attempting to master them. Therefore, an object relations therapist who finds herself feeling stressed and confused during a session with an anxious child, or who feels hurt and angered by the jibes and insults of a conduct-disordered child, might wonder, "What do these feelings tell me about this child's internal world?" As therapy progresses, the therapist's ability to tolerate the child's negative emotions helps the child to overcome the need to use the defense mechanism of splitting in order to keep those feelings from consciousness.

Object Relations in the Family Context

Selma Fraiberg (1980) is another psychoanalyst who exemplifies the object relations approach. She takes to heart the idea that relationships are causal in the development of psychopathology and that they provide the key to ameliorating it. Accordingly, Fraiberg recommends treating relationships rather than individuals. *Parent–infant psychotherapy* (Lieberman & Pawl, 1993) strives to prevent psychopathology in young children through banishing from the nursery the "ghosts" of the mother's troubled childhood. Through remembering and resolving their childhood traumas, adults can avoid reenacting them with their own children. "In each case, when our therapy has brought the parent to remember and reexperience his childhood anxiety and suffering, the ghosts depart, and the afflicted parents become the protectors of their children against the repetition of their own conflicted past" (p. 196). (See Box 17.1.)

Erickson, Korfmacher, and Egeland (1992) have continued this line of work by providing home-based interventions for at-risk mothers and young children. The *STEEP* (Steps Toward Effective, Enjoyable

Box 17.1   **A Psychoanalytic Infant–Parent Psychotherapy Session**

Annie, age 16, came to the attention of the Infant Mental Health Program when she refused to care for her baby, Greg. She avoided physical contact with him, often forgot to buy milk, and fed him on Kool-Aid and Tang. Annie herself was the product of an abusive upbringing, and while she could remember the facts of what had occurred to her, she blocked off all awareness of the emotions she suffered—just as she seemed unable to empathize with her baby's distress. The team speculated that Annie's abusive parenting arose from a defense mechanism—identification with the aggressor—that allowed her to keep from awareness her childhood feelings of anxiety and terror. Her therapist, Mrs. Shapiro, visited her at home.

Greg, 17 months old, was in his high chair eating his breakfast. Mother kept up a stream of admonitions while he ate: "Don't do that. Don't drop the food off." Then suddenly, responding to some trivial mishap in the high chair, Annie screamed, "Stop it!" Both Greg and Mrs. Shapiro jumped. Annie said to

the therapist, "I scared you, didn't I?" Mrs. Shapiro, recovering from shock, decided this was the moment she was waiting for. She said, "Sometimes, Annie, the words and sounds that come out of your mouth don't even sound like you. I wonder who they do sound like?" Annie said immediately, "I know. They sound just like my mother. My mother used to scare me." "How did you feel?" Annie said, "How would you feel if you were in with a bull in a china shop? . . . Besides, I don't want to talk about that. I've suffered enough. That's behind me."

But Mrs. Shapiro persisted, gently, and made the crucial interpretation. She said, "I could imagine that as a little girl you might be so scared, that in order to make yourself less scared, you might start talking and sounding like your mother." Annie said again, "I don't want to talk about it right now." But she was deeply affected by Mrs. Shapiro's words.

The rest of the hour took a curious turn. Annie began to collapse before Mrs. Shapiro's eyes. Instead of a

tough, defiant, aggressive girl, she became a helpless, anxious little girl for the entire hour. Since she could find no words to speak of the profound anxiety which had emerged in her, she began to speak of everything she could find in her contemporary life that made her feel afraid, helpless, alone.

In this way, and for many hours to come, Mrs. Shapiro led Annie back into the experiences of helplessness and terror in her childhood and moved back and forth, from the present to the past, in identifying for Annie the ways in which she brought her own experiences to her mothering of Greg, how identification with the feared people of her childhood was "remembered" when she became the frightening mother to Greg. It was a moment for therapeutic rejoicing when Annie was able to say, "I don't want my child to be afraid of me."

Source: Fraiberg (1980), pp. 192–193

Parenting) program is designed to offset the risk of an insecure attachment. The target population is mothers pregnant with their first child who are at risk for parenting problems due to poverty, youth, lack of education, social isolation, and stressful life circumstances. Individual sessions are offered with the goal of helping the mother achieve insight into how her own early experiences of being inadequately cared for triggered her current feelings of sadness, loss, and anger and then to help her deal with these feelings. The therapist also serves an educative function by providing information about child care and helping the mother with issues regarding personal

growth, education, work, and general life management. There are also group sessions, which allow the mothers to confront their defense mechanisms, air problems, and gain confidence from mutual support.

Psychodynamic Developmental Therapy

One of the most recent developments in psychoanalytic psychotherapy is Fonagy and colleagues' (1996) *psychodynamic developmental therapy for children (PDTC)*. Their work is conducted at the Anna Freud Center in London, which, as the name implies, is inspired by Anna Freud's thinking. Fonagy and colleagues were particularly interested in developing a treatment model that would lend itself to the demands of empirical investigation. Their program of research represents a step forward in terms of its clarification of the underlying theory, its operationalization of slippery psychoanalytic concepts, and its explicit links between theory and intervention techniques.

The Conceptual Model

Influenced by the work of John Bowlby, Fonagy and colleagues consider disturbed *self-development* to lie at the heart of childhood psychopathology. Failures in the early attachment relationship with the parent deprive the child of the kind of social experiences that lead to a positive, undistorted view of self and relationships.

Further, Fonagy and Target (1996) utilize concepts from the social cognitive literature to describe the ways children's assumptions about themselves and others are internally represented. For example, they use the term *theory of mind*, which we encountered in relation to autism (see Chapter 4) to refer to the child's capacity to understand mental states in the self and others. This capacity is deficient in children whose parents lacked empathy and emotional responsiveness. Other important mental functions that are disrupted in psychopathology include the ability to *tolerate emotions* and *control impulses* rather than being overwhelmed by them, a *reality organization* that allows the child to explore the world and act in it, and *stable representations* of the self and others.

The Therapeutic Process

The focus of PDTC is to remove the obstacles that prevent children from progressing on a healthy developmental course. This is accomplished by providing children with *corrective experiences* that help them to develop more complete and accurate representations of self and other. The therapist strives to increase children's capacity to reflect on mental states in self and others, to bring their feelings and actions under conscious control, and to develop a "metacognitive mode"—that is, to be able to think about their own thought processes. We now turn to describing how these aims are accomplished.

In order to *enhance reflective processes*, the therapist helps children to observe their own emotions, to understand and label them, and to recognize the relationship between their behavior and their feelings. Next, in order to *strengthen impulse control* the therapist may employ a variety of techniques. One such technique involves the use of metaphor. For example, one child acted out the part of the "most powerful train engine in the world," going so far as to threaten to jump out the window in order to prove his indestructibility. The therapist suggested that really powerful trains have good brakes, and interested the child in the challenge of finding his.

Next, the psychoanalytic relationship gives the PDTC therapist the opportunity to help the child develop *awareness of others*, such as an understanding of the motivations underlying people's actions. Children who have experienced disturbed attachment relationships may find the mental states of adults to be confusing or frightening. The supportive and accepting environment of the therapy relationship provides children with a safe place to explore their ideas about interpersonal relationships and correct their faulty internal models. Lastly, PDTC aims to help children develop the *capacity to play*. The capacity to play is central to the acquisition of metacognitive capacities because it requires the child to hold in mind two different realities: the pretend and the actual. The therapist facilitates playfulness by exaggerating actions in order to indicate that they are "just pretend," and by encouraging the use of play materials (e.g., wooden blocks) that do not make reference to real-world concerns.

Empirical Support

Psychoanalytically oriented psychotherapies do not lend themselves readily to empirical research. Neither the technique nor the outcome it strives to achieve is easily standardized. For example, the mechanism of change is the creation of an intense relationship between patient and therapist; interpretations must be timed just so, so that the patient is ready to receive them. The subtleties of these techniques are not easily put into a treatment manual for therapists to follow in a uniform way. Further, the outcome of a successful psychoanalysis is a change in such hypothetical constructs as defense mechanisms, ego strengths, and internal representations that are difficult to observe or quantify. Thus, it comes as no surprise that efforts to empirically test the effectiveness of psychoanalysis with children are few and far between. By the same token, the difficulties inherent in research on psychoanalysis with children make the efforts that have been made all the more noteworthy.

Psychodynamic developmental therapy is the only psychoanalytically oriented child treatment to be subjected to rigorous and programmatic research. To date, Fonagy and colleagues (1996) have documented the success of their approach with a wide range of disorders, including depression, anxiety, phobias, posttraumatic stress disorder, oppositional-defiant disorder, conduct disorder, and ADHD. As described in Chapter 9, children and adolescents with *internalizing disorders* tend to respond to psychodynamic developmental therapy better than those with externalizing disorders. For example, Fonagy and Target (1994) found that over 85 percent of children treated for anxiety and depression were no longer diagnosable at outcome, whereas this was the case for only 69 percent of children with conduct disorder and 30 percent of those with obsessive-compulsive disorder. *Younger* children (less than 12 years old) benefited the most, particularly when therapy was *intensive* (four to five times per week.)

Next, research on the *STEEP* program (Erickson, Korfmacher, & Egeland, 1992) for preventing attachment disorders (described earlier) is worth consideration, since it approximates a test of the object relations model. A follow-up evaluation conducted a year after the intervention ended, when the children were 2 years old, showed that the treated mothers provided a more appropriately stimulating and organized home environment for their child than did mothers in the control group. In addition, mothers had fewer symptoms of depression and anxiety and better life management skills. Attachment security was not increased in the first year, but a trend in that direction was detected in the second year. Finally, van IJzendoorn, Juffer, and Duyvesteyn (1995) conducted a *meta-analysis* of a number of attachment-based interventions for mothers and young children. Results indicated that they were effective, especially when treatment was intensive and long-lasting.

The Humanistic Approach

The **humanistic** approach, also called client-centered or nondirective, differs radically from the psychoanalytic and behavior therapies. The humanistic therapist never interprets as does the analyst, and never tells clients how to solve their problems as does the behavior therapist. Instead, the therapist strives to create a nonjudgmental and nurturing atmosphere in which the client can grow. While on the face of it the humanistic approach seems simple, in reality, the therapy is based on an explicit developmental model of psychopathology and is one of the most demanding for its practitioners.

The Conceptual Model

Our discussion is based on the ideas of Carl Rogers (1959), founder of humanistic therapy. Rogers stresses the primacy of the individual's *self*, the concept of who one is and of one's relations with others. As awareness of the self emerges in the toddler period, the individual develops the universal need for warmth, respect, sympathy, and acceptance. It is essential that the people the child loves and values foster the child's need to experience and decide things for himself or herself. This can be done only if the child receives **unconditional positive regard**. Here, no aspect of the child is perceived as more or less worthy of positive regard. Children are intrinsically valued, and their experiences are not viewed judgmentally as being "good" or "bad" by adult standards.

Normal development goes awry because of what Rogers calls **conditions of worth**. Instead of unconditional positive regard, significant adults, particularly parents, say, in essence, "I will love you on the condition that you behave as I want you to." Because of the strong need for positive regard, children eventually make parental values into self values. At this point children are no longer in touch with their true selves, no longer open to experience and capable of deciding for themselves whether an experience is growth-promoting. By incorporating alien values they become alienated from themselves. Because of alienation, children begin to distort experiences in order to fit the imposed model of a "good boy" or a "good girl": perhaps the aesthetic boy believes he has to be a competitive go-getter because this is his father's ideal, or the bright girl is hounded by feelings of inadequacy because her mother disparages intellectual achievement.

The Therapeutic Process

In light of what we have explored in our discussions we can understand how the humanistic therapist, by offering the child unconditional positive regard, can help undo the damage of conditional love. The focus is continually on feelings, because these hold the key to maturity. In addition, the process of therapy is client-centered, allowing the child to take the lead in choosing the themes to be explored.

Virginia Axline (1969) is the figure most closely associated with the application of Rogers's principles to child therapy. The major change in the client-centered procedure is the introduction of *play material* for children below the preadolescent age range. The material is simple and conducive to self-expression—dolls, animals, clay, sand, building materials. Construction toys and games of skill are avoided as being too structured to produce varied and individualized behavior. While the formal arrangement resembles that of psychoanalysis, the purpose is quite different. Rather than using play as the basis for interpretation, therapists limit their activity to reflecting the themes and affects the child introduces. (See Box 17.2 for an example of Axline's technique.)

The technique of *reflection* of the child's feelings is at the heart of the humanistic approach. While easily parodied in the form of mindlessly parroting back what another person says, reflection is a powerful technique, especially for working with children. Children often have the experience of talking with adults who are busy, distracted, or listen with only half an ear. The therapists' reflection of the child's own thoughts and feelings communicates that the therapist is actively listening and taking the child's concerns seriously. What is more, in the per-

missive atmosphere of the therapeutic session, the child begins to explore feelings that formerly had to be banished from conscious awareness. In fact, some of these feelings may never have been clearly recognized for what they were. Thus, reflection also serves a defining function rather than being a mere echo of what the child already knows.

The therapist's nonjudgmental reflection also communicates *acceptance* of formerly banished feelings, which encourages the child's self-acceptance. As feelings are explicitly defined and accepted, they become congruent. As the boy realizes his resentment for being pushed into the alien role of a go-getter and as the girl can face her fear of being rejected by a nonintellectual mother, such feelings become part of the self. The once-divided self is whole again.

The therapist has complete confidence in the client's ability to solve his or her own problems with the minimum of direction—hence, the humanistic child therapist is *nondirective*. After discussing the ground rules for the therapeutic hour and describing the procedure in general terms, humanistic therapists leave the direction of the sessions up to the child. As we have seen, therapists do not interpret the meaning of the child's behavior, nor do they introduce any material from the child's past, from the reality of the child's present situation, or from previous sessions. If, for example, they learn that the child has started setting fires, they wait until the child is ready to make such behavior part of the therapeutic session. Thus responsibility is always on the child's shoulders. What therapists communicate implicitly is a faith in the child's ability to decide what is best for his or her own growth.

Understandably, it is demanding to be a nondirective therapist. First it means relinquishing the role of the authoritative adult who "knows better." Moreover, the therapist's acceptance of and respect for the child must be *genuine*. However, when children are given freedom to do what they like, many of them begin to gravitate toward destructive acting out. Not only that, but they also have a genius for finding ways of teasing, testing, and provoking adults. For the therapist to maintain an attitude of acceptance and understanding rather than self-defense and retaliation requires a forbearing disposition and self-discipline.

Box 17.2 | **A Humanistic Play Therapy Session**

Joanne, age 6, comes into the play-room. She sits quietly at the table and uses clay to make the same thing she does every session: a figure of a man carrying a cane [Joanne's mother's new boyfriend also carries a cane]. Each time, after he is finished, awful things happen to him.

Therapist: Here comes that man again.

Joannne: Yes. *(her voice is tense, de-termined)*

Therapist: The man with the cane.

Joannne: Yes. *(she begins to punch him full of holes)*

Therapist: You're putting holes in the clay man.

Joannne: Stab! Stab! Stab!

Therapist: You're stabbing him.

Joannne (in a small voice): Ouch, you hurt me. *(voice changes)* I don't care. I want to hurt you.

Therapist: The clay man is crying be-cause he is hurt.

Joannne: (interrupting): I *want* to hurt him.

Therapist: You want to hurt him.

Joannne: I don't *like* him.

Therapist: You don't like him.

Joannne: I don't like him. I hate him. Look this hole went clear through him. It went in his front and out his back.

Therapist: He gets holes punched clear through him. You'll fix him.

Joannne: Yes. I'll tear his head off.

Therapist: You'll even tear his head off.

Joannne: I know, I know. I'll put him clear down in the bottom of the jar and then I'll put the clay in on top of him and he'll smother.

Therapist (following child's actions): You tore him into little pieces and buried him in the bottom of the jar.

Joanne nods and smiles at the ther-apist. Then she goes over to the baby doll, pretends to feed it, holds it tenderly in her arms, puts it to bed, and plays house very quietly.

Source: Axline (1969), pp. 179–180

Empirical Support   While Rogers had an inter-est in assessing the effectiveness of his therapeutic approach, little programmatic research has been car-ried out on humanistic therapy with children. How-ever, psychotherapy process research is consistent in showing that therapist-offered conditions, such as warmth, empathy, and acceptance, are related to positive outcomes with children. (See Shirk and Russell, 1996, for a review of the research.)

Behavior Therapies

The Conceptual Model

Behavior therapies are characterized by attention to specific, *currently observable behaviors* of the client, by a concern with *objective measures* of the outcomes of their interventions, and by a reliance on the research laboratory to provide *general prin-ciples of behavior change* that can be used as the basis of therapeutic intervention and as a place to put clinical findings to rigorous experimental tests. Rather than being a special set of techniques, be-

havior therapies are "an *approach* to abnormal be-havior . . . characterized by [an] empirical method-ology" (Ross and Nelson, 1979, p. 303).

To elaborate: Pragmatic considerations have dic-tated the emphasis on current behaviors, since these are most amenable to change. Behavior therapists would not deny that such behaviors may be rooted in the past, but the past cannot be altered, whereas the present and the future can. Among ongoing be-haviors, the therapists deal with three response sys-tems: *overt-motor*, *physiological-emotional*, and *cognitive-verbal*. All must be considered in a com-prehensive treatment program, since they are not necessarily correlated; for example, a boy who is constantly fighting in school may tell the therapist that "everything is OK" and he only fights "a little every now and then."

In the constant interplay between the clinic and the laboratory, principles of learning have been ex-tensively used to generate therapeutic procedures, while both social and developmental psychology have provided conceptual underpinnings for thera-peutic techniques, although to a lesser degree. Per-haps even more significant than the application of laboratory findings is the incorporation of *experimental procedures* into psychotherapeutic practice. The behavior therapist reasons very much like his or her experimental counterpart: If behavior X is due to antecedent Y and consequent Z, then as Y and Z are changed, so should X. The therapeutic intervention, like an experiment, consists of testing out the hypothesis, the crucial measure being a change in the base rate of the target behavior X in the desired direction.

The simplest design in evaluating therapeutic effectiveness is the *A-B design*, in which the dependent measure is evaluated both before intervention (baseline, or A) and during intervention (B). If, for example, a therapist hypothesized that temper tantrums in a 3-year-old were being sustained by maternal attention, he might advise the mother to ignore them. If the base rate went down, the therapist would have evidence that the hypothesis was correct. Such a design is adequate for clinical work because it demonstrates whether change occurs. However, for a more stringent test of the hypothesis that change was caused by the intervention rather than by other variables, the reversal, the *A-B-A-B design*, is used, in which the therapeutic procedure is repeatedly applied and withdrawn. If change in the target behavior occurs only in the presence of the intervention, then a causal relationship can be more readily assumed (see Figure 17.1).

The Developmental Dimension

We have integrated discussion of developmental issues into our description of other forms of therapy. However, behavioral thinking is by definition *ahistorical*—current contingencies for behavior are all that matters, and the past is irrelevant. Are developmental considerations irrelevant to behavior therapy? While roundly criticizing behaviorists for their insensitivity to developmental issues in their conceptualization and treatment of psychopathology, leading figures in the field have taken on the task of filling the gap. For example, Forehand and Wierson (1993) present an overview of developmental factors to be considered in designing behavioral interventions for children. They review the literature on stage-salient issues and emotional,

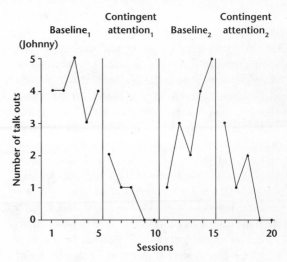

Figure 17.1   A record of talking out behavior of an educable mentally challenged student. Baseline1—before experimental conditions. Contingent Teacher Attention1—systematic ignoring of talking out and increased teacher attention to appropriate behavior. Baseline2—reinstatement of teacher attention to talking out behavior.

Source: Hall et al., 1971, p. 143, Figure 2. Reproduced by permission.

cognitive, social, and moral development, as well as considering changes in the environmental context of development from infancy to adolescence.

From their review, Forehand and Wierson derive three major areas for the behavioral therapist to consider. The first of these is the *cognitive capacity* of the child. For example, younger children require concrete, present-oriented language and cope best with nonverbal modes of interaction, such as drawings and play. With the onset of more sophisticated cognitive abilities, older children may be able to benefit from learning more sophisticated, verbally based control techniques, such as problem-solving skills.

The second area concerns the child's *developmental tasks*. For behavior therapy to be maximally effective, the behaviors targeted for change should be consistent with the developmental tasks the child is currently facing, such as to achieve mastery in middle childhood or to achieve individuation in adolescence. In addition, intervention must target tasks the child has failed to accomplish at previous developmental transitions. This means that the child therapist may need to go beyond the simple presenting problem in order to determine what might have gone awry in earlier developmental periods.

Third is the *developmental context*. It is not only children who change over the course of development; their environments change also, as the social world broadens from the family to include peers, school, and the larger society. The individuals in each of these settings provide contingencies for children's behavior, acting as reinforcers, punishers, and models. Individuals outside the family increasingly have the capacity to either contribute to problem behavior or help to reduce it. Thus, over the course of development, behavior therapists need to widen their scope of intervention from the narrow focus on parent–child relationships in order to incorporate peers and teachers into the intervention plan.

The Therapeutic Process

Principles of learning—specifically, classical conditioning, operant learning, and imitation—form the bases of behavior therapy procedures. We examine here exemplars of the application of each principle. (For an account of how behavior therapies are applied to various psychopathologies, see Morris and Kratochwill, 1998.)

Classical Conditioning   **Systematic desensitization**, as developed by Wolpe (1973), is a procedure for eliminating anxiety-mediated problems. In such problems, initially neutral stimuli come to elicit powerful anxiety responses as a result of classical conditioning. The bond between the conditioned stimulus and the anxiety response can be broken, however, by **reciprocal inhibition**, in which the stronger of two incompatible responses tends to inhibit the weaker. The therapist's task, therefore, becomes one of pairing anxiety-eliciting stimuli with a more powerful, incompatible response. The response Wolpe uses is deep muscle relaxation, since an individual cannot simultaneously anxious and relaxed.

Two preliminary steps are needed to implement the therapy. First, the child must be instructed in the technique of relaxing various muscle groups through-

out the body. The child is also required to make up a graduated sequence of anxiety-eliciting stimuli, going from the least to the most intense. A girl with a school phobia, for example, may feel no anxiety when she awakens and dresses, mild anxiety at breakfast, increasingly strong anxiety while waiting for the bus and approaching school, and the most intense anxiety during the free period before classes start.

In the therapy proper, the children imagine each of the steps, pairing them with the relaxation response. If the anxiety is too strong at any particular step and they cannot relax, they return to the preceding step. Over a series of sessions the children gradually are able to relax in response to even the most intense anxiety-producing stimuli. While Wolpe's rationale has been questioned and the specific variables responsible for improvement have not been satisfactorily isolated, the therapy itself has been successful in treating a host of problems, including school and hospital phobias, examination anxiety, fear of authority, maternal separation anxiety, and asthma.

Operant Conditioning   Behavior therapists have made extensive use of the operant principle that behavior is controlled by specific antecedent and consequent stimulus events. **Contingency management**, or the manipulation of rewards and punishments that follow or are contingent upon the response, is particularly potent in decreasing the strength of undesirable behaviors or increasing the strength of adaptive ones. There are two kinds of positive consequences: reward, or **positive reinforcement**, and removal of an aversive stimulus, or **negative reinforcement**. There are also two kinds of negative consequences: *positive punishment*, or the administering of an aversive stimulus, and *negative punishment*, or the removal of a pleasant stimulus.

Examples of the application of operant principles are legion, with some involving a therapist, and others involving parents, who not only can be taught how to implement a therapeutic program with relative ease but who also are in a position to control a wider range of behaviors than can be elicited in a therapeutic setting. (The examples are from Ross and Nelson, 1979.) The language skills of 2- and 3-year-old children were enhanced when their mothers reinforced naming of objects with praise or bits of food, while the tantrums of a 21-month-old were extinguished when the mother ignored them, thereby withdrawing the attention that had been sustaining them.

Instead of direct reinforcement, a child can be given a *token*, which subsequently can be redeemed for rewards such as prizes or privileges. In one therapeutic program children were given tokens for cooperative behavior and doing chores but lost them for undesirable social behavior. In **time out**, the child is isolated for a brief period, thereby being punished by the withdrawal of reinforcers. In one complex program an acting-out boy was isolated for two minutes when he was aggressive and disobedient, while less severe misbehavior was ignored and cooperative behavior was rewarded by special attention and treats.

Observational Learning   Observational learning, or **modeling**, has not been extensively employed as a primary therapeutic technique. However, having fearful children observe fearless children interacting with a phobic stimulus, such as a snake or a dog, has successfully eliminated some phobias. The model may be presented either in real life or on film. Modeling is often combined with reinforcement of the desired behavior; for example, in teaching verbal behavior to children with autism, the child is immediately rewarded with food upon each successful imitation of the therapist's vocalization. Another good example of this technique is the pain management modeling described in Chapter 13.

Behavior Therapy in the Family Context

Behavior therapists have also begun expanding their interventions to include various contexts in their treatment plan, such as the family, the school, and peers. It makes little sense to change a deviant behavior while leaving a child in a disharmonious or dysfunctional setting.

Parent management training (PMT), introduced in Chapter 9, is one of the most successful and best-documented programs based on social learning principles. PMT was developed by Patterson (1982), who saw maladaptive parent–child relationships as central to the etiology of conduct disorder. PMT focuses on altering the interactions between parent and child so that prosocial behavior, rather than coercive behavior, is reinforced. As the name implies, this is accomplished by training the parents to respond more effectively to the child.

First, parents learn how to think about their child-rearing problems in *behavioral terms*. They are trained to identify, define, and observe problem behavior, as well as its precipitants and consequences. In this way, they are better able to perceive their roles in perpetuating child misbehavior and to abandon such unhelpful attributions as personalizing the problem ("I'm a lousy parent") or psychopathologizing their children ("He's a bad seed").

Second, parents learn a number of behavior modification techniques, including the use of *positive reinforcement*. Often, parents who have become caught in repetitive cycles of coercive exchanges neglect the need to provide any sort of positive feedback to their children and seldom spend pleasurable time with them. The fundamental goals of behavior modification are not only to reduce problem behavior but to increase prosocial behavior as well. Therefore, parents learn to use social praise ("Good job!") and tokens that can be exchanged for rewards when children have behaved well. Reinforcement for positive behavior ("Try to catch the child doing something good") also counteracts the child's experience of the family as a kind of boot camp.

As a parallel to increasing positive reinforcement, parents are also trained to use *mild punishment*. Rather than using such aversive techniques as yelling, hitting, or "nattering" (repetitive nagging complaints without any follow-through) that only exacerbate the problem, parents are encouraged to provide *time out* from reinforcement or *loss of privileges* in response to misbehavior. Typically, these skills are first applied to relatively simple, easily observed behavioral sequences. As parents become more adept, the focus shifts to more difficult and involved behaviors. As children's behavior improves, parents learn higher-level skills such as *negotiation* and mutual problem solving with children. In this way, the overall tone of family relationships becomes more positive and collaborative, as well as being more supportive of children's increasing self-control over their own behavior.

Empirical Support

Behavior therapists have been the most active in documenting the effectiveness of their approach. Outcome studies report success with a wide variety of child behavior problems, ranging from phobias to bed-wetting to conduct disorder.

For example, many outcome studies conducted over the past two decades attest to the effectiveness of parent management training (PMT) (Kazdin, 1997c). Marked improvement is shown in the behavior of conduct-disordered children, which is sustained as long as four and a half years after treatment ends. In addition, the impact of PMT is broad, with many other problem behaviors improving in addition to the specific ones targeted for treatment. Sibling behavior also improves, and ratings of maternal psychopathology, particularly depression, decrease after PMT. Overall, family members report feeling more positive emotions with one another. Thus, PMT seems to alter multiple aspects of dysfunctional family relationships.

Despite its proven effectiveness, there are *limitations* to PMT (Patterson, 1982). For one thing, the treatment is relatively time-consuming: 50 to 60 hours seems to be optimal. Further, not everyone benefits equally. Patterson finds that he is unable to help about a third of the families who come to his clinic. Often these are parents who have serious psychopathology or families that are in crisis. PMT is also relatively demanding: parents must be willing and able to engage in the extensive training, to implement a consistent routine, and to work intensively with the behavior therapists. A considerable number of parents are too disturbed or too despairing to make such a commitment. Finally, the failure of several studies to find treatment effects has led to the suggestion that parent training should be supplemented by other techniques, such as those that address academic problems or cognitive skill deficits. (See Vuchinich, Wood, and Angelelli, 1996, for an innovative intervention program that integrates Patterson's approach to parent training with cognitive problem-solving skills training for children.) It is to those therapies inspired by the cognitive model that we turn next.

Cognitive Therapies

The Conceptual Model

Cognitive therapies can be distinguished from behavior therapies by their attention to the *mental processes* that mediate between stimulus and response. Rather than changing the environmental contingencies that reinforce child behavior problems, cognitive therapists target the dysfunctional and maladaptive *beliefs* that guide behavior. The basic goal is to change the way the child thinks. When this has been accomplished, behavior will also change.

There is not actually a strict dichotomy between behavior and cognitive therapies. Behavior therapists employ cognitive elements as a means of achieving behavioral change; in desensitization, for example, children imagine various situations and instruct themselves to relax, both of which are cognitive activities. For their part, cognitive therapies are consistent with their behaviorist roots in that they concern themselves with changing specific observable behaviors, systematically monitor the relation between intervention and behavioral change, and retain allegiance to the scientific method. Many therapists combine the techniques under the rubric of "cognitive-behavioral therapy." For the sake of clarity, however, we limit our discussion here to the specifically cognitive dimension of these therapies.

The Therapeutic Process

Cognitive therapies have been developed to address a wide variety of childhood psychopathologies, including depression, substance abuse, ADHD, anxiety, sexual abuse, conduct disorder, and autism, among others. We select for presentation two treatment programs—one for an internalizing problem, separation anxiety, and the other for an externalizing problem, conduct disorder. (For presentations of cognitive techniques applied to various disorders in children, see Reinecke, Dattilio, and Freeman, 1996.)

Cognitive Therapy for Separation Anxiety Disorder Kendall and his colleagues (Kendall & Treadwell, 1996; Levin et al., 1996) developed a cognitive intervention program for treating anxiety disorders in children. The core principle underlying the model is that *cognitive representations* of the environment determine children's response to it. In the case of anxiety disorders, exaggerated perceptions of *threat*—the fear of devastating loss, harsh criticism, or catastrophic harm—dominate the child's reactions to events. The therapist's job is to alter these maladaptive cognitions, as well as the behavioral patterns and emotional responses that accompany them, by designing new *learning experiences* for the child.

The therapists' goals are to teach children to identify anxious feelings and to calm themselves when anxious, to modify their thoughts, to develop a plan for coping with anxiety-arousing situations, and to reward themselves for coping well. Children are taught to accomplish these goals in a series of steps identified with the acronym *FEAR*.

The first step in the FEAR sequence—*Feeling Frightened*?—focuses on helping children to recognize when they are experiencing anxiety. (See Box 17.3 for an example.) Often children do not perceive the connection between physical sensations—trembling, stomachache, and so forth—and their emotional distress in a given situation. Recognizing that they are anxious cues them to the fact that it is time to put into place their problem-solving skills.

The second stage is *Expecting Bad Things to Happen*? Here the child is helped to identify the negative expectancies that generate the fear. For example, a child might fear riding an elevator because a "bad man" might get on it or because her parents might disappear while she is gone. However, many young children have difficulty with this step. Their cognitive capacities are limited such that it is difficult for them to observe their own thought processes. The therapist might assist by suggesting possible expectations rather than requiring the child to come up with them (e.g., "Some kids are afraid that the elevator will get stuck").

The third stage is *Attitudes and Actions That Can Help*. Here the therapist helps the child to come up with more realistic attitudes about the feared event, as well as actions to cope with it. For example, the therapist might ask the child to think about the like-

lihood of being locked in an elevator or to conduct a poll to find how many times others have ridden in an elevator without incident. Then the child is encouraged to generate possible solutions to the problem. For example, the child might be encouraged to talk about how she could differentiate "bad men" from harmless ones; alternatively, the child might be taught how to use the emergency phone to bring help. New coping strategies are tried out as "experiments," which has a playful and non-threatening air.

The fourth stage is *Results and Rewards*. Here children evaluate the success of their problem-solving attempts and are encouraged to think of possible rewards for coping with the anxiety-arousing situation, such as having a snack, telling parents about their accomplishment, or praising themselves for doing a "good job."

After children have learned the FEAR steps, the next phase of treatment involves *practicing* their new skills in imaginary and real-life situations. Exercises are tailored to the specific fears of a child and are called *Show That I Can* tasks. For example, the child who is anxious about riding an elevator might be exposed to one in increasingly proximal steps, while a child who believes he alone worries might be assigned to interview classmates and report back regarding what they worry about. *Reinforcements* are provided for children who complete their "homework" assignments. The completion of treatment is celebrated with a special session in which child and therapist create a videotaped "commercial" for the FEAR steps they have learned. Not only does this activity introduce an element of fun and creativity, but it also helps to reinforce the collaborative and positive relationship that is an important component of the therapy.

While the focus on the intervention is with children, *parents* play an important role as well. Parents often inadvertently reinforce children's withdrawal from anxiety-arousing situations by giving in to their fears. The therapist works with parents to help them support their child's independence from them and to increase their capacity to tolerate the child's short-term discomfort with facing the feared situation. The therapist is also sensitive to the ways in which the parents' own concerns—such as their own

Box 17.3   A Cognitive Therapy Session for Childhood Anxiety

Allison, aged 9, was referred to treatment for separation anxiety disorder. During this session Allison and her therapist discuss how she coped with an anxiety-provoking situation one morning when she forgot to bring her homework to school. Annotations identify the FEAR steps.

Therapist: So tell me, how did you know that you were feeling frightened? *(Feeling Frightened?)*

Allison: My heart started pounding.

Therapist: What else?

Allison: Umm . . . let's see. I started biting my nails.

Therapist: Uh-huh. That's a sign isn't it?

Allison: Yeah.

Therapist: So then what did you notice? What were you thinking about? *(Expecting Bad Things to Happen?)*

Allison: I could get in real big trouble here—get punished.

Therapist: That's what you were thinking about. Well, what bad things were going to happen to you? What were you worried about?

Allison: I was gonna get yelled at.

Therapist: You were gonna get yelled at, and if you got yelled at, what?

Allison: I would probably have to stay in for recess.

Therapist: Okay, what about your teacher? What would your teacher be thinking if you lost your health homework?

Allison: Boy, is she forgetful. He'd say, "Why did you take it home in the first place?"

Therapist: He would think you were forgetful?

Allison: Yeah, and he yells. You can hear him all the way down the hall. And when he yells, the kids down the hall can

---

anxieties or marital difficulties—might contribute to the child's problems. Consequently, Kendall has expanded the scope of his approach in the form of cognitive-behavioral family therapy (see Howard and Kendall, 1996).

Interpersonal Problem-Solving Skills Training (IPS)   IPS was introduced in Chapter 9 as a treatment of choice for conduct disorder. As described, Shure and Spivack (1988) focus on building competence in five skills found to be deficient in aggressive children. The first of these is to *generate alternative solutions* to a problem. Children are encouraged to brainstorm and explore different ideas without fear of censorship or premature closure. The goals are to assemble a repertoire of solutions that children can draw from and to develop the habit of thinking before acting. (See Box 17.4 for an example of IPS techniques.) One of the hallmarks of ICPS training is that the focus is not so much on *what* children think but on *how* they think. Rather than relying on external support for their behavior, the idea is to bring behavior under children's control by helping them think through interpersonal problems and arrive at solutions on their own.

Second, children are trained to *consider the consequences* of social acts. Aggressive children do not generally think beyond the present to consider the possible negative consequences of misbehavior or, for that matter, the positive consequences of prosocial behavior. Therefore, children learn to consider the consequences of acts of self and other and to develop a less impulsive response style. The third goal is to develop *means-ends thinking*, to learn to engage in the step-by-step process needed to carry out a particular solution. This may require considering several possible actions and their consequences along the way. The next stage involves the development of *social-causal thinking*, an understanding of how the people in a problem situation feel and what motivates them to act the way they do. For example, this may involve recognizing the fact that aggressive behavior may anger other children and cause them to retaliate.

Fourth, children are helped to develop *sensitivity to interpersonal problems*. Children with poor social skills lack the sensitivity to the cues that indicate that there is a relational conflict between themselves and another person, and they often fail to recognize when a problem is an interpersonal one. Finally, at the highest level of ICPS skills hear him.

Therapist: You might get yelled at, and other kids would know. What would they think?

Allison: They'd just think I was weird.

Therapist: They'd think you were weird. Well, no wonder you were feeling a little scared! Okay, so what did you do about that? How else could you have thought about that? *(Attitudes and Actions That Can Help)*

Allison: Maybe he won't want to go over them today, be-

cause he didn't. I asked him at lunch, and he said he didn't want to go over them until tomorrow.

Therapist: That was an action you took to help yourself out. Good for you, Allison; you went and asked the question! How could you have changed your scary thoughts around a little bit?

Allison: I don't know. Maybe he'll just forget about going over them or something, and maybe if he doesn't,

he won't yell at me.

Therapist: Well, I think that you should really be congratulated for that action that you took! That's like the best idea I could have thought of—go check it out, you found out what's going to happen. *(Results and Rewards)*

Allison: Before you start worrying your head off.

Therapist: Before you start getting so upset and worried. Yeah, that was excellent!

Source: Levin et al. (1996), pp. 166–167

training, children develop a *dynamic orientation.* This refers to the ability to look beyond the surface of human behavior and to appreciate that there may be underlying motives that arise from the unique perspective of that person, based on his or her experience in life. For example, a bully may be construed as a bad person who likes to hurt others, as someone who is insecure and trying to prove he is good enough, or as someone who is mistreated at home and is taking his frustrations out on others. The issue is not the validity of the interpretation but rather the ability to see that surface behavior often masks underlying concerns and motivations, an understanding of which can guide a more effective response.

Empirical Support   The cognitive therapies described above have received empirical support. For example, Kendall and Gerow (1996) randomly assigned forty-seven anxiety-disordered children to cognitive treatment or a wait-list control group. Those children who underwent treatment showed significant decreases in anxiety on self-report measures, as well as on measures obtained from parents, teachers, and observers. Two-thirds of the treated children were no longer diagnosable after

treatment, and treatment gains were maintained at follow-ups conducted one year and then three and a half years later.

Even more impressive, Kazdin's (1996) studies of cognitive problem-solving skills training have been singled out as a model of research into therapeutic effectiveness. He and his colleagues randomly assigned a sample of school-age boys with conduct disorder to one of three treatments. The first group received problem-solving skill training. The second group received the same training, but it was supplemented by in vivo practice; for example, they were given "homework" involving applying what they learned in the treatment session to situations with parents, peers, and teachers. The third group received relationship therapy that emphasized empathy, warmth, and unconditional positive regard on the therapists' part, along with helping the boys express their feelings and discuss their interpersonal problems.

The children in the two cognitive problem-solving skill training groups showed significantly greater reductions in antisocial behavior and overall behavior problems and greater increases in prosocial behavior than did the children in the relationship group. The effects were present in a one-year follow-up in

Box 17.4 | **An Interpersonal Problem-Solving Skills Training Session**

The following is a dialogue between a kindergarten-age child and a teacher trained in IPS. Annotations identify the IPS techniques used at each step in the process.

Teacher: What's the matter? What happened? *(eliciting child's view of problem)*

Child: Robert won't give me the clay!

Teacher: What can you do or say so he will let you have the clay? *(eliciting a problem solution)*

Child: I could ask him.

Teacher: That's one way. And what might happen next when you ask him? *(guiding means-end thinking)*

Child: He might say no.

Teacher: He might say no. What else could you try? *(guiding child to think of alternative solutions)*

Child: I could snatch it.

Teacher: That's another idea. What might happen if you do that? *(not criticizing child's solution; continuing to guide consequential thinking)*

Child: He might hit me.

Teacher: How would that make you feel? *(encouraging social-causal thinking)*

Child: Mad.

Teacher: How would Robert feel if you grabbed the clay? *(en-*

couraging social-causal thinking)

Child: Mad.

Teacher: Can you think of something different you can do or say so Robert won't hit you and you both won't be mad? *(guiding child to think of further solutions)*

Child: I could say, "You keep some and give me some."

Teacher: That's a different idea. *(reinforcing idea as different rather than "good," thus avoiding adult judgment)*

Source: Spivack and Shure (1982), p. 343

the home and at school. In spite of their improvement, however, the children were still outside the normal range for antisocial behavior. Further, gains of this kind of intervention do not always generalize beyond the treatment situation (Southam-Gerow et al., 1997).

Meta-analyses demonstrate that, taken as a whole, the various cognitive therapies for children are effective. However, some questions remain as to how this effectiveness comes about. For example, Durlak, Fuhrman, and Lampman (1991) analyzed sixty-four studies of various kinds of cognitive therapies. Most of the studies involved 9-year-old boys with externalizing problems in brief treatment. The results showed that treated children changed significantly as compared with untreated controls, although their behavior was still not within normal limits. Improvement was maintained over a four-month follow-up period. Effectiveness was a function of the children's cognitive level, those functioning at the formal operational level (ages 11 to 13) showing twice as much change as those at less advanced stages (ages 5 to 10). However, contrary to what the rationale of cognitive

behavior therapy would predict, improvement was not related to changes in cognition. Thus, the underlying mechanism responsible for change remains to be discovered.

Further, in general, cognitive treatments are more effective with adolescents than with younger children, perhaps because cognitive treatments are modeled on those developed for adults. Indeed, Weisz and colleagues (1995) argue that the effectiveness of cognitive treatments could be improved if they were better integrated with what is known about child development. For example, sensitivity to children's cognitive and language development could help to increase their capacity to understand and utilize the skills being taught to them.

The Family Systemic Approach

Given the importance of the family system in the etiology of psychopathology, it is not surprising that therapists from most schools of psychotherapy, including behaviorists, cognitive therapists, and psychoanalysts, have adapted their techniques to treating families. However, these approaches to working with individuals in the context of the family can be distinguished from approaches that specifically treat the whole family as a system. Our discussions of anorexia nervosa (Chapter 11) and schizophrenia (Chapter 10) introduced the basic premise and some of the concepts generated by the family systemic approach. Here we will examine both in greater detail.

The Conceptual Model

The basic premise is that the family is a *dynamic system*, an entity over and above the interaction of its individual members. Further, the family system has certain characteristics that define whether it is functioning adequately. As we saw in Chapter 1, Minuchin's structural approach (1974; Minuchin, Lee, & Simon, 1996) introduces two important concepts, those of boundaries and triangulation. For example, in malfunctioning families, *boundaries* may be blurred, resulting in an enmeshed system in which family members are overly involved with one another in an intrusive way; or *triangulation* may result when rigid patterns have formed in which certain family members ally with one another to the exclusion of other family members.

These patterns, once established, are difficult to change. The reason for this resistance to change, however, lies at the heart of the systemic theory of psychopathology: these troublesome patterns serve a *function* in the family system. To take a concrete example, consider the child in the *detouring-attacking* family (see Chapter 1). This is the child whose misbehavior serves the function of distracting the parents from their marital problems. Because there is such a significant payoff for the child's symptoms—the family stays intact—there will be strong ambivalence on the part of family members about relinquishing them.

The disturbed child is merely the *identified patient*—the symptom, as it were, that something has gone wrong. The pathology itself is in the system. Consequently, treatment of one individual within the family system is not going to be effective in bringing about change, because the family will tend to reorganize in order to reestablish the old pattern. Thus, the focus of treatment must be the entire family.

The Therapeutic Process

How does the therapist facilitate change? First, in order to change the system, the therapist must become a part of it. The initial step in the process of forming a therapeutic system is *joining*. Minuchin himself joins the family through his use of self. He emphasizes aspects of his personality and life experience that are consistent with the family's, such as by sharing with an immigrant family the fact that he, too, had to struggle with adapting to life in the United States. He accepts the family's organization and style and accommodates to them, showing respect for their way of doing things. In this way, the family therapist behaves much like an anthropologist taking the role of participant-observer, accepting the way that people define their problems, using their language, and openly enjoying their humor.

The next stage in the process is *enacting transactional patterns*. Here the family therapist encourages family members to show, rather than to tell, so that the therapist can observe their interactions directly. This can be informative in diagnosing the problem. For example, the therapist might note the small smile on the father's face as the conduct-disordered boy describes his pranks, or the way the mother always interrupts to qualify her anxious daughter's comments. The therapist might recreate problematic family scenarios by instructing family members to enact them in the therapy session: for example, if a child is complaining that his father never spends time with him, Minuchin might ask him to turn to his father and talk with him about it.

A family therapy session.

Box 17.5   A Family Therapy Session

The therapist has been called in to consult with the family of 7-year-old Mandy, who was caught setting fire to her mother's bed. Present are Mandy, her mother, and siblings Morris, age 10; Joyce, age 8; and Debbie, age 4. First, the therapist joins with and engages the family.

Mother: I—yesterday I was so upset.

Therapist: You were very upset. *(acknowledges and calms mother's anxiety)*

Mother: Yeah, because this could be very dangerous. And she has done it before. And if Morris had called me on the job and told me that the house was on fire again and the fire department

was there, I don't know what I would have done.

Therapist: You were on the job and Morris called.

Mother: He didn't call because he had gotten it out.

Therapist *(to Morris):* I see. So you handled the fire yourself? Who set the fire?

Morris: Mandy.

Therapist *(to Mandy):* Mandy? Was he pretty good with the— what did he use? Water? Mandy? *(shifts focus to how problem was solved rather than who was to blame)*

Mother *(to Mandy):* Speak up.

Therapist: What did he use? Water? *(asks questions in a concrete*

manner a frightened 7-year-old can answer with monosyllables)

Mandy: Yes.

Therapist: Was it a really big fire?

Mandy: Yes.

Therapist: About this big? *(holds his hand up)* Or about this big?

Mandy: About this.

Therapist: That big? Hoo, boy. *(to mother)* Did you find out from Mandy how it got started?

Mother: She got some matches and lit them. She didn't say what she lit.

Therapist: Could you ask her? Talk with her now. *(gestures, directing Mrs. Gordon to speak*

Enacting patterns in the therapy session not only allows the therapist to see family members in action but also can help family members to experience their own interactions with a heightened awareness. A prototypical example of this technique is the family lunch session used in treating families of adolescents in anorexia, which was described in Chapter 11.

Once accepted into the family system, and with sufficient observation to develop a formulation of the problem, the therapist moves into action. **Restructuring techniques** are the tools of the trade used to alter family patterns of interaction. For example, the therapist acts to *recreate communication channels* among family members who resist talking directly to one another and attempt to route all their comments through the therapist. The therapist may avoid making eye contact, refuse to respond when addressed, insist that family members talk to one another, or even leave the room and observe behind a one-way mirror. Like an orchestra conductor, the therapist signals family members when to speak or be silent. The family therapist also uses

repositioning, which involves manipulating the physical space between family members in order to alter their interactions, perhaps by moving chairs to physically separate family members who need more psychological distance from one another. For example, the therapist may sit between a mother and parentalized child so as to block the child from interfering while the mother and the identified patient talk. (See Box 17.5 for an example of this and other structural techniques.)

Another restructuring technique is called *marking boundaries*. The therapist may promote clear boundaries between individuals by ensuring that family members refrain from talking for one another. In addition, the therapist encourages differentiation of individual family members by interacting differently with each of them according to their age and developmental status. The therapist may also work so as to emphasize boundaries between subsystems, such as between the marital and child subsystems. For example, a boy was referred for therapy because of a dog phobia so severe he could not leave the house. After interacting with the

	directly to Mandy)	*Mandy:*	I was trying—		helpful. But Mandy didn't
Mother:	What exactly did you do? How did you catch the spread on fire?	*Mother:*	With Morris's chemistry set?		have a chance to finish her story. *(reframing Morris's in-*
Mandy:	I struck the match.	*Mandy:*	Yes! *(Mandy begins to cry. The therapist gestures for the mother to change seats with him so that she can sit next to Mandy. Again, Morris intervenes.)*		*terference in a positive way, while still blocking it; later, Morris once again attempts to interfere when mother and Mandy are doing a task together)*
Mother:	And just lit the spread. *(mother's tone becomes negative, admonitory)*				
Mandy:	Yes.	*Morris:*	And then you said you wanted a drink of water. And you went out. *(to mother)* She stayed a long time. So I went to see what she was doing. And when I got to the room, she came running in there and said "Mommy's bed is on fire."	*Therapist:*	Morris, you're out of a job. Hey, Morris—come over here, Morris. This guy works so much for you.
Mother:	You meant to light the spread?				
Mandy:	I was doing an experiment.			*Mother:*	Right.
Mother:	Well, what happened? I can't hear you. You were doing an experiment?			*Therapist:*	Relax, man. You have a vacation now. Okay? *(moves Morris to a chair near him)*
Morris:	She was—	*Therapist:*	Morris is trying to be helpful, and he is. You are very		
Therapist:	Excuse me, Morris. Because—go ahead, Mandy. *(blocks interference by Morris)*				

Source: Excerpted from Minuchin (1974)

family, the therapist's formulation was that the mother and son were enmeshed and that the father was being excluded from their intimate twosome. The therapist decided to restructure the family interaction by increasing the affiliation between father and son. Recall that this boy had a dog phobia. As it happened, the father was a mailman, and therefore an expert in dealing with dogs. Therefore, the therapist assigned the father the task of teaching his son how to cope with strange dogs. The intervention was a great success. Ultimately, the child, who was himself adopted, asked to adopt a dog, and the father and son spent time together training their new pet. As the father–son bond strengthened, a healthy separation between mother and son was promoted, and the parents embarked on marital therapy.

The therapist can also use *positive reframing* to give family members a new perspective on the problem and new lenses through which to see themselves. For instance, the therapist might praise overprotective parents for their desire to be supportive and nurturing, reframing their behavior in positive terms. In this way, the therapist underlines the good intentions behind problematic interaction patterns, thus reducing resistance to finding new and better ways to achieve those ends.

Empirical Support Kurtines and Szapocznik (1996) have initiated a program of research into the effectiveness of structural family therapy in contexts of cultural diversity. In particular, their work focuses on treatment of Hispanic families with drug-abusing adolescents. In one study, families were randomly assigned to either structural family therapy or to a control condition in which they received "treatment as usual" as it would be delivered in an outpatient setting. Results showed that youths in both conditions improved significantly, with no differences between the types of intervention. However, there were dramatic differences in retention rates. Families in the family therapy condition were overwhelmingly more likely to complete the treatment program: only 17 percent dropped out of treatment as compared to 44 percent of those in the control condition.

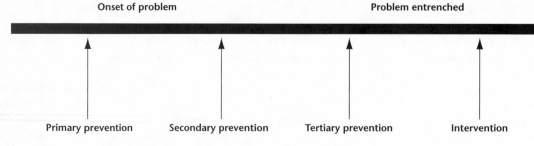

Figure 17.2   The Continuum of Prevention and Intervention.

In regard to the effectiveness of family therapies overall, Hazelrigg, Cooper, and Borduin's (1987) review of the available research showed that family therapy had positive effects when compared with no treatment and with alternative treatment controls. Follow-up studies showed that positive effects continued over time, but the effects were weaker and more variable than at the end of treatment. Again, however, family therapies were more effective than alternative treatments in reducing recidivism.

Prevention

Definition   First, we need to define **prevention**. Preventive efforts can be conceptualized along a continuum. (See Figure 17.2.) At one end are those programs put into place before a problem develops, designed to prevent it from occurring in the first place. This is known as **primary prevention**. An example of this is the home-based visiting program for first-time mothers, designed to prevent child abuse, as described in Chapter 14. In contrast, **secondary prevention** efforts focus on early identification of problems in order to prevent them from blossoming into full-blown disorders. An example of this would be a crisis line for stressed parents who are demonstrating poor parenting skills. Lastly, **tertiary prevention** intervenes somewhat later, in order to prevent a burgeoning problem from getting worse or reoccurring. In fact, the line between tertiary prevention and intervention is not a strict one, as most child therapies also have the goal of preventing problems from intensifying or relapsing.

Recall that when we first discussed developmental psychopathology in Chapter 1 we noted that the concepts of risk and developmental pathways could furnish guides for prevention. Developmentally oriented research has been sufficiently fruitful that some of those guides are now available. We have already discussed one prevention program, STEEP, designed to prevent insecure attachment (Erickson, Korfmacher, & Egeland, 1992). Here we will present another preventive program informed by the research on the developmental psychopathology of conduct disorder.

The Fast Track Program   *Fast Track* (Conduct Problems Prevention Research Group, 1992) is based on the developmental pathway that identifies the early signs of conduct disorder and the contribution of parents, school, and peers to its fruition (see Chapter 9). The target population is first-graders evidencing disruptive behaviors such as noncompliance, aggression, impulsivity, and immaturity. The techniques used are ones that had been tried already with some degree of success. However, the unique feature of the program is the integration of such techniques. In this way the separate components, such as dealing with parents and teachers, can be coordinated and can reinforce one another, and the chances of generalizing across settings can be maximized.

We have already presented two of the interventions: changing parents' ineffectual disciplinary practices and increasing the child's social skills so as to circumvent peer rejection (see Chapter 9). Therefore, in this discussion we concentrate on the more novel components of the program aimed at avoiding school failure. Sessions with the family focused on setting up a structured learning environment in the home and encouraged parental involvement in the child's learning as well as communication with the school. The importance of establishing a positive relation with the child's teacher was particularly emphasized. At school, teachers were trained by Fast Track staff in strategies for effective management of disruptive behaviors, such as establishing clear rules, rewarding appropriate behavior, and not rewarding—or punishing—inappropriate behavior. Teachers also implemented special classroom programs designed to strengthen the children's self-control, to build and maintain friendships, and to enhance problem-solving abilities. Finally, children who needed it were tutored, especially in reading.

Fast Track, along with recognizing the multidetermined nature of conduct disorder, is both integrated and solidly based on research. Thus it avoids the rather piecemeal, improvisational quality of many previous attempts at prevention. While studies of effectiveness are not available at present, it is a prime example of the practical application of developmental psychopathology.

abilities tests Tests designed to evaluate abilities directly related to academic achievement.

accelerated longitudinal approach (also known as the longitudinal, cross-sectional approach) A research technique in which data on the origins of a psychopathology are obtained from different age groups which are subsequently followed until the children in the younger groups are the same age as those in the next older group.

achievement tests Tests designed to assess academic achievement.

adaptive behavior The ability to cope with environmental demands, such as those for self-care, conventional social interactions, and independent functioning in the community, at an age-appropriate level.

adjustment disorder Deviant behavior that is a reaction to a specific event or events, such as parental death or divorce.

adjustment disorder with depressed mood A short-term dysphoric reaction to a recent identified stressor.

aggression Behavior whose goal is physical or psychological injury or destruction; anger or hatred may be the accompanying affect.

anaclitic depression The infant's reaction of despair following the loss of a loved and needed caregiver.

anal stage In Freud's psychosexual theory, the second stage of development, in which pleasure is derived from retaining and evacuating feces and the toddler confronts the issue of autonomy versus compliance.

anorexia nervosa A voluntary restriction of food and/or an involvement in purging in an active pursuit of thinness that results in at least a 15 percent loss of body weight. The *restricting* type relies solely on strict dieting to lose weight; the *binge-eating/purging* type alternates between dieting and binge eating, followed by self-induced vomiting or purging.

anoxia Deprivation of oxygen during or immediately following birth; may cause damage to or destroy brain cells.

anxiety As used here, the anticipation of a painful experience.

anxiety disorders A group of disorders characterized by intense, chronic anxiety. Formerly called psychoneurotic disorders.

asynchrony Disjointed or markedly uneven rates of progression among developmental variables.

attachment The bond of love that develops between infant and caregiver.

attention-deficit/hyperactivity disorder Developmentally inappropriate inattention accompanied by motor restlessness and impulsivity.

attribution theory A theory dealing with the inferences individuals make concerning the causes of behavior.

attrition Attrition is the loss of subjects during longitudinal studies.

authoritarian parenting Discipline requiring strict, unquestioning obedience.

authoritative parenting Discipline requiring compliance with standards for mature behavior, accompanied by love, communication, and respect for the child.

autism A severe disorder of the infancy and toddler period marked by extreme aloneness, a pathological need for sameness, and mutism or noncommunicative speech.

avoidance learning A form of learning in which an organism, having experienced an aversive stimulus, behaves so as to prevent future encounters with that stimulus.

avoidant attachment A form of insecure attachment marked by precocious independence from the caregiver.

baseline In behavioral assessment, the frequency of the natural occurrence of behavior targeted for change by behavioral techniques.

behavior deficit or excess The behaviorists' conceptualization of psychopathology as behaviors occurring at a lower or at a higher frequency or intensity than is expected within a given society.

behavior inhibition A temperamental predisposition for children to react to novelty with avoidance or distress and to be shy and fearful.

behavior therapies A group of therapies characterized by attention to specific, current behaviors, objective measurement, and reliance on principles of behavior change derived from the laboratory.

behavioral assessment Procedures designed to locate specific behaviors—along with their antecedents and consequences—that subsequently can serve as targets for modification through behavioral techniques.

behaviorism A theory inaugurated by John B. Watson according to which the study of overt behavior is the sole basis for a scientific psychology.

bipolar disorder (Also known as manic-depression.) A severe form of psychopathology characterized by depression alternating with states of euphoria or overactivity.

boundaries The separation between individuals or sub-systems within the family, such as between marital and parent–child relationships.

brain damage Damage to the brain can be defined neurologically in terms of the nature, site and size of the damage, behaviorally in terms of impaired functions, or etiologically in terms of the source of the damage.

brain injury There are either penetrating head injuries caused by a penetration of the skull, dura and actual brain tissue, or closed head injuries when a blow to the head does not penetrate the dura.

bulimia nervosa An eating disorder characterized by recurrent episodes of binge eating (i.e., the rapid consumption of large quantities of food in a brief time), followed by attempts to prevent weight gain either through self-induced vomiting or misuse of laxatives in the purging type or through fasting or excessive exercise in the nonpurging type.

case formulation A succinct description of the child that incorporates the clinician's interpretation of how the problem came about and how it might be remediated.

castration anxiety In Freud's psychosexual theory, the universal fear among preschool boys in the oedipal stage that the rivalrous father will emasculate them for wanting to possess the mother.

central nervous system (CNS) The part of the nervous system that includes the spinal cord and the brain.

child abuse See *maltreatment*.

childhood schizophrenia A psychosis appearing in middle childhood characterized by marked withdrawal, bizarre thinking and behavior, loss of reality contact, and inappropriate affect.

classical conditioning The pairing of a neutral stimulus with one that elicits a given response so that the neutral stimulus will come to elicit that response.

client-centered therapy See *humanistic therapy*.

clinical disorder As defined by DSM-IV, a clinical disorder is a clinically significant behavioral or psychological syndrome or pattern that occurs in an individual and that is associated with present distress or disability, or with significantly increased risk of suffering death, pain, disability, or an important loss of freedom.

coercion theory A pattern of parent–child interaction in which a series of attacks and counterattacks are negatively reinforced by cessation, thus increasing the likelihood of their reoccurrence.

cognitive behavior therapy Behavior therapy aimed at changing cognitions so as to make behavior more adaptive.

cognitive restructuring A behavioral technique aimed at substituting adaptive for maladaptive cognitions through a logical analysis of the latter and the assignment of specific tasks putting the new understanding into practice.

cognitive therapies Therapies that aim to change behavior by altering the dysfunctional and maladaptive beliefs that guide such behavior.

cohort effect The possibility that childrens' behavior might be different because they were born in different eras and therefore had different experiences.

comorbidity The co-occurrence of two or more psychopathologies.

compulsion An irrational act that an individual is compelled to do.

computerized axial tomography (CAT scan) (Also called computer-assisted tomography or CT scan.) Computerized axial tomography (CAT scan), uses computer-driven x-ray machines to produce detailed images both of the brain's surface and of the levels below, making it possible to locate lesions at any level of the brain.

concrete-operational stage In middle childhood, the emergence of the ability to understand the world in terms of reason rather than naive perception.

conditions of worth Carl Rogers's term for conditions set by parents under which they will grant their love and respect for the child.

conduct disorders Behaviors in which children act out their feelings or impulses toward others in an antisocial or destructive fashion. Also called undersocialized, aggressive type.

contingency management Contingency management decreases the strength of undesirable behaviors and increases the strength of adaptive ones by manipulating the rewards and punishments that follow or are contingent upon such behaviors.

controlling behaviors A form of insecure attachment marked by a reversal of roles in that the child takes over the adult's functions.

corrective emotional experience In psychoanalytic therapy, the discovery that expression of anxiety-laden feelings does not lead to punishment or rejection.

critical period The assumption that early experiences have disproportionately potent influence on later development.

cross-sectional strategy A research technique in which the origins of a psychopathology are reconstructed by obtaining data from different age groups at a single point in time.

culture   Culture involves a shared set of learning experiences, beliefs, and behavioral norms as well as physical objects unique to the group such as tools, art, and buildings.

defense mechanisms   Stratagems for reducing anxiety. See also *repression, reaction formation, projection*, and *displacement*.

delinquency   A legal term for offenses that are criminal if committed by an adult.

delusion   A firmly held, irrational belief that runs counter to reality and to the individual's culture or subculture.

depression   In its psychopathological form, depression is marked by a depressed mood, loss of self-esteem, intense self-deprecation, and guilt. Eating and sleeping disturbances as well as agitation may also occur.

detachment   The final phase of an infant's reaction to the loss of a loved caregiver when socially acceptable but superficial contact is established when the caregiver returns. Also called *restitution*.

detouring   Salvador Minuchin's term for parents' avoidance of their own conflicts by regarding their child as their sole problem.

developmental crises   Crises inherent in normal development.

developmental delay   Development that proceeds at a significantly slower pace than normal.

developmental pathway   The risk and protective factors responsible for diverting development from its normal course, maintaining in the deviation or returning development to its normal course.

developmental psychopathology   The study of the developmental processes that contribute to the formation of, or resistance to, psychopathology.

diathesis-stress hypothesis   The hypothesis that abnormal behavior results from a genetic predisposition combined with environmental stress.

differentiation phase   In object relations theory, the ability of the infant to recognize the mother as a separate person.

discrepancy model   Defining learning disability as the difference between what students should achieve in terms of their ability and their actual achievement.

disorganized/disoriented attachment   A form of insecure attachment marked by inconsistent and odd behavior.

disorganized or catatonic behavior   In schizophrenia, behavior marked by extreme deviance, such as grimacing, odd posturing, long periods of immobility, or self-mutilation.

disorganized speech   In schizophrenia, speech characterized by loose associations, illogical reasoning, fragmentation, and bizarreness.

displacement   A mechanism of defense in which an impulse is directed toward a target that is safer than the original one.

double bind   A communication pattern that traps the recipient between two negative and inescapable injunctions. There is also a prohibition against drawing attention to the bind itself.

Down syndrome   A form of mental retardation caused by having three number 21 chromosomes instead of the normal two.

drug abuse   See *substance abuse*.

DSM   The *Diagnostic and Statistical Manual of Mental Disorders*, published by the American Psychiatric Association, providing diagnostic criteria for mental disorders. The latest edition is DSM-IV.

dysthymic disorder   Dysthymic disorder is characterized either by a depressed mood or by irritability in children, along with at least two other specific symptoms of depression. The disturbance persists for at least a year.

ecology   The study of children in their natural environment.

ego   In Freud's structural theory, the psychic component responsible for learning the nature of reality in order to gratify the id's demands for maximal pleasure, on the one hand, and to avoid the painful censure of the superego, on the other hand.

egocentrism   In Jean Piaget's theory, the tendency to view the physical and social world exclusively from one's own point of view.

ego ideal   In Freudian theory, the individual's idealized self-image.

ego psychology   In psychoanalytic theory, the study of the adaptive functions of the ego and the interpersonal context of development.

electroencephalogram (EEG)   A device for recording the electric activity of the brain.

emotion regulation   The ability to monitor, evaluate, and modify one's emotional reactions in order to achieve one's goals.

emotional maltreatment   See *psychological maltreatment*.

empathy   Awareness of the feelings of others and a vicarious affective response to those feelings.

enmeshment   Salvador Minuchin's term for excessive involvement by individual members of a family with one another so that there is no strong sense of individuality.

enuresis (also called functional enuresis)   Involuntary urination during the day or night in children 5 years of age or older.

equifinality   The fact that a number of different pathways may lead to the same outcome, such as a given psychopathology.

ethnic group   A group that shares certain practices, values, and beliefs based on exposure to a common culture.

ethnic identity   Knowledge about one's ethnic group and a sense of belonging to that group.

ethnic socialization   The process of acquiring the behaviors, perceptions, values, and attitudes of an ethnic group and seeing the self and others as members of such groups.

etiology   The study of the causes or of the necessary and sufficient conditions for producing various psychopathologies.

event-related potential (ERP)   Event-related potential (ERP) is an electroencephalographic technique that records the brain response to a given stimulus so that one can tell whether the response is characteristic (normal) or deviant.

executive functions   The functions underlying flexible, goal-directed behavior; specifically, planning, working memory, set shifting, and inhibition of competing behaviors.

externalization   See *internalization-externalization*.

extinction   The gradual disappearance of a learned behavior through the removal of reinforcements.

fading   In behavior therapy, the gradual removal of reinforcements so that the desired behavior may become autonomous.

false belief   The cognitive task assessing how well a child can infer what another person knows and does not know.

familial or familial cultural retardation   Retardation characterized by a mild degree of retardation with no clear organic cause, a greater prevalence among minorities and individuals of low socioeconomic status, and a tendency to blend in with the general population after school.

family system   The conceptualization of the family as a dynamic

whole that is greater than the sum of its parts.

family therapies   A group of specific techniques based on the assumption that it is necessary to treat the entire family to correct the faulty pattern responsible for producing a disturbance in single members.

fixation   The persistence of normal behavior beyond the point where it is developmentally appropriate. This arrest of development may be psychopathological, depending on the degree or intensity.

follow-back strategy   A research technique in which the origins of a psychopathology are reconstructed by obtaining data from records made at a previous time period, such as school or court records.

follow-up strategy   A research technique involving following children for a considerable period of time in order to obtain data on the antecedents of various psychopathologies.

formal operational stage   In adolescence, the ability to think in terms of general ideas and abstract concepts.

fragmentation   A thought disorder in which tangentially related or unrelated ideas disrupt the chain of thought.

free association   The basic psychoanalytic technique for uncovering unconscious material by encouraging the patient to say whatever comes to mind.

functional disorder   A designation given to disturbances that are primarily psychological rather than primarily organic in origin.

functional magnetic resonance imaging (fMRI)   Functional magnetic resonance imaging (fMRI) tracks increases and decreases in oxygen in the brain as an individual performs a given task and subsequently can locate where the greatest areas of activation occur.

GAP report   A diagnostic classification system devised especially for children by the Group for the Advancement of Psychiatry.

gender identity   Self-classification as male or female.

gender role   Society's prescriptions for appropriate behaviors and feelings for boys and girls.

group therapies   Therapeutic techniques in which individuals work together to solve their problems through social interaction guided by a trained leader.

guilt   The painful affect accompanying judgment of oneself as bad.

hallucination   A sensory perception occurring in the absence of any appropriate external stimulus.

hierarchical development   The view that psychological growth involves increasing complexity and organization with new structures emerging out of those that have come before.

humanistic therapy (Also called *nondirective* or *client-centered therapy*.)   Carl Roger's therapeutic procedure that utilizes warmth, acceptance, and reflection of the client's ideas and feelings to remove the obstacles to self-actualization.

hyperactivity (or hyperkinetic syndrome)   See *attention-deficit hyperactivity disorder*.

id   In Freud's structural theory, the biologically based pleasure-seeking source of all psychic energy.

identity   In Erik Erikson's theory, the search for inner continuity and interpersonal mutuality that begins in adolescence and is evidenced by a vocational choice.

imitation (Also called *modeling*.)   Learning by observing the behavior of others (models).

induction discipline   Discipline based on reasoning that appeals to the child's pride and concern for others.

information processing The step-by-step conversion of sensory input into knowledge by means of operations such as attention, memory, organization, and retrieval.

initiative Self-reliant expansiveness.

insecure attachment There are three types: in *resistant attachment* there is an ambivalent mixture of demands for and rejection of maternal attention; in *avoidant attachment*, the child ignores the mother; and in *disorganized/disoriented attachment* there are contradictory responses to the mother such as approaching her with depressed or flat affect.

insight In psychoanalytic psychotherapy, the patient's conscious awareness of anxiety-producing thoughts and feelings that had been in the unconscious.

intelligence quotient (IQ) A measure of intelligence derived either (1) from the relation between the child's mental age and chronological age or (2) from the deviation of a child's score from the mean score of children his or her age.

intelligence tests Standardized techniques for measuring intellectual functioning.

internalization The process by which behavior that was once dependent on environmental factors for its maintenance comes to be maintained by intraindividual factors.

internalization-externalization A classification of psychopathologies based on whether the child suffers (internalization) or the environment suffers (externalization).

internalizers See *internalization-externalization*.

interpersonal context Variables necessary for understanding various psychopathologies that have their locus within the individual;

e.g., cognition, affect, the self, conscience.

interpersonal problem-solving skills training Helping conduct-disordered children achieve greater self-control by generating alternative solutions to problems, anticipating consequences of their behavior, and planning.

interpretation In psychoanalytic theory, interpretation consists of the therapist pointing out the meaning of material the patient is not aware of.

invulnerables Children who manage to adjust well in spite of being exposed to a significant number of risk factors.

joint attention behavior This is the infant's use of gaze or gesture to attract the caregiver's attention in order to share an interest.

learned helplessness Nonresponsiveness to a noxious stimulus that had previously occurred independently of the organism's efforts to avoid it and was therefore inescapable.

learning disabilities (also called learning disorders) Learning problems due to a disorder in one or more of the basic psychological processes involved in understanding or in using spoken or written language and not due to mental retardation, emotional disturbance, environmental disadvantage, or specific perceptual or motor handicaps.

libido Freud's term for the biologically based drive to obtain erotic bodily sensations; also equated with sexual drive.

magnetic resonance imaging (MRI) Magnetic resonance imaging (MRI) generates three-dimensional images of various brain structures by using images from successive layers of the brain.

mainstreaming The term given to placing retarded children in regular classes.

major depression An acute, debilitating disorder characterized by five or more symptoms, one of which is depressed mood in adults or irritability in children.

maltreatment Behavior that is outside the norms of conduct and entails a substantial risk of causing physical or emotional harm.

masked depression Underlying depression in children in middle childhood that is masked by a wide variety of deviant but non-depressive behaviors.

medical model A model of psychopathology emphasizing the role of organic dysfunction in the etiology of psychopathologies as well as classification and interpretation of psychopathological behaviors in terms of diagnostic entities.

mental retardation A condition characterized by subnormal intelligence, deficits in adaptive behavior, and onset typically below the age of 18 years.

minority group Minority group can be defined simply as a group having fewer members than the majority group. Some definitions add two other characteristics—powerlessness or subordination and being the object of discrimination.

modeling See *imitation*.

multiaxial classification A diagnostic system whereby individuals are assessed in terms of a number of dimensions rather than in terms of a single classification.

multiculturalism The comparative study of ethnic minority groups.

multideterminism The idea that psychopathology is determined by a number of causes rather than a single cause.

multifinality The idea that a single risk factor may have a number of different consequences depending upon contextual and intraindividual factors.

mutism   Refusal to speak despite an ability to do so.

narcissistic disorders   Within psychoanalytic theory, disorders resulting from an inability to form true object relations owing to faulty early parenting.

negative affectivity   Subsuming anxiety and depression under their shared negative affects such as fear, sadness, and guilt.

negative reinforcement   Increasing the probability that behavior will occur by removing unpleasant or aversive consequences.

negativism   A heightened state of opposition to adults that flourishes in the toddler and early preschool period.

neglect   Deficiencies in provision of caregiving that compromise the child's physical and/or psychological health.

neglectful parenting   Parents who are indifferent to their children or uninvolved and self-centered.

neurotransmitters   These are the "chemical messengers" responsible for communication among nerve cells.

object constancy   In Mahler's theory, the final stage of separation-individuation that involves the ability to integrate both positive and negative feelings toward the caregiver; e.g., the child now can be angry at the caregiver but still love her. In Piaget's theory, object constancy means the ability to grasp the idea that physical objects exist independent of the child's involvement with such objects.

object permanence   In Jean Piaget's cognitive theory, the infant's separation of the self from the physical world and the realization that objects have independent existence.

object relation   In Freudian theory, the term used for an emotional attachment to another person.

obsession   An irrational thought, the repeated occurrence of which is beyond the individual's conscious control.

obsessive-compulsive disorder   See *obsession* and *compulsion*.

Oedipus complex   In Freud's psychosexual theory, the universal desire of the preschool boy to take possession of the mother and eliminate the rivalrous father.

omnipotent thinking   Belief that one can control events that, in reality, lie beyond one's power.

operant conditioning (instrumental conditioning)   A form of conditioning in which the persistence of a response depends on its effects on the environment.

oppositional-defiant disorder   Purposeful defiance of adults' requests resulting in violation of minor rules. See *negativism.*

oral stage   In Freud's psychosexual theory, the first stage of development, in which pleasure is derived from sucking and biting and attachment to the caregiver is formed.

organic context   Variables necessary for understanding various psychopathologies that involve characteristics of the human body; e.g., genetics, brain structure and functioning.

overinclusiveness   A thought disorder in which ideas flit from one tangential association to another.

overprotection   Excessive and unrealistic concern over another's welfare.

parent–child coalition   Salvador Minuchin's term for a family pattern in which a child sides with one parent against the other.

parent management training (PMT)   The use of social learning principles such as positive reinforcement and mild punishment to alter parent–child interactions in a prosocial direction.

parent training   Behavioral techniques designed to teach parents positive, effective ways of dealing with their children's disturbed behavior.

pediatric psychology   The study of the interplay between organic factors on the one hand and psychological, social, and cultural factors on the other in the etiology, course, and treatment of disease. Pediatric psychology is also concerned with prevention and health maintenance.

pedophilia   A state of being sexually aroused by children.

permissive parenting   Parents who are undemanding, accepting, and child-centered but who make few attempts at control.

perseveration   A thought disorder in which the individual dwells on a single idea.

personality disorders   Deeply ingrained, maladaptive behaviors that, while more pervasive than the anxiety disorders, still do not significantly diminish the individual's reality contact.

personality inventories   Personality assessment techniques in which a series of statements is judged as characteristic or not characteristic of the individual.

perspective taking   The cognitive ability to see the physical environment and social situations from the point of view of another person or persons.

phallic stage   In Freud's psychosexual theory, the third stage of development, in which the preschooler is expansive and assertive and derives pleasure from stimulating the genitals.

phobia   An intense, persistent, irrational fear of an animate or inanimate object or of a situation.

phonemes   The sound units of speech. *Phonological awareness* is the awareness that words are made up of separate sounds.

physical maltreatment   Physical maltreatment involves the presence of injuries from acts of commission or omission in which the child's life, health, or safety are endangered.

play therapy   Using play to encourage the child to express important ideas, conflicts, and feelings symbolically rather than through direct verbal communication. The procedure depends on the kind of psychotherapy being used, such as psychoanalytic or nondirective.

positive reinforcement   Use of rewards to increase the probability that a desired behavior will occur.

positron emission tomography (PET scan)   Positron emission tomography (PET scan) detects abnormal functioning in brains that might look structurally intact by recording the rate of metabolizing radioactive glucose that has been introduced into cerebral arteries.

posttraumatic stress disorder   A disorder resulting from experiencing an event involving actual or threatened death or injury to the self or others.

practicing   In Mahler's theory, the phase in which infants actively experiment with independence from the caregiver while still maintaining an attachment to that caregiver.

pragmatics   This is the social context of language which involves learning when to say what to whom in order to communicate effectively.

precausal thinking   In Jean Piaget's theory, the tendency to view the physical world in animistic terms, as having life and purpose, for example.

precocity   As applied to psychopathology, precocity is an accelerated rate of development that leads to an attempt to take on adult roles and responsibilities before the child is prepared to do so successfully.

preoperational stage   In the preschool period, the literal belief in what is seen so that, for example, things that look different are in fact different.

prevention   Programs initiated before a problem develops (**primary** prevention), in the early stages of a problem to forestall its development into a full-blown disorder (**secondary** prevention), or to prevent a problem from worsening or reoccurring (**tertiary** prevention).

primary-process thinking   In Freudian theory, unrealistic thinking based on immediate need for gratification rather than on reality.

projection   A mechanism of defense in which anxiety-provoking impulses are denied in oneself and attributed to others.

projective techniques   Personality assessment methods using ambiguous or unstructured stimuli. The most popular are the *Rorschach*, consisting of a series of ink blots; the *Thematic Apperception Test (TAT)*, consisting of a series of ambiguous pictures; and human figure drawing.

prompting   In operant conditioning, the use of instructions, modeling, or guidance to elicit a desired response.

protective factors   Factors that promote healthy development and counteract the negative effects of risks.

protective mechanisms   Processes that account for the effectiveness of protective factors.

pseudo-mutuality   L. C. Wynne's term for a facade of harmony used by families to cover pervasive feelings of futility.

psychoactive drugs   Drugs that affect the central nervous system so as to alter subjective states of feeling.

psychoanalysis   A psychotherapeutic technique relying upon free

association, dream interpretation, play, and the analysis of resistance and transference to provide insights into the unconscious roots of disturbed behavior.

psychodynamic theory   The Freudian and neo-Freudian theories that aim to understand the basic motivations of human behavior. Both emotions and unconscious motivations play a major role.

psychological maltreatment   Acts of commission and omission which are judged on the basis of community standards and professional expertise to be psychologically damaging. Such acts damage immediately or ultimately the behavioral, cognitive, affective, or physical functioning of the child.

psychoneurotic disorders   See *anxiety disorders*.

psychopath   A psychopathology marked by callousness, egocentricity, shallow emotions, superficial charm, manipulativeness, impulsiveness, and an absence of meaningful relations.

psychopathology   Abnormal behavior that may have psychological and/or biological causes.

psychosexual theory   Freud's developmental theory in which each stage—the oral, anal, and phallic—is marked by a change in the source of erotic bodily sensations and a distinct personality development.

psychosis   A disorder so severe and pervasive as to interfere with the individual's capacity to meet the ordinary demands of life.

punishment   Presentation of an aversive stimulus that decreases the probability that the response leading to it will occur.

race   Race involves grouping of individuals based on genetic inheritance and/or physical characteristics.

rapprochement   In Mahler's theory, the rapprochement phase is marked by ambivalence toward the caregiver, the infant alternating between clinging to and pushing the caregiver away.

rational emotive therapy   Albert Ellis's cognitive restructuring therapy in which the client is helped to identify and correct irrational ideas responsible for disturbed behavior.

reaction formation   A mechanism of defense in which a child's thoughts and feelings are diametrically opposed to an anxiety-provoking impulse.

reading disability   Failure to learn to read or to make appropriate progress despite normal intelligence and adequate instruction.

reciprocal determinism   In social learning theory, the idea that both the individual and the environment influence one another rather than the individual's being the passive recipient of environmental influences.

reciprocal inhibition   The inhibition of the weaker of two incompatible responses by the stronger one. Utilized in systematic desensitization.

regression   The return of behaviors that once were developmentally appropriate but no longer are. Whether or not the behaviors are psychopathological depends on the degree or intensity of regression.

reinforcement   An increase in the probability that a response will occur to a contiguously presented stimulus.

reliability   The consistency with which an assessment instrument performs.

repression   The basic mechanism of defense in which anxiety-provoking impulses and ideas are banished from consciousness.

resilience   A child's ability to make a good adjustment in spite of being at high risk for developing a disturbance.

resistance   In psychoanalytic therapy, devices used by patients to avoid bringing painful material to consciousness.

resistant attachment   A form of insecure attachment in which the infant is preoccupied with the caregiver while relating in an ambivalent manner.

restitution   See *detachment*.

restructuring techniques   Techniques for altering faulty patterns of family interaction.

retrospective strategy   A research technique involving reconstructing the origins of a psychopathology through inquiring about the past history of the disturbed child.

rigidity   Excessive and unrealistic resistance to change.

risks   Factors that increase the probability that development will be diverted from its normal path, resulting either in clinically significant problem behavior or psychopathology.

schema (plural, schemata)   For Piaget: cognitive structures comprising children's developing understanding of their experience of the environment and of themselves. For social cognitive theories: stable mental structures incorporating perceptions of self and others and including past experiences and future expectations.

schismatic family   Theodore Lidz's term for families characterized by overt conflict between parents, mutual depreciation, and competition for the child's loyalty.

schizophrenia   A severe, pervasive disorder consisting of delusions, hallucinations, disorganized speech, inappropriate affect, disorganized or bizarre behavior, and the negative symptoms of flat affect, avolition, alogia, and anhedonia.

school phobia   An irrational dread of school. Also called school refusal.

selective attention   The ability to filter out irrelevant stimuli in order to focus on stimuli specifically relevant to the task at hand.

self-control   The ability of the child to behave in a socially acceptable rather than a socially unacceptable manner when the two are in conflict.

self-efficacy   An individual's estimation of the likelihood of achieving a given outcome.

self-instruction   A behavioral therapy designed to increase self-control by teaching impulsive children how to guide their behavior by first talking out loud and then to themselves.

self-psychology   Within psychoanalytic theory, the belief that the self has a more central role in development than that provided for by the classical theory.

semantics   Semantics is concerned with the meaning of words and sentences.

sensitive periods   Times when particular developments come to the fore and are both most vulnerable to disruption and open to amelioration.

sensorimotor stage   The infant's and toddler's reliance on sensations and motor actions as vehicles for understanding the environment.

separation anxiety   The anxiety engendered by the caregiver's departure after an attachment has been formed in infancy.

separation anxiety disorder   Excessive anxiety concerning separation from those to whom the child is attached.

separation-individuation   In object relations theory, the development of a sense of the self as distinct from the caregiver and the achievement of a sense of uniqueness.

serotonin   A neurotransmitter that is either excitatory or inhibitory in nature and may be involved in emotional arousal.

sex role See *gender role*.

sexual abuse Involving children in incest, sexual assault, fondling, exposure to sexual acts, and pornography.

shaping An operant-conditioning technique in which responses that successively approximate the desired one are reinforced.

situational crises Crises that, while not inherent in normal development, are frequently encountered and are typically weathered.

skewed family Theodore Lidz's term for families in which the mother is dominating and overprotective and the father is weak and passive.

social problem solving The application of the information-processing model specifically to coping with social situations.

social skills training A behavioral therapy applying techniques such as modeling, reinforcement, coaching, and interpersonal problem solving to the substitution of adaptive for maladaptive social behavior.

splitting In object relations theory, the splitting of the image of the mother and of the self into a good and a bad image.

stage theories Theories that assume that development proceeds by qualitatively distinct reorganizations of behavior and that the sequence of such reorganizations is invariant.

status offense Behavior regarded as illegal in children but not in adults, such as drinking alcoholic beverages.

stimulus generalization The tendency of an organism, conditioned to a particular stimulus, subsequently to respond to similar stimuli.

strange situation A sequence of prearranged separations and reunions between infant and caregiver that reveal patterns of attachment.

substance abuse A pattern of excessive use of a chemical substance to the extent that it interferes with work or school and interpersonal relationships.

superego The moral component, or conscience, in Freud's structural theory. Initially, it is perfectionistic, requiring absolute obedience and punishing transgressions with guilt feelings.

superordinate context Variables necessary for understanding various psychopathologies that aggregate individuals into a unit; e.g., the gang, an ethnic minority, the poor.

sustained attention The ability to continue a task until it is completed.

symbiotic phase In object relations theory, the infants' experiencing of the self and the caregiver as two parts of the same organism.

symptom A psychological, behavioral, or biological manifestation of a psychopathology.

syndrome A group of behaviors or symptoms that tend to occur together in a particular disorder.

syntax Syntax concerns the way words are combined to produce meaningful sentences.

systematic desensitization A behavior therapy for extinguishing anxiety by pairing a graded series of anxiety stimuli with the incompatible response of relaxation.

theory of mind A child's understanding of the content and function of mental life, such as perception, memory, and dreams.

therapeutic alliance In psychoanalytic therapy, the positive bond between patient and therapist.

time out In behavior therapy, isolating the child for brief periods in order to extinguish undesirable behaviors.

token economy A behavioral therapy in which socially desirable behavior is rewarded by tokens that can subsequently be exchanged for rewards of the client's choosing.

transaction A series of dynamic, reciprocal interactions between the child, the family, and the social context.

transference In psychoanalytic therapy, the projection onto the therapist of intense feelings once directed toward significant figures, typically the parents.

transformations The continuity of an underlying variable even while its behavioral manifestations change over time.

triangulation Salvador Minuchin's term for a family pattern in which the child is forced to side with one parent against the other.

unconditional positive regard In Carl Rogers's theory, the parents' intrinsic valuing and acceptance of the child.

unconscious In Freudian theory, the region of the mind that contains material that has been repressed or has never been conscious.

validity The degree to which an instrument evaluates what it intends to evaluate.

vulnerability Factors that intensify the effects of risks.

work The ability to do what is required to be done; task orientation.

working through In psychoanalytic theory, the process by which the patient gains insight into the many ways in which a single conflict is expressed.

References

AACAP Official Action (1997). Practice parameters for assessment and treatment of children, adolesents and adults with attention-deficit/hyperactivity disorder. *Journal of the American Academy of Child and Adolescent Psychiatry, 36* (Suppl. 10), 85S–114S.

Aboud, F. E. (1987). The development of ethnic self-identification and attitudes. In J. S. Phinney & M. J. Rotheram (Eds.), *Children's ethnic socialization: Pluralism and development* (pp. 32–55). Newbury Park, CA: Sage Publications.

Abramson, L. Y., Seligman, M. E. P., & Teasdale, J. D. (1978). Learned helplessness in humans: Critique and reformulation. *Journal of Abnormal Psychology, 87*, 49–74.

Achenbach, T. M. (1966). The classification of children's psychiatric symptoms: A factor-analytic study. *Psychological Monographs 80* (7, whole no. 609).

Achenbach, T. M. (1990). Conceptualization of developmental psychopathology. In M. Lewis & S. M. Miller (Eds.), *Handbook of developmental psychopathology* (pp. 3–14). New York: Plenum.

Achenbach, T. M. (1991). *Manual for the Child Behavior Checklist/4-18 and 1991 Profile.* Burlington, VT: University of Vermont Department of Psychiatry.

Achenbach, T. M. (1995). Developmental issues in assessment, taxonomy, and diagnosis of child and adolescent psychopathology. In D. Cicchetti & D. J. Cohen (Eds.), *Developmental psychopathology. Vol. I: Theory and methods* (pp. 57–80). New York: Wiley.

Achenbach, T. M., Conners, C. K., Quay, H. C., Verhults, F. C., & Howell, C. T. (1989). Replication of empirically derived syndromes as a basis for a taxonomy of child/adolescent psychopathology. *Journal of Abnormal Child Psychology, 17*, 299–323.

Achenbach, T. M., & Edelbrock, C. S. (1981). Behavioral problems and competencies reported by parents of normal and disturbed children aged four through sixteen. *Monographs of the Society for Research in Child Development 1* (46, series no. 188).

Achenbach, T. M., & Edelbrock, C. (1991). *Manual for the Youth Self-Report and Profile.* Burlington, VT: University of Vermont Department of Psychiatry.

Achenbach, T. M., & Howell, C. T. (1993). Are American children's problems getting worse? A 13-year comparison. *Journal of the American Academy of Child and Adolescent Psychiatry, 32*, 1145–1154.

Achenbach, T. M., Howell, C. T., McConaughy, S. H., & Stanger, C. (1995a). Six-year predictors of problems in a national sample of children and youths: I. Cross-informant syndromes. *Journal of the American Academy of Child and Adolescent* Psychiatry, 34, 336–347.

Achenbach, T. M., Howell, C. T., McConaughy, S. H., & Stranger, C. (1995b). Six-year predictors of problems in a national sample of children and youth: II. Signs of disturbance. *Journal of the American Academy of Child and Adolescent* Psychiatry, 34, 488–498.

Achenbach, T. M., & McConaughy, S. H. (1997). *Empirically based assessment of child and adolescent psychopathology: Practical applications.* Newbury Park, CA: Sage Publications.

Achenbach, T. M., McConaughy, S. H., & Howell, C. T. (1987). Child/adolescent behavioral and emotional problems: Implications of cros-informant correlations for situational specificity. *Psychological Bulletin, 101*, 213–232.

Adrien, J. L., Faure, M., Perrot, A., Hameury, L., Garreau, B., Barthelemy, C., & Sauvage, D. (1991). Autism and family home movies: Preliminary findings. *Journal of Autism and Developmental Disorders 21*, 43–50.

Ainsworth, M. D. S., & Bell, S. M. (1969). Some contemporary patterns of mother-infant interaction in the feeding situation. In A. Ambrose (ed.), *Stimulation in early infancy* (pp. 133–162). New York: Academic Press.

Akiskal, H. S. (1995). Developmental pathways to bipolarity: Are juvenile-onset depressions pre-bipolar? *Journal of the American Academy of Child and Adolescent* Psychiatry, 34, 754–763.

Albano, A. M., Chorpita, B. F., & Barlow, D. H. (1996). Childhood anxiety disorders. In E. J. Mash & R. A. Barkley (Eds.), *Child psychopathology* (pp. 196–241). New York: Guilford.

Alexander, J. F., Holtzworth-Munroe, A., & Jameson, P. B. (1994). The process and outcome of marital and family therapy research: Review and evaluation. In A. E. Bergin & S. L. Garfield (Eds.), *Handbook of psychotherapy and behavior change* (pp. 595–630). New York: Wiley.

Alexander, J. F., & Parsons, B. V. (1982). *Functional family therapy.* Monterey, CA: Brooks/Cole.

Alfieri, T., Ruble, D. N., & Higgins, E. T. (1996). Gender stereotypes during adolescence: Developmental changes and the transition to junior high school. *Developmental Psychology, 32*, 1129–1137.

Allen, A. J., Leonard, H., & Swedo, S. E. (1995). Current knowledge of medications for the treatment of childhood anxiety disorders. *Journal of the American Academy of Child and Adolescent* Psychiatry, 34, 976–987.

Altman, H., Collins, M., & Mundy, P. (1997). Subclinical hallucinations and delusions in nonpsychotic adolescents. *Journal of Child Psycology and* Psychiatry, *38*, 413–420.

Altmann, E. O., & Gotlib, I. H. (1988). The social behavior of depressed children: An observational study. *Journal of Abnormal Child Psychology*, *16*, 29–44.

Alvarado, N. (1994). Empirical validity of the Thematic Apperception Test. *Journal of Personality Assessment*, *63*, 59–79.

Aman, M. G., & Singh, N. N. (1991). Pharmacological intervention. In J. L. Matson & J. A. Mulick (eds.) *Handbook of mental retardation* (pp. 347–372). New York: Pergamon.

Amato, P. R. (1994). Lifespan adjustment of children to their parent's divorce. *Children and Divorce*, *4*, 143–164.

Amato, P. R., & Booth, A. (1996). A prospective study of divorce and parent–child relationships. *Journal of Marriage and the Family*, *58*, 356–365.

American Association on Mental Retardation (AAMR). (1992). *Mental retardation: Definition classification and systems of support* (9th ed). Washington, DC: Author. American Association on Mental Retardation.

American Psychiatric Association (APA) (1968). *Diagnostic and statistical manual of mental disorders.* 2nd ed. Washington, DC.

American Psychiatric Association (APA). (1980). *Diagnostic and statistical manual of mental disorders.* 3d ed. Washington, DC.

American Psychiatric Association (APA). (1987). *Diagnostic and statistical manual of mental disorders* (3rd ed., revised). Washington, DC: American Psychiatric Association.

American Psychiatric Association (APA) (1994). *Diagnostic and statistical manual of mental disorders* (4th ed.) Washington, DC: Author.

American Psychological Association. (1985). *Standards for educational and psychological testing.* Washington, DC: Author.

American Psychological Association. (1992). Ethical principles of psychologists and code of conduct. *American Psychologist*, *47*, 1597–1611.

Anastopoulos, A. D., Guevremont, D. C., Shelton, T. L., & DuPaul, G. J. (1992). Parenting stress among families of children with attention deficit hyperactivity disorder. *Journal of Abnormal Child Psychology*, *20*, 503–518.

Anderson, C. A., & Hammen, C. (1993). Psychosocial outcomes of children of unipolar depressed, bipolar, medically ill, and normal women: A longitudinal study. *Journal of Consulting and Clinical Psychology*, *61*, 448–454.

Anderson, J. C. (1994). Epidemiological issues. In T. H. Ollendick, N. J. King, & W. Yule (Eds.), *International handbook of phobia and anxiety disorders in children and adolescents* (pp. 43–65). New York: Plenum.

Anderson-Inman, L., Knox-Quinn, C., & Horney, M. A. (1996). Computer-based study strategies for students with learning disabilities: Individual differences associated with adoption level. *Journal of Learning Disabilities*, *5*, 461–484.

Andrews, J. A., Hops, H., & Duncan, S. C. (1997). Adolescent modeling of parent substance use: The moderating effect of the relationship with the parent. *Journal of Family Psychology*, *11*, 259–270.

Angold, A., & Costello, J. (1996). Toward establishing an empirical basis for the diagnosis of oppositional defiant disorder. *Journal of the American Academy of Child and Adolescent Psychiatry*, *35*, 1205–1212.

Angold, A., & Rutter, M. (1992). Effects of age and pubertal status on depression in a large clinical sample. *Development and Psychopathology*, *4*, 5–28.

Applegate, B., Lahey, B. B., Hart, E. L., Biederman, J., Hynd, G. W., Barkley, R. A., Ollendick, T., Frick, P. J., Greenhill, L., McBurnett, K., Newcorn, J. H., Kerdyk, L., Garfinkel, B., Waldman, I., & Shaffer, D. (1997). Validity of the age-of-onset criterion for ADHD: A report from the *DSM-IV* field trials. *Journal of the American Academy of Child and Adolescent* Psychiatry, *36*, 1211–1221.

Arnold, L. E., (1996). Sex differences in ADHD: Confernce summary. *Journal of Abnormal Child Psychology*, *24*, 555–567.

Arroyo W. (1997). Children and families of Mexican descent. In G. Johnson-Powell & J. Yamamoto (Eds.), *Transcultural child development: Psychological assessment and treatment* (pp. 290–304). New York: Wiley.

Arroyo, W., & Cervantes, R. C. (1997). The Mexican American child. In J. Noshpitz (Ed.), *Handbook of child and adolescent* psychiatry. (Vol. 4, pp. 532–543). New York: Wiley.

Asarnow, J. R. (1994). Annotation: Childhood-onset schizophrenia. *Journal of Child Psychology and* Psychiatry, *35*, 1345–1371.

Asarnow, J. R., & Asarnow, R. F. (1996). Childhood-onset schizophrenia. In E. J. Mash & R. A. Barkley (Eds.), *Child psychopathology* (pp. 340–361). New York: Guilford.

Asarnow, R. F., Brown, W., & Standburg, R. (1995). Children with a schizophrenic disorder: Neurobehavioral studies. *European Archives of* Psychiatry, *and Clinical Neurology*, *245*, 70–79.

Asarnow, J. R., Goldstein, M. J., Thompson, M., & Guthrie, D. (1993). One-year outcomes of depressive disorders in child psychiatric inpatients: Evaluation of the prognostic power of a brief measure of emotion. *Journal of Child Psychology and* Psychiatry, *34*, 129–137.

Asarnow, J. R., Tompson, M., Hamilton, E. B., Goldstein, M. J., & Guthrie, D. (1994). Family-expressed emotion, childhood-onset depression, and childhood-onset schizophrenia spectrum disorders: Is expressed emotion a nonspecific correlate of child psychopathology or a specific risk factor for depression? *Journal of Abnormal Child Psychology*, *22*, 129–146.

Attie, I., & Brooks-Gunn, J. (1995). The development

of eating regulation across the life span. In D. Cicchetti & D. J. Cohen (Eds.), *Developmental psychopathology: Vol 2. Risk disorder and adaptation* (pp. 332–368). New York: Wiley.

Attwood, A., Frith, U., & Hermelin, B. (1988). The understanding and use of interpersonal gestures by Down's syndrome children. *Journal of Autism and Developmental Disabilities, 18*, 241–257.

Axline, V. (1969). *Play therapy.* New York: Ballantine.

Azar, S. T. (1997). A cognitive behavioral approach to understanding and treating parents who physically abuse their children. In D. A. Wolfe, R. J. McMahon, and R. D. Peters (Eds.), *Child abuse: New directions in prevention and treatment across the lifespan* (pp. 79–101). Thousand Oaks, CA: Sage Publications.

Bailey, A., Phillips, W., & Rutter, M. (1996). Autism: Toward an integration of clinical, genetic, neuropsychological, and neurobiological perspectives. *Journal of Child Psychology and Psychiatry, 37*, 89–126.

Bakwin, H., & Bakwin, R. M. (1972). *Behavior disorders in children* (4th ed.). Philadelphia: Saunders.

Baltaxe, C. A. M., & Simmons, J. Q., III (1995). Speech and language disorders in children and adolescents with schizophrenia. *Schizophrenia Bulletin, 21*, 677–687.

Bandura, A. (1968). A social learning interpretation of psychological dysfunctions. In P. London & D. Rosenhan (Eds.), *Foundations of abnormal psychology.* New York: Holt, Rinehart & Winston.

Bandura, A. (1977). *Social learning theory.* Englewood Cliffs, N.J.: Prentice-Hall.

Bandura, A. (1986). *Social foundations of thought and action: A social cognitive theory.* Englewood Cliffs, N.J.: Prentice-Hall.

Barakat, L. P., & Linney, J. A. (1992). Children with physical handicaps and their mothers: The interrelation of social support, maternal adjustment, and child adjustment. *Journal of Pediatric Psychology, 17*, 725–239.

Barbarin, O. A. (1993). Coping and resilience: Exploring the inner lives of African American children. *Journal of Black Psychology, 19*, 478–492.

Bardone, A. M., Moffitt, T. E., Avshalom, C., Dickson, N., & Silva, P. A. (1996). Adult mental health and social outcomes of adolescent girls with depression and conduct disorder. *Development and Psychopathology, 8*, 811–829.

Barker P. (1990). *Clinical interviews with children and adolescents.* New York: Norton.

Barkley, R. A. (1982). Guidelines for defining hyperactivity in children: Attention deficit disorder with hyperactivity. In B. B. Lahey & A. E. Kazdin (Eds.), *Advances in clinical child psychology* (Vol. 5, pp. 137–180). New York: Plenum.

Barkley, R. A. (1990). *Attention-deficit hyperactivity disorder: A handbook for diagnosis and treatment.* New York: Guilford.

Barkley, R. A. (1996). Atten-tion-deficit/hyperactivity disorder. In E. J. Mash & R. A. Barkley (Eds.), *Child psychopathology* (pp. 63–112). New York: Guilford.

Barkley, R. A. (1997a). Attention-deficit/hyperactivity disorder. In E. J. Mash & L. G. Terdal (Eds.), *Assessment of childhood disorders,* (pp. 71–129). New York: Guilford.

Barkley, R. A. (1997b). Behavior inhibition, sustained attention, and executive function. *Psychological Bulletin, 121*, 65–94.

Barlow, D. H. & Durand, V. M. (1995). *Abnormal psychology. An integrative approach.* Pacific Grove, CA: Brooks/Cole Publishers.

Barnett, D., Manly, J. T., & Cicchetti, D. (1993). Defining child maltreatment: The interface between policy and research. In D. Cicchetti, S. L. Toth, & I. E. Sigel (Eds.), *Child abuse, child development, and social policy: Advances in applied developmental psychology* (pp. 7–73). Norwood, NJ: Ablex.

Baron-Cohen, S. (1988). Social and pragmatic deficits in autism: Cognitive or affective? *Journal of Autism and Developmental Disorders, 18*, 379–401.

Baron-Cohen, S. (1991). Do people with autism understand what causes emotion? *Child Development, 62*, 385–395.

Baron-Cohen, S. Theory of mind and face-processing: How do they interact in development and psychopathology? In D. Cicchetti & D. J. Cohen (Eds.), *Developmental psychopathology Vol. I: Theory and methods* (pp. 343–356).

New York: John Wiley & Sons.

Baron-Cohen, S., Leslie, A. M., & Frith, U. (1985). Does the autistic child have a "theory of mind"? *Cognition, 21*, 37–46.

Baumrind, D. (1991). The influences of parenting style on adolescent competence and substance use. *Journal of Early Adolescence, 11*, 56–95.

Bayley N. (1993). *Bayley Scales of Infant Development* (2nd ed.). San Antonio, TX: Psychological Corporation.

Beautrais, A. L., Joyce, P. R., & Mulder, R. T. (1996). Risk factors for serious suicide attempts among youths aged 13 through 24 years. *Journal of the American Academy of Child and Adolescent Psychiatry,, 35*, 1174–1182.

Beeghly, M., & Cicchetti, D. (1994). Child maltreatment, attachment, and the self system: Emergence of an internal state lexicon in toddlers at high social risk. *Development and Psychopathology, 6*, 5–30.

Beeghly, M., Weiss-Perry, B., & Cicchetti, D. (1991). Beyond sensorimotor functioning: Early comunicative and play development of children with Down syndrome. In D. Cicchetti and M. Beeghly (Eds.), *Children with Down syndrome: A developmental perspective,* pp. 329–368. Cambridge: Cambridge University Press.

Beitchman, J. H., & Young, J. R. (1997). Learning disorders with a special emphasis on reading disorders: A review of the past 10 years. *Journal of the American Academy of*

Child and Adolescent Psychiatry, 36, 1020–1031.

Belitz, J., & Valdez, D. M. (1997). A sociocultural context for understanding gang involvement among Mexican-American youth. In J. J. Garcia & M. C. Zea (Eds.), *Psychological interventions and research with Latino populations* (pp. 56–72). Boston: Allyn & Bacon.

Bell, C., & Jenkins, E. (1993). Community violence and children on Chicago's southside. *Psychiatry, 56,* 46–53.

Bell-Dolan, D. J., Reaven, N. M., & Peterson, L. (1993). Depression and social functioning: A multidimensional study of the linkages. *Journal of Clinical Child Psychology, 22,* 306–315.

Bemporad, J. R., & Schwab, M. E. (1986). The DSM-III and clinical child psychiatry. In T. Millon & G. L. Klerman (Eds.), *Contemporary directions in psychopathology: Toward the DSM-IV* (pp. 135–151). New York: Guilford.

Bender, S. L., Ponton, L. E., Crittenden, M. R., & Word, C. O. (1995). For underprivileged children, standardized intelligence testing can do more harm than good: Reply. *Journal of Developmental and Behavioral Pediatrics, 16,* 428–430.

Benes, F. M. (1995). A neurodevelopmental approach to the understanding of schizophrenia and other mental disorders. In D. Cicchetti & D. J. Cohen (Eds.), *Development and psychopathology: Vol. 1. Theory and methods* (pp. 227–253). New York: Wiley.

Bennett, D. S. (1994). Depression among children with chronic medical problems: A meta-analysis. *Journal of Pediatric Psychology, 19,* 149–169.

Bennett, D. S., & Bates, J. E. (1995). Prospective models of depressive symptoms in early adolescence: Attributional style, stress, and support. *Journal of Early Adolescence, 15,* 299–315.

Berger, J. (1991). Interaction between parents and their infants with Down syndrome. In D. Cicchetti & M. Beeghly (Eds.), *Children with Down syndrome: A developmental perspective* (pp. 101–146). Cambridge: Cambridge University Press.

Berk, L. E. (1999). *Infants, children, and adolescents.* Boston: Allyn & Bacon.

Berkowitz, L. (1990). On the formation and regulation of anger and aggression: A cognitive-neoassociationistic analysis. *American Psychologist, 45,* 494–503.

Berliner, L., & Elliott, D. M. (1996). Sexual abuse of children. In J. Briere, L. Berliner, J. A. Bulkley, C. Jenny, & T. Reid (Eds.), *The APSAC handbook on child maltreatment* (pp. 51–71). Thousand Oaks, CA: Sage.

Berman, A. L., & Jobes, D. A. (1991). *Adolescent suicide: Assessment and intervention.* Washington, DC: American Psychological Association.

Bernal, E. M. (1990). Increasing the interpretative validity and diagnostic utility of Hispanic children's scores on tests of achievement and intelligence. In F. C. Serafica, A. I. Schwebel, R. K. Russell,

P. D. Isaac, & L. B. Myers (Eds.), *Mental health of ethnic minorities* (pp. 108–138). New York: Praeger.

Bernal, M. E. (1989). Ethnic minority mental health training: Trends and issues. In F. C. Serafica, A. I. Schwebel, R. K. Russell, P. D. Isaac, & L. B. Myers (Eds.), *Mental health of ethnic minorities* (pp. 249–274). New York: Praeger.

Bernal, M. E., & Knight, G. P. (1997). Ethnic identity of Latino children. In J. G. Garcia & M. C. Zea (Eds.), *Psychological interventions and research with Latino populations* (pp. 15–38). Boston: Allyn & Bacon

Bernal, M. E., Knight, G. P., Ocampo, K. A., Garza, C. A., & Cota, M. K. (1993). Development of Mexican American identity. In M. E. Bernal & G. P. Knight (Eds.) *Ethnic identity: Formation and transmission among Hispanic and other minorities* (pp. 31–46). Albany, NY: State University of New York Press.

Berry, S. L., Hayford, J. R., Ross, C. K., Pachman, L. M. & Lavigne, J. V. (1993). Conceptions of illness by children with juvenile rheumatoid arthritis: A cognitive developmental approach. *Journal of Pediatric Psychology, 18,* 83–97.

Beyer, H. A. (1991). Litigation involving people with mental retardation. In J. L. Matson & J. A. Mulick (Eds.), *Handbook of mental retardation* (pp. 451–467). New York: Pergamon.

Biederman, J., Faraone, S. V., Milberger, S., Jetton, J. G., Chen, L., Mick, E.,

Greene, R. W., & Russell, R. L. (1996). Is childhood oppositional defiant disorder a precursor to adolescent conduct disorder? Findings from a four-year follow-up study of children with ADHD. *Journal of the American Academy of Child and Adolescent Psychiatry, 35,* 1193–1204.

Biederman, J., Santangelo, S. L., Faraone, S. V., Kiely, K., Guite, J., Mick, E., Reed, E. D., Kraus, I., Jellinek, M., & Perrin, J. (1995). Clinical correlates of enuresis in ADHD and non-ADHD children. *Journal of Child Psychology and Psychiatry, 36,* 865–877.

Bifulco, A., Harris, T., & Brown, G. W. (1992). Mourning or early inadequate care? Reexamination of the relation of maternal loss in childhood with adult depression and anxiety. *Development and Psychopathology, 4,* 433–449.

Bigler, E. D. (1996). Brain imaging and behavioral outcome of traumatic brain injury. *Journal of Learning Disabilities, 29,* 515–530.

Bigler, E. D., Nilsson, D. E., Burr, R. B. & Boyer, R. S. (1996). Neuroimaging in pediatric neuropsychology. In C. R. Reynolds & E. F. Fletcher-Janzen (Eds.), Handbook of clinical child neuropsychology, (2nd ed., pp. 342–358). New York: Plenum.

Blagg, N., & Yule, W. (1994). School phobia. In T. H. Ollendick, N. J. King, & W. Yule (Eds.), *International handbook of phobia and anxiety disorders in children and adolescents* (pp. 169–186). New York: Plenum.

Blatt, S. J., & Homann, E. (1992). Parent–child interaction in the etiology of dependent and self-critical depression. *Clinical Psychology Review, 12,* 47–91.

Blatt, S. J., Zohar, A., Quinlan, D. M., & Luthar, S. (1996). Levels of relatedness within the dependency factor of the Depression Experience Questionnaire for Adolescents. *Journal of Personality Assessment, 67,* 52–71.

Block, J., Block, J. H., & Keyes, S. (1988). Longitudinally foretelling drug usage in adolescence: Early childhood personality and environmental processes. *Child Development, 59,* 336–355.

Block J., & Gjerde P. F. (1990). Depressive symptoms in late adolescence: A longitudinal perspective on personality antecedents. In J. Rolf, A. S. Masten, D. Cicchetti, K. H. Nuechterlein, & S. Weintraub (Eds.), *Risk and protective factors in the development of psychopathology* (pp. 334–360). Cambridge, MA: Cambridge University Press.

Block, J., & Haan, N. (1971). *Lives through time.* Berkeley, CA: Bancroft.

Boetsch, E. A., Green, P. A., & Pennington, B. F. (1996). Psychological correlates of dyslexia across the life span. *Development and Psychopathology, 8,* 539–562.

Boll, T. J., & Stanford, L. D. (1997). Pediatric brain injury. In C. R. Reynolds & E. F. Fletcher-Janzen (Eds.), *Handbook of clinical child neuropsychology* (2nd ed., pp. 140–157). New York: Plenum.

Bolton, D. (1996). Annotation: Developmental issues in obsessive-compulsive disorder. *Journal of Child Psychology and Psychiatry, 37,* 131–137.

Bond, M. P. (1995). The development and properties of the Defense Style Questionnaire. In H. R. Conte & R. Plutchik (Eds.), *Ego defenses: Theory and measurement* (pp. 202–220). New York: Wiley.

Boney-McCoy, S., & Finkelhor, D. (1995). Prior victimization: A risk factor for child sexual abuse and for PTSD-related symptomatology among sexually abused youth. *Child Abuse and Neglect, 19,* 1401–1421.

Bools, C. N., Neale, B. A., & Meadow, S. R. (1994). Munchausen syndrome by proxy: A study of psychopathology. *Child Abuse and Neglect, 18,* 773–788.

Borkowski, J. G., Peck, V. A., & Damberg, P. R. (1983). Attention, memory, and cognition. In J. L. Matson & J. A. Mulick (Eds.), *Handbook of mental retardation* (pp. 479–498). New York: Pergamon.

Botvin, G. J., Baker, E., Dusenbury, L., Botvin, E. M., & Diaz, T. (1995). Long-term follow-up results of a randomized drug abuse prevention trial in a white middle-class population. *Journal of the American Medical Association, 273,* 1106–1112.

Boucher, J., Lewis, V., & Collis, G. (1998). Familiar face and voice matching and recognition in children with autism. *Journal of Child Psychology and Psychiatry, 39,* 171–181.

Bourdin, C. M., Mann, B. J., Cone, L. T., Henggeler, S. W., Fucci, B. R., Blaske, D. M., & Williams, R. A. (1995). Multisystemic treatment of serious juvenile offenders: Long-term prevention of criminality and violence. *Journal of Consulting and Clinical Psychology, 63,* 569–578.

Bowlby, J. (1960). *The psychoanalytic study of the child: Vol. 15. Grief and mourning in infancy and early childhood.* New York: International Universities Press.

Bowlby, J. (1973). *Attachment and loss: Vol. 2. Separation: Anxiety and anger.* New York: Basic Books.

Bowlby, J. (1988). Developmental psychiatry comes of age. *American Journal of Psychiatry, 145,* 1–10.

Bregman, J. D., & Hodapp, R. (1991). Current developments in the understanding of mental retardation. Part 1: Biological and phenomenological perspectives. *Journal of the American Academy of Child and Adolescent Psychiatry 30,* 707–719.

Brent, D. A., Roth, C. M., Holder, D. P., Kolko, D. J., Birmaher, B., Johnson, B. A., & Schweers, J. A. (1996). Psychosocial interventions for treating adolescent suicidal depression: A comparison of three psychosocial interventions. In E. D. Hibbs & P. S. Jensen (Eds.), *Psychosocial treatments for child and adolescent disorders* (pp. 187–206). Washington, DC: American Psychological Association.

Bretherton, I. (1996). Internal working models of attachment relationships as related to resilient coping. In G. G. Noam & K. W.

Fischer (Eds.), *Development and vulnerability in close relationships.* Hillsdale, NJ: Erlbaum.

Briere, J., & Conte, J. (1993). Self-reported amnesia for abuse in adults molested as children. *Journal of Traumatic Stress, 6,* 21–31.

Broman, S. H. & Michel, M. E. (eds.) (1995). *Traumatic head injury in children.* New York: Oxford University Press.

Brooks-Gunn, J., & Duncan, G. J. (1997). The effects of poverty on children. *The future of children: Children and poverty, 7,* 55–71.

Brown, C. A., & Kerig, P. K. (1998, August). *Parent-child boundaries as mediators of the effects of maternal distress on children's adjustment.* Presented at the American Psychological Association, San Francisco.

Brown, G. W., Bifulco, A., & Harris, T. O. (1987). Life events, vulnerability and onset of depression: Some refinements. *British Journal of Psychiatry, 150,* 30–42.

Brown, G. W., Harris, T. O., & Bifulco, A. (1986). Long-term effects of early loss of parent. In M. Rutter, C. E. Izard, & P. B. Read (Eds.), *Depression in young people: Developmental and clinical perspectives* (pp. 251–296). New York: Guilford.

Brown, S. A. (1993). Recovery patterns in adolescent substance abusers. In J. S. Baer, G. A. Marlatt, & R. J. McMahon (Eds.), *Addictive behaviors across the lifespan: Prevention, treatment and policy issues* (pp. 161–183). Newbury Park, CA: Sage Publications.

Brown, S. A., Gleghorn, A. A., Shuckit, M. A., Myers, M. G., & Mott, M. A. (1996). Conduct disorder among adolescent substance abusers. *Journal of Studies on Alcohol, 57,* 314–324.

Bruch, H. (1973). *Eating disorders: Obesity, anorexia nervosa, and the person within.* New York: Basic Books.

Bruck, M., Ceci, S. J., & Hembroke, H. (1998). Reliability and credibility of young children's reports: From research to policy and practice. *American Psychologist, 53,* 136–151.

Buchanan, C. M., Maccoby, E. E., & Dornbusch, S. M. (1991). Caught between parents: Adolescents' experience in divorced homes. *Child Development, 62,* 1008–1029.

Buchanan, R. W., Stevens, J. R. & Carpenter, Jr., W. T., (1997). The neuroanatomy of schizophrenia: Editor's introduction. *Schizophrenia Bulletin, 23,* 365–366.

Buitelaar, J. K., van Engeland, H., de Kogel, K. H., de Vries, H., & van Hooff, J. A. R. A. M. (1991). Differences in the structure of social behaviour of autistic children and nonautistic retarded controls. *Journal of Child Psychology and Psychiatry, 32,* 995–1015.

Bukowski, W. M., & Cillessen, A. (1998). Sociometry, then and now. *New directions for child development,* No. 80. San Francisco: Jossey Bass.

Burns, R. C. (1982). *Self-growth in families: Kinetic Family Drawings, research and application.* New York: Brunner/Mazel.

Buss, D. M., Block, J. H., & Block, J. (1980). Preschool activity level:

Personality correlates and developmental implications. *Child Development, 51,* 401–408.

Butcher, J. N., Williams, C. L., Graham, J. R., Archer, R. P., Tellegen, A., Ben-Porath, Y. S., & Jaemmer, B. (1992). *MMPI-A. Minnesota Multiphasic Personality Inventory—Adolescent: Manual for administration, scoring, and interpretation.* Minneapolis: University of Minnesota.

Cahill, B. M., & Glidden, L. M. (1996). Influence of child diagnosis on family and parental functioning: Down syndrome versus other disabilities. *American Journal of Mental Retardation, 101,* 149–160.

Campbell, S. B. (1989). Developmental perspectives. In T. H. Ollendick & M. Hersen (Eds.), *Handbook of child psychopathology* (2nd ed., pp. 5–25). New York: Plenum.

Campbell, S. B. (1990). The socialization and social development of hyperactive children. In M. Lewis & S. M. Miller (Eds.), *Handbook of developmental psychopathology* (pp. 77–92). New York: Plenum.

Campbell, S. B. (1990). *Behavior problems in preschool children.* New York: Guilford.

Campbell, S. B. (1995). Behavior problems in preschool children: A review of recent research. *Journal of Child Psychology and Psychiatry, 36,* 113–149.

Campbell, S. B. (1997). Behavior problems in preschool children: Developmental and family issues. In T. H. Ollendick & R. J. Prinz (Eds.), *Advances in*

clinical child psychology. (Vol 9, pp. 1–26). New York: Plenum.

Campbell, S. B., March, C. L., Pierce, E. W., Ewing, L. J., & Szumowski, E. K. (1991). Hard-to-manage preschool boys: Family context and the stability of externalizing behavior. *Journal of Abnormal Child Psychology, 19,* 301–318.

Canino, I. A. & Spurlock, J. (1994). *Culturally diverse children and adolescents: Assessment, diagnosis, and treatment.* New York: Guilford.

Cannon, T. D., Barr, C. E., & Mednick, S. A. (1991). Genetic and perinatal factors in the etiology of schizophrenia. In E. F. Walker (Ed.), *Schizophrenia: A life-course developmental perspective* (pp. 9–31). San Diego: Academic Press.

Cantor, S. (1988). *Childhood schizophrenia* New York: Guilford.

Cantwell, D. P. (1996). Attention deficit disorder: A review of the past 10 years. *American Journal of the Academy of Child and Adolescent Psychiatry, 35,* 978–987.

Cantwell, D. P. (1996). Classification of child and adolescent psychopathology. *Journal of Child Psychology and Psychiatry and Allied Disciplines, 37,* 3–12.

Capaldi, D. M. (1991). Co-occurrence of conduct problems and depressive symptoms in early adolescent boys: Part I. Familial factors and general adjustment at Grade 6. *Development and Psychopathology, 3,* 277–300.

Capaldi, D. M. (1992). Co-occurrence of conduct

problems and depressive symptoms in early adolescent boys: Part II. A 2-year follow-up at Grade 8. *Development and Psychopathology, 4,* 125–144.

Capaldi, D. M., & Patterson, G. R. (1994). Interrelated influences of contextual factors on antisocial behavior in childhood and adolescence for males. In D. C. Fowles, P. Sutker, & S. H. Goodman (Eds.), *Progress in experimental personality and psychopathology research* (pp. 165–198). New York: Springer.

Caplan, R., Foy, J. G., Asarnow, R. F., & Sherman, T. (1990). Information processing deficits of schizophrenic children with formal thought disorder. *Psychiatric Research, 31,* 169–177.

Caplan, R., & Sherman, T. 1990. Thought disorder in the childhood psychoses. In B. B. Lahey & A. E. Kazdin (Eds.), *Advances in clincal child psychology* (Vol. 13, pp. 175–206). New York: Plenum.

Capps, L., Sigman, M., & Mundy, P. (1994). Attachment security in children with autism. *Development and Psychopathology, 6,* 249–262.

Carlat, D. J., Camargo, C. A., & Herzog, D. B. (1997). Eating disorders in males: A report on 135 patients. *American Journal of Psychiatry, 154,* 1127–1132.

Carlson, E. A., & Sroufe, L. A. (1995). Contribution of attachment theory to developmental psychopathology. In D. Cicchetti, & D. J. Cohen (Eds.), *Developmental psychopathology: Vol. 1. Theory and methods* (pp. 581–617). New York: Wiley.

Carlson, G. A., & Garber, J. (1986). Developmental issues in the classification of depression in children. In M. Rutter, C. E. Izard, & P. B. Read (Eds.), *Depression in young people* (pp. 399–434). New York: Guilford.

Carpenter, M., Nagell, K., & Tomasello, M. (1998). Social cognition, joint attention, and communicative competence from 9 to 15 months of age. *Monographs of the Society for Research in Child Development, 63* (4, Serial No. 255).

Carr, J. (1975). *Young children with Down's syndrome: Their development, upbringing and effect on their families.* London: Butterworth.

Casper, R. C., Hedeker, D., & McClough, J. F. (1992). Personality dimensions in eating disorders and their relevance for subtyping. *Journal of the American Academy of Child and Adolescent Psychiatry, 31,* 830–840.

Caspi, A., Lynam, D., Moffitt, T. E., & Silva, P. A. (1993). Unraveling girls' delinquency: Biological, dispositional, and contextual contributions to adolescent misbehavior. *Developmental Psychology, 29,* 19–30.

Cassidy, J. (1996). Attachment and generalized anxiety disorder. In D. Cicchetti & S. Toth (Eds.), *Rochester symposium on developmental psychopathology: Vol. 6. Emotion, cognition, and representation* (pp. 1–56). Rochester, NY: University of Rochester Press.

Cassidy, J., Kirsh, S. J., Scolton, K. L., & Parke, R. D. (1996). Attachment and representations of peer relationships. *Developmental Psychology, 32,* 892–904.

Castillo, R. J. (1997). *Culture and mental illness. A client-centered approach.* Pacific Grove, CA: Brooks/Cole.

Catalano, R. F., & Hawkins, J. D. (1995). The social development model: A theory of antisocial behavior. In J. D. Hawkins (Ed.), *Some current theories of delinquency and crime.* New York: Springer-Verlag.

Cauffman, E., & Steinberg, L. (1996). Interactive effects of menarcheal status and dating on dieting and disordered eating among adolescent girls. *Developmental Psychology, 32,* 631–635.

Ceci, S. J., & Bruck, M. (1995). *Jeopardy in the classroom: A scientific analysis of children's testimony.* Washington, DC: American Psychological Association.

Celano, M., Hazzard, A., Webb, C., & McCall, C. (1996). Treatment of traumagenic beliefs among sexually abused girls and their mothers: An evaluation study. *Journal of Abnormal Child Psychology, 24,* 1–17.

Centers for Disease Control. (1995). Suicide among children, adolescents, and young adults—United States, 1980–1992. *Morbidity and Mortality Weekly Report, 44,* 289–291.

Charman, R., & Baron-Cohen, S. (1997). Brief report: Prompted pretend play in autism. *Journal of Autism and Developmental Disorders, 27,* 325–335.

Chase-Lansdale, L. C., Cherlin, A. J., & Kiernan, K. E. (1995). The long-term effects of parental divorce on the mental health of young adults: A developmental perspective, *Child Development, 66,* 1614–1634.

Chavez, J. M., & Rodney, C. E. (1990). Psychocultural factors affecting the mental health status of Mexican American adolescents. In A. R. Stiffman & L. E. Davis (Eds.), *Ethnic issues in adolescent mental health* (pp. 73–91). Newbury Park, CA: Sage Publications.

Chodorow, N. J. (1978). *The reproduction of mothering.* Berkeley: University of California Press.

Christiano, B., & Tarbell, S. E. (1998). Brief report: Behavioral correlates of postoperative pain in toddlers and preschoolers. *Journal of Pediatric Psychology, 23,* 149–154.

Christoffel, K. K., Scheidt, P. C., Agran, O. F., Kraus, J. F., McLoughlin, E., & Paulson, J. A. (1992). Standard definitions for childhood injury research: Excerpts of a conference report. *Pediatrics, 89,* 1027–1034.

Christophersen, E. R., & Edwards, K. J. (1992). Treatment of elimination disorders: State of the art, 1991. *Applied and Preventive Psychology, 1,* 15–22.

Cicchetti, D. (1991). Defining psychological maltreatment: Reflections and future directions. *Development and Psychopathology, 3,* 1–2.

Cicchetti, D. (1993). Developmental psychopathology:

Reaction, reflections, projections. *Developmental Review, 13,* 471–502.

Cicchetti, D., & Beeghly, M. (1991). An organizational approach to the study of Down syndrome: Contributions to an integrative theory of development. In D. Cicchetti & M. Beeghly (Eds.), *Children with Down syndrome: A developmental perspective* (pp. 29–62). Cambridge: Cambridge University Press.

Cicchetti, D., & Bukowski, W. M. (eds.) (1995). Special issue: Developmental processes in peer relations and psychopathology. *Development and Psychopathology 7(4),* 587–874.

Cicchetti, D., & Cohen, D. J. (1995). Perspectives on developmental psychopathology. In D. Cicchetti & D. J. Cohen (Eds.), *Developmental psychopathology: Vol. I. Theory and methods* (pp. 3–20). New York: Wiley.

Cicchetti, D., & Garmezy, N. (Eds.). (1993). Special issue: Milestones in the study of resilience. *Development and Psychopathology, 5(4),* 497–783.

Cicchetti, D., & Howes, P. W. (1991). Developmental psychopathology in the context of the family: Illustrations from the study of child maltreatment. *Canadian Journal of Behavioural Science, 23,* 257–281.

Cicchetti, D., & Izard, C. E. (Eds.). (1995). Special issue: Emotions in developmental psychopathology. *Development and Psychopathology, 7(1),* 1–226.

Cicchetti, D., & Lynch, M. (1995). Failures in the expectable environment and their impact on individual development: The case of child maltreatment. In D. Cicchetti & D. J. Cohen (Eds.), *Developmental psychopathology: Vol. 2. Risk, disorder, and adaptation* (pp. 32–71). New York: Wiley.

Cicchetti, D., & Olsen, K. (1990). The developmental psychopathology of child maltreatment. In M. Lewis & S. M. Miller (Eds.), *Handbook of developmental psychopathology* (pp. 261–279). New York: Plenum.

Cicchetti, D., & Rogosch, F. A. (1996). Editorial: Equifinality and multifinality in developmental psychopathology. *Development and Psychopathology, 8,* 597–600.

Cicchetti, D., Rogosch, F. A., & Toth, S. L. (1997). Ontogenesis, depressotypic organization, and the depressive spectrum. In S. S. Luthar, J. A. Burack, D. Cicchetti, & J. R. Weisz (Eds.), *Developmental psychopathology: Perspectives on adjustment, risk, and disorder* (pp. 273–315). Cambridge: Cambridge University Press.

Cicchetti, D., & Toth, S. L. (1992). The role of developmental theory in prevention and intervention. *Development and Psychopathology, 4,* 489–494.

Cicchetti, D., & Toth, S. L. (1995a). Developmental psychopathology and disorders of affect. In D. Cicchetti & D. J. Cohen (Eds.), *Developmental psychopathology: Vol. 2. Risk, disorder, and adaptation* (pp. 369–420). New York: Wiley.

Cicchetti, D., & Toth, S. L. (1995b). A developmental psychopathology perspective on child abuse and neglect. *Journal of the American Academy of Child and Adolescent Psychiatry, 34,* 541–565.

Cicchetti, D., & Toth, S. L. (1998). The development of depression in children and adolescents. *American Psychologist, 53,* 221–241.

Cicchetti, D., Toth, S. L., Bush, M. A., & Gillespie, J. F. (1988). Stage-salient issues: A transactional model of intervention. In E. D. Nannis & P. A. Cowan (Eds.), *Developmental psychopathology and its treatment* (pp. 123–146). San Francisco: Jossey-Bass.

Cicchetti, D., & Wagner, S. (1990). Alternative assessment strategies for the evaluation of infants and toddlers: An organizational perspective. In S. J. Meisels & J. P. Shonkoff (Eds.), *Handbook of early childhood intervention* (pp. 246–277). Cambridge: Cambridge University Press.

Claussen, A. H., & Crittenden, P. M. (1991). Physical and psychological maltreatment: Relations among types of maltreatment. *Child Abuse and Neglect, 15,* 5–18.

Clay, R. A. (1997). Are children being overmedicated? *APA monitor, 29,* 1, 27.

Clinton, D. N., & Glant, R. (1992). The eating disorders spectrum of DSM-III-R: Clinical features and psychosocial concomitants of 86 consecutive cases from a Swedish urban catchment area. *Journal of Nervous and Mental Disease, 180,* 244–250.

Cohen, D., Nisbett, R. E., Bowdle, B. F., & Schwarz, N. (1996). Insult, aggression, and the Southern culture of honor: An "experimental ethnography." *Journal of Personality and Social Psychology, 70,* 945–960.

Cohen, D., & Strayer, J. (1996). Empathy in conduct-disordered and comparison youth. *Developmental Psychology, 32,* 988–998.

Cohen, H. J., Grosz, J., Ayoob, K., & Schoen, S. (1997). Early intervention for children with HIV infection. In M. J. Guralnick (Ed.) *Effectiveness of early intervention* 2nd ed. (pp. 193–203). Baltimore, MD: Paul H. Brooks.

Cohen, P., Cohen, J., Kasen, S., Velez, C. N., Hartmark, C., Johnson, J., Rojas, M., Brook, J., & Streuning, E. L. (1993). An epidemiological study of disorders in late childhood and adolescence: I. Age- and gender-specific prevalence. *Journal of Child Psychology and Psychiatry, 34,* 851–867.

Cohler, B. J. (1987). Adversity, resilience, and the study of lives. In E. J. Anthony & B. J. Cohler (Eds.), *The invulnerable child* (pp. 363–424). New York: Guilford.

Cohler, B. J., Stott, F. M., & Musick, J. S. (1995). Adversity, vulnerability, and resilience: Cultural and developmental perspectives. In D. Cicchetti & D. J. Cohen (Eds.), *Developmental psychopathology: Vol. 2. Risk, disorder and adaptation* (pp. 753–800). New York: Wiley.

Coie, J., Terry, R., Lenox, K., Lochman, J., & Hyman, C. (1995). Childhood peer rejection and aggression as predictors of stable patterns of adolescent disorder. *Development and Psychopathology, 7,* 697–714.

Cole, D. A., Truglio, R., & Peeke, L. (1997). Relation between symptoms of anxiety and depression in children: a multitrait-multimethod-multigroup assessment. *Journal of Consulting and Clinical Psychology, 65,* 110–119.

Cole, P. M., Michel, M. K., & Teti, L. O. (1994). The development of emotion regulation and dysregulation: A clinical perspective. In N. A. Fox (Ed.), The development of emotion regulation: Biological and behavioral considerations. *Monographs of the Society for Research in Child Development, 59,* 73–102.

Cole, P. M., Zahn-Waxler, C., Fox, N. A., Usher, B. A., & Welsh, J. D. (1996). Individual differences in emotion regulation and behavior problems in preschool children. *Journal of Abnormal Psychology, 105,* 518–529.

Cole, P. M., Zahn-Waxler, C., & Smith, K. D. (1994). Expressive control during a disappointment: Variations related to preschoolers' behavior problems. *Developmental Psychology, 30,* 835–846.

Comas-Diaz, L. (1997). Mental health needs of Latinos with professional status. In J. G. Garcia & M. C. Zea (Eds) *Psychological interventions and research with Latino populations.* (pp. 142–165). Boston: Allyn & Bacon.

Compas, B. E. (1997). Depression in children and adolescents. In E. J. Mash & L. G. Terdal (Eds.),

Assessment of childhood disorders (pp. 197–229). New York: Guilford.

Compas, B. E., Oppedisano, G., Connor, J. K., Gerhardt, C. A., Hinden, B. R., Achenbach, T. M., & Hammen, C. (1997). Gender differences in depressive symptoms in adolescence: Comparison of national samples of clinically referred and nonreferred youths. *Journal of Consulting and Clinical Psychology, 65,* 617–626.

Conduct Problems Prevention Research Group. (1992). A developmental and clinical model for the prevention of conduct disorder: The FAST Track Program. *Development and Psychopathology, 4,* 509–528.

Conger, J. J., & Galambos, N. L. (1997). *Adolescence and youth.* New York: Longman.

Conte, J. R. (1992). Has this child been sexually abused? Dilemmas for the mental health professional who seeks the answer. *Criminal Justice and Behavior, 19,* 54–73.

Copans, S. A., & Kinney, J. (1996). Adolescents. In J. Kenney (Ed.), *Clinical manual of substance abuse* (pp. 288–300). St. Louis: Mosby.

Corah, N. L., Anthony, E. J., Painter, P., Stern, J. A. & Thurston, D. (1965). Effects of perinatal anoxia after seven years. *Psychological Monographs 79* (3, whole no. 596).

Costello, A. J., Edelbrock, L. S., Dulcan, M. K., Kalas, R., & Klaric, S. H. (1984). *Report on the NIMH Diagnostic Interview Schedule for Children (DISC).* Washington, DC: National Institute of Mental Health.

Costello, E. J., Loeber, R., & Stouthamer-Loeber, M. (1991). Pervasive and situational hyperactivity: Confounding effect of informant. A research note. *Journal of Child Psychology and Psychiatry, 32,* 367–376.

Courchesne, E., Yeung-Courchesne, R., Press, G. A., Hesselink, J. R. & Jernigan, T. L. (1988). Hypoplasia of cerebellar vermal lobules VI and VII in autism. *New England Journal of Medicine, 381,* 1349–1354.

Cowan, P. A. (1978). *Piaget with feeling.* New York: Holt, Rinehart & Winston.

Craig, K. D., & Grunau, R. V. E. (1991). Developmental issues: Infants and toddlers. In J. P. Bush & S. W. Harkins (Eds.), *Children in pain: Clinical and research issues from a developmental perspective* (pp. 171–193). New York: Springer-Verlag.

Cramer, P. (1991). *The development of defense mechanisms: Theory, research, and assessment.* New York: Springer-Verlag.

Creer, T. L., & Bender, B. G. (1995). Pediatric asthma. In M. C. Roberts (Ed.), *Handbook of pediatric psychology* (2nd ed., pp. 219–240). New York: Guilford.

Crews F. (1997). *The memory wars: Freud's legacy in dispute.* New York: New York Review of Books.

Crick, N. R., & Dodge, K. A. (1994). A review and reformulation of social information-processing mechanisms in children's social adjustment. *Psychological Bulletin, 115,* 74–101.

Crick N. R., & Grotpeter, J. K. (1995). Relational aggression, gender, and social-psychological adjustment. *Child Development, 66,* 710–722.

Crisp, J., Ungerer, J. A., & Goodnow, J. J. (1996). The impact of experience on children's understanding of illness. *Journal of Pediatric Psychology, 21,* 57–72.

Crittenden, P. M. (1992). Treatment of anxious attachment in infancy and early childhood. *Development and Psychopathology, 4,* 575–602.

Crittenden, P. M. (1993). An information-processing perspective on the behavior of neglectful parents. *Criminal Justice and Behavior, 20,* 27–48.

Crnic, K. A. (1991). Families of children with Down syndrome: Ecological contexts and characteristics. In D. Cicchetti & M. Beeghly (Eds.), *Children with Down syndrome: A developmental perspective* (pp. 399–423). Cambridge: Cambridge University Press.

Crockenberg, S., & Litman, C. (1990). Autonomy as competence in 2-year-olds: Maternal correlates of child defiance, compliance, and self-assertion. *Developmental Psychology, 26,* 961–971.

Crow, T. J., Done, D. J., & Sacker, A. (1995). Childhood precursors of psychosis as clues to its evolutionary origins. *European Archives of Psychiatry and Clinical Neurology, 245,* 61–69.

Crowell, J. A., & Waters, E. (1990). Separation anxiety. In M. Lewis & S. M. Miller (Eds.), *Handbook of developmental psychopathology,* pp. 209–218. New York: Plenum.

Cuddy-Casey, M., & Orvaschel, H. (1997). Children's understanding of death in relation to child suicidality and homicidality. *Clinical Psychology Review, 17,* 33–45.

Cummings, E. M., & Davies, P. T. (1994a). Maternal depression and child development. *Journal of Child Psychology and Psychiatry, 35,* 73–112.

Cummings, E. M., & Davies, P. (1994b). *Children and marital conflict: The impact of family dispute and resolution.* New York: Guilford.

Dadds, M. R., Spence, S. H., Holland, D. E., Barrett, P. M., & Laurens, K. R. (1997). Prevention and early intervention for anxiety disorders: A controlled trial. *Journal of Consulting and Clinical Psychology, 65,* 627–635.

Dana, R. H. (1996). Culturally competent assessment practice in the United States. *Journal of Personality Assessment, 66,* 472–487.

Davidson, L. M., & Baum, A. (1990). Posttraumatic stress in children following natural and human made trauma. In M. Lewis & S. M. Miller (Eds.), *Handbook of developmental psychopathology,* (pp. 252–260). New York: Plenum.

Davies, P. T., & Windle, M. (1997). Gender-specific pathways between maternal depressive symptoms, family discord, and adolescent adjustment. *Developmental Psychology, 33,* 657–668.

Dawes, R. M. (1994). *House of cards: Psychology and psychotherapy built on myth.* New York: Free Press.

Dawson, G. (1991). A psychobiological perspective on the early socio-emotional development of children with autism. In D. Cicchetti and S. L. Toth (Eds.), *Models and integrations. Rochester symposium on developmental psychopathology,* vol. 3, pp. 207–234. Rochester, NY: University of Rochester Press.

Dawson, G. (1996). Brief report: Neuropsychology of autism: A report of the state of the science. *Journal of Autism and Developmental Disorders, 26,* 179–184.

Dawson, G., & Galpert, L. (1986). A developmental model for facilitating the social behavior in autistic children. In E. Schopler & G. B. Mesibov (Eds.), *Social behavior in autism* (pp. 237–261). New York: Plenum.

Dawson, G., Hill, D., Spencer, A., Galpert, L., & Watson, L. (1990). Affect exchange between young autistic children and their mothers. *Journal of Abnormal Child Psychology, 18,* 335–345.

Dawson, G., & Levy, A. (1989). Arousal, attention, and the socioemotional impairment of individuals with autism. In G. Dawson (Ed.), *Autism: Nature and diagnosis* (pp. 49–74). New York: Guilford.

Dawson, G., & Osterling, J. (1996). Early intervention in autism: Effectiveness and common elements of current approaches. In M. J. Guralnick (Ed.), *The effectiveness of early interventions: Second generation research* (pp. 307–326). Baltimore: Paul H. Brooks.

Deitz, D. E. D., & Repp, A. C. (1989). Mental retardation. In T. H. Ollendick & M. Hersen (Eds.), *Handbook of child psychopathology,* 2nd ed., pp. 75–92. New York: Plenum.

DeKlyen, M. (1996). Disruptive behavior disorder and intergenerational attachment patterns: A comparison of clinic-referred and normally functioning preschoolers and their mothers. *Journal of Consulting and Clinical Psychology, 64,* 357–365.

del Carmen, R. (1990). Assessment of Asian-Americans for family therapy. In F. C. Serafica, A. I. Schwebel, R. K. Russell, P. D. Isaac, & L. B. Myers (Eds.), *Mental health of ethnic minorities* (pp. 139–166). New York: Praeger.

Daleiden, E. L., & Vasey, M. W. (1997). An information-processing perspective on childhood anxiety. *Clinical Psychology Review, 17,* 407–429.

Daleiden, E. L., Vasey, M. W., & Brown, L. M. (in press). Internalizing disorders. In W. K. Silverman & T. H. Ollendick (Eds.), *Developmental issues in the clinical treatment of children and adolescents.* New York: Allyn & Bacon.

DePanfilis, D. (1996). Social isolation of neglectful families: A review of social support assessment and intervention models. *Child Maltreatment, 1,* 37–52.

DeVane, C. L., & Sallee, F. R. (1996). Serotonin selective reuptake inhibitors in child and adolescent psychopharmacology: A review of published experience. *Journal of Clinical Psychiatry, 57,* 55–66.

De Wolff, M. S. & IJzendoorn, M. H. (1997). Sensitivity and attachment: A meta-analysis on parental antecedents of infant attachment. *Child Development, 68,* 571–591.

Diaz-Guerrero, R. (1990). Commentary on "Limits to the use and generalizability of the views of life questionnaire." *Hispanic Journal of Behavioral Sciences, 12,* 322–327.

Diaz-Guerrero, R., & Szalay, L. B. (1991). *Understanding Mexicans and Americans: Cultural perspectives in conflict.* New York: Plenum.

Didden, R., Duker, P. C., & Korzilius, H. (1997). Meta-analytic study on treatment effectiveness for problem behaviors with individuals who have mental retardation. *American Journal of Mental Retardation, 101,* 387–399.

Dishion, T. J., French, D. C., & Patterson, G. R. (1995). The development and ecology of antisocial behavior. In D. Cicchetti & D. J. Cohen (Eds.), *Developmental psychopathology: Vol. 2. Risk, disorder, and adaptation* (pp. 421–471). New York: Wiley.

Dissanayake, C., & Crossley, S. A. (1997). Autistic children's responses to separation and reunion with their mothers. *Journal of Autism and Developmental Disorders, 27,* 295–312.

Dodge, K. A. (1986). A social information process model of social competence in children. In M. Perlmutter (Ed.), *Eighteenth annual Minnesota symposium on child psychology* (pp. 77–125). Hillsdale, NJ: Erlbaum.

Dodge, K. A. (1990). Nature versus nurture in child conduct disorder: It is time to ask a different question. *Developmental Psychology, 26,* 698–701.

Dodge, K. (1993). Social-cognitive mechanisms in the development of conduct disorder and depression. *Annual Review of Psychology, 44,* 559–584.

Dodge, K. A., Pettit, G. S., & Bates, J. E. (1994). Effects of physical maltreatment on the development of peer relations. *Development and Psychopathology, 6,* 43–56.

Dodge, K. A., Pettit, G. S., Bates, J. E., & Valente, E. (1995). Social information-processing patterns partially mediate the effect of early physical abuse on later conduct problems. *Journal of Abnormal Psychology, 104,* 632–643.

Dolgin, M. J. & Jay, S. M. (1989). Childhood cancer. In T. H. Ollendick & M. Hersen (Eds.), *Handbook of child psychopathology,* 2nd ed., pp. 327–340. New York: Plenum.

Douglas, V. I. (1983). Attention and cognitive problems. In M. Rutter (Ed.), *Developmental neuropsychiatry* (pp. 280–329). New York: Guilford.

Douglass, H. M., Moffitt, T. E., Dar, R., McGee, R., & Silva, P. (1995). Obsessive-compulsive disorder in a birth cohort of 18-year-olds: Prevalence and prediction. *Journal of the American Academy of Child and Adolescent Psychiatry, 34,* 1424–1430.

Drake, B., & Pandey, S. (1996). Understanding the relationship between neighborhood poverty and specific types of child maltreatment. *Child Abuse and Neglect, 20*, 1003–1018.

Drotar, D. (1995). Failure to thrive (growth deficiency). In M. C. Roberts (Ed.), *Handbook of pediatric psychology* (2nd ed., pp. 518–536). New York: Guilford.

Drotar, D. (1997). Relating parent and family functioning to the psychological adjustment of children with chronic health conditions: What have we learned? What do we need to know? *Journal of Pediatric Psychology, 22*, 149–165.

Drotar, D., Stein, R. E. K., & Perrin, E. C. (1995). Methodological issues in using the Child Behavior Checklist and its related instruments in clinical child psychology research. *Journal of Clinical Child Psychology, 24*, 184–192.

Dujovne, V. F., Barnard, M. U., & Rapoff, M. A. (1995). Pharmacological and cognitive-behavioral approaches in the treatment of childhood depression: A review and critique. *Clinical Psychology Review, 15*, 589–611.

Dukewich, T. L., Borkowski, J. G., & Whitman, T. L. (1996). Adolescent mothers and child abuse potential: An evaluation of risk factors. *Child Abuse and Neglect, 20*, 1031–1047.

Dumas, J. E., LaFreniere, P. J., & Serketich, W. J. (1995). "Balance of power": A transactional analysis of control in mother-child dyads involving socially competent, aggressive, and anxious children. *Journal of Abnormal Psychology, 104*, 104–113.

Duncan, R. D., Saunders, B. E., Kilpatrick, D. G.,

Rochelle, F., & Resnick, H. S. (1996). Childhood physical assault as a risk factor for PTSD, depression, and substance abuse: Findings from a national survey. *American Journal of Orthopsychiatry, 66*, 437–448.

Dupree, D., Spencer, M. B., & Bell, S. (1997). African American children. In G. Johnson-Powell & J. Yamamoto (Eds.), *Transcultural child development: Psychological assessment and treatment* (pp. 237–268). New York: Wiley.

Durlak, J. A. (1997). Primary prevention programs in the schools. In T. H. Ollendick & R. J. Prinz (Eds.), *Advances in clinical child psychology* (Vol. 19, pp. 283–318). New York: Plenum.

Durlak, J. A., Fuhrman, T., & Lampman, C. (1991). Effectiveness of cognitive-behavior therapy for maladapting children: A meta-analysis. *Psychological Bulletin, 110*, 204–214.

Dworkin, R. H., Cornblatt, B. A., Friedmann, R., Kaplansky, L. M., Lewis, J. A., Rinaldi, A., Shilliday, C., & Erlenmeyer-Kimling, L. (1993). Childhood precursors of affective vs. social deficits in adolescents at risk for schizophrenia. *Schizophrenia Bulletin, 19*, 563–574.

Dykens, E. M., Hodapp, R. M., & Leckman, J. F. (1994). *Behavior and development in fragile X syndrome.* London: Sage Publications.

Dykens, E. M., & Kasari, C. (1997). Maladaptive behavior in children with Prader-Willi syndrome, Down syndrome, and non-

specific mental retardation. *American Journal of Mental Retardation, 102*, 228–237.

Dykens, E. M., Ort, S., Cohen, I., Finucane, B., Spiridigliozzi, G., Lachiewicz, A., Reiss, A., Freund, L., Hagerman, R., & O'Connor, R. (1996). Trajectories and profiles of adaptive behavior in males with fragile X syndrome. *Journal of Autism and Developmental Disorders, 26*, 287–303.

Ebata, A. T., Peterson A. C., & Conger, J. J. (1990). The development of psychopathology in adolescence. In J. Rolf, A. S. Masten, D. Cicchetti, K. H. Nuechterlein, & S. Weintraub (Eds.), *Risk and protective factors in the development of psychopathology* (pp. 308–333). Cambridge, MA: Cambridge University Press.

Echeverry, J. J. (1997). Treatment barriers: Accessing and accepting professional help. In J. J. Garcia & M. C. Zea (Eds.), *Psychological interventions and research with Latino populations*, (pp. 94–107). Boston: Allyn & Bacon.

Edelbrock, C., Rende, R., Plomin, R., & Thompson, L. A. (1995). A twin study of competence and problem behavior in childhood and early adolescence. *Journal of Child Psychology and Psychiatry, 35*, 775–785.

Egeland, B. (1988). Breaking the cycle of abuse: Implications for prediction and intervention. In K. D. Browne, C. Davies, & P. Stratton (Eds.), *Early prediction and prevention of child abuse* (pp. 87–99). New York: Wiley.

Egeland, B. (1991). A longitudinal study of high-risk families. In R. Starr & D. Wolfe (Eds.), *The effects of child abuse and neglect: Issues and research* (pp. 43–46). New York: Guilford.

Egeland, B., Kalkoske, M., Gottesman, N., & Erickson, M. E. (1990). Preschool behavior problems: Stability and factors accounting for change. *Journal of Child Psychology and Psychiatry, 31*, 891–909.

Eggers, C., & Bunk, D. (1997). The long-term course of childhood-onset schizophrenia: A 42-year followup. *Schizophrenia Bulletin, 23*, 105–116.

Einfeld, S. L., & Tonge, B. J. (1996). Population prevalence of psychopathology in children and adolescents with intellectual disability: II. Epidemiological findings. *Journal of Intellectual Disability Research, 40*, 99–109.

Eisenberg, N., Fabes, R. A., Shepard, S. A., Murphy, B. C., Guthrie, I. K., Jones, S., Friedman, J., Poulin, R., & Maszk, P. (1997). Contemporaneous and longitudinal prediction of children's social functioning from regulation and emotionality. *Child Development, 68*, 642–664.

Elliot, D. S., Huizinga, D., & Menard, S. (1989). *Multiple problem youth: Delinquency, substance use, and mental health problems.* New York: Springer-Verlag.

Eme, R. F., & Kavanaugh, L. (1995). Sex differences in conduct disorder. *Journal of Clinical Child Psychology, 24*, 406–426.

Emery, R. E., & Kitzmann, K. M. (1995). The child in the family: Disruptions in family functions. In D. Cicchetti & D. J. Cohen (Eds.), *Developmental psychopathology: Vol. I. Theory and methods* (pp. 3–31). New York: Wiley.

Emery, R. E., & Laumann-Billings, L. (1998). An overview of the nature, causes, and consequences of abusive family relationships: Toward differentiating maltreatment and violence. *American Psychologist, 53*, 121–135.

Emery, R. E., Matthews, S. G., & Kitzmann, K. M. (1994). Child custody mediation and litigation: Parents' satisfaction and functioning one year after settlement. *Journal of Consulting and Clinical Psychology, 62*, 124–129.

Emslie, G. J., Kennard, B. D., & Kowatch, R. A. (1995). Affective disorders in children: Diagnosis and management. *Journal of Child Neurology, 10*, 42–49.

Erickson, M. F., & Egeland, B. (1996). Child neglect. In J. Briere, L. Berliner, J. A. Bulkley, C., Jenny, & T. Reid (Eds.), *The APSAC handbook on child maltreatment* (pp. 4–20). Thousand Oaks, CA: Sage Publications.

Erickson, M. F., Korfmacher, J., & Egeland, B. R. (1992). Attachment past and present: Implications for therapeutic intervention with mother-infant dyads. *Development and Psychopathology, 4*, 495–508.

Erikson, E. H. (1950). *Childhood and society.* New York: Norton.

Erikson, E. H. (1964a). Play and cure. In M. R. Haworth (Ed.), *Child psychotherapy* (pp. 475–485). New York: Basic Books.

Erikson, E. H. (1964b). Clinical observation of play disruption in young children. In M. R. Haworth (Ed.), *Child psychotherapy* (pp. 264–276). New York: Basic Books.

Erikson, E. H. (1968). *Identity: Youth and crisis.* New York: Norton.

Erickson, M. F., Sroufe, L. A., & Egeland, B. (1985). The relationship between quality of attachment and behavior problems in preschool in a high-risk sample. In I. Bretherton & E. Waters (Eds.), *Growing points of attachment theory and research. Monographs of the Society for Research in Child Development, 50* (1-2 Series No. 209), 147–166.

Eron, L. D., & Huesmann, L. R. (1990). The stability of aggressive behavior—Even unto the third generation. In M. Lewis & S. M. Miller (Eds.), *Handbook of developmental psychopathology* (pp. 147–155). New York: Plenum.

Eron, L. D., Huesmann, L. R., Monroe, M., & Walder, L. O. (1996). Does television violence cause aggression? In D. F. Greenberg (Ed.), *Criminal careers: Vol. 2. The international library of criminology, criminal justice and penology* (pp. 311–321). Aldershot, England: Dartmouth.

Exner, J. E. (1993). *The Rorschach: A comprehensive system: Vol. 1.* New York: Wiley.

Exner, J. E. (1994). *The Rorschach: A comprehensive system: Vol. 3. Assessment of children and adolescents.* New York: Wiley.

Fairburn, C. G., Norman, P. A., Welch, S. L., O'Connor, M. E., Doll, H. A., & Peveler, R. C. (1995). A prospective study of outcome in bulimia nervosa and the long-term effects of three psychological treatments. *Archives of General Psychiatry, 52*, 304–312.

Fairburn, C. G., Welch, S. L., Doll, H. A., Davies, B. A., & O'Connor, M. E. (1997). Risk factors for bulimia nervosa: A community-based case-control study. *Achives of General Psychiatry, 54*, 509–517.

Farrell, A. D., & White, K. S. (1998). Peer influences and drug use among urban adolescents: Family structure and parent-adolescent relationship as protective factors. *Journal of Consulting and Clinical Psychology, 66*, 248–258.

Farrington, D. P. (1995). The development of offending and antisocial behavior from childhood: Key findings from the Cambridge study in delinquent development. *Journal of Child Psychology and Psychiatry, 360*, 929–964.

Farrington, D. P., Loeber, R., & Van Kammen, W. B. (1990). Long-term criminal outcomes of hyperactivity-impulsivity-attention deficit and conduct problems in childhood. In L. N. Robins & M. Rutter (Eds.), *Straight and devious pathways from childhood to adulthood* (pp. 62–81). Cambridge: Cambridge University Press.

Feigelman, S., Stanton, B. F., & Ricardo, I. (1993). Perceptions of drug selling and drug use among urban youths. *Journal of Early Adolescence, 13*, 267–284.

Feldman, M. A. (1997). The effectiveness of early intervention for children of parents with mental retardation. In M. J. Guralnick (Ed.), *The effectiveness of early intervention* (pp. 171–192). Baltimore MD: Paul H. Brooks.

Fennell, E. B., & Bauer, R. M. (1997). Models of inference in evaluating brain-behavior relationships in children. In C. R. Reynolds & E. Fletcher-Janzen (Eds.), *Handbook of clinical child neuropsychology* (2nd ed., pp. 204–215). New York: Plenum.

Fergusson, D. M., Horwood, L. J., & Lynskey, M. T. (1993). Early dentine lead levels and subsequent cognitive and behavioural development. *Journal of Child Psychology and Psychiatry, 34*, 215–227.

Fergusson, D. M., Horwood, L. J., & Lynskey, M. T. (1995). The stability of disruptive childhood behaviors. *Journal of Abnormal Child Psychology, 23*, 379–396.

Fergusson, D. M., & Horwood, L. J. (1996). The role of adolescent peer affiliations in the continuity between childhood behavioral adjustment and juvenile offending. *Journal of Abnormal Child Psychology, 24*, 205–221.

Fergusson, D. M., Lynskey, M. T., & Horwood, L. J. (1996). Factors associated with continuity and changes in disruptive behavior patterns between childhood and adolescence. *Journal of Abnormal Child Psychology, 24*, 533–553.

Ferretti, R. P., & Okolo, C. M. (1996). Authenticity in learning: Multimedia design projects in the social studies for students with disabilities. *Journal of Learning Disabilities, 29,* 450–460.

Field, T. (1992). Infants of depressed mothers. *Development and Psychopathology, 4,* 49–66.

Field, T. (1996). Attachment and separation in young children. *Annual Review of Psychology, 47,* 541–561.

Finkelhor, D. (1984). *Child sexual abuse: New theories and research.* New York: Free Press.

Finkelhor, D., & Berliner, L. (1995). Research on the treatment of sexually abused children: A review and recommendations. *Journal of the American Academy of Child and Adolescent Psychiatry, 34,* 1408–1423.

Finkelhor, D., & Browne, A. (1988). Assessing the long-term impact of child sexual abuse: A review and reconceptualization. In L. Walker (Ed.), *Handbook on sexual abuse of children* (pp. 55–71). New York: Springer.

Finkelhor, D., & Dziuba-Leatherman, J. (1995). Victimization prevention programs: A national survey of children's exposure and reactions. *Child Abuse and Neglect, 19,* 129–140.

Finkelhor, D., Hotaling, G. T., Lewis, I. A., & Smith, C. (1990). Sexual abuse in a national survey of adult men and women: Prevalence, characteristics, and risk factors. *Child Abuse and Neglect, 14,* 19–28.

Fisher, P., Schaffer, D., Piacentini, J., Lapkin, J., Wicks, J., & Rojas, M. (1991). *Completion of revisions of the NIMH Diagnostic Interview*

Schedule for Children (DISC-2). Washington, DC: Epidemiology and Psychopathology Research, National Institute for Mental Health.

Fisher, R. L., & Fisher, S. (1996). Antidepressants for children: Is scientific support necessary? *Journal of Nervous and Mental Disease, 184,* 99–102.

Fitzgerald, H. E., Davies, W. H., Zucker, R. A., & Klinger, M. T. (1994). Developmental systems theory and substance abuse: A conceptual and methodological framework for analyzing patterns of variation in families. In L. L'Abate (Ed.), *Handbook of developmental family psychology and psychopathology* (pp. 350–372). New York: Wiley.

Fleming, J., Mullen, P., & Bammer, G. (1997). A study of potential risk factors for sexual abuse in childhood. *Child Abuse and Neglect, 21,* 49–58.

Fletcher, K. E. (1996). Childhood posttraumatic stress disorder. In E. J. Mash & R. A. Barkley (Eds), *Child psychopathology* (pp. 242–276). New York: Guilford.

Fonagy, P., & Target, M. (1994). The efficacy of psychoanalysis for children with disruptive disorders. *Journal of the American Academy of Child and Adolescent Psychiatry, 33,* 45–55.

Fonagy, P., & Target, M. (1996). A contemporary psychoanalytical perspective: Psychodynamic developmental therapy. In E. D. Hibbs & P. S. Jensen (Eds.), *Psychosocial treatments for child and adolescent disorders: Empiri-*

cally based strategies for clinical practice (pp. 619–638). Washington, DC: American Psychological Association.

Fonagy, P., Target, M., Steele, M., & Gerber, A. (1995). Psychoanalytic perspectives on developmental psychopathology. In D. Cicchetti & D. J. Cohen (Eds.), *Developmental psychopathology: Vol. I. Theory and methods* (pp. 504–554). New York: Wiley.

Forehand, R. (1977). Child noncompliance to parental requests: Behavioral analysis and treatment. In M. Hersen, R. M. Eisler, & P. M. Miller (Eds.), *Progress in behavior modification* (Vol. 5, pp. 111–148). New York: Academic Press.

Forehand, R., & McMahon, R. (1981). *Helping the noncompliant child: A clinician's guide to parent training.* New York: Guilford.

Forehand, R., & Wierson, M. (1993). The role of developmental factors in planning behavioral interventions for children: Disruptive behavior as an example. *Behavior Therapy, 24,* 117–141.

Foreyt, J. P., & Mikhail, C. (1997). Anorexia nervosa and bulimia nervosa. In E. J. Mash & L. G. Terdal (Eds.), *Assessment of childhood disorders* (pp. 683–716). New York: Guilford.

Forgatch, M. S. (1994, June). The two faces of Janus: Conflict and cohesion in the development of antisocial behavior. Santa Fe, New Mexico: Family Research Consortium Summer Institute.

Forth, A. E., Hart, S. D., & Hare, R. D. (1990). Assessment of psychopathy in male young offenders. *Psychological Assessment, 3,* 342–344.

Fosson, A., Knibbs, J., Bryant-Waugh, R., & Lask, B. (1987). Early onset anorexia nervosa. *Archives of Disease in Childhood, 62,* 114–118.

Foster, S. L., & Martinez, Jr., C. R. (1995). Ethnicity: Conceptual and methodological issues in clinical child research. *Journal of Clinical Child Psychology, 24,* 214–226.

Foy, D. W., Madvig, B. T., Pynoos, R. S., & Camilleri, A. J. (1996). Etiological factors in the development of posttraumatic stress disorder in children and adolescents. *Journal of School Psychology, 34,* 133–145.

Fraiberg, S. (1980). *Clinical studies in infant mental health.* New YorK: Basic Books.

Franklin, M. E., Kozak, M. J., Cashman, L. A., Coles, M. E., Rheingold, A. A., & Foa, E. B. (1998). Cognitive-behavioral treatment of pediatric obsessive-compulsive disorder: An open clinical trial. *Journal of the American Academy of Child and Adolescent Psychiatry, 37,* 412–419.

Freud, A. (1965). *Normality and pathology in childhood. Assessment of development.* New York: International Universities Press.

Frick, P. J., & Jackson, Y. K. (1993). Family functioning and childhood antisocial behavior: Yet another reinterpretation. *Journal of Clinical Child Psychology, 22,* 410–419.

Frick, P. J., Lahey, B. B., Loeber, R., Tannenbaum, L., Van Horn, Y., Christ, M. A., Hart, E. L., & Hanson, K. (1993). Oppositional defiant disorder and conduct disorder: A meta-analytic review of factor analyses and cross-validation in a clinic sample. *Clinical Psychology Review, 13,* 319–340.

Frick, P. J., O'Brien, B. S., Wootton, J. M., & McBurnett, K. (1994). Psychopathy and conduct problems in children. *Journal of Abnormal Psychology, 103,* 700–707.

Friedrich, W. (1997). Psychotherapy with sexually abused boys. In D. A. Wolfe, R. J. McMahon, & R. D. Peters (Eds.), *Child abuse: New directions in prevention and treatment across the lifespan* (pp. 205–222). Thousand Oaks, CA: Sage Publications.

Friedrich, W. N. (1996). An integrated model of psychotherapy for abused children. In J. Briere, L. Berliner, J. A. Bulkley, C. Jenny, & T. Reid (Eds.), *The APSAC handbook on child maltreatment* (pp. 104–118). Thousand Oaks, CA: Sage Publications.

Frith, U. (1989). *Autism: Explaining the enigma.* Cambridge, MA: Basil Blackwell.

Frith, U., & Baron-Cohen, S. (1987). Perception in autistic children. In D. J. Cohen, A. M. Donnellan, & R. Paul (Eds.), *Handbook of autism and developmental disabilities* (pp. 85–102). New York: Wiley.

Fritz, G. K., Rockney, R. M., & Yeung, A. S. (1994). Plasma levels and efficacy of imipramine treatment for enuresis. *Journal of the American Academy of Child and Adolescent Psychiatry, 33,* 60–66.

Fugita, S. S. (1990). Asian/Pacific American mental health: Some needed research in epidemiology and service utilization. In F. C. Serafica, A. I. Schwebel, R. K. Russell, P. D. Isaac, & L. B. Myers (Eds.), *Mental health of ethnic minorities* (pp. 66–86). New York: Praeger.

Fuller, R. L. (1997). The African American child. In J. D. Noshpitz (Ed.), *Handbook of child and adolescent psychiatry.* (Vol. 4, pp. 484–492). New York: Wiley.

Gabel, S. (1997). Oppositional defiant disorder. In J. D. Noshpitz, (Ed.), *Child and adolescent psychiatry.* (Vol. 2, pp. 351–359). New York: Wiley.

Gaines, S., & Reed, E. (1995). Prejudice from Allport to DuBois. *American Psychologist, 50,* 96–103.

Gallimore, R., Coots, J., Weisner, T., Garnier, H., & Guthrie, D. (1996). Family responses to children with early developmental delays: II. Accommodaton intensity and activity in early and middle childhood. *American Journal on Mental Retardation, 101,* 215–232.

The Gallup Organization (1995). *Disciplining children in America.* Princeton, NJ: Author.

Ganiban, J., Wagner, S., & Cicchetti, D. (1991). Temperament and Down syndrome. In D. Cicchetti & M. Beeghly (Eds.), *Children with Down syndrome: A developmental perspective* (pp. 63–100).

Cambridge: Cambridge University Press.

Garbarino, J., Stott, F. M., & Faculty of the Erikson Institute (1992). *What children can tell use: Eliciting, interpreting, and evaluating information from children.* San Francisco, Jossey-Bass.

Garber, J. (1984). Classification of childhood psychopathology: A developmental perspective. *Child Development, 55,* 30–48.

Garber, J., Braafladt, N., & Weiss, B. (1995). Affect regulation in depressed and nondepressed children and young adolescents. *Development and Psychopathology, 7,* 93–116.

Garcia, J. G., & Marotta, S. (1997). Characterization of the Latino population. In J. G. Garcia & M. C. Zea (Eds.), *Psychological interventions and research with Latino populations* (pp. 1–14). Boston: Allyn & Bacon.

Gard, G. C., & Berry, K. K. (1986). Oppositional children: Taming tyrants. *Journal of Clinical Child Psychology, 15,* 148–158.

Garfinkel, P. E., & Garner, D. M. (1986). Anorexia nervosa and adolescent mental health. In R. A. Feldman & A. R. Stiffman (Eds.), *Advances in adolescent mental health* (Vol. 1, pp. 163–204). Greenwich, CT: JAI Press.

Garland, A. F., & Zigler, E. (1993). Adolescent suicide prevention: Current research and social policy implications. *American Psychologist, 48,* 169–182.

Garnefski, N., & Arends, E. (1998). Sexual abuse and adolescent maladjustment: Differences between male and female victims. *Journal of Adolescence, 21,* 99–107.

Garrison, W. T., & McQuiston, S. (1989). *Chronic illness during childhood and adolescence: Psychological aspects.* Newbury Park, CA: Sage Publications.

Gaub, M., & Carlson, C. I. (1997). Gender differences in ADHD: A meta-analysis and critical review. *Journal of the American Academy of Child and Adolescent Psychiatry, 36,* 1036–1045.

Ge, X., Conger, R. D., Cadoret, R. J., Nedierhiser, J. M., Yates, W., Troughton, E., & Stewart, M. A. (1996). The developmental interface between nature and nurture: A mutual influence model of child antisocial behavior and parent behaviors. *Developmental Psychology, 32,* 574–589.

Gedaly-Duff, V. (1991). Developmental issues: Preschool and school-age children. In J. P. Bush & S. W. Harkins (Eds.), *Children in pain: Clinical and research issues from a developmental perspective* (pp. 195–230). New York: Springer-Verlag.

Gelfand, D. M., Teti, D. M., Seiner, S. A., & Jameson, P. B. (1996). Helping mothers fight depression: Evaluation of a home-based intervention program for depressed mothers and their infants. *Journal of Clinical Child Psychology, 25,* 406–422.

Geller, D., Biederman, J., Jones, J., Park, K., Schwartz, S., Shapiro, S., & Cofey, B. (1998). Is juvenile obsessive-compulsive disorder a developmental subtype of disorder? A review of the pediatric literature. *Journal of the*

American Academy of Child and Adolescent Psychiatry, 37, 420–427.

Gelman, R., & Baillargeon, R. (1983). A review of some Piagetian concepts. In P. H. Mussen (Series 8 J. H. Flavell and E. M. Markman Vol. Ed.), *Handbook of child psychology* (Vol. 3, pp. 167–230). New York: Wiley.

Gerring, J. P. (1997). Closed head injuries. In J. D. Noshpitz (Ed.), *Handbook of child and adolescent psychiatry* (Vol. 4, pp. 319–330). New York: Wiley.

Gesell, A., Ilg, F. L., Ames, L. B., & Bullis, G. E. (1946). *The child from five to ten.* New York: Harper.

Gibbs, J. T. (1990). Mental health issues of black adolescents: Implications for policy and practice. In A. R. Stiffman & L. E. Davis (Eds.), *Ethnic issues in adolescent mental health* (pp. 21–52). Newbury Park, CA: Sage Publications.

Gillberg, C. (1988). Annotation. The neurobiology of infantile autism. *Journal of Child Psychology and Psychiatry, 29,* 257–266.

Gillberg, C. (1991). Outcome in autism and autistic-like conditions. *Journal of the American Academy of Child and Adolescent Psychiatry, 30,* 375–382.

Gjerde, P. F. (1995). Alternative pathways to chronic depressive symptoms in young adults: Gender differences in developmental trajectories. *Child Development, 66,* 1277–1300.

Gjerde, P. F., & Block, J. (1991). Preadolescent antecedents of depressive symptomatology at age 18: A prospective study.

Journal of Youth and Adolescence, 20, 217–231.

Goldberg, S. (1997). Attachment and childhood behavior probems in normal, at-risk, and clinical samples. In L. Atkinson & K. J. Zuker (Eds.), *Attachment and psychopathology* (pp. 171–195). New York: Guilford.

Goldstein, M. J. (1990). Family relations as risk factors for the onset and course of schizophrenia. In J. Rolf, A. S. Masten, D. Cicchetti, K. H. Nuechterlein, & S. Weintraub (Eds.), *Risk and protective factors in the development of psychopathology* (pp. 408–423). Cambridge: Cambridge University Press.

Goldsmith, H. H., Gottesman, I. I., & Lemery, K. S. (1997). Epigenetic approaches to developmental psychopathology. *Development and Psychopathology, 9,* 365–387.

Golombok, S., & Fivush, R. (1994). *Gender development.* Cambridge: Cambridge University Press.

Gooding, D. C., & Iacono, W. G. (1995). Schizophrenia through the lens of a developmental psychopathology perspective. In D. Cicchetti & D. J. Cohen (Eds.), *Developmental psychopathology: Vol. 1. Theory and methods* (pp. 535–580). New York: Wiley.

Gottlieb, J., Alter, M., & Gottlieb, B. W. (1991). Mainstreaming mentally retarded children. In J. L. Matson & J. A. Mulick (Eds.), *Handbook of mental retardation* (pp. 63–73). New York: Pergamon.

Graham, F. K., Ernhart, C. B., Thurston, D., & Craft, M. (1962). Development three

years after perinatal anoxia and other potentially damaging newborn experiences. *Psychological Monographs 76,* (3, whole no. 522).

Graham, S. (1992). "Most of the subjects were White and middle class." Trends in published research on African Americans in selected APA journals. 1970-1989. *American Psychologist, 47,* 629–639.

Greenberg, J. R., & Mitchell, S. A. (1983). *Object relations in psychoanalytic theory.* Cambridge, MA: Harvard University Press.

Greenberg, M. T., DeKlyen, M., Speltz, M. L., & Endriga, M. C. (1997). The role of attachment processes in externalizing psychopathology in young children. In L. Atkinson & K. J. Zuker (Eds.), *Attachment and psychopathology* (pp. 196–222). New York: Guilford.

Greenberg, M. T., Speltz, M. L., & DeKlyen, M. (1993). The role of attachment in the early development of disruptive behavior problems. *Development and Psychopathology, 5,* 191–213.

Greenberg, R. P., & Fisher, S. (1996). *Freud scientifically reappraised.* New York: Wiley.

Greenspan, S. I., & Greenspan, N. T. (1991). *The clinical interview of the child.* D.C. American Psychiatric Press.

Group for the Advancement of Psychiatry Committee on Child Psychiatry. (1974). *Psychopathological disorders in childhood: Theoretical considerations and a proposed classification.* New York: J. Aronson.

Grusec, J. E., & Goodnow, J. J. (1994). Impact of parental discipline methods on the child's internalization of values: A reconceptualization of current points of view. *Developmental psychology, 30,* 4–19.

Grych, J. H., & Fincham, F. D. (1992). Interventions for children of divorce: Toward greater integration of research and action. *Psychological Bulletin, 111,* 434–454.

Grych, J. H., & Fincham, F. D. (1997). Children's adaptation to divorce: From description to explanation. In S. A. Wolchik & I. N. Sandler (Eds.), *Handbook of children's coping: Linking theory and intervention* (pp. 159–193). *New York: Plenum.*

Grych, J. H., & Fincham, F. (Eds.) (in press). *Child development and interparental conflict.* New York: Cambridge University Press.

Guidubaldi, J., Perry, J. D., & Nastasi, B. K. (1987). Growing up in a divorced family: Initial and long-term perspectives on children's adjustment. In S. Oskamp (Ed.), *Applied social psychology annual: Vol. 7. Family processes and problems* (pp. 202–237). Newbury Park, CA: Sage Publications.

Guntrip, H. (1986). My experience of analysis with Fairbairn and Winnicott (How complete a result does psycho-analytic therapy achieve?). In P. Buckley (Ed.), *Essential papers on object relations* (pp. 447–468). New York: New York University Press.

Guralnick, M. J. (1986). The peer relations of young handicapped and non-handicapped children. In P. S. Strain, M. J. Guralnick, & H. M. Walker (Eds.), *Children's social behavior: Development, assessment and modification* (pp. 93–140). New York: Academic Press.

Guralnick, M. J. (1998). Effectiveness of early intervention for vulnerable children: A developmental perspective. *American Journal of Mental Retardation, 102,* 319–345.

Guterman, N. B. (1997). Early prevention of physical child abuse and neglect: Existing evidence and future directions. *Child Maltreatment, 2,* 12–34.

Hadwin, J., Baron-Cohen, S., Howlin, P., & Hill, K. (1997). Does teaching theory of mind have an effect on the ability to develop conversations in children with autism? *Journal of Autism and Developmental Disorders, 27,* 519–536.

Häfner, H. (1995). Special issue "Schizophrenia in childhood and adolescence." *European Archives of Psychiatry and Clinical Neuroscience, 245,* 57–60.

Häfner, H., & Nowotny, B. (1995). Epidemiology of early-onset schizophrenia. *European Archives of Psychiatry and Clinical Neuroscience, 245,* 80–92.

Hale, C. A., & Borkowski, J. G. (1991). Attention, memory, and cognition. In J. L. Matson & J. A. Mulick (Eds.), *Handbook of mental retardation,* (pp. 505–528). New York: Pergamon.

Hall, N. W., & Zigler, E. (1997). Drug-abuse prevention efforts for young children: A review and critique of existing programs. *American Journal of Orthopsychiatry, 67,* 134–143.

Hall, R. V., Fox, R., Willard, D., Goldsmith, L., Emerson, M., Owen, M., Davis, T., & Porcia, E. (1971). The teacher as observer and experimenter in the modification of disputing and talking-out behaviors. *Journal of Applied Behavioral Analysis, 4,* 141–149.

Halperin, J. M., Matier, K., Bedi, G., Sharma, V., & Newcorn, J. H. (1992). Specificity of inattention, impulsivity, and hyperactivity to the diagnosis of attention-deficit hyperactivity disorder. *Journal of the American Academy of Child and Adolescent Psychiatry, 31,* 190–196.

Halstead Neuropsychological Test Battery for Children. 1969. Indianapolis: Reitan.

Hammen, C. (1991). The family-environmental context of depression: A perspective on children's risk. In Cicchetti, D., & Toth, S. L. (Eds.), *Rochester symposium on developmental psychopathology, 4,* 251–281.

Hammen, C. (1992). Cognitive, life stress, and interpersonal approaches to a developmental psychopathology model of depression. *Development and Psychopathology, 4,* 189–206.

Hammen, C., Burge, D., & Adrian, C. (1991). Timing of mother and child depression in a longitudinal study of children at risk. *Journal of Consulting and Clinical Psychology, 59,* 341–345.

Hammen, C., Burge, D., Daley, S. E., Davila, J., Paley, B., & Rudolph, K. D. (1995). Interpersonal attachment cognitions and prediction of symptomatic responses to interpersonal stress. *Journal of Abnormal psychology, 104,* 436–443.

Hammen, C., Burge, D., & Stansbury, K. (1990). Relationship of mother and child variables to child outcomes in a high-risk sample: A casual modeling analysis. *Developmental Psychology, 26,* 24–30.

Hammen, C., & Compas, B. E. (1994). Unmasking unmasked depression in children and adolescents: The problem of comorbidity. *Clinical Psychology Review, 14,* 585–603.

Hammen, C., & Rudolph, K. D. (1996). Childhood depression. In E. J. Mash & R. A. Barkley (Eds.), *Child psychopathology* (pp. 153–195). New York: Guilford.

Hammer, E. F. (1958). *The clinical application of projective drawings.* Springfield, IL: Charles C Thomas.

Hammill, D. D. (1993). A brief look at the learning disabilities movement in the United States. *Journal of Learning Disabilities, 26,* 295–310.

Handler, L., & Habenicht, D. (1994). The Kinetic Family Drawing Technique: A review of the literature. *Journal of Personality Assessment, 62,* 440–464.

Hankin, B. L., Abramson, L. Y., Moffitt, T. E., Silva, P. A., McGee, R., & Angell, K. E. (1998). Development of depression from preadolescence to young adulthood: Emerging gender differences in a 10-year longitudinal study. *Journal of Abnormal Psychology, 107,* 128–140.

Hanna, G. L. (1995). Demographic and clinical features of obsessive-compulsive disorder in children and adolescents. *Journal of the American Academy of Child and Adolescent Psychiatry, 34,* 19–25.

Hanson, D. R., Gottesman, I. I., & Heston, L. L. (1990). Long-range schizophrenia forecasting: Many a slip twixt the cup and the lip. In J. Rolf, A. S. Masten, D. Cicchetti, K. H. Nuechterlein, & S. Weintraub (Eds.), *Risk and protective factors in the development of psychopathology* (pp. 242–444). Cambridge: Cambridge University Press.

Happe, F., & Frith, U. (1996). Theory of mind and social impairment in children with conduct disorder. *British Journal of Developmental Psychology, 14,* 385–398.

Harbeck-Weber, C., & McKee, D. H. (1995). Prevention of emotional and behavioral distress in children experiencing hospitalization and chronic illness. In M. C. Roberts (Ed.), *Handbook of pediatric psychology* (2nd ed., pp. 167–184). New York: Guilford.

Harbeck-Weber, C., & Peterson, L. (1993). Children's conceptions of illness and pain. *Annals of Child Development, 9,* 133–161.

Harbeck-Weber, C., & Peterson, L. (1996). Health-related disorders. In E. J. Mash & R. A. Barkley (Eds.), *Child psychopathology* (pp. 572–601). New York: Guilford.

Hare, R. D. (1993). *Without conscience: The disturbing*

world of the psychopaths among us. New York: Pocket Books.

Hare, R. D. (1996). Psychopathy: A clinical construct whose time has come. *Criminal Justice and Behavior, 23,* 25–54.

Harrington, R., Bredenkamp, D., Groothues, C., Rutter, M., Fudge, H., & Pickles, A. (1994). Adult outcomes of childhood and adolescent depression: III. Links with suicidal behaviours. *Journal of Child Psychology and Psychiatry, 35,* 1309–1319.

Harrington, R., Fudge, H., Rutter, M., Pickles, A., & Hill, J. (1991). Adult outcomes of childhood and adolescent depression: II. Risk for antisocial disorders. *Journal of the American Academy of Child Psychiatry, 30,* 434–439.

Harrington, R., Rutter, M., & Fombonne, E. (1996). Developmental pathways in depression: Multiple meanings, antecedents, and endpoints. *Development and Psychopathology, 8,* 601–616.

Hart, C. H., Germain, R., & Brassard, M. (1987). The challenge: To better understand and combat psychological maltreatment of children and youth. In M. Brassard, R. Germain, & S. Hart (Eds.), *Psychological maltreatment of children and youth* (pp. 3–24). New York: Pergamon.

Hart, E. L., Lahey, B. B., Loeber, R., Applegate, B., & Frick, P. J. (1995). Developmental changes in Attention-Deficit Hyperactive Disorders in boys: A four-year longitudinal study. *Journal of Abnor-*

mal Child Psychology, 23, 729–750.

Hart, S. N., Binggeli, N. J., & Brassard, M. R. (1998). Evidence for the effects of psychological maltreatment. *Journal of Emotional Abuse, 1,* 27–56.

Harter, S. (1986). Processes underlying the construction, maintenance, and enhancement of the self-concept in children. In J. Suls & A. G. Greenwald (Eds.), *Psychological perspectives on the self* (Vol. 3, pp. 137–180). Hillsdale, NJ: Erlbaum.

Harter, S. (1988). Developmental and dynamic changes in the nature of the self-concept: Implications for child psychotherapy. In S. Shirk (Ed.), *Cognitive development and child psychotherapy.* New York: Plenum.

Harter, S. (1990). Causes, correlates, and the functional role of global self-worth: A life-span perspective. In R. J. Sternberg & J. Kolligian (Eds.), *Competence considered* (pp. 67–97). New Haven, CT: Yale University Press.

Harter, S., Bresnick, S., Bouchey, H. A., & Whitesell, N. R. (1997). The development of multiple role-related selves during adolescence. *Development and Psychopathology, 9,* 835–853.

Harter, S., & Marold, D. (1991). A model of the determinants and mediational role of self-worth: Implications for adolescent depression and suicidal ideation. In G. R. Goethals & J. Strauss (Eds.), *The self: An interdisciplinary approach* (pp. 66–92). New York: Springer-Verlag.

Harter, S., & Marold, D. B. (1994). Psychosocial risk factors contributing to adolescent suicidal ideation. In G. G. Noam & S. Borst (Eds.), *Children, youth, and suicide: Developmental perspectives* (pp. 71–92). San Francisco: Jossey-Bass.

Harter, S., Marold, D. B., & Whitesell, N. R. (1992). A model of psychosocial risk factors leading to suicidal ideation in young adolescents. *Development and Psychopathology, 4,* 167–188.

Harter, S., & Whitesell, N. R. (1996). Multiple pathways to self-reported depression and psychological adjustment among adolescents. *Development and Psychopathology, 8,* 761–777.

Hartup, W. W. (1974). Aggression in childhood: Development perspectives. *American Psychologist, 29,* 336–341.

Harvey, P. D. (1991). Cognitive and linguistic functions of adolescent children at risk for schizophrenia. In E. F. Walker (Ed.), *Schizophrenia: A life-course developmental perspective* (pp. 139–156). San Diego, CA: Academic Press.

Haywood, H. C., Meyers, C. E., & Switzky, H. N. (1982). Mental retardation. In M. R. Rosenzweig & L. W. Porter (Eds.), *Annual review of psychology,* Vol. 33, pp. 309–342. Palo Alto, CA: Annual Reviews.

Hazan, C., & Shaver, P. R. (1994). Attachment as an organizational framework for research on close relationships. *Psychological Inquiry, 5,* 1–22.

Hazelrigg, M. D., Cooper, H. M., & Borduin, C. M.

(1987). Evaluating the effectiveness of family therapies: An integrative review and analysis. *Psychological Bulletin, 101,* 428–442.

Heatherton, T. F., & Baumeister, R. F. (1991). Binge eating as escape from self-awareness. *Psychological Bulletin, 110,* 86–108.

Helfer, M. E., Kempe, R. S., & Krugman, R. D. (1997). *The battered child* (5th ed.). Chicago: University of Chicago Press.

Helms, J. E. (1990). Three perspectives on counseling and psychotherapy with visible racial/ethnic group clients. In F. C. Serafica, A. I. Schwebel, R. K. Russell, P. D. Isaac, & L. B. Myers (Eds.), *Mental health of ethnic minorities* (pp. 171–201). New York: Praeger.

Henggeler, S. W., & Bourdin, C. M. (1990). *Family therapy and beyond: A multisystemic approach to treating behavior problems of children and adolescents.* Pacific Grove, CA: Brooks/Cole.

Henin, A., & Kendall, P. C. (1997). Obsessive-compulsive disorder in childhood and adolescence. In T. H. Ollendick & R. J. Prinz (Eds.), *Advances in clinical child psychology* (Vol. 19, pp. 75–131). New York: Plenum.

Henry, B., Moffitt, T. E., Caspi, A., Langley, J., & Silva, P. A. (1994). On the "remembrance of things past": A longitudinal evaluation of the retrospective method. *Psychological Assessment, 6,* 92–101.

Hermelin, B. (1976). Coding and sense modalities. In L. Wing (Ed.), *Early childhood autism: Clinical edu-*

cational and social aspects. New York: Pergamon.

Herrenkohl, R. C., Egolf, B. P., & Herrenkohl, E. C. (1997). Preschool antecedents of adolescent assaultive behavior: A longitudinal study. *American Journal of Orthopsychiatry, 67*, 422–432.

Herzog, D. B., & Beresin, E. V. (1991). Anorexia nervosa. In A. M. Nicholi (Ed.), *Textbook of child and adolescent psychiatry* (pp. 362–375). Washington, DC: American Psychiatric Association.

Herzog, D. B., Keller, M. B., Sacks, N. R., Yeh, C. J., & Lavori, P. W. (1992). Psychiatric comorbidity in treatment-seeking anorexics and bulimics. *Journal of the American Academy of Child and Adolescent Psychiatry, 31*, 810–818.

Herzog, D. B., Sacks, N. R., Keller, M. B., Lavori, P. W., von Ranson, K. B., & Gray, H. N. (1993). Patterns and predictors of recovery in anorexia nervosa and bulimia nervosa. *Journal of Child Psychology and Psychiatry, 32*, 962–966.

Hetherington, E. M. (1991). The role of individual differences and family relationships in children's coping with divorce and remarriage. In P. A. Cowan & E. M. Hetherington (Eds.), *Family transitions* (pp. 165–194). Hillsdale, NJ: Erlbaum.

Hetherington, E. M. (1993). An overview of the Virginia Longitudinal Study of Divorce and Remarriage with a focus on early adolescence. *Journal of Family Psychology, 7*, 39–56.

Hetherington, E. M., Bridges, M., & Insabella, G. M.

(1998). What matters? What does not? Five perspectives on the association between marital transitions and children's adjustment. *American Psychologist, 53*, 167–184.

Hibbs, E. D., & Jensen, P. S. (1996). *Psychosocial treatments for child and adolescent disorders: Empirically based strategies for clinical practice.* Washington, DC: American Psychological Association.

Higgins, K., & Boone, R. (1996). Special series on technology: An introduction. *Journal of Learning Disabilities, 29*, 340–343.

Hines, A. M. (1997). Divorce-related transitions, adolescent development, and the role of the parent-child relationship: A review of the literature. *Journal of Marriage and the Family, 59*, 375–388.

Hinshaw, S. P., & Anderson, C. A. (1996). Conduct and oppositional defiant disorders. In E. J. Mash & R. A. Barkley (Eds.), *Child psychopathology* (pp. 113–152). New York: Guilford.

Hinshaw, S. P., Zupan, B. A., Simmel, C., Nigg, J. T., & Melnick, S. (1997). Peer status in boys with and without attention-deficit hyperactivity disorder. Predictions from overt and covert antisocial behavior, social isolation, and authoritative parenting beliefs. *Child Development, 68*, 880–896.

Ho, M. K. (1992). *Minority children and adolescents in therapy.* Newbury Park, CA: Sage Publications.

Hobson, R. P. (1986a). The autistic child's appraisal of expressions of emotion. *Journal of Child Psychol-*

ogy and Psychiatry, 27, 321–342.

Hobson, R. P. (1986b). The autistic child's appraisal of expression of emotions: A further study. *Journal of Child Psychology and Psychiatry, 27*, 671–680.

Hobson, R. P., Ouston, J., & Lee, A. (1988). What's in a face? The case of autism. *British Journal of Psychology, 79*, 441–453.

Hodapp, R. M. (1994). Cultural-familial mental retardation. In R. Sternberg (Ed.), *Encyclopedia of intelligence* (pp. 711–717). New York: Macmillan.

Hodapp, R. M., & Dykens, E. M. (1944). The two cultures of behavioral research in mental retardation. *American Journal of Mental Retardation, 97*, 675–687.

Hodapp, R. M., & Dykens, E. M. (1996). Mental retardation. In E. J. Mash & R. A. Barkley (Eds.), *Child psychopathology* (pp. 362–389). New York: Guilford.

Hodapp, R. M., Dykens, E. M., & Masino, L. L. (1997). Families of children with Prader-Willi syndrome: Stress-support and relations to child characteristics. *Journal of Autism and Developmental Disorders, 27*, 11–24.

Hodapp, R. M., & Zigler, E. (1995). Past, present, and future issues in the developmental approach to mental retardation and developmental disabilities. In D. Cicchetti & C. J. Cohen (Eds.), *Developmental psychopathology: Vol. 2. Risk, disorder, and adaptation* (pp. 299–331). New York: Wiley.

Hodges, K. (1993). Structured interviews for assessing

children. *Journal of Child Psychology and Psychiatry, 34*, 49–68.

Hoge, R. D., Andrews, D. A., & Leschied, A. W. (1996). An investigation of risk and protective factors in a sample of youthful offenders. *Journal of Child Psychology and Psychiatry, 37*, 419–424.

Holden, E. W., Chmielewski, D., Nelson, C. C., Kager, V. A., & Foltz, L. (1997). Controlling for general and disease-specific effects in child and family adjustment to chronic childhood illness. *Journal of Pediatric Psychology, 22*, 15–27.

Holland, A. J., Treasure, J., Coskeran, P., & Dallow, J. (1995). Characteristics of eating disorder in Prader-Willi syndrome: Implications for treatment. *Journal of Intellectual Disability Research, 39*, 373–381.

Hops, H. (1992). Parental depression and child behaviour problems: Implications for behavioural family intervention. *Behaviour Change, 9*, 126–138.

Howard, B. L., & Kendall, P. C. (1996). Cognitive-behavioral family therapy for anxiety-disordered children: A multiple-baseline evaluation. *Cognitive Therapy and Research, 20*, 423–443.

Howlin, P. (1998). Practitioner Review: Psychological and educational treatment for autism. *Journal of Child Psychology and Psychiatry, 39*, 307–322.

Hughes, C. C. (1996). The culture-bound syndromes and psychiatric diagnosis. In J. E. Mezzich, A. Kleinman, H. Fabrega, & D. L.

Parron (Eds.), *Culture and diagnosis: A DSM-IV perspective* (pp. 289–308). Washington, DC: American Psychiatric Association Press.

Hughes, C. C. (1997). The culture-bound syndromes and psychiatric diagnosis. In J. E. Messich, A. Kleinman, H. Fabrega, & D. L. Parron, (Eds.) *Culture and psychiatric diagnosis. A DSM-IV perspective*, (pp. 289–308). Washington DC: American Psychiatric Association Press, Inc.

Huguenin, N. H., Weidenman, L. E., & Mulick, J. A. (1991). Programmed instruction. In J. L. Matson & J. A. Mulick (Eds.), *Handbook of mental retardation* (pp. 451–467). New York: Pergamon.

Humphrey, L. (1989). Observed family interactions among subtypes of eating disorders using structural analysis of social behavior. *Journal of Consulting and Clincial Psychology, 57,* 206–214.

Hundleby, J. D., & Mercer, G. W. (1987). Family and friends as social environments and their relationship to young adolescents' use of alcohol, tobacco, and marijuana. *Journal of Marriage and the Family, 49,* 151–164.

Hurley, A. D., Pfadt, A., Tomasulo, D., & Gardner, W. I. (1996). Counseling and psychotherapy. In J. W. Jacobson & J. A. Mulick (Eds.), *Manual of diagnosis and professional practice in mental retardation* (pp. 371–378). Washington, DC: American Psychological Association.

Hutchinson, G., Takei, N., Fahy, T. A., Bhugra, D., Gilvarry, C., Moran, P.,

Mallett, R., Sham, P., Leff, J. & Murray, R. M. (1996). Morbid risk of schizophrenia in first-degree relatives of White and African-Caribbean patients with psychosis. *British Journal of Psychiatry, 169,* 776–780.

Ialongo, N., Edelsohn, G., Werthamer-Larsson, L., Crockett, L., & Kellam, S. (1993). Are self-reported depressive symptoms in first-grade children developmentally transient phenomena? A further study. *Development and Psychopathology, 5,* 433–457.

Ingraham, L. J., Kugelmass, S., Frenkel, E., Nathan, M., & Mirsky, A. F. (1995). Twenty-five-year followup of Israeli high-risk study: Current and lifetime psychopathology. *Schizophrenia Bulletin, 21,* 183–192.

Jacobs, J. (1971). *Adolescent suicide.* New York: Wiley.

Jacobsen, L. K., & Rapoport, J. L. (1998). Research update: Childhood-onset schizophrenia: Implications for clinical and neurobiological research. *Journal of Child Psychology and Psychiatry, 38,* 101–111.

Jakab, I. (1993). Pharmacological treatment. In F. B. Van Hasselt & M. Hersen (Eds.), *Handbook of behavior therapy and pharmacotherapy for children: A comparative analysis.* Boston: Allyn & Bacon.

Jay, S. M. (1988). Invasive medical procedures: Psychological intervention and assessment. In D. J. Routh (Ed.), *Handbook of pediatric psychology,* pp. 401–425. New York: Guilford.

Jay, S. M., Elliot, C. H., Katz, E., & Siegel, S. E. (1987). Cognitive behavioral and pharmacologic intervention for children's distress during painful medical procedures. *Journal of Consulting and Clinical Psychology, 55,* 860–865.

Jensen, P. S., & Hoagwood, K. (1997). The book of names: DSM-IV in context. *Development and Psychopathology, 9,* 231–249.

Jensen, P. S., Martin, D., & Cantwell, D. P. (1997). Comorbidity in ADHD: Implications for research, practice, and *DSM-V. Journal of the American Academy of Child and Adolescent Psychiatry, 36,* 1065–1079.

Jessor, R., Donovan, J. E., & Costa, R. M. (1991). *Beyond adolescence: Problem behavior and young adult development.* New York: Cambridge University Press.

Jessor, R., & Jessor, S. L. (1977). *Problem behavior and psychosocial development: A longitudinal study of youth.* New York: Academic Press.

Jessor, R., Van Den Bos, J., Vanderryn, J., Costa, F. M., & Turbin, M. S. (1995). Protective factors in adolescent problem behavior: Moderate effects and developmental change. *Developmental Psychology, 31,* 923–933.

Jimerson, D. C., Wolfe, B. E., Metzger, E. D., & Finkelstein, D. M. (1997). Decreased serotonin function in bulimia nervosa. *Archives of General Psychiatry, 54,* 529–534.

Johnson, C., & Larson, R. (1982). Bulimia: An analysis of mood and behavior.

Psychosomatic Medicine, 44, 341–351.

Johnson, C. A., MacKinnon, D. P., & Pentz, M. A. (1996). Breadth of program and outcome effectiveness in drug abuse prevention. *American Behavioral Scientist, 39,* 884–896.

Johnson, J. H., & Goldman, J. (1990). *Developmental assessment in clinical child psychology: A handbook.* Boston: Allyn & Bacon.

Johnson, S. B. (1995). Insulin-dependent diabetes mellitus in childhood. In M. C. Roberts (Ed.), *Handbook of pediatric psychology* (2nd ed., pp. 263–285). New York: Guilford.

Johnson W. G., Tsoh J. Y., & Varnado P. J. (1996). Eating disorders: Efficacy of pharmacological and psychological interventions. *Clincial Psychology Review, 16,* 457–478.

Johnson-Powell, G. (1997a). The culturologic interview: Cultural, social, and linguistic issues in the assessment and treatment of children. In G. Johnson-Powell & J. Yamamoto (Eds.), *Transcultural child development: Psychological assessment and treatment* (pp. 349–364). New York: Wiley.

Johnson-Powell, G. (1997b). A portrait of America's children: Social, cultural, and historical context. In G. Johnson-Powell & J. Yamamoto (Eds.), *Transcultural child development: Psychological assessment and treatment* (pp. 3–33). New York: Wiley.

Johnson-Powell, G., & Yamamoto, J. (Eds.). (1997). *Transcultural child devel-*

opment: Psychological assessment and treatment. New York: Wiley.

Johnston, J. R., Campbell, L. E., & Mayes, S. S. (1985). Latency children in post-separation and divorce disputes. *Journal of the American Academy of Child Psychiatry*, 24, 563–574.

Johnston, L. D. (1985). The etiology and prevention of substance use: What can we learn from recent historical changes? In C. L. Jones & R. J. Battjes (Eds.), *Etiology of drug abuse: Implications for prevention* (pp. 155–177). NIDA Research Monograph 56. Rockville, MD: National Institute on Drug Abuse.

Johnston, L. D., O'Malley, P. M., & Bachman, J. G. (1998). *National survey results on drug use from the Monitoring the Future study, 1975–1995: Vol. I. Secondary school students.* Washington, DC: National Institute on Drug Abuse.

Johnston, L. D., O'Malley, P. M., & Bachman, J. G. (1988). *National survey results on drug use from the Monitoring the Future study, 1975–1994: Vol. II. College students and young adults.* Washington, DC: National Institute on Drug Abuse.

Joiner, T. E., Jr., Catanzaro, S. J., & Laurent, J. (1996). Tripartite structure of positive and negative affect, depression, and anxiety in children and adolescent psychiatric inpatients. *Journal of Abnormal Psychology*, 105, 401–409.

Jouriles E. N., Norwood W. D., McDonald, R., Vincent, J. P., & Mahoney, A. (1996). Physical violence

and other forms of marital aggression: Links with children's behavior problems. *Journal of Family Psychology*, 10, 223–234.

Kaffman, M., & Elizur, E. (1977). Infants who become enuretics: A longitudinal study of 161 kibbutz children. *Monographs of the Society for Research in Child Development*, Vol. 42, no. 2.

Kagan, J., Reznick, J. S., & Snidman, N. (1988). Temperamental influences on reactions to unfamiliarity and challenge. In G. P. Chruousos, K. L. Louriaux, & P. W. Gold (Eds.), *Mechanisms of physical and emotional stress. Advances in experimental medicine and biology* (pp. 319–339). New York: Plenum.

Kahn, T. J., & Chambers, H. J. (1991). Assessing reoffense risk with juvenile sexual offenders. *Child Welfare*, 70, 333–345.

Kalish, C. (1996). Causes and symptoms in preschoolers' conceptions of illness. *Child Development*, 67, 1647–1670.

Kaminer, R., & Vig, S. (1995). Standardized intelligence testing: Does it do more good than harm? Comment. *Journal of Developmental and Behavioral Pediatrics*, 16, 425–427.

Kamphaus R. W., & Frick P. J. (1996). *Clinical assesment of child and adolescent personality and behavior.* Boston: Allyn & Bacon.

Kanfer, R., Eyberg, S. M., & Krahn, G. L. (1992). Interviewing strategies in child assessment. In C. E. Walker & M. C. Roberts (Eds.), *Handbook of clinical child*

psychology (pp. 49–62). New York: Wiley.

Kanner, L. (1943). Autistic disturbances of affective contact. *Nervous Child*, 2, 217–250.

Kanner, L. (1977). *Child Psychiatry* (4th ed.). Springfield, IL: Charles C. Thomas.

Kanner, L., Rodriguez, A., & Ashenden, B. (1972). How far can autistic children go in matters of social adaptation? *Journal of Autism and Childhood Schizophrenia*, 2, 9–33.

Kasari, C., Sigman, M., Mundy, P., & Yirmiya, N. (1990). Affective sharing in the context of joint attention interactions in normal, autistic, and mentally retarded children. *Journal of Autism and Developmental Disorders*, 20, 87–100.

Kasen, S., Johnson, J., & Cohen, P. (1990). The impact of school emotional climate on student psychopathology. *Journal of Abnormal Child Psychology*, 18, 165–177.

Kaslow, N. J., Deering, C. G., & Racusin, G. R. (1994). Depressed children and their families. *Clinical Psychology Review*, 14, 39–59.

Katzev, A. R., Warner, R. L., & Acock, A. C. (1994). Girls or boys? Relationship of child gender to marital instability. *Journal of Marriage and the Family*, 56, 89–100.

Kaufman, J., Jones, B., Steiglitz, E., Vitulano, L., & Mannarino, A. P. (1994). The use of multiple informants to assess children's maltreatment experiences. *Journal of Family Violence*, 9, 227–248.

Kaufman, J., & Zigler, E. (1989). The intergenera-

tional transmission of child abuse and the prospect of predicting future abusers. In D. Cicchetti & B. Carlson (Eds.), *Child maltreatment: Research and theory on the causes and consequences of child abuse and neglect* (pp. 129–150). New York: Cambridge University Press.

Kavale, K. A. (1990a). A critical appraisal of empirical subtyping research in learning disabilities. In H. L. Swanson & B. Keogh (Eds.), *Learning disabilities: Theoretical and research issues* (pp. 215–230). Hillsdale, NJ: Erlbaum.

Kavale, K. A. (1990b). Variance and verities in learning disability intervention. In T. E. Schruggs & B. Y. L. Wong (Eds.), *Intervention research in learning disabilities* (pp. 3–33). New York: Springer-Verlag.

Kavale, K. A., & Forness, S. R. (1996). Social skill deficits and learning disabilities: A meta-analysis. *Journal of Learning Disabilities*, 29, 226–237.

Kazak, A. E. (1992). The social context of coping with childhood chronic illness: Family systems and social support. In A. M. La Greca, L. J. Siegel, J. L. Wallander, & C. E. Walker (Eds.), *Stress and coping in child health* (pp. 262–278). New York: Guilford.

Kazak, A. E., Segal-Andrews, A. M., & Johnson, K. (1995). Pediatric psychology research and practice: A family systems approach. In M. C. Roberts (Ed.), *Handbook of pediatric psychology* (2nd ed., pp. 84–103). New York: Guilford.

Kazdin, A. E. (1996). Problem solving and parent management in treating aggressive and antisocial behavior. In E. D. Hibbs & P. S. Jensen (Eds.), *Psychosocial treatments for child and adolescent disorders* (pp. 377–408). Washington, DC: American Psychological Association.

Kazdin, A. E. (1997a). Conduct disorder across the life-span. In S. S. Luthar, J. A. Burack, D. Cicchetti, & J. R. Weisz (Eds.), *Developmental psychopathology: Perspectives on adjustment, risk, and disorder* (pp. 248–272). Cambridge: Cambridge University Press.

Kazdin, A. E. (1997b). Practitioner review: Psychosocial treatments for conduct disorder in children. *Journal of Child Psychology and Psychiatry and Allied Disciplines, 38*, 161–178.

Kazdin, A. E. (1997c). A model for developing effective treatments: Progression and interplay of theory, research, and practice. *Journal of Clinical Child Psychology, 26*, 114–129.

Kazdin, A. E., Kraemer, H. C., Kessler, R. C., Kupfer, D. J., & Offord, D. R. (1997). Contributions of risk-factor research to developmental psychopathology. *Clinical Psychology Review, 17*, 375–406.

Kazdin, A. E., & Weisz, J. R. (1998). Identifying and developing empirically supported child and adolescent treatments. *Journal of Consulting and Clinical Psychology, 66*, 19–36.

Kearney, C. A., Eisen, A. R., & Silverman, W. K. (1995). The legend and myth of school phobia. *School Psychology Quarterly, 10*, 65–85.

Keller, M. B., Herzog, D. B., Lavori, P. W., Bradburn, I. S., & Mahoney, E. M. (1992). The natural history of bulimia nervosa: Extraordinarily high rates of chronicity, relapse, recurrence and psychosocial morbidity. *International Journal of Eating Disorders, 12*, 1–9.

Kendall, P. C. (1994). Treating anxiety disorders in children: Results of a randomized clinical trial. *Journal of Consulting and Clinical Psychology, 62*, 100–110.

Kendall, P. C., & Gerow, M. (1996). Long-term follow-up of a cognitive-behavioral therapy for anxiety-disordered youth. *Journal of Consulting and Clinical Psychology, 64*, 724–730.

Kendall, P. C., & Ronan, K. R. (1990). Assessment of children's anxieties, fears, and phobias: Cognitive-behavioral models and methods. In C. R. Reynolds & R. W. Kamphaus (Eds.), *Handbook of psychological and educational assessment of children* (Vol. 2, pp. 223–244). New York: Guilford.

Kendall, P. C., & Treadwell, K. R. (1996). Cognitive-behavioral treatments for childhood anxiety disorders. In E. D. Hibbs & P. S. Jensen (Eds.), *Psychosocial treatments for child and adolescent disorders: Empirically based strategies for clinical practice* (pp. 23–42). Washington, DC: American Psychological Association.

Kendall-Tackett, K. A., Williams, L. M., & Finkelhor, D. (1993). Impact of sexual abuse on children: A review and synthesis of recent empirical studies. *Psychological Bulletin, 113*, 164–180.

Keogh, B. K., Bernheimer, L. P., & Guthrie, D. (1997). Stability and change over time in cognitive level of children with delays. *American Journal on Mental Retardation, 101*, 365–373.

Kerig, P. K. (1995). Triangles in the family circle: Effects of family structure on marriage, parenting, and child adjustment. *Journal of Family Psychology, 9*, 28–43.

Kerig, P. K. (in press). Coping with interparental conflict. In J. H. Grych & F. Fincham (Eds.), *Child development and interparental conflict.* New York: Cambridge University Press.

Killen, J. D., Hayward, C., Wilson, D. M., Taylor, C. B., Hammer, L. D., Litt, I., Simmonds, B., and Haydel, F. (1994). Factors associated with eating disorder symptoms in a community sample of 6th and 7th grade girls. *International Journal of Eating Disorders, 15*, 357–367.

King, B. H., State, M. W., Shah, B., Davanzo, P., & Dykens, E. (1997). Mental retardation: A review of the past 10 years: Part I. *Journal of the American Academy of Child and Adolescent Psychiatry, 36*, 1656–1663.

King, N. J., & Ollendick, T. H. (1997). Annotation: Treatment of childhood phobias. *Journal of Child Psychology and Psychiatry, 38*, 389–400.

Klein, R. G., & Last, C. G. (1989). *Anxiety disorders in children.* Newbury Park, CA: Sage Publications.

Klein, R. G., & Mannuzza, S. (1991). Long-term outcome of hyperactive children: A review. *Journal of the American Academy of Child and Adolescent Psychiatry, 30*, 383–387.

Klinger, L. G., & Dawson, G. (1996). Autistic disorder. In E. J. Mash & R. A. Barkley (Eds.), *Child psychopathology* (pp. 311–339). New York: Guilford.

Knight, R. A., & Roff, J. D. (1985). Affectivity in schizophrenia. In M. Alpert (ed.), *Controversies in schizophrenia: Changes and constancies* (pp. 280–313). New York: Guilford.

Knoff, H. M. (1990). Evaluation of projective drawings. In C. Reyonlds & R. Kamphaus (Eds.), *Handbook of psychological and educational assessment of children* (pp. 89–146). New York: Guilford.

Kochanska, G. (1995). Children's temperament, mothers' discipline, and security of attachment: Multiple pathways to emerging internalization. *Child Development, 66*, 597–615.

Kochanska, G. (1997). Multiple pathways to conscience for children with different temperaments: From toddlerhood to age 5. *Developmental Psychology, 33*, 228–240.

Kochanska, G., & Aksan, N. (1995). Mother-child mutually positive affect, the quality of child compliance to requests and prohibitions, and maternal control as correlates of early internalization. *Child Development, 66*, 236–254.

Kochanska, G., Aksan, N., & Koenig, A. L. (1995). A

longitudinal study of the roots of preschooler's conscience: Commited compliance and emerging internalization. *Child Development, 66,* 1752–1769.

Kochanska, G., Murray, K., Jacques, T. Y., Koenig, A. L., & Vandgeest, K. A. (1996). Inhibitory control in young children and its role in emerging internalization. *Child Development, 67,* 490–507.

Kohlberg, L. (1976). Moral stages and moralization: The cognitive-developmental approach. In T. Lickona (Ed.), *Moral development and behavior: Theory, research and social issues.* New York: Holt, Rinehart & Winston.

Kohn, M. (1977). *Social competence, symptoms and underachievement in childhood: A longitudinal perspective.* Silver Spring, MD: V. H. Winston.

Kolko, D. J. (1996). Child physical abuse. In J. Briere, L. Berliner, J. A. Bulkley, C. Jenny, & T. Reid (Eds.), *The APSAC handbook on child maltreatment* (pp. 21–50). Thousand Oaks, CA: Sage Publications.

Kolvin, I., Miller, F. J. W., Fleeting, M., & Kolvin, P. A. (1989). Risk/protective factors for offending with particular reference to deprivation. In M. Rutter (Ed.), *Studies in psychosocial risk: The power of longitudinal studies* (pp. 77–95). Cambridge: Cambridge University Press.

Kovacs M. (1992). *Children's Depression Inventory manual.* Toronto: Multi-Health Systems.

Kovacs, M., Akiskal, H. S., Gatsonis, C., & Parrone, P. L. (1994). Childhood-onset dysthymic disorder:

Clincial features and prospective naturalistic outcome. *Archives of General Psychiatry, 51,* 365–374.

Kovacs, M., & Beck, A. T. (1977). An empirical-clinical approach toward a definition of childhood depression. In J. G. Schulterbrandt & A. Raskin (Eds.), *Depression in childhood: Diagnosis, treatment and conceptual models.* New York: Raven Press.

Kovacs, M., & Devlin, B. (1998). Internalizing disorders in childhood. *Journal of Child Psychology and Psychiatry and Allied Disciplines, 39,* 47–63.

Kraus, J. F. (1995). Epidemiological features of brain injury in children: Occurrence, children at risk, causes and manner of injury, severity, and outcomes. In S. H. Broman & M. E. Michel (Eds.), *Traumatic head injury in children* (pp. 22–39). New York: Oxford University Press.

Kronenberger, W. G., & Meyer, R. G. (1996). Elimination disorders. *The child clinician's handbook* (pp. 119–154). Boston: Allyn & Bacon.

Kruttschnitt, C., & Dornfeld, M. (1993). Exposure to family violence: A partial explanation for initial and subsequent levels of delinquency? *Criminal Behaviour and Mental Health, 3,* 63–75.

Kuczynski, L., & Kochanska, G. (1990). Development of children's noncompliant strategies from toddlerhood to age 5. *Developmental Psychology, 26,* 398–408.

Kuhne, M., Schachar, R., & Tannock, R. (1997). Im-

pact of comorbid oppositional or conduct problems on attention-deficit hyperactivity disorder. *Journal of the American Academy of Child and Adolescent Psychiatry, 36,* 1715–1725.

Kupersmidt, J. B., Burchinal, M., & Patterson, C. J. (1995). Developmental patterns of childhood peer relations as predictors of externalizing behavior problems. *Development and Psychopathology, 7,* 825–844.

Kurtines, W. M., & Szapoczalnik, J. (1996). Family interaction patterns: Structural family therapy within contexts of cultural diversity. In E. D. Hibbs & P. S. Jensen (Eds.), *Psychosocial treatments for child and adolescent disorders: Empirically based strategies for clinical practice* (pp. 671–697). Washington, DC: American Psychological Association.

Kye, C., & Ryan, N. (1995). Pharmacologic treatment of child and adolescent depression. *Child and Adolescent Psychiatric Clinics of North America, 4,* 261–281.

Lachar D., & Gruber C. P. (1994). *The Personality Inventory for Youth.* Los Angeles: Western Psychological Services.

LaFromboise, T., Coleman, H. L. K., & Gerton, J. (1993). Psychological impact of biculturalism: Evidence and theory. *Psychological Bulletin, 114,* 395–412.

La Greca, A. M., & Schuman, W. B. (1995). Adherence to prescribed medical regimens. In M. C. Roberts (Ed.), *Handbook of pediatric psychology* (2nd ed.,

pp. 55–83). New York: Guilford.

La Greca, A. M., & Stone, G. (1992). Assessing children through interviews and behavioral observations. In C. E. Walker & M. C. Roberts (Eds.), *Handbook of clinical child psychology* (pp. 63–83). New York: Guilford.

Lahey, B. B., Hart, E. L., Pliszka, S., Applegate, B., & McBurnett, K. (1993). Neurophysiological correlates of conduct disorder: A rationale and review of current research. *Journal of Clinical Child Psychology, 22,* 141–153.

Lahey, B. B., Loeber, R., Hart, E. L., Frick, P. J., Applegate, B., Zhang, Q., Green, S. M., & Russo, M. F. (1995). Four-year longitudinal study of conduct disorder in boys: Patterns and predictors of persistence. *Journal of Abnormal Psychology, 104,* 83–93.

Lamb, M. E. (ed.). (1997). *The role of the father in child development.* New York: Wiley.

Landrine, H. (1992). Clinical implications of cultural differences: The referential versus the indexical self. *Clinical Psychology Review, 12,* 401–415.

Last, C. G., & Francis, G. (1988). School phobia. In B. B. Lahey & A. E. Kazdin (Eds.), *Advances in clinical child psychology* (Vol. 11, pp. 193–222). New York: Plenum.

Last, C. G., Hansen, C., & Franco, N. (1998). Cognitive-behavioral treatment of school phobia. *Journal of the American Academy of Child and Adolescent Psychiatry, 37,* 404–411.

Last, C. G., Perrin, S., Hersen, M., & Kazden, A. E. (in press). A prospective study of childhood anxiety disorders. *Journal of the American Academy of Child and Adolescent Psychiatry.*

Lau, E. (1995, July 21–28). An insatiable emptiness. *The Georgia Straight,* pp. 13–14.

Ledingham, J. E. (1990). Recent developments in high-risk research. In B. B. Lahey & A. E. Kazdin (Eds.), *Advances in clinical child psychology* (Vol. 13, pp. 91–137). New York: Plenum.

Leffert, J. S., & Siperstein, G. N. (1996). Assessment of social-cognitive processes in children with mental retardation. *American Journal on Mental Retardation, 100,* 441–455.

Lee, A., Hobson, R. P., & Chiat, S. (1994). I, you, me, and autism: An experimental study. *Journal of Autism and Developmental Disorders, 24,* 155–176.

Leon, G. R., Fulkerson, J. A., Perry, C. L., & Dube, A. (1994). Family influences, school behaviors, and risk for the later development of an eating disorder. *Journal of Youth and Adolescence, 23,* 499–515.

Leon, G. R., Fulkerson, J. A., Perry, C. L., & Early-Zald, M. B. (1995). Prospective analysis of personality and behavioral vulnerabilities and gender influences in the later development of disordered eating. *Journal of Abnormal Psychology, 104,* 140–149.

Leon, G. R., Lucas, A. R., Colligan, R. C., Ferdinande, R. J., & Kamp. J. (1985). Sexuality, body-image, and personality attitudes in anorexia nervosa. *Journal of Abnormal Child Psychology, 13,* 245–258.

Leonard, H. L., Swedo, S. E., Allen, A. J., & Rapoport, J. L. (1994). Obsessive-compulsive disorder. In T. H. Ollendick, N. J. King, & W. Yule (Eds.), *International handbook of phobic and anxiety disorders in children and adolescents* (pp. 207–222). New York: Plenum.

Levin, M. R., Ashmore-Callahan, S., Kendall, P. C., & Ichii, M. (1996). Treatment of separation anxiety disorder. In M. A. Reinecke, M. Dattilio, & A. Freeman (Eds.), *Cognitive therapy with children and adolescents* (pp. 153–174). New York: Guilford.

Levine, M., Compaan, C., & Freeman, J. (1995). Maltreatment-related fatalities: Issues of policy and prevention. *Law and Policy, 16,* 449–471.

Levy, D. M. (1955). Oppositional syndrome and oppositional behavior. In P. H. Hoch & J. Zubin (Eds.), *Psychopathology of childhood* (pp. 204–226). New York: Grune & Stratton.

Levy, F. (1980). The development of sustained attention (vigilance) and inhibition in children: Some normative data. *Journal of Child Psychology and Psychiatry, 21,* 77–84.

Levy, F., Hay, D. A., McStephen, M., Wood, C., & Waldman, I. (1997). Attention-deficit hyperactivity disorder: A category or a continuum? Genetic analysis of a large-scale twin study. *Journal of the American Academy of Child and Adolescent Psychiatry, 36,* 737–744.

Lewandowski, L. M., Gebing, T. A., Anthony, J. L., & O'Brien, W. H. (1997). Meta-analysis of cognitive-behavioral treatment studies for bulimia. *Clinical Psychology Review, 17,* 703–718.

Lewine, R. R. J. (1984). Stalking the schizophrenia marker: Evidence for a general vulnerability model of psychopathology. In N. F. Watt, E. J. Anthony, L. C. Wynne, & J. E. Rolf (Eds.), *Children at risk for schizophrenia: A longitudinal perspective* (pp. 545–550). Cambridge: Cambridge University Press.

Lewinsohn, P. M., Clarke, G. N., Rohde, P., Hops, H., & Seeley, J. R. (1996). A course in coping: A cognitive-behavioral approach to the treament of adolescent depression. In E. D. Hibbs & P. S. Jensen (Eds.), *Psychosocial treatments for child and adolescent disorders* (pp. 109–135). Washington, DC: American Psychological Association.

Lewinsohn, P. M., Clarke, G. N., Seeley, J. R., & Rohde, P. (1994). Major depression in community adolescents: Age at onset, episode duration, and time to recurrence. *Journal of the American Academy of Child and Adolescent Psychiatry, 33,* 809–818.

Lewinsohn, P. M., Gotlib, I. H., & Seeley, J. R. (1997). Depression-related psychosocial variables: Are they specific to depression in adolescents? *Journal of Abnormal Psychology, 106,* 365–375.

Lewinsohn, P. M., Gotlib, I. H., Lewinsohn, M., Seeley, J. R., & Allen, N. B.

(1998). Gender differences in anxiety disorders and anxiety symptoms in adolescence. *Journal of Abnormal Psychology, 107,* 109–117.

Lewis, M. H. (1996). Brief report: Psychopharmacology of autism spectrum disorders. *Journal of Autism and Developmental Disorders, 26,* 231–235.

Lidz, T. (1973). *The origin and treatment of schizophrenic disorders.* New York: Basic Books.

Lieberman, A. F. (1992). Infant-parent psychotherapy with toddlers. *Development and Psychopathology, 4,* 559–574.

Lieberman, A. F., & Pawl, J. H. (1993). Infant-parent psychotherapy. In C. H. Zeanah (Ed.), *Handbook of infant mental health.* New York: Guilford.

Limber, S. P., & Wilcox, B. L. (1996). Application of the U.N. Convention on the rights of the child to the United States. *American Psychologist, 51,* 1246–1250.

Liu, W. T., Yu, E. S. H., Chang, C., & Fernandez, M. (1990). The mental health of Asian-American teenagers: A research challenge. In A. R. Stiffman & L. E. Davis (Eds.), *Ethnic issues in adolescent mental health* (pp. 92–112). Newbury Park, CA: Sage Publications.

Lizardi, H., Klein, D. N., Ouimette, P. C., Riso, L. P., Anderson, R. L., & Donaldson, S. K. (1995). Reports of the childhood home environment in early-onset dysthymia and episodic major depression. *Journal of Abnoral Psychology, 104,* 132–139.

Loeber, R. (1988). Natural histories of conduct problems, delinquency, and associated substance use. Evidence for developmental progression. In B. B. Lahey & A. E. Kazdin (Eds.), *Advances in clinical child psychology* (Vol. 11, pp. 73–118). New York: Plenum.

Loeber, R. (1991). Questions and advances in the study of developmental pathways. In D. Cicchetti and S. L. Toth (Eds.), *Models and integrations. Rochester symposium on developmental psychopathology* (Vol. 3, pp. 97–116). Rochester, NY: University of Rochester Press.

Loeber, R., & Farrington, D. P. (1994). Problems and solutions in longitudinal and experimental treatment studies of child psychopathology and delinquency. *Journal of Consulting and Clinical Psychology, 62,* 887–900.

Loeber, R., Green, S. M., Lahey, B. B., Christ, M. A., & Frick, P. J. (1992). Developmental sequences in the age of onset of disruptive child behaviors. *Journal of Child and Family Studies, 1,* 21–41.

Loeber, R., & Hay, D. (1997). Key issues in the development of aggression and violence from childhood to early adulthood. *Annual Review of Psychology, 48,* 371–410.

Loeber, R., & Keenan, K. (1994). Interaction between conduct disorder and its comorbid conditions: Effects of age and gender. *Clinical Psychology Review, 14,* 497–523.

Loeber, R., Lahey, B. B., & Thomas, C. (1991). Diagnostic conundrum of oppositional defiant disorder and conduct disorder. *Journal of Abnormal Psychology, 100,* 379–390.

Loeber, R., & Stouthamer-Loeber, M. (1998). Development of juvenile aggression and violence: Some common misconceptions and controversies. *American Psychologist, 53,* 242–259.

Loeber, R., Wung, P., Keenan, K., Giroux, B., Stouthamer-Loeber, M., VanKammen, W. B., & Maughan, B. (1993). Developmental pathways in disruptive child behavior. *Development and Psychopathology, 5,* 103–134.

Lonigan, C. J., Anthony, J. L., & Shannon, M. P. (1998). Diagnostic efficacy of posttraumatic symptoms in children exposed to disaster. *Journal of Clinical Child Psychology, 27,* 255–267.

Lonigan, C. J., Carey, M. P., & Finch, A. J., Jr. (1994). Anxiety and depression in children and adolescents: Negative affectivity and the utility of self-report. *Journal of Consulting and Clinical Psychology, 62,* 1000–1008.

Lorion, R. L., & Satzman, W. (1995). Children's exposure to community violence: Following a path from concern to research to action. *Psychiatry, 56,* 55–65.

Losche, G. (1990). Sensorimotor and action development in autistic children from infancy to early childhood. *Journal of Child Psychology and Psychiatry 31,* 749–761.

Lotter, V. (1978). Follow-up studies. In M. Rutter & E. Schopler (Eds.), *Autism: A reappraisal of concepts and treatment.* New York: Plenum.

Lourenco, O., & Machado, A. (1996). In defense of Piaget's theory: A reply to 10 common criticisms. *Psychological Review, 103,* 143–164.

Lovaas, O. I. (1977). The autistic child: *Language development through behavior modification.* New York: Irvington.

Luborsky, L., Singer, B., & Luborsky, L. I. (1975). Comparative studies of psychotherapies: Is it true that "Everyone has won and all must have prizes?" *Archives of General Psychiatry, 32,* 995–1008.

Luthar, S. S. (1993). Annotation: Methodological and conceptual issues in research on childhood resilience. *Journal of Child Psychology and Psychiatry, 34,* 441–453.

Luthar, S. S., Cushing, G., & McMahon, T. J. (1997). Interdisciplinary interface: Developmental principles brought to substance abuse research. In S. S. Luthar, J. A. Burack, D. Cicchetti, & J. R. Weisz (Eds.), *Developmental psychopathology: Pespectives on adjustment, risk, and disorder* (pp. 437–456). Cambridge: Cambridge University Press.

Lynam, D. R. (1997). Pursuing the psychopath: Capturing the fledgling psychopath in a nomological net. *Journal of Abnormal Psychology, 106,* 425–438.

Lyon, G. R. (1996a). Learning disabilities. In E. J. Mash & R. A. Barkley (Eds.), *Child Psychopathology,* (pp. 390–435). New York: Guilford.

Lyon, G. R. (1996b). Learning disabilities. In *The Future of Children: Special Education for Students with Disabilities,* (Vol. 6, pp. 54–76). The Center for the Future of Children, The David and Lucille Packard Foundation, 300 Second Street, Los Altos, CA.

Lyon, M., Chatoor, I., Atkins, D., Silber, T., Mosimann, J., & Gray, J. (1997). Testing the hypothesis of the multidimensional model of anorexia nervosa in adolescents. *Adolescence, 32,* 101–111.

Lyons-Ruth, K., Zeanah, C. H., & Benoit, D. (1996). Disorder and risk for disorder during infancy and toddlerhood. In E. J. Mash & R. A. Barkley (Eds.), *Child psychopathology* (pp. 457–491). NY: Gilford Press.

Lytton, H. (1990). Child and parent effects in boys' conduct disorder: A reinterpretation. *Developmental Psychology, 26,* 683–697.

Maccoby, E. E. (1990). Gender and relationships: a developmental account. *American Psychologist, 45,* 513–520.

Machover, K. (1949). *Personality projection in the drawing of the human figure.* Springfield, IL: Charles C Thomas.

MacMillan, D. L., Gresham, F. M., & Forness, S. R. (1996). Full inclusion: An empirical perspective. *Behavioral Disorders, 21,* 145–159.

Madonna, P. G., Van Scoyk, S., & Jones, D. P. H. (1991). Family interactions within incest and nonincest families. *American Journal of Psychiatry, 148,* 46–49.

Maggs, J. L., & Galambos, N. L. (1993). Alternative

structural models for understanding adolescent problem behavior in two-earner families. *Journal of Early Adolescence, 13,* 79–101.

Magnusson, D., & Bergman, L. R. (1990). A pattern approach to the study of pathways from childhood to adulthood. In L. Robins & M. Rutter (Eds.), *Straight and devious pathways from childhood to adulthood* (pp. 101–115). Cambridge: Cambridge University Press.

Mahler, M. S., Pine, F., & Bergman, A. (1975). *The psychological birth of the human infant.* New York: Basic Books.

Main, M. (1996). Introduction to the special section on attachment and psychopathology: 2. Overview of the field of attachment. *Journal of Consulting and Clinical Psychology, 64,* 237–243.

Malphurs, J. E., Field, T. M., Larraine, C., Pickens, J., Pelaez-Nogueras, M., Yando, R., & Bendell, D. (1996). Altering withdrawn and intrusive interaction behaviors of depressed mothers. *Infant Mental Health Journal, 17,* 152–160.

Manly, J. T., Cicchetti, D., & Barnett, D. (1994). The impact of subtype, frequency chronicity, and severity of child maltreatment on social competence and behavior problems. *Development and Psychopathology, 6,* 121–143.

Mannarino, A. P., & Cohen, J. A. (1990). Treating abused children. In R. T. Ammerman & M. Hersen (Eds.), *Children at risk: An evaluation of factors contributing to child abuse and neglect* (pp. 249–268). New York: Plenum.

Mannarino, A. P., & Cohen, J. A. (1996). A follow-up study of factors that mediate the development of psychological symptomatology in sexually abused girls. *Child Maltreatment, 1,* 246–260.

Mannuzza, S., Klein, R. G., Bessler, A., Malloy, P., & Hynes, M. E. (1997). Educational and occupational outcome of hyperactive boys grown up. *Journal of the American Academy of Child and Adolescent Psychiatry, 36,* 1222–1227.

March, J. S. (1995). Cognitive-behavioral psychotherapy for children and adolescents with OCD: A review and recommendations for treatment. *Journal of the American Academy of Child and Adolescent Psychiatry, 34,* 7–18.

Marcia, J. E. (1993). *Ego identity: A handbook for psychosocial research.* New York: Springer-Verlag.

Marcotte, D. (1997). Treating depression in adolescence: A review of the effectiveness of cognitive-behavioral treatments. *Journal of Youth and Adolescence, 26,* 273–283.

Mariani, M., & Barkley, R. A. (1997). Neuropsychological and academic functioning. *Developmental Neuropsychology, 13,* 111–129.

Markus, H. R., & Kitayama, S. (1991). Culture and the self: Implications for cognition, emotion, and motivation. *Psychological Review, 98,* 224–253.

Marshall, S. (1995). Ethnic socialization of African American children: Implications for parenting, identity development, and academic achievement. *Journal of Youth and Adolescence, 24,* 377–396.

Martinez, K. J. (1994). Cultural sensitivity in family therapy gone awry. *Hispanic Journal of Behavioral Sciences, 16,* 75–89.

Mash, E. J., & Barkley, R. A. (1998). *Treatment of childhood disorders.* New York: Guilford.

Masia, C. L., & Morris, T. L. (1998). Parental factors associated with social anxiety: Methodological limitations and suggestions for integrated behavioral research. *Clinical Psychology Science and Practice, 5,* 211–228.

Masten, A. S., & Coatsworth, J. D. (1995). Competence, resilience, and psychopathology. In D. Cicchetti & D. J. Cohen (Eds.), *Developmental psychopathology: Vol. 2. Risk, disorder and adaptation* (pp. 715–752). New York: Wiley.

Masten, A. S., & Coatsworth, J. D. (1998). The development of competence in favorable and unfavorable environments. *American Psychologist, 53,* 205–220.

Masterson, J. F., Tolpin, M., & Sifneos, P. E. (1991). *Comparing psychoanalytic psychotherapies: Developmental, self, and object relations; self psychology; short-term dynamic.* New York: Brunner/Mazel.

Matarazzo, J. D. (1990). Psychological assessment versus psychological testing: Validation from Binet to the school, clinic, and courtroom. *American Psychologist, 45,* 999–1017.

Mattis, S. G., & Ollendick, T. H. (1997). Children's cognitive responses to the academic achievement. *Journal of Youth and Adolescence, 24,* 377–396.

academic achievement. *Journal of Youth and Adolescence, 24,* 377–396.

somatic symptoms of panic. *Journal of Abnormal Child Psychology, 25,* 47–57.

Maughan, B. (1995). Annotation: Long-term outcomes of developmental reading problems. *Journal of Child Psychology and Psychiatry, 36,* 357–371.

Maughan, B., & Hagell, A. (1996). Poor readers in adulthood: Psychosocial functioning. *Development and Psychopathology, 8,* 457–476.

Maughan, B., Pickles, A., Hagell, A., Rutter, M., & Yule, W. (1996). Reading problems and antisocial behaviour: Developmental trends in comorbidity. *Journal of Child Psychology and Psychiatry, 37,* 405–418.

Max, J. E., Sharma, A., & Qurashi, M. I. (1997). Traumatic brain injury in a child psychiatry inpatient population: A controlled study. *Journal of the American Academy of Child and Adolescent Psychiatry, 36,* 1595–1601.

Max, J. E., Smith W. L., Yutaka, S., Mattheis, P. J., Castillo, C. S., Lindgren, S. D., Robin, D. A., & Stierwalt, J. A. G. (1997). Traumatic brain injury in children and adolescents: Psychiatric disorders in the first three months. *Journal of the American Academy of Child and Adolescent Psychiatry, 36,* 94–102.

Mayes, S. D., Hanford, H. A., Schaefer, J. H., Scogno, C. A., Neagley, S. R., Michael-Good, L., & Pelco, L. E., (1996). The relationship of HIV status, type of coagulation disorder, and school absenteeism to cognition, educational performance, mood, and behavior of boys with hemophilia. *Journal of Genetic Psychology*, *157*(2), 137–151.

Mayseless, O. (1998). Maternal caregiving strategy: A distinction between the ambivalent and disorganized profile. *Infant Mental Health Journal*, *19*, 20–33.

McAdoo, W. G., & DeMyer, M. K. (1978). Personality characteristics of parents. In M. Rutter & E. Schopler (Eds.), *Autism: A reappraisal of concepts and treatment* (pp. 251–267). New York: Plenum.

McArdle, P., O'Brien, G., & Kolvin, I. (1995). Hyperactivity: Prevalence and relationship with conduct disorder. *Journal of Child Psychology and Psychiatry*, *36*, 279–303.

McArthur, D. S., & Roberts, G. E. (1982). *Roberts Apperception Test for Children.* Los Angeles: Western Psychological Services.

McClellan, J., McCurry, C., Ronnei, M., & Adams, J. (1996). Age of onset of sexual abuse: Relationship to sexually inappropriate behaviors. *Journal of the American Academy of Child and Adolescent psychiatry*, *35*, 1375–1383.

McConaughy, S. H., & Achenbach, T. M. (1994). *Manual for the Semistructured Clinical Interview for children and adolescents.* Burlington, VT: University Associates in Psychiatry.

McCord, J. (1990). Long-term perspectives on parental absence. In L. Robins & M. Rutter (Eds.), *Straight and devious pathways from childhood to adult-*

hood (pp. 116–135). Cambridge: Cambridge University Press.

McCord, J., Tremblay, R. E., Vitaro, F., & Desmarais-Gervais, L. (1994). Boys' disruptive behaviour, school adjustment, and delinquency: The Montreal Prevention Experiment. *International Journal of Behavioral Development*, *17*, 739–752.

McGee, R., Feehan, M., Williams, S., & Anderson, J. C. (1992). DSM-III disorders from age 11 to age 15 years. *Journal of the American Academy of Child and Adolescent Psychiatry*, *31*, 50–59.

McGee, R. A., Wolfe, D. A., & Wilson, S. K. (1997). Multiple maltreatment experiences and adolescent behavior problems: adolescent's perspectives. *Development and Psychopathology*, *9*, 131–150.

McGhie, A., & Chapman, J. (1969). Disorders of attention and perception in early schizophrenia. In A. H. Buss & E. H. Buss (Eds.), *Theories of schizophrenia* (pp. 47–75). New York: Atherton.

McGoldrick, M., & Gerson, R. (1985). *Genograms in family assessment.* New York: W. W. Norton.

McGrath, P. J., & Pisterman, S. (1991). Developmental issues: Adolescent pain. In J. P. Bush & S. W. Harkins (Eds.), *Children in pain: Clinical and research issues from a developmental perspective* (pp. 231–250). New York: Springer-Verlag.

McGue, M. (1995). Evidence for causal mechanisms from human genetics data bases. In R. A. Zucker, J. Howard, and G. M.

Boyd (Eds.), *The development of alcohol problems: Exploring the biopsychosocial matrix of risk.* Rockville, MD: National Institute on Alcohol Abuse and Alcoholism.

McHale, J. P., & Cowan, P. A. (1996). Understanding how family-level dynamics affect children's development: Studies of two-parent families. *New directions in child development, No. 74,* San Francisco: Jossey-Bass.

McLoyd, V. C., Ceballo, R., & Mangelsdorf, S. C. (1997). The effects of poverty on children's socioemotional development. In J. D. Noshpitz (Ed.), *Handbook of child and adolescent psychiatry* (Vol. 4, pp. 191–206). New York: Wiley.

McMahon, R. J., & Estes, A. M. (1997). Conduct problems. In E. J. Mash & L. G. Terdal (Eds.), *Assessment of childhood disorders* (pp. 130–193). New York: Guilford.

McMahon, R. J., & Wells, K. C. (1989). Conduct disorders. In E. J. Mash & R. A. Barkley (Eds.), *Treatment of childhood disorders* (pp. 39–134). New York: Guilford.

Meadow, S. R. (1993). False allegations of abuse and Munchausen syndrome by proxy. *Archives of Disease in Childhood, 68,* 444–447.

Mednick, S. A., Huttunen, M. O., & Machon, R. A. (1994). Prenatal influenza infections and adult schizophrenia. *Schizophrenia Bulletin, 20,* 263–267.

Mejia, D. (1983). The development of Mexican-American children. In G. J. Powell (Ed.), *The*

psychological development of minority group children (pp. 77–114). New York: Brunner/Mazel.

Mellin, L. M., Irwin, C., & Scully, S. (1992). Prevalence of disordered eating in girls: A survey of middle class children. *Journal of the American Dietetic Association, 92,* 851–853.

Melton, G. B. (1992). The improbability of prevention of sexual abuse. In D. J. Willis, G. W. Holden, & M. Rosenberg (Eds.), *Prevention of child maltreatment: Developmental perspectives* (pp. 168–179). New York: Wiley.

Menzies, R. G., & Clarke, J. C. (1995). The etiology of phobias: A nonassociative account. *Clinical Psychology Review, 15,* 23–48.

Merckelbach, P. J., de Jong, P. J., Muris, P., & van den Hout, M. A. (1996). The etiology of specific phobias: A review. *Clinical Psychology Review, 16,* 337–361.

Messer, S. C., & Gross, A. M. (1995). Childhood depression and family interaction: A naturalistic observation study. *Journal of Clinical Child Psychology, 24,* 77–88.

Miklowitz, D. J. (1994). Family risk indicators in schizophrenia. *Schizophrenia Bulletin, 20,* 137–147.

Miller, L. C., Barrett, C. L., & Hampe, E. (1974). Phobias of childhood in a prescientific era. In A. Davids (Ed.), *Child personality and psychopathology: Current topics,* (Vol. 1). New York: Wiley.

Miller, L. C., Barrett, C. L., Hampe, E., & Noble, H. (1972). Comparison of reciprocal inhibition, psychotherapy and waiting list control for phobic children. *Journal of Abnormal Psychology, 79,* 269–279.

Minnes, P. (1988). Family stress associated with a developmentally handicapped child. *International Review of Research on Mental Retardation, 15,* 195–226.

Minuchin, S. (1974). *Families and family therapy.* Cambridge, MA: Harvard University Press.

Minuchin, S., Lee, W. Y., & Simon, G. (1996). *Mastering family therapy: Journeys of growth and transformation.* New York: Wiley.

Minuchin, S., Rosman, B. L., & Baker, L. (1978). *Psychosomatic families: Anorexia nervosa in context.* Cambridge: Cambridge University Press.

Mirsky, A. F., Kugelmass, S., Ingraham, L. J., Frenkel, E., & Nathan, M. (1995). Overview and summary: Twenty-five-year follow up of high-risk children. *Schizophrenia Bulletin, 21,* 227–238.

Mishler, E. G., & Waxler, N. E. (1965). Family interaction and schizophrenia: A review of current theories. *Merrill-Palmer Quarterly, 11,* 269–316.

Mitchell, P., Saltmarsh, R., & Russell, H. (1997). Overly literal interpretations of speech in autism: Understanding that messages arise from minds. *Journal of Child Psychology and Psychiatry, 38,* 685–691.

Moffitt, T. E. (1993). Life-course persistent and adolescence-limited antisocial behavior: A developmental taxonomy. *Psychological Review, 100,* 674–701.

Moffitt, T. E., Caspi, A., Dickson, N., Silva, P., & Stanton, W. (1996). Childhood-onset versus adolescent-onset antisocial conduct problems in males: Natural history from ages 3 to 18 years. *Development and Psychopathology, 8,* 399–424.

Moffitt, T. E., & Lynam, D. (1994). The neuropsychology of conduct disorder and delinquency: Implications for understanding antisocial behavior. In D. C. Fowles, P. Sutker, & S. H. Goodman (Eds.), *Progress in experimental personality and psychopathology research* (pp. 233–262). New York: Springer.

Moldin, S. O., & Gottesman, I. J. (1997). At issue: Genes, experience, and chance in schizophrenia: Positioning for the 21st century. *Schizophrenia Bulletin, 23,* 547–561.

Morris, R. J., & Kratochwill, T. R. (1998). *The practice of child therapy.* Boston: Allyn & Bacon.

Mundy, P. (1995). Joint attention and social-emotional approach behavior in children with autism. *Development and Psychopathology, 7,* 63–82.

Mundy, P., & Sigman, M. (1989a). The theoretical implications of joint-attention deficit in autism. *Development and Psychopathology, 1,* 173–183.

Mundy, P., & Sigman, M. (1989b). Specifying the nature of the social impairment in autism. In G. Dawson (Ed.), *Autism: Nature and treatment* (pp. 3–21). New York: Guilford.

Mundy, P., Sigman, M., & Kasari, C. (1994). Joint attention, developmental level, and symptom presentation in autism. *Development and Psychopathology, 6,* 389–402.

Murphy, L. M. B., Thompson, R. J., & Morris, M. A. (1997). Adherence behavior among adolescents with type I insulin-dependent diabetes mellitus: The role of cognitive appraisal processes. *Journal of Pediatric Psychology, 22,* 811–825.

Musun-Miller, L. (1993). Social acceptance and social problem solving in preschool children. *Journal of Applied Developmental Psychology, 14,* 59–70.

Nabors, L. (1997). Playmate preferences of children who are typically developing for their classmates with special needs. *Mental Retardation, 35,* 107–113.

Nagata, D. K. (1989). Japanese-American children and adolescents. In J. T. Gibbs & L. N. Huang (Eds.), *Children of color: Psychological intervention with minority youth* (pp. 67–113). San Francisco: Jossey-Bass.

Nagera, H. (1966). Early childhood disturbances, the infantile neurosis, and the adult disturbances: Problems of a developmental psychoanalytic psychology. *The psychoanalytic study of the child* (Monograph No. 2). New York: International Universities Press.

Naglieri, J. A., LeBuffe, P. A., & Pfeiffer, S. I. (1994). *Devereux scales of mental disorders.* New York: The Psychological Corporation.

Naglieri, J. A., & Pfeiffer, S. I. (1992). Performance of disruptive behavior disordered and normal samples on the Draw A Person: Screening procedure for emotional disturbance. *Psychological Assessment, 4,* 156–159.

Nassau, J. H., & Drotar, D. (1997). Social competence among children with central nervous system-related chronic health conditions: A review. *Journal of Pediatric Psychology, 22,* 771–793.

National Center on Child Abuse and Neglect (1995). *Child maltreatment 1993: Reports from the states to the National Center on Child Abuse and Neglect (Contract Number ACF-105-91-1802).* Washington, DC: U.S. Government Printing Office.

National Joint Committee on Learning Disabilities (1988, April). (Letter from NJCLD to member organizations.) Austin, TX: NJCLD.

National Research Council. (1993). *Understanding child abuse and neglect.* Washington, DC: National Academy Press.

Nellis, L., & Gridley, B. E. (1994). Review of the Bayley Scales of Infant Development—Second Edition. *Journal of School Psychology, 32,* 201–209.

Nelson, C. A., & Bloom, F. E. (1997). Child development and neuroscience. *Child Development, 68,* 970–987.

Newcomb, M. D., & Bentler, P. M. (1988). *Consequences of adolescent drug use: Impact on the lives of young adults.* Newbury Park, CA: Sage Publications.

Newman, D. L., Caspi, A., Moffitt, T. E., & Silva, P. A. (1997). Antecedents of adult interpersonal functioning: Effects on individual differences in age 3 temperament. *Developmental Psychology, 33,* 206–217.

Nihira, K. (1976). Dimensions of adaptive behavior in institutionalized mentally retarded children and adults: Developmental perspectives. *American Journal of Mental Deficiency, 81,* 215–226.

Nihira, K., Foster, R., Shellhaas, M., & Leland, H. 1974. *AAMD Adaptive Behavior Scale* (1974 revision). Washington, D.C.: American Association on Mental Deficiency.

Nolen-Hoeksema, S., & Girgus, J. S. (1994). The emergence of gender differences in depression during adolescence. *Psychological Bulletin, 115,* 424–443.

Ocampo, K. A., Bernal, M. E., & Knight, G. P. (1993). Gender, race, and ethnicity: The sequencing of social constancies. In M. E. Bernal & G. P. Knight (Eds.), *Ethnic identity: Formation and transmission among Hispanics and other minorities* (pp. 11–30). Albany, NY: State University of New York Press.

Ocampo, K. A., Garza, C. A., Dabul, A. J., & Ruiz, S. Y. (1991). Ethnic identity and school achievement in Mexican-American youths. *Hispanic Journal of Behavioral Sciences 13,* 234–235.

O'Donnell, J., Hawkins, J. D., & Abbott, R. D. (1995). Predicting serious delinquency and substance use among aggressive boys. *Journal of Consulting and Clinical Psychology, 63,* 529–537.

Offord, D. R., Boyle, M. H., & Racine, Y. A. (1991). The epidemiology of antisocial behavior in childhood and adolescence. In D. J. Pepler & K. H. Rubin (Eds.), *The development and treatment of childhood aggression* (pp. 31–54). Hillsdale, NJ: Erlbaum.

Ohta, M. (1987). Cognitive disorders in infantile autism: A study employing the WISC, spatial relationships, conceptualization, and gesture imitation. *Journal of Autism and Developmental Disorders, 17,* 45–62.

Oldenburg, C. M., & Kerns, K. A. (1997). Associations between peer relationships and depressive symptoms: Testing moderator effects of gender and age. *Journal of Early Adolescence, 17,* 319–337.

Olds, D. (1997). The prenatal early infancy project: Preventing child abuse and neglect in the context of promoting maternal and child health. In D. A. Wolfe, R. J. McMahon, & R. D. Peters (Eds.), *Child abuse: New directions in prevention and treatment across the lifespan* (pp. 130–154). Thousand Oaks, CA: Sage Publications.

Ollendick, T. H., & King, N. J. (1991). Developmental factors in child behavioral assessment. In P. R. Martin (Ed.), *Handbook of behavior therapy and psychological science: An integrative approach* (pp. 57–72). New York: Pergamon.

Ollendick, T. H., & King, N. J. (1994). Diagnosis, assessment, and treatment of internalizing problems in children: The role of longitudinal data. *Journal*

of Consulting and Clinical Psychology, 62, 918–927.

Ollendick, T. H., & King, N. J. (1998). Empirically supported treatment for children with phobic and anxiety disorders: Current status. *Journal of Clinical Child Psychology, 27,* 156–167.

Olin, S. S., & Mednick, S. A. (1996). Risk factors of psychosis: Identifying vulnerable populations permorbidly. *Schizophrenia Bulletin, 22,* 223–240.

Olweus, D. (1979). Stability of aggressive reaction patterns in males: A review. *Psychological Bulletin, 86,* 852–875.

O'Neill, M., & Jones, R. S. P. (1997). Sensory-perceptual abnormalities in autism: A case for more research? *Journal of Autism and Developmental Disorders, 27,* 283–293.

Ornstein, P. A., Baker-Ward, L., Myers, J., Principe, G. F., & Gordon, B. N. (1995). Children's long-term retention of medical experiences: Implications for testimony. In F. E. Weinert & W. Schneider (Eds.), *Memory performance and competencies: Issues in growth and development* (pp. 349–371). Hillsdale, NJ: Erlbaum.

Osofsky, J. D. (1995). The effects of exposure to violence on young children. *American Psychologist, 50,* 782–788.

Overholser, J., Hemstreet, A. H., Spirito, A., & Vyse, S. (1989). Suicide awareness programs in the schools: Effects of gender and personal experience. *Journal of the American Academy of Child and Adolescent Psychiatry, 28,* 925–930.

Ozonoff, S., & McEvoy, R. E. (1994). A longitudinal study of executive function and theory of mind development in autism. *Development and Psychopathology, 6,* 415–432.

Ozonoff, S., Pennington, B. F., & Rogers, S. J. (1990). Are there emotion perception deficits in young autistic children? *Journal of Child Psychology and Psychiatry, 31,* 343–361.

Ozonoff, S., & Strayer, D. L. (1997). Inhibitory function in nonretarded children with autism. *Journal of Autism and Developmental Disorders, 27,* 59–76.

Parke, R. D., & Slaby, R. G. (1983). The development of aggression. In P. H. Mussen (Series Ed.) & E. M. Hetherington (Vol. Ed.), *Handbook of child psychology,* Vol. 4, Socialization, personality and social development. New York: Wiley.

Parker, J. G., Rubin, K. H., Price, J. M., & DeRosier, M. E. (1995). Peer relationships, child development, and adjustment: A developmental psychopathology perspective. In D. Cicchetti & D. J. Cohen (Eds.), *Developmental psychopathology: Vol. 2. Risk, disorder, and adaptation,* (pp. 96–161). New York: Wiley.

Pate, J. E., Pumariega, A. J., Hester, C., & Garner, D. M. (1992). Cross-cultural patterns in eating disorders: A review. *Journal of the American Academy of Child and Adolescent Psychiatry, 31,* 802–808.

Patterson, C. J., Kupersmidt, J. B., & Vaden, N. A. (1990). Income level, gender, ethnicity, and household composition as predictors of children's school-based competence. *Child Development, 61,* 485–494.

Patterson, G. R. (1982). *Coercive family process: A social learning approach.* Eugene, OR: Castalia.

Patterson, G. R., & Capaldi, D. M. (1990). A mediational model for boys' depressed mood. In J. Rolf, A. S. Masten, D. Cicchetti, K. H. Nuechterlein, & S. Weintraub (Eds.), *Risk and protective factors in the development of psychopathology* (pp. 141–163). Cambridge: Cambridge University Press.

Patterson, G. R., DeBaryshe, B. D., & Ramsey, E. (1989). A developmental perspective on antisocial behavior. *American Psychologist, 44,* 329–335.

Patterson, G. R., Reid, J. B., & Dishion, T. J. (1992). *Antisocial boys.* Eugene, OR: Castalia.

Paul, R. (1987). Natural history. In D. J. Cohen, A. M. Donnellan, & R. Paul (Eds.), *Handbook of autism and pervasive developmental disorders* (pp. 121–130). New York: Wiley.

Pavel, D., Sanchez, T., & Machamer, A. (1994). Ethnic fraud. Native peoples, and higher education. *Thought and Action, 10,* 91–100.

Pelham, W. E., Jr., Wheeler, T., & Chronis, A. (1998). Empirically supported psychosocial treatments for attention deficit hyperactive disorder. *Journal of Clinical Child Psychology, 27,* 190–205.

Pellegrino, E. D. (1996). Clinical judgment, scientific

data, and ethics: antidepressant therapy in adolescents and children. *Journal of Nervous and Mental Disease, 184,* 106–108.

Pellegrino, J. W., & Goldman, S. R. (1990). Cognitive science perspective on intelligence and learning disabilities. In H. L. Swanson & B. Keogh (Eds.), *Learning disabilities: Theoretical and research issues* (pp. 41–58). Hillsdale, NJ: Erlbaum.

Pennington, B. F., & Ozonoff, S. (1996). Executive functions and developmental psychopathology. *Journal of Child Psychology and Psychiatry, 37,* 51–87.

Pennington, B. F., & Welsh, M. (1995). Neuropsychology and developmental psychopathology. In D. Cicchetti & D. J. Cohen (Eds.), *Developmental psychopathology: Vol. 1. Theory and methods* (pp. 254–290). New York: Wiley.

Perner, J., Frith, U., Leslie, A. M., and Leekam, S. R. (1989). Exploration of the autistic child's theory of mind: Knowledge, belief and communication. *Child Development, 60,* 689–700.

Perry, C. L., Williams, C. L., Veblen-Mortenson, S., Toomey, T. L., Komro, K. A., Anstine, P. S., McGovern, P. G., Finnegan, J. R., Forster, J. L., Wagenaar, A. C., & Wolfson, M. (1996). Project Northland: Outcomes of a community wide alcohol use prevention program during adolescence. *American Journal of Public Health, 86,* 956–965.

Peterson, A. C., Compas, B. E., Brooks-Gunn, J., Stemmler, M., Ey, S., & Grant, K. E. (1993). Depression in adolescence.

American Psychologist, 48, 155–168.

Peterson, B. S. (1995). Neuroimaging in child and adolescent neuropsychiatric disorders. *Journal of the American Academy of Child and Adolescent Psychiatry, 34,* 1560–1576.

Peterson, L., & Bell-Dolan, D. (1995). Treatment outcome research in child psychology: Realistic coping with the "Ten Commandments of Methodology." *Journal of Clinical Child Psychology, 24,* 149–162.

Peterson, L., & Brown, D. (1994). Integrating child injury and abuse-neglect research: Common histories, etiologies, and solutions. *Psychological Bulletin, 116,* 293–315.

Peterson, L. & Roberts, M. C. (1986). Community intervention and prevention. In H. C. Quay and J. S. Werry (Eds.), *Psychopathological disorders of childhood,* 3rd ed., pp. 622–660. New York: Wiley.

Pfeffer, C. R., Hurt, S. W., Kakuma, T., Peskin, J. R., Siefker, C. A., & Nagabhairava, S. (1994). Suicidal children grow up: Suicidal episode and effects of treatment during follow-up. *Journal of the American Academy of Child and Adolescent Psychiatry, 33,* 225–230.

Pfefferbaum, B. (1997). Posttraumatic stress disorder in children: A review of the past 10 years. *Journal of the American Academy of Child and Adolescent Psychiatry, 36,* 1503–1511.

Phillips, W., Baron-Cohen, S., & Rutter, M. (1995). To what extent can children with autism understand desire? *Development and Psychopathology, 7,* 151–169.

Phillips, W., Gómez, J. C., Baron-Cohen, S., Laá, V., & Riviere, A. (1995). Treating people as objects, agents, or "subjects": How young children with and without autism make requests. *Journal of Child Psychology and Psychiatry, 36,* 1383–1398.

Phinney, J. S. (1990). Ethnic identity in adolescents and adults: Review of research. *Psychological Bulletin, 108,* 499–514.

Phinney, J. S. (1993). A three-stage model of ethnic identity development in adolescence. In M. E. Bernal & G. P. Knight (Eds.), *Ethnic identity: Formation and transmission among Hispanics and other minorities* (pp. 61–80). Albany, NY: State University of New York Press.

Phinney, J. S. (1996). When we talk about American ethnic groups, what do we mean? *American Psychologist, 51,* 918–927.

Phinney, J. S., & Kohatsu, E. L. (1997). Ethnic and racial identity development and mental health. In J. Schulenberg, J. L. Maggs, & K. Hurrelmann (Eds.), *Health risks and developmental transitions during adolescence* (pp. 420–333). Cambridge, UK: Cambridge University Press.

Phinney, J. S., & Rosenthal, D. S. (1992). Ethnic identity in adolescence: Process, context, and outcome. In G. R. Adams, T. P. Gullotta, & R. Montemayor (Eds.), *Adolescent identity formation* (pp. 145–172). Newbury Park, CA: Sage Publications.

Piaget, J. (1932). *The moral judgment of the child.* London: Kegan Paul.

Piaget, J. (1967). *Six psychological studies.* New York: Random House.

Piaget, J. (1981). *Intelligence and affectivity: Their relationship during child development.* Palo Alto, CA: Annual Reviews.

Pianta, R. C., Egeland, B., & Sroufe, L. A. (1990). Maternal stress and children's development: Prediction of school outcomes and identification of protective factors. In J. Rolf, A. S. Masten, D. Cicchetti, K. H. Nuechterlein, & S. Weintraub (Eds.), *Risk and protective factors in the development of psychopathology* (pp. 215–235). Cambridge: Cambridge University Press.

Pierce, K., Glad, K. S., & Schreibman, L. (1997). Social perception in children with autism: An attentional deficit? *Journal of Autism and Developmental Disorders, 27,* 265–282.

Pike, A., Hetherington, E. M., McGuire, S., Reiss, D., & Plomin, R. (1996). Family environment and adolescent depressive symptoms and antisocial behavior: A multivariate genetic analysis. *Developmental Psychology, 32,* 590–603.

Piran, N., Lerner, P., Garfinkel, P. E., Kennedy, S. H., & Brouillette, C. (1988). Personality disorders in anorexic patients. *International Journal of Eating Disorders, 7,* 589–599.

Plomin, R. (1989). Environment and genes: Determinants of behavior. *American Psychologist, 44,* 105–111.

Plummer, D. L. (1995). Patterns of racial identity development of African American adolescent males and females. *Journal of Black Psychology, 21,* 168–180.

Pogue-Geile, M. F. (1991). The development of liability to schizophrenia: Early and late developmental models. In E. F. Walker (Ed.), *Schizophrenia: A life-course developmental perspective* (pp. 277–299). San Diego: Academic Press.

Pollock, M. H., Otto, M. W., Sabatino, S., Matcher, D., Worthington, J. J., McArdle, E. T., & Rosenbaum, J. F. (1996). Relation of childhood anxiety to adult panic disorder: Correlates and influences on course. *American Journal of Psychiatry, 153,* 376–381.

Pope, K. S. (1996). Memory, abuse, and science: Questioning claims about the false memory syndrome epidemic. *American Psychologist, 51,* 957–974.

Post, R. M., & Weiss, S. R. (1997). Emergent properties of neural systems: How focal molecular neurobiological alterations can affect behavior. *Development and Psychopathology, 9,* 907–929.

Powers, S. W., Vannatta, K., Noll, R. B., Cool, V. A., & Stehbens, J. A. (1995). Leukemia and other childhood cancers (1995). In M. C. Roberts (Ed.), *Handbook of pediatric psychology* (2nd ed., pp. 310–326). New York: Guilford.

Preciado, J., & Henry, M. (1997). Linguistic barriers in health education and services. In J. G. Garcia & M. C. Zea (Eds.), *Psychological interventions and research with Latino populations* (pp. 235–254). Boston: Allyn & Bacon.

Prior, M., & Werry, J. S. (1986). Autism, schizophrenia and allied disorders. In H. C. Quay & J. S. Werry (Eds.), *Psychopathological disorders of childhood* (3rd ed., pp. 156–210). New York: Wiley.

Pueschel, S. M., & Goldstein, A. (1991). Genetic counseling. In J. L. Matson & J. A. Mulick (Eds.), *Handbook of mental retardation* (pp. 279–307). New York: Pergamon.

Puig-Antich, J., & Chambers, W. (1978). *The Schedule for Affective Disorders and Schizophrenia for School-Age Children (Kiddie-SADS).* New York: New York State Psychiatric Institute.

Quay, H. C. (1993). The psychobiology of undersocialized aggressive conduct disorder: A theoretical perspective. *Development and psychopathology, 5,* 165–180.

Quiggle, N. L., Garber, J., Panak, W. F., & Dodge, K. A. (1992). Social information processing in aggressive and depressed children. *Child Development, 63,* 1305–1320.

Radke-Yarrow, M., McCann, K., DeMulder, E., Belmont, B., Martinez, P., & Richardson, D. T. (1995). Attachment in the context of high-risk conditions. *Development and Psychopathology, 7,* 247–265.

Ramey, C. T., & Ramey, S. L. (1992). Effective early intervention. *Mental Retardation, 30,* 337–345.

Ramirez, O. (1989). Mexican-American children and adolescents. In J. T. Gibbs & L. N. Huang (Eds.), *Children of color: Psychological intervention with minority youth* (pp. 224–250). San Francisco: Jossey-Bass.

Rapoport, J. L., & Ismond, D. R. (1996). *DSM-IV training guide for diagnosis of childhood disorders.* New York: Runner/Mazel.

Rastam, M. (1992). Anorexia nervosa in 51 Swedish adolescents: Premorbid problems and comorbidity. *Journal of the American Academy of Child and Adolescent Psychiatry, 31,* 819–828.

Rastam, M., & Gillberg, C. (1991). The family background in anorexia nervosa: A population-based study. *Journal of the American Academy of Child and Adolescent Psychiatry, 30,* 283–289.

Reed, T., & Peterson, C. (1990). A comparative study of autistic subjects' performance at two levels of visual and cognitive perspective taking. *Journal of Autism and Developmental Disorders, 20,* 555–567.

Reeker, J., Ensing, D., & Elliott, R. (1997). A meta-analytic investigation of group treatment outcomes for sexually abused children. *Child Abuse and Neglect, 21,* 669–680.

Reich, W., Welner, Z., & Herjanic, B. (1997). *Diagnostic Interview for Children and Adolescents-IV (DICA-IV).* North Tonawanda, NY: Multi-Health Systems.

Reid, J. B. (1978). *A social learning approach to family intervention: Observations in the home setting.* Eugene, OR: Castalia.

Reinecke, M. A., Dattilio, F. M., & Freeman, A. (1996). *Cognitive therapy with children and adolescents: A casebook for clinical practice.* New York: Guilford.

Reinhertz, H. Z., Gianconia, R. M., Pakiz, B., Silverman, A., Frost, A. K., & Lefkowitz, E. S. (1993). Psychological risks for major depression in late adolescence: A longitudinal community study. *Journal of the American Academy of Child and Adolescent Psychiatry, 32,* 1155–1163.

Reitan-Indiana Neuropsychological Test Battery. (1969). Indianapolis: Reitan.

Remschmidt, H. E., Schulz, E., Martin, M., Warnke, A., & Trott, G. (1994). Childhood-onset schizophrenia: History of the concept and recent studies. *Schizophrenia Bulletin, 20,* 727–744.

Rende, R., & Plomin, R. (1995). Nature, nurture, and development of psychopathology. In D. Cicchetti & D. J. Cohen (Eds.), *Developmental psychopathology: Vol. 1. Theory and methods* (pp. 291–314). New York: Wiley.

Rende, R. D., Plomin, R., Reiss, D., & Hetherington, E. M. (1993). Genetic and environmental influences on depressive symptomatology in adolescence: Individual differences and extreme scores. *Journal of Child Psychology and Psychiatry, 8,* 1387–1398.

Rey, J. M. (1993). Oppositional defiant disorder. *American Journal of Psychiatry, 150,* 1769–1777.

Reynolds, C. A., Hewitt, J. K., Erickson, M. T., Silberg, J. S., Rutter, M., Simonoff, E., Meyer, J., & Eaves, L. J. (1996). The genetics of children's oral reading performance. *Journal of Child Psychology and Psychiatry, 37,* 425–434.

Reynolds, C. R., & Fletcher-Janzen, E. (1997). *Handbook of clinical child neuropsychology.* New York: Plenum.

Reynolds, C. R., & Kamphaus, R. W. (1992). *Behavior assessment system for children (BASC).* Circle Pines, MN: American Guidance Services.

Reynolds, C. R., & Richmond, B. O. (1985). *Revised Children's Manifest Anxiety Scale (RCMAS).* Los Angeles: Western Psychological Services.

Ricardo, I. B., & Holden, E. W. (1994). Multicultural training in pediatric and clinical child psychology predoctoral internship programs. *Journal of Clinical Child Psychology, 23,* 32–38.

Richards-Colocino, N., McKenzie, P., & Newton, R. R. (1996). Project success: Comprehensive intervention services for middle school high-risk youth. *Journal of Adolescent Research, 11,* 130–163.

Richters, J. E., Arnold, L. E., Jensen, P. S., Abikoff, H., Conners, C. K., Greenhill, L. L., Hechtman, L., Hinshaw, S. P., Pelham, W. E., & Swanson, J. M. (1955). NIMH collaborative multisite multimodal treatment study of children with ADHD: I. Background and rationale. *Journal of the American Academy of Child and Adolescent Psychiatry, 34,* 987–1000.

Richters, J. E., & Cicchetti, D. (1993). Mark Twain meets DSM-III-R: Conduct disorder, development, and the concept of harmful dysfunction. *Development and Psychopathology, 5,* 5–30.

Rind, B., Tromovitch, P., & Bauserman, R. (1998). A meta-analytic examination of assumed properties of child sexual abuse using college samples. *Psychological Bulletin, 124,* 22–53.

Rispens, J., Aleman, A., & Goudena, P. P. (1997). Prevention of child sexual abuse victimization: A meta-analysis of school programs. *Child Abuse and Neglect, 21,* 975–987.

Risk factors for suicide attempts. (1987). *Adolinks, 4*(2).

Roberts, M. C. (Ed.), (1995). *Handbook of pediatric psychology, 2nd ed.* NY: The Guilford Press.

Robertson, J., & Robertson, J. (1971). Young children in brief separation. *Psychoanalytic Study of the Child, 26,* 264–315.

Robin, A. L., Bedway, M., Siegel, P. T., & Gilroy, M. (1996). Therapy for adolescent anorexia nervosa: Addressing cognitions, feelings, and the family's role. In E. D. Hibbs & P. S. Jensen (Eds.), *Psychosocial treatments for child and adolescent disorders: Empirically based strategies for clinical practice* (pp. 239–259). Washington, DC: American Psychological Association.

Robins, L. N. (1972). Follow-up studies of behavior disorders in children. In H. C. Quay & J. S. Werry (Eds.), *Psychopathological disorders of childhood.* New York: Wiley.

Robins, L. N., & McEvoy, L. (1990). Conduct problems as predictors of substance abuse. In L. E. Robins & M. Rutter (Eds.), *Straight and devious pathways from childhood to adulthood* (pp. 182–204). Cambridge: Cambridge University Press.

Rodin, J., Striegel-Moore, R. H., & Silberstein, L. R. (1990). Vulnerability and resilience in the age of eating disorders: Risk and protective factors for bulimia nervosa. In J. Rolf, A. S. Masten, D. Cicchetti, K. H. Nuechterlein, & S. Weintraub (Eds.), *Risk and protective factors in the development of psychopathology* (p. 361–383). Cambridge: Cambridge University Press.

Rodriguez, N., Ryan, S. W., Vande Kemp, H., & Foy, D. W. (1997). Posttraumatic stress disorder in adult female survivors of childhood sexual abuse: A comparison study. *Journal of Consulting and Clinical Psychology, 65,* 53–59.

Roeyers, H., Van Oost, P., & Bothuyne, S. (1998). Immediate imitation and joint attention in young children. *Development and Psychopathology, 10,* 441–450.

Rogers, C. R. (1959). A theory of therapy, personality, and interpersonal relationships as developed in the client-centered framework. In S. Koch (Ed.), *Psychology: Study of a science: Vol. 3. Formulations of the person and the social context.* New York: McGraw-Hill.

Rogers, S., & Pennington, B. F. (1991). A theoretical approach to the deficits in infantile autism. *Development and Psychopathology, 3,* 137–162.

Rogers, S. J. (1998). Empirically supported comprehensive treatments for young children with autism. *Journal of Clinical Child Psychology, 27,* 168–179.

Rogers, S. J. (1996). Brief report: Early intervention in autism. *Journal of Autism and Developmental Disorders, 26,* 243–246.

Rose, D. R., & Abramson, L. Y. (1991). Developmental predictors of depressive cognitive style: Research and theory. In Cicchetti, D., & Toth, S. L. (Eds.), *Rochester symposium on developmental psychopathology, No. 4,* 323–349.

Rosenblith, J. F., & Sims-Knight, J. (1992). *In the beginning: Development in the first two years of life.* Monterey, CA: Brooks/Cole.

Rosenthal, P. A., & Rosenthal, S. (1984). Suicidal behavior by preschool children. *American Journal of Psychiatry, 141,* 520–525.

Ross, A. O., & Nelson, R. O. (1979). Behavior therapy. In H. C. Quay & J. S. Werry (Eds.), *Psychopathological disorders of childhood* (2nd ed.). New York: Wiley.

Rossini, E. D., & Moretti, R. J. (1997). Thematic Apperception Test (TAT) interpretation: Practice recommendations from a survey of clinical psychology doctoral programs accredited by the American Psychological Association. *Professional Psychology: Research and Practice, 28,* 393–398.

Rossman, B. B. R., & Rosenberg, M. S. (1997). *Multiple victimization of children: Conceptual, research, and treatment issues.* New York: Haworth Press.

Roth, A., & Fonagy, P. (1996). *What works for whom: A critical review of psychotherapy research.* New York: Guilford.

Rothbart, M. K., Posner, M. I., & Hershey, K. L. (1995). Temperament, attention, and developmental psychopathology. In D. Cicchetti & D. J. Cohen (Eds.), *Developmental psychopathology: Vol. 1. Theory and methods* (pp. 315–340). New York: Wiley.

Rotheram, M. J., & Phinney, J. S. (1987). Ethnic behavior patterns as an aspect of identity. In J. S. Phinney & M. J. Rotheram (Eds.), *Children's ethnic socialization: Pluralism and development* (pp. 180–200). Newbury Park, CA: Sage Publications.

Rounsaville, B. J., Kosten, T. R., Weissman, M. M., Prusoff, B., Pauls, D., Foley, S., & Merikangas, K. (1991). Psychiatric disorders in the relatives of probands with opiate addiction. *Achives of General Psychiatry, 48,* 33–42.

Rubin, K. H. (1993). The Waterloo longitudinal project: Correlates and consequences of social withdrawal from childhood to adolescence. In K. H. Rubin & J. B. Asendorpf (Eds.), *Social withdrawal, inhibition, and shyness* (pp. 291–314). Hillsdale, NJ: Earlbaum.

Ruble, D. N., & Martin, C. L. (1998). Gender development. In W. Damon & N. Eisenberg (Eds.), *Handbook of child psychology* (5th ed., Vol. 3).

Social, emotional, and personality development. New York: Wiley.

Rudolph, K. D., Hammen, C., & Burge, D. (1994). Interpersonal functioning and depressive symptoms in childhood: Addressing the issues of specificity and comorbidity. *Journal of Abnormal Child Psychology, 22,* 355–371.

Ruiz, R. A., & Padilla, A. M. (1983). Counseling Latinos. In D. R. Atkinson, G. Morten, & D. W. Sue (Eds.), *Counseling American minorities: A cross-cultural perspective* (2nd ed., pp. 213–236). Dubuque, IA: W. C. Brown.

Russell, A. T., Bott, L., & Sammons, C. (1989). The phenomenology of schizophrenia occurring in childhood. *Journal of the American Academy of Child and Adolescent Psychiatry, 28,* 399–407.

Rutter, M. (1977). Brain damage syndromes in childhood: Concepts and findings. *Journal of Child Psychology and Psychiatry, 18,* 1–21.

Rutter, M. (1981). Psychological sequelae of brain-damaged children. *American Journal of Psychiatry, 138,* 1533–1544.

Rutter, M. (1990). Psychosocial resilience and protective mechanisms. In J. Rolf, A. S. Masten, D. Cicchetti, K. H. Nuechterlein, & S. Weintraub (Eds.), *Risk and protective factors in the development of psychopathology* (pp. 181–214). Cambridge: Cambridge University Press.

Rutter, M. (1994). Beyond longitudinal data: Causes, consequences, changes, and continuity. *Journal of*

Consulting and Clinical Psychology, 62, 928–940.

Rutter, M. (1996). Autism: Research—Prospects and priorities. *Journal of Autism and Developmental Disorders, 26,* 257–274.

Rutter, M. (1996). Transitions and turning points in developmental psychopathology: As applied to the age span between childhood and mid-adulthood. *International Journal of Behavioral Development, 19,* 603–626.

Rutter, M., Bailey, A., Bolton, P., & LeCouteur, A. (1993). Autism: Syndrome definition and possible genetic mechanisms. In R. Plomin & G. E. McClean (Eds.), *Nature, nurture, and psychology* (pp. 269–284). Washington, DC: APA Books.

Rutter, M., Dunn, J., Plomin, R., Simonoff, E., Pickles, A., Maughan, B., Ormel, J., Meyer, J., & Eaves, L. (1997). Integrating nature and nurture: Implications of person-environment correlations and interactions for developmental psychopathology. *Development and Psychopathology, 9,* 335–364.

Rutter, M., & Garmezy, N. (1983). Developmental psychopathology. In P. H. Mussen (Ed.), *Handbook of child psychology* (Vol. 4, pp. 775–911). New York: Wiley.

Safyer, A. W., & Hauser, S. T. (1995). A developmental view of defenses: Empirical approaches. In H. R. Conte & R. Plutchik (Eds.), *Ego defenses: Theory and measurement* (pp. 120–138). New York: Wiley.

Salzinger, S., Feldman, R. S., Hammer, M., & Rosario, M. (1993). The effects of physical abuse on children's social relationships. *Child Development, 64,* 169–187.

Sameroff, A. J. (1990). Neoenvironmental perspectives on developmental theory. In R. M. Hodapp, J. A. Burack, & E. Zigler (Eds.), *Issues in the developmental approach to mental retardation,* pp. 93–113. Cambridge: Cambridge University Press.

Sameroff, A. J. (1994). Models of development and developmental risk. In C. H. Zeanah (Ed.), *Handbook of infant mental health* (pp. 3–13). New York: Guilford.

Sameroff, A. J. (1995). General systems theories and developmental psychopathology. In D. Cicchetti & D. J. Cohen (Eds.), *Developmental psychopathology: Vol. I. Theory and methods* (pp. 659–695). New York: Wiley.

Sandler, I. N., Tein, J., & West, S. G. (1995). Coping, stress, and the psychological symptoms of children of divorce: A cross-sectional and longitudinal study. *Child Development, 65,* 1744–1763.

Sanson, A., Prior, M., & Smart, D. (1996). Reading disabilities with and without behaviour problems at 7-8 years: Prediction from longitudinal data from infancy to 6 years. *Journal of Child Psychology and Psychiatry, 37,* 529–541.

Santa, L. S. (1983). Mental health issues of Japanese-American children. In G. J. Powell (Ed.), *The psychosocial development of minority group children* (pp. 362–372). New York: Brunner/Mazel.

Satterfield, J. H., & Schnell, A. (1997). A prospective study of hyperactive boys with conduct problems and normal boys: Adolescent and adult criminality. *Journal of the American Academy of Child and Adolescent Psychiatry, 36,* 1726–1735.

Sattler, J. M. (1992). *Assessment of children.* San Diego: Author.

Saywitz, K. J., & Goodman, G. S. (1996). Interviewing children in and out of court: Current research and practical implications. In J. Briere, L. Berliner, J. A. Bulkley, C. Jenny, & T. Reid (Eds.), *The APSAC handbook on child maltreatment* (pp. 297–318). Thousand Oaks, CA: Sage Publications.

Saywitz, K. J., Goodman, G., Nicholas, G., & Moan, S. (1991). Children's memory of a physical examination involving genital touch: Implications for reports of child sexual abuse. *Journal of Consulting and Clinical Psychology, 59,* 682–691.

Schopler, E. (1994). Behavioral priorities for autism and related developmental disorders. In E. Schopler & G. B. Messibov (Eds.), *Behavioral issues in autism* (pp. 55–77). New York: Plenum.

Schopler, E. (1998). Behavioral priorities for autism and related developmental disorders. In E. Schopler & G. B. Mesibov (Eds.), *Behavioral issues in autism* (pp. 55–77). New York: Plenum.

Schopler, E., Lansing, M., & Waters, L. (1983). *Individualized assessment and treatment for autistic and developmentally disabled children: Vol. 3. Teaching activities for autistic children.* Austin, TX: Pro-Ed.

Schopler, E., & Mesibov, G. B. (Eds.) (1985). *Communication problems in autism.* New York: Plenum.

Schreier, H. A., & Libow, J. A. (1993). *Hurting for love: Munchausen by proxy syndrome.* New York: Guilford.

Schwalberg, M. D., Barlow, D. H., Alger, S. A., & Howard, L. J. (1992). Comparison of bulimics, obese binge eaters, social phobics, and individuals with panic disorder on comorbidity across DMS-II-R anxiety disorders. *Journal of Abnormal Psychology, 101,* 675–681.

Scott, B. S., Atkinson, L., Minton, H. L., & Bowman, T. (1997). Psychological distress of parents of infants with Down syndrome. *American Journal of Mental Retardation, 102,* 161–171.

Seidman, L. J., Biederman, J., Faraone, S. V., Weber, W., & Ouellette, C. (1997). Toward defining a neuropsychology of attention deficit-hyperactivity disorder: Performance of children and adolescents from a large clinically referred sample. *Journal of Counseling and Clinical Psychology, 65,* 150–160.

Seiner, S. H., & Gelfand, D. M. (1995). Effects of mothers' simulated withdrawal and depressed affect on mother-toddler interactions. *Child Development, 66,* 1519–1528.

Seligman, M., & Peterson, C. (1986). A learned helplessness perspective on childhood depression: Theory and research. In M. Rutter, C. E. Izard, & P. B. Read (Eds.), *Depression in young people* (pp. 223–249). New York: Guilford.

Selman, R. L., & Schultz, L. H. (1988). Interpersonal thought and action in the case of a troubled early adolescent: Toward a developmental model of the gap. In S. R. Shirk (Ed.), *Cognitive development and child psychotherapy* (pp. 207–246). New York: Plenum.

Selman, R. L., Schultz, L. H., & Yeates, K. O. (1991). Interpersonal understanding and action: A development and psychopathology perspective on research and prevention. In D. Cicchetti & S. L. Toth (Eds.), *Models and integrations: Rochester symposium on developmental psychopathology* (Vol. 3, pp. 389–326). Rochester, NY: University of Rochester Press.

Shaffer, D., Garland, A., Vieland, V., Underwood, M., & Busner, C. (1991). The impact of curriculum-based suicide prevention programs for teenagers. *Journal of the American Academy of Child and Adolescent Psychiatry, 30,* 588–596.

Shafii, M., & Shafii, S. L. (1992). *Clinical guide to depression in children and adolescents.* Washington, DC: American Psychiatric Press.

Shapiro, S. (1973). Disturbances in development and childhood neurosis. In S. L. Copel (Ed.), *Behavior pathology of childhood and adolescence.* New York: Basic Books.

Shaw, D. S., & Bell, R. Q. (1993). Developmental

theories of parental contributors to antisocial behavior. *Journal of Abnormal Child Psychology, 21,* 493–518.

Shaw, D. S., Owens, E. B., Vondra, J. I., Keenan, K., & Winslow, E. B. (1996). Early risk factors and pathways in the development of early disruptive behavior problems. *Development and Psychopathology, 8,* 679–699.

Shaw, D. S., Vondra, J. I., Hommerding, K. D., Kennan, K., & Dunn, M. (1994). Chronic family adversity and early behavior problems: A longitudinal study of low income families. *Journal of Child Psychology and Psychiatry, 35,* 1109–1122.

Shaw, S. F., Cullen, J. P., McGuire, J. M., & Brinckerhoff, L. C. (1995). Operationalizing a definition of learning disabilities. *Journal of Learning Disabilities, 26,* 586–597.

Shaywitz, B. A. (1995). Implications for clinical care and cognitive neuroscience. In S. H. Broman & M. E. Michel (Eds.), *Traumatic head injury in children* (pp. 271–280). New York: Oxford University Press.

Shaywitz, S. E., Shaywitz, B. A., Pugh, K. R., Fulbright, R. K., Constable, R. T., Mencl, W. E., Shankweiler, D. P., Liberman, A. M., Skudlarski, P., Fletcher, J. M., Katz, L., Marchione, K. E., Lacadie, C., Gatenby, C., & Gore, J. C. (1998). Functional disruption in the organization of the brain for reading and dyslexia. *Proceedings of the National Academy of Science, USA, 95,* 2636–2641.

Shedler, J., & Block, J. (1990). Adolescent drug use and psychological health. *American Psychologist, 45,* 612–630.

Shirk, S. R. (1988). *Cognitive development and child psychotherapy.* New York: Plenum.

Shirk, S. R., & Russell, R. L. (1996). *Change processes in child psychotherapy: Revitalizing treatment and research.* New York: Guilford.

Shure, M. B., & Spivack, G. (1988). Interpersonal cognitive problem-solving. In R. H. Price, E. L. Cowen, R. P. Lorion, & J. Ramos-McKay (Eds.), *Fourteen ounces of prevention: a casebook for practioners* (pp. 69–82). Washington, DC: American Psychological Association.

Sigman, M., Ungerer, J. A., Mundy, P., & Sherman, T. (1987). Cognition in autistic children. In D. J. Cohen, A. M. Donnellan, & R. Paul (Eds.), *Handbook of autism and developmental disabilities* (pp. 103–120). New York: Wiley.

Silverman, W. K., & Kurtines, W. M. (1996). *Anxiety and phobic disorders.* New York: Plenum.

Silverman, W. K., & Rabian, B. (1994). Specific phobias. In T. H. Ollendick, N. J. King, & W. Yule (Eds.), *International handbook of phobic and anxiety disorders in children and adolescents* (pp. 87–110). New York: Plenum.

Simmons, R. G., & Blyth, D. (1987). *Moving into adolescence: The impact of pubertal change and school context.* Hillsdale, NJ: Erlbaum.

Simon, E. W., Rappaport, D. A., Papka, M., &

Woodruff-Pak, D. S. (1995). Fragile-X and Down syndrome: Are there syndrome-specific cognitive profiles at low IQ levels? *Journal of Intellectual Disability Research, 39,* 326–330.

Singh, N. N., Osborne, J. G., & Huguenin, N. H. (1996). Applied behavioral intervention. In J. W. Jacobson & J. A. Mulick (Eds.), *Manual of diagnosis and professional practice in mental retardation* (pp. 341–353). Washington DC: American Psychological Association.

Siperstein, G. N., & Leffert, J. S. (1997). Comparison of socially accepted and rejected children with mental retardation. *American Journal of Mental Retardation, 101,* 339–351.

Siperstein, G. N., Leffert, J. S., & Wenz-Gross, M. (1997). The quality of friendships between children with and without learning problems. *American Journal of Mental Retardation, 102,* 111–125.

Skodol, A. E., Oldham, J. M., Hyler, S. E., Kellman, H. D., Doidge, N., & Davies, M. (1993). Comorbidity of DSM-III-R eating disorders and personality disorders. *International Journal of Eating Disorders, 14,* 403–416.

Smart, D., Sanson, A., & Prior, M. (1996). Connections between reading disability and behavior problems: Testing temporal and causal hypotheses. *Journal of Abnormal Child Psychology, 24,* 363–375.

Smetana, J. G. (1990). Morality and conduct disorders. In M. Lewis & S. M. Miller (Eds.), *Handbook of developmental psycho-*

pathology (pp. 157–180). New York: Plenum.

Sommers-Flanagan, J., & Sommers-Flanagan, R. (1996). Efficacy of antidepressant medication with depressed youth: What psychologists should know. *Professional Psychology: Research and Practice, 27,* 145–153.

Sonuga-Barke, E. J. S., Williams, E., Hall, M., & Saxton, T. (1996). Hyperactivity and delay aversion: III. The effects on cognitive style of imposing delay after errors. *Journal of Child Psychology and Psychiatry, 37,* 189–194.

Southam-Gerow, M. A., Henin, A., Chu, B., Marrs, A., & Kendall, P. C. (1997). Cognitive-behavioral therapy with children and adolescents. *Child and Adolescent Psychiatric Clinics of North America, 6,* 111–136.

Speier, P. L., Sherk, D. L., Hirsch, S., & Cantwell, D. P. (1995). Depression in children and adolescents. In E. E. Beckham & W. R. Leber (Eds.), *Handbook of depression* (pp. 467–493).

Speight, S. L., Vera, E. M., & Derrickson, K. B. (1996). Racial self-designation, racial identity, and self-esteem revisited. *Journal of Black Psychology, 22,* 37–52.

Speltz, M. L., DeKlyen, M., Greenberg, M. T., & Dryden, M. (1995). Clinic referral for oppositional defiant disorder: Relative significance of attachment and behavioral variables. *Journal of Abnormal Child Psychology, 23,* 487–505.

Spence, S. H. (1997). Structure of anxiety symptoms

among children: A confirmatory factor-analytic study. *Journal of Abnormal Psychology, 106,* 280–297.

Spencer, M. B. (1991). Identity, minority development of. In R. M. Lerner, A. C. Petersen, & J. Brooks-Gunn (Eds.), *Encyclopedia of adolescence,* (Vol. 1, pp. 525–528). New York: Garland.

Spencer, T., Biederman, J., Wilens, T., Harding, M., O'Donnell, D., & Griffin, S. (1996). Pharmacotherapy of attention-deficit-hyperactivity disorder across the life cycle. *Journal of the American Academy of Child and Adolescent Psychiatry, 35,* 409–432.

Spiker, D., & Hopmann, M. R. (1997). The effectiveness of early intervention for children with Down syndrome. In M. J. Guralnick (Ed.), *The effectiveness of early intervention* (pp. 271–306). Baltimore: Paul H. Brooks.

Spirito, A., Francis, G., Overholser, J., & Frank, N., (1996). Coping, depression, adolescent suicide attempts. *Journal of Clinical Child Psychology, 25,* 147–155.

Spitz, R. A. (1945). Hospitalism: An inquiry into the genesis of psychiatric conditions in early childhood. *Psychoanalytic study of the child, 1,* 53–74.

Spivack, G., & Shure, M. B. (1982). The cognition of social adjustment: Interpersonal cognitive problem-solving thinking. In B. Lahey & A. E. Kazdin (Eds.), *Advances in child clinical psychology* (pp. 323–372). New York: Plenum.

Springer, K. (1994). Beliefs about illness causality

among preschoolers with cancer: Evidence against immanent justice. *Journal of Pediatric Psychology, 19,* 91–101.

Sroufe, L. A. (1990). Considering normal and abnormal together: The essence of developmental psychopathology. *Development and Psychopathology, 2,* 335–348.

Sroufe, L. A. (1996). *Emotional development: The organization of emotional life in the early years.* New York: Cambridge University Press.

Sroufe, L. A. (1997). Psychopathology as an outcome of development. *Development and Psychopathology, 9,* 251–268.

Sroufe, L. A., & Rutter, M. (1984). The domain of developmental psychopathology. *Child Development, 55,* 17–29.

Stanger, C., Achenbach, T. M., & McConaughy, S. H. (1993). Three-year course of behavioral/emotional problems in a national sample of 4- to 16-year-olds: Predictors of signs of disturbance. *Journal of Consulting and Clinical Psychology, 61,* 839–848.

Stanger, C., Achenbach, T. M., & Verhulst, F. C. (1997). Accelerated longitudinal comparisons of aggressive versus delinquent syndromes. *Development and Psychopathology, 9,* 43–58.

Stanton, M. D., & Shadish, W. R. (1997). Outcome, attrition, and family-couples treatment for drug abuse: A meta-analysis and review of the controlled, comparative studies. *Psychological Bulletin, 122,* 170–191.

Stark, K. D. (1990). *Childhood depression: School-*

based interventions. New York: Guilford.

Stark, K. D., Swearer, S., Kurowski, C., Sommer, D., & Bowen, B. (1996). Targeting the child and family: A holistic approach to treating child and adolescent depressive disorders. In E. D. Hibbs & P. S. Jensen (Eds.), *Psychosocial treatments for child and adolescent disorders* (pp. 207–238). Washington, DC: American Psychological Association.

State, M. W., King, B. H., & Dykens, E. (1997). Mental retardation: A review of the past 10 years (Part II). *Journal of the American Academy of Child and Adolescent Psychiatry, 36,* 1664–1671.

Steinberg, L., Lamborn, S. D., Darling, N., Mounts, N. S., & Dornbusch, S. M. (1994). Over-time changes in adjustment and competence among adolescents from authoritative, authoritarian, indulgent, and neglectful families. *Child Development, 65,* 754–770.

Stern, D. N. (1985). *The interpersonal world of the infant.* New York: Basic Books.

Stevens, J. R. (1997). Anatomy of schizophrenia revisited. *Schizophrenia Bulletin, 23,* 373–383.

Stevenson, H. W., Chen, C., & Uttal, D. H. (1990). Beliefs and achievement: A study of black, white, and Hispanic children. *Child Development, 16,* 508–523.

Steward, M. S., Bussey, K., Goodman, G. S., & Saywitz, K. J. (1993). Implications of developmental research for interviewing children. *Child Abuse and Neglect, 17,* 25–37.

Stice, E., Ziemba, C., Margolis, J., & Flick, P. (1996). The dual pathway model differentiates bulimics, subclinical bulimics, and controls: Testing the continuity hypothesis. *Behavior Therapy, 27,* 531–549.

Stone, N. (1993). Parental abuse as a precursor to childhood onset depression and suicidality. *Child Psychiatry and Human Development, 24,* 13–24.

Stone, W. L., & Lemanek, K. L. (1990). Developmental issues in children's self-reports. In A. M. La Greca (Ed.), *Through the eyes of the child: Obtaining self-reports from children and adolescents* (pp. 18–56). Boston: Allyn & Bacon.

Stone, W. S., & Gottesman, I. I. (1993). A perspective on the search for the causes of alcoholism: Slow down the rush to genetical judgments. *Neurology, Psychiatry, and Brain Research, 1,* 123–132.

Straus, M. A., Sugarman, D. B., & Gile-Sims, J. (1997). Spanking by parents and subsequent antisocial behavior of children. *Archives of Pediatrics and Adolescent Medicine, 151,* 761–767.

Straus, M. A., & Yodanis, C. L. (1996). Corporal punishment in adolescence and physical assaults on spouses in later life: What accounts for the link? *Journal of Marriage and the Family, 58,* 825–841.

Striegel-Moore, R. H. (1993). Etiology of binge eating: A developmental perspective. In C. G. Fairburn & G. T. Wilson (Eds.), *Binge eating: Nature, assessment, and treatment* (pp. 144–172). New York: Guilford.

Strober, M. (1995). Family-genetic perspectives on anorexia nervosa and bulimia nervosa. In K. Brownell & C. G. Fairburn (Eds.), *Eating disorders and obesity: A comprehensive handbook* (pp. 212–218). New York: Guilford.

Strober, M., & Humphrey, L. (1987). Familial contributions to the etiology and course of anorexia nervosa and bulimia. *International Journal of Eating Disorders, 5,* 654–659.

Stuckey, S. (1987). *Slave culture.* New York: Oxford University Press.

Sullivan, H. S. (1953). *The interpersonal theory of psychiatry.* New York: Norton.

Swarr, A. E., & Richards, M. H. (1996). Longitudinal effects of adolescent girls' pubertal development, perceptions of pubertal timing, and parental relations on eating problems. *Developmental Psychology, 32,* 636–646.

Swisher, L., & Demetras, M. J. (1985). The expressive language characteristics of autistic children compared with mentally retarded or specific language-impaired children. In E. Schopler & G. B. Mesibov (Eds.), *Communication problems in autism* (pp. 147–162). New York: Plenum.

Szapocznik, J., Kurtines, W., Santiesteban, D. S., Pantín, H., Scopetta, M., Mancilla, Y., Aisenberg, S., McIntosh, S., Pérez-Vidal, A., & Coatsworth, J. D. (1997). The evolution of a structural ecosystemic theory for working with Latino families. In J. G. Garcia & M. C. Zea (Eds.) *Psychological interventions and research with Latino populations* (pp. 166–190). Boston: Allyn & Bacon.

Tager-Flusberg, H. (1985). Psycholinguistic approaches to language and communication in autism. In E. Schopler & G. B. Mesibov (Eds.), *Communication problems in autism* (pp. 89–92). New York: Plenum.

Tager-Flusberg, H. (1989). A psycholinguistic perspective on language development in the autistic child. In G. Dawson (Ed.), *Autism: Nature, diagnosis and treatment* (pp. 92–115). New York: Guilford.

Tager-Flusberg, H., Calkins, S., Nolin, T., Baumberger, T., Anderson, M., & Chadwick-Dias, A. (1990). A longitudinal study of language acquisition in autistic and Down syndrome children. *Journal of Autism and Developmental Disorders, 20,* 1–20.

Tager-Flusberg, H., & Sullivan, K. (1994). A second look at second-order belief attribution in autism. *Journal of Autism and Developmental Disorders, 24,* 577–588.

Tangney, J. P., & Fischer, K. W. (1995). *Self-conscious emotions: The psychology of shame, guilt, embarrassment, and pride.* New York: Guilford.

Tarter, R. E., Moss, H. B., & Banukov, M. W. (1996). Behavior genetic perspective of alcoholism etiology. In H. Begleiter & B. Kissin (Eds.), *Alcohol and alcoholism* (Vol. 1). New York: Oxford University Press.

Taylor, E. (1994). Syndromes of attention deficit and hyperactivity. In M. Rutter, E. Taylor, & L. Hersov (Eds.), *Child and adolescent psychiatry: Modern approaches.* New York: Blackwell Scientific.

Taylor, E. (1995). Dysfunctions of attention. In D. Cicchetti & D. J. Cohen (Eds.), *Developmental psychopathology* (pp. 243–273). New York: Wiley.

Taylor, H. G., Drotar, D., Wade, S., Yeates, K., Stancin, T., & Klein, S. (1995). Recovery from traumatic brain injury in children: The importance of the family. In S. H. Broman & M. E. Michel (Eds.), *Traumatic head injury in children* (pp. 188–217). New York: Oxford University Press.

Teti, D. M., Gelfand, D. M., Mesinger, D. S., & Isabella, R. (1995). Maternal depression and the quality of early attachment: An examination of infants, preschoolers, and their mothers. *Developmental Psychology, 31,* 364–376.

Thapar, A., & McGuffin, P. (1996). The genetic etiology of childhood depressive symptoms: A developmental perspective. *Development and Psychopathology, 8,* 751–760.

Thapar, A., & McGuffin, P. (1997). Anxiety and depressive symptoms in childhood: A genetic study of comorbidity. *Journal of Child Psychology and Psychiatry, 38,* 651–656.

Tharinger, D., & Stark, K. (1990). A qualitative versus quantitative approach to evaluating the Draw-A-Person and Kinetic Family Drawing: A study of mood- and anxiety-disorder children. *Psychological Assessment, 2,* 365–375.

Theander, S. (1996). Anorexia nervosa with an early onset: Selection, gender, outcome, and results of a long-term follow-up study. *Journal of Youth and Adolescence, 25,* 419–429.

Thomas, A. M., Peterson, L., & Goldstein, D. (1997). Problem solving and diabetes regimen adherence by children and adolescents with IDDM in social pressure situations: A reflection of normal development. *Journal of Pediatric Psychology, 22,* 541–561.

Thomas, C. S., & Schandler, S. L. (1996). Risk factors in adolescent substance abuse: Treatment and management implications. *Journal of Child and Adolescent Substance Abuse, 5,* 1–16.

Thompson, M. C., Asarnow, J. R., Goldstein, M. J. & Miklowitz, D. J. (1990). Thought disorders and communication problems in children with schizophrenia spectrum disorders and their parents. *Journal of Clinical Child Psychology 19,* 159–168.

Thompson, R. A. (1987). Empathy and emotional understanding. The early development of empathy. In N. Eisenberg & J. Strayer (Eds.), *Empathy and its development* (pp. 119–145). Cambridge: Cambridge University Press.

Thompson, R. A. (1994). Emotion regulation: A theme in search of definition. In Fox, N. A. (Ed.), The development of emotion regulation: Biological and behavioral considerations. *Monographs of the Society for Research in Child Development, 59,* 25–52.

Thompson, R. J., & Gustafson, K. (1996). *Adaptation to chronic childhood illness* (pp. 271–287). Washington, DC: American Psychological Association.

Thompson, S., & Rey, J. (1995). Functional enuresis: Is desmopressin the answer? *Journal of the American Academy of Child and Adolescent Psychiatry, 34,* 266–271.

Thorndike, R. L., Hagen, E. P., & Sattler, J. M. (1986). *Guide for administering and scoring the Stanford-Binet Intelligence Scale.* (4th ed.). Chicago: Riverside.

Tienari, P., Lahti, I., Sorri, A., Naarala, M., Moring, J., Kaleva, M., Wahlberg, K., & Wynne, L. C. (1990). Adopted-away offsprings of schizophrenics and controls: The Finnish adoptive family study of schizophrenia. In L. E. Robins & M. Rutter (Eds.), *Straight and devious pathways from childhood to adulthood* (pp. 365–379). Cambridge: Cambridge University Press.

Tienari, P., Sorri, A., Naarala, M., Lahti, I., Pohjola, J. (1983). The Finnish adoptive study: Adopted-away offsprings of schizophrenic mothers. In H. Stierlin, L. C. Wynne, & M. Wirsching (Eds.), *Psychosocial intervention in schizophrenia* (pp. 21–34). Berlin: Springer-Verlag.

Tonge, B. (1994). Separation anxiety disorder. In T. H. Ollendick, N. J. King, & W. Yule (Eds.), *Interna-*

tional handbook of phobic and anxiety disorders in children and adolescents (pp. 145–168). New York: Plenum.

Toth, S. L., Manly, J. T., & Cicchetti, D. (1992). Child maltreatment and vulnerability to depression. *Development and Psychopathology, 4,* 97–112.

Tremblay, R. E., Pagani-Kurtz, L., Masse, L. C., Vitaro, F., & Pihl, R. O. (1995). A bimodal preventive intervention for disruptive kindergarten boys: Its impact through mid-adolescence. *Journal of Consulting and Clinical Psychology, 63,* 560–568.

Trickett, P. K., & McBride-Chang, C. (1995). The developmental impact of different forms of child abuse and neglect. *Developmental Review, 15,* 311–337.

Tucker, J. S., Schwartz, J. E., Tomlinson-Keasey, C., Friedman, H. S., Criqui, M. H., & Wingard, D. L. (1997). Parental divorce: Effects on individual behavior and longevity. *Journal of Personality and Social Psychology, 73,* 381–391.

Turner, S. M., Beidel, D. C., & Wolff, P. L. (1996). Is behavioral inhibition related to the anxiety disorders? *Clinical Psychology Review, 16,* 157–172.

United Nations. (1989). *Adoption of a convention on the rights of the child.* (U.N. Document No. A/44/736). New York: Author.

Vaden-Kiernan, N., Ialongo, N. S., Pearson, J., & Kellam, S. (1995). Household family structure and children's aggressive behavior: A longitudinal study

of urban elementary school children. *Journal of Abnormal Child Psychology, 23,* 553–568.

van IJzendoorn, M. H., Juffer, F., & Duyvesteyn, M. G. C. (1995). Breaking the integenerational cycle of insecure attachment: A review of the effects of attachment-based interventions on maternal sensitivity and infant security. *Journal of Child Psychology and Psychiatry and Allied Disciplines, 36,* 225–248.

Vargas, L. A. (1997). Psychopathology in Hispanic children: What should we be looking for? In S. B. Campbell (Chair), *Psychopathology in ethnic minority children: A developmental-cultural perspective.* Symposium conducted at the meeting of the American Psychological Association, Chicago, IL, August 15–19.

Vargas, L. A., & Koss-Chioino, J. D. (Eds.). (1992). *Working with culture: Psychotherapeutic interventions with ethnic minority children and adolescents.* San Francisco: Jossey-Bass.

Vargas, L. A., & Willis, D. J. (1994). Introduction to the special section—New directions in the treatment and assessment of ethnic-minority children and adolescents. *Journal of Clinical Child Psychology, 23,* 2–4.

Varni, J. W., Blount, R. L., Waldron, S. A., & Smith, A. J. (1995). Management of pain and distress. In M. C. Roberts (Ed.), *Handbook of pediatric psychology,* (2nd ed., pp. 105–122). New York: Guilford.

Vasey, M. W., Crnic, K. A., & Carter, W. G. (1994). Worry in childhood: A developmental perspective. *Cognitive Therapy and Research, 18,* 529–549.

Vasey, M. W., & Dadds, M. R. (in press). An integrative perspective on the developmental psychopathology of anxiety. In M. W. Vasey & M. R. Dadds (Eds.), *The developmental psychopathology of anxiety.* New York: Oxford University Press.

Vasey, M. W., & Ollendick, T. H. (in press). Anxiety. In M. Lewis & A. Sameroff (Eds.), *Handbook of developmental psychopathology* (2nd ed.). New York: Plenum.

Vicker, B., and Monahan, M. 1988. The diagnosis of autism by state agencies. *Journal of Autism and Developmental Disorder 26,* 55–75.

Vik, P. W., Brown, S. A., & Myers, M. G. (1997). Adolescent substance abuse problems. In E. J. Mash & L. G. Terdal (Eds.), *Assessment of childhood disorders* (pp. 717–748). New York: Guilford.

Vitaro, F., Tremblay, R., Kerr, M., Pagani, L., & Bukowski, W. M. (1997). Disruptiveness, friends' characteristics, and delinquency in early adolescence: A test of two competing models of development. *Child Development, 68,* 676–689.

Vizard, E., Monch, E., & Misch, P. (1995). Child and adolescent sex abuse perpetrators: A review of the research literature. *Journal of Child Psychology and Psychiatry, 36,* 731–756.

Volkmar, F. R. (1986). Compliance, noncompliance, and negativism. In E. Schopler & G. B. Mesibov (Eds.), *Social behavior in autism* (pp. 171–188). New York: Plenum.

Volkmar, F. R. (1987). Social development. In D. J. Cohen, A. M. Donnellan, & R. Paul (Eds.), *Handbook of autism and pervasive developmental disorder* (pp. 41–60). New York: Wiley.

Volkmar, F. R. (1996). The disintegrative disorders: Childhood disintegative disorders and Rett's disease. In F. R. Volkmar (Ed.), *Psychoses and pervasive developmental disorders in childhood and adolescence* (pp. 223–248). Washington, DC: American Psychiatric Press, Inc.

Volkmar, F. R., & Mayes, L. C. (1990). Gaze behavior in autism. *Development and Psychopathology, 2,* 61–69.

Volkmar, F. R., & Schwab-Stone, M. (1996). Annotation: Childhood disorders in DSM-IV. *Journal of Child Psychology and Psychiatry and Allied Disciplines, 37,* 779–784.

Vondra, J. I., Barnett, D., & Cicchetti, D. (1989). Perceived and actual competence among maltreated and comparison school children. *Development and Psychopathology, 1,* 237–255.

Vondra, J. I., Kolar, A. B., & Radigan, B. L. (1992). Psychological maltreatment of children. In R. T. Ammerman & M. Hersen (Eds.), *Assessment of family violence: A clinical and legal sourcebook* (pp. 253–290). New York: Wiley.

Vuchinich, S., Wood, B., & Angelelli, J. (1996). Coalitions and family problem solving in the psychosocial treatment of preadolescents. In E. D. Hibbs & P. S. Jensen (Eds.), *Psychosocial treatments for child and adolescent disorders* (pp. 497–520). Washington, DC: American Psychological Association.

Vurpillot, E. (1968). The development of scanning strategies and their relation to visual differentiation. *Journal of Experimental Child Psychology, 6,* 632–650.

Wachtel, E. F. (1994). *Treating troubled children and their families.* New York: Guilford.

Wagner, B. M. (1997). Family risk factors for child and adolescent suicidal behavior. *Psychological Bulletin, 121,* 246–298.

Walco, G. (1994). Sounding Board: Pain, hurt, and harm—The ethics of pain control in infants and children. *New England Journal of Medicine, 331,* 541–544.

Waldron, H. B. (1997). Adolescent substance abuse and family therapy outcome: A review of randomized trials. In T. H. Ollendick & R. J. Prinz (Eds.), *Advances in clinical child psychology* (Vol. 9, pp. 199–234). New York: Plenum.

Walker, C. E. (1995). Elimination disorders: Enuresis and encopresis. In M. C. Roberts (Ed.), *Handbook of pediatric psychology* (2nd ed., pp. 537–557). New York: Guilford.

Walker, E. F., Davis, D. M., Gottlieb, L. A., & Weinstein, J. A. (1991). Developmental trajectories in schizophrenia: Elucidating the divergent pathways. In E. F. Walker (Ed.), *Schizophrenia. A life-course developmental perspective* (pp. 299–331). San Diego, CA: Academic Press.

Walker, E. F., Neumann, C. C., Baum, K., Davis, D. M., DiForio, D., & Bergman, A. (1996). The developmental pathways to schizophrenia: Potential moderating effects of stress. *Development and Psychopathology, 8,* 647–666.

Walker, E. F., Savole, T., & Davis, D. (1994). Neuromotor precursors of schizophrenia. *Schizophrenia Bulletin, 20,* 441–451.

Wallander, J. L. & Thompson, R. J., Jr. (1995). Psychological adjustment of children with chronic physical conditions. In M. J. Roberts (Ed.), *Handbook of pediatric psychology* (2nd ed., pp. 124–141). New York: Guilford.

Wallander, J. L., & Varni, J. W. (1998). Effects of pediatric chronic physical disorders on child and family adjustment. *Journal of Child Psychology and Psychiatry, 39,* 29–46.

Wallerstein, J. S. (1991). The long-term effects of divorce on children: a review. *Journal of the American Academy of Child and Adolescent Psychiatry, 30,* 349–360.

Walsh, T., & Menvielle, E. (1997). Disorders of elimination. In J. M. Weiner (Ed.), *Textbook of child and adolescent psychiatry* (2nd ed., pp. 613–615). Washington, DC: The American Psychiatric Association.

Warren, S. L., Huston, L., Egeland, B., & Sroufe, L. A. (1997). Child and adolescent anxiety disorders and early attachment. *Journal of the American Academy of Child and Adolescent Psychiatry, 36,* 637–644.

Watkins, J. M., Asarnow, R. F., & Tanguay, P. E. (1988). Symptom development in childhood schizophrenia. *Journal of Child Psychology and Psychiatry, 29,* 865–878.

Watson, J. S., & Ramey, C. T. (1972). Reactions to responsive-contingent stimulation in early infancy. *Merrill-Palmer Quarterly, 18,* 219–227.

Watson, L. R., Lord, C., Schaffer, B., & Schopler, E. (1989). *Teaching spontaneous communication to autistic and developmentally handicapped children* New York: Pro-Ed.

Watt, N. F. (1984). In a nutshell: The first two decades of high-risk research in schizophrenia. In N. F. Watt, E. J. Anthony, L. C. Wayne, & J. E. Rolf (Eds.), *Children at risk for schizophrenia: A longitudinal perspective,* pp. 572–595. Cambridge: Cambridge University Press.

Watt, N. F., Anthony, E. J., Wynne, L. C., & Rolf, J. E. (Eds.) (1984). *Children at risk for schizophrenia: A longitudinal prospective.* Cambridge: Cambridge University Press.

Watt, N. F., & Saiz, C. (1991). Longitudinal studies of premorbid development of adult schizophrenics. In E. F. Walker (Ed.), *Schizophrenia: A life-course developmental perspective* (pp. 157–192). San Diego, CA: Academic Press.

Wechsler, D. (1989). *Wechsler Preschool and Primary Scale of Intelligence—Revised*. San Antonio, TX: The Psychological Corporation.

Wechsler, D. (1991). *Manual for the Wechsler Intelligence Scale for Children—Third Edition*. San Antonio: The Psychological Corporation.

Weinberger, D. R. (1987). Implications of normal brain development for the pathogenesis of schizophrenia. *Archives of General Psychiatry, 44*, 660–669.

Weiner, I. B. (1992). *Psychological disturbances in adolescence* (2nd ed.). New York: Wiley.

Weiner, I. B. (1996). Some observations on the validity of the Rorschach Inkblot method. *Psychological Assessment, 8*, 206–213.

Weisz, J. R., & Weiss, B. (1991). Studying the "referability" of child clinical problems. *Journal of Consulting and Clinical Psychology, 59*, 266–273.

Weisz, J. R., Weiss, B., Han, S. S., Granger, D. A., & Morton, T. (1995). Effects of psychotherapy with children and adolescents revisited: A meta-analysis of treatment outcome studies. *Psychological Bulletin, 117*, 450–468.

Wekerle, C., & Wolfe, D. A. (1996). Child maltreatment. In E. J. Mash & R. A. Barkley (Eds.), *Child psychopathology* (pp. 492–537). New York: Guilford.

Weller, R. A., Weller, E. B., Fristad, M. A., & Bowes, J. M. (1991). Depression in recently bereaved prepubertal children. *American Journal of Psychiatry, 148*, 1536–1540.

Wellman, H. M. (1988). First steps in the child's theorizing about the mind. In J. W. Astington, P. L. Harris, & D. R. Olson (Eds.), *Developing theories of mind* (pp. 64–92). Cambridge: Cambridge University Press.

Wellman, H. M. (1993). Early understanding of mind: The normal case. In S. Baron-Cohen, H. Tager-Flusberg, & D. J. Cohen (Eds.), *Understanding others minds: Perspectives from autism* (pp. 10–39). Oxford, UK: Oxford University Press.

Wenar, C. (1982). On negativism. *Human Development, 25*, 1–23.

Werner, E. E., & Smith, R. S. (1992). *Overcoming the odds: High risk children from birth to adulthood*. Ithaca, NY: Cornell University Press.

Werry, J. S. (1986). Biological factors. In H. C. Quay & J. S. Werry (Eds.), *Psychopathological disorders of childhood* (3rd ed., pp. 294–331). New York: Wiley.

Wertlieb, D. (1989). The psychological test report: An instrument of therapy and advocacy for the child with learning problems. In M. C. Roberts & C. E. Walker (Eds.), *Casebook of child and pediatric psychology* (pp. 16–36). New York: Guilford.

Westat Inc. (1993). *A report on the maltreatment of children with disabilities*. Washington, DC: National Center on Child Abuse and Neglect.

Westen, D. (1990). *Social cognition and object relations scale (SCORS): Manual for coding TAT data*. Unpublished manuscript,

Department of Psychology, University of Michigan.

Westerman, M. A. (1990). Coordination of maternal directive with preschoolers' behavior in compliance-problem and healthy dyads. *Developmental psychology, 26*, 621–630.

Wetzel, K. (1996). Speech-recognizing computers: A written-communication tool for students with learning disabilities? *Journal of Learning Disabilities, 29*, 371–380.

Whaley, A. L. (1993). Self-esteem, cultural identity, and psychosocial adjustment in African American children. *Journal of Black Psychology, 19*, 406–422.

White, R. W. (1959). Motivation reconsidered: The concept of competence. *Psychological Review, 66*, 297–333.

Widaman, K. F., & McGrew, K. S. (1996). The structure of adaptive behavior. In J. W. Jacobson & J. A. Mulick (Eds.), *Manual of diagnosis and professional practice in mental retardation* (pp. 97–110). Washington, DC: American Psychological Association.

Wiener, J. M. (1997). Oppositional defiant disorder. In J. M. Wiener (Ed.), *Textbook of child & adolescent psychiatry* (2nd ed., pp. 459–463). Washington, DC: American Psychiatric Press.

Wilens, T. E., Biederman, J., Abrantes, A. M., & Spencer, T. J. (1997). Clinical characteristics of psychiatrically referred adolescent outpatients with substance use disorder. *Journal of the American Academy of Child and Adolescent Psychiatry, 36*, 941–947.

Williams, L. M. (1994). Recall of childhood trauma: A prospective study of women's memories of child sexual abuse. *Journal of Consulting and Clinical Psychology, 62*, 1167–1176.

Williamson, S. E., Harpur, T. J., & Hare, R. D. (1991). Abnormal processing of affective words by psychopaths. *Psychophysiology, 28*, 260–273.

Wilson, G. T., Heffernan, K., & Black, C. M. (1996). Eating disorders. In E. J. Mash & R. A. Barkley (Eds.), *Child psychopathology* (pp. 541–571). New York: Guilford.

Wilson, R., Majsterek, D., & Simmons, D. (1996). The effects of computer-assisted versus teacher-directed instruction on the multiplication performance of elementary students with learning disabilities. *Journal of Learning Disabilities, 29*, 382–390.

Windle, R. C., & Windle, M. (1997). An investigation of adolescents' substance use behaviors, depressed affect, and suicidal behaviors. *Journal of Child Psychology and Psychiatry and Allied Disciplines, 38*, 921–929.

Winnicott, D. W. (1975). *Through paediatrics to psycho-analysis*. New York: Basic Books.

Wirt, R. D., Lachar, D., Klinedinst, J. K., & Seat, P. S. (1990). *Personality Inventory for Children—1990 edition*. Los Angeles: Western Psychological Services.

Wissick, C. A. (1996). Multimedia: Enhancing instruction for students with learning disabilities. *Jour-*

nal of Learning Disabilities, 29, 494–503.

Wolfe, D. A. (1987). Child abuse: Implications for child development and psychopathology. *Developmental Clinical Psychology and Psychiatry, 10,* Newbury Park, CA: Sage Publications.

Wolfe, D. A., & McEachran, A. (1997). Child physical abuse and neglect. In E. J. Mash & L. G. Terdal (Eds.), *Assessment of childhood disorders* (pp. 523–568). New York: Guilford.

Wolfe, D. A., Wekerle, C., Reitzel-Jaffe, D., & Lefebvre, L. (1998). Factors associated with abusive relationships among maltreated and nonmaltreated youth. *Development and Psychopathology, 10,* 61–85.

Wolpe, J. (1973). *The practice of behavior therapy* (2nd ed.). New York: Pergamon.

Woodcock, R. W., Johnson, M., Mather, N., McGrew, K. S., & Werder, J. K. (1989). *Woodcock-Johnson Psycho-Educational Battery-Revised.* Chicago: Riverside.

Wooden, W., Leon, J., & Toshima, M. (1988). Ethnic identity among Sansei and Yonsei church-affiliated youth in Los Angeles and Honolulu. *Psychological Reports, 62,* 268–270.

Wootton, J. M., Frick, P. J., Shelton, K. K., & Silverthorn, P. (1997). Ineffective parenting and childhood conduct problems: The moderating role of callous-unemotional traits. *Journal of Consulting and Clinical Psychology, 65,* 301–308.

World Health Organization. (1997). *Mulitaxial classifi-*

cation of child and adolescent psychiatric disorder. New York: Cambridge University Press.

Wren, F. J., & Tarbell, S. E. (1998). Feeding and growth disorders. In R. T. Ammerman & J. V. Campo (Eds.), *Handbook of pediatric psychology and psychiatry: Vol. II. Disease, injury and illness* (pp. 133–165). Boston: Allyn & Bacon.

Wurtele, S. K. (1997). Sexual abuse. In R. T. Ammerman & M. Hersen (Eds.), *Handbook of prevention and treatment with children and adolescents* (pp. 357–384). New York: Wiley.

Wyly, M. V. (1997). *Infant assessment.* Boulder, CO: Westview Press.

Wynne, L. C. (1984). Communication patterns and family relations of children at risk for schizophrenia. In N. F. Watt, E. J. Anthony, L. C. Wynne, & J. E. Rolf (Eds.), *Children at risk for schizophrenia: A longitudinal perspective* (pp. 572–595). Cambridge: Cambridge University Press.

Yamamoto, J., & Iga, M. (1983). Emotional growth of Japanese-American children. In G. J. Powell (ed.), *The psychosocial development of minority group children* (pp. 167–180). New York: Brunner/Mazel.

Yamamoto, J., & Kubota, M. (1983). The Japanese-American family. In G. J. Powell (Ed.), *The psychosocial development of minority group children* (pp. 237–246). New York: Brunner/Mazel.

Yamamoto, J., Silva, J. A., Ferrari, M., & Nukar-

iya, K. (1997). Culture and psychopathology. In G. Johnson-Powell & J. Yamamoto (Eds.), *Transcultural child development: Psychological assessment and treatment* (pp. 34–60). New York: Wiley

Yamamoto, J., Yeh, J. W., Yeh, M., & Hifumi, S. S. (1997). Japanese American children. In J. Noshpitz, (Ed.), *Handbook of child and adolescent psychiatry.* (Vol. 4, pp. 579–585). New York: Wiley.

Yee, A. H., Fairchild, H. H., Weizmann, G., & Wyatt, G. E. (1993). Addressing psychology's problems with race. *American Psychologist, 48,* 1132–1140.

Yirmiya, N., Erel, O., Shaked, M., & Solomonica-Levi, D. (1998). Meta-analyses comparing theory of mind abilities of individuals with autism, individuals with mental retardation, and normally developing individuals. *Psychological Bulletin, 124,* 283–307.

Yirmiya, N., Sigman, M. D., Kasari, C., & Mundy, P. (1992). Empathy and cognition in high-functioning children with autism. *Child Development, 63,* 150–160.

Yule, W. (1994). Posttraumatic stress disorder. In T. H. Ollendick, N. J. King, & W. Yule (Eds.), *International handbook of phobic and anxiety disorders in children and adolescents* (pp. 223–240). New York: Plenum.

Zahn-Waxler, C. (1993). Warriors and worriers: Gender and psychopathology. *Development and Psychopathology, 5,* 79–89.

Zahn-Waxler, C. (1996). Special issue: Development, transitions, and adjustment in adolescence. *Developmental Psychology, 32*(4), 571–801.

Zahn-Waxler, C., Friedman, R. J., Cole, P. M., Mizuta, I., & Hiruma, N. (1996). Japanese and United States preschool children's responses to conflict and distress. *Child Development, 67,* 2462–2477.

Zea, M. C., Garcia, J. G., Belgrave, F. Z., & Quezada, T. (1997). Socioeconomic and cultural factors in rehabilitation of Latinos with disabilities. In J. G. Garcia & M. C. Zea (Eds.), *Psychological interventions and research with Latino populations* (pp. 217–234). Boston: Allyn & Bacon.

Zeanah, C. H. (1996). Beyond insecurity: A reconceptualization of attachment disorders of infancy. *Journal of Consulting and Clinical Psychology, 64,* 42–52.

Zeanah, C. H., Boris, N. W., & Scheeringa, M. S. (1997). Psychopathology of infancy. *Journal of Child Psychology and Psychiatry, 38,* 81–99.

Zeanah, C. H., Mammen, O. K., & Lieberman, A. F. (1993). Disorders of attachment. In C. H. Zeanah (Ed.), *Handbook of infant mental health* (pp. 332–349). New York: Guilford.

Zero to Three. (1994). *Diagnostic classification of mental health and developmental disorders of infancy and early childhood.* Arlington, VA: Zero to Three/National Center for Clinical Infant Programs.

Zimmerman, M. A., & Arunkumar, R. (1994). Resiliency research: Implications for schools and policy. *Social Policy Report: Society for Research in Child Development, 8,* 1–18.

Zoccolillo, M. (1997). Conduct disorder, substance dependence, and adolescent motherhood. *American Journal of Orthopsychiatry, 67,* 152–157.

Zohar, A. H., & Bruno, R. (1997). Normative and pathological obsessive-compulsive behavior and ideation in childhood: A question of timing. *Journal of Child Psychology and Psychiatry, 38,* 993–999.

Zupan, B. A., Hammen, C., & Jaenicke, C. (1987). The effects of current mood and prior depressive history on self-schematic processing in children. *Journal of Experimental Child Psychology, 43,* 149–158.

Name Index

Subject Index

Note: Italicized letters *b, f,* and *t* following page numbers indicate boxes, figures, and tables, respectively.